Although biblical texts were known in Church Slavonic as early as the ninth century, translation of the Bible into Russian came about only in the nineteenth century. Modern scriptural translation generated major religious and cultural conflict within the Russian Orthodox Church. The resulting divisions left church authority particularly vulnerable to political pressures exerted upon it in the twentieth century. *Russian Bible Wars* illuminates the fundamental issues of authority that have divided modern Russian religious culture. Set within the theoretical debate over secularization, the volume clarifies why the Russian Bible was issued relatively late and amidst great controversy. Stephen K. Batalden's study traces the development of biblical translation into Russian and of the "Bible wars" that then occurred in the nineteenth and twentieth centuries in Russia. The annotated bibliography of the Russian Bible identifies the different editions and their publication history.

STEPHEN K. BATALDEN is Professor of History and Director of the Melikian Center for Russian, Eurasian, and East European Studies at Arizona State University.

RUSSIAN BIBLE WARS

Modern Scriptural Translation and Cultural Authority

BY

STEPHEN K. BATALDEN

CAMBRIDGE
UNIVERSITY PRESS

University Printing House, Cambridge CB2 8BS, United Kingdom

Cambridge University Press is part of the University of Cambridge.

It furthers the University's mission by disseminating knowledge in the pursuit of education, learning and research at the highest international levels of excellence.

www.cambridge.org
Information on this title: www.cambridge.org/9781316600924

First published 2013
First paperback edition 2015

A catalogue record for this publication is available from the British Library

Library of Congress Cataloguing in Publication data
Batalden, Stephen K.
Russian Bible wars : modern scriptural translation and cultural authority / Stephen K. Batalden.
pages cm
Includes bibliographical references and index.
ISBN 978-1-107-03211-8
1. Bible – Translating – Russia – History. 2. Bible – Translating – Soviet Union – History. 3. Russian language. 4. Russia – Church history – 1801–1917. 5. Russia – Church history – 20th century. 6. Soviet Union – Church history. I. Title.
BS460.R7B37 2013
220.5′9171–dc23
2012032891

ISBN 978-1-107-03211-8 Hardback
ISBN 978-1-316-60092-4 Paperback

To Sandy

Contents

Acknowledgments

Although all the chapters here are original to this volume, portions of several chapters have appeared before as parts of separate articles in journals and edited anthologies. This work has benefited greatly from the critical review of those earlier publications, as well as from the reading of portions of this work by colleague friends. I am particularly appreciative of the comments of Alexander Agadjanian, Kathleen Cann, Gregory Freeze, Mark von Hagen, Alexei Lalo, and the late historian and theologian Fairy von Lilienfeld. I have been fortunate also to draw upon the insights of several of my former and current graduate students with whom I have been able to discuss portions of this work – among them Melissa Jones, Kate Harrie, and Andrew Reed. From the earliest stages of this project, the research has been aided by the support of devoted professional archivists in St. Petersburg and Cambridge. For the assistance of Agnessa Mukhtan (Russian State Historical Archive), the late Evgeniia Granstrem (Russian National Library), and especially Kathleen Cann (British and Foreign Bible Society Archive), I am deeply grateful. It is a pleasure also to acknowledge the support of research fellowships from the International Research and Exchanges Board and the Fulbright-Hays Faculty Research Abroad Program, as well as sabbatical leave support from Arizona State University. At Arizona State University, I have been inspired by a distinguished group of colleagues in Russian and East European studies – notably, Eugene Clay, Lee Croft, Laurie Manchester, and Mark von Hagen – all of whom share a special concern for interpreting modern Russian cultural history. It has been an honor to be associated with these colleagues and with the remarkable staff of the ASU Melikian Center for Russian, Eurasian, and East European Studies. The Melikian Center and its devoted patrons, Gregory and Emma Melikian, have contributed to this study in ways great and small. This volume is dedicated to Sandra Batalden, whose loving partnership and selfless collaboration extend far beyond her professional bibliographical and editorial guidance.

Introduction

The modern Russian Bible, like all such sacred texts, is a political and cultural document. One of the axioms of modern text criticism is that all texts, including such sacred texts as the Hebrew Bible and the Arabic Qur'an, reflect the historical circumstances surrounding their creation, translation, and dissemination. Within the three main Abrahamic traditions (Judaism, Islam, and Christianity), Christianity has arguably placed greatest emphasis upon the translation of its sacred text into local languages. That translation process, in turn, has added to the local significance of the Bible as a political and cultural artifact.

A hallmark of the process of biblical translation in the Eastern Orthodox world is its unusual timing. In Eastern Orthodoxy, biblical translation occurred both earlier *and* later than elsewhere in Europe – earlier in the case of the Slavonic world because the original Slavonic translation of scripture took place as a part of the missions of Sts. Cyril and Methodius in the ninth century; and later because translation into modern languages, in contrast to the German and English translations of the Reformation era, came to the Orthodox world only from the nineteenth century. The relatively late translation of the Bible into Russian reflected, in part, the persistence of linguistic diglossia in Russian culture, a situation that exists to the present in which the historical evolution of the modern Russian language was paralleled by the continued authority of the old Slavonic biblical text for liturgical worship.

Modern Russian biblical translation in the nineteenth century was from the outset highly politicized. The title for this work draws upon the language of "culture wars," framing the politics of modern scriptural translation in figurative terms as Russian Bible wars. It is the thesis of this work that the debates over modern scriptural translation in nineteenth-century Russia contributed to the transformation of modern Russian religious culture by posing fundamental questions of authority within Eastern Christian tradition. These debates reached well beyond the confines of the religious culture into the wider public sphere. How and why did modern biblical translation become such a contested issue for nineteenth- and twentieth-century Russia? That is the question this volume seeks to answer. It may have been inevitable that modern Russian biblical translation would become politically charged, having been launched as it was by formal imperial proclamation in 1816. The fact that the establishment of the Russian Bible Society in the reign of Alexander I was closely identified with the work of the British and Foreign Bible Society ultimately heightened the controversy over biblical translation, and made the politics of the Russian Bible an issue also involving Russian cultural ties with the West. But the politics of modern Russian biblical translation extended well beyond its occasional imperial blessings and proscriptions, and the perceptions of western influence. Russian biblical translation was politically charged – and remained so at least to the end of the Soviet era – because it posed for modern Russian religious culture fundamental, unresolved issues of authority. At stake in these issues was the very arbitration of modern Russian religious culture itself. Who should be authorized to translate Holy Scripture? What texts should be considered authoritative? What linguistic medium should be used, and for what purposes? Who should have the authority to publish and disseminate Holy Scripture? These questions of authority invariably left the traditional arbiters of Russian religious culture – the Russian church hierarchy and its emperor – divided. Indeed, the failure of the religious culture to resolve these fundamental issues of authority left the church all the more vulnerable in the twentieth century.

Two assumptions have guided this framing of the problem of Russian biblical translation. First, traditional Russian religious culture, while it necessarily responded to the interests of the wider believing community, invested official authority in a hierarchical elite.[1] Russian religious culture was not intended to be brokered on the basis of "market" forces, but was rather subjected to the controls of the Russian state and the church hierarchy. In subordinating church administration to state authority, the Petrine church reform of 1721, while it did little to challenge the church hierarchy's official authority in matters of faith and doctrine, demonstrated the power of the state over religious institutions. The Petrine reform

[1] The relationship between elite ecclesiastical authority and the wider believing community has been well addressed for Orthodox Slavs in Eve Levin's, *Sex and Society in the World of the Orthodox Slavs, 900–1700* (Ithaca, New York: Cornell University Press, 1989). Levin's point is that "the gap between ecclesiastical and community norms was not great" (302). But the ultimate arbitration of religious authority in early modern Russia, particularly in matters of biblical texts, translation, and distribution, continued to rest in the hands of elite ecclesiastical and political authorities.

also reinforced imperial authority over official episcopal appointments. Catherine II's subsequent secularization of monastic properties in 1764, while it may have limited the church's economic independence from the state, drawing the state directly into local diocesan financing, reconfirmed the longstanding shared authority of church and state in matters pertaining to Russian religious culture. The capacity of the post-Petrine church and state to identify and label "heresy," as in the case of the Old Believer communities, was an indication that this prescriptive, hierarchical authority continued to be embedded in modern Russian religious culture. Slavophile critics would argue that this hierarchical control became even greater, and more impersonal, in the aftermath of the Petrine reforms than it had been in traditional Russian religious life. Modern Russian biblical translation, by generating market demand and a modernized supply system for Holy Scripture, and by introducing modern text criticism, fundamentally challenged the prevailing traditional elite arbitration of authority in modern Russian religious culture.

The second assumption underlying this study is that religious authority in Russia, as elsewhere, has always been culturally conditioned. H. Richard Niebuhr noted many years ago in his classic study, *Christ and Culture*, that religious traditions are never independent of culture.[2] The transmission of religious tradition has always occurred within a cultural context. Religious traditions may challenge prevailing cultural norms, but they do so within concrete social or political contexts. Thus, as Elaine Pagels demonstrated so convincingly for early Christianity, even such basic matters as the establishment of the biblical canon were conditioned by specific political issues facing the early church, notably its confrontation with Gnosticism.[3]

In western Christian tradition, canon lawyers and inquisitorial judges served as the arbiters of church authority, interpreting with greater or lesser scholastic skill the norms of religious tradition. Such canonists, however, operated within clearly identifiable cultural and political constraints, despite their occasional claim to operate above culture at the direct command of divine authority. The contested politics of religious culture was often concealed in this arbitration and interpretation of divinely ordained authority. Whether it be papal bulls, hagiography, confessional literature, or even Holy Scripture, all such religious texts, like their secular counterparts, were constructed representations arising out of specific, contested circumstances. The fact that sacred texts have arisen out of concrete political contexts

[2] H. Richard Niebuhr, *Christ and Culture* (New York: Harper Row, 1951).
[3] Elaine Pagels, *The Gnostic Gospels* (New York: Random House, 1979).

merely defines their status as texts, and does not address their divine authority. This book, in focusing upon the contextual issues surrounding Russian biblical translation, recognizes modern Russian religious culture as a domain of contested authority worthy of scholarly study. As such, this is a work of history, not a guide to biblical exegesis or textology.

In the absence of a more rigid canon law, Eastern Christendom developed alternative vehicles for defining a normative Christian tradition. These vehicles included a wealth of confessional, hagiographic, and patristic literature, as well as the aesthetically rich iconographic, musical, and sacramental resources of Orthodox liturgical worship. A most important part of that tradition was the transmission of sacred scriptural texts. For Eastern Orthodoxy, the Bible remained not only the repository of God's divine word, but was also venerated as an icon, a witness to God's saving grace. The Bible's iconic character, reinforced by the seventeenth-century controversies over changes in liturgical texts – the source of the Old Believer schism – lent a heightened note of caution to those who would engage in the revision of sacred texts.[4] Nevertheless, the Orthodox Slavonic scriptures, as texts, continued to be refashioned to meet very specific historical circumstances. By the end of the eighteenth century, the Russian Orthodox Church had adopted as the standardized Slavonic biblical text a translation first published in 1751 during the reign of Empress Elizabeth. The process and the politics surrounding that Elizabeth Slavonic text, a work launched in the reign of Peter the Great, has been well recorded in secondary accounts.[5] Artificial separation of text from context is no more justified for earlier periods of Slavonic textology than for the nineteenth-century translation of the Bible into Russian.

Fortunately, the documentation for the history of the Russian Bible has been well preserved. The primary archival sources for this study are found in St. Petersburg, Russia, and Cambridge, UK. In St. Petersburg, the Russian State Historical Archive (Rossiiskii gosudarstvennyi istoricheskii arkhiv, hereinafter RGIA) houses most of the extant papers of the Russian Bible

[4] On the conflict between Old Believers and Nikonian reformers over the use of language, see Boris A. Uspensky, "The Schism and Cultural Conflict in the Seventeenth Century," in *Seeking God: The Recovery of Religious Identity in Orthodox Russia, Ukraine, and Georgia*, ed. Stephen K. Batalden (DeKalb: Northern Illinois University Press, 1993), 106–43.

[5] On the revisions incorporated into the Elizabeth Bible, see I. A. Chistovich, "Ispravlenie slavianskogo perevoda Biblii pered izdaniem 1751 g.," *Pravoslavnoe obozrenie*, 1860, chast' 1: 499–507; also the publications of I. E. Evseev on the Slavonic Bible, including his *Ocherki po istorii slavianskogo perevoda Biblii* (Petrograd, 1916); Henry R. Cooper's *Slavic Scriptures: The Formation of the Church Slavonic Version of the Holy Bible* (Madison, NC: Fairleigh Dickinson University Press, 2003); and A. A. Alekseev, *Tekstologiia slavianskoi Biblii* (St. Petersburg, 1999).

Society (*fond* 808), as well as the papers of the Holy Synod (*fond* 796) and its lay administrator, the ober-prokuror (chief procurator) (*fond* 797). These Holy Synod papers document, among other matters, the Pavskii affair recounted in Chapter 3 and the internal workings of the Russian Bible Society addressed in Chapter 2. In Cambridge, the archive and the Bible collection of the British and Foreign Bible Society (hereinafter BFBS) remain preserved on permanent loan to the Cambridge University Library. BFBS papers pertaining to Russian biblical translation, including the "Paterson Deposited Papers," the "BFBS Agents Books," and a wealth of other indexed correspondence and deposited papers from its agents in Russia, have been well catalogued and are readily accessible.[6]

There is also an abundance of published work on Russian biblical translation. Most of these studies have tended to focus upon one small period of the translation process, and have generally failed to utilize the archival record of biblical translation in St. Petersburg and Cambridge. Particularly systematic, however, has been the attention to the earliest decades of modern translation during the Bible Society era of the early nineteenth century. The pioneering study by social historian A. N. Pypin, *Religioznyia dvizheniia pri Aleksandre I* (Religious Movements in the Period of Alexander I) (1868), was complemented a century later by the doctoral thesis of Judith Cohen Zacek, "The Russian Bible Society, 1812–1826."[7] The Bible Society era has also left a wealth of published memoir and related documentary literature, ranging from the first-person accounts of the British agents, John Paterson and Ebenezer Henderson, to the correspondence of the most prominent Russian translator, Metropolitan Filaret (Drozdov) of Moscow.[8]

[6] See the published catalogue of the BFBS archive prepared by Kathleen Cann found in *Sowing the Word: The Cultural Impact of the British and Foreign Bible Society, 1804–2004*, ed. Stephen K. Batalden, Kathleen Cann, and John Dean (Sheffield: Phoenix Press, 2004), 344–59. For collections bearing specifically on the Russian Bible, see Stephen K. Batalden, "Revolution and Emigration: The Russian Files of the British and Foreign Bible Society, 1917–1970," in *The Study of Russian History from British Archival Sources*, ed. Janet M. Hartley (London: Mansell Publishing for the University of London School of Slavonic and East European Studies, 1986), 147–71.

[7] Pypin's study was first published under the title, "Rossiiskoe bibleiskoe obshchestvo," in *Vestnik Evropy*, 1868. The third edition, published in 1916 in Petrograd, bears the title, *Religioznye dvizheniia pri Aleksandre I.* The Zacek thesis was defended at Columbia University in 1964.

[8] For Paterson's published memoir, see *The Book for Every Land: Reminiscences of Labour and Adventure in the Work of Bible Circulation in the North of Europe and in Russia*, ed. William Lindsay Alexander (London: John Snow, 1858). For the Henderson memoir, see *Biblical Researches and Travels in Russia* (London: James Nisbet, 1826). Among the voluminous papers of Metropolitan Filaret, see in particular *Sobranie mnenii i otzyvov Filareta, Mitropolita Moskovskogo i Kolomenskogo, po uchebnym i tserkovno-gosudarstvennym voprosam*, vol. IV (Moscow, 1886); also I. N. Korsunskii, *Pamiati Sviatitelia Filareta, Mitropolita Moskovskogo. K istorii redaktsii russkogo perevoda Sviashchennago Pisaniia* (Moscow, 1894).

In addition to the many memoirists and contributors to nineteenth-century Russian religious journals, there have been several historical accounts of the Russian Bible in the century following its 1876 publication. The most widely cited of these is the work of Ilarion Alekseevich Chistovich, whose standard history of the Russian Bible, *Istoriia perevoda Biblii na russkii iazyk* (A History of the Translation of the Bible into Russian), covers the period from the Russian Bible Society to the publication of the completed synodal translation (*sinodal'nyi perevod*) in 1876. Chistovich's study has been augmented by the biographical accounts of Metropolitan Filaret (Drozdov) prepared by Moscow Theological Academy librarian Ivan Nikolaevich Korsunskii. Often overlapping the coverage of Chistovich and Korsunskii has been the work of Nikolai A. Astaf'ev, whose history of the Russian Bible reflected the evangelical interest and involvement of Astaf'ev in the nineteenth-century Society for the Dissemination of Holy Scripture in Russia. Finally, there has been a flurry of late Soviet and post-Soviet writing on the Russian Bible, including the work of Mikhail Iosifovich Rizhskii, *Istoriia perevodov Biblii v Rossii* (The History of Translations of the Bible in Russia). The Rizhskii study appropriately refocused scholarly attention on modern biblical translation after fifty years of Soviet rule, but tended to do so in such a reductionist way as to discredit the authority of the Russian Bible by dismissing it simply as a product of petty scholarly conflicts.[9] More promising has been the recovery of interest in biblical studies in post-Soviet Russia symbolized by the publication of the late Aleksandr Men', *Bibliologicheskii slovar'* (Dictionary of Biblical Studies).[10] Despite the tragic assassination of Aleksandr Men' in 1990, the recovery of Russian scholarly interest in biblical studies has continued to advance.[11]

[9] See I. A. Chistovich, *Istoriia perevoda Biblii na russkii iazyk*, 2nd edn (St. Petersburg: Tip. M. M. Stasiulevicha, 1899). The volume was reissued in a 1997 rotoprint edition in Moscow. Korsunskii's work, *O podvigakh*, was published as vol. II of *Sbornik izdannyi obshchestvom liubitelei dukhovnogo prosveshcheniia, po sluchaiu prazdnovaniia stoletnego iubileia so dnia rozhdeniia (1782–1882) Filareta, Mitropolita Moskovskogo* (Moscow: Tip. Snegireva, 1883), 215–666. Astaf'ev's work cited here was published in the *Zhurnal ministerstva narodnogo prosveshcheniia* in 1888 and then separately in St. Petersburg in 1892. Rizhskii's monograph appeared in Novosibirsk in 1978.

[10] Aleksandr Men', *Bibliologicheskii slovar'*, 3 vols. (Moscow: Fond im. Aleksandra Menia, 2002).

[11] See in particular the multivolume *Pravoslavnaia entsiklopediia* begun in 2000 (Moscow: Tserkovno-nauchnyi tsentr). On Russian biblical studies, see Anatolii Alekseev's *Tekstologiia slavianskoi Biblii* (St. Petersburg, 1999) and his essays on the Russian Bible, including "Pervyi russkii perevod Novogo Zaveta v izdanii 1823 goda," in *Rol' perevodov Biblii v stanovlenii i razvitii slavianskikh literaturnykh iazykov* (Moscow: Institut slavianovedeniia, 2002), 7–38, and "Bibliia: Perevody na russkii iazyk," in *Pravoslavnaia entsiklopediia*, V: 153–61.

While the rich legacy of published and unpublished sources on the Russian Bible illumines the critical issues of authority that biblical translation and publication posed for modern Russian religious culture, the Russian Bible itself, throughout its many editions, has also served to guide this study. Because of the significance of these nineteenth- and twentieth-century biblical imprints, an extended, annotated guide to Russian biblical imprints has been appended. The bibliography of the Russian Bible documents the rare Russian Bible holdings of the British and Foreign Bible Society Library in Cambridge, the Russian National Library in St. Petersburg, the British Library in London, and the Bodleian Library in Oxford.

In assessing the wider significance of the politics of modern Russian biblical translation, this study draws upon an eclectic body of theory that today rests at the center of the sociology of religion and religious history – namely, the widening debate over religion, secularism, and modernity. Forty years ago the paradigm of "secularization" and its link with "modernization" commanded widespread authority in academic circles. Drawing upon Max Weber's association of secularization with the passage from traditional to modern society, the paradigm presented a historical process in which religious institutions were fundamentally being transformed, marginalized from the public sphere. As a consequence, religious belief in the modern age was inevitably privatized in a broadly universal process of modernization and rationalization affecting all societies. This largely Eurocentric and reductionist secularization theory – what Charles Taylor calls the "subtraction story"[12] – remains a part of the sociology of religion, but has been largely superseded by theoretical currents that offer far greater saliency in addressing the politics of the Russian Bible.

Three such currents – what I refer to as post-secularization theory – provide an interpretive framework for this study. The first of these has been the effort of sociologists, beginning already in the 1960s, to reformulate the theory of secularization.[13] Claiming that the original framing of secularization theory was simply wrong, sociologists such as Peter Berger and David Martin effectively sought to separate the modern theory of the differentiation of the secular and religious spheres from the accompanying thesis that the end result would be the inevitable decline and eventual disappearance of

[12] Charles Taylor, *A Secular Age* (Cambridge, MA: Harvard University Press, 2007).

[13] Peter Berger, *The Sacred Canopy* (Garden City, NJ: Doubleday, 1967); David Martin, *On Secularization: Towards a Revised General Theory* (Burlington, VT: Ashgate Publishing, 2005); and José Casanova, *Public Religions in the Modern World* (University of Chicago Press, 1994).

religion. Instead, Berger argued that in confronting modernity and the secular or public sphere, religious institutions develop a range of strategies extending from confrontation to accommodation in a process that he called "cognitive bargaining."[14] In assessing the range of responses arising within Russian religious culture to the process of modern Russian biblical translation, it is this "cognitive bargaining" that allows us to appreciate the "wars" that occurred within Russian culture – for example, over the Pavskii affair or the related controversy over the abortive Russian attempt to canonize the Greek Septuagint Old Testament text, as opposed to the Hebrew Masoretic counterpart. These were highly charged disputes over authority in the arbitration of modern Russian religious culture, and the divisions that ensued reflected the kind of "cognitive bargaining" that Berger and others have addressed in their critique of traditional secularization theory.

What this early critique of secularization theory did was to restore agency to religious institutions as these institutions addressed issues of modernity and the secular. A further refinement of the critique has particular relevance for this study – namely, the work of José Casanova in his *Public Religions in the Modern World.* Casanova's focus is particularly on the privatization argument accompanying traditional secularization theory. He argues that, rather than religion having been removed from the public sphere as a consequence of modernity, such "privatization is not a modern structural trend," but rather one of several historical options.[15] The Russian church of the nineteenth century represented, in this Casanova sense, a "public religion," a state-supported monopoly. This remained the case even when the dissemination of the Russian Bible began to open up alternative "options" of private devotional piety in late Imperial Russia. In his most recent treatment of the "post-secular," Casanova once again recasts the secularization of modern Europe as a "de-confessionalization" that followed distinctly different patterns across a European state system that offered a variety of statist religious institutional forms.[16] In this Casanova sense, the Russian Bible wars constituted a defensive effort of the established Russian Orthodox Church, buttressed by the state, to withstand the pressures of

[14] Peter Berger, "Modernisation and Religion," Fourteenth Geary Lecture (Dublin: Economic and Social Research Council, 1981), 20.

[15] Casanova, *Public Religions in the Modern World*, 215.

[16] José Casanova, "Exploring the Post-Secular: Three Meanings of 'the Secular' and their Possible Transcendence," in *Habermas and Religion*, ed. Craig Calhoun, Eduardo Mendieta, and Jonathan VanAntwerpen (Cambridge: Polity Press, 2013).

de-confessionalization posed by modern scriptural translation. At stake was the arbitration of authority in modern Russian religious culture.

A second major "post-secularization" theoretical current informing this study is the body of writing associated with Charles Taylor's work, *A Secular Age*, and the commentaries generated by this work in the Social Science Research Council's blog, "The Immanent Frame."[17] In his volume, Taylor sets out to answer the question of how there came to be the "shift to secularity" in western Christendom between the years 1500 and 2000. The rise of modernity and secularity for Taylor involved far more than a story of subtraction – the retreat of religion from the public sphere – or the simple absence of God in what he calls a "post-cosmic universe" or "disenchanted world." Rather, Taylor argues that the precondition for the shift to secularity involved the growing disaffection of elites, including those who might be considered traditional religious elites. This is the transition Taylor sees from the "enchanted universe" of medieval Christendom to alternative forms of spiritual and moral aspiration – what he calls "the great disembedding." It was this turn that, for Taylor, marked the movement toward an "exclusive humanism" in which ultimately the "God-reference" becomes but one option in the modern world.

While Taylor's treatment is intended primarily to address the cultural world of Latin Christendom and its post-Reformation descendants, there are important points of reference that link his theoretical framework with deeper threads of Russian history and, indeed, the story of modern Russian biblical translation. Most clearly is this the case in his discussion of the "rise of the disciplinary society," a discussion of the "well-ordered police state" that draws explicitly on Marc Raeff's study of cameralist legal and bureaucratic institutions.[18] What Taylor has in mind by the "rise of the disciplinary society" is the movement within Christendom, particularly in seventeenth-century German Protestantism, toward a more secular view of statecraft that set forth bureaucratic and legal demands for obedience to state authority separate from appeals to divine authority. For Taylor, what is significant about the "rise of the disciplinary society" is that, however much it may have contributed to the abandonment of an enchanted medieval world,

[17] For the SSRC blog, see http://blogs.ssrc.org/tif/, "The Immanent Frame: Secularism, Religion, and the Public Sphere," accessed 26 May 2012. See also the essays relating to the Taylor volume in *Varieties of Secularism in a Secular Age*, ed. Michael Warner, Jonathan VanAntwerpen, and Craig Calhoun (Cambridge, MA: Harvard University Press, 2010). The reference to the "great disembedding" is from Taylor, *A Secular Age*, 146–58.

[18] Marc Raeff, *The Well-Ordered Police State: Social and Institutional Change through Law in the Germanies and Russia, 1600–1800* (New Haven, CT: Yale University Press, 1983). On "the rise of the disciplinary society," see Taylor, *A Secular Age*, 90–145.

the disciplinary society was fundamentally a movement championed by religious elites themselves. In Taylor's view, the elite arbiters of traditional Christian culture in western European religious culture gave critical impetus to the rise of a new secular order.

Similarly, and even more directly relevant to this study, Taylor assesses the role of evangelicalism in the coming of "a secular age." He points out that the wave of evangelicalism of the late eighteenth and nineteenth centuries – what he calls the "age of mobilization" – sought to bring order to "forms of behavior that were idle, irresponsible, undisciplined and wasteful."[19] Citing the impact of evangelicals on the anti-slavery movement, Taylor identifies evangelicalism as an "anti-hierarchical force," a part of the drive for democracy. By appealing to democracy and the marketplace, early nineteenth-century evangelicals became a causal force driving the engine of modernity. In depicting this commercial, market-oriented "mobilization" of evangelicals, Taylor's work captures the dynamism of the British and Foreign Bible Society whose operatives in St. Petersburg effectively launched the Russian Bible Society (Rossiiskoe bibleiskoe obshchestvo) in 1812. It was this Russian Bible Society that embarked upon the most effective commercial publication and dissemination of Holy Scripture then known to Eastern Christendom. Taylor's assertion that the engines of secularity lay within the religious culture itself is an important point of departure for understanding the highly charged politics of modern Russian biblical translation.

Finally, a third current of post-secularization theory informing this study comes, perhaps surprisingly, from the contributions of rational choice theory to the sociology of religion.[20] Rational choice theory (RCT) begins with the simple assumption that human beings seek what they perceive to be rewards, and avoid what they perceive to be costs. As Michael Hechter puts it, "people are rational to the degree that they pursue the most efficient means available to attain their most preferred ends."[21] While I am not persuaded by other aspects of RCT regarding religion, especially as they relate to the pre-modern period, rational choice theorists in addressing "supply-side explanations for religious change" turn out to have provided an unintended explanation for the critical opening moment in the history of the modern Russian Bible. Roger Finke has noted in his essay,

[19] Taylor, *A Secular Age*, 451.

[20] Lawrence A. Young, ed., *Rational Choice Theory and Religion: Summary and Assessment* (New York: Routledge, 1997).

[21] Michael Hechter, "Religion and Rational Choice Theory," in Young, ed., *Rational Choice Theory and Religion*, 148.

"The Consequences of Religious Competition," that the secularization model was based largely "on the premise that religion will decline as modernity erodes the demand for traditional religious beliefs." But he proceeds to demonstrate not only that such a model fails to accommodate increases in religious activity, but also that it neglects the impact of what he calls "changing supply." "What happens," he asks, "when the number and type of available religions change?"[22]

In line with Finke's post-secularization supply-side argument, the first major political crisis over modern Russian biblical translation arose because of the potential for the Russian Bible indirectly to threaten the monopoly position of the Russian Orthodox Church in the arbitration of modern Russian religious culture. As is noted in Chapter 2, the Russian Bible Society during the reign of Alexander I not only launched comprehensive translation of the Bible into modern Russian, it also established with the support of the BFBS a state-of-the-art stereotype printing facility in Petersburg that would publish over the course of a decade nearly one million copies of Holy Scripture in more than two dozen languages spoken within the Russian Empire. With its system of local affiliated chapters and associations, the Russian Bible Society also built the first empire-wide modern publication distribution system. So successful was this publishing enterprise that, by the 1820s, the supply of scripture effectively exceeded the demand of a literate following. As a result, the architects of the Bible Society movement sought to stimulate demand by urging a system of Lancaster schooling and literacy campaigns, and encouraging free distribution of Bibles in prisons as part of what would become a more far-reaching prison reform movement. In short, for a brief, anomalous period in modern Russian history, technology and the marketplace had begun to drive the politics of Russian religious culture – a supply-side explanation for religious change strikingly similar to the RCT argument. As I argue, the demise of the Russian Bible Society and its closure by imperial edict in 1826 reflected, in part, the recognition by the arbiters of Russian religious culture of how dangerous this precedent was for the traditional hierarchy of the Russian Orthodox Church.

22 Roger Finke, "The Consequences of Religious Competition: Supply-Side Explanations for Religious Change," ibid., 47.

CHAPTER I

Origins of the Russian Bible Society

Translation of the Bible into modern Russian, as distinct from the Slavonic translation used in liturgical worship, began in the second decade of the nineteenth century with the 1812 establishment of the "Bible Society in St. Petersburg," as it was initially labeled. Earlier attempts to render scripture in a more common Russian language had been undertaken by individuals operating alone, such as Avramii Firsov who prepared the unpublished Psalter of 1683, or Archbishop Mefodii (Smirnov) who translated the book of Romans in a first published edition of 1794. The more freely rendered Psalms of the eighteenth-century spiritual ode (*dukhovnaia oda*) were also isolated contributions, but were not, strictly speaking, translations. All these attempts to translate scripture constituted efforts by single individuals whose completed texts were consequently limited both in their scope and in the far smaller audience they reached. While the poetic odes of the eighteenth century never were intended to be read as sacred texts, the projects of Avramii Firsov and Archbishop Mefodii failed to secure the kind of religious and political support needed to sustain more comprehensive publication of biblical texts in modern Russian.[1]

In this respect, the work of the Bible Society, from its founding in St. Petersburg in 1812 to its mandated closure in 1826, was unprecedented. With support from the highest religious and political authorities, the Bible Society generated a well-funded societal effort to translate and publish the Bible in Russian. Within little more than a decade, the Bible Society in St. Petersburg had translated and published in Russian complete editions of the New Testament, the Psalter, and the first eight books of the Old

[1] On the translation by Firsov, see the *kandidat* dissertation of E. A. Tselunova, "Psaltir' 1683 goda v perevode Avramiia Firsova" (Moscow State University, 1985); and her article, "Psaltir' 1683 g. 'na prostom slovenskom' iazyke," *Kalbotyra*, 39, no. 2 (1988): 112–18. On Archbishop Mefodii (1761–1815), see *Nachertanie zhizni i deianii arkhiepiskopa Mefodiia* (Moscow, 1823). For the Epistle to the Romans, see "Annotated Bibliography of the Russian Bible" (hereinafter Appendix), no. 1.

Testament (this "Octateuch," though printed in sheets, was forbidden by the authorities to be circulated). The Bible Society Press had also printed, during this period, biblical translations in an additional twenty-six languages spoken throughout the Russian Empire and the Orthodox East. In all, close to one million copies of scripture, in whole or in part, were published by the Russian Bible Society between 1812 and 1826.[2] The society, in turn, built a large supply pipeline for disseminating its published editions of Holy Scripture. Within a decade of its founding, the Bible Society headquartered in St. Petersburg had established 57 branch chapters and 232 local auxiliaries, thereby effectively extending the reach of the Bible Society movement to all corners of the Russian Empire.[3]

At least four sets of circumstances on the eve of the Napoleonic invasion combined to generate this explosive growth of the Russian Bible Society in the second decade of the nineteenth century: (1) the ascetic piety, or new religion of the heart, that found a ready home in the freemasonic societies that were reopened in the reign of Alexander I; (2) Russian Orthodox ecclesiastical support for the new piety; (3) critical imperial patronage afforded by Emperor Alexander and his closest confidants; and (4) the timely intervention of representatives from the British and Foreign Bible Society (BFBS). Taken together these conditions provide the historical context for the politics of biblical translation in the reign of Alexander I.

FREEMASONRY AND ITS RELATIONSHIP TO THE BIBLE SOCIETY MOVEMENT

The first such explanation for the popularity and growth of the Bible Society movement relates to the prominent freemasonic societies that reopened in the reign of Alexander I. Freemasonry in Russia dates from the first half of the eighteenth century when British and later French,

[2] On RBS imprints, see D. A. Khvol'son, "Bibleiskie obshchestva v Rossii," in *Entsiklopedicheskii slovar'* (St. Petersburg: Brokgauz-Efron, 1891), VI: 696–708. Drawing upon RBS statistics provided in its own *Otchety*, Khvol'son notes a total RBS circulation of approximately 700,000 copies by January 1, 1823. This figure also conforms to the January 1823 total of 704,831 cited in *The Twenty-first Annual Report of the BFBS* (London, 1825). Final publication totals for RBS imprints, including numerous Russian NT and Psalter printings in 1823, brought circulation closer to one million volumes.

[3] The 289 figure comes from the BFBS representative in Russia, Robert Pinkerton, in his memoir, *Russia; or, Miscellaneous Observations on the Past and Present State of the Country and its Inhabitants* (London, 1833), 381. See also *Twenty-first Annual Report of the BFBS*, 87–9. These figures correspond to the RBS's own annual reports (*Otchety rossiiskogo bibleiskogo obshchestva*, 1814–23), which list fifty-seven different *otdeleniia* of the RBS, and 232 separate auxiliaries, each tied to a specific *otdelenie* of the society.

German, and Swedish masonic lodges entered Russia.[4] The impact of freemasonry upon the Russian nobility became substantially greater in the last third of the eighteenth century, when Russian freemasonry, partly under the influence of new Rosicrucian lodges, incorporated elements of mysticism into its practice. Freemasonry became for many Russian noblemen in Moscow and Petersburg a new interior "true" Christianity, a religion of the heart supplanting more traditional dogmatic and liturgical formalities of the official Russian church. Responding to appeals from an older generation of freemasons whose formative period dated from the reign of Catherine II, who had ultimately closed the lodges in 1792, Alexander I restored official sanction for masonic lodges in Russia. The masonic lodges that then flourished for two decades prior to their closure again in 1822 combined, as Aleksandr Pypin noted long ago, the more "simple-hearted," civic-minded traditions of eighteenth-century masonic orders with the more rigorous "ascetic pietism" of a new generation.[5] This revitalized Russian freemasonry of the nineteenth century drew its inspiration from an eclectic group of writers, frequently German, who had abandoned the natural religion of the Enlightenment for a new Christian pietism. This pietism was personified in the teachings of Ignaz Aurelius Fessler (1756–1839), a German transplant to Petersburg who, grounded in the Enlightenment and able to explicate clearly the philosophical world of Immanuel Kant, was also very much a product of late eighteenth-century German pietism. For some Russian masons the appeal of the new pietism went well beyond a revived religion of the heart to an open embrace of the occult. Such ascetic pietism combined the new religious awakening with explorations in esoteric or occult literature. Despite occasional synodal proscriptions on publication, the works of Johann Arndt, Karl von Eckartshausen, Johann Heinrich Jung-Stilling, Claude de Saint-Martin, and Russia's own Ivan Lopukhin – all associated with the idea of an interior "true" Christian piety – circulated both in

[4] On freemasonry in the reign of Alexander I, see the classic study of A. N. Pypin in *Obschestvennoe dvizhenie v Rossii pri Aleksandre I* (St. Petersburg, 1870). Pypin's work went through several editions, most recently the 2001 version (St. Petersburg: Gumanitarnoe agentstvo "Akademicheskii proekt") used in this study. See in particular Pypin's discussion on the reopening of the lodges, 314–60. See also Pypin, *Masonstvo v Rossii XVIII i pervaia chetvert' XIX v.* published in 1867 and reissued in Moscow ("Vek," 1997). For a more recent account, see the work of Raffaella Faggionato, *A Rosicrucian Utopia in Eighteenth-Century Russia: The Masonic Circle of N. I. Novikov* (Dordrecht: Springer, 2005), translated from Italian by Michael Boyd and Brunello Lotti; and Faggionato's article, "From a Society of the Enlightened to the Enlightenment of Society: The Russian Bible Society and Rosicrucianism in the Age of Alexander I," *Slavonic and East European Review*, 79, no. 3 (2001), 459–87.

[5] Pypin, *Obshchestvennoe dvizhenie*, 314–15.

published and unpublished popular editions in the first two decades of the nineteenth century.[6]

Until roughly 1813, there appears to have been one common directorate for the masonic lodges, wherein many of the original eighteenth-century lodge names were retained (Sphinx, Phoenix, for example). A major division in the ranks of Russian freemasonry came with the second decade of the nineteenth century, and this division reflected in good measure the wider international patterns present within Russian freemasonry. In the older, eighteenth-century pattern of Russian freemasonry, considerable prominence was given to a system of multiple steps or gradations in status within the lodge, such that men were honored for the high step they had reached by dint of philanthropy or other work and/or expense. By the second decade of the nineteenth century, that pattern of higher degrees or steps was effectively challenged by the so-called Johannine (*Ioannovskie*) lodges wherein only three steps were recognized – *uchenik* (apprentice), *tovarishch* (fellow craftsman), and *master*. By 1818, the popular Russian Johannine masonic order or directorate, Astreia, had eighteen lodges within it; by 1819 that number had swelled to twenty-three.[7] The attraction of the new simplified masonic order was that it tended to level the differences in masonic rank, readily incorporating new professionals – teachers, doctors, merchants, and craftsmen – into ranks previously accessible only to those of higher noble rank. The new system, conforming to the internalized piety of the age, implied that masonic orders were not for the purpose of reinforcing exclusivity. Rather, all freemasons were encouraged to seek their own higher level of internal understanding. Advanced levels of internal understanding were, in principle, accessible to all who passed the first steps within the masonic order.

The simplified Johannine or English system of three masonic steps was introduced into Russia from central Europe in the first decade of the nineteenth century. In Germany, where it was widely adopted, this reformed masonic system with its abolition of higher degrees was associated

[6] On the Russian reception of this interior Christianity, including its influence on St. Tikhon, see Avgustin (Nikitin), "Iogann Arndt i russkaia pravoslavnaia tserkov'," *Vestnik russkogo khristianskogo gumanitarnogo universiteta*, 1999, no. 3: 73–88; also, Natal'ia Dmitrievna Kochetkova, "Pietizm i russkoe masonstvo," in *Eighteenth-Century Russia: Society, Culture, Economy*, ed. R. Bartlett and Gabriela Lehmann-Carli (Berlin: LIT Verlag, 2007), 229–36; Stefan Reichelt, "Retseptsiia tvorchestva Ioanna Arndta v Rossii," in *Eighteenth-Century Russia*, ed. Bartlett and Lehmann-Carli, 221–8; and D. Čyževśkyj, "Arndts 'Wahres Christentum' in Russland," in *Aus zwei Welten: Beiträge zur Geschichte der slavisch-westlichen literarischen Beziehungen* (The Hague: Mouton, 1956), 220–30.

[7] Pypin, *Obshchestvennoe dvizhenie*, 329. See also *Masonstvo v ego proshlom i nastoiashchem*, ed. S. P. Mel'gunov and N. P. Sidorov, 2 vols. ([Moscow]: Izdanie "Zadrugi" i K. F. Nekrasova, [1914–15]).

with the efforts of the dramatist Friedrich-Ludwig Schroeder (1744–1816). Equally prominent, however, was Ignaz Fessler, the distinguished orientalist from whom the "Fessler system," a variant of the Johannine or English masonic order, took its name. The Fessler system extended the three-stage continental system into a modified English system, clearly spelling out stages of advancement ranging from "Apprentice" to "Perfection."

The central message of this esoteric, moral-spiritual literature was that an invisible spiritual world paralleled the material world. God's spirit dwelt within the invisible universe of the spirit, and was accessible to those with interior understanding (what Lopukhin, drawing upon Eckartshausen, called the "interior church").[8] In his "Theory of Pneumatology," Heinrich Jung-Stilling (who met with Emperor Alexander I in Germany in 1814) presented in a more or less systematic way this division between visible and invisible worlds:

> Presentiments, visions, and apparitions of spirits testify of an invisible world of spirits, which is the abode of departed souls, and of good and evil angels and spirits . . . Our bodies belong to the visible, and our spirits to the invisible world; we do not feel with our senses the substance of our spirits, but we feel their influence upon our bodies. Now as we find in our own beings that a rational spirit can act upon matter, and does so without ceasing, how can anyone venture to deny the influence of invisible beings, angels and spirits, on the visible world? . . . Man, by means of his body, is organized for the existing visible world; but his human soul, or its spirit, with its immortal luminous body, is organized for the invisible world.[9]

What followed in Jung-Stilling's account was a lively set of recorded examples of extra-sensory experiences that testified to the human ability, guided by the light of the soul, to apprehend this invisible world. The invisible world, since it also was occupied by evil spirits, lay at the base of witchcraft. The task of the pious Christian was to focus upon the invisible good spiritual world to which Holy Scripture bore witness. The Bible, in this sense, was the initiate's guide to God's supernatural powers – powers

[8] See I. V. Lopukhin, "Nekotorye cherty o vnutrennei tserkvi, o edinom puti istiny i o razlichnykh putiakh zabluzhdeniia i gibeli," written in 1789 and published in multiple editions beginning in St. Petersburg, 1798. For D. H. S. Nicholson's English translation of Lopukhin's work, see *Some Characteristics of the Interior Church* (London: Theosophical Publishing Society, 1912). On Lopukhin, see Ia. Barskov, "Lopukhin, Ivan Vladimirovich (1756–1816)," in *Russkii biograficheskii slovar'* (St. Petersburg, 1914), [x]: 650–82.

[9] Johann Heinrich Jung-Stilling, *Theory of Pneumatology: In Reply to the Question, What Ought to be Believed or Disbelieved concerning Presentiments, Visions, and Apparitions according to Nature, Reason, and Scripture*, trans. Samuel Jackson (New York: Redfield, Clinton Hall, 1851), 5, 22, 81. See also *The Autobiography of Heinrich Stilling*, trans. Samuel Jackson, 3rd edn (London: John Wright & Co., 1844).

that, in contradistinction to the views of eighteenth-century deists, continued to be felt within the troubled revolutionary world of Napoleonic Europe.

For the educated masons who read the popular journal of Aleksandr Labzin, *Messenger of Zion* (*Sionskii vestnik*), there was nothing incompatible between this esoteric religion of inner understanding and Russian Orthodox spirituality. On one level the new "ascetic pietism," with its occasional admixture of occult esoterica, could be readily conflated with the popular piety of saints' miracles, faith healing, and sacramental mysteries. Indeed, examples from popular piety contributed to a heightened sense of universalism within the otherwise elite professional and noble-dominated freemasonic circles. All ranks, from grave diggers (thought to be peculiarly attuned to the invisible world of spirits) to women of high society, had access to this world of "inner" enlightenment.

The universalist nature of this inner understanding no doubt also contributed to the remarkable outpouring of philanthropy that came to be associated with the post-Napoleonic decade. The Society for the Supervision of Prisons, the Committee for the Establishment of Schools for Mutual Instruction (the Lancaster school movement), and the Imperial Philanthropic Society were all launched in Russia after 1815 with support from leading freemasonic circles.[10] Such philanthropy spoke to a spiritual world in which *soslovnost'* (one's social estate or status) appeared less salient. It was, in the end, to such followers of the new piety that the Russian Bible Society would provide a natural vehicle for their moral and spiritual quest. The Bible was, after all, the supreme source of moral and spiritual enlightenment. Equally important, the rank-neutral mission of providing Holy Scripture for all – men and women, capital and province, Russian and non-Russian, imprisoned and free – spoke to the universalism, or ecumenism, embedded in the new piety.

[10] On the role of women in early nineteenth-century Russian philanthropy, see Iuliia Zhukova, "Pervaia zhenskaia organizatsiia v Rossii (Zhenskoe patrioticheskoe obshchestvo v Peterburge v period 1812–1826)," *Vse liudi – sestry: Biulleten' peterburgskogo tsentra gendernykh problem*, 5 (1996): 38–56; also Adele Lindenmeyr, *Poverty Is Not a Vice: Charity, Society and the State in Imperial Russia* (Princeton University Press, 1996); Wendy Rosslyn, *Deeds, Not Words: The Origins of Women's Philanthropy in the Russian Empire*, Birmingham Slavonic Monographs, XXXVII (Birmingham: Centre for Russian and East European Studies, 2007); and Judith Cohen Zacek, "The Prison Reform Movement in the Reign of Alexander I," *Canadian Slavic Studies*, 1 (1967): 196–211; and "The Lancasterian School Movement in Russia," *Slavonic and East European Review*, 45, no. 105 (July 1967): 343–67; and "The Imperial Philanthropic Society in the Reign of Alexander I," *Canadian-American Slavic Studies*, 9 (1975): 427–36.

Although some historians of freemasonry see a major break between eighteenth- and nineteenth-century freemasonries, Russian freemasons who embraced the new religion of the heart continued the commitment of eighteenth-century Russian freemasonry to human dignity, moral self-improvement, and brotherhood – the latter involving civic-minded regard for one's neighbor. It was not necessarily egalitarian in the current sense of advocacy for human rights, but its values included a commitment to philanthropy. Critiquing this universalist religion of the heart, the twentieth-century neo-patristic theologian Georges Florovsky saw the Alexandrine period as "the apogee of Russia's westernism," "the seduction of pietism at the outset of the nineteenth century."[11] But, for others, freemasonry was by no means inimical to Russian Orthodoxy. When Catherine the Great closed the masonic lodges in 1792 in the aftermath of the French Revolution, more than two dozen Russian clergy turned out to be members of these lodges.[12] Addressing this phenomenon within a wider European context, Charles Taylor in his *Secular Age* sees this as part of the "great disembedding," in which religious elites often became self-conscious agents of a new secularism. For Taylor, this was part of a commitment within the religious culture to the values of education and self-discipline in an "age of mobilization."[13]

Raffaella Faggionato has argued recently that there was an essential congruence between the interior religion of the Russian Rosicrucians and the evangelicalism of the Bible Society movement, in effect linking the late eighteenth-century "society of the enlightened" with the Bible Society's commitment "to enlighten society."[14] Florovsky finds a similar linkage of the new religion of the heart and the Bible Society movement, arguing that the "swing toward mystical literature occurred only after the Great Fatherland War in connection with the activities of the Bible Society." His point is that the "renunciation of Reason" and the appeal to Revelation was not so much a historical or written Revelation as an "inner one," a certain interior enlightenment or "illumination," corresponding to the evangelical appeal to "conversion." The intolerance of some Bible Society adherents rested, according to Florovsky, on a rejection of "the pride of

[11] Georges Florovsky, *Puti russkogo bogosloviia*, 2nd edn (Paris: YMCA Press, 1981), 128. Translation here from Robert Nichols, *Ways of Russian Theology*, vol. v of *The Collected Works of Georges Florovsky* (Belmont, MA: Nordland Press, 1979), 162.

[12] Tatiana Bakounine, *Répertoire biographique des francs-maçons russes (XVIIIe et XIXe siècles)*, Collection historique de l'Institut d'Études slaves, XIX (Paris: Institut d'Études Slaves, 1967), 33–4. This is a second edition of the biographical index of Russian freemasons first issued in Brussels in 1940.

[13] Taylor, *A Secular Age*, 423–72. [14] Faggionato, "From a Society of the Enlightenment," 459–87.

Reason," and a belief that the "true" church was not reflected in superficial confessional divisions, but in a religion of the heart that encompassed the whole human race. Indeed, the freemasons' desire for initiation and higher degrees of perfection arose from this fraternal aspiration. Only the "lowest orders of men," in this view, could be satisfied with the pious rituals of historical churches.[15]

Such a conflation of freemasonry with the Bible Society movement runs the risk of turning evangelicals into mystics. It was true that in both Britain and Russia it was not uncommon for some of the leading Bible Society activists to hold membership in masonic lodges. In Russia, this was possible only until 1822 when Alexander I again closed masonic lodges during the Arakcheevshchina, the later repressive years of the emperor's reign named for War Minister Aleksei Arakcheev. The point, however, is not that the Bible Society movement was in some sense the logical operational extension of early nineteenth-century freemasonry, but rather that the interior piety, philanthropy, and commitment to brotherhood of many well-placed masons could be marshaled for the advancement of similar interconfessional, if more narrow, Bible Society goals. Two of the masons who became active supporters of the Bible Society, Ignaz Fessler and Aleksandr Labzin, illustrate particularly well this ability of the Bible Society to draw strength from such freemasonic piety, the interior religion of the heart.

Ignaz Fessler

One of the most renowned of the early Bible Society supporters in Russia was the German Catholic convert to Lutheranism, Ignaz Aurelius Fessler.[16] Fessler not only demonstrated the ability of the Bible Society movement to draw upon the support of freemasons, but he also reflected the interconfessional support for the Russian Bible Society. Fessler was born in Hungary into a modest German family. Guided by his devout mother into a church career, Ignaz Fessler entered a Capuchin monastery at the age of seventeen. Following careful training in classical languages and philosophy, he was tonsured in 1779 as a monk in the Capuchin order. He incurred the wrath of his order, however, for his defense of Joseph II and the Habsburg monarchy

[15] Florovsky, *Ways of Russian Theology*, 172.

[16] On Fessler, see Peter F. Barton, *Ignatius Aurelius Fessler: Vom Barockkatholizismus zur Erweckungsbewegung* (Vienna/Cologne: Hermann Böhlaus, 1969). Fessler's Russian career is addressed in Pypin, *Obshchestvennoe dvizhenie*. See also, S[ergei] Tr[ubetskoi], "Fessler, Ignatii Avrelii," in *Russkii biograficheskii slovar'* (St. Petersburg, 1901), [XXI]: 59–60.

in instituting religious toleration and reform.[17] Cast out of his monastic residence near Vienna, Fessler assumed a position in the 1780s as lecturer and later professor in Lemberg (L'vov), where he published his major texts on Hebrew and oriental languages – works that would ultimately land him a position in St. Petersburg. His Capuchin order continued to challenge what they considered to be Fessler's disloyalty toward the papacy, with the result that Fessler abandoned Lemberg for Silesia in 1791, at the same time converting from Catholicism to Lutheranism.

Throughout the following two turbulent decades of the French Revolution, Fessler remained in Silesia and Berlin, publishing his many translations from classical languages, as well as original literary and historical works, which ultimately included a multivolume history of Hungary.[18] Although his masonic lodge activity began in L'vov in 1783, when he joined the Phoenix lodge and passed through the higher degrees of the Swedish system, Fessler would break with what he considered to be the barrenness of that Swedish system. His authority within masonic circles dated from his activity in Berlin, where he renounced his Catholicism, founded the Society of the Friends of Humanity, and wrote a history of masonic orders that circulated in manuscript. Fessler's published collection of letters on freemasonry went through two printings, establishing the "Fessler system" with its hallmark concern for moral and philosophical awakening. Although Fessler was briefly affiliated with a lodge that sought to propagandize for political freedoms, he abandoned those connections, in the end maintaining the monarchist sympathies that characterized his earlier ties with Joseph II.[19]

Fessler was invited to Russia in 1809 to teach oriental languages and philosophy at St. Petersburg Theological Academy. The invitation came from Alexander I's state secretary, Mikhail Speranskii, in his capacity as a leading figure within the Commission on Ecclesiastical Schools, which had been established in 1808 to reform the church's diocesan seminaries and district schools. An active freemason and one of the most prominent reform figures of the first half of Alexander I's reign, Mikhail Speranskii was a guiding force in the early years of the commission, arranging for Fessler's invitation and settlement in Petersburg.[20] Fessler was an immediate success at the academy. Not only did he bring a fresh voice to the academy's rigid

[17] Pypin, *Obshchestvennoe dvizhenie*, 321–8. [18] S. Tr., "Fessler."

[19] Pypin, *Obshchestvennoe dvizhenie*, 322; and S. Tr., "Fessler."

[20] Pypin, *Obshchestvennoe dvizhenie*, 325. For Speranskii's position on the Commission on Ecclesiastical Schools, see Marc Raeff, *Michael Speransky: Statesman of Imperial Russia, 1772–1839*, 2nd edn (The Hague: Martinus Nijhoff, 1969), 58.

scholastic training, recommending a thorough overhaul of the curriculum (much of which would later be adopted), but he also showed the capacity to lay out clearly and systematically for students and colleagues the world of German Kantian and post-Kantian philosophy. Other foreigners were then teaching in Petersburg, notably the Hebraist Jean de Horn,[21] but many of these foreign instructors remained almost invisible, yielding marginal public impact. Fessler, however, was different. As Pypin notes, he was "a person who was really able to have influence upon the mind."[22]

Such instruction by foreign academics was potentially threatening to longstanding academy professors whose reputation among the Petersburg seminarians seemed to be correspondingly diminished. And Fessler, in turn, suffered the consequences of his popularity. Archbishop Feofilakt (Rusanov), an ambitious church leader and instructor in literature at the St. Petersburg Academy, used the pretext of Fessler's non-Orthodox confessional identity to challenge Fessler's ability to teach Hebrew at the academy, claiming that Fessler was a Socinian who denied the divinity of Jesus Christ. These charges escalated in the minds of others to equate with an accusation of atheism, such that Fessler was driven from the academy at the end of the academic year in 1810. By 1813, Fessler was forced to leave the Russian capital, much like his reform-minded patron, Mikhail Speranskii, but not before he became identified with the newly established Bible Society in St. Petersburg. Fessler would later return to Petersburg as the superintendent of the Lutheran communities in St. Petersburg, where he died in 1839. His time in Russia, however, had included extended periods working in the Moravian community of Sarepta and in Saratov, where he completed his history of Hungary and served as a faithful superintendent for the German Lutheran churches of the Volga region.[23]

It was during Fessler's brief early period in Petersburg, and again when he returned to the capital a decade later, that he became an important point of linkage between freemasonry and the incipient Bible Society movement. Gathering around him figures such as Speranskii, Aleksandr Labzin, and Aleksandr Turgenev, Fessler challenged the rigidity of a freemasonic order tied to higher masonic steps or degrees, and rather encouraged the development of a more vibrant freemasonry marked by religious and moral

[21] On Horn, see his autobiographical account, *Mémoire sur ma carrière civile et militaire en Russie* (London, 1843).

[22] Pypin, *Obshchestvennoe dvizhenie*, 322.

[23] See Gregory L. Freeze, "Die Lutherisch-Evangelische Kirche in Russland, 1800–1914," in *Handbuch der baltischen Geschichte*, ed. Konrad Maier, Karsten Brueggerman, and Ralph Tuchtenhagen, vol. II (Stuttgart: A Hiersemann, forthcoming).

awakening. Out of this new, more vibrant freemasonry would emerge the Astreia masonic order, an order commanding the loyalty of three out of every four lodges in Russia by 1820. Of some thirty masonic lodges active in Russia at the end of the second decade of the nineteenth century, twenty-three fell within the masonic order of Astreia. Among the followers were initiates of the earlier Novikov school, such as Aleksandr Labzin, the editor of *Messenger of Zion* (*Sionskii vestnik*).

Aleksandr Fedorovich Labzin

Perhaps more than any other freemason active in the Russian Bible Society, Aleksandr Labzin became a lightning rod for those who saw in his *Messenger of Zion* dangerous mystical and illuminationist currents – what the historian Pypin has referred to as the less readily controlled "ascetic piety" of the new masonic orders. A graduate of Moscow University and one of the founders of the St. Petersburg lodge of the Dying Sphinx, Labzin was drawn into freemasonry early in his life by the famous German masonic figure in Moscow, I. G. Schwartz, who in the 1780s introduced Rosicrucian masonic lodges into Russia. At the turn of the century, Labzin assumed a position in Petersburg as secretary of the Academy of Arts. From that period and at the reopening of masonic lodges, he became a leader within the Dying Sphinx, an exclusive and separate Rosicrucian lodge. *Sionskii vestnik* began in 1806 and featured translations of western mystical literature, including the works of Jung-Stilling, Boehme, and Eckartshausen, among others. The journal was suspended shortly after its inauguration because of complaints about the mystical tenor of its publication. The broader interest in mystical literature, however, developed with renewed strength after the Napoleonic invasion, with the result that the popularity of Labzin and his journal expanded greatly in the second half of Alexander I's reign. *Sionskii vestnik* was allowed to be published again in 1817 under an imperial order secured by the emperor's minister, Aleksandr Golitsyn. The reestablished *Sionskii vestnik* gave Labzin a renewed platform for his message of moral awakening and religious conversion.[24] From the time of the founding of the

[24] Among the most avid readers of *Sionskii vestnik* were Russian clerics. Bezsonov in "A. F. Labzin," *Russkii arkhiv*, 1868: 833, notes that of the ninety-three copies of *Sionskii vestnik* first issued, thirty-three went to clerical figures. Recipients included leading church hierarchs. Reopened in 1817, Labzin's journal was read by all ranks of the Russian clergy. The St. Petersburg Theological Academy, then under the rectorship of Filaret Drozdov, subscribed to eleven copies (see Tsvetkov, *Dukhovnyi vestnik*, 1862, II: 404, as cited in N. Stelletskii, *Kniaz' A. N. Golitsyn i ego tserkovno-gosudarstvennaia deiatel'nost'* [Kiev: I. I. Gorbunov, 1901], 151).

Bible Society in St. Petersburg, Alexander Labzin was among its greatest supporters, serving as one of the initial members of the managing "Committee" or Russian Bible Society board of directors. He later served also on the society's critical translation subcommittee overseeing publication of Russian biblical texts.

As Florovsky noted in his *Puti russkogo bogosloviia*, Labzin was not a biblicist. For theologians of the Russian church such as Florovsky, Labzin was a negative example of the age of illumination. Florovsky calls Labzin "extremely immodest, willful, and annoying." When in the 1820s, the opponents of Labzin's mysticism used his presence to undermine imperial support for the Russian Bible Society, Archimandrite Fotii, the arch-enemy of the RBS, labeled Labzin "one of the chief instigators of heresy."[25] But, for Labzin, Russian biblical translation was always of secondary, instrumental importance in what he saw as a universalist Christianity. The importance of scriptural texts was not how they informed church tradition. Rather, for Labzin, sacred texts were mute instruments, offering symbols and signs that informed the internal teacher residing in the heart of the believer. Labzin remained, in that sense, one of the clearest examples of the marriage of early nineteenth-century Russian mystical "ascetic piety" and Bible Society evangelicalism.

This marriage of mysticism and evangelicalism constituted an important, if temporary, reorientation of Russian religious culture during the Napoleonic and immediate post-Napoleonic era. It was a univeralist, interconfessional reorientation that many mainstream Russian clerics also embraced.

THE NEW PIETY AND RUSSIAN ORTHODOX CHURCHMEN

Translation of the modern Russian Bible in the second decade of the nineteenth century was not just the cause of the Labzins and the Fesslers, but also of the most distinguished mainstream Russian churchmen of the day, including leading prelates of Petersburg and Moscow, not the least of whom was St. Filaret (Drozdov). First as rector of the St. Petersburg Theological Academy and subsequently as Moscow archbishop and metropolitan, Filaret championed modern Russian biblical translation alongside his more "illuminationist" masonic countrymen. As noted in the account of the membership of Russian churchmen in freemasonic lodges, the "awakening" within official Orthodox circles of the late eighteenth and

[25] On Archimandrite Fotii's antipathy to Labzin, see Florovsky, *Ways of Russian Theology*, 172.

early nineteenth century tended to parallel developments within official Russian society.[26]

For the overwhelming ranks of Russia's parish clergy, however, there was one major institutional barrier that stood in the way of the new awakening. The eighteenth century had bequeathed to the Russian church a system of religious schools badly disorganized and enslaved to scholastic, Latinized curriculum.[27] Peter the Great's spiritual reform of 1721 had provided for a system in which each Russian diocese would have its own seminary, a secondary institution intended for the training of priests' sons. That institution, alongside a haphazard combination of lower parish and district schools, as well as higher theological academies, had grown out of the reforms. But the curriculum of those schools and seminaries constituted a rigid classical training, with instruction largely in Latin, except for studies in Church Slavonic. Aside from the elite few who managed to thrive under such rote classical learning, the resulting seminary instruction was frequently marked by failure. Graduates often owed their survival as much to their payment of bribes as to their scholastic success.[28] Little wonder then that clergy in the capitals of Petersburg and Moscow, with access to Russian-language moral and spiritual literature such as that published by Labzin, welcomed the reorientation of the religious culture.

Not only did the new piety meet a ready reception from more inquiring urban clergy, but the widespread expectation of reform in ecclesiastical education in the early nineteenth century also served initially to weaken potential opposition within the Russian church hierarchy to the sudden outpouring of Russian-language religious publication. The expectations for reform initially arose out of Emperor Alexander I's establishment in 1807 of a Committee for the Improvement of Ecclesiastical Schools (Komitet po usovershenstvovaniiu dukhovnykh uchilishch). That joint lay/clerical committee was composed of some of the most powerful figures in St. Petersburg – Prince Aleksandr Golitsyn (who proposed its formation), Mikhail Speranskii, St. Petersburg Metropolitan Amvrosii (Podobedov), Bishop Feofilakt (Rusanov), Father Ioann Derzhavin (overseer of military chaplains and member of the Holy Synod), and Archpriest Pavel Krinitskii

[26] The term "awakening" follows the usage by Robert L. Nichols in his Ph.D. dissertation, "Metropolitan Filaret of Moscow and the Awakening of Orthodoxy" (University of Washington, 1972).

[27] On Russian theological education, see Nichols, "Metropolitan Filaret"; Gregory L. Freeze, *The Parish Clergy in Nineteenth-Century Russia: Crisis, Reform, Counter-Reform* (Princeton University Press, 1983), 103–25; and B. V. Titlinov, *Dukhovnaia shkola v Rossii v XIX st.*, 2 vols. (Vil'na, 1908–9).

[28] On such abuse in the training of priests, see Ivan S. Belliustin, *Description of the Clergy in Rural Russia: The Memoir of a Nineteenth-Century Parish Priest*, trans. with an introduction by Gregory L. Freeze (Ithaca, NY: Cornell University Press, 1985).

(chief priest of the court chapel, Alexander I's confessor, and member of the Holy Synod). The committee's members, with the exception of Prince Golitsyn, were all products of seminary education. The four members of clerical rank were prominent figures in the Holy Synod.[29]

Within a year of its formation, the committee proposed an ambitious program for the reform of ecclesiastical schools. Along with its suggestions to streamline and clarify the levels of ecclesiastical schooling, the committee proposed the thoroughgoing transformation of the curriculum in schools. Specifically, it sought to eliminate scholasticism and reduce the role of Latin in seminary instruction, while emphasizing subjects such as theology and church history, and adding secular subjects befitting a modern professional clergy.[30] Emperor Alexander approved the program of reform in 1808, providing for experimental testing of the proposal in St. Petersburg. Following its report to the emperor, the committee was transformed into the Commission on Ecclesiastical Schools (Komissiia dukhovnykh uchilishch) and was placed under the authority of the Holy Synod. The renamed commission would remain in St. Petersburg throughout the Bible Society era, continuing to play an important role in clerical affairs until its replacement by synodal Ober-prokuror Protasov in 1838. The commission's final set of ecclesiastical school regulations, less ambitious than the original committee had envisioned, was issued in 1814 for empire-wide reform of ecclesiastical schools.

In approving the 1808 plan for a trial implementation of commission reforms in St. Petersburg, the emperor ended up giving considerable latitude to leading commission members for the introduction of a new religious and secular curriculum, particularly at the Aleksandr Nevskii Seminary and the newly formed Theological Academy in Petersburg. It was within such latitude that Mikhail Speranskii, reformist state secretary and original committee member, arranged for the invitation of Ignaz Fessler to Petersburg. Fessler would join there a number of other western scholars holding prominent positions in both religious and secular educational institutions in Petersburg. The effect of the enlivened ecclesiastical training in Petersburg was quickly felt. Leading Russian churchmen of the first half

[29] For the imperial decree establishing the commission, see *Polnoe sobranie zakonov rossiiskoi imperii* (hereinafter *PSZ*), [November 1807], XXIII: 122. The two parish priests on the panel held significant posts in the capital. On Derzhavin, see "Derzhavin, Ioann Semenovich," in *Russkii biograficheskii slovar'* (St. Petersburg, 1905), [V]: 323. On Krinitskii, see S. G. R., "Krinitskii, Pavel Vasil'evich," in *Russkii biograficheskii slovar'* (St. Petersburg, 1903), [IX]: 444. See also I. A. Chistovich, *Rukovodiashchie deiateli dukhovnogo prosveshcheniia v Rossii v pervoi polovine tekushchego stoletiia* (St. Petersburg, 1894).

[30] Titlinov, *Dukhovnaia shkola v Rossii v XIX st.*, I: 23–7; see also Freeze, *Parish Clergy*, 106.

of the nineteenth century, notably the Hebraic scholar and biblical translator Gerasim Petrovich Pavskii, received in St. Petersburg their formal training from these western orientalists, notably Jean de Horn and Ignaz Fessler. From Moscow came the talented young graduate of the Moscow Theological Academy, Filaret Drozdov, who assumed the post of St. Petersburg Seminary rector in 1809, later being appointed inspector of the Theological Academy by the Commission on Ecclesiastical Schools. What the commission provided was an institutionalized locus for reform that was subordinated to the Holy Synod – an important consideration in later debates over the authority of biblical translation inasmuch as it was the commission that was assigned to review the actual translation of scriptural texts. In short, the Commission on Ecclesiastical Schools contributed not only to the reform of priestly training, but also to the broader reorientation and awakening of religious life in Petersburg. Its broad scope of activity provided an important legitimizing cover for the new piety surfacing in Russian religious culture in the capital.

More than any other clerical leader of the early nineteenth century, Vasilii Mikhailovich Drozdov, 1782–1867 (subsequently Moscow Metropolitan Filaret, canonized St. Filaret in 1994) reflected the energy, as well as the complexity, of the new religious awakening within Russian Orthodoxy. After receiving his early childhood and seminary training at Kolomna and Moscow, the young Drozdov came under the guidance of the eminent Moscow Metropolitan, Platon (Levshin), who supported the seminary graduate as much for his gifted preaching as for his outstanding academic talents. Platon was known within church leadership for his own erudition, a learning that extended well beyond the narrow world of Russian church life to secular scholarly circles in Moscow. Metropolitan Platon's treatises on Orthodox doctrine and theology, written in a clearly accessible Russian language, reflected the prelate's departure from Latin scholasticism and his concern for the training of Russian clergy.[31] Metropolitan Platon's ties to the Moscow freemason Nikolai Novikov also reflected the diversity of worlds encompassed by the esteemed hierarch. Under the wing of Platon, the young Vasilii Drozdov was quickly promoted from Moscow seminary instructor in Greek and Hebrew (1803) to seminary instructor in poetry and preacher at the St. Sergius Holy Trinity Monastery (1806). At Platon's urging, Drozdov took monastic vows in 1808, assuming thereafter the name Filaret.

[31] On Metropolitan Platon (Levshin), see S. Runkevich, "Platon (Levshin)," in *Russkii biograficheskii slovar'* (St. Petersburg, 1905), [XIV]: 49–54; also I. M. Snegirev, *Zhizn' Moskovskogo mitropolita Platona*, 4th edn (Moscow, 1891).

Hierodeacon Filaret's arrival in St. Petersburg in early 1809 was directly tied to the work of the Commission on Ecclesiastical Schools. Despite Metropolitan Platon's desire to retain Filaret's talents in Moscow, the Moscow prelate had recommended Filaret's appointment to the commission. From this appointment, the young Filaret came to be assigned by the commission itself to the post of inspector of the St. Petersburg Theological Academy, a post he initially combined with teaching responsibilities in the philosophy chair at the Aleksandr Nevskii Seminary. Little more than a year later, in 1809, he was appointed rector of the Seminary, retaining his other responsibilities as academy inspector for the commission and instructor in philosophy. In 1811, Filaret was asked by the Commission on Ecclesiastical Schools to undertake a thoroughgoing structural and curricular revision at both the St. Petersburg Seminary and its higher academy. In 1812, he was elevated to rector and professor of theology at the St. Petersburg Theological Academy. Thus, at the relatively young age of thirty, Archimandrite Filaret had assumed administrative authority over (and an important chair within) one of the most prestigious religious training institutions of the Russian Empire – and at a time of profound reorientation and reform of ecclesiastical education in the capital. As academy professor, Filaret also continued to teach courses in biblical hermeneutics, ancient church history, church law, and dogmatic theology. Throughout his early years in Petersburg, Filaret was supported by the venerable St. Petersburg Metropolitan Amvrosii (Podobedov, 1742–1818), who shared Filaret's commitment to religious awakening.

While the intellectual roots of Filaret's own training at the St. Sergius Monastery incorporated elements of the new German piety, Filaret was also very much a product of the church, steadfastly holding to the authority of the church's dogmatic teachings. For Filaret, Holy Scripture did not just open up access to inner spiritual enlightenment. The Bible was a direct witness to God's revelation, a revelation that could only be comprehended through the dogmas and traditions of the church. Thus, when Fessler was accused by Bishop Feofilakt (Rusanov) of being unable to provide appropriate instruction at St. Petersburg Theological Academy because he was not confessionally Orthodox, the newly arrived Filaret could sympathize with some of that concern. Filaret would nevertheless have his own falling out with Feofilakt, whose charges against Fessler may well have been motivated as much by personal jealousy as by confessional purity. For Filaret, the importance of confessional and dogmatic integrity needed to be integrated into the new piety. Operating in the midst of a Napoleonic crisis that seemed to intensify religious concerns, it was critical for Filaret that this religious awakening in Russia be appropriately grounded in Orthodox dogmatic theology – a theology that he sought to link with early Christian patristic traditions.[32]

The curricular reforms introduced under Filaret's tenure as rector of St. Petersburg Theological Academy were subsequently institutionalized throughout the empire after 1814. The structure of the seminary and academy curricula, in particular, came to be overhauled. Under the new system, a six-year program of study was instituted at the seminary. The six years were divided into three two-year divisions (*otdeleniia*) – rhetoric, philosophy, and theology – each of which also incorporated church history and scriptural study. Although some russification of instruction occurred, Latin remained a part of seminary training. At the higher theological academies, which added four additional years on top of seminary training, only the upper two forms of seminary instruction were continued, and they were accompanied by greater academic rigor.[33]

Such structural changes sought to break with traditional rote, classical training. It was during Filaret's rectorship that the Commission on Ecclesiastical Schools, under Mikhail Speranskii's lead, invited Ignaz Fessler and Jean de Horn to the St. Petersburg Academy to teach oriental languages. Although Filaret's own instruction was never directly challenged, the commitment he shared for the reform of ecclesiastical schools, demonstrated by his acceptance of non-Orthodox instructors such as Fessler, led to the formal accusation by Petersburg Academy professor and Riazan Archbishop Feofilakt (Rusanov), who brought charges against the popular Fessler before the Commission on Ecclesiastical Schools.[34] The challenges to innovation at the St. Petersburg Seminary and Academy were not lost on the young rector Filaret, who moved easily within the contested, politicized world of Russian religious culture. Filaret's effectiveness in working with state authorities, even when on rare occasions he crossed swords with them, dated from these early years in Petersburg. Archbishop Feofilakt was less effective in that regard. Following his intervention in the Fessler affair and his subsequent conflicts with Filaret, Feofilakt would be dispatched to distant Georgia in 1817, where he became the first Russian exarch of the Georgian Church then being integrated into synodal administration.

[32] Filaret Drozdov's role in advancing Russian interest in patristic writings is critical for Florovsky, *Puti russkogo bogosloviia*, 228–9.

[33] See Freeze, *Parish Clergy*, 102–25.

[34] K. Zdravomyslov, "Feofilakt," in *Russkii biograficheskii slovar'* (St. Petersburg, 1913), [xxv]: 466–69.

Reflecting on those days of transition at the St. Petersburg seminary and academy, the linguist Gerasim Pavskii (1787–1863) captured the sense of the old and the new. On the one hand, he wrote, all students in a given division had to proceed in lock step through the old mandated, scholastic curriculum, resulting in large boring classes such as the one he had attended with some one hundred other students. On the other hand, it was possible to take up one's own "favorite sciences," which in Pavskii's case were theology and languages. Many seminarians failed to meet the test, but others, such as Pavskii, took their place among Russia's outstanding academicians of the first half of the nineteenth century. In 1814, Pavskii was awarded the first graduate master's degree ever issued by the St. Petersburg Theological Academy, at which point he was appointed to the chair of Hebrew vacated by the expulsion of Ignaz Fessler.[35]

Meanwhile, Archimandrite Filaret proceeded to infuse the capital with his own energy, combining the new piety with well-placed contacts in Russian high society. Frequently accepting offers to give homilies at the home of the synodal ober-prokuror and imperial favorite, Prince Aleksandr N. Golitsyn, Filaret fitted easily into the new religious awakening. Filaret probably never attended a masonic lodge meeting, but he read the translations of Labzin and was sensitive to the new religion of the heart. His alliance with Prince Golitsyn, while it set the pattern for Filaret's future role as a prominent state (as well as church) figure, also reflected the shared commitment of the prelate and the emperor's minister to spiritual renewal. More than any other leading Russian Orthodox churchman, Filaret Drozdov became an unequivocal supporter of the Bible Society movement. In 1822, a decade after his appointment to the rectorship of the St. Petersburg Academy, Filaret, then archbishop of Moscow, would summarize before the local Bible Society in Moscow what he saw among the greatest achievements of a decade of work in ecclesiastical reform and religious awakening:

> Behold! In all our seminaries and schools the word of God is now read; people who formerly never read anything, or read only what was useless and hurtful, now read the word of God. In prisons, where convicts used to teach each other new crimes, they begin to read the word of God, and to recognize their Saviour. Nations that hardly knew the name of Jesus Christ, or were entirely ignorant of him, begin also to read the word of God and to know their Saviour … May God, the Word,

[35] S. V. Protopopov, *Protoierei G. P. Pavskii* (St. Petersburg, 1876). The Protopopov biography incorporates excerpts from Pavskii's unpublished papers. See also Arsenii Vol'skii, "Gerasim Petrovich Pavskii," in *Russkii biograficheskii slovar'* (St. Petersburg, 1902), [XIII]: 103–9.

vouchsafe his powerful blessing upon every benevolent effort to propagate among mankind the word of salvation, to the understanding of the truth according to godliness.[36]

More than sixteen hundred people were in attendance in February 1822 when Filaret delivered his speech to the ninth annual assembly of the Moscow Bible Society. In the months that followed, Filaret and his fellow Orthodox supporters of the new piety and of the Bible Society movement would come under sustained challenge. Nevertheless, in the decade after the Napoleonic invasion of Russia, leading clerical arbiters of Russian Orthodox religious culture, while launching a movement for reform of ecclesiastical schools, embraced much of this new piety.

ALEXANDER I AND IMPERIAL PATRONAGE OF THE BIBLE SOCIETY

In the end, the reorientation of Russian religious culture in the first quarter of the nineteenth century, even with the support of leading Russian Orthodox churchmen, would have been of marginal consequence for Russian biblical translation had it not been for the active support of a more significant arbiter of the Russian religious culture of the day – namely, Emperor Alexander I. It was ultimately the patronage of Alexander I and his close ministerial confidant Aleksandr Nikolaevich Golitsyn that fueled the explosive growth of the Bible Society movement in Russia, and with it the first round of modern Russian biblical translation. The "politics" of modern Russian biblical translation reflected in good measure the critical importance of this imperial patronage.

The story of Alexander I's own religious reorientation has been widely recounted in the historical literature. Drawing upon the first-person memoirs of one of Empress Elizabeth's attendants, Countess Roksandra Edling (née Sturdza), and others, historians have noted that Alexander underwent a profound existential crisis at the time of the Napoleonic invasion of Russia.[37] Amidst the deepening gloom of Petersburg in the fall of 1812,

[36] "Speech of His Eminence, the Archbishop of Moscow, Philaret," in "Letters from the Rev. Dr. Pinkerton," to BFBS, May 2, 1822, in *The Nineteenth Report of the BFBS* (London: BFBS, 1823), 87–8.

[37] See, for example, N. K. Shil'der, *Imperator Aleksandr Pervyi, ego zhizn' i tsarstvovanie*, 4 vols. (St. Petersburg, 1897–8); Pypin, *Religioznye dvizheniia*; and Stelletskii, *Kniaz' A. N. Golitsyn i ego tserkovno-gosudarstvennaia deiatel'nost'*, esp. 65–126. For the memoirs of Roksandra Edling, see *Mémoires de la Comtesse Edling (née Stourdza), Demoiselle d'Honneur de Sa Majesté L'Impératrice Élisabeth Alexéevna* (Moscow: Archives Russes, 1888).

Alexander found comfort in the counsel of his childhood companion and court advisor Aleksandr Golitsyn. Golitsyn, who had been drawn to the new religious and moral literature since his rather unexpected elevation to head of the Holy Synod (the post of ober-prokuror) in 1803, recommended to the emperor that he seek comfort in Holy Scripture. Reading the Bible in French, rather than in the Slavonic, Alexander seemed to find solace in the readings, underlining passages that he found particularly relevant to his own troubles.[38] Roksandra Edling would later write that the emperor's appeal to religious inspiration had a profound and visible effect, altering Alexander's personal manner and convincing him that his own salvation, as well as that of Russia, was only to be found in God's divine providence.[39] By the time Alexander traveled to western Europe in 1814 for the Congress of Vienna, his religious awakening had marked him as a follower of the new piety. During these travels he gave priority to extended meetings with such apostles of the new piety as Jung-Stilling and the Baroness von Krüdener – meetings that were occasionally attended also by Roksandra Edling.[40]

The best-documented manifestation of Emperor Alexander I's newfound piety was, of course, the famous Holy Alliance advanced by the Russian emperor at the close of the Vienna peace negotiations. Believing that he was to be the providential catalyst for a new sacred union that superseded previous diplomatic alliances, Alexander put forth the curious idea that all the nations of Europe should enter into a union that would recognize the omnipotence of the Lord Jesus Christ. Advanced on the Orthodox feast day of the Elevation of the Holy Cross (September 14 on the Eastern Christian calendar), the Fraternal Christian Alliance – the so-called Holy Alliance – was ultimately signed in 1815, only by Russia, Prussia, and Austria. On the face of it, the idea was quite bizarre, and surely did not carry with it the expectation that the Ottoman sultan's representative at Vienna would sign

[38] According to Florovsky, Emperor Alexander read a popular French Bible prepared by Louis-Issac Lemaistre de Sacy (1613–84), who with his fellow inmates translated the Bible into French while imprisoned in the Bastille for Jansenist loyalties (*Ways of Russian Theology*, 189, 360n.). Owing to the opposition to the Port Royalists, the Sacy translation of the NT from the Vulgate could not be issued in France and was first published in 1667 at the press of Daniel Elzevir in Amsterdam. The Sacy Bible was first published in a Port Royal edition in 1701, and was frequently reissued, both as NT and complete biblical text. See T. H. Darlow and H. F. Moule, *Historical Catalogue of the Printed Editions of Holy Scripture in the Library of the BFBS* (London: BFBS, 1911), II: 400–1.

[39] *Mémoires de la Comtesse Edling*, 77–80.

[40] Ibid. The Countess Edling was from the prominent Moldavian Phanariot Sturdza family. She recounts how in childhood she was influenced by the poetry and hymns of Friedrich Gottlieb Klopstock (1724–1803), the German romantic poet, whose classic work, "Messiah," reflected the new piety of the age. Edling's memoir, published posthumously, reflects this impact of German pietism and recounts the author's experiences with the imperial family.

the accord. Behind the idea was the millenarian notion that the Holy Alliance would somehow prepare the way for a thousand-year reign of the Kingdom of God on earth. As the emperor's confidant, Aleksandr Golitsyn, indicated, "It will be apparent to anyone who wishes to see that this act can only be understood as a preparation for that promised Kingdom of the Lord on earth, even as it is in heaven." The Holy Synod ordered that the act of the Holy Alliance be posted in all churches. Mikhail Speranskii called the act "the greatest governmental act since the introduction of the Christian faith." The subsequent establishment of the "dual ministry" of Religious Affairs and Public Enlightenment (see below), a ministry to be headed by Aleksandr Golitsyn, was allegedly part of the effort to instrumentalize this idea domestically by enlisting the service of all to "the One Lord and Savior."[41]

In the decade following the Napoleonic war, such Russian court interest in the new piety found its champion in the emperor's mentor, Prince Aleksandr Nikolaevich Golitsyn. The wide latitude accorded Golitsyn in state affairs reflected his longstanding personal friendship with the emperor. That friendship dated to the reign of Alexander's grandmother, when in the 1780s, the young Golitsyn left his Moscow birthplace for Petersburg to live under the guardianship of Mariia Perekusikhina, an attendant to Catherine II. On weekends and holidays, Aleksandr Nikolaevich would accompany his guardian to the Winter Palace, where he became a boyhood acquaintance of Catherine's grandson, the future Emperor Alexander I. Recognizing the affection of the young grand prince for Aleksandr Golitsyn, Catherine II saw first to Golitsyn's early promotion in the Preobrazhenskii Regiment, and then, in 1794, to his appointment as a court chamberlain (*kamer-iunker*). Golitsyn continued in that capacity until 1798, when he was relieved of his position during the reign of Emperor Paul, and retired to Moscow.

With the assassination of Emperor Paul and the accession to power of Alexander I, Golitsyn was invited back to Petersburg, where he remained among the closest confidants of the young emperor. In 1802 he was named an officer in the State Senate, and in 1803 the emperor prevailed upon Golitsyn to take the combined posts of state secretary and ober-prokuror of the Holy Synod. Although Golitsyn was hesitant to assume the *ober-prokurorstvo* because of his inexperience in religious affairs, he nevertheless held the post for more than a decade. His administration of the Holy Synod

41 The quotes are internally cited in Florovsky, *Ways of Russian Theology*, 166.

was marked by the initial efforts at church reform under the aegis of the Commission on Ecclesiastical Schools.

Prince Golitsyn's growing authority within the Russian court corresponded to his own and the emperor's increasing preoccupation with matters of spiritual and moral enlightenment. In the decade following the Congress of Vienna, this conjunction of court influence and newfound religious zeal was institutionalized in Golitsyn's 1817 appointment as head of the so-called "dual ministry" – the new Ministry of Spiritual Affairs and Public Instruction. This post combined the former Ministry of Public Instruction with oversight of the Holy Synod and of non-Orthodox religious confessions of the empire. The occasion for this reordering of Russian state administration was the resignation in 1816 of the Minister of Public Instruction, Count A. K. Razumovskii. Rather than appoint a new minister, Alexander I left the post vacant, asking Golitsyn to assume temporary responsibility for the ministry of public instruction. Thus, the dual ministry in effect began to function from 1816, although it was not formalized until 1817. While Golitsyn's dual ministry continued to oversee matters in the Holy Synod, Golitsyn abandoned the post of synodal ober-prokuror upon assuming his new ministerial office. Petr S. Meshcherskii, a fellow advocate for the new piety, became ober-prokuror of the Holy Synod in November 1817.[42]

The elevation of Golitsyn to head the new dual ministry marked more than a mere consolidation of bureaucratic offices into one streamlined ministry. It also marked the high point in the personal authority and court access of Prince Golitsyn. The patronage network of Golitsyn favorites came to dominate Russian educational, cultural, and ecclesiastical affairs in the years during and after the Napoleonic wars. That did not mean, however, that Golitsyn was alone among court favorites. Sharing patronage and access, particularly in the domain of military and foreign affairs, was the emperor's ambitious minister of war, Count Aleksei Arakcheev. While Golitsyn's dual ministry is commonly seen as one of participation with

[42] On the dual ministry, see James T. Flynn, *The University Reform of Tsar Alexander I, 1802–1835* (Washington, DC: Catholic University Press of America, 1988), 71–157. Flynn uses the term "Bible Society reform" rather broadly to include the repressive efforts of figures like M. L. Magnitskii to root out evil and instill morality, as in the case of Kazan University. Similarly, the crackdown of Dmitrii Runich directed against alleged atheist professors at St. Petersburg University has often been identified, as in the Flynn volume, with "the Bible Society decade" because of the association of these repressive activities with Golitsyn's dual ministry. While the Golitsyn ministry and the overlapping loyalties of some Golitsyn lieutenants active in the RBS serve as a point of linkage between the new piety and repressive efforts to root out atheism and impose moral order on universities, strictly speaking the RBS had nothing to do with the dual ministry's administration of public instruction.

Arakcheev in the wider politics of reaction characterizing the aftermath of the Congress of Vienna in Russia, in fact Golitsyn and Arakcheev headed rival patronage networks. Arakcheev strongly opposed Golitsyn's support for freemasonic societies and the mystical currents in contemporary Russian religious culture. In his commitment for restored law and order, Arakcheev implemented the dreaded military settlement policy that sought to guarantee a pacified countryside by maintaining Russian regiments in armed camps. Both of these prominent post-Napoleonic court favorites were censorious – Golitsyn in the name of moral and spiritual awakening, Arakcheev in the name of resolute absolutism. The contested world of court patronage in the last decade of the reign of Alexander I thus became, as the publisher Nikolai Grech put it, a showdown between rival Arakcheev and Golitsyn parties.[43]

In this showdown, Prince Golitsyn should not be confused with civil libertarian free-thinking. While he was a patron of the new piety and an advocate of spiritual renewal, his ministry also served as the cover for censorious crackdowns on universities in Kazan and St. Petersburg. His dual ministry both patronized the new piety and enforced confining terms of moral instruction. Each side of the Golitsyn dual ministry had its own directorship. The director for the Department of Education was V. M. Popov. The director for the Department of Religious Affairs was A. I. Turgenev. Both Popov and Turgenev served prominently on the governing RBS committee. Thus, the dual ministry could be, on the one hand, the public guardian of morals and "right" instruction, and, on the other, a cover for freemasonic and philanthropic activity quite unprecedented in Russian history. The same Golitsyn whose lieutenants implemented a crackdown on new secular universities subsequently came to patronize the Imperial Philanthropic Society. The Golitsyn who supported Labzin, Fessler, and Russia's revived freemasonic societies, corresponded with Archimandrite Fotii and the arch-opponents of such free societies. So, while Golitsyn should not be viewed as a civil libertarian, he was a powerful arbiter of religious awakening and the new piety in post-Vienna Russian religious culture who served in that capacity until he was deposed from office in 1824. To challenge the authority of Prince Golitsyn within the domain of Russian religious culture required a frontal assault on the new piety. The Arakcheev

[43] Nikolai Grech writes of "two parties" at court. See the memoirs of Grech, published in many editions beginning in 1838. The edition used here is the Moscow re-publication of 2002, *Zapiski o moei zhizni* (Moscow: I. Zakharov, 2002), 244–7. In her history of the RBS, Zacek, "The Russian Bible Society, 1812–1826," sees the conflict between these rival parties as central to the ultimate downfall of the Bible Society.

party would ultimately rise to that challenge. But, while it lasted, the financial and political patronage of Emperor Alexander I and Prince Golitsyn remained critically instrumental in the success of the Bible Society movement in Russia.[44]

THE COMING OF THE BIBLE SOCIETY

Critics of the Russian Bible Society have been quick to point out that the Bible Society was foreign or alien in its inspiration, and had developed from a model first established in Britain. While such criticism carries an implied anti-foreigner message, its basic claim is undeniable. In the formation of the Bible Society in St. Petersburg in 1812 (it only became the Russian Bible Society in 1814), the British and Foreign Bible Society (BFBS) played a seminal role. Founded in 1804 for the purpose of providing scripture without note or comment to all people in their own language, the BFBS fostered through its agents the development of national Bible Societies and local Bible Society chapters throughout Europe. It became one of the most dynamic and successful global institutions arising out of the evangelical awakening of the late eighteenth and early nineteenth centuries. Appealing to an expanded literate audience, the BFBS launched market-oriented mass publication and circulation of Holy Scripture. To use the language of supply-side rational choice theorists, the BFBS transformed the commercial world of biblical translation, publication, and distribution – and with it modern religious culture.[45]

The roots of the Bible Society movement lay in the great awakening of evangelical circles in late eighteenth-century Britain. The evangelical movement spawned a flurry of institutional development – the Society for Promoting Religious Knowledge among the Poor (established 1750),

[44] For more recent Russian historical writing on Alexander I and religious awakening, see especially Andrei Zorin, *Kormia dvuglavogo orla: Literatura i gosudarstvennaia ideologiia v Rossii v poslednei treti XVIII – pervoi treti XIX veka* (Moscow: Novoe literaturnoe obozrenie, 2001); and Mariia Maiofis, *Vozzvanie k evrope: Literaturnoe obshchestvo "Arzamas" i rossiiskii modernizatsionnyi proekt 1815–1818 godov* (Moscow: Novoe literaturnoe obozrenie, 2008). Alexander Martin, *Romantics, Reformers, Reactionaries: Russian Conservative Thought and Politics in the Reign of Alexander I* (DeKalb: Northern Illinois University Press, 1997) distinguishes between three separate streams of conservative ideology in the reign of Alexander I – what he calls romantic nationalists, reactionary gentry conservatives, and reform-oriented religious conservatives. While the loyalties of individual protagonists changed over the course of Alexander's reign and while individual figures often fit into more than one category, it was the support by Prince Golitsyn of "reform-oriented religious conservatives" that rested behind the rise of the RBS.

[45] See, "Introduction: Two Hundred Years of the British and Foreign Bible Society," in Batalden *et al.*, *Sowing the Word*, 2; also Leslie Howsam, *Cheap Bibles: Nineteenth-Century Publishing and the British and Foreign Bible Society* (Cambridge University Press, 1991).

the Sunday School Society (1785), the London Missionary Society (1795), and the Religious Tract Society (1799), among others.[46] While committed to a message of personal salvation, the movement extended across a wide spectrum of British society, including both low-church Anglicanism and non-conformist breakaway churches that challenged the hegemony of the state Church of England. The movement's message of individual salvation was, at its foundation, egalitarian. This egalitarianism was reflected in the Bible Society's vision that all people should have direct access to Holy Scripture in their own spoken language. Its message was also reflected in the commitment of Bible Society leaders, such as William Wilberforce, to the anti-slavery movement. Thus, the BFBS was an extension of both the philanthropic and missionary spirit of the era of evangelicalism, the "age of mobilization." It was a piety that would readily fuse with the religion of the heart in the religious culture of post-Napoleonic Alexandrine Russia.

The BFBS representative most responsible for the expansion of the Bible Society movement into Russia was John Paterson (Figure 1), a Scot by birth. Representing the BFBS, Paterson traveled widely in Scandinavia and northern Europe assisting in the organization there of local Bible Societies following the BFBS model. Preceding Paterson to Russia was another BFBS correspondent and later employee of the Russian Bible Society, Robert Pinkerton, who served as an English tutor at the Meshcherskii estate in Moscow on the eve of the Napoleonic war. It was the Reverend John Paterson, however, who initiated the Bible Society effort in Petersburg.[47]

During Paterson's 1812 journey to Sweden and Finland (Finland already being a part of the Russian Empire from 1809), he arranged for travel to Petersburg ostensibly to secure official blessing for BFBS publication of the Bible in Finnish. He arrived in Petersburg in August 1812, just as preparations were underway for the empire's defense against invading Napoleonic forces. Paterson's initial round of activities involved meetings with the emperor's trusted confidant and then ober-prokuror of the Holy Synod, Prince Golitsyn, as well as with other highly placed officials at court. Given the reason behind Paterson's travel to Petersburg, the BFBS representative's turn to Golitsyn was particularly appropriate, for among

[46] On the rise of evangelicalism, see Roger H. Martin, *Evangelicals United: Ecumenical Stirrings in Pre-Victorian Britain, 1795–1830* (Metuchen, NJ, and London: Scarecrow Press, 1983).

[47] See Paterson's memoir, *The Book for Every Land* (London: John Snow, 1858); also the unedited manuscript of the memoir in the BFBS Archive, "BSA Deposited Papers" (F3/Paterson: Memoirs and Papers, 1805–50). The BFBS Archive is in Cambridge University Library, Cambridge, UK.

Figure 1. John Paterson, 1776–1855, executive officer of the Russian Bible Society's committee, 1813–26.
Source: C. R. Bawden, *Shamans, Lamas, and Evangelicals: The English Missionaries in Siberia* (London: Routledge and Kegan Paul, 1985).

his other duties Golitsyn oversaw the administration of non-Orthodox confessions in the empire.

The linkage with Golitsyn would prove to be of defining importance for the future development of the Bible Society in Petersburg. Paterson, for his part, harbored wider goals beyond the printing of scripture in Finnish. At his first August 1812 meeting with Golitsyn, Paterson unveiled his ambition to form a local Bible Society for the purpose of "circulation of the Scripture among the members of foreign religions in the empire."[48] He had already secured the support of Interior Minister Viktor Kochubei and other well-placed figures at court for such an effort. By December 1812, he returned to Prince Golitsyn with a formal proposal for the establishment of a Bible Society in Petersburg. Sensitive to the potential concerns of Russian church hierarchs – concerns that he had previously encountered in working with the state churches of Scandinavia – Paterson formulated a limited goal for the proposed Bible Society, of circulating scripture among the members of foreign religions in the empire. Avoided was any mention of

[48] Paterson, *The Book for Every Land*, 164–6.

Slavonic, much less Russian, scripture circulation among Russian Orthodox believers of the empire. Golitsyn took Paterson's proposal directly to Emperor Alexander. On December 6, 1812, the emperor gave his signature to the proposal, formally decreeing the establishment of the St. Petersburg Bible Society.[49]

The first meeting of the St. Petersburg Bible Society was convened in January 1813 at the residence of Aleksandr Golitsyn, who personally invited representative members of the Orthodox clergy to join the assembled group. In all, forty people attended the opening session, including a mix of highly placed clerical and lay officials, Orthodox and non-Orthodox. Its ecumenical, universalist appeal across confessional lines was readily apparent from the outset. The society was organized along lines parallel to that of the BFBS, with a general committee composed of a president, vice-presidents, officers, and directors. Functioning committees or sub-committees, named for "translations," "printing," and "finance," were later formed. Golitsyn was chosen to be president of the society, and the two secretarial positions went to the director of Golitsyn's chancellery, A. I. Turgenev, and to Minister Kochubei's privy counselor, Vasilii Popov – the same Turgenev and Popov who would from 1817 direct the two departments of Golitsyn's dual ministry. Jacob Schmidt of the Moravian Brethren's Sarepta House in Petersburg was elected treasurer, and Paterson became the staff officer or managing director for the society. In the management of the St. Petersburg Society, Paterson was initially aided by Robert Pinkerton, his fellow BFBS correspondent who had a greater command of Russian, although Paterson subsequently developed considerable ability in Russian alongside his command of German and Scandinavian languages. Responding to the encouragement of those Orthodox clergy who were present at the opening session of the society, the committee of the St. Petersburg Bible Society decided at its first meeting in late January 1813 to add the circulation of Slavonic scripture within its charge, arranging for the purchase of such scripture initially from the Holy Synod.[50] The commitment to distribute the Slavonic Bible thus had the immediate effect of expanding the original remit of the Bible Society beyond that of servicing just the non-Russian confessions of the empire.

[49] For Alexander I's decree, see *PSZ* (no. 25287 of December 6, 1812), series 1, vol. XXXII: 471–6. The proposal is referenced in Paterson, *The Book for Every Land*, 185–9; and Zacek, "The Russian Bible Society, 1812–1826," 42. For an English edition of the Golitsyn proposal, see "Most Submissive Memorial to his Imperial Majesty from the Director-General of the Clerical Concerns of Members of Foreign Faiths," in *Religious Intelligence* (London: BFBS, 1813), 193–8. This English edition of Golitsyn's memorial includes Emperor Alexander's formal confirmation, "Thus be it," 193.

[50] Paterson, *The Book for Every Land*, 190–1.

The dispatch with which the St. Petersburg Society moved to print Finnish and German editions and circulate the Synod's Slavonic text reflected both the leadership of Paterson and the sudden popularity of the society that followed Emperor Alexander's public display of support. The financial success of the society was guaranteed by Alexander I's contribution of 25,000 rubles in January 1813, and the promise of subsequent imperial endowment of 10,000 rubles annually thereafter. The emperor's generosity was quickly followed by subscription commitments from the society's governing committee, as well as from its expanding general membership. Membership in and contribution to the St. Petersburg Bible Society became a mark of social distinction as thousands of rubles flowed into the Bible Society's operation.

Despite the setback associated with the illness and death of his wife in early 1813, Paterson managed to secure type, paper, and the ultimate publication of Finnish and German editions of scripture in 1813, even commissioning a special type font for a proposed edition of the Gospel of Matthew in Kalmyk. In addressing the circulation and marketing of scripture, Paterson had to overcome significant problems confronting the publishing industry in Petersburg. As he had expressed already in the first months of his stay in Russia, he was dismayed over the state of the facilities:

> There was not a single type-foundry worthy of the name. Lead was not to be got: what little had been in the country was all used for making musket balls ... Antimony was not to be had, as it could be obtained only from Germany and Holland, which were in possession of the French, who forbade its transport to either Russia or England. Paper in large quantities was not to be obtained from any one manufactory, so that it had to be got from several, and if of the same size, of different qualities and colors. The printing office was tolerable, but still far from being what could be wished. In short, I saw that if my plans were to succeed, I must lay my account with having everything to create.[51]

From the outset, Paterson recognized that the key to the Bible Society's success in the Russian Empire would be its ability to develop a modern printing and circulation capacity beyond the limits of existing facilities. Alongside the problems confronted in preparing Finnish and German editions in the Russian Empire, the additional frustrations encountered in purchasing Slavonic scripture from the Holy Synod in sufficient quantity and at reduced prices contributed to Paterson's ultimate decision to establish the Bible Society's own publishing arm, or press (*tipografiia*). In order to

[51] Ibid., 166.

fashion such an enterprise, Paterson departed his new home of Petersburg for Britain in the spring of 1814. What had begun in late 1812 as a modest proposal to provide scripture to non-Russian citizens of the empire had, within a year, mushroomed into a plan for the modernization of printing technology in Petersburg itself.

Thus, by the time of the founding of the Bible Society in St. Petersburg all the conditions were in place for the explosive growth of the society in Russia. The reorientation of Russian religious culture introduced a new "ascetic piety" from within the reopened freemasonic societies and from "awakened" Russian church officials who sought reform of ecclesiastical schools. That new religion of the heart, broadly interconfessional or ecumenical in spirit, benefited in turn from the powerful patronage of a Russian court and a network of Golitsyn loyalists whose commitment to the new piety preceded the Napoleonic invasion of Russia. Finally, in the depths of that war crisis, the arrival of entrepreneurial representatives of British evangelicalism offered a modern supply-side, market-oriented vision for mass circulation of Holy Scripture in the Russian Empire. The result was the founding of the Bible Society in St. Petersburg, headed by an interconfessional committee of elite government officials, prominent noblemen (many holding membership in local freemasonic lodges), Orthodox and non-Orthodox prelates, and international expatriates working in the Russian capital.

CHAPTER 2

Technology and textology

Slavonic translation and publication projects – notably the Moscow Bible of the seventeenth century and the Elizabeth Bible of the eighteenth century – had successfully utilized imperial and churchly patronage to issue new texts of the Bible in the Slavonic language.[1] But before the nineteenth century there had never been a comprehensive effort to translate the entire Bible into modern Russian. The Russian Bible Society, 1812–26, not only launched such a translation project with imperial support, but did so as part of a social movement and a technological innovation whose impact was felt well beyond the confines of the Russian Orthodox Church and the Holy Synod.

In addition to the obvious precedent of translating Holy Scripture into modern Russian, there were three features of the Russian Bible Society (hereinafter RBS) project that best explain the dynamism of this unique experiment in Russian biblical translation. First, the RBS managed to establish a state-of-the-art commercial publishing enterprise that was as advanced for its time as any comparable press on the European continent. The Russian Bible Society Press fundamentally altered the dynamics of modern Russian religious culture in the decade following the Congress of Vienna. Second, in their appeal to original Greek and Hebrew biblical texts, the society's Russian translators carved out entirely new ground in Orthodox biblical textology, significantly expanding the textual authority that lay behind the Slavonic Bible. Finally, in its commercial and ecumenical appeal to a wider public audience in more than 250 chapters and auxiliary units throughout the Russian Empire, the RBS created a form of social organization – an NGO (non-governmental organization), to use the contemporary terminology – that was completely new to modern Russian religious culture. The market orientation and modern technology of the RBS not only contributed to its dynamism in Alexandrine Russia, but the resulting threat that Russian biblical translation posed to the established

[1] Cooper, *Slavic Scriptures.*

religio-political order ultimately led to the society's forcible closure little more than a decade after its auspicious opening. To capture the dynamism of the RBS, it is necessary to address not only its linguistic and textological innovations, but also the commercial success of its organization and its state-of-the-art stereotype printing operations.

THE INTRODUCTION OF STEREOTYPE PRINTING IN RUSSIA

Although John Paterson had earlier assessed the limitations of print technology in Russia when arriving in Petersburg in 1812, the problems surrounding Bible Society purchase and distribution of Slavonic Bibles one year after its founding became the occasion for introducing a new technology into Petersburg that would revolutionize Russian printing. Having committed itself to circulating the Slavonic Bible alongside scriptural texts in other languages of the Russian Empire, the Bible Society in St. Petersburg confronted the deficiencies in the Holy Synod's publishing practices. In his October 1813 memorandum to the Bible Society's governing committee, Paterson reported that the Holy Synod "could furnish no more than 1,000 copies of the Holy Scripture to the Bible Society, and that a farther supply could not be expected before the expiration of two years." In addition to the problem of supply, Paterson noted the costs resulting from the existing antiquated methods of production:

> The Russian [i.e. Slavonic] Bible printed as at present cannot be furnished for less than 17 rubles and even thereover [i.e. for more]. It is indeed sold by the Holy Synod at the moderate price of about 7 r[ubles], not much more than what the binding costs. But altho' the Synod may be able to sell the Bible at a loss of 10 rubles or more a copy when not more than 1,000 copies, or thereabouts, are disposed of yearly, yet if it should happen that the demand shall require that 10,000 copies shall be furnished yearly, the loss will be greater than perhaps the Synod, even when assisted by the Bible Society, can bear. And at any rate this would absorb those funds which are designed for other pious purposes.[2]

To answer this problem, Paterson proposed for the first time in his October 1813 memorandum the use of stereotype plates in printing the Bible, a technology that had been developed in Britain, but was nowhere to be found in the Russian Empire. Troubled by the lack of such printing technology in Russia, Paterson initially considered the possibility of

[2] Paterson's October 1813 memorandum is located in RGIA (Rossiiskii gosudarstvennyi istoricheskii arkhiv [Russian State Historical Archive]), *fond* 808 ("Rossiiskoe bibleiskoe obshchestvo"), *opis'* 1, *delo* 34 ("Delo ob izdanii knig Sviashchennago Pisaniia na slavianskom iazyke"), *ll.* 34–5.

preparing stereotype plates in Britain for subsequent use in the Russian Empire. This would require that a person "perfectly acquainted with the language [be] sent to correct the proofs."[3] Paterson also proposed reducing the type size for less expensive and wider distribution. He envisioned a small New Testament (12mo) to be sold for as little as two rubles. To accomplish the size reduction, Paterson proposed that the Bible Society committee commission new typefaces, including an improved, more attractive Cyrillic typeface that Bible Society committee member Filaret (Drozdov) would design. While a smaller typeface might solve part of the problem of pricing, Paterson cautioned that such a change would not alone solve the problem of small print runs that resulted from antiquated production methods. The 1813 proposal to prepare type fonts for the Bible Society, whether the German fonts commissioned from the Academy of Sciences or the separate Kalmyk and Slavonic types designed by the type founder Johan Winheber (Iogan Vingeber), anticipated the society's ultimate development of its own autonomous printing capacity.[4] At its November 1813 meeting, the committee of the Bible Society received and approved Paterson's plan.

Concerned over the loss of time and money entailed in Russian printing, Paterson sought a more innovative commercial answer. He wrote to the committee that "the only means to prevent entirely this great loss of time [at the Synodal Press] would be to print ... with Stereotype." Paterson bemoaned the fact that, while it "would certainly be much preferable, and perhaps even cheaper, if there was a possibility of having them [i.e. the plates] prepared here, there is reason to fear that this is at present impossible."[5]

In January 1814, one year after the founding meeting of the St. Petersburg Bible Society and two months after the committee's decision to modernize its publishing capacity, John Paterson set off for England to address the issue of modern printing technology.[6] When he returned nine months later, in early October 1814, he brought a comprehensive recommendation before the society's committee. The recommendation was intended to address the impediments to more efficient publication and distribution of scripture. But, as historians of the RBS have largely overlooked, the Paterson plan also

[3] Ibid., *l.* 35.

[4] RGIA, *fond* 808, *opis'* 1, *delo* 10 ("Uspekhi v knigopechatnykh rabotakh i zaniatiia komiteta dlia pechatnykh del"), *l.* 77. This file contains a later November 1814 Paterson memorandum to the RBS printing subcommittee summarizing the commitment to Winheber. Reference to Filaret's approval in the design and cutting of new letters is clarified in Paterson's later memoranda of February and December 1815 in the same *delo* 10, *ll.* 86 and 117. See also Paterson, *The Book for Every Land*, 233.

[5] RGIA, *fond* 808, *opis'* 1, *delo* 34, *l.* 35.

[6] For a description of his travel to England, see Paterson, *The Book for Every Land*, 215–32.

sought to turn the society into the most ambitious European publishing house of the first quarter of the nineteenth century. Drawing upon printing technology newly developed in Britain and upon the model of "factory community" functioning in his native Scotland, Paterson proposed the "establishment of a stereotype printing office under the direction of the society in St. Petersburg."[7] In the decade that followed, the Bible Society thus added a major mission for itself – publication of the modern Russian Bible – but its unprecedented productivity, its dynamism, was based upon the successful implementation of the new stereotype printing office in Petersburg. The RBS stereotype publishing house became a classic counter-example, rarely evidenced in modern Russia, in which newly imported technology would drive the political culture, rather than the other way around.[8] It is for this reason that the Russian Bible Society Press remains such a source of curiosity for students of early nineteenth-century Russian religious culture.

Stereotype printing was a revolutionary new technology patented in Britain in the first decade of the nineteenth century. The technology, as initially conceived, involved the preparation of gypsum (plaster of Paris) molds onto which was imprinted a form of standing type. An alloy of molten lead was then poured into the mold, forming a single-piece metal stereotype ("stereo" here meaning hard) plate. The contemporary word "stereotype" derives from this early printing term for typecasting hardened plates. The plates, unlike traditional locked-up forms of individual letters, withstood the pressures of the press better. In traditional printing, the extreme pressure applied to a form of type at the moment of printing meant that individual letters at the edge of a form invariably began to fragment or collapse after a few thousand imprints. The ability to use single-piece hardened stereotype plates eliminated the problem of type fragmentation such that there was virtually no limit to the size of a print run. Moreover, the type could be redistributed after the plate was cast and the plates could be stored for future reprintings, thereby saving the amount of type needing to be held in forms. By reducing labor costs in recomposition, stereotype printing also saved money for publishers.

[7] Ibid., 232–3.

[8] One of the arguments of this study is that, for a brief period during the Bible Society era, there was the unusual phenomenon of technology driving culture, rather than the more common Russian pattern of the political culture driving technological development. Elizabeth Eisenstein addresses a comparable moment in the transition from scribal culture to print culture. See her classic work, *The Printing Press as an Agent of Change: Communications and Cultural Transformations in Early Modern Europe*, 2 vols. (Cambridge University Press, 1979); and Sabrina Alcorn Baron, Eric N. Lindquist, and Eleanor F. Shevlin, *Agent of Change: Print Culture Studies after Elizabeth L. Eisenstein* (Amherst: University of Massachusetts Press; Washington, DC: Center for the Book, 2007).

Understandably, the process was kept secret in its infancy, some printers fearing labor unrest from potentially disaffected compositors.[9] While the invention of the process appears to have been spurred in Britain by the desire to eliminate counterfeit paper money, one of the greatest early uses for the process was in the publication of scripture, where the uniformity of text lent itself to stereotype reprintings.

When Paterson returned to Russia in the fall of 1814, he brought before the Bible Society committee a plan for the outfitting of a modern stereotype printing facility in St. Petersburg – the Russian Bible Society Press.[10] For expertise on stereotyping, Paterson had turned to J. Thomas Rutt of Shacklewell, the highly regarded English stereotype printing firm used by the BFBS. Under terms worked out in cooperation with the BFBS, and with RBS funding, Rutt agreed to dispatch his son Thomas with all necessary materials to the RBS in the spring of 1815 to head up a stereotype printing branch office of the parent Rutt firm. Paterson made an initial payment to J. Thomas Rutt of two hundred pounds from the RBS to seal the agreement. Rutt, in turn, promised to return the two hundred pounds if his son Thomas was prevented from coming to Petersburg the next spring. The terms of the agreement with Rutt, as spelled out in Rutt's attestation of August 10, 1814, were that the Rutt stereotype printing operation in Petersburg would remain at least three years, and that the son Thomas Rutt would secure, above the costs of production for the society, a 5 percent profit for his labors. All movable property tied to the junior Rutt's operations in Petersburg would remain under the ownership of the Rutt firm.[11]

The accord Paterson had reached with J. Thomas Rutt concealed the issue of ownership of the new press. Paterson indicated in his October 1814 report to the RBS committee that the younger Rutt, with his assistants and their equipment, would "establish an English printing office here to print for the Bible Society." Paterson's references to "an English printing office," but "for the Bible Society," left some ambiguity over the position of the younger Rutt. Was Thomas Rutt to be an employee of the RBS, or was Paterson creating an independent English printing company as a subsidiary to the Bible Society in

[9] On stereotyping, see T. C. Hansard, *Typographia* (London, 1825); also Herbert G. Smart, *Electrotyping and Stereotyping: A Record of Effort and Achievement Spread over the Generations* (London: St. Bride Printing Library, 1984); and C. S. Partridge, *Stereotyping* (Chicago and New York: Inland Printer, 1909). For the BFBS introduction of stereotype printing, see Howsam, *Cheap Bibles*, 79–81. For the comparable, market-oriented vision of the American Bible Society and its stereotype printing operations, see David Nord, "Free Grace, Free Books, Free Riders: The Economics of Religious Publishing in Early Nineteenth-Century America," in *Religion, Media, and the Marketplace*, ed. L. S. Clark (New Brunswick, NJ: Rutgers University Press, 2007), 37–66; also Peter J. Wosh, *Spreading the Word: The Bible Business in Nineteenth-Century America* (Ithaca, NY: Cornell University Press, 1990).

[10] RGIA, *fond* 808, *opis'* 1, *delo* 10 (October 9, 1814). [11] Ibid., *l.* 59 ob.

Petersburg? From the perspective of the elder Rutt in Shacklewell, the latter was the case. For, in his will, probated in 1821, he referred to joint ownership with his son Thomas of their own Petersburg branch:

My dear son Thomas being already provided for by having a half share of the stereotype printing business at St. Petersburg is not considered as having any share in the arrangements herein specified tho' sharing my sincere affection equally with the rest of my children.[12]

Despite the elder Rutt's understanding of the co-ownership of their own branch operations in Petersburg, all publications issued by the society in Petersburg bore the sole imprint of the "Press of the Russian Bible Society" (Tipografiia rossiiskago bibleiskago obshchestva).

In retrospect, both the Rutt claims and the proprietary interests of the RBS Press were maintained. The unique status of the Bible Society Press assured Rutt's freedom from both secular and spiritual censorship. This freedom was demonstrated in 1815 when Golitsyn's intervention was required to mollify local police inspectors who questioned by what authority or formal certification Rutt and his apprentices were carrying on such a publishing venture.[13] Operating without official registration, the RBS Press shielded an English stereotype printing firm – among the earliest and finest such establishments in the world – that was in effect functioning independently as a subcontractor for profit. In the contemporary idiom, this was a subcontracted "joint venture" (*sovmestnoe predpriiatie*). What was striking about the joint publishing venture was not just that it escaped censorial review, but that it did so on such a substantive matter as that of biblical texts – an area of longstanding controversy dating from the seventeenth-century schism and earlier. For the time being, the political culture and official court protection afforded the Bible Society and its English printer a unique window of opportunity. Paterson had decided to meet the challenges of printing technology in the Russian Empire by creating "an English printing company" in Petersburg as a central subsidiary to the expanding Bible Society operations.

The young Thomas Rutt arrived in May 1815 with an assistant by the name of Astbury. Together the two of them brought all the equipment needed for making stereotype plates, including a new printing press.[14]

[12] British Public Record Office, PROB 11/1645, RC/8387 ("J. Thomas Rutt"), 60.

[13] RGIA, *fond* 808, *opis'* 1, *delo* 49 ("O tipografskom zavedenii pri Obshchestve i o T. Rutte"), *ll.* 15–16. This file contains correspondence from July 1815 in which Golitsyn instructs the police not to intervene with the functioning of the press.

[14] RGIA, *fond* 808, *opis'* 1, *delo* 10, *ll.* 95–6. This large file on the operations of the RBS Press includes Paterson's "Memorial" to the RBS committee on May 24, 1815 announcing the arrival of Rutt.

Figure 2. Applegath and Cowper's cylindrical printing machine imported to St. Petersburg for use in the Russian Bible Society Press, 1817.
Source: *The Penney Magazine* (Society for the Diffusion of Useful Knowledge), 2, no. 112 (1833): 509.

A second press followed by separate ship. Six modern presses were in operation by 1817, with ten presses functioning by 1819, including the latest in machine printing presses – the cylindrical press patented in 1816 by Edward Cowper (1790–1852), which employed curved stereotype plates. At its peak, the Applegath and Cowper machine (see Figure 2), which was driven from an attached horse mill, could print between 500 and 800 sheets on both sides in a single hour.[15] At the July 1815 meeting, Paterson was able to show the RBS committee the first specimen stereotype plate made for use in printing the society's own first Slavonic New Testament (1816). He remarked on the occasion:

It is the first stereotype plate made in Russia and we may indulge the hope that the introduction of this beautiful art into the country under the auspices of the Russian Bible Society will prove a powerful means of spreading the light of Divine truth over the whole extensive Empire.[16]

[15] On RBS printing innovations, see V. V. Zakharov, "Svedeniia o nekotorykh peterburgskikh tipografiiakh (1810–1830-e gody)," *Kniga: Issledovaniia i materialy* 26 (1973): 71–5.

[16] RGIA, *fond* 808, *opis'* 1, *delo* 10, *l.* 100.

Paterson's innovations were not limited to stereotyping. In order to secure proper paper at a reasonable price, he worked with the Ol'khin paper mills in Petersburg, creating out of the Ol'khin establishment the Peterhof Paper Mill (Petergofskaia bumazhnaia fabrika), the first mill to produce "machine-made paper" in Russia. The machine-made paper introduced at the Peterhof Paper Mill on behalf of the RBS preceded by more than forty years the gradual abandonment of hand-made paper milling, which otherwise continued throughout the Russian Empire into the 1880s. Paterson's goal was the production of lightweight, thinner English paper that would reduce the size of the society's bound scripture.[17]

In the binding of Bible Society editions, Paterson encountered numerous delays, and at one point asked the Petersburg binder Richter to work solely for the society. Ultimately, Paterson again turned to Britain for the establishment of a professional bindery within the RBS Press. In 1818, Ebenezer Rennie and five accompanying workmen, including Rennie's immediate assistant and future son-in-law Luke Dixon, arrived in Petersburg with their modern equipment. As in the case of the Rutt stereotyping business, Rennie functioned as a subcontractor for the RBS Press, but with free space in the larger Bible Society complex.[18]

To house such elaborate printing and binding operations, Paterson appealed for more adequate facilities. When Rutt arrived in Petersburg in the spring of 1815, the society rented space for one year in a building facing the Fontanka Canal, near the Old Kalinkin (Staro-Kalinkin) Bridge. Those facilities quickly became inadequate for the expanding operations of the press, and Paterson sought a larger building. In 1816, Alexander I authorized the search for a more permanent structure for the society large enough to house its staff and accommodate the press. Paterson located such a large vacant structure just off Nevskii Prospekt immediately north of the old Jesuit House. The building was conveniently located on the Catherine Canal (Ekaterininskii Canal, now the Griboedov Canal), directly opposite the summer gardens. Because the Mikhailovskii Palace (now the Russian Museum on Art Square) was not yet under construction and the Church of the Resurrection was yet to be built along the canal site of Alexander II's assassination, the building chosen by

[17] Ibid., *l.* 116. On the Ol'khin paper mills, see Z. V. Uchastkina, *A History of Russian Hand Paper-mills and their Watermarks*, ed. and adapted for English by J. S. G. Simmons, Collection of Works and Documents Illustrating the History of Paper, IX, ed. E. J. LaBarre (Hilversum, Holland: Paper Publications Society, 1962), 57. Uchastkina argues that, until the emancipation act made it more difficult and costly to conscript serf labor into hand-made papermilling, there was little financial incentive for the machine production of paper.

[18] RGIA, *fond* 808, *delo* 10, *ll.* 239–45. Announcement of Rennie's arrival, along with his family and five workmen (including Dixon), heard before the RBS committee, June 1818.

Paterson afforded full access to the summer gardens. In June 1816, Alexander I formally gave over to the Bible Society "the stone house in Petersburg on Catherine Canal (No. 47) attached to the Mikhailovskii Gardens ... [with access to the gardens' grounds] from the embankment street to the orangery."[19] The substantial grounds included a separate office behind the house. Ebenezer Henderson, a biblical scholar and BFBS colleague of Paterson who came to assist in Petersburg, described in some detail the accommodation provided to the society by Alexander I:

It is a fine stone building, three stories and a half in height, and stands quite insulated, on the east side of St. Catharine's canal, on a portion of ground attached to the garden of the summer palace ... In the interior of the house are two divisions, to which there is a separate entrance from either end, as well as a staircase in the middle from the court. In the one end is the depot, on the first floor; on the second are the principal apartments, one of which will be appropriated to the meetings of Committee; and the third floor contains the room for the depositary, etc. The other end of the house is at present occupied by the printing office, but will be chiefly appropriated to dwellings for the printers, when the new office is ready. This office stands directly behind the house, and consists of a ground and upper floor, the one for the stereotype foundry, and the other for the printing. There is also a considerable piece of ground allotted to the house, which will make an excellent garden.[20]

Securing a suitable building for the expanded Bible Society operations proved to be the easiest part of the organizational effort. To run the new machines and equipment, Rutt and later the binder Rennie needed an army of workers whom they commonly referred to as "stout lads." At its high point of production, in the years 1819–21, the press and bindery comprised a daily working staff of approximately ninety people.[21] In his effort to locate such workers, Paterson turned to Aleksandr Golitsyn, requesting that able personnel from the Moscow Synodal Press be depositioned temporarily to Petersburg for assistance with the new presses.[22] The appeal to the Synod for

[19] On Alexander's grant of the house, see RGIA, *fond* 808, *opis'* 1, *delo* 70, *l.* 7. On May 31, 1816, Paterson wrote to the BFBS offices in London: "His Imperial Majesty has this week presented the Society with a house for their depot, printing office, etc. It is worth more than 100,000 rubles, in the centre of the town, and situated on one of the canals in the midst of the Imperial Gardens." Paterson further indicated that the Bible Society committee had instructed him to make his own residence in the building. For this letter, see John Paterson and Ebenezer Henderson, *Extracts of Letters from the Rev. John Paterson and the Rev. Ebenezer Henderson during their respective tours through the East Sea Provinces of Russia, Sweden, Denmark, Jutland, Holstein, Swedish Pomerania, etc.* (London: BFBS, 1817).

[20] Internally quoted in Paterson, *The Book for Every Land*, 257–8.

[21] Zakharov, "Svedeniia o nekotorykh peterburgskikh tipografiiakh," 73.

[22] RGIA, *fond* 808, *opis'* 1, *delo* 49, *ll.* 1–2. Copies of correspondence between Aleksandr Golitsyn and Pavel Levashev of the Moscow Synodal Press, July 1815. For the case involving RBS use of Synodal Press corrector Konstantin Nekrasov, see RGIA, *fond* 808, *opis'* 1, *delo* 55.

assistance proved to be of long-term importance in staffing the Bible Society Press. For, as the society added more and more presses, the personnel needs mushroomed. To meet these needs Paterson secured the approval of Prince Golitsyn and the Holy Synod to use the young sons of rural parish clergy as workers at the Bible Society publishing house. Later, Golitsyn also secured approval from the Empress Mariia Fedorovna to employ young lads from the St. Petersburg Foundling Home for the Bible Society Press.[23]

Between 1818 and 1820, more than one hundred young sons of parish clergy and recruits from the Petersburg Foundling Home were at one time employed by the society's press.[24] These "stout lads" were brought into the press between the ages of ten and sixteen, and were theoretically obliged to remain until the age of twenty-one. The assistants were divided into two ranks – learners (*ucheniki*) and apprentices (*podmaster'ia*). Learners received their clothing, linens, room and board, and a modest salary of about twenty rubles per month, with bonuses for good work. Apprentices received a higher salary and their own private room. Dormitory facilities were provided within the society's enlarged compound. Ebenezer Rennie and Thomas Rutt initially also started a formal school for the recruits so that the young workers would have literacy and numeracy training.[25] The young lads followed a rigorous schedule that involved an eleven-hour work day broken twice for lunch and dinner. The work day was shorter on Saturday, Sunday was a day of rest, and the young men were obliged to attend religious services and observe church festivals.[26]

[23] For Golitsyn's appeal to the Foundling Home to provide up to ten persons aged fifteen to eighteen to staff the RBS bindery and press, see copies of the 1818 correspondence in RGIA, *fond* 808, *opis'* 1, *delo* 104, *ll.* 1–7.

[24] RGIA, *fond* 808, *opis'* 1, *delo* 110, *ll.* 364–467. This large file identifies the "tserkovniki" who were employed at the RBS Press, as well as the problems associated with their employment.

[25] For the complete file regarding the establishment of the school house (*vospitatel'nyi dom*) attached to the bindery of the RBS Press, see RGIA, *fond* 808, *opis'* 1, *delo* 104. Golitsyn arranged for the school to take up to twenty learners, aged ten to fifteen, at RBS expense, under the royal authority of Empress Mariia Fedorovna. For Golitsyn's description of the provisions accorded each student and the formal approval of the empress, see his exchange with Grigorii Vallamov, June 29 and August 24, 1818, *delo* 104, *ll.* 2–6. This arrangement for "charity schooling" followed a pattern familiar to Paterson from the remarkable New Lanark cotton mill near Glasgow. There, David Dale and his son-in-law, the notable Robert Owen, developed schooling attached to the cotton mill to serve the advancement of poor children working in the mills. New Lanark was later among the sites visited by Grand Duke Nicholas (later Nicholas I) during his travels to Scotland. On this model of charity schooling at New Lanark, see Ian Donnachie and George Hewitt, *Historic New Lanark: The Dale and Owen Industrial Community since 1785* (Edinburgh University Press, 1993).

[26] For a copy in Paterson's own hand of the "Rules" governing the employment of priests' sons and other assistants at the RBS Press, see RGIA, *fond* 808, *delo* 75, *ll.* 19–21. The rules were approved by the Holy Synod in a decree of September 1817 (*delo* 75, *ll.* 15–18).

From the perspective of the English artisans Rutt and Rennie, the basic problem was that of keeping apprentices long enough so that the skills learned on the job could be retained in their workforce. In the end, the initial requirement that a young man remain at the press for five or more years frequently came to be appealed and the lengthy term was difficult, though not impossible given the wage incentives, to enforce. Responding to Rutt's chronic complaint on this score, the Bible Society secretary and Golitsyn aide, Vasilii Popov, responded in 1818:

You know well that we have kept every one of those working boys who have petitioned for leaving the office as long as we could possibly do; some of them have also in consequence of it abandoned their project of going away; but to retain them always against their will is merely impossible, as they are free people, and cannot be disposed of by anybody.[27]

By 1819, Rutt began to recommend that "no more lads come marching in from outside dioceses," a reflection that the supply at last had met the press's substantial demand.[28]

The effort to replicate a modern English printing establishment in Petersburg succeeded in its major task – that of publishing large quantities of scripture at dramatically lower prices. Paterson also managed to overcome difficulties in dealing with suppliers. Indeed, in the preparation of fonts, including those in the Turkic languages of the Russian Empire, the press was well served by the excellent matrices produced by Petersburg artisan Winheber. But the press was not without problems. Most difficult to resolve were disciplinary problems with the young learners and apprentices. It was not unusual, particularly on pay days, for the priests' sons to become drunk. In cases where chronic drunkenness and other unspecified bad conduct interrupted the work of the press, Rutt decided, as in the 1820 case of three priests' sons Platon Smirnov, Ivan Stroganov, and Aleksei Protopopov, to recommend dismissal with a severance pay adequate to return them to their diocese – in the case of these three, to Moscow.[29] Disciplinary problems recorded by the British artisans ranged from venereal disease, public drunkenness, indecency, and gambling to chronic complaints regarding poor work habits and lack of industriousness. Referring to his apprentice Ivan Smirnov, the bookbinder Ebenezer Rennie reported to the society's secretary Vasilii Popov:

He is not very strong and that he is, now and then, a little indisposed . . . has originated from his having the Venereal Disease last June . . . and I am very sorry to

[27] Popov to Rutt, RGIA, *fond* 808, *opis'* 1, *delo* 49, *l.* 32. [28] Ibid., *ll.* 53–4.

[29] RGIA, *fond* 808, *opis'* 1, *delo* 10, *l.* 345.

say that this disease is very prevalent among my people – which is a disgrace to the Bible Society Establishment.[30]

By 1819, with the pressures of production under control, the stereotyper Rutt increasingly advocated release of the problem cases. In a hefty file containing reports on the *tserkovniki* (largely sons of ordained clergy) working at the press, over fifty worker petitions were forwarded to secretary Popov or the society's president Golitsyn calling for outright release or punitive action. By way of contrast, many petitioners were judged by Rutt or the bookbinder Rennie to have been attentive and sober – often receiving bonuses ("overmoney") or increased wages of up to thirty or forty rubles monthly – and their petitions reflected merely a desire to return early to their diocese for family reasons. But, not infrequently, disciplinary problems yielded a recommendation of formal dismissal without severance pay. Not all of the disciplinary problems involved the *tserkovniki.* According to the society's records, by late 1821 there were thirty-two workers employed at the society's press also from the Imperial Foundling Home.[31]

It was apparent from the reaction of the British artisans Thomas Rutt and Ebenezer Rennie that the society's concern for discipline was as much a concern for the reputation of the Bible Society as it was for the efficiency of their own operation. In perhaps the most celebrated case bearing on the image of the society, Ebenezer Rennie, a strong disciplinarian, noted the problem with one particularly troublesome employee and the need to secure ultimate authority from the society's committee for disciplining workers:

On Sunday being much intoxicated he [the apprentice in question] went into the Kazan Church and being there unruly he was turned out and inquiry was made where he belonged – to the Bible Society House was the answer. In the evening coming near home he met a Gentleman [nobleman] whom he began to abuse. The Gentleman naturally made the above enquiry and received the same answer. What a disgrace to a house from whence issues the Word of God. But this is not all. Last Sunday night he came home much intoxicated, presented himself naked before the women in the building, broke two panes and conducted himself in a shocking manner . . . and finding we have not ourselves full authority to punish and that they may escape, they bid defiance and only laugh at all remonstrances.[32]

Worker reaction to the regimen of strict order and discipline reached a high point of disaffection in a celebrated protest of nineteen assistants under the

[30] RGIA, *fond* 808, *opis'* 1, *delo* 110, *l.* 82 (Rennie–Popov, November 22, 1819).
[31] The most complete record regarding the *tserkovniki* is in RGIA, *fond* 808, *opis'* 1, *delo* 110. On the number of foundling home workers as of December 15, 1821, see the same file, *l.* 281.
[32] Ibid., *l.* 294.

master bookbinder Rennie. The nineteen prepared a formal list of charges against Rennie, and filed a complaint with Prince Golitsyn in late 1818. In addition to vague accusations that Rennie was tyrannizing the assistants and reporting them unfairly to supervisors, they charged that he was deducting from their salary when they were sick, and that aside from clothes and food, they had yet to see their monthly salary. In March 1819, the RBS committee reviewed the charges, noting that each grievant had been interviewed. The final official determination on the matter was that a core group of five lads had pressured others to sign the petition, that the charges were completely unfounded, and that the five perpetrators were routine troublemakers.[33]

Despite such occasional disciplinary problems, the best evidence for the success of the society's mobilization to publish scripture – all of it outside normal publishing, censorship, and bureaucratic channels – were the impressive results. Between 750,000 and 1,000,000 copies of scripture were published in Petersburg at the RBS Press in the decade following 1815. Most of this publishing, including editions in twenty-six languages, occurred between 1816 and 1823. At the height of production, the RBS was printing, binding, and circulating more than 100,000 copies of scripture a year – figures that are in stark contrast with previous book circulation figures in the Russian Empire. Based upon careful examination of circulation figures and readership in the eighteenth century, historians of Russian printing and readership patterns have concluded that only in the case of the most popular calendars and special elementary primers did circulation runs exceed 10,000 copies before the nineteenth century – and then only because of additional reprintings, owing to the absence of stereotype technology.[34] By comparison, the RBS Russian Psalter went through multiple stereotype reprintings between 1822 and 1824 in a total circulation run exceeding 100,000 copies. More than twice as many copies of scripture in the Russian language were published by the RBS Press in just the two-year period, 1821–3, than the Holy Synod had circulated (in Slavonic) from its own presses for the whole period from Peter the Great to 1820.

[33] RGIA, *fond* 808, *opis'* 1, *delo* 52, *ll.* 12–22.

[34] Gary Marker, *Publishing, Printing, and the Origins of Intellectual Life in Russia, 1700–1800* (Princeton University Press, 1985). Max Okenfuss notes similarly modest print runs for Slavic primers in his *Discovery of Childhood: The Evidence of the Slavic Primer* (Newtonville, MA: Oriental Research Partners, 1980). Marker documents unusual cases of print runs as high as 12,000 copies, and one edition up to 36,000 in the reign of Peter the Great, the latter almost surely issued in multiple printings because of the type damage to page corners prior to stereotyping. For these high print runs, which still do not compare with Bible Society Press figures, see Marker, "Primers and Literacy in Muscovy," *Russian Review*, 48, no. 1 (1989): 1–19.

What the RBS Press had done in one decade was to revolutionize the publication and circulation of the printed word. Its stereotype printing operation was the finest on the European continent, and was only superseded by publishing enterprises in Britain. Part of the explanation for this revolution was to be found in the ability of Paterson and his publishing operation to function outside the accepted local conventions (including censorship) governing the world of Russian book publication. The RBS was printing and circulating in stereotyped editions copies of Holy Scripture that had hitherto been the sole responsibility and right of the Holy Synod. Mainly, however, the dramatic circulation figures reflected the successful application in the Russian Empire of the same organizational strategies used in Britain by the BFBS.

AFFILIATED BRANCH CHAPTERS AND AUXILIARIES OF THE BIBLE SOCIETY: MARKETING THE WORD

What this meant in practice was the development of affiliated branch chapters of the Bible Society outside of Petersburg – chapters that served as allies in marketing the biblical texts produced in Petersburg. By 1814, the Bible Society in St. Petersburg had renamed itself the Russian Bible Society. Under its new name it proceeded to establish affiliated chapters throughout the Russian Empire, capitalizing in this effort on the imperial patronage it had secured from Emperor Alexander I. Leadership of local chapters was often shouldered by the diocesan bishop, a provincial governor-general, or a local nobleman. Like the counterpart Bible Society chapters in Britain, membership was restricted to males. Unlike the English model, however, Russian Bible Society chapters did not maintain separate women's auxiliaries, although women did attend the large annual meetings of local Bible Society branch chapters. Bible Society chapters became so popular that invitation to membership was often considered a social necessity. To foster the development of these local chapters, occasional visits were scheduled to keep them in close communication with the Petersburg RBS committee. Robert Pinkerton, a BFBS colleague of Paterson in Petersburg, traveled south to Kishinev in the spring of 1816, returning through central Europe. At each stop in the Russian Empire, Pinkerton met with members of local Bible Society chapters (Tver, Moscow, Tula, Voronezh, Novo-Cherkassk, Taganrog, Feodosiia, Odessa, and Kishinev), sending back inspirational letters to be read aloud at the monthly meetings of the Bible Society's governing committee in Petersburg.[35]

[35] RGIA, *fond* 808, *opis'* 1, *delo* 65 ("O pervom i vtorom puteshestviiakh Pinkertona [On the first and second journeys of Pinkerton]"), *ll.* 36–96. Copies of the correspondence from Pinkerton's second journey follow in later sections of the same file.

With rising membership rolls, there also came increasing donations to the Bible Society. Total contributions to the society over the ten-year period of its greatest activity reached 3,500,000 rubles, *not* counting sales receipts and annual BFBS contributions. Income from the sale of scripture by the various local chapters and auxiliaries amounted to another 1,924,362 rubles. Thus, the total RBS income between 1812 and 1826 approximated 5.5 million rubles, not counting the estimated 2 million rubles' worth of back-stock in volumes left unsold in the Bible Society depot at the time of its closure in 1826.[36] This substantial Bible Society income was all the more striking when compared to the total state revenue generated by the Russian Empire at the beginning of the century, estimated to have been little more than 100 million rubles annually.[37] Even those who would later turn against the society felt obliged in the period of its greatest growth to support its efforts and purchase its publications of scripture. M. A. Magnitskii, the reactionary educational curator of the Kazan district who has occasionally been identified with the Bible Society, even though he later aligned himself against it in the 1820s, bought ten thousand rubles' worth of scripture from the society, insisting that all students of Kazan University read these works.[38]

Not only did the affiliated chapters serve as a strong source of financial contribution to the society, but they also became vital instruments for circulation of the Bible Society's scripture. Stretching from the Baltic provinces to the remote parts of Siberia, these local chapters were drawn into a wider plan for expanded circulation. Routinely invoking their want of the scripture, Paterson cited the growth of local chapters as the rationale for increased publication. As inventory began to outstrip demand, especially in the case of the more remote chapters such as the one in Irkutsk, Paterson tried to stimulate a call for scripture by supporting gratis distribution in prisons and, more generally, by encouraging improved education and literacy among the population at large. Thus, if demand should ever slacken, the Bible Society was prepared indirectly to forge new sources or markets through literacy campaigns and prison distribution. As noted

[36] The membership donation figure is from D. A. Khvol'son, "Bibleiskie obshchestva v Rossii," in *Entsiklopedicheskii slovar'* (St. Petersburg, 1891), VI: 701, who provides a total figure based on adding contributions cited each year in the RBS annual *Otchet*, and covering receipts through 1822 (the last *Otchet* was published in 1823, for 1822). Sales figures are reported by the RBS depot manager, H. M. Andresen, as of the closure of RBS operations. See, Andresen to BFBS, St. Petersburg, June 18/30, 1827, BFBS Foreign Correspondence Inwards, 1827, no. 3, 28.

[37] For a reliable 1801 estimate of 107 million rubles for total Russian state revenue, see "Dokhody (gosurdarstvennye)," in *Entsiklopedicheskii slovar'* (St. Petersburg, 1893), XI: 85. Total state revenue in 1851 was still less than 225 million rubles annually.

[38] Khvol'son, "Bibleiskie obshchestva," 701.

above, at the time of the final RBS closure in 1826, the number of affiliated chapters or sections had reached two hundred and eighty-nine (289) – the most widespread network of voluntary organizations of this type known to the Russian Empire in the first half of the nineteenth century.[39]

TRANSLATING THE BIBLE

RBS commercial successes – namely, its technologically advanced printing establishment and unprecedented system of affiliated local chapters – remained in the eyes of John Paterson and the governing Petersburg committee only the means toward a higher goal: the provision of scripture for the whole of the Russian Empire. That goal was dramatically advanced in 1816, when little more than three years after its founding and two years after the Petersburg Society had renamed itself the *Russian* Bible Society (Rossiiskoe bibleiskoe obshchestvo), Alexander I issued a decree that transformed the role of the Bible Society movement throughout the Russian Empire. Alexander's decree of February 23, 1816 called for the Bible Society to undertake translation and publication of the Bible into modern Russian. RBS technological and organizational innovation, under cover of imperial patronage and freedom from censorship, had given the society an unprecedented production and distribution capacity, but the emperor's decision to entrust to the Bible Society the task of translating and publishing the Bible in Russian thrust the society into a situation in which fundamental issues of authority in modern Russian religious culture had no clear precedent. Who had the authority to translate scripture into the common language? What textual bases were to be authoritative in modern biblical translation? Who had the authority to distribute sacred texts? These questions would command the attention of the Russian Bible Society for the decade from the emperor's 1816 decree until its closure, again by imperial decree, in 1826.

While the combination of the Bible Society's remarkable publishing capacity and the imperial decree permitting translation and publication of the Bible in Russian secured for the Bible Society the authority it needed to proceed, within a decade a bitter division within Russian religious culture ultimately led to closure of the society. Nevertheless, in the intervening decade, the Bible Society issued the *textus primus* of the Russian NT and

[39] Ibid., 703. See also the *Entsiklopedicheskii slovar'* entry, "Lankasterskiia Shkoly." The involvement of British expatriates in the prison reform movement and in the development of the Lancaster school movement is documented in Judith Cohen Zacek: "The Prison Reform Movement in the Reign of Alexander I," *Canadian Slavic Studies*, 1 (1967): 196–211, and "The Lancasterian School Movement in Russia," *Slavonic and East European Review*, 45, no. 105 (July 1967): 343–67.

Psalter, as well as an unbound edition of the first eight books of the OT, or Hebrew Bible (the Octateuch), and it did so at a level of circulation far greater than that of any prior publication project in the history of Eurasia.

The emperor's decree of 1816 fundamentally altered the purpose of the Bible Society, which had been founded in 1812 to provide scripture for non-Russian peoples and confessions of the empire (with the further purpose later added to provide Slavonic scripture for more general distribution). The significance of the new imperial charge – one openly sought by the Bible Society committee and Prince Golitsyn – was clear from the wording of the emperor's mandate:

His Imperial Majesty, by the inner divine worth of the Holy Scripture and from his own experience, being persuaded how useful is its reading for all people for instilling the integrity and righteousness that constitute the true good of people and nations; and turning attention to the activities of the Russian Bible Society, regrets to observe that many Russians by reason of their upbringing have been cut off from the Old Slavonic dialect and are able only with extreme difficulty to use the Holy Books published for them only in this dialect, so that some resort in such a case to the help of foreign translations, and the greater number are not able to have such. But, according to the Report [*Otchet*] of the Russian Bible Society for 1814 it is known to His Imperial Majesty that in similar circumstances the Greek Patriarchal Church by decree approved for the nation the reading of the New Testament of Holy Scripture in modern Greek together with the ancient Greek. So, therefore, His Imperial Majesty finds in accordance with these circumstances that also for the Russian nation there be undertaken, under the review of clerical figures [*dukhovnykh lits*], a translation of the New Testament from Old Slavonic into modern Russian to be published with the Old Slavonic text by the Russian Bible Society for those desiring it, just as was already published with the permission of the Holy Synod the Epistle to the Romans in Slavonic and Russian parallel text [the Mefodii Smirnov translation]. It goes without saying that church [i.e. liturgical] use of the Slavonic text must remain inviolable.[40]

The society's president, Aleksandr Golitsyn, no doubt provided much of the wording for the emperor's February decree. The subject of Russian biblical translation was not entirely new to the Bible Society's committee. At the time of the Bible Society's founding, Golitsyn had been cautious about the potential political ramifications of extending the reach of the society beyond non-Russians of the Russian Empire. But the early caution of the years 1812–13 was abandoned by 1816 after Russian Orthodox prelates

40 Alexander I's decree is from the preface, "Vozglashenie k khristoliubivym chitateliam," introducing the RBS Slavonic/Russian NT diglot – *Gospoda Nashego Iisusa Khrista Novyi Zavet, na slavianskom i russkom iazyke* (St. Petersburg: RBS, 1821 [1822]), v.

became so prominently involved in the Bible Society's own governing committee.

In the end, the decision to endorse Russian biblical translation conformed to the emperor's own views. His reference to those who were forced to read Holy Scripture in foreign languages carried with it a personal ring inasmuch as Alexander's own introduction to scripture involved the use of a French translation. In the immediate aftermath of the Napoleonic wars, Alexander I was increasingly motivated by personal religious piety. The interconfessional character of the Bible Society coincided well with his own goal of an empire united by broad Christian principles – a goal that was extended to all of Europe in his 1815 Holy Alliance. His concerns were not limited to the preservation of Orthodox traditions and the authority of the Holy Synod, but extended rather to the more ambitious idea of "religious awakening" for his increasingly complex multinational empire. The decision to authorize the Bible Society to publish such a text, while it was accompanied by reference to oversight by "clerical figures," constituted a significant circumvention of Holy Synod authority at a moment when the new religion of the heart held its greatest appeal for both the emperor and official Russian society. In commissioning Russian biblical translation and publication through the auspices of the Russian Bible Society, Alexander I was exercising his authority as the ultimate arbiter of Russian religious culture in an extra-bureaucratic manner that assured the most rapid advance of the project.

Of particular interest within the emperor's decree was the reference to the Ecumenical Patriarch's encouragement of modern Greek translation of the Bible. The appeal to patriarchal support for a modern Greek text offered Alexander I the opportunity to demonstrate that modern translation was canonically in conformity with the direction taken by those leaders traditionally most respected in the wider Orthodox East. Having heard through BFBS representatives Pinkerton and Paterson of Patriarch Kyrillos VI's support for the 1810 modern Greek NT diglot (with the *koinē* Greek text), Golitsyn arranged for Alexander to link his own support for modern Russian translation to the wider authority of Eastern Christendom represented by the Ecumenical Patriarchate. This effort to extend legitimacy to the project under cover of patriarchal authority mirrored a similar appeal to the Orthodox East made by Patriarch Nikon a century and a half earlier when defending his reform of church service books.[41]

[41] Ecumenical Patriarch Kyrillos VI issued his imprimatur on December 13, 1814, granting support for reading and distribution of the 1810 BFBS NT diglot edition "in Greek and Romaic [i.e. modern Greek]." The Patriarch's sanction extended only to that diglot edition, not to general publication of

To offset those who might think he was imposing his will upon matters that were more traditionally under the purview of the church, Alexander proclaimed that the translation was to be subject to ecclesiastical review, and he reaffirmed the authority of the Slavonic text in Orthodox liturgical worship. From the emperor's perspective what was at stake in the proposed translation project was not so much a challenge to the church hierarchy and religious tradition as a pious appeal for the Christianization of the empire. In terms of its implementation, the most important clause of the decree, aside from the grant of publishing authority to the Russian Bible Society, was the provision for clerical oversight of the project. Alexander decreed that the translation be "under the review of clerical figures," but he did so without calling for synodal review or oversight. His wording anticipated action already prepared by Prince Golitsyn in his capacity as ober-prokuror of the Holy Synod. Five days after Alexander's decree launching the modern Russian translation, the Holy Synod responded by delegating translation oversight to its Commission on Ecclesiastical Schools. That commission would "select from the local [St. Petersburg] Academy those with ability for this important work." A select committee chosen from within the Commission on Ecclesiastical Schools, sometimes referred to as the "special committee" (*osobyi komitet*), was charged with the responsibility for revising the translated texts submitted to it. When the translation was completed and reviewed by the commission's select committee, it would be turned over to the Russian Bible Society for ongoing examination by the society's clerical members serving as a "translations subcommittee." Translations approved by the Bible Society's translations subcommittee would then be published.[42]

The decision to assign primary spiritual oversight on the translation project to the Commission on Ecclesiastical Schools (Komissiia dukhovnykh uchilishch), while it reflected the need for expertise from the theological academies, also had the effect of positioning Archbishop Filaret (Drozdov, 1782–1867; subsequently Metropolitan of Moscow, canonized St. Filaret in 1994 – see Figure 3), the Petersburg Theological Academy rector, at the center of the translation effort.

the Bible in modern Greek. On this issue, see Richard Clogg, "Enlightening 'A Poor, Oppressed, and Darkened Nation': Some Early Activities of the BFBS in the Levant," in *Sowing the Word*, ed. Batalden *et al.*, 237–9. The Clogg article includes a lithographic reproduction of this patriarchal imprimatur, 238, drawn from the *Eleventh Report of the BFBS* (London: BFBS, 1915), 164. See also Geōrgios Metallinos, *To zētēma tēs metaphraseōs tēs Agias Graphēs eis tēn neoellēnikēn kata ton 19 aiōna* (Athens, 1977). See also, Nomikos Michael Vaporis, *Translating the Scriptures into Modern Greek* (Brookline, MA: Holy Cross Orthodox Press, 1994).

[42] RGIA, *fond* 808, *opis'* 1, *delo* 64 ("O perevode i izdanii knig Sviashchennago Pisaniia na rossiiskom iazyke so slavenskim tekstom"), *ll.* 1–2 (copy of the synodal resolution, February 28, 1816).

Figure 3. St. Filaret (Drozdov), Metropolitan of Moscow, 1782–1867.
Source: See http://fr.wikipedia.org/wiki/Fichier:Filaret.jpg, "Graviury ispolneny na medi professorom-akademikom Ivanom Pozhalostinym i khudozhnikom F. A. Merkinym," in *Russkie deiateli v portretakh, izdannykh redaktsiei istoricheskogo zhurnala "Russkaia starina"* (St. Petersburg: Tip. V. S. Balasheva, 1890).

Established by Alexander I in 1807 to oversee and reform the training of the sons of clergy in ecclesiastical schools, the commission had from its outset been concerned with liberating clerical training from its deadly Latin scholasticism. Serving both on the commission and as an active member of the Bible Society's governing committee, the young Filaret was vaulted into a critical position of leadership in both the commission's and the Bible Society's committees overseeing the translation and publication of the modern Russian NT.[43]

Aleksandr Golitsyn as president of the Bible Society and lay head of the Holy Synod knew that in the figure of Filaret Drozdov he had located the person most appropriate by predilection, as well as position, to advance the modern Russian translation. Committed to overcoming the scholastic educational

[43] B. V. Titlinov, *Dukhovnaia shkola v Rossii v XIX st.*, vol. I (Vil'na, 1908). On the commission's plans for reform of ecclesiastical schools, see Freeze, *Parish Clergy*, 103–41. On Filaret's role in biblical translation, see Chistovich, *Istoriia perevoda Biblii*; and Ivan Korsunskii, "O podvigakh Filareta, mitropolita moskovskogo, v dele perevoda Biblii na russkii iazyk," in *Sbornik izdannyi obshchestvom liubitelei dukhovnogo prosveshcheniia, po sluchaiu prazdnovaniia stoletnego iubileia so dnia rozhdeniia* (1782–1882) *Filareta, Mitropolita Moskovskogo* (Moscow: Snegirev Press, 1883), II: 215–666.

traditions of Russian seminary studies, Filaret spearheaded the efforts of the Commission on Ecclesiastical Schools to focus upon the professional religious training of priests' sons. He recognized that one of the barriers to that religious training had been the inordinate emphasis upon Latin and strictly scholastic grammatical studies. A consistent theme drawing the distinguished prelate Filaret to support modern Russian biblical translation was that of the need for parish clergy to be able more readily to understand and explicate the biblical text as an integral function of seminary training. Moreover, as an academy administrator and able Greek scholar in his own right, he was well prepared to address the textual issues and personalities bearing on the translation process.

Filaret was also more than a nominal member of the Bible Society's standing committee. As noted in connection with the society's preparation of its own Slavonic stereotype edition, Filaret had overseen the design and preparation of Johan Winheber's Slavonic typeface. He also headed up the Bible Society's translations subcommittee. This committee became the central point of review for the many translations published by the society in non-Russian languages of the Russian Empire, as well as in those Balkan and other languages brought under the society's expanding publication program. While the British biblical scholar Ebenezer Henderson, then resident in Petersburg, occasionally joined John Paterson in meeting with the translations committee, the internal leadership of the committee was dominated by Russian clergy, including Filaret and his former student, Gerasim Petrovich Pavskii, who also taught at the Petersburg Theological Academy. It was this translations committee that would oversee the final correction, proofreading, and publication of the Russian NT.[44] The path had been prepared for the rapid implementation

[44] The Bible Society's internal translations subcommittee – the Committee for Oversight of Translations of Holy Scripture (Komitet po razsmotreniiu perevodov Sv. Pisaniia) – was composed primarily of Orthodox prelates on the society's governing committee. See the biographical article on an RBS director and translations committee member, Bishop Innokentii (d. 1819), by A. I. Brilliantov, "Preosviashchennyi Innokentii (Smirnov), episkop penzenskii i saratovskii," *Khristianskoe chtenie* (December 1912): 1383. According to S. M. Sol'skii, "Obozrenie trudov po izucheniiu Biblii v Rossii s xv veka do nastoiashchago vremeni," *Pravoslavnoe obozrenie* 1, n.s. (1869): 804, this RBS *komitet* also included among its clerical members Metropolitans Mikhail (St. Petersburg), Serafim (then of Moscow), and Archbishop Filaret (Drozdov, then of Tver). These latter three prelates from the committee signed the preface to the first Bible Society Russian NT of 1821. From the earliest years of the society's translations subcommittee, the Hebraic scholar G. P. Pavskii served on the *komitet*, as did two non-ecclesiastical RBS committee members, Vasilii Popov and Aleksandr Labzin. See Chistovich, *Istoriia perevoda Biblii*, 29. Ebenezer Henderson, who attended translations meetings, referred to Pavskii as "a liberal and enlightened clergyman," later collaborating with him in the preparation of a Hebrew translation of the NT. See Henderson to Bishop Frederick Munter, September 20, 1822, "Ny Kgl. Samling," fol. 1698, Royal Library of Copenhagen.

of Alexander I's February 1816 decree. Because the Bible Society's printing operations were authorized to circumvent normal censorship procedures, including an ecclesiastical censorship exercised by faculty conferences from the theological academies, no further structural impediment stood in the way of fulfilling the imperially authorized mandate for Russian biblical translation.

In accordance with the authority granted to it by the Holy Synod, the Commission on Ecclesiastical Schools proceeded to assign portions of the New Testament for translation at the respective theological academies. The majority of the work was undertaken directly in Petersburg, where Filaret reserved for himself the translation of the Gospel of John. Although the rector provided guidelines for translators and remained in close contact with the full NT translation effort until its completion in 1821, his appointment in 1817 to the vacant archbishopric of Tver and Kashin meant that his personal supervision of the text through the press at the Bible Society was occasionally delegated to others on the revision committees. In the assignment of other NT texts for translation, the Commission on Ecclesiastical Schools turned also to the Moscow and Kiev Theological Academies for assistance. Draft translations were submitted through the Commission on Ecclesiastical Schools for revision, and on to the translations committee of the Bible Society. Although the specific identity of first-draft translators from the academies is not recorded for each of the NT books, it is known that, in addition to the translation of the Gospel of John by Archimandrite Filaret (Drozdov), Archpriest Gerasim Pavskii of the St. Petersburg Theological Academy translated the Gospel of Matthew; Archimandrite Polikarp (Petr Gaitannikov, 1787–1837), inspector of the St. Petersburg Theological Academy (subsequently rector of Moscow Theological Academy), translated the Gospel of Mark; and Archimandrite Moisei (Bogdanov-Platonov), rector of the Kiev Theological Academy, rendered the initial translation of the Gospel of Luke.[45]

A complete Russian text of the Gospels was submitted for publication to the society in 1818, little more than two years after the emperor's decree authorizing the translation. Printed in 1818, but with an issue date of early

[45] Chistovich, *Istoriia perevoda Biblii*, 28–9; see also *Chetvertyi otchet rossiiskogo bibleiskogo obshchestva* (St. Petersburg, 1817), 73–82. Aleksandr Vasil'evich Gorskii, long-time rector of Moscow Theological Academy and a close associate of Metropolitan Filaret, recalled his conversations with the late metropolitan in which Filaret also credited Grigorii Postnikov and Bishop Kirill (Konstantin Bogoslovskii-Platonov, 1788–1840, former Moscow Theological Academy rector and Bishop of Viatka) with contributing to the NT translation. See Gorskii, "Iz vospominanii pokoinogo Filareta, mitropolita moskovskogo," *Pravoslavnoe obozrenie*, 26 (August 1868): 507–42.

1819, the first Slavonic/Russian diglot of the Gospels included the emperor's original decree authorizing the Russian translation. The emperor's decree was preceded by a separate preface to the reader, "Proclamation to Christ-loving Readers" (*Vozglashenie k khristoliubivym chitateliam*), dated March 30, 1819, and signed by Metropolitan Mikhail of Novgorod and St. Petersburg, Metropolitan Serafim of Moscow and Kolomna, and Archbishop Filaret of Tver and Kashin. The prelates' preface constituted a carefully worded defense for translation of scripture into modern Russian. Noting that in the pre-Christian era there was just "one nation to whom God's Word was entrusted, the Jews, and then the sacred books were written in a single Hebrew language," the prelates pointed to what they called the divinely providential division of the treasure of God's Word among other peoples, even before the advent into the world of Jesus Christ – a reference to the Greek Septuagint translation of the Hebrew Bible. Subsequent translations by "shepherds and teachers of the Christian Church" had brought the holy books into many languages, "in whose number also was our native Slavonic." Then, in the critical point of their preface, the bishops intoned:

> But, while the language in books is able to remain unchanged for many centuries, the oral language of the people changes greatly in a single century; and what has been written for several centuries past in our native [Slavonic] language is now little understood by us without special study ... From this it follows that for the unhindered use and dissemination of God's Word there is need not only to translate Holy Scripture into a native language, but also to renew [*vozobnovliat'*] the translation from time to time according to the condition of the language in its popular usage.[46]

In their appeal for a more modern text, the authors of the preface noted by way of precedent how, in the past, those who copied the Slavonic biblical texts often replaced antiquated words in the text with more readily understood language.

But the Bible Society's Russian NT went far beyond the cosmetic removal of archaisms. The authors of the *Vozglashenie* sought to address more fundamental textological issues in the preface. In appealing to the use of the original Greek text alongside the Slavonic, the prelates noted, for example, that the fourteenth-century Metropolitan of Moscow Aleksei, in his Slavonic manuscript of the Holy Gospels, had used an original Greek text as the basis for corrections. Reflecting their commitment to a new

[46] "Vozglashenie k khristoliubivym chitateliam," in *Gospoda Nashego Iisusa Khrista Sviatoe Evangelie ot Matfeia, Marka, Luki i Ioanna, na slavianskom i russkom narechii* (St. Petersburg: Printed at the Press of Nikolai Grech for the RBS, 1819), iv.

translation, rather than simply a russification of the Slavonic text, the three prelates concluded:

> The Russian dialect in popular use is so cut off from the Slavonic used in the old translation of Holy Scripture that, in order to facilitate popular understanding, it would now be inadequate simply to exchange some old archaisms for new, more commonly used wording. What is required is an entirely fresh translation corresponding to the present condition of the Russian language.[47]

The prelates were in effect acknowledging that the Bible Society's Russian NT was a fresh translation drawing upon the Greek as well as the Slavonic text. Their justification for this bold departure, alongside the appeal to Emperor Alexander I's own decree, was that of the fourteenth-century precedent and the popular need for scripture in a more understandable Russian language.

In practice, the translators were guided by the Slavonic text, but they also employed original Greek textology, using as their base an 1811 Greek NT text published in Moscow. This text, far from being unique to the Byzantine or Eastern Orthodox world, was in a long line of Greek NT textology identified with the *textus receptus*, a compilation evolving from the scholarship of the western Renaissance scholar, Desiderius Erasmus.[48] For the Slavonic text, the translators accepted the authority of the standardized Elizabeth 1751 Slavonic Bible.

The authority of the Erasmian *textus receptus* has been a source of considerable controversy in subsequent Russian biblical studies. In an occasional effort to dramatize the difference between "eastern" and "western" NT textology, Russian biblical scholars, especially during the Soviet period, seized upon the Erasmian *textus receptus* used in nineteenth-century translation, claiming it as an authentically "Orthodox" rendering of the Greek NT in contrast to western critical Greek NT textology represented in the so-called Nestle/Aland critical editions of the late nineteenth and twentieth centuries.[49]

[47] Ibid., iv–v.

[48] Coined by the Leiden printer Abraham Elzevir, the term *textus receptus* was used in the preface to the second Leiden edition of the Greek NT (1633) to refer to a text received without change. What had been "received" both in the Leiden case and in the Moscow 1811 Greek edition used by Russian translators was not an uncorrupted "original" text, but rather one of the numerous more or less identical Greek editions published after the model of Erasmus's first published Greek edition of 1516. On the *textus receptus* and the genealogy of Greek NT textology, see Bruce M. Metzger, *The Text of the New Testament, its Transmission, Corruption, and Restoration*, 2nd edn (Oxford University Press, 1968).

[49] The effort to christen the Erasmian Greek NT as an "Orthodox" text is one of the textological curiosities arising out of the debate over the authority of texts in Russian biblical translation. In contrast to the Erasmian *textus receptus* based on a handful of Greek texts, the critical editions of the Greek NT today reflect hundreds of variant Greek textual readings. Advances in critical Greek NT textology of the nineteenth and twentieth century are documented in the multiple editions of the *Novum Testamentum*

Despite all the Slavonic and Greek texts used in the translation effort, it is hard to escape the conclusion when examining the Bible Society's Slavonic/Russian NT diglot that the major, though not exclusive, task became that of transforming the Slavonic into a more understandable Russian. As in the selection from 1 Corinthians, Chapter 13 – a frequently cited passage on faith, hope, and love – the Slavonic structure was invariably retained, alongside shifts in vocabulary and word order. However, the passage from 1 Corinthians reflected also an attempt by the translators to appeal beyond the Slavonic text in seeking fidelity to the Greek. For example, the translators inserted the word *dar* (gift) in the second verse of the 1 Corinthians passage ("If I have *the gift of* prophecy . . ."). Such changes of nuance, intended either to correct the Slavonic text or render its meaning more accurately in Russian, were printed in italicized type in Bible Society editions, a practice that continued in later synodal editions into the twentieth century. The italicized changes were to be found in virtually every chapter of the new Russian translation. As a result the final product documented the degree to which the new Russian text was not a mere russification of the Slavonic text, but, as indicated in the preface, a genuinely new translation.

Responding in 1823 to apparent charges leveled by those challenging the differences between the Slavonic and Russian texts, Archbishop Filaret (by then in the diocese of Moscow and Kolomna), Metropolitan Serafim of St. Petersburg, and Archbishop Ioann of Tver openly acknowledged in a new preface accompanying the 1823 Russian NT (without the Slavonic diglot) that the differences in the Russian text were accounted for by the need to be true to the Greek original.[50]

Despite the central role of the Russian Bible Society in launching the new Russian translation, the actual printing of the Slavonic/Russian NT began at the press of Nikolai Grech, the conservative Petersburg publicist. Preoccupied with its own stereotype publications in Slavonic and several other languages, the Bible Society paid Grech's press to produce the initial NT books for the society's own distribution. In waiting two years to produce its own Slavonic/Russian stereotype edition, the Bible Society was able immediately to stereotype the 1821 first complete NT edition (the *editio princeps* of the Russian NT) at the reduced price of "four rubles

graece, cum apparatu critico, ed. Eberhard Nestle, Erwin Nestle, and Kurt Aland. See, for example, the 1945 edition published in Stuttgart. The Soviet campaign directed against the Nestle/Aland critical Greek NT arose after World War II in response to a new Russian émigré translation of the NT that sought to employ the Nestle/Aland critical Greek text in its version. For this opposition campaign waged in the pages of *Zhurnal moskovskoi patriarkhii*, see the "Afterword," n. 24.

50 "K khristoliubivym chitateliam po sluchaiu izdaniia vsego Novogo Zaveta na odnom russkom narechii," in *Gospoda Nashego Iisusa Khrista Novyi Zavet* (St. Petersburg: RBS, 1823), xi–xiv.

bound." This delay meant it could avoid the financial risk of producing stereotype plates before the earlier diglot printings of separate books had been subjected to criticism and the elimination of typographical errors.[51]

From 1821 to 1823, the Russian Bible Society issued at least six printings of the Slavonic/Russian NT diglot (see Figures 4 and 5), with an approximate

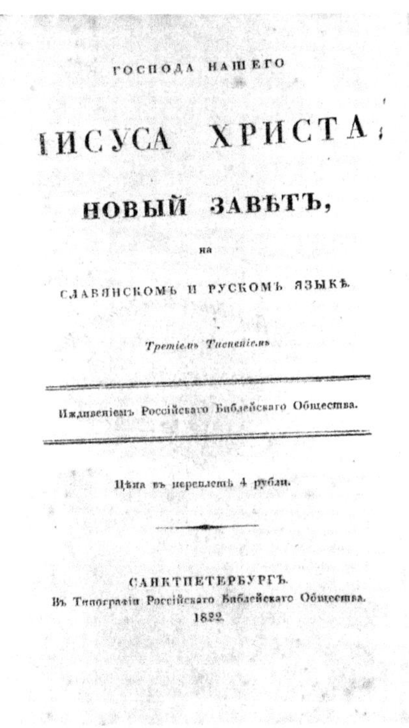

ГОСПОДА НАШЕГО

ІИСУСА ХРИСТА,

НОВЫЙ ЗАВѢТЪ,

на

СЛАВЯНСКОМЪ И РУСКОМЪ ЯЗЫКѢ.

Третіемъ Тисненіемъ

Иждивеніемъ Россійскаго Библейскаго Общества.

Цѣна въ переплетѣ 4 рубли.

САНКТПЕТЕРБУРГЪ.
Въ Типографіи Россійскаго Библейскаго Общества.
1822.

Figure 4. Third printing of the Slavonic/Russian New Testament diglot issued by the Russian Bible Society, 1822 (Annotated Bibliography, no. 9).
Source: Photograph from author's personal copy.

[51] *Gospoda Nashego Iisusa Khrista Novyi Zavet, na slavianskom i russkom iazyke* (St. Petersburg: RBS, 1821 [1822]) – no. 7, Appendix. Even the delay in stereotyping the RBS Russian NT did not entirely avoid the need for recasting part of the text, as can be seen from the two separate editions of the NT diglot appearing in 1822. Such recasting demonstrated the urgent need for early standardization, or "fixity," of the text. Archbishop Filaret (Drozdov), who faced major delays in the internal meetings of the NT revision committee, at one point cautioned the RBS not to establish stereotype plates too quickly because of the endless debate over text that was delaying the revision committee. He asked the RBS to request that his own commission's revision committee move more quickly in completing the review of the final books of the NT. See Filaret to Golitsyn (May 5, 1820), and the RBS Publishing Committee resolution requesting

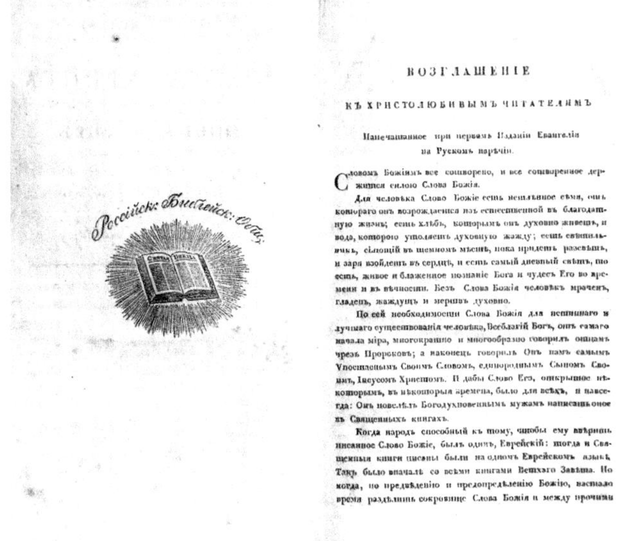

ВОЗГЛАШЕНІЕ

КЪ ХРИСТОЛЮБИВЫМЪ ЧИТАТЕЛЯМЪ

Напечатанное при первомъ Изданіи Евангелія на Рускомъ нарѣчіи.

Словомъ Божіимъ все сотворено, и все сотворенное держится силою Слова Божія.

Для человѣка Слово Божіе есть нетлѣнное сѣмя, отъ котораго онъ возрождается изъ естественной въ благодатную жизнь; есть хлѣбъ, которымъ онъ духовно живетъ, и вода, которою утоляетъ духовную жажду; есть свѣтильникъ, сіяющій въ темномъ мѣстѣ, пока придетъ разсвѣтъ, и заря взойдетъ въ сердцѣ, и есть самый дневный свѣтъ, то есть, живое и блаженное познаніе Бога и чудесъ Его во времени и въ вѣчности. Безъ Слова Божія человѣкъ мраченъ, гладенъ, жаждущъ и мертвъ духовно.

По сей необходимости Слова Божія для истиннаго и лучшаго существованія человѣка, Всеблагій Богъ, отъ самаго начала міра, многократно и многообразно говорилъ отцамъ чрезъ Пророковъ; а наконецъ говорилъ Онъ намъ самымъ Ѵпостаснымъ Своимъ Словомъ, единороднымъ Сыномъ Своимъ, Іисусомъ Христомъ. И дабы Слово Его, открытое нѣкоторымъ, въ нѣкоторыя времена, было для всѣхъ, и навсегда: Онъ повелѣлъ Богодухновеннымъ мужамъ написать оное въ Священныхъ книгахъ.

Когда народъ способный къ тому, чтобы ему ввѣрить писанное Слово Божіе, былъ одинъ, Еврейскій: тогда и Священныя книги писаны были на одномъ Еврейскомъ языкѣ. Такъ было вначалѣ со всѣми книгами Ветхаго Завѣта. Но когда, по предвѣдѣнію и предопредѣленію Божію, настало время раздѣлить сокровище Слова Божія и между прочими

Figure 5. Slavonic/Russian 1822 diglot New Testament internal pages: verso is the seal of the Russian Bible Society; recto is the proclamation to readers regarding the new Russian edition. Source: Photograph from author's personal copy.

circulation of 100,000 copies.[52] The subsequent decision to publish the NT in an exclusively Russian text yielded at least another two printings in 1823 at the reduced price of two rubles, twenty-five kopecks.[53] Thus, exclusive of the NT books published separately by the press of Nikolai Grech and the Moscow Synodal Press, total Bible Society circulation of the Russian NT in diglot and monolingual editions exceeded 150,000 copies in the two-year period from the end of 1821 through 1823. As noted above, that two-year figure exceeded the total circulation run of the Slavonic Bible for the entire period (1672–1825) from Peter the Great through the reign of Alexander I.[54]

expedited completion of the NT in RGIA, *fond* 808, *opis'* 1, *delo* 10 ("Uspekhi v knigopechatnykh rabotakh i zaniatiia Komiteta dlia pechatnykh del"), *ll.* 301–3.

52 See Appendix, nos. 7–10 and 19. The circulation estimate is based upon 20,000 copies per printing after the smaller first RBS edition of 1821 [1822] (Appendix, no. 7). The BFBS representative in Petersburg, Robert Pinkerton, identifies the second edition of 1822 (Appendix, no. 8) as having been issued in 20,000 copies.

53 See Appendix, nos. 20 and 21. The second printing of this Russian-only edition includes the printed price on the title page.

54 For a bibliography that includes most of these eighteenth-century Slavonic printings in small circulation runs, see A. S. Zernova, ed., *Svodnyi katalog russkoi knigi kirillovskoi pechati XVIII veka* (Moscow, 1968).

The Russian Bible Society's landmark first edition of the Russian New Testament was followed by translation and publication of the equally popular Russian Psalter. The issue of the textual authority resting behind the Russian Old Testament proved to be far more complicated than had been the case for the New Testament. The Slavonic OT had been translated largely from the Greek Septuagint, a text for which the extant manuscripts date from the fourth century CE. Although the oldest extant manuscripts of the Hebrew Masoretic text date six hundred years later to the ninth and tenth centuries CE, the Hebrew text occupies a special place in OT studies as the original text and the source from which the Greek Septuagint (the text of the seventy translators, or LXX) was derived. Owing to the fact that the Hebrew canon had not yet become standardized at the time of the Septuagint translation, the LXX contains whole books and some variant readings not found in the extant Hebrew Masoretic manuscript tradition. The books found in the LXX, but not in the Hebrew Masoretic text, are commonly referred to as the deuterocanonical books, or the Apocrypha.[55]

Despite the Slavonic biblical tradition and its LXX authority, the ascendant strength of Hebraic studies in Petersburg led Russian Old Testament scholars, notably the lead translator of the Psalter, Gerasim Petrovich Pavskii, to draw upon the rich tradition of Hebrew Masoretic studies. An added factor that no doubt weighed in favor of the authority of the Hebrew text was BFBS ideological opposition to inclusion in their OT translations of the deuterocanonical books of the Bible, or the Apocrypha. Like much of Protestant biblical scholarship at the time and like the King James OT version (which attached the Apocrypha separately from the other OT books), the BFBS took an increasingly strong stand in support of OT translation from the Hebrew original.

The debate over the textual base for the modern Russian Old Testament would continue to inflame Russian biblical studies throughout the nineteenth century, and remains largely unresolved to the present. At stake in the case of the Russian Bible Society's translation of the Psalter were the differing numbering systems for the Psalms in the Hebrew Masoretic and LXX traditions, and the absence of the 151st Psalm in the Hebrew text. Pragmatically, the issue of the authority of OT textology came to be resolved by virtue of the person

[55] Deuterocanonical books most commonly included in the Orthodox Slavic tradition include Tobit, Judith, the Wisdom of Solomon, Ecclesiasticus, Baruch, Song of the Three Young Men (an addition to Daniel), Maccabees, two of the three books of Esdras, the Prayer of Manasseh, Susanna, Bel and the Dragon, Enoch, and the 151st Psalm.

who ultimately translated most of the Psalter. Gerasim Petrovich Pavskii, professor of Hebrew at the St. Petersburg Theological Academy, prepared the original Russian translation of the Psalter. Archbishop Filaret (Drozdov), who continued to serve on the Bible Society's translations subcommittee when in Petersburg, edited the final revision of the Psalter, but the hand of the future academician, Archpriest Pavskii, lay behind the original translation. A student of Filaret from the latter's days as Petersburg Academy rector, Gerasim Pavskii had also studied under the tutelage of visiting scholars Ignaz Fessler and Johan von Horn. Pavskii was an able translator from both Greek and Hebrew, and had already undertaken the translation of the Gospel of Matthew. Pavskii's Russian Psalter was based upon a working assumption that OT translation should be based upon the Hebrew Masoretic text, as well as the Greek Septuagint. In addition to Pavskii's recognized authority in biblical languages, his standing within the Bible Society was significant. He was a member of the society's governing committee and a collaborator with the British biblical scholar Ebenezer Henderson, who provided technical assistance in the preparation of RBS publications for press.[56] Pavskii also assisted the society in handling the large body of correspondence that developed between Petersburg and the outlying chapters or sections (*otdeleniia*) of the Russian Bible Society.[57]

The first edition of the Russian Psalter, published in 1822, followed what would be the pattern in modern Russian OT translation – specifically, translation from the Hebrew original, but with incorporation of Septuagint readings, Septuagint numeration, and inclusion of the 151st Psalm.[58] In order to clarify and arbitrate the textological issue, the Bible Society asked leading Russian prelates to prepare a special preface for this first edition. The preface, "To the Christ-Loving Reader" (*K khristoliubivomu chitateliu*), clarified the textological thinking behind the translation. It noted that the

56 Pavskii is profiled in Chapter 3. Alongside his command of Hebrew, Pavskii was proficient in Greek, as reflected in his translation of Greek patristic writings published from the 1820s in the St. Petersburg Theological Academy's journal, *Khristianskoe chtenie*.

57 Pavskii's role in day-to-day RBS operations is documented in the work of his biographer, S. V. Protopopov, *Protoierei G. P. Pavskii* (St. Petersburg, 1876); and "Protoierei Gerasim Petrovich Pavskii (Materialy dlia ego biografii)," *Strannik*, 17 (1876), no. 1: 3–45; no. 2: 101–37; and no. 3: 213–24.

58 *Kniga Khvalenii ili Psaltir' na rossiiskom iazyke* (St. Petersburg: Tip. Nikolaia Grecha [for the RBS]), 1822 (Appendix, no. 11). As with the Russian NT, the first edition of the Russian Psalter was published at the press of Nikolai Grech, with the RBS stereotype edition awaiting the identification of errors in the first edition. By publishing the Psalter outside the Bible Society it was also possible to mute potential objections from BFBS representatives over the inclusion of the 151st Psalm. This first edition was followed immediately by printings of the text in Moscow at the Synodal Press and in stereotype edition directly by the RBS Press. Each of the initial printings, as well as the RBS stereotype printings, carried the preface ("K khristoliubivomu chitateliu"), i–xi.

translation drew from both the Greek Septuagint (the basis for the Slavonic Psalter) and the Hebrew "original." It also provided examples of cases in which the Hebrew text was given precedence in translation. Given the traditional authority of the Greek Septuagint text in the Orthodox church, this appeal to the Hebrew "original" was a particularly significant turn in the history of Russian biblical studies.

There were several explanations for this new direction. On the one hand, Pavskii's own training in Hebrew reflected the new access at St. Petersburg Theological Academy to western textual scholarship. Although some of this western scholarship would later be tarred in the campaigns to root out masonic and other mystical currents at the Petersburg Academy, the foundations had been laid for modern biblical scholarship in nineteenth-century Russia. In the years prior to the death of Alexander I and the closure of the Russian Bible Society, there was remarkable openness in biblical text studies, particularly in Petersburg where the tradition of outstanding Hebraic scholarship established in the early nineteenth century extended well into the twentieth century. While Filaret would later write a defense of the use of the Septuagint in biblical translation, his defense consistently bore witness to the authority of both Greek and Hebrew OT textology.[59]

Although the BFBS sought to adopt a Protestant canon based on the Hebrew text, its more rigid stance against the inclusion of Apocryphal readings came somewhat later. In 1813, the London BFBS offices had agreed that foreign Bible societies, even those operating with support funding from the BFBS, could publish scriptures in their own canonical tradition. Of more immediate influence in this matter may have been BFBS representative Ebenezer Henderson in St. Petersburg. An OT scholar, Henderson was more clearly fixated on a Protestant canon drawn from the Hebrew Masoretic text. Moreover, the early BFBS flexibility over the publication of deuterocanonical texts in Bible Society editions was soon abandoned in the wake of a storm of evangelical opposition known as the "Apocrypha controversy." By 1825, British evangelicals effectively forced the BFBS to remove all deuterocanonical texts from its published editions in Britain and abroad.[60]

59 The controversy over the attempted canonization of the Greek Septuagint text in OT translation was the context for Metropolitan Filaret's carefully qualified defense of the Septuagint. Penned in the 1840s, Filaret's defense was first published openly in 1858 after the resumption of modern Russian biblical translation. See "O dogmaticheskom dostoinstve i okhranitel'nom upotreblenii grecheskogo semidesiati tolkovnikov," *Pribavleniia k tvoreniiam sviatykh ottsov v russkom perevode*, 32 (1858): second pagination 452–84.

60 On the Apocrypha controversy, see George Browne, *A History of the BFBS, from its Institution in 1804, to the Close of its Jubilee in 1854*, 2 vols. (London: BFBS, 1859); also Martin, *Evangelicals United*, 123–31.

Never directly drawn into the Aprocrypha controversy, the Russian Bible Society steered a careful middle ground with respect to Greek and Hebrew Old Testament textological traditions. A seasoned translator from Greek, Pavskii had at the same time prepared his own Hebrew grammar for use by his Russian students. According to Pavskii's most reliable biographer, S. V. Protopopov, Pavskii had already translated for himself the Psalter from Hebrew into Russian in his free time. Motivated to translate out of a curiosity concerning what he allegedly considered the unclear, "dark places" in the Slavonic text of the Psalter, Pavskii accordingly presented his translation to the "special committee" (*osobyi komitet*) of the Commission on Ecclesiastical Schools. The special committee, headed by Filaret Drozdov, transmitted the revised text to the Russian Bible Society's Committee for Oversight of Translation of Holy Scripture (Komitet po razsmotreniiu perevodov Sv. Pisaniia), which undertook the final review prior to publication. With Filaret increasingly drawn to diocesan matters in Moscow, and Pavskii playing an ever more prominent role within the Bible Society as a corrector of translations, the Psalter rapidly advanced to publication.[61]

This did not mean that the Hebrew textology behind the Pavskii Russian Psalter went unchallenged. Indeed, Pavskii's corrections in the third printing of the Psalter, including his recommended bracketing of the 151st Psalm because of its absence from the Hebrew Masoretic text, met with a storm of protest from Moscow Archbishop Filaret, who insisted that the Bible Society's edition (the stereotype edition first printed in 1822) be changed to accord with the first printing that had included the 151st Psalm without bracketing.[62]

Such textological conflicts presaged a far more acrimonious battle (see Chapter 3) over the Russian OT in the 1840s. In the Russian Bible Society's Old Testament translation – namely, the Octateuch containing the OT books Genesis through Ruth – the compromise reached was to print variant Septuagint readings in bracketed passages footnoted at the bottom margin of the page. This compromise inclusion of both Hebrew and Greek readings was continued in virtually all subsequent nineteenth-century Russian OT translation, including the authorized *sinodal'nyi perevod*, or synodal translation, the most common text issued by the Russian Orthodox Church up to the present day.

In the era of Alexander I, the Russian Psalter became the single most popular volume published by the society, going through at least thirteen

[61] Protopopov, *Protoierei G. P. Pavskii*, 46.
[62] Archbishop Filaret to Vasilii Popov, September 7, 1822, RGIA, *fond* 808, *opis'* 1, *delo* 159 ("O napechatanii knigi psalmov na russkom iazyke"), *l.* 78.

printings between 1822 and 1824. As in the case of the NT diglot, the initial printings of the Russian Psalter were done outside the Bible Society's own establishment – the first printing at the press of Nikolai Grech, the second at the Holy Synod's own Moscow press. Only with the third printing in St. Petersburg was the text stereotyped and printed at the Bible Society Press.[63] Based upon the unusually large print run of fifteen thousand copies of the first Grech edition, the total circulation of the Russian Psalter in all its printings matched and probably exceeded the 150,000 NT copies circulated by the Russian Bible Society. As in the case of the Russian NT, the Bible Society in this instance had issued another popular, landmark *editio princeps* – a Russian Psalter that constituted the first published edition of an OT book in modern Russian.

Publication of the Russian Psalter notably extended the Bible Society's reach beyond the intent of the emperor's February 1816 decree calling for publication of a Russian New Testament. Nevertheless, the popularity of the Bible Society and the influence of its president, Aleksandr Golitsyn, made it possible for the society to proceed with publication in the absence of any formal decree. As in the case of the Bible Society's freedom from censorship, the expanding authority of the Bible Society to publish and circulate Holy Scripture initially went without much notice. The society proceeded to prepare translations of other OT books in a manner similar to that followed in connection with the NT. Filaret Drozdov, who had readied his own commentary on the book of Genesis, assumed primary responsibility for the first draft of the translation of Genesis. Assignments were made to the theological academies for the translation of other OT books. Exodus was assigned to the Moscow Theological Academy, Leviticus to the Kiev Academy, and the remaining books of the so-called Octateuch were assigned to the Petersburg Academy.[64]

Despite the division of labor, Gerasim Pavskii continued to play the primary role in translation of the Octateuch, as he had in the preparation of the Russian Psalter. Even in the case of the book of Leviticus, officially

[63] All RBS Psalters bear the same title, *Kniga Khvalenii ili Psaltir' na rossiiskom iazyke*. The third printing, a stereotype edition, is the first to bear the RBS imprint, St. Petersburg, 1822 (Appendix, no. 13).

[64] Chistovich, *Istoriia perevoda Biblii*, 34–5. Each of the academies developed its own internal review of the translations assigned to it. At the Moscow Academy, Hebrew Professor Tiazhelov completed the initial translation of Exodus. On the broader issue of the Moscow Academy's engagement with OT translation, see Ivan Korsunskii, "Trudy moskovskoi dukhovnoi akademii po perevodu Sv. Pisaniia i tvorenii Sv. Ottsev na russkii iazyk za 75 let eia sushchestvovaniia (1814–1889 gg.)," *Pribavleniia k tvoreniiam Sv. Ottsev v russkom perevode*, 56 (1889), kn. 4: 419–587; 57 (1890), ch. 1, kn. 2: 341–405; and 57 (1891), ch. 2, kn. 2: 483–614. For Korsunskii's reference to Filaret's translation of the book of Genesis, see 56 (1889), kn. 4: 445.

assigned to the Kievan Academy, Pavskii's own former Petersburg Academy students, Spiridon V. Guliaev and Aleksandr A. Maksimovich, completed the draft translation in Kiev before submitting it to the translations revision committee set up by the Commission on Ecclesiastical Schools.[65] Following review by this revision committee, or what Protopopov identifies as the special committee, a Bible Society translations committee composed of ecclesiastical members of the Bible Society met to review the translations. Pavskii's presence was felt throughout the process, from the Commission on Ecclesiastical Schools' revision committee, which was dominated by representatives from the Petersburg Theological Academy, to the meetings he also attended of the translations oversight committee of the society. As Protopopov recounts, Pavskii took upon himself the difficult responsibility of preparing for each meeting of the committee the given section of translation scheduled for review.

> This preparation consisted of making sure that the translation was done accurately [*verno*] from the Hebrew and was checked [*slichen*] with the Septuagint. In such a manner the translation of the Pentateuch, Joshua, Judges, Ruth and the first book of Kings [this last book not printed by the Bible Society] took on their form under the editorship of Pavskii.[66]

Pavskii's primary concern for fidelity or accuracy with respect to the Hebrew was coupled with an obligatory comparison with the Septuagint reading. The description by Protopopov, a priest who had close family ties to Pavskii and who was one of a select group to set eyes on Pavskii's unpublished autobiography, confirmed the special role assigned to the Hebrew text in the Bible Society's OT translations. This authority given to the Hebrew text in Russian OT translation was a significant legacy of the Bible Society era. As in the Octateuch readied for publication by Pavskii and the Bible Society's translations committee, so also, in subsequent synodal translations of the 1860s and 1870s, bracketed Russian readings from the Septuagint were inserted into the margins in all Russian OT translations to designate text based solely on the Septuagint for which there was no Hebrew Masoretic equivalent.

[65] Maksimovich taught Hebrew at the Kiev Academy and was joined in the translation of Leviticus not only by Guliaev, but also by instructors in literature (Professor Sokolov) and math and sciences (Professor Kolerov), all of whom participated in the review of the text. For the careers of Guliaev and Maksimovich, including their study at the Petersburg Academy, see Aleksei Rodosskii, *Biograficheskii slovar' studentov pervykh xxviii-li kursov sanktpeterburgskoi dukhovnoi akademii, 1814–1869 gg.* (St. Petersburg, 1907), 123, 258. On the working of the translations committee at the Kievan Academy, see the memoir of F. F. Ismailov, "Zapiski," *Pravoslavnoe obozrenie*, 1870 (February): 114; also Chistovich, *Istoriia perevoda Biblii*, 34–5.

[66] Protopopov, *Protoierei G. P. Pavskii*, 46.

This process of OT translation and revision yielded, in the end, the successful Bible Society publication of the Russian Psalter, as well as the additional OT translation through the book of Ruth. But the society's printing of the Russian translation of the Octateuch, OT books Genesis through Ruth, remained in sheets and was not bound, foreshadowing the Bible Society's own perilous fate in the 1820s. Printed in the years 1824–5 in ten thousand copies, these sheets of the Octateuch remained in storage and were never bound.[67] Binding and distribution of the Octateuch, despite the absence of any official proscription, were effectively thwarted following the forced resignation of the Bible Society's president, Aleksandr Golitsyn, in 1824. While the Bible Society's Octateuch never circulated openly and much of the printing was destroyed, it continued to play a significant role in subsequent OT translation. As the *textus primus* for the Russian OT books Genesis through Ruth, it resurfaced in foreign editions and in the published Pavskii translations of the 1860s. The Bible Society's Octateuch also remained a point of reference in the preparation of the Holy Synod's authorized OT of the 1870s.

CLOSURE OF THE RUSSIAN BIBLE SOCIETY

The fate of the Russian Octateuch begged the much larger question of why the popular Russian Bible Society and its prominent president had become so politically vulnerable by 1824 following a decade of unprecedented publication and circulation of Holy Scripture. Traditional accounts of the demise of Aleksandr Golitsyn and the Bible Society have offered four sets of overlapping arguments. The first of these, which draws upon the commentaries of the day by leading publicists such as Nikolai Grech, is that the Bible Society fell victim to the intense struggle for power and influence that pitted against each other two major patronage/clientele groups of the latter half of Alexander I's reign – namely, the Arakcheev and Golitsyn "parties."[68] According to this view, the so-called Arakcheevshchina ultimately doomed the Bible Society. The coalition of forces associated with Arakcheev and the reactionary publicist Admiral Aleksandr Shishkov managed to gather a constellation of court insiders and Orthodox prelates – notably, the Archimandrite Fotii and St. Petersburg Metropolitan Serafim – sufficient

[67] [*Vos'miknizhie.*] [St. Petersburg: RBS, 1825] – Appendix, no. 23. Printed in 1824–5 in unbound sheets, most of the 10,000 copies were destroyed at the time of RBS closure in 1826. According to BFBS records (Ellerby to Knolleke, May 25/June 26, 1850, BFBS Foreign Correspondence Inwards, 1850, no. 1, 257), circulation of the remaining undestroyed Octateuch copies remained forbidden into the 1850s.

[68] See Chapter 1, n. 43.

to advance their own interests and to persuade Emperor Alexander that Golitsyn and the Bible Society were a danger to Russia.

In making their case to the emperor, the "Arakcheevtsy" specifically appealed to a second, more substantive argument for why the Russian Bible Society and its president posed a threat to Russia. Their appeal drew upon the well-known international opposition of Austrian Foreign Minister Klemens von Metternich, who had warned the emperor about incendiary groups that could threaten the forces of legitimacy in post-Napoleonic Europe. This appeal to law and order no doubt carried far greater weight following the outbreak of revolutionary events in Spain and, from 1821, the Greek peninsula. Faced also with rebellion from within his own Semenovskii military regiment in 1820, Emperor Alexander, in this view, was prepared to yield to the wider post-Congress of Vienna counter-revolutionary mood. The crackdown on free-masonic lodges, which were closed in 1822, and the sacking of Prince Golitsyn in the spring of 1824 reflected this perception that Bible Society activism was part of a potentially uncontrollable threat to public order.

Curiously, the Russian Bible Society's director, John Paterson, lent his own credence to such an international argument, adding a conspiratorial twist. Reflecting on the Bible Society's demise, Paterson noted in his unpublished memoirs that his internal BFBS rival, Robert Pinkerton, had foolishly compromised the Russian Bible Society by bringing its activities to the attention of the Austrian foreign minister.[69] Commenting on Pinkerton's 1816 meeting with Metternich, Patterson alleges that it was Pinkerton who first instilled in the Austrian minister a fear of the Bible Society:

> Pinkerton's visit to Vienna was worse than a failure. The least reflection ought to have taught him that if anything was to be done for priest-ridden, papistical Austria it must be done in a quiet manner and from the surrounding countries. Metternich was too much of a Jesuit for him [Pinkerton]. By smooth promises he [Metternich] got information from him which he meant to turn against the Bible Society as soon as Pinkerton's back was turned. Pinkerton was foolish enough to tell the Prince that he could not keep out the Bible, but that we would hustle them in from all quarters.

[69] The conflict between Paterson and Henderson, on the one hand, and Pinkerton, on the other, ultimately led to Paterson's and Henderson's departure from the BFBS in late 1821. The precipitating occasion was the BFBS publication of a Turkish NT trumpeted by Pinkerton, but considered unworthy by Paterson and Henderson. Underlying the disagreement was a long-simmering personality conflict that pitted the practical, pragmatic Paterson against the sophisticated and polished Robert Pinkerton. After the formal severance of Paterson and Henderson from the BFBS, Prince Golitsyn, with the support of the RBS committee, arranged for Paterson to receive an annual salary from the RBS – a salary that would be continued in perpetuity by Emperor Nicholas I following closure of the society in 1826. For the Paterson/Henderson letter announcing the severance of their ties with the BFBS, see Paterson and Henderson to the Rev. John Owen (Mozdok, December 1, 1821, O.S.), BFBS Foreign Correspondence Inwards, 1822, no. 192, 21.

Having got all he [Metternich] wished out of his dupe [Pinkerton], he wished him to depart as soon as possible, and immediately after issued a proclamation absolutely prohibiting the entrance of the Bible into the Austrian states. But even this was not the worst of it. Metternich made use of what he had learned from Mr. Pinkerton to prejudice the mind of Alexander thro' his tools in Russia, no doubt by giving a false and Jesuitical colouring to what had passed between them. It is my firm conviction that here we have the key to all that happened in Russia years after.[70]

In short, Paterson believed rather conspiratorially that Pinkerton's meeting with Metternich not only poisoned the Austrian minister against the Bible Society, but also was used indirectly by the Austrian foreign minister to turn Emperor Alexander I against his Bible Society favorites in Petersburg. From this rather jaundiced and anti-papal point of view, the key to understanding Alexander I's change of heart with respect to Golitsyn and the Bible Society was to be found in the counter-revolutionary forces that reasserted themselves in the Concert of Europe. The logic of this argument was grounded in the reality that the imperial government and War Minister Arakcheev were by the end of the second decade of the nineteenth century increasingly guided by European-wide concerns for public order and security – concerns that led to the crackdown on freemasonic societies in 1822.

The perception of threat from mystical and freemasonic movements constituted a third major argument for why Aleksandr Golitsyn and the Russian Bible Society were put on the defensive. According to this view, the society and its president were discredited by their association with sectarian and other fringe religious and mystical movements. Bible Society membership, after all, included many freemasons, and the society's governing committee included among its directors the religious mystic, Aleksandr Labzin. As editor of the controversial journal *Sionskii vestnik*, Labzin did not hesitate to share with readers his zeal for religious awakening, a zeal that came to be associated with heterodoxy in the minds of some Orthodox leaders within the church hierarchy. Labzin's denigrating comments about the emperor's minister of war, Arakcheev, ultimately landed the controversial editor in a monastery far removed from Petersburg affairs.[71] In hindsight, the historian Pypin and the theologian Florovsky both see the Bible Society as having been tarred by association with such mystical currents.

[70] Paterson Memoirs, pt. 2, 271, in BSA, F3/Paterson: Memoirs and Papers, 1805–50.

[71] On Labzin's fate, see M. A. Dmitriev, "Vospominaniia o Labzine (iz zapisok M. A. Dmitrieva)," *Russkii arkhiv*, 4 (1866): 837–60. On Labzin's journal, see N. F. Dubrovin, "Nashi mistiki-sektanty: A. F. Labzin i ego zhurnal *Sionskii vestnik*," *Russkaia starina*, 82 (1894), no. 9: [145]–203, no. 10: [101]–26, no. 11: [58]–91 and no. 12: [98]–132; and 83 (1895), no. 1: [56]–91 and no. 2: [35]–52; and I. A. Galakhov, "Obzor misticheskoi literatury v tsarstvovanie Aleksandra I," *Zhurnal ministerstva narodnogo prosveshcheniia*, 182 (November 1875): [87]–175.

A fourth line of argument heard ever more widely in the waning years of the Russian Bible Society was related to the concerns over mystical literature and freemasonry – namely, the suspicion that the Bible Society in its universalist Christian appeal was guilty of heterodoxy and therefore alien to Russian Orthodox interests. This last argument in particular resonated with an increasingly disaffected church hierarchy represented in the Holy Synod. The growing synodal opposition to the Bible Society was reflected in the turnabout of Metropolitan Serafim, a one-time loyal member of the society's governing committee who turned against the society despite being named to succeed Golitsyn as president of the RBS in the spring of 1824. More vocal opposition to the Bible Society within church circles was expressed by Archimandrite Fotii, Emperor Alexander I's confessor, who openly plotted against the society in league with Aleksei Arakcheev. Even Metropolitan Filaret, stalwart defender of the Bible Society, came to harbor second thoughts about the society's legacy for Russian Orthodoxy. In the aftermath of the Bible Society era, this consistent champion of modern Russian biblical translation accepted the implied judgment that biblical translation had become associated with "neologists," the protagonists of heterodoxy and non-Orthodox doctrinal formulations.

THE GOSSNER AFFAIR

The argument pointing to the Bible Society's association with heterodoxy and non-Orthodox religious movements came into sharper focus during the so-called Gossner affair. Two of the focal points for the discontent over heterodoxy were the popular revivalist Roman Catholic clergymen Ignaz Lindl and Johannes Gossner. Lindl, the first of the pair to arrive in Petersburg, came from Bavaria in 1819. Alexander I had earlier shown interest in this Catholic awakener. Following the restrictions put in place against Lindl in Munich – namely, that he could not convene worship services for more than five persons at a time – Alexander invited the cleric to Petersburg, where he was given imperial protection and a small Catholic chapel. Later, the emperor permitted Lindl and those loyal to him safe passage to Bessarabia where Lindl continued to attract a following to his increasingly more sectarian, evangelical movement.[72]

Before Lindl left Petersburg one year later in 1820, he arranged to have his place taken by a fellow Bavarian Catholic evangelical, Johannes Gossner.

[72] On Ignaz Lindl and his Lindlianer following, see Hans Petri, *Ignaz Lindl und die Bauernkolonie Sarata in Bessarabien* (Munich: R. Oldenbourg, 1965); and Franz Heinrich Reusch, "Lindl, Ignaz," in *Allgemeine deutsche Biographie* (Leipzig, 1883), XVIII: 698–9.

Eventually, Gossner's popularity in Petersburg so far exceeded that of his predecessor that the small Catholic chapel was unable to contain those who gathered for services. Under the circumstances, Alexander permitted Gossner the use of a large Catholic church formerly occupied by the Jesuits for services on weekday and Sunday evenings when the building was not in use by local Catholic clergy. John Paterson noted that Gossner's flock numbered around five hundred faithful. This substantial following, while galling to the established Catholic clergy in Petersburg, ultimately led Gossner to find an even larger hall for his meetings, holding as many as eight hundred people. As Paterson noted, "many were brought to the knowledge of the truth by Gossner's preaching so that we began to reckon the converts by the hundreds. This created quite a stir in Petersburg."[73] Although it would later be held against the Bible Society, Paterson's support for this Bavarian Catholic evangelist led to Gossner's appointment to the governing committee of the Russian Bible Society.

Ultimately, Gossner, like Lindl before him, was banished from Petersburg, but not before he was used by General Arakcheev and Archimandrite Fotii to discredit Aleksandr Golitsyn and the Bible Society with which Gossner had been associated. Adding fuel to the opposition generated against Gossner by the longstanding Catholic clergy of Petersburg were rumors regarding the private lives of the two Bavarian Catholic priests. These rumors were not without foundation. As John Paterson noted, "both of them, as it is usual with Catholic priests, had their nieces with them." Paterson further noted that, before departing for Bessarabia, Lindl had called upon him and indicated that "he was thinking of marrying the young woman." In the end, shortly before heading south, Lindl was married at a secret ceremony performed by his successor Gossner. The birth of a baby boy to the Lindls followed in Bessarabia. As Paterson concluded, "This, as might be expected, afforded a fine handle to his enemies of which they were not slow to take advantage."[74]

For Aleksandr Golitsyn and the Bible Society, the fallout from the Lindl–Gossner affair became ever more serious as charges against Gossner mounted. A further charge related to the publication of Gossner's New Testament biblical commentary. Having earlier published and circulated among the Catholics of

[73] Paterson's account of the Gossner affair is incomplete in the published memoirs. For a more complete account, see BSA Deposited Papers: F3/Paterson: Memoirs and Papers (1805–50), Memoirs, pt. 3, 107–8. On Archimandrite Fotii and synodal reaction, see K. D. Popov, "Iur'evskii arkhimandrit Fotii i ego tserkovno-obshchestvennaia deiatel'nost'," *Trudy kievskoi dukhovnoi akademii*, 1875 (February): 373–84 and (June): 696–817.

[74] BSA Deposited Papers, F3/Paterson: Memoirs and Papers (1805–50), pt. 3, 108.

Bavaria a German translation of the Bible – a translation circulated also by BFBS agents – Gossner proceeded to prepare in St. Petersburg a commentary on the Gospel of St. Matthew in German. Although the Russian Bible Society had nothing to do with the publication of biblical commentaries, the society's secretary Vasilii Popov, Prince Golitsyn's close aide, agreed to assist in the final revisions of the Russian translation of the commentary, and Paterson's own friend, Karl von Poll of the Office of Censorship for Foreign Publications, took charge of overseeing circulation of the Russian version. Golitsyn himself personally patronized the project.

With such interlocking associations, it was not unpredictable that when controversy began to swirl around the Gossner commentary in 1824, friends of the Bible Society who were connected with the project came to suffer as well. The immediate occasion for the attention given to the commentary had nothing to do with the content of the work itself. Rather, the unidentified Russian translator of Gossner's commentary mysteriously slumped over dead following prayers at the Gossner home in Petersburg in early 1824. Those who sought to utilize this event quickly interpreted the death as an act of God, and investigations were launched into the Gossner commentary. The accusers claimed that the Gossner work was filled with allegorical interpretations of scripture. Moreover, it was also their contention that these allegories contained hidden references to the state of affairs in Russia – including one charge that Gossner's references to Pontius Pilate (who delivered Jesus Christ to be crucified) were really hidden references to Emperor Alexander. Gossner's work in both Russian and German was seized, he was placed under house arrest, and criminal proceedings were drawn up against those most directly involved in the commentary, including Paterson's friend Karl von Poll and RBS secretary Vasilii Popov.[75] Although Paterson was not directly implicated in the affair, it was not lost upon the enemies of the Bible Society that Gossner was a member of the society's governing committee, and that others implicated in the Gossner commentary and translation were deeply involved in Bible Society affairs.

In the end, the Gossner affair became part of the campaign to undermine Golitsyn and the Russian Bible Society. Gossner later returned to a successful career in Germany following his appeal to the emperor. But seizing upon the

[75] Underlying the complaint was also the opposition to a biblical commentary that referenced biblical passages in modern Russian – a practice that was new to publications of the time. Such opposition factored in the effort to discredit Metropolitan Filaret Drozdov's Catechism, an issue from the same period. On the Gossner affair, see "Gossner, Ioann, 1773–1858," *Entsiklopedicheskii slovar'* (St. Petersburg, 1893), XVII: 388. See also Paterson, *The Book for Every Land*, 382, and the more extended account in his memoirs, BSA Deposited Papers, F3/Paterson: Memoirs and Papers, 1805–50, pt. 3, 107.

surface issues of the Bible Society's alleged mystical and sectarian associations, the campaign ultimately crippled the society's influence and standing by 1824. Collaborating with conservative War Minister Arakcheev, the publicist and naval admiral Aleksandr Shishkov launched a set of public charges against the Bible Society in that year, condemning the society more for its associations than for the substance of its activity. Shishkov claimed that the Bible Society was brought to Russia by an English Methodist (Paterson was a Scot and a Congregationalist, neither English nor Methodist). Shishkov pointed out that it was quite abnormal that "our hierarchs should be sitting down on these matters with Lutherans, Catholics, Calvinists, and Quakers – in a word, with members of foreign creeds [*inovertsami*]."[76]

Shishkov and Arakcheev were able to enlist in their campaign the support of church hierarchs Serafim (Glagolevskii), Metropolitan of St. Petersburg, and Evgenii (Bolkhovitinov), Metropolitan of Kiev. Their success in this effort was reflected in a formal written piece, "Opinion Regarding the Bible Society," composed by the two conservative hierarchs in 1824. According to this joint opinion, Bible Society publishing efforts were unnecessary because the 1751 Slavonic edition had been routinely published in St. Petersburg, Moscow, and Kiev, and no assistance on that score was needed. As regarded the modern language editions of the society, the two prelates argued, not without some foundation, that there was enough backstock of Bible Society editions out in the provinces such that the demand could easily be met for years to come. Alluding to the arguments of Aleksandr Shishkov regarding association with foreigners, Metropolitans Serafim and Evgenii found that the mixture of Orthodox believers with those of foreign creeds in such a society was "non-canonical." In addressing the issue of the modern Russian Bible, the two metropolitans argued further that the failure to include explanatory matter with the translations fueled sectarianism, even as the Russian text more generally weakened adherence to the Slavonic text in liturgical worship. Finally, they found that the commercial means used for sale of the volumes encouraged profit-taking from the sale of Bibles. In the end, Metropolitans Serafim and Evgenii concluded that the society, for all these reasons, should be closed.[77]

[76] "Sobstvennoruchnaia zapiska A. S. Shishkova o bibleiskikh obshchestvakh," in *Sbornik istoricheskikh materialov, izvlechennykh iz arkhiva sobstvennoi ego Imperatorskago Velichestva Kantseliarii*, ed. N. F. Dubrovin (St. Petersburg, 1903), XII: 339–47. For Shishkov's opposition to the Bible Society, see also the documents in "Razsuzhdenie A. S. Shishkova o bibleiskikh obshchestvakh voobshche i v osobennosti o rossiiskom bibleiskom obshchestve," in *Sbornik istoricheskikh materialov*, ed. Dubrovin, 348–76.

[77] "Mnenie preosviashchennykh mitropolitov novgorodskogo Serafima i kievskogo Evgeniia o bibleiskom obshchestve," in *Sbornik istoricheskikh materialov*, ed. Dubrovin, 376–8. The three concerns

Metropolitan Serafim followed up the "Opinion" with two letters of his own and a personal visit to Alexander I in December 1824.[78] In the letters Serafim presented what would be a recurring theme directed against Bible Society adherents – namely, that the continued existence of the Bible Society threatened Russia with church schism. "It is impossible not to agree," intoned Metropolitan Serafim, "that the general turning to the Bible without other means toward instilling piety in the people has contributed to such a schism." By "schism," Serafim was not referring to the Old Believer schism of the seventeenth century. Rather his objection was to the rise of sectarianism (non-Orthodox Christian confessions within the Russian Empire) and the divisions within Russian religious culture occasioned by the mystical turn toward a new "religion of the heart." Responding to this combined challenge from among Orthodox prelates and high-placed advisors such as War Minister Arakcheev, Emperor Alexander I finally dismissed Aleksandr Golitsyn from his ministerial posts and from the presidency of the Russian Bible Society in the spring of 1824, ironically naming Metropolitan Serafim as the new president of the society. Metropolitan Serafim had sat on the Bible Society's governing committee for most of the prior decade, but in the new circumstances of mounting court and synodal opposition to the religious awakening, he did not wish to be drawn into the Bible Society presidency. On December 28, 1824, Serafim penned a second note to the emperor, claiming that it would be inappropriate for him to be serving both as a senior member of the Holy Synod and president of the Bible Society. Instead, Serafim called for the outright closure of the society, an action that Alexander I refused to take. As a result, the publishing and organizational efforts of the Russian Bible Society devolved into an uneasy limbo status in 1825, lacking the imperial patronage and support of the immediate post-Vienna period. The fact that the society's presidency was to be held by a prelate who had declared his unwillingness to hold such office foreshadowed its ultimate closure.

The limbo status of the Russian Bible Society ended with the November 1825 death of Emperor Alexander I and the abortive Decembrist uprising. In

articulated by Metropolitans Serafim and Evgenii were relatively new to the debate on Russian biblical translation – namely, that the Bible Society's failure to attach notes or commentary fueled sectarianism, that the Russian text weakened the authority of the Slavonic text used in liturgical worship, and that the commercial success of the society was a problem. Notably absent from the critique was any discussion of the RBS texts and their textology.

[78] Metropolitan Serafim's two letters are included in M. Ia. Moroshkin, "K istorii bibleiskikh obshchestv," *Russkii arkhiv*, 6 (1868): 940–51 – "Pis'mo mitropolita Serafima k imperatoru Aleksandru 1-mu, ot 11-ogo dekabria 1824 g." (940–2); and "Vtoroe pis'mo mitropolita Serafima k imperatoru Aleksandru o tom zhe predmete, ot 28-ogo dekabria 1824 goda" (943–4).

April 1826, Emperor Nicholas I issued a formal rescript closing the society and its press, and distributing its assets.[79] The printing establishment launched by the Bible Society was turned over to the Engineering Corps. Stereotype printing was abandoned, not to begin again in Russia for another generation. Translation of Holy Scripture into Russian was proscribed. Some of the unbound copies of the Octateuch were burned, but most of the unsold stock remained for subsequent sale. Nicholas I's rescript said nothing to preclude circulation of the remaining stock of the society's bound scripture, which was given over to the Holy Synod.[80] In the absence of any specific proscription directed against circulation of scriptural texts, the unsold stock of the Bible Society continued to be purchased from the Synod, much of it for distribution under the aegis of a new Protestant Bible Society founded after the collapse of the Russian Bible Society. The London Missionary Society's Congregational minister, Rev. Richard Knill, who had arrived in Petersburg in 1820 at the urging of John Paterson to minister to the small expatriate evangelical community, remained in St. Petersburg, lending a minor element of continuity with the Bible Society era of Alexandrine Russia.

All of the reasons traditionally given for the collapse of the Russian Bible Society are plausible and offer a measure of explanatory power – the divisive patronage politics of the Arakcheevshchina, the resurgent European-wide counter-revolutionary forces of Metternichean legitimism, the perceived dangers of the new mystical pietism and freemasonic currents in Russian religious culture, and the concerns over sectarian heterodoxy in traditionally Orthodox Russia. However, by focusing on the issues of authority posed in the politics of modern Russian biblical translation, it is possible to reach beyond these traditional arguments to a more deep-seated explanation for the Bible Society's demise. For what the politics of Russian biblical translation had generated in Alexandrine Russia was a fundamental challenge to the traditional arbitration of authority in Russian religious culture. What the Russian Bible Society and its modern press had done was to introduce for the first time into Russian religious culture the role of the marketplace. The threat of Johannes Gossner, after all, was not to be found in the content of his commentary on the Gospel of St. Matthew, but rather in the popular,

79 For the decree, see *PSZ*, sobr. 2, vol. 1 (1826), no. 475.

80 In his separate notification to Metropolitan Serafim, Nicholas I gave to the Holy Synod the remaining stock of unsold scripture, which was to be held under Serafim's oversight. In his note, the emperor places a value on the remaining stock of up to 2,000,000 rubles (see Nicholas I to Metropolitan Serafim of St. Petersburg, July 15, 1826, in RGIA, *fond* 808, *opis* 1, *delo* 242, *l.* 1).

public appeal of his preaching. Similarly, the goal of stereotype printing was to provide scripture at commercially viable prices far below anything that could be offered by the Holy Synod. The Russian Bible Society succeeded in this mission far beyond what anyone in authority could have anticipated. It was also the commercial appeal of scripture available in the common languages of the Russian Empire, and for the first time in Russian itself, that was unique to the society's operation. Freed from the constraints of censorial review, the Bible Society also challenged the traditional textual authority of the Slavonic Bible in ways that could hardly have been anticipated by the forty clerics and laymen who attended the first meeting of the Bible Society in Petersburg in January 1813.

This introduction of the market and supply-side innovations corresponded closely to the role played also by the BFBS in early nineteenth-century Britain. As in the case of the Russian Bible Society, the BFBS was a commercial enterprise whose mission was to sell "cheap Bibles" to an expanded literate audience, to use the phrase coined by Leslie Howsam. It, too, could challenge established authority, whether it was the challenge posed by some BFBS non-conformists to high-church Anglicanism, or the leadership of some BFBS committee members in the anti-slavery movement.

Unwitting agents of modernity, the market-oriented enthusiasts of the Russian Bible Society and their supporters in scores of Bible Society chapters throughout the Russian Empire evidenced at times also the kind of raw self-assurance that separates them today from postmodern skeptics. When Aleksandr Labzin wrote confidently about the interior religion of the heart, when Aleksandr Golitsyn spoke of a broadly Christian empire, or when Paterson spoke in black-and-white terms about "priest-ridden, papistical" forces arrayed against God's light, there was a self-confident air that we commonly associate with the dawn of modernity.

Ultimately, this introduction of the market and supply-side innovations into modern Russian religious culture was unable to be sustained. The Bible Society had developed a novel supply-side marketing of biblical literature in a domain that had hitherto been under the exclusive purview of the Holy Synod. In this sense, the Russian Bible Society was undermined by its own remarkable success. The opposition within official court and church circles that developed in the 1820s – from Admiral Shishkov, General Arakcheev, Metropolitan Serafim, Archimandrite Fotii, and others – would almost surely have been mollified had the Bible Society and its printing establishment not been such a remarkable commercial success.

So relatively efficient was this new publishing enterprise that circulation totaling close to one million copies of scripture printed in Petersburg in twenty-six languages had begun to outstrip demand. Paterson complained at the end of 1823 that the auxiliary branch chapters or sections were not selling enough copies.[81] Warehouse inventories consequently began to build in the 1820s. Thomas Rutt, concerned about his profits, had earlier approached Aleksandr Golitsyn about the possibility of using his excess stereotyping capacity to do publishing work for the government.[82] Along with some of his western friends in the capital, Paterson had tried to generate additional readership by providing copies gratis to prisoners and by encouraging through the establishment of Lancaster schools the wider development of literacy.[83] In short, if there was a lack of readership, then the indefatigable Paterson simply needed to forge such a readership. In all these ways, the architects of the Russian Bible Society had become unwitting agents of modernity, commercial agents appealing to the demand of an evolving religious marketplace.

Paterson, Golitsyn, and the Bible Society committee in Petersburg had developed the Bible Society's publishing capacity by introducing into Petersburg "an English printing company" that completely circumvented normal registrations and censorship oversight. Yet the new reality of the 1820s in which supply exceeded demand revealed deeper conflicts that set the Bible Society on a collision course with powerful elements in Alexandrine Russia. As the Bible Society sought an ever broader readership, the society's own visibility – its very success – alarmed those conservative Orthodox prelates who had initially supported the Bible Society out of loyalty to the emperor. The opposition that arose from Metropolitans Serafim and Evgenii, as well as from the reactionary Archimandrite Fotii, reflected the growing alienation of the Russian Church hierarchy from the Bible Society, as the society's operations came increasingly to be perceived as a threat to what was formerly the Synod's hegemonial prerogative to publish and disseminate scripture. In the highly structured traditional religio-political culture of Orthodox Russia, the

[81] RGIA, *fond* 808, *opis'* 1, *delo* 10, *ll.* 395–6 (Paterson's memorandum to the printing subcommittee, [December 1823]). Paterson also noted that circulation of the Slavonic/Russian diglot had slowed owing to the printing of the NT in Russian only. He recommended that unsold copies of the diglot be distributed gratis to the poor and to prisoners.

[82] Rutt to Golitsyn, February 1819, RGIA, *fond* 808, *opis'* 1, *delo* 49, *ll.* 51–2.

[83] Paterson recounts in *The Book for Every Land*, 302–5 and 309–10, that already in late 1818 he had introduced the Quaker advocates of Lancaster schools, Messrs. Allen and Grellet, to Interior Minister Kochubei, who added support to the cause. Concern for education ultimately led Paterson and like-minded British residents in Petersburg to prepare with the support of the emperor a set of scripture readings for use in the schools – readings that continued to be used after the closure of the RBS and the official proscription on publication of modern Russian scripture. See Appendix, nos. 27 (1843) and 28 (1845). Paterson's *Book for Every Land* documents the commitment of Walter Venning and other collaborators in prison reform, a commitment shared by Prince Golitsyn who also headed the Prison Reform Society. For this philanthropic activity during the reign of Alexander I, see n. 39 above.

marketplace was not supposed to determine the fate of the word, especially in such a traditionally sensitive area as that of sacred texts. Behind the new protestations directed, for example, against Bible Society committee member Aleksandr Labzin lay not just the surface issues of Labzin's journal *Messenger of Zion* and the editor's ties with religious mystics, but also the unspoken issue of his leadership in a Bible Society that had succeeded in reaching an ever larger audience while circumventing the conventions, sanctions, and institutions normally limiting such marketable activities.

Even more pernicious from this perspective was Bible Society President Aleksandr Golitsyn. Golitsyn's access to Alexander I had assured a favorable interpretation of the activities of the Bible Society before an emperor whose commitment to a more Christian empire tended to obscure such subtleties as canon law, church tradition, or textual authority. War Minister Arakcheev, who also had the ear of the emperor, loathed such unpredictable religious influences upon Alexander I. Meanwhile, the commitment to a more Christian empire could also become censorious. After all, in Golitsyn's dual ministry his lieutenants in the field of education, Dmitrii Runich and Mikhail Magnitskii, sought to impose ever narrower forms of moral education on the curriculum of newly established institutions of higher education. It is clear that the Bible Society's success generated opposition from all sides.

Most interesting was the opposition that arose from within the Russian intelligentsia, as typified by the sarcastic wit of Alexander Pushkin's epigrams directed against the "Bible men." On the one hand, Pushkin used his witty epigrams to attack Prince Golitsyn's repressive lieutenants and their crackdown on secular higher education. Noting the deepening conflicts at court and relishing the predicament of the one-time agnostic Golitsyn, Pushkin capitalized on the growing disaffection with Golitsyn to attack this pious imperial advisor who had provided cover for the opponents of modern higher education. On the eve of Golitsyn's forced "resignation" in 1824, Pushkin penned the epigram, "On Prince A. N. Golitsyn":

Here we have the soul of a slave,
Education's chief destructor . . .
For God's sake, put pressure on him,
From all sides attack withal!
From behind shall we not try him?
That's his weakest side of all.[84]

[84] Translation is by Cynthia Whittaker, ed., *Alexander Pushkin: Epigrams and Satirical Verse* (Ann Arbor, MI: Ardis, 1986), 36.

In light of the modernist commercial agenda of the Bible Society, perhaps Pushkin's challenge to the "Bible men" anticipated a yet deeper reality. Was it not possible that Pushkin, in his challenge to the self-assurance of the Bible men, was also airing an early anti-modernist message, repelled as he was by the raw self-confidence of these agents of the marketplace? Pushkin captured not only this self-assurance, but also the sycophancy of Bible Society followers and Orthodox prelates who had earlier pandered to imperial patronage at a time when the Bible Society commanded the loyalties of much of high society. As Pushkin writes in this untitled epigram of 1819:

> The Bible men enjoy such bliss,
> Their asses boast such cleanliness;
> The monks just lick their sirs –
> The holy low-down curs![85]

When the tide began to turn against the Russian Bible Society and its remarkable printing operation, it had nowhere to go – court, nobility, church, or intelligentsia. Paterson's instinctive appeal to a broader audience – his concern for expanded literacy, for example – revealed the central problem. Operating in a highly structured and hierarchical political and religious culture, the more egalitarian, market-oriented Bible Society movement in Russia, despite the early support of the emperor and his favorites, lacked an independent constituency that could uphold it under fire. Bible reading had not been a traditional form of Orthodox piety. Beyond the clergy and intelligentsia, literacy was still largely confined to the more secular, urban population for many of whom the activities of the Russian Bible Society were of marginal interest.

In short, the Russian Bible Society met its demise not because it provided a vehicle for religious mystics and freemasons, although it may have done that as well. Rather, it collapsed because, in seeking to extend its appeal, it turned to a nascent marketplace, circumventing those religious and bureaucratic authorities which traditionally maintained control over and access to spiritual and political authority. Given the potential power of the publishing establishment that the Russian Bible Society had created, it was notable that even the technology of stereotyping itself fell into abeyance after the fall of the Bible Society. When stereotyping resurfaced in Russian printing a quarter-century later, it was no longer as an independent technology propelling change, but as a carefully managed component of a publishing industry that conformed to the dictates of official censorship.

[85] Ibid., 34.

Within a few months of Nicholas I's accession to power the Russian Bible Society was officially closed by imperial decree. According to the April 1826 decree, not only was the Bible Society to close its operations, but the publication of scripture was to be permitted solely in the Slavonic language. The decree, however, expressly permitted the ongoing circulation of Russian scripture published by the Bible Society.[86] Circulation of modern Russian scripture was neither prohibited by law nor restricted to the offices of the Holy Synod. As a result, western Bible Societies, as well as a Protestant Bible Society in Russia, continued to distribute biblical literature in the reign of Nicholas I. John Paterson, who had abandoned his ties with the BFBS while serving as director of the Russian Bible Society, returned to Scotland, having been granted by the emperor an annual pension of six thousand rubles, which he continued to receive until his death in 1854.[87]

The Russian Bible Society, from its founding in 1812 to its closure in 1826, set important precedents for the subsequent course of modern Russian biblical translation and publication. It established the importance of the Hebrew Masoretic text in Russian Old Testament translation. It addressed the issue of biblical translation and distribution for non-Russian nationals of the empire. Politically, it appealed beyond the structures of the Holy Synod both in its publishing program and in its unexpectedly large constituency of local sections or affiliated chapters. Most significantly, with the support of a sympathetic Orthodox Christian emperor who shared the Bible Society's vision of religious awakening in a more Christian empire, it launched for the first time systematic translation and publication of the Bible in modern Russian. Its success in these matters was in good measure a result of its unique printing establishment that operated outside the constraints of official censorship and corporate registration. Within a matter of months, the Russian Bible Society created in Petersburg the largest press in Eurasia using the most modern western stereotype technology and managerial organization available. There was, however, a supreme irony to these precedents. For in securing its broad authority to translate and publish scripture, the Russian Bible Society appealed outside normal religious and social/estate structures to the highest levels of imperial court politics. But the very politics that were so instrumental in creating the Russian Bible Society's unique status after its founding left the society vulnerable a decade

86 For a copy of Nicholas I's rescript (April 12, 1826) closing the RBS, see "Vysochaishii reskript mitropolitu Serafimu," in *Sbornik istoricheskikh materialov*, ed. Dubrovin, 379. It is also copied in Paterson to Reyner (St. Petersburg, April 16/28, 1826), BFBS Foreign Correspondence Inwards, 1826, 81.

87 On Paterson's pension, see the instructions issued in 1826 and again in 1827 by synodal Ober-prokuror Meshcherskii, RGIA, *fond* 808, *opis'* 1, *delo* 291, *ll.* 17, 35, and 43.

later when the shifting politics of the Russian court undermined the position and authority of the society and its president Aleksandr Golitsyn. Precisely because of the extraordinary technological success of its independent publishing establishment, the Bible Society had become by then a powerful threat to the very institutions, such as the Holy Synod, whose support was needed in the shifting politics of biblical translation. After Russian biblical translation was officially proscribed in 1826, the politics of the Russian Bible in the reign of Nicholas I shifted to unofficial clandestine and foreign publication.

CHAPTER 3

Foreign and clandestine publishing in Nikolaevan Russia

Despite the Russian Bible Society's closure in 1826, the Bible continued to be translated into Russian, and editions of Russian scripture continued to be published and disseminated throughout the reign of Nicholas I. Because of the emperor's 1826 decree, however, translation and publication shifted abroad and to unofficial, clandestine venues.[1] While distribution of the remaining Bible Society stock was permitted under the emperor's 1826 rescript, the Holy Synod and other official organs of the Russian Orthodox Church did not participate in the sale or dissemination of Russian translated editions of scripture. For the thirty-year period of the reign of Nicholas I, Russian biblical translation moved underground, with circulation handled unofficially and through largely non-Orthodox religious channels. The unintended consequence of the 1826 rescript was the opening of a period of semi-clandestine biblical activity during which the more repressive atmosphere of the day nevertheless witnessed renewed, politically charged interest in the Russian Bible.

This unofficial nature of Russian biblical translation and circulation was reflected in a new locus of support for the Russian Bible. While the Russian Bible Society had received imperial patronage, post-1826 support for Russian biblical translation came almost exclusively from outside the ranks of the nobility and the church hierarchy – that is, from laypeople, seminarians, missionaries, parish clergy, and academy professors. In this regard, the Russian Bible served as a barometer for the disaffection between a synodal bureaucracy and hierarchy, on the one hand, wedded largely to support for the old regime, and a growing, articulate group of church laypeople and

[1] Notable exceptions were the extracts of Russian scripture published for school use and an 1840 Aleut/Russian diglot of the Gospel of St. Matthew (Appendix, nos. 26–30). The Aleut-Fox translation, done under the supervision of Alaskan missionary, Ioann Veniaminov (later Innokentii, Metropolitan of Moscow), was probably able to be published because of its exclusive missionary use in North America.

clerics, on the other, who saw access to the Russian Bible as a symbol of the need for the Russian church to be more attuned to the problems of contemporary society. Amidst this growing polarity of positions, Metropolitan Filaret (Drozdov) of Moscow sought the untenable middle ground position. Committed to the cause of modern translation since his days on the Bible Society committee, Metropolitan Filaret nevertheless sought to avoid an open confrontation with church leadership over the issue. Filaret tried with minimal success to postpone the issue, responding bureaucratically or evasively to appeals for modern translation. Frustrated in the end, he added his voice to those of official reaction in the celebrated Pavskii affair, at which point he withdrew altogether from participation in the Holy Synod in the 1840s. The intensified politics of modern biblical translation in the reign of Emperor Nicholas I recognized very little middle ground, Filaret's withdrawal from synodal affairs reflecting this polarization of positions.

WHO HAD THE RIGHT TO DISTRIBUTE RUSSIAN SCRIPTURE?

In the impasse between official church circles and the defenders of modern biblical translation, the issue of authority once again was tested, but in the aftermath of the Russian Bible Society it was the authority to distribute that first ignited controversy. The question of the authority to distribute Holy Scripture arose in connection with the disposition of the remaining stock of RBS scripture remaining in the society's Petersburg depot. The 1826 decree closing the Bible Society specified that the remaining assets, including the unsold stock of scripture, were to go to the Holy Synod. Faced with the storage of tens of thousands of volumes of bound and unbound scripture, the Synod initially chose to retain use of the Bible Society's building as a depot, even employing the former depot custodian, H. M. Andresen.

Actual distribution of the back-stock, however, awaited the intervention of one of the holdovers from the Bible Society era, the Rev. Richard Knill (see Figure 6).[2] Richard Knill had come to Petersburg in 1820 at the invitation of John Paterson to meet the needs of a small community of

[2] On Knill and his service to the London Missionary Society, see his autobiographical reflections compiled by Charles Birrell, *The Life of the Rev. Richard Knill of St. Petersburgh*, 3rd edn (London: James Nisbet & Co., 1860). The depot superintendant H. M. Andresen reported having heard that Emperor Nicholas I was prepared to give over all the Protestant editions of the Bibles and NTs (i.e. those published in German or Baltic languages by the RBS) for delivery to the Protestants in Russia. See Andresen to BFBS (St. Petersburg, June 18/30, 1827), BFBS Foreign Correspondence Inwards, 1827, no. 3, 28.

Figure 6. Richard Knill (1787–1857), London Missionary Society Congregational pastor and BFBS St. Petersburg agent, 1820–33.
Source: Charles M. Birrell, *The Life of Richard Knill of St. Petersburgh, Being Selections from his Reminiscences, Journals, and Correspondence*, 3rd edn. (London: James Nisbet & Co., 1860).

British evangelicals who were not otherwise served by the official Anglican chaplaincy of the British Company in Petersburg. The British community in St. Petersburg numbered approximately two thousand at the time. Salaried by both the London Missionary Society and the Scottish Missionary Society, the Congregationalist Knill not only took over as pastor for the expatriate evangelical community in Petersburg, but also became the liaison person for the field operations of these missionary societies in Eurasia, including the London Missionary Society's trans-Baikal mission in Selenginsk and the Scottish Missionary Society's Karass mission in the Caucasus.[3] Knill also launched an English-language primary school for both girls and boys whose parents might not otherwise have funding for private tutors.[4] It is in the context of this continuing British evangelical presence in Petersburg that distribution of the Bible Society's back inventory began.

[3] Birrell, *The Life of the Rev. Richard Knill*, 101. On the Selenginsk mission, see Charles Bawden, *Shamans, Lamas, and Evangelicals: The English Missionaries of Siberia* (London: Routledge & Kegan Paul, 1985).

[4] Supported by Princess Meshcherskaia (wife of Ober-prokuror Petr Meshcherskii), whom Knill calls a "nursing mother" to the school, and with instruction offered by the two Meshcherskii daughters, Sofiia and Mariia, this British evangelical primary school in Petersburg reached an enrollment of 270

By the end of 1827, within months of John Paterson's departure from Petersburg, Knill began a series of appeals to BFBS for funds "to purchase Russian, Armenian and other such Biblical Books as can be got from the Russian Bible Society depot and which are wanted here."[5] John Paterson added his own voice in early 1828, attaching a letter he had received from Archbishop Tengstrom of Finland, requesting BFBS purchase of 2,000 Finnish New Testaments, so that they could be provided to the Protestant Bible Society in Petersburg for transmittal onward to Finland.[6] What followed was a pattern in which the BFBS and other international donor agencies offered financial support for Richard Knill to purchase Bible Society back-stock from the Holy Synod for subsequent resale or gratis distribution either directly by Knill himself or through the aegis of the newly established Protestant Bible Society.

The Protestant Bible Society (PBS) in Petersburg was founded in November 1827 under the presidency of Count Karl von Lieven, a prominent Baltic German Lutheran who served in the courts of Alexander I and Nicholas I, and had been active in the RBS. He was Minister of Public Instruction in the early years of Nicholas I's administration. In order to secure access to the back-stock of scripture for Protestants of the empire, the newly formed PBS sought to bring John Paterson back to St. Petersburg to handle the negotiations with the Holy Synod.[7] Paterson, having been given

boys and 70 girls in 1823. Another approximately 300 students had to be refused admission owing to limits of space. See Birrell, *The Life of the Rev. Richard Knill*, 97. Having begun informally before Knill's arrival in Petersburg, the school continued to be attached to the local evangelical church up to the Russian Revolution of 1917. The school's archive, 470 files dating from 1818 to 1917, is located in the Tsentral'nyi gosudarstvennyi istoricheskii arkhiv Sankt-Peterburga (TsGIA SPb – Central State Historical Archive of St. Petersburg), *fond* 499 ("Uchilishche pri reformatskikh tserkvakh v g. Petrograde" ["School attached to reformed churches in the city of Petrograd"]). For a description of the archive, see A. Kh. Gorfunkel' and L. E. Strel'tsova, *Gosudarstvennyi istoricheskii arkhiv Leningradskoi oblasti: Kratkii putevoditel'* (Leningrad, 1960), 69.

5 Knill to Robert Pinkerton (St. Petersburg, December 27, 1827), BFBS Foreign Correspondence Inwards, 1828, no. 1, 68.

6 Paterson to Rev. Andrew Brandram (Edinburgh, January 2, 1828), BFBS Foreign Correspondence Inwards, 1828, no. 1, 8.

7 Writing on behalf of Count Lieven, John Venning appealed to Paterson. See Venning to Paterson (St. Petersburg, November 12, 1827), in BSA Deposited Papers, F3/Paterson: Memoirs and Papers, 1805–50, 130. Regarding Nicholas I's permission for the founding of the Protestant Bible Society in November 1827, see Venning to Joseph Tarn/BFBS (London, October 4, 1830), BFBS Home Correspondence Inwards, 1830. Known informally as the Protestant Bible Society, its official title in 1831 became the Evangelical Bible Society in Russia (Evangelicheskoe bibleiskoe obshchestvo v Rossii, EBOR). Alongside Lieven, other EBOR officers with RBS experience included its secretary, Karl von Poll, and its treasurer, Pomian Pezarovius. Pezarovius, editor of *Russkii invalid*, served subsequently as president of the Petersburg Evangelical Lutheran Consistory (1833–47). Like its RBS predecessor, the EBOR had a governing main committee (*glavnyi komitet*), with branches or sections (*otdeleniia*) operating in major urban centers and provinces inhabited by the empire's Protestant population. Within several of these *otdeleniia*, there were individual associations or affiliates (*sotovarishchestva*).

a generous pension by Nicholas I, was unwilling to return to Petersburg for such a purpose. Instead, Richard Knill became the central intermediary, procuring through the Holy Synod the back-stock of Russian and other biblical texts, including the occasional purchase of German and other non-Russian biblical texts from abroad.

Knill's operation extended beyond the mere distribution of biblical texts. Princess Meshcherskaia had given over to Knill some 70,000 of her published tracts, which Knill also added to his retail circulation. By September 1830, Knill recorded in his autobiographical journal that he had distributed 14,000 copies of scripture since beginning his circulation efforts two years previously. Adding prayer books, school books, and tracts, he estimated a total circulation of approximately 120,000 imprints.[8] By October 1832, shortly before his final departure from St. Petersburg in 1833, Knill reported that the unsold stock of Russian New Testaments from the Bible Society era had dwindled to just 300 copies. Lest that generate London home office interest in the republication of Bible Society Russian editions, Knill expressed concern over any possible BFBS foreign publication of the Russian NT for subsequent sale in Russia. His comments reflected the new realities governing the publication of Russian scripture in the aftermath of the RBS – "it is not at all likely that strangers will be given the right to issue [such an] edition, that being the sacred privilege of the Holy Synod."[9]

Thus, in the period from the 1826 RBS closure to Richard Knill's 1833 departure from St. Petersburg, the precedent was established for BFBS-subvented purchase from the Holy Synod of Russian scripture for sale and

EBOR assumed jurisdiction over thirty-nine such former RBS *otdeleniia* and *sotovarishchestva*. Despite the operation of these EBOR subdivisions and auxiliaries prior to 1831, the imperial charter establishing the society was not issued until 1831, and anniversaries of the organization were marked from that date. EBOR eventually received the right to draw upon the remaining stock of RBS-published scripture. When supplies in non-Russian languages of the empire dwindled, EBOR purchased scripture from Bible Societies in the West, particularly the Canstein Bible Society of Halle. The Halle ties were important for those Lutherans of the Baltic provinces who had never adopted the restrictive BFBS exclusion of deuterocanonical texts from printed editions of the Bible. In the last half of the nineteenth century, the Latvian and Estonian sections of EBOR were able to publish their own Baltic-language texts of scripture, and the EBOR main committee established in Petersburg a warehouse for Bibles within its own Evangelicheskaia Biblioteka, a library containing more than 50,000 volumes, including scripture in German, French, English, Finnish, Swedish, Danish, and Russian. On the Evangelical Bible Society, see "Bibleiskie obshchestva," in *Khristianstvo: Entsiklopedicheskii slovar'* (Moscow: "Bol'shaia Rossiiskaia entsiklopediia," 1993), 1: 229–30; also Freeze, "Die Lutherisch-Evangelische Kirche in Russland."

8 Birrell, *The Life of the Rev. Richard Knill*, 165. By 1846, Knill's successor reported that total circulation of scripture from the onset of renewed circulation, 1828 to 1846, was 191,896 copies (see T. S. Ellerby to John Jackson [St. Petersburg, British and American Chapel, February 28/March 12, 1846], BFBS Foreign Correspondence Inwards, 1846, no. 1, 186).

9 Knill to Rev. Jackson/BFBS (Sarepta House, St. Petersburg, October 5, 1832 N.S.), BFBS Foreign Correspondence Inwards, 1832, no. 4, 18.

gratis distribution, often in cooperation with the new Protestant Bible Society, and exclusively among the non-Russian population of the empire. That pattern would continue unbroken right up to the Russian Revolution of 1917. The Holy Synod, for its part, agreed to permit outlets such as that of Knill to distribute Russian scripture so long as the financial returns warranted it. What the Holy Synod did not concede was its sole authority to publish scripture. This claim to exclusive synodal authority – a break with the more market-oriented Russian Bible Society – was to be tested in three separate incidents during the reign of Nicholas I.

FOREIGN PUBLICATION OF RUSSIAN SCRIPTURE

The first of these tests to synodal authority involved foreign republication of RBS modern Russian biblical translations. Rev. Knill's successor as pastor to the English evangelical community in Petersburg, Rev. J. C. Brown, and the British commercial importer in Petersburg who served as a frequent intermediary with the BFBS London offices, Archibald Mirrielees, both cautioned London about the inadvisability of republishing the RBS Russian NT abroad.[10] But Robert Pinkerton, who had abandoned Petersburg in 1823 and was by the 1830s repositioned in Germany as a BFBS agent, argued otherwise. Citing the absence of Russian scriptures in Moscow – a concern brought to his attention by Aleksandr Turgenev, one of the former Golitsyn aides and an RBS secretary – and noting the ability to spirit such texts through border stations in the Baltic, through Poland, and through the Black Sea, Pinkerton argued for BFBS funding of a foreign edition that could be camouflaged as a speculative venture by a private publisher.[11] In the end, Pinkerton's willingness to defy synodal hegemony on the matter trumped the more cautious position of BFBS representatives in Petersburg. The resulting 1838 edition printed at the publishing house of Karl Tauchnitz in Leipzig was

[10] Mirrielees to Rev. Jackson/BFBS (St. Petersburg, September 17/29, 1837), BFBS Foreign Correspondence Inwards, 1837, no. 3: 178. Mirrielees writes: "We are all of the opinion that it would be a very inadvisable step to get an edition of the Modern Russ NT published at Leipzig, even were it quite practicable." Fearing that the suspicions raised by such an edition would threaten all other operations in Petersburg, they argued strongly against such an effort. Archibald Mirrielees served as intermediary for the BFBS in St. Petersburg during much of the period between the departure of Richard Knill and the outbreak of the Crimean War. On the Mirrielees family and its evangelical and entrepreneurial ventures in Russia, see Harvey Pitcher, *Muir and Mirrielees: The Scottish Partnership that Became a Household Name in Russia* (Cromer, Norfolk: Swallow House Books, 1994).

[11] See Pinkerton to A. Brandram/BFBS (Berlin, July 22, 1837), BFBS Foreign Correspondence Inwards, 1837, no. 3, 54; and Pinkerton to Jackson/BFBS (Frankfurt, October 23, 1837), BFBS Foreign Correspondence Inwards, no. 3, 199.

the first Russian New Testament ever printed abroad.[12] Identical to the text of the RBS NT, it was issued in 2,000 copies, 500 of which were to be sent to Constantinople and secreted into southern Russia.[13]

Despite the difficulties of circulating such externally published texts within the Russian Empire, the Leipzig edition did not mark the end of Russian biblical publication abroad during the reign of Nicholas I. The Leipzig edition was reprinted by Tauchnitz in 1850. More curious was the subsequent fate of the Leipzig edition. Using stereotype plates provided by the Tauchnitz Press in Leipzig, the BFBS republished this Russian NT in two large reprintings in 1854 for gratis distribution among Russians taken prisoner in the Crimean War.[14] In addition to these Russian New Testaments, the BFBS sponsored publication of a revised 1852 edition of the popular RBS Psalter. In the case of the Psalter, significant revision was required to meet what had become the more rigid BFBS policy proscribing publication of deutero-canonical texts, as well as any "note or comment" in their editions. For this purpose the BFBS hired its translations consultant from the days of the Russian Bible Society, Ebenezer Henderson, to oversee revision of the text. Henderson eliminated the original introductory preface to readers and the 151st Psalm, but otherwise followed the text of the RBS Psalter in what became the Leipzig 1852 Psalter. So as not to identify the publication with the work of its agency in St. Petersburg, the BFBS removed any reference to its sponsorship in this 1852 Leipzig Russian Psalter.[15]

Published only at the very end of the nineteenth century, one other significant translation of Russian scripture undertaken abroad during the reign of Nicholas I has invariably been lost in the wider history of Russian biblical translation – namely, the NT translation of the nineteenth-century romantic poet Vasilii Zhukovskii (1783–1852). A contemporary of Alexander Pushkin and member of the "Arzamas" circle, Zhukovskii was mainly

[12] *Gospoda Nashego Iisusa Khrista Novyi Zavet* (Leipzig: Karl Tauchnitz Press, 1838) – Appendix, no. 24.

[13] The 500 copies were sent to London for binding, and then onward to Constantinople. The BFBS agent in Smyrna, Benjamin Barker, initially assured London offices that "we shall never be destitute of Christian coworkers in Russia to receive and dispose of the books in a judicious manner" (B. Barker to John Jackson [Smyrna, January 10, 1838], BFBS Foreign Correspondence Inwards, 1838, no. 1, 58). Later, Barker was forced to concede on advice from representatives on the ground in Odessa: "I think it will be better not to make the experiment here for the present" (Barker to Brandram/BFBS [Smyrna, February 29, 1840], BFBS Foreign Correspondence Inwards, 1840, no. 1, 140). In the end, few copies of the Leipzig edition made it through Russian customs, circulation rather being limited to Russian travelers in Germany or on the Black Sea.

[14] The 1850 reprinting (Appendix, no. 31) was issued in 1,000 copies. On the 1854 reprintings, see Appendix, no. 33.

[15] *Kniga Khvalenii ili Psaltir' na rossiiskom iazyke* (Leipzig: Karl Tauchnitz Press [for the BFBS], 1852) – Appendix, no. 32.

known for his sentimental poetry and his many translations, including Homer's *Odyssey* and works by Walter Scott and Goethe. Well placed in Russian society, he served for several years as an assisting tutor to the tsarevich, Alexander Nikolaevich (the future Emperor Alexander II).[16] His translation of the NT, undertaken during one of his many travels in German lands, was intended as a direct Russian translation from the Slavonic NT, which explains its occasional archaisms. Published posthumously in Berlin in 1895, the Zhukovskii Russian NT failed to enter into the politics of modern Russian translation, reaching a limited Russian audience only in the early twentieth century well after publication of the Holy Synod's authorized Russian translation.[17]

THE PAVSKII AFFAIR

In the aftermath of the Russian Bible Society's closure, the single most celebrated incident involving Russian biblical translation in the reign of Nicholas I was the so-called Pavskii affair. Archpriest Gerasim Petrovich Pavskii (see Figure 7) was both a former member of the Bible Society's governing committee and the society's most deeply engaged translator of the Old Testament or Hebrew Bible into modern Russian.[18] Instructor of Hebrew at the St. Petersburg Theological Academy, Pavskii used his academy instruction as the occasion for completing his Russian translation of the Hebrew Bible. In a practice that was not uncommon for the day, students in the Hebrew class arranged for publication of the resulting Russian text as a lithographic edition for their Hebrew class. When this Pavskii translation of the Hebrew Bible later began to circulate more widely in clandestine lithographed editions at the end of the 1830s, the archpriest and seminary

[16] See B. Glinskii, "Zhukovskii, Vasilii Andreevich," in *Russkii biograficheskii slovar'* (Petrograd, 1916), VII: 60–117.

[17] For selections from the Zhukovskii translation, *Novyi Zavet Gospoda nashego Iisusa Khrista*, see the journal *Strannik* (1902), no. 4. For reference to the Zhukovskii translation, including a facsimile page from the Gospel of John, see "Zhukovskii," in Men', *Bibliologicheskii slovar'*, I: 449–50.

[18] The most complete biographical works on Pavskii are those of Protopopov, *Protoierei G. P. Pavskii*; and N. I. Barsov, "Protoierei Gerasim Petrovich Pavskii: Ocherk ego zhizni po novym materialam," *Russkaia starina*, 27 (1880), kn. 1–4 and 28 (1880), kn. 1–2 (discontinuous pagination). Barsov and Protopopov had access to a Pavskii autobiography that was never published and is no longer extant. Standard accounts of the translation of the Russian Bible also contain a lengthy treatment of Pavskii. See, particularly, Chistovich, *Istoriia perevoda Biblii*; and Nikolai Astaf'ev, *Opyt istorii Biblii v Rossii v sviazi s prosveshcheniem i nravami* (St. Petersburg: V. V. Komarov, 1892). For a published account of the Pavskii affair based on Holy Synod archival holdings, see the relevant sections of A. Kotovich, *Dukhovnaia tsenzura v Rossii, 1799–1855 gg.* (St. Petersburg: "Rodnik,"1909); also S. K. Batalden, "Gerasim Pavskii's Clandestine Old Testament: The Politics of Nineteenth-Century Russian Biblical Translation," *Church History*, 57, no. 4 (1988): 486–99.

Figure 7. Archpriest Gerasim Petrovich Pavskii (1787–1863), professor of biblical studies, St. Petersburg Theological Academy, and translator of the *textus primus* of the Russian Old Testament from the Hebrew.
Source: http://dic.academic.ru/dic.nsf/ruwiki/1083477.

professor of Hebrew was drawn into one of the most extraordinary Russian church interrogations of the nineteenth century. Not only did the interrogation yield one of the most dramatic book burnings of that century, bringing down the full censorial force of the church hierarchy and synodal chancellery against modern Russian translation, but in the process the issue of the Russian Bible also became for a time the central focus in the wider arena of Russian religious politics - who had the right to translate and publish modern Russian scripture? In the politically charged atmosphere of Nikolaevan Russia, the official answer arising out of the Pavskii affair was quite simple: no one had such a right.

Gerasim Pavskii was arguably the brightest pupil of Metropolitan Filaret (Drozdov). Pavskii's work under the tutelage of Filaret dated from the period of Filaret's rectorate at the St. Petersburg Theological Academy, 1812–17. Yet in the twenty-five years following Filaret's appointment to the episcopate in 1817, the young theologian and philologist broke decisively with his former rector. This break culminated in the celebrated Pavskii affair (*delo Pavskogo*) of 1841–4, a far-reaching synodal investigation that dramatized the deep divisions within the religious culture of Orthodox Russia. On one level, these divisions involved issues of modern biblical textology.

Alongside those textological issues, however, there existed deep-seated differences over Orthodox piety and church polity that conditioned the responses of the esteemed metropolitan and the erudite theologian. This fundamental divide within Russian religious culture was never reconciled, and indeed has continued to the present in modified form both in Russia and within religious circles of the Russian emigration.

Gerasim Pavskii entered St. Petersburg Theological Academy in 1809 as a member of its first class. He excelled in ancient languages as well as theology, and was offered the post of baccalaureate instructor in Hebrew upon graduation. He continued at the St. Petersburg Academy throughout the 1820s, where he developed a reputation as an outstanding teacher and the most gifted Russian Hebraist of the first half of the nineteenth century. His work at the academy was soon combined with lectures in comparative religion at St. Petersburg University. As the leading Russian Hebraist of his day, Pavskii served as an RBS director from 1814 until its closure in 1826. As noted, during the Bible Society era, Pavskii translated for the first time into Russian the Gospel of Matthew (1819) and the Psalter (1822), while also overseeing through the Bible Society translations committee the Russian Octateuch (1825), the first eight books of the Hebrew Bible or OT.[19] In 1815, Pavskii also assumed the post of archpriest at Kazan Cathedral. By the 1820s, he had become a member of the St. Petersburg Academy's spiritual censorship committee, and, most significantly, he became in 1826 the religious tutor (*zakonouchitel'*) and confessor to the Grand Prince Alexander Nikolaevich (the future Emperor Alexander II). Pavskii formally left his post at the academy upon becoming tutor to the grand prince and princess, although he apparently continued to work informally with academy students.

Not unexpectedly, given the range of his appointments and official duties, Pavskii found himself under close scrutiny from the Russian church leadership. This was especially the case when he expressed his reservations on pedagogical grounds to Metropolitan Filaret's Catechism. Later, in 1835, when his own religious instruction of the tsarevich was challenged, Pavskii resigned the post of religious tutor and confessor.[20]

19 Pavskii's work on the RBS Octateuch is confirmed by Barsov, "Protoierei Pavskii," 505–7.

20 The early Filaret-Pavskii dispute anticipated the later events of the Pavskii affair. Pavskii had been critical of Filaret's Catechism for failing to address the practical concerns of everyday believers, and in turn Filaret in the pages of *Khristianskoe chtenie* openly criticized the liberal views of Pavskii as represented in the latter's guide to instruction of the tsarevich. For Pavskii's rejoinder, defending his position on religious instruction, see "Ob"iasnenie na primechaniia, sdelannyia protiv knizhek: 'Khristianskoe uchenie v kratkoi sisteme' i 'Nachertanie tserkovnoi istorii,'" *Chteniia v imperatorskom obshchestve istorii i drevnostei rossiiskikh pri moskovskom universitete*, 1870, kn. 2, otd. 5: 175–208. Pavskii's proposal for instruction of the tsarevich was published posthumously, "Mysli zakonouchitelia

The Pavskii affair began at the end of 1841, almost seven years after the archpriest had resigned as *zakonouchitel'* to the tsarevich and well after he had left his post as professor of Hebrew at the St. Petersburg Theological Academy. In the decade following Pavskii's departure from the St. Petersburg Academy, his Russian translations of the Hebrew Bible had continued to circulate in semi-clandestine lithographed editions. As noted in connection with his instruction in Hebrew, Pavskii had completed a full translation of the Hebrew Masoretic text – a Russian translation that he, in turn, had routinely used in the course of his theological academy instruction. Between 1838 and 1841, academy students undertook publication of Pavskii's Hebrew lecture notes in three separate lithographic editions.[21] These notes constituted, in effect, Pavskii's translation into Russian of the Hebrew Bible, or the Masoretic text of the OT. Lithographic reproduction of lecture notes was commonly undertaken by academy students, and could be done without recourse to censorial review. (The practice has its current counterpart in the reproduction and sale of faculty lecture notes by industrious fraternity or sorority undergraduates.)

The enterprising St. Petersburg divinity students undoubtedly recognized a market for the notes inasmuch as there was no other published Russian OT edition. Circulation of the lithographed editions ultimately extended to the other theological academies and to virtually every diocese of the empire. Based upon the subsequent investigation – an exhaustive synodal effort to interrogate all persons in the distribution network and recover all lithographed copies – the total circulation run for all three lithographed editions, not counting the many manuscript reproductions, was judged to be only 490 copies. Of these, 308 copies were either recovered or otherwise accounted for. Of the 308 located, 305 were burned.[22]

protoiereia G. P. Pavskogo o religioznom uchenii i vospitanii e. i. v. gosudaria velikago kniazia . . . Aleksandra Nikolaevicha, izlozhennyia v 1826 godu," *Sbornik imperatorskago russkago istoricheskago obshchestva*, 30 (1881): 61–8.

21 RNB holds five distinct sets of the lithographed collection. The most complete collection (no. 18.173.3.8) contains the books of Job, Proverbs, Ecclesiastes, the Song of Songs, and the books of the major and minor prophets. Because of the earlier Bible Society publication of the Psalter and the "non-circulating" Octateuch, these other Russian translations were never among the lithographed texts. Owing to the nature of the investigation that followed, the focus has always been on the prophetic books, which were lithographed in each of the three editions. See Appendix, no. 25.

22 Documentation of the synodal investigation is preserved in 4,000 leaves of once secret files within the Holy Synod archive, RGIA, *fond* 796, *opis'* 205, *dela* 192–213. The opening *delo* 192 bears the characteristic title, "O nelegal'nom izdanii i rasprostranenii studentami Peterburgskoi akademii litografirovannogo perevoda nekotorykh knig Biblii (Vetkhogo Zaveta) na russkii iazyk s 'prevratnymi tolkovaniiami'" ("On the illegal publication and dissemination by students of the Petersburg Academy of the lithographed translation of several books of the Bible (the OT) in Russia with 'false interpretations'"). For total print runs, see *delo* 192, *l.* 59. For the register of recovered copies and confirmation of their burning, see RGIA, *fond* 796, *opis'* 205, *delo* 195, *ll.* 28–28 ob. and *delo* 213, *l.* 2.

Previously unaware of this notable samizdat circulation within their own ecclesiastical establishment, the metropolitans of Moscow, St. Petersburg, and Kiev, as well as the synodal chancellery, were informed of the matter in late 1841 by a high-placed leak in the distribution network – Ieromonakh Agafangel (Aleksei Fedorovich Solov'ev, 1812–76), who was then serving as inspector of the Moscow Theological Academy.[23]

The matter of the erroneous translation (*nepravil'nyi perevod*) was then brought before the full Holy Synod by Ober-prokuror Protasov in February 1842.[24] In a decree signed by the six attending bishops, including Moscow Metropolitan Filaret, the Holy Synod created a formal investigatory commission with the following assignments:

1. To monitor the results of an instruction sent out to all diocesan bishops. The query to bishops was for the purpose of recovering lithographed or manuscript copies of the translation for return to the Holy Synod, and for the purpose of determining if diocesan seminary teachers owning copies held any non-Orthodox beliefs. This diocesan inquiry was to be conducted secretly without the bishops' report of the Synod's inquiry to either their diocesan chancery or their seminary.
2. To gather information on any laity holding copies.
3. To secure complete information regarding the translation, preparation, and dissemination of the work; and to determine why this was not reported earlier by the superintending authorities.
4. To oversee the strictest interrogation of students at the Moscow, Petersburg, and Kiev theological academies.
5. To submit monthly reports to the ober-prokuror regarding the progress of the investigation.

[23] RGIA, *fond* 796, *opis'* 205, *delo* 192, *ll.* 2–9. The account of Agafangel's report is standard in all secondary accounts. See, Florovsky, *Ways of Russian Theology*, 249–50. Agafangel was appointed rector of Kazan Theological Academy in 1854 and later served as bishop in several dioceses following his appointment to Revel in 1857. Although he claimed not to have any principled opposition to modern Russian biblical translation, only to the translation done by Pavskii, he submitted his report to Metropolitan Filaret (Amfiteatrov) of Kiev, a vocal opponent of modern translation, rather than to his immediate Moscow diocesan authority, Metropolitan Filaret (Drozdov). A Hebraist and later a translator in his own right, Agafangel translated the book of Job from Hebrew into modern Russian (Viatka, 1860 – see Appendix, no. 41) and the deuterocanonical book of the Wisdom of Jesus, Son of Sirakh, from Greek to Russian. See also, "Agafangel," in Men', *Bibliologicheskii slovar'*, I: 32–3.

[24] RGIA, *fond* 796, *opis'* 205, *delo* 192, *l.* 1. Moscow Metropolitan Filaret referred to the translation already in early February 1842 as a "nepravoslavnyi perevod [non-Orthodox translation]." See Filaret to Holy Synod, February 11, 1842, RGIA, *fond* 796, *opis'* 205, *delo* 192, *ll.* 10–11. Filaret's subsequent exchanges within the Synod over the matter, February-July 1842, have been published in *Sobranie mnenii i otzyvov Filareta* (St. Petersburg: Sinodal'naia tip., 1885), III: 54–81.

6. To secure a special report from Bishop Nikolai of Tambov who appeared to be the highest spiritual authority openly cooperating in the distribution.
7. To conduct [independently of the investigatory commission] a formal hearing for Archpriest Pavskii to inquire into the details of the case. The hearing was to be conducted by Moscow Metropolitan Filaret (Drozdov), Kiev Metropolitan Filaret (Amfiteatrov) and Synod Ober-prokuror Protasov.[25]

Ober-Prokuror Protasov and the synodal chancellery organized the investigation, the first stage of which involved the identification and confiscation of extant copies, along with the interrogation of those found to be in possession of the Pavskii translation. Employing a synodal decree of March 31, 1842, Ober-prokuror Protasov sent out a notice to all bishops calling for them to report the discovery of any lithographed copies they were able to locate. The Synod's decree yielded a flood of dutiful episcopal responses that were followed, in turn, by synodally directed interrogation of all those identified as having held copies of the lithographed Russian OT books.

Petr Simonovich Kazanskii, later professor of history at Moscow Theological Academy, recalled the circumstances surrounding his own interrogation in 1842 when he was a student at the Moscow academy. The interrogation was conducted by two Synod members (Bishop Agapit and Archbishop Feofan) along with an official (Balabin) from the Synod chancellery, all of whom arrived to question those students found in possession of the lithographed copies. Petr Simonovich and his fellow Moscow Theological Academy students were marshaled into a secure room from which they were individually ushered to the interrogation, a process that ran from 8:00 a.m. until 4:00 p.m. They were each questioned initially on the identity of the person through whom they had secured their own copy of the lithographed text. Kazanskii noted that, upon being called into the interrogation, the questioning in his case included the following exchange:

Q: Why did you order two copies?
A: Because it was a good book.
Q: Ah! You consider it good?
A: What book is possibly better than the Holy Scripture?
Q: But, even now (you consider it so)?

[25] RGIA, *fond* 796, *opis'* 205, *delo* 192, *ll.* 20–6.

A: When I saw that there were some additions (comments), I showed it to the rector.
Q: Did you give it to anyone else?
A: I did not keep it from anyone.

Summarizing his experience, Kazanskii observed that "none of us considered ourselves guilty, but the unusual way in which we were confined and the expectation of the interrogation had us all trembling." He added, "no one was charged."[26]

The initial hearing of Pavskii himself was conducted in March 1842, before the Moscow and Kiev metropolitans. Prepared questions were submitted by the two hierarchs for Pavskii's response. As a follow-up to the March hearing, Pavskii was called to two separate interrogations by Metropolitan Filaret (Drozdov), on April 24 and 30, 1842. A summary report on the Pavskii hearings was issued to the Holy Synod in May 1842, by Metropolitan Filaret (Drozdov) and Archbishop Gavriil of Riazan.[27] At the conclusion of the entire investigation, some two and a half years later in August 1844, Pavskii was again queried by Archbishop Gedeon of Poltava, at which time Pavskii complied with a request that he issue a confession of faith.[28] The Pavskii hearings of 1842 and 1844 served as a border to thirty months of intensive investigation and interrogation, alongside the feverish hunt for extant copies of Pavskii's Russian translation of the Masoretic text.

In the initial hearing of 1842, Pavskii recounted how and when he had undertaken his translations from the Hebrew. He claimed, as came to be generally accepted, that he had had no prior knowledge that students were clandestinely lithographing his translations, and that he had not even availed himself of the opportunity to secure a lithographed copy after the fact. From the outset of the interrogations, Moscow Metropolitan Filaret was clearly preoccupied with the narrowly textual/philological explanations located at the head of chapters, particularly in the case of Pavskii's translations of key prophetic books such as Isaiah and Daniel. Filaret inquired

[26] P. Kazanskii, "Mysli i chuvstvovaniia m. Filareta po delu otobraniia litogr. perevoda knig Vetkhago Zaveta po pis'mam ego k o. Antoniiu," *Pravoslavnoe obozrenie*, 1878, no. 1 (January): 106–18. Kazanskii claims that the interrogation was primarily the doing of Ober-prokuror Protasov, who sought to use the matter to weaken the position of Moscow Metropolitan Filaret, who had been in conflict with Protasov on synodal efforts to take over the work of the Commission on Ecclesiastical Schools. As insightful as the Kazanskii narrative is, its interpretation of the Pavskii affair minimizes the real differences that divided Metropolitan Filaret Drozdov and Archpriest Gerasim Pavskii.

[27] For the transcript of the March 20 interrogation, see RGIA, *fond* 796, *opis'* 205, *delo* 192, *ll.* 283–301 ob.; for that of April 24, see ibid., *ll.* 287–96; for April 30, see ibid., *ll.* 297–300.

[28] RGIA, *fond* 796, *opis'* 205, *delo* 198, *ll.* 64–6.

whether Pavskii considered the messianic prophecies in the book of Isaiah to refer to Jesus Christ, and if so, why he had not so noted explicitly in the relevant chapter headings (as, for example, in the seventh chapter of Isaiah). Pavskii's response was that he considered the prophecies to relate directly or indirectly to Jesus Christ, but that his own task as translator was a philological one – that of translating a Hebrew text. That task was complementary to, but distinct from, the concerns of dogmatic theology:

> In my inscriptions on the prophetic passages, I constantly follow the rule that I need not relate dogmatic explanations to my subject. As a translator, I am not obliged to do this. Dogmatic explanations relate to dogmatic theology.[29]

In short, even if Orthodox theology, for interpretive dogmatic reasons, assumed that the messianic prophecy of Isaiah entailed an explicit reference to Jesus Christ, Pavskii felt no obligation to bring dogmatic theological considerations into his philological and historical text-critical rendering of the Hebrew Masoretic text.

By the time of the final April 30 session, Moscow Metropolitan Filaret had, in effect, been drawn into a line of questioning over chapter headings and inscriptions that only served to confirm Pavskii's historical and philological command of the prophetic books. Pavskii defended at length his estimated dating of the fall of Babylon to ca. 540 BCE, his dating of specific chapters of Isaiah based upon the content of the prophecy in question, and his division of the book of Daniel into nine parts on philological, contextual grounds.[30] Pavskii had effectively turned the hearings away from claims of dogmatic laxity and non-Orthodox belief to the very philological and historical-critical text issues that he believed vindicated his position as an innocent, if learned, translator.

At the end of the 1842 hearings, Pavskii's only regret was that his translation with the scholarly notes or apparatus had fallen into the hands of those for whom it was inappropriate. If that should happen again – specifically, the distribution of his translations to those for whom they were not intended – he invited the authorities to circumscribe his pastoral privileges.[31] This last concession on Pavskii's part has been widely misinterpreted to mean that Pavskii, in the end, disavowed his work in an appeal for Filaret's support.[32] The gratuitous appeal to Filaret's "wisdom" was clearly there, but there was no disavowal of his translation effort. In this, Pavskii stood firm.

[29] RGIA, *fond* 796, *opis'* 205, *delo* 192, *l.* 286. [30] Ibid., *ll.* 297–8 ob. [31] Ibid., *l.* 300 ob.
[32] Chistovich, *Istoriia perevoda Biblii*, 133–207.

Far from marking any reconciliation between the two men, the hearings proved to be the final break between them. In Filaret's May 1842 report to the Holy Synod on the interrogation, he recognized Pavskii's innocence in the distribution of the lithographed editions, but concluded that the translator's "attestations and explanations bearing on the Orthodoxy of the translation and its introductions and notes are inadequate and unsatisfactory."[33] Frustrated in his confrontation with the gifted Hebraic scholar and archpriest, Filaret returned to Moscow absenting himself from most proceedings of the Holy Synod throughout the remainder of the reign of Nicholas I.

How is one to interpret this conflict between the metropolitan and the Hebrew Bible translator? Why should Filaret, an active collaborator and supporter of modern Russian biblical translation during the years of the Russian Bible Society and again in the reign of Alexander II, turn against such a gifted Russian Hebraic scholar? Filaret's conflict with Pavskii surely cannot be attributed to simple expediency on the part of the metropolitan in the repressive atmosphere of Nikolaevan Russia. On the one hand, Filaret was able to rise above such narrow statist considerations. The Pavskii affair was never a burning issue for the state – indeed, Pavskii had been in the 1820s a popular tutor to the tsarevich, and the learned archpriest continued to be held in the affections of imperial family members. On the other hand, the animus generated by the conflict suggested more than a dispassionate scholarly debate over how, if at all, to register Christian dogma in OT translation.

The most common interpretation of the Filaret–Pavskii conflict has been that put forward by supporters of the metropolitan. Included in such company was the late émigré church historian and patristics scholar, Georges Florovsky.[34] Focusing upon the theological debates of the first quarter of the nineteenth century, Florovsky identified with, indeed lionized, the biblicist position of Metropolitan Filaret. For Florovsky, the main concern was the perceived cleavage in early nineteenth-century Russian theological circles over matters of divine revelation and holy tradition. Filaret, in Florovsky's view, always took the point of departure in theological discourse to be the historical manifestation of divine revelation. Moral, scholastic, or logical argumentation in matters of theology was always subordinate to the historical revelation of scripture, which was the foundation of holy tradition. Thus, on the one hand, Filaret parted company with mystics, such as Aleksandr Labzin or more exotic cult followers, who made

[33] RGIA, *fond* 796, *opis'* 205, *delo* 192, *l.* 301 ob. [34] Florovsky, *Ways of Russian Theology*, 212–20.

scripture into an allegory rather than a book of divine history. On the other hand, Filaret also rejected moral or abstract theology that was guided by logic rather than divine revelation. This latter school of rationalist theologians Filaret identified as "neological."[35]

Accordingly, Metropolitan Filaret's conflict with Archpriest Gerasim Pavskii was, in the metropolitan's own eyes, a conflict between a biblicist seeking to uphold holy tradition and a neologist. There had been an earlier anticipation of this conflict in the controversy over the religious instruction of the tsarevich. Filaret had challenged the archpriest's published guide to the Christian teaching of Grand Duke Alexander Nikolaevich on the grounds that Pavskii was appealing to the innate religious feelings of his young charge as the point of departure for Christian instruction. Such neological thinking was, in Filaret's view, pernicious, and needed to be replaced by traditional rote catechetical instruction. In a similar fashion, Pavskii's textual notes accompanying his OT translation had sought to enhance the meaning and significance of the prophetic books by providing strictly philological or historical-critical context. Filaret considered Pavskii's historical-critical concern for the relation between text and context to be neological. What was rather needed to illumine the OT text was the clarity and firm application of Orthodox doctrine as formulated by the early church fathers.

In light of Filaret's perception of Pavskii, was the "neologist" charge against the Russian Hebraist valid – even within its own frame of reference? And, if not, how can one interpret Metropolitan Filaret's intense personal involvement in the 1842 interrogations? Filaret was by no means the first to raise concerns about "neological," "rationalistic" theology. It is possible, in fact, that the metropolitan borrowed his use of the term from earlier BFBS representatives in Petersburg with whom he had been closely affiliated. BFBS agent Robert Pinkerton, for example, in his memoirs from Russia uses the term to refer to those who were challenging continental millenarian and mystical Protestant writers, such as Professor Jung-Stilling. Seeking to defend such writing, Pinkerton decried the opposition to them, arguing that the works of Jung-Stilling "contained most powerful and popular arguments in defense of the inspiration and authority of the Scriptures against the attacks of the *Neologian* [italics added] literati and clergy of Germany."[36]

[35] On Filaret's perception of this neologism, see Nichols, "Metropolitan Filaret of Moscow," 122.

[36] Robert Pinkerton, *Russia: Or, Miscellaneous Observations on the Past and Present State of that Country and its Inhabitants* (London, 1833), 144. The *Oxford English Dictionary* (1933), VII: 89, identifies the term as originating with Pinkerton.

Thus, in decrying "neologists," Filaret found himself in common alliance with BFBS evangelicals appealing to the priority of divine revelation in scriptural interpretation against what commonly came to be referred to as "neologisms."

Yet, those same BFBS agents of the Russian Bible Society era who were quick to identify what they perceived to be dangerous rationalistic or neological thought regarded Gerasim Petrovich Pavskii as one of their own. Ebenezer Henderson, the BFBS assistant to John Paterson in RBS translation and publication efforts, wrote of Pavskii in 1822:

> The Psalms have been translated by the Rev. Dr. Paffsky of the Kazan Church in this city, a liberal and enlightened clergyman who has also furnished his countrymen with a Hebrew Grammar in their own language. I [am] happy in having him for my coadjutor in the Revision of the New Translation of the N[ew] T[estament] into Hebrew, which, you will see from the Report, has been undertaken by the R[ussian] B[ible] Society.[37]

Henderson's highly favorable judgment of Pavskii is all the more curious coming, in this context, from someone who considered himself a biblicist whose point of departure, like Filaret's, was the authority of divine revelation. In short, although Filaret found Pavskii to be neological in his failure to subordinate his translation work to Orthodox dogmatic theology, others found nothing in Pavskii's philological rigor or in his historical-critical methodology conflicting with the church's traditional teaching on divine revelation. For BFBS agents, the absence of Christian apologetics in Old Testament or Hebrew Bible translation was simply an appropriate adherence to the dictum that biblical translation ought to be done "without note or comment."

Moreover, if the "neologist" charge was meant to convey the idea that Pavskii had strayed from the patristic foundations of Eastern Christian dogmatics – a charge implied in Florovsky's defense of Metropolitan Filaret – that too was difficult to sustain in the context of Pavskii's substantial contribution to Russian patristics. Alongside his biblical translations into Russian, Pavskii was perhaps the single most significant translator of patristic writings into modern Russian in the 1820s, when his translations of early Christian writers filled the pages of the newly established journal of the St. Petersburg Theological Academy, *Khristianskoe chtenie* (Christian Reading). Pavskii's preoccupation with patristic literature stemmed from

[37] Henderson to Bishop Frederick Munter (St. Petersburg, September 20, 1822 O.S.), Royal Library of Copenhagen, "Ny Kgl. Samling," fol. 1698. I am indebted to the Rev. Felix Olafsson of Stenlose, Denmark, for sharing the Henderson correspondence.

concern ostensibly shared with Filaret that the interpretive foundations of holy tradition be made accessible to Russian clergy. Pavskii's immersion in historical-critical western philological and theological writings presumably ought not to have posed a problem for Filaret so long as there could be agreement on the sources of holy tradition.

The absence of any such agreement, however, begs the question of whether, alongside the genuine theological conflict between Metropolitan Filaret and Archpriest Gerasim Pavskii, there were other sources of discord between the two distinguished churchmen. Was the charge of "neologism" something of a red herring, motivated by factors beyond that of the fear over the absence of explicit Christian dogmatics in OT translation?[38] If the charge of "neologism" was arguably inflated by Filaret in its application to Pavskii, were there other conditions that may have lain behind the charges? Indeed, it is the position here that the conflict between the metropolitan and the archpriest was exacerbated by two related issues on which the metropolitan and the archpriest were irreconcilably opposed – modern text criticism and the institution of monasticism.

What Filaret's 1842 interrogation of Pavskii revealed was a fundamental impasse between the two over how to approach the scriptural text. For Pavskii, the text, especially in OT prophetic writing, needed to be understood in its historical and philological *context* so as to make the translation alive and meaningful. Pavskii saw no conflict between that modern

[38] Writing on the development of Russian theological thought during the era of Nicholas I, A. N. Kotovich dismisses this charge of "neologism" in the case of Pavskii, seeing the learned archpriest in a line of innovative theologians of the nineteenth century, such as Innokentii Borisov, A. V. Gorskii, and Filaret Gumilevskii, all of whom held that there was no necessary conflict between the freely exercised interpretation of Holy Scripture, divine revelation, and dogmatic theology. As Kotovich noted in the case of Innokentii Borisov, Russian religious culture in the era of Nicholas I could accommodate innovative new theologians who saw revelation and the formation of holy tradition as ongoing processes in which God reveals himself in ever new creative ways. Such theological innovation, however, was opposed by Filaret Drozdov, and subsequently by Father Georges Florovsky, both of whom viewed dogmatic theology through the prism of early Christian patristic writing, and sought to interpret scripture accordingly. See A. N. Kotovich, "Cherty i usloviia razvitiia russkoi bogoslovskoi mysli v epokhu Nikolaia I," *Khristianskoe chtenie* (November 1906): 644–68 and (December 1906): 854–77. In his doctoral dissertation, Arthur Repp defends the "neologist" charge against Pavskii, noting the way in which the term was used in the early nineteenth century to denote those who gave priority to OT grammatical and philological exegesis over traditional Christian doctrine. See Arthur C. Repp, "In Search of an Orthodox Way: The Development of Biblical Studies in Late Imperial Russia" (Ph.D. dissertation, University of Illinois at Chicago, 1999), 65–6. While Repp is right to note how the term "neologist" was employed at that time, the point is rather that such usage was itself part of the polemic of the day, reflecting one side of a nascent divide in nineteenth-century Russian theology between traditional interpreters of Orthodox Christian dogma and those like Pavskii who were prepared to use new historical-critical methodology in reinterpreting Holy Scripture.

textological task and the parallel labor of the dogmatic theologian interpreting from a doctrinal point of view the meaning of texts. Texts, after all, lent themselves to different levels of interpretive meaning. As Pavskii responded at length in the interrogation:

> It is known that in the circle of academic theological sciences there is a special class for studying Holy Scripture, a special class for hermeneutics, and likewise a special class for dogmatics. For each of these sciences a special teacher is provided. My students heard all about the interpretation of Holy Scripture and all dogmatic positions of the church in those other classes, so that in my class it was not necessary to deal with dogmatics and hermeneutical forms. This doesn't mean that I did not know and did not accept any kind of dogmas of my church, but rather that I strictly separated one science from the other, and very well remembered that from the circle of my science I ought not stray.
>
> As professor of Hebrew and philology, I had to teach these students the Hebrew language ... and lead them to the clearest possible understanding of the Bible. In the compiling of my lectures, I had before me only the finest contemporary dictionaries of Hebrew, the best grammars, the best archeological books in which are explained the life of God's people in various relations. From these lectures, compiled according to purely philological guidelines, there came my translation of the prophetic and other biblical books. As a philological translation, it was not able and was not meant to bear upon anything non-philological. [So, for example] in a prophetic utterance when the point is about "the king," I noted that here it is written about "the king," not adding indeed about which king ... Dogmatics entered into my philological translation only negatively, that is, I did not permit myself to bring to my translation anything opposing the clear positions of the Orthodox church. But to introduce into it dogmatic instructions directly favorable, I had neither the right nor the obligation.
>
> In the matter of not including dogmatic instructions in my translation, I followed the path of former editors of the Bible. Neither in the Slavonic Bible nor in the Russian Psalter [1822] do we have inscriptions with dogmatic instructions. Are we to conclude from this that editors of the Psalter [a clear reference to Metropolitan Filaret himself] did not accept the prophetic meaning in many Psalms, and that the Psalms (for example, the 21st) do not relate to the long awaited Messiah?[39]

Pavskii's interrogator in this case came to the scriptural text with a markedly different perspective. For Metropolitan Filaret, the meaning of the scriptural text lay primarily, if not exclusively, in its correct doctrinal and dogmatic interpretation – interpretations laid down by the early church fathers, the creedal formulations, and the acts of ecumenical councils. That was the essence of holy tradition. Translation of scripture into modern

[39] RGIA, *fond* 796, *opis'* 205, *delo* 194, *ll.* 292 ob.–294.

Russian must be done with attention to the dogmas of the church so as to make explicit, as for example in the prophetic writings of Isaiah, potential messianic references to Jesus Christ. Even though Filaret was sensitive to western textual developments, including use of the Hebrew Masoretic text in OT translation, his fear was that modern philological text criticism, if uncontrolled, would create interpretive ambiguity unacceptable to the teachings of the church. Thus translation became for Filaret a political issue in which control must be in the hands of the church and its anointed leaders. Moreover, correct translation had not only to be churchly translation – a formula developed in the aftermath of the Russian Bible Society – but it must be guided by doctrinal standards set forth in the early Greek and Byzantine patristic tradition.

Pavskii, whose command of patristic writings was just as impressive as that of Metropolitan Filaret, entertained no such fear of conflict between philological and theological tasks. Filaret's fundamental conservatism on this issue of modern text criticism was to be reflected in the narrow textual base – the *textus receptus* – used in the synodal NT translation published under Filaret's oversight, 1860–2. For his part, Pavskii predictably turned to other philological pursuits after departing the Theological Academy. Even though he remained a parish clergyman to the end of his life, his reputation as a philologist and grammarian earned him full membership in the Russian Academy of Sciences in 1858.[40]

Had the only difference between the metropolitan and the archpriest been over modern text criticism, perhaps the conflict between the two would have been less politically charged. But alongside the textological issue there lay the sensitive issue of Pavskii's rejection of monasticism. As archpriest of Kazan Cathedral, Pavskii held one of the leading posts for a married white, or parish, clergyman in the capital. He was a devoted husband and father. When, in 1824, his wife died, Pavskii was enjoined to take monastic vows. Not only did he refuse to do so, but he was openly disdainful of a monastic hierarchy that he believed was preoccupied with the accumulation of power. In his autobiography Pavskii wrote:

> It is not difficult to guess why they sought to induce me to enter into monasticism. They wanted to hold everyone in their grasp. From the time when the tsars began to select as religious tutors and confessors for their children persons from the white

[40] Pavskii's major contribution from this later period, in addition to his translation of the Igor tale, was his *Filologicheskie nabliudeniia nad sostavom russkago iazyka*, 2nd edn, 4 vols. (St. Petersburg, 1850). On the politics of the delay in Pavskii's admission to the Academy of Sciences, a matter not unrelated to the earlier conflicts with Filaret, see Barsov, "Protoierei Pavskii," 113–14.

clergy, it seemed to the monastic hierarchs that power (in the church) was slipping away from them, and correspondingly passing to the white clergy. And for them that was murder.[41]

Pavskii's disdain for the monastic life yielded an obvious point of friction with Filaret, for here the two churchmen represented the polarities of Russian spirituality. Metropolitan Filaret equated the highest form of Orthodox piety with the ascetic tradition of cenobitic Byzantine monastic community. Pavskii, on the other hand, held to the less heroic vision of Russian piety expressed in the spirituality of the Russian parish. For Pavskii, despite his formidable erudition, Christian piety was to be found in Galilean fishermen, Russian Orthodox peasants, and parish clergymen.

This fundamental difference of perspective, while perhaps not utterly irreconcilable, mirrored a growing chasm in the Russian Church between black and white clergy. Gregory Freeze has identified this split as the condition leading toward "clerical liberalism," a movement for reform of the white clergy in the second half of the nineteenth century.[42] The importance of the Pavskii affair, in this context, is that it reinforced an underlying, deep-seated conflict between parish and monastic ranks (white and black clergy) within Russian religious culture. The breeding grounds of this conflict were found in the theological academies and, to a lesser extent, in the diocesan seminaries. The interrogations of theological academy students undertaken during the Pavskii affair elicited their uniformly righteous defense that distribution of the lithographed text was necessary because it was the only way to get access to an understandable Russian text otherwise withheld from students by the religious authorities.[43]

Professor Florovsky has argued that Pavskii had only "a few direct disciples," a charge that cannot be sustained.[44] The Pavskii phenomenon

41 Pavskii internally quoted in Barsov, "Protoierei Pavskii," 510.

42 On "clerical liberalism," see Freeze, *Parish Clergy*, and the introduction to his translation of Belliustin, *Description of the Clergy in Rural Russia* (Ithaca, NY: Cornell University Press, 1985).

43 For examples of these interrogations, see RGIA, *fond* 796, *opis'* 205, *delo* 200, *ll.* 11–191 ("Materialy sledstvennogo komiteta po delu o nelegal'nom izdanii i rasprostranenii studentami Peterburgskoi dukhovnoi akademii perevoda nekotorykh knig perevoda Biblii [Vetkhogo Zaveta] na russkii iazyk s 'prevratnymi tolkovaniiami'" [Materials of the investigative committee on the matter of the illegal publication and dissemination by students of the Petersburg Theological Academy of the translation of several books of the translation of the Bible (Old Testament) into Russian with 'erroneous interpretations']).

44 Florovsky, *Ways of Russian Theology*, 232. Florovsky writes that "only S. K. Sabinin (1787–1863), a priest with the diplomatic mission in Copenhagen and then in Weimar, did any independent work." Florovsky exaggerates here. A wide circle of leading Russian churchmen of the nineteenth century acknowledged their identification with Gerasim Pavskii, among them figures such as the Altai missionary Makarii (Glukharev) and the biblical scholars P. I. Gorskii-Platonov and Ivan E. Evseev.

drew unprecedented loyalties from a broad cross-section of academy students. While he was under interrogation in 1842, Pavskii referred rather modestly to the number of his students, saying simply, "of them there was not a small number."[45] The samizdat distribution of Pavskii's translation continued Pavskii's influence in academy life and his concern for Russian biblical translation well beyond his departure from the Petersburg Theological Academy in the 1820s. Most of the academy students interrogated between 1842 and 1844 came from the thirteenth and fourteenth graduating classes. Several of the key leaders in the distribution network ended up serving in strategic urban parishes where they became, alongside more outspoken figures such as Ivan Belliustin, the quiet champions of clerical reform. Having left his mark upon subsequent generations of Russian biblical scholars, many of them academy professors, the larger impact of Gerasim Pavskii may have been among the Russian white clergy with whom he so closely identified himself.[46]

The issues dividing Metropolitan Filaret and Gerasim Pavskii remained very much alive after their deaths in the 1860s. What Metropolitan Filaret was arguing, in effect, was that biblical translation must be subordinate to church doctrine. Pavskii, on the other hand, saw no conflict between the philological task and what he interpreted to be the broad outline of church doctrine, including the interpretation of prophetic texts. As noted in Chapter 4, the position of Metropolitan Filaret was readily seized upon by conservatives in the years after the publication of the synodal Russian Old Testament in the 1870s to claim that strict conformity to the Septuagint Greek text ought to have prevailed in Russian OT translation. According to such a view, Orthodox doctrine was uniquely tied to the Slavonic Bible and the Greek text upon which it was primarily based. Nevertheless, Pavskii's effectiveness as a translator and his seminal role in the development of Hebraic studies at the theological academies ultimately insured the continued appeal to the Hebrew Masoretic text in Russian OT translation. Pavskii's text became the *editio princeps* of the Russian OT. Despite the interrogations and the burning of most extant copies, the Pavskii text continued to exert a powerful influence upon subsequent translations, including the Russian OT translation of one of

45 RGIA, *fond* 796, *opis'* 205, *delo* 192, *l.* 294.

46 The careers of students interrogated in the Pavskii affair may be traced using Rodosskii, *Biograficheskii slovar' studentov sanktpeterburgskoi dukhovnoi akademii.* Many of those implicated in the distribution network during the Pavskii affair (graduates of the thirteenth and fourteenth classes) found placement in major parishes of the capital.

Figure 8. St. Makarii (Glukharev), 1792–1847, missionary to the Altai and translator of the Russian Old Testament from Hebrew. Source: http://orthodoxwiki.org/Makarii_%28Glukharev%29.

the most idiosyncratic Orthodox figures of the nineteenth century, the Altai missionary St. Makarii (Glukharev).

OLD TESTAMENT TRANSLATIONS OF THE ALTAI MISSIONARY, ST. MAKARII (GLUKHAREV)

Canonized by the Russian Orthodox Church in August 2000, Archimandrite Makarii (Mikhail Glukharev – see Figure 8) has long been known for his pioneering Orthodox missionary efforts from 1830 to 1844 among the Telengit and other Altai Turkic indigenous peoples of the Russian frontier region adjoining Mongolia and Turkestan.[47] Son of an Orthodox priest from Vladimir province, Makarii received traditional seminary training in Smolensk before undertaking his advanced study at

[47] There is a substantial secondary literature on St. Makarii and the Altai Mission, as well as a published collection of his correspondence. The best biography is that of D. D. Filimonov, *Materialy dlia biografii osnovatelia altaiskoi missii Arkhimandrita Makariia* (Moscow: V. F. Rikhter, 1892). The Filimonov work was serialized (1887–8) in the journal *Pravoslavnoe obozrenie*. For the letters of Makarii, see K. V. Kharlampovich, ed., *Pis'ma arkhimandrita Makariia Glukhareva, osnovatelia altaiskoi missii* (Kazan: Tsentral'naia tipografiia, 1905). Kharlampovich adds to the edition of letters his own extended biographical essay, "Biograficheskii ocherk," which complements the Filimonov

the St. Petersburg Theological Academy, from which he graduated in 1818. Makarii was a product of the Russian Bible Society era, having been at the academy when Filaret (Drozdov) was its rector, and having taken Hebrew under the tutelage of Gerasim Pavskii, who was five years his senior. Combining the ascetic and mystical strains of early nineteenth-century Orthodox piety, Makarii read widely from western writers such as Johann Arndt and Johann Heinrich Jung-Stilling, while also being drawn to the hesychast tradition of Eastern Orthodox monasticism. It is from this period that his close associations with both the cleric Filaret Drozdov and the emperor's minister, Aleksandr Golitsyn, date. The formative influence of the Bible Society era was also to be seen in Makarii's identification with the more ecumenical, cross-confessional, inter-religious spirit of the time.

An articulate and outspoken advocate of modern Russian biblical translation, and well connected both to the church hierarchy and to leading figures in the Russian capital, Makarii advanced rapidly within the ecclesiastical estate (*dukhovnoe soslovie*). Tonsured into monastic vocation upon graduation from the academy, Makarii was quickly elevated to *ieromonakh* and assumed a position in the cathedral church of the Kievo-Pecherskaia Lavra in Ukraine, among the most revered sites of early Eastern Slavic Christianity. In 1819, he briefly assumed a position as instructor of church history and inspector at the Ekaterinoslav Seminary, but unable to abide the censorious views of the Ekaterinoslav bishop, Iov (Potemkin), he managed to secure a position in 1821 as rector of the diocesan seminary in Kostroma. Dissatisfied with the administrative responsibilities and unwilling to assume a position in the episcopate, Makarii moved several times in the following years – back to the Kievo-Pecherskaia Lavra and ultimately to the Glinskii Monastery in Kursk province.

Finally, in 1829, Makarii petitioned the Synod to appoint him to the Tobol'sk diocese in Siberia, where Bishop Evgenii (Kazantsev) was seeking to enlist missionaries for service among the indigenous Shamanist Tatar Turkic population of the region. Arriving in Tobol'sk in 1829, Makarii prepared to establish a missionary station in the distant outpost of Biisk, a frontier city on the slopes of the Altai mountains, to which he traveled in 1830. In Biisk, he founded the first of several missionary settlements,

study. The Kharlampovich work has been translated into English, with an interpretive essay, by James Haney, *Archimandrite Makarii Glukharev: Founder of the Altai Mission*, Studies in Russian History, VI (Lewiston, NY: Edwin Mellen Press, 2001). See also Paul Valliere, "Russian Orthodoxy and the Challenge of Modernity: The Case of Archimandrite Makary," *St. Vladimir's Theological Quarterly*, 22, no. 1 (1978): 3–15.

including one that later became his residence in Maima. What Makarii brought to his new missionary appointment was not just a solid grounding in Orthodox dogmatic theology, but also a remarkable capacity to identify with "the other," a throwback perhaps to the ecumenical orientation of his days in Petersburg when Quakers, Lutherans, and Catholics could sit down together in interconfessional assemblies with Orthodox clergy and laymen alike. He also brought a commitment to Russian translation of early Christian literature, having previously translated St. Augustine's *Confessions*, the *Discourses* of St. Gregory the Great, and the sermons of St. Theodore the Studite.

The success of Makarii Glukharev's missionary efforts in the Altai region has typically been measured by the 675 converts to Orthodox Christianity that he generated over the course of his fourteen years there. Traditionally observing Shamanist practices, the Turkic peoples of the Altai region were historically nomadic until, under the influence of Russian colonization, there came to be fixed settlements. The relatively new fixed settlements – sites also for the new mission stations – served as the location for Russian acculturation and religious reorientation of Telengit and other Altai Turkic elites. The conversion to Christianity of Altai peoples continued well after Makarii's departure from the region, with approximately half of the indigenous Altai population embracing Christianity by the time of the 1917 Russian Revolution. In this missionary effort Makarii worked with local elites to translate key passages of scripture into local Turkic dialects – passages that, in their Russian edition, constituted the basis for his *Alfavit Biblii*, biblical excerpts intended for use by the newly converted.[48] Complicating the translation process in the case of OT translation was the absence of a readily accessible Russian base text that could be used for the reliable translation of OT passages into native dialects. What followed was Makarii's major effort to complete his own translation into Russian of the Hebrew Bible, or Old Testament.

Among the unique features of this translation and missionary effort was Makarii's close collaboration with two Russian women who became his coworkers (*sotrudnitsy*) in the Altai, Ekaterina Fedorovna Nepriakhina (d. 1872) and Sofiia Gustavovna de Val'mon. The daughter of a local Russian official in Tobol'sk, Nepriakhina was an icon painter with close ties to exiled Decembrists, several of whom also became attached to Makarii's mission and to the translation effort (these included, among others, M. A. Fonvizin, P. S. Bobrishchev-Pushkin, and P. N. Svistunov). Viewing Makarii

[48] Filimonov, "Materialy," 425.

as her confessional *starets* or spiritual elder, Nepriakhina not only painted icons for all new converts, working most closely with female converts, but she also assisted Makarii with the transcription of all biblical translations. Sofiia de Val'mon, the daughter of a military officer who died in the 1812 Battle of Borodino, was a well-educated young woman from the Smol'ny Institute who had ties to higher St. Petersburg society, including her connection to Prince Aleksandr Golitsyn. Following Makarii's visit to St. Petersburg in 1839, Val'mon joined him at the Altai mission to work with women and children. The presence of these close female collaborators with Makarii at the Altai mission was a source of concern for Makarii's former mentor, Moscow Metropolitan Filaret, who expressed dismay over the matter. Filaret inquired whether the young Sofiia de Val'mon, in particular, would not be in Makarii's way, but the underlying message was clearly that of concern about the appearance of a prominent monastic figure working so closely with female counterparts.[49] Over Filaret's objection Makarii invited Sofiia de Val'mon to join the mission, while continuing to collaborate also with Ekaterina Nepriakhina throughout his period in the Altai region.

Makarii's idea for biblical translation was first presented to Moscow Metropolitan Filaret in an 1834 proposal entitled, "On the necessity for the Russian Church of a translation of the entire Bible from the original languages into contemporary Russian" (O potrebnosti dlia Rossiiskoi tserkvi prelozheniia vsei Biblii s original'nykh iazykov na sovremennyi russkii iazyk).[50] In his missive to Filaret, Makarii articulated the rationale for modern Russian biblical translation. First, he asked, what are the clergy of our contemporary church to do, many of them unable to understand the Slavonic text themselves? He claimed that a Russian Bible would even help to clarify and make more meaningful the Slavonic Bible. Second, responding to Filaret's claim that the time would not be right until the Russian people had matured and were properly prepared for such a translation, Makarii writes, "I say that when the language has matured, the people have matured." Third, Makarii, noting the biblical refrain that "God spoke by the prophets," proceeded to inquire of Filaret whether those prophets did

49 On Decembrist ties to the Altai mission, see K. V. Kharlampovich, "Makarii Glukharev i tobol'skie dekabristy," *Russkii arkhiv*, 42 (February 1904): 235–43. On Ekaterina Nepriakhina, to whom Makarii addressed more than fifty letters during his Altai period, see Kharlampovich, *Archimandrite Makarii Glukharev*, 116 n. 73. On Sofiia de Val'mon and Filaret's concern, see Filimonov, "Materialy," 459–62.

50 Arkhimandrit Makarii, *Pis'mo pokoinago missionera Arkhimandrita Makariia, byvshago nachal'nikom altaiskoi dukhovnoi missii, k sinodal'nomu chlenu, vysokopreosviashchenneishemu Filaretu mitropolitu moskovskomu, ot 23 dnia marta 1834 goda, o potrebnosti dlia rossiiskoi tserkvi*, ed. K. V. Kharlampovich (Moscow, 1861).

not speak in Hebrew or another Semitic tongue of their own day. Finally, responding to Filaret's claim that "our forefathers held fast the Slavonic Bible in the simplicity of their hearts, and were saved," Makarii asked whether this meant that it would not be possible to be saved if people held in the simplicity of their hearts both the Slavonic and the Russian, to say nothing of the Greek and the Hebrew. Georges Florovsky claims that, given the opposition to Russian biblical translation in the aftermath of the Bible Society era, Metropolitan Filaret concealed the letter to protect Makarii, whom Florovsky rather patronizingly calls "the romantic missionary."[51] In any case, not receiving a response to his 1834 proposal, Makarii nevertheless launched his translations, first the book of Job (1837), then of Isaiah (1839), and ultimately all of the Hebrew Bible or Old Testament, except for the Psalter, which had circulated openly from the time of the Russian Bible Society.

In rendering his Russian OT translations from the Hebrew Masoretic text, Makarii was aided by three basic resources that he secured for work on the project. Two of these were western sources, the first being the French translation and commentary on the Bible by Jean Frédéric Osterwald (1663–1747). The Swiss Reformed Pastor Osterwald's *La Sainte Bible ... avec les nouveaux argumens & les nouvelles reflexions* (1724), with its accompanying exegetical "Notes," constituted a revision of the Geneva Bible that was republished throughout the eighteenth century, and later adopted for circulation by the BFBS. The second western resource used by Makarii was the monumental OT commentary (*Scholia in Vetus Testamentum* [24 parts, 1788–1835]) done by Ernst Friedrich Karl Rosenmüller (1768–1835), one of the more prominent German orientalists and theologians of his day.[52] Rosenmüller was a pioneer in using historico-critical methodology in OT scholarship, as for example in his argument on contextual grounds for possible multiple authorship of the book of Isaiah.

Neither of these two western resources matched in importance Makarii's appeal to the Russian OT *editio princeps*, the clandestine lithographed text of Gerasim Pavskii's translation. Although Makarii had been a student of Hebrew under Pavskii's tutelage at St. Petersburg Theological Academy, it appears that, far removed from the Russian center, Makarii was unaware of the existence of the lithographed edition until 1839 when he traveled to St. Petersburg and Moscow, ostensibly to raise funds for the mission and to

[51] Florovsky, *Ways of Russian Theology*.

[52] K. V. Kharlampovich, "Ucheno-literaturnye trudy arkhim. Makariia Glukhareva," *Khristianskoe chtenie*, 1905 (December): 794.

pursue possible publication outlets for his biblical translation work. From 1839 onward, Makarii drew heavily on the Pavskii text for revision of his own OT translations, revising the Pavskii text that then remained as the lithographed notes of seminary students. The Makarii text frequently paralleled word for word the Pavskii text.[53]

Makarii's effort to publish his Russian OT translations drew him into a series of dramatic confrontations with religious and political authorities that ultimately demonstrated how threatened and defensive official Russian religious culture had become over biblical translation in the era of Nicholas I. As noted above, the first such confrontation was with Metropolitan Filaret, and dated from Makarii's initial 1834 proposal to publish an edition of the whole Bible in Russian. In addition to the arguments noted above, Makarii added a compelling account of his encounter with a semi-literate Russian cleric whose need of an understandable Russian text was clear:

> If we fear the whole Bible in Russian, then there shall enter into the number of our missionaries someone like the cleric who came up to me announcing that he wanted to serve the sacred church with the propagation of the divine Word to unbelievers. Fine, my friend, I say, but tell me how many gods we have, so as to know what faith we intend to propagate. And what happens? He counted them for me – not only three, but also four, and five, and perhaps it would have stretched further if I did not cut him short at that count . . . We poor missionaries, unworthy of such a name, pray above all that we be given the Bible in Russian, faithfully translated from the original languages of Hebrew and Greek.[54]

Appealing to national honor as well as divine providence, Makarii claimed that failure to launch this translation effort would mean that "the British Bible Society shall preempt this honorable work needed by the shepherds of the Orthodox Church."[55] Failing to get a response to his 1834 letter, Makarii would subsequently issue more strident appeals concerning biblical translation – appeals that carried dire apocalyptic warnings.

Frustrated by the lack of response to his appeal, Makarii wrote a long letter to Synod Ober-prokuror Nechaev in June 1836, reiterating his concerns on behalf of the translation of the whole Bible into Russian from the Greek and Hebrew original sources. Again, there was a long period of silence. Finally, in August 1837, fourteen months later, Metropolitan Filaret wrote to Makarii, apologizing for not responding earlier, but

[53] Following the reopening of official Russian biblical translation, Makarii's OT translations were posthumously serialized in *Pravoslavnoe obozrenie*, 1860–8 (see Appendix, nos. 47, 57–9, 78, 83, and 92).

[54] Cited in Filimonov, "Materialy," 467. [55] Makarii's appeal is cited ibid., 438.

indicating that what Makarii was "sowing" was not falling on "prepared soil." Filaret wrote that now was "not the time for sowing." He coupled his response with an appeal "to preserve in the general understanding the liturgical [i.e. Slavonic] language."[56] Such an appeal did little to mollify Makarii, whose new converts in Biisk and Maima had difficulty enough with Russian, to say nothing of the Church Slavonic.

In 1837, having completed his translation of the book of Job, Makarii sent his translation directly to the Commission on Ecclesiastical Schools, the unit that had provided a pre-publication review of biblical translations prior to their publication during the Bible Society era. Aware of the backlash that had led to the closure of the Russian Bible Society, he decided to couple his appeal to the commission with a letter sent directly to Emperor Nicholas I, asking for the emperor's intervention to support the publication of Job. In his appeal to the emperor, Makarii wrote:

> At the time of St. Vladimir's baptism, the Scriptures had been received in a Slavonic tongue which could not have been more clear or adequate for that day. But, today the Slavonic language has become dead, for millions not understandable, including among them the servants of the church.[57]

Repeating his concern that the English might take on the matter of Russian biblical translation in the absence of such an initiative, Makarii noted how important the translation was also for missionary work among the newly converted. To make sure that the manuscript and letter reached the emperor, Makarii appears to have transmitted the documents through Prince Aleksandr Golitsyn, whom Makarii had known during the days of the Russian Bible Society.[58] He also wrote directly to the Holy Synod, appealing on behalf of missionaries, priests, and other subdeacons and readers, noting that "many missionaries and most *tserkovnosluzhiteli* [service assistants, such as readers, deacons, cantors] are not able to understand the Old Testament in Slavonic, which is already a dead tongue among us."[59]

The Commission on Ecclesiastical Schools, for its part, turned the translation over to the person who was then teaching Hebrew at St. Petersburg

[56] The exchanges between Makarii, Metropolitan Filaret, and Ober-prokuror Nechaev are found ibid., 438, 476–7.

[57] Cited ibid., 443–4. Makarii's letter to Emperor Nicholas I was published in its entirety in *Pravoslavnoe obozrenie*, 1887–8: 106–43.

[58] RGIA, *fond* 797, *opis'* 8, *delo* 24178, *ll.* 1–2. This file includes the January 1838 letter from Prince Golitsyn to Ober-prokuror Protasov in which Golitsyn indicates he had received from the missionary Makarii in Siberia a letter together with a manuscript for the emperor. Golitsyn informs Protasov that he transmitted this to the emperor, and that the emperor had asked to retain the letter, but Golitsyn forwarded the manuscript to the Synod for its review.

[59] Cited in Filimonov, "Materialy," 445.

Theological Academy, Archpriest Ivanov, who returned the manuscript to the commission, providing what was probably the commission's desired answer – namely, that, although the translation was "satisfactorily correct," nevertheless parts were not clear or clean, and sometimes the translation was too literal or too long-winded, with the result that the translation would not be useful in church schools.[60]

Undaunted, in January 1839 Makarii sent his next installment to Emperor Nicholas I and to the Commission on Ecclesiastical Schools, indicating again his desire to have his translation of the book of the prophet Isaiah published. In the case of the letter to the emperor, Makarii was uncertain whether the emperor had actually received and read his first letter, and so he added a summary of that. The appeal to the emperor in this second instance was far more forceful in its tone, including Makarii's reminder to the emperor of a passage from James 4:17, "to him that knoweth to do good, and doeth it not, to him it is sin." As in his subsequent letter to the Holy Synod, Makarii alluded to divine retribution or punishment if the Word of God is kept from the Russian people. Indeed, he claimed that the 1824 flood in St. Petersburg and the cholera epidemic of the 1830s foreshadowed this divine retribution for failure to provide God's Word.[61]

Makarii continued his correspondence with the Holy Synod following his travel to St. Petersburg where he hoped to secure additional funding for the Altai mission and arrange publication of his translations. His December 1840 letter to the Holy Synod was, if anything, even more apocalyptic in character:

> I recall that after the great punishment and great deliverance which the Lord sent to his people in 1812, there appeared in the living, popular, understood-by-all language the New Testament and Psalter, and there were ready to appear Moses and all the prophets, but suddenly all was concealed and became dark. The prophetical Old Testament books circulate in Russian among just a few in manuscript [a reference to the clandestine Pavskii translation]; and the Pentateuch of Moses is translated into clear Russian from the Hebrew, but now lies at the hands of some special persons in a simple storage place [reference to the 1824 Russian Bible Society Octateuch remaining in unpublished sheets].
>
> Since when does the Word of God in the cloudiness of the Slavonic letter exceed the Divine Word in the clothing of the all-Russian language? In the unpleasant events that have befallen Russia there will be seen the wrath of God over the discontinuation of the translation and publication of the Word of God in Russian.[62]

60 Cited ibid.

61 Cited ibid., 446–8; also Kharlampovich, *Archimandrite Makarii Glukharev*, 147–50.

62 Quoted in Filimonov, "Materialy," 479. Makarii's December 1840 letter to the Holy Synod is published in *Chteniia v imp. obshchestve istorii i drevnostei rossiiskikh pri moskovskom universitete*,

Alluding to the Ararat earthquake, Makarii concluded: "What do the underground shocks of God, having yielded such an awful transformation, tell us?" Quoting from Luke 13, Makarii answered, "Do you think that these Galileans suffered because they were the most sinful of all Galileans? No, I say to you, but if you do not repent, so also shall you perish." He closed with a request for ten copies of the RBS Pentateuch in sheets for the use of the Altai mission.[63]

The Synod's response to this was as predictable as it was swift. Makarii had earlier in St. Petersburg had an unpleasant meeting with St. Petersburg Metropolitan Serafim, one of the prelates who had been most deeply involved in the RBS closure. It was at that meeting, prior to Makarii's letter of December 1840, that it had become clear to Serafim that there was nothing that could be done to change Makarii's thinking on the matter of modern Russian biblical translation. When the Synod met in April 1841 to take up Makarii's epistolary challenge, it issued a formal reproach. In the first place, it indicated that by continuing his translations of the Holy Scripture into Russian, Makarii was violating the limits of his calling and his responsibilities. Second, it judged that in his "unconsidered zeal" he failed to take into account that the all-Russian church did indeed have the whole of Holy Scripture in a natural language of the all-Russian people – namely, the Slavonic Bible. Finally, it considered Makarii's specific reference to disasters that would serve as divine punishment for not proceeding with modern biblical translation "absurd" and contemptible.[64]

As a consequence, the Synod decided to punish Makarii by requiring that he remove himself to the residence of the bishop of Tomsk where for three to six weeks he would be obliged to read the prayers daily under the observation of the bishop. Given the nature of the offense to the sensibilities of the Synod, the penalty was remarkably modest, and no doubt reflected the hand of Moscow Metropolitan Filaret, who was still at that time serving in the Holy Synod. Tomsk Archbishop Afanasii had been one of Makarii's students when the latter had been rector of the seminary in Kostroma. Moreover, as emerged at the time of the Pavskii affair, the diocese at Tomsk was one of the locations where several copies of the clandestine lithographed

1862, kn. 3, smes': 167–78 ("Predstavlenie nachal'nika tserkovnoi altaiskoi missii, arkhimandrita Makariia, sviateishemu sinodu"). The letter includes Makarii's earlier reference to the use of the Hebrew language and Masoretic text: "If we believe in the Holy Spirit 'who spoke through the prophets,' in the living language of those prophets and of the Hebrew Jewish people, but do not ourselves desire that the Russian language be the language of prophets and the spirit of prophecy, then some of us, not wishing to oppose the Holy Spirit, wish not to contradict ourselves. Others, not contradicting themselves, will they persist against the Holy Spirit?"

63 From Filimonov, "Materialy," 479–80.

64 The Holy Synod's response to Makarii is recounted ibid., 479–83.

edition of the Pavskii OT translation were found. Indeed, as Makarii's biographer noted, Makarii considered the sentence a sign of God's providence, for at the archbishop's residence there was a rich library of Greek and Hebrew editions of the Bible, as well as lexicons and commentaries, all of which allowed Makarii to continue his translation efforts. Makarii's departure for Tomsk and his subsequent return to the Altai mission effectively ended the two years of travel that had taken him to St. Petersburg, Moscow, and Kazan – Kazan having increasingly become a focal point for Siberian missionary efforts. The travel had been highly successful in securing contributions for the Altai mission, but had failed to advance Makarii's goal of publishing his Russian OT translation.

How should one interpret this quite remarkable and unprecedented clash over the Russian Bible between the arbiters of official Russian religious culture and the Altai missionary? First, the Makarii affair served to reconfirm the importance of Gerasim Pavskii's first Russian translation of the Hebrew Bible. Makarii openly acknowledged that it was in St. Petersburg that he initially encountered the lithographed Pavskii text, which in turn led to the revision of Makarii's own translations. Makarii was emboldened by the presence of the Pavskii text. His flaunting of synodal authority on the matter of modern biblical translation reflected the continuity of Makarii's work (and Pavskii's) with the era of the Russian Bible Society. The apocalyptic strain and appeal to divine providence in Makarii's correspondence were also features of the more mystically inspired writing of early nineteenth-century Russian piety.

The showdown between Makarii and the Synod over Russian and Slavonic editions of Holy Scripture also helped to sharpen the quite different perspectives of the Russian center and the Eurasian periphery, because the Slavonic Bible, despite its continuing authority as a liturgical text for the Russian heartland, did little to advance the Christianization of the indigenous non-Russian peoples of Eurasia. In raising this question, Makarii anticipated a debate that arose in the 1850s at the time of the resumption of modern Russian biblical translation when the imperial nature of the Slavonic text resurfaced as an issue.

Finally, on a related level, there was the question of Makarii's inflated, providence-flaunting language, which some might see as evidence of his possible disconnect with the real religio-political world of the imperial center. Although Makarii's own health suffered during his travels to St. Petersburg and Moscow – health problems that some of his biographers attribute to his conflict with the Synod – his use of language, especially after the earlier synodal rejection of his translations in 1837 and 1839, was almost surely carefully considered. What Makarii sought to do was to clarify the sharp differences that existed between the spiritual world he inhabited on the periphery of empire and the official world of St. Petersburg religious culture. In doing so, moreover, he captured what the prelates of the Holy Synod intuitively understood – namely, that they could do little to punish a simple monk who was willing to serve with impunity as an independent Russian missionary in remote Biisk on the Altai frontier of Turkestan and Mongolia.

Makarii's last years continued to be consumed with his translation efforts. When he finally petitioned the Synod to leave the Altai region, it appears that his goal was to travel to Jerusalem, stopping long enough in Leipzig to seek publication of his Russian OT.[65] He left the Altai region for good in July 1844, ultimately becoming archimandrite of Bolkhov Monastery. Fearing that he would use travel abroad to publish his OT translations, the Synod refused to authorize his requested travel to Jerusalem until it turned out to be too late. Archimandrite Makarii Glukharev died in July 1847.

For thirty years, following RBS closure in 1826, the translation and distribution of modern Russian biblical texts inhabited the shadowy world of clandestine lithography, foreign republication, unofficial distribution through third-party intermediaries, and creative work destined for the desk drawer. What this reflected was not so much the repressive political world of Nikolaevan Russia, although Nicholas I's *ancien régime* did nothing to encourage religious dissent. Rather, with the closure of the Russian Bible Society and its stereotype printing operations, the market orientation temporarily driving Russian religious culture in the early nineteenth century was supplanted by an official Russian religious culture under the arbitration of a Holy Synod bureaucracy that saw its mission increasingly in more rigid administrative terms. Under these circumstances, the important questions of authority posed during the Bible Society era – the authority of the original biblical textual base, the authority to disseminate scripture, and the spiritual authority of the modern Russian language itself – were temporarily subordinated to the new religio-political realities. But alongside the synodal bureaucracy, there remained beneath the surface significant tensions – the tension between white

[65] Filimonov notes how he met with Makarii during the latter's visit to Moscow, at which time they discussed the fate of RBS editions, including the continuing "dissemination by the English Bible Society of the Bible in Russian translation," a topic that greatly interested Makarii, who had come to realize that the Pavskii affair made it politically impossible for him to publish his translations in Russia. Filimonov indicates that he broached with Makarii the idea of publishing his translations abroad, referring in his conversations to the Leipzig republication of the RBS NT and to the fact that the BFBS still had not been able to publish a comparable OT edition. See Filimonov, "Materialy," 590–4.

parish clergy and their more powerful black monastic, episcopal counterparts; the tension between the religious traditions of the Russian heartland and those of the non-Russian Eurasian frontier; and the tension between modern theological academy scholarship and the rote Latinized seminary and theological academy training of the eighteenth and early nineteenth centuries. In each of these tensions, the politics of the Russian Bible invariably sharpened the lines of division.

Despite his involvement in the Pavskii affair, Metropolitan Filaret Drozdov of Moscow remained the most prominent clerical figure able to operate across the religio-political divisions in modern Russian religious culture. When Russian biblical translation was reopened in the reign of Alexander II, Filaret led the way. Perhaps anticipating such an arbitrating role, he had penned in 1845, following the contentious Pavskii affair, an important treatise on the Septuagint and Slavonic translations, "O dogmaticheskom dostoinstve i okhranitel'nom upotreblenii grecheskogo semidesiati tolkovnikov i slavenskogo perevodov Sviashchennogo Pisaniia" (Concerning the dogmatic value and conserving function of the Greek Septuagint and the Slavonic translation of Holy Scripture).[66] The treatise was issued in the context of an abortive effort by synodal Ober-prokuror Protasov to declare the Greek Septuagint text inviolable, effectively canonizing the Greek text in the aftermath of the Pavskii affair. Opposed to such an effort, Metropolitan Filaret sought to recognize the authority of both the Hebrew and Greek texts in OT translation. In acknowledging the authority of the Septuagint (LXX) in Orthodox biblical translation, Filaret argued that its authority was founded on three fundamental principles. First, the authority of the LXX was based on its recognized use for liturgical purposes since the earliest centuries of the church. Second, the LXX, despite its having been at the time a translation from the Hebrew, remained the oldest extant OT translation containing many superior readings, some of which were no longer present in the Hebrew Masoretic text (e.g. the ending of Psalm 144). Third, in those cases in which the NT referred to a passage from the Septuagint OT reading, the LXX clearly needed to take precedence.[67] Nevertheless, having struggled with several Slavonic passages where the appeal to the Septuagint in the Elizabeth Bible of 1751 had left the meaning unclear or obscure, the metropolitan recognized the need to use the Hebrew Masoretic text in OT translation, particularly in cases where it

[66] Filaret, "O dogmaticheskom dostoinstve." Although prepared in 1845, Filaret's essay was published only in 1858 following the official reopening of modern Russian biblical translation.

[67] Ibid., 469–70.

served to clarify the Greek text, or in those specific cases where the NT reference was to wording in the Hebrew original.

There was an irony in this conservative restatement on the dogmatic value of the Septuagint text in Orthodox biblical translation, for when efforts to translate the Bible into Russian were begun anew after 1856, the pathbreaking precedents set by Gerasim Pavskii and Makarii Glukharev would, in effect, be honored by Metropolitan Filaret, who sanctioned what became essentially a hybrid text, employing a Hebrew Masoretic textual base, but with parenthetical alternative Septuagint readings, and with the inclusion of deuterocanonical texts found only in the LXX. Clandestine Russian biblical translation in the era of Nicholas I had created the foundation for renewed Russian biblical translation in the reign of Alexander II.

CHAPTER 4

The synodal Bible

In May 1858, following two years of intense internal debate within the Russian Orthodox Church, Emperor Alexander II formally approved the Holy Synod's petition to resume Russian translation of the Bible. The two-year debate over the renewal of Russian biblical translation would be defining for modern Russian religious culture not only because it determined the manner in which publication of the Russian Bible would proceed, but also because it set the stage for the reception that would ultimately greet the synodal translation (*sinodal'nyi perevod*). The openness of the debate and the renewal of Russian biblical translation reflected the reformist impulse at work in Russia after the Crimean War when, during the reign of Alexander II, issues long shielded from public debate, including serf emancipation, could be openly aired. Over the course of the twenty years following Emperor Alexander II's coronation, renewed translation and publication of variant editions of Russian Old and New Testaments culminated in the 1876 publication of a complete Russian Bible authorized by the Russian Orthodox Church – the so-called synodal translation. That synodal translation, although it never replaced the Old Slavonic text in Orthodox liturgical worship, remains to this day the most commonly circulated edition of modern Russian scripture.

The renewal of Russian biblical translation also reflected the ascendancy of Moscow Metropolitan Filaret (Drozdov), whose absentee leadership within the Holy Synod following the death in 1855 of Ober-prokuror Nikolai Aleksandrovich Protasov altered the dynamics of official church power. Although the Moscow metropolitan never returned to formal synodal meetings, he would ultimately prevail not only in the internal Holy Synod debate over whether to reopen biblical translation, but he put his own stamp on the translation process, guiding its development until his death in 1867. Having earlier led the Commission on Ecclesiastical Schools during the reign of Alexander I when the commission worked with the Russian Bible Society in overseeing modern Russian biblical translation,

Metropolitan Filaret reassumed church leadership of the translation process forty years later in the reign of Alexander II.

To understand what prompted the mid-century turnabout in the fortunes of modern Russian biblical translation, how the renewed translation effort proceeded, and how once again the BFBS became involved in the effort, is to enter into the changing dynamics of Russian religious culture itself. For it was in the engagement with modern biblical translation, biblical text criticism, and the open circulation of such sacred texts that nineteenth-century Russian religious culture entered, however tentatively, what Jürgen Habermas has termed the "public sphere" – the print-mediated public realm that began to function with a measure of independence from narrow state, autocratic authority in the last decades of the Russian Empire. Western involvement marginally accelerated the translation process itself, contributing to the Russian church's adaptation to a more market-oriented modern religious consciousness – a distinctively reflexive religious consciousness that recognized competing communities of faith and alternative claims to truth. In short, the issues of authority reopened by modern biblical translation – the authority of texts, the authority to publish and disseminate scripture, and the authority of the linguistic medium – became a critical part of Russian religious culture's fledgling engagement with modernity.

THE INITIAL DEBATE

The reopening of modern Russian biblical translation in the 1850s was prefaced by a significant church dispute that prefigured the engagement of the Russian church with issues of modernity and the public sphere. Internal Synod debate over whether to resume Russian biblical translation revolved around three central questions: (1) what would be the impact of any new translation effort upon the authority and liturgical use of the Slavonic Bible?; (2) what would be the ecclesiological significance of a renewed modern translation – specifically, how would any such translation affect the relationship of the Russian church to its Slavic and Near East Orthodox neighbors, the wider Orthodox East?; and (3) how would the translation effort intersect with the missionary efforts of the Russian church? Each of these questions posed problems of authority for the Russian church of the nineteenth century, problems that have remained very much at the center of modern Russian religious culture. The debate that ensued from 1856 to 1876 was notable for its openness as well as for its substance.

The debate began within the Holy Synod in 1856 during meetings held at the time of the coronation of Alexander II. While one of the observers of the process, nineteenth-century church historian I. A. Chistovich, has noted the initial agreement within the Synod over the need for a Russian translation, there continued to be disagreement about the textual base to be used in OT translation.[1] Moscow Metropolitan Filaret, who had earlier sought to carve out a balanced position on the use of both the original Hebrew and Greek texts for OT translation in his treatise "On the Dogmatic Value . . . of the Greek Septuagint," argued once again in 1856 that OT and NT translation should be based on "original" texts. One Synod member expressed the concern that, while a synodally authorized Russian NT might be able to be advanced more rapidly, the process could not be rushed in the case of the OT. Concern over the OT base text ultimately led to a compromise position wherein Russian OT translation would occur over an extended time period during which there could be discussion of the matter within the theological academies and the publication of variant editions. The provision for the open-ended publication of variant OT editions permitted publication during the 1860s of the Pavskii *editio princeps* and the Makarii (Glukharev) translations, thus indirectly reinforcing the use of the Hebrew Masoretic text in OT translation. Although Filaret's support for the use of both the Hebrew and Greek texts in Russian OT translation was a minority position within the Synod, it was to the Moscow metropolitan that the Synod ultimately deferred in the development of guidelines for renewed Russian biblical translation. In those guidelines Filaret appealed to the sentiments of his Synod colleagues, indicating that while the Russian Bible Society Psalter had been translated with insufficient attention to the Greek text, it could be rectified.[2] But OT translation would need to be undertaken with reference to the Hebrew as well as the Greek text.

Moscow Metropolitan Filaret's advocacy of renewed Russian biblical translation was strongly supported within the Holy Synod by Kherson and Tavride Archbishop Innokentii (Borisov, 1800–57), as well as by imperial confessor Vasilii Borisovich Bazhanov (1800–83) and the future Metropolitan of St. Petersburg and Novgorod, Isidor (Nikol'skii, 1799–1892). Metropolitan Isidor, having been appointed to the diocesan seat of St. Petersburg in 1860,

[1] Chistovich, *Istoriia perevoda Biblii*, 261–323; see also *Serdechnyi privet: Sbornik statei, izdannykh S.-Peterburgskoi dukhovnoi akademiei v pamiat' piatidesiatiletiia sviatitel'skogo sluzheniia vysokopreosviashchenneishago Isidora Mitropolita Novgorodskago, S-Peterburgskago i Finliandskago* (St. Petersburg, 1884). For the unpublished exchange between the two most prominent prelates of Kiev and Moscow, see "Sbornik statei o raznykh predmetakh," Rukopisnyi Otdel, Rossiiskaia natsional'naia biblioteka (RORNB, Manuscript Room, Russian National Library), *fond* S.-Peterburgskaia dukhovnaia akademiia, *delo* A.I.80, 381 leaves.

[2] Chistovich, *Istoriia perevoda Biblii*, 265. Filaret's reference may also relate to the RBS debate over Septuagint readings in the translation of the Psalter.

assumed the leadership of the translation effort upon the death of Filaret in 1867. Indeed, his outspoken championing of modern Russian biblical translation may explain in part why Metropolitan Isidor was never awarded the doctoral degree. Archbishop Innokentii, in turn, had been a correspondent and devoted supporter of Archpriest Pavskii during the Pavskii affair, and Bazhanov had succeeded Pavskii as tutor to the tsarevich Alexander Nikolaevich after Pavskii resigned from the position. So the conflicts attending the issue of the Russian Bible from the time of the RBS closure were well known to the synodal supporters of a renewed biblical translation.

At the same time, the opposition to a renewed translation generated a significant body of anonymous petitions to the Synod, and the Synod's lay ober-prokuror, Aleksandr Petrovich Tolstoi, was known to be opposed to the matter. At the center of the opposition stood Synod stalwart, Metropolitan of Kiev Filaret (Amfiteatrov, 1779–1857). The Synod's decision in 1856 to proceed with translation predictably elicited a major reaction from the Kievan metropolitan, who had been unable to attend the Synod's September session in Moscow where the decision to proceed was taken. The ensuing polemic over a renewed Russian biblical translation pitted against one another the two most formidable conservative prelates in the Holy Synod – the two Filarets – Metropolitan Filaret of Moscow versus Metropolitan Filaret of Kiev.

Canonized in 1994, St. Filaret, the metropolitan of Moscow, was the most significant Russian churchman of the nineteenth century. A close observer and defender of Orthodox churches in the Near East and an apologist for imperial autocracy and the institution of Russian serfdom at home, he had been a guiding member of the RBS governing committee forty years previously, serving also on the society's crucial translations and publications subcommittee. Anxious to preserve the authority of the church and its institutions, particularly the institution of monasticism which he sought to reinvigorate, Metropolitan Filaret advocated the reopening of Russian biblical translation and publication in order to address the growing public disaffection of the Russian laity and parish clergy, many of whom could not comprehend the Slavonic biblical text. The Moscow prelate had no interest in undermining the longstanding diglossia existing in Russia wherein there was both a churchly Slavonic liturgical language and a separate modern Russian literary language operating in tandem. Rather, Filaret Drozdov sought to provide a modern Russian text to accompany the Slavonic, especially for the private use of believers as they sought to understand and interpret the difficult-to-read Slavonic scripture used in liturgical worship.

The other Filaret (Amfiteatrov) was the founder of St. Vladimir's Cathedral in Kiev, and followed in a long line of distinguished Kievan prelates that included the early nineteenth-century church leader and scholar Evgenii Bolkhovitinov. Metropolitan Filaret of Kiev was sensitive to the controversies aroused by earlier Russian biblical translation. He had supported Ober-prokuror Protasov's effort to declare the Greek Septuagint and Slavonic biblical texts inviolate. Positioning himself as the defender of holy tradition, Filaret of Kiev believed that renewed translation would threaten the spiritual inheritance of Russia, especially the authority of the Slavonic Bible. In the ensuing conflict between the two Filarets, the political context was firmly established for Russian biblical translation in the last half of the nineteenth century.

In responding to the Synod's 1856 proposal to resume modern Russian biblical translation, Metropolitan Filaret Amfiteatrov took the fundamentalist or essentialist position, arguing again for the infallibility of the Slavonic text and the rejection of a modern Russian translation. In his "Zapiska" of 1857, penned shortly before his death, the Kievan prelate offered a series of challenging arguments against a modern Russian translation. His most basic line of attack was the charge that translation and dissemination of the Bible in modern Russian would undermine the authority of the Slavonic text.[3] What was needed in his view was not a renewed Russian translation, but more diligent training in the sacred Slavonic tongue. All that was needed for those who might be struggling with the Slavonic text was a Russian biblical commentary. The Kievan metropolitan argued that the Old Believer schism of the seventeenth century and the controversy spawned by biblical translation in the early nineteenth century developed out of a basic disregard for the holy and infallible Slavonic text. The Kievan metropolitan was essentially continuing a line of attack that he had put forward in the 1840s, when after the celebrated Pavskii affair he supported efforts to canonize the Slavonic text.

Anticipating this opposition, Moscow Metropolitan Filaret had earlier counseled his Synod colleagues that the Russian translation ought not to be represented as a liturgical text, but should rather be offered as an aid for those believers who were unable to understand the more obscure passages of the Slavonic text. Among the number of such believers he also included those from the ranks of Russia's own parish clergy. His

[3] "Otvetnaia zapiska," RORNB, *fond* S.-Peterburgskaia dukhovnaia akademiia, *delo* A.I.80, *ll.* 95–104; also Chistovich, *Istoriia perevoda Biblii*, 269–83.

subsequent formal rejoinder to Filaret Amfiteatrov took the form of a response to the Holy Synod in July 1857, shortly before the Kievan metropolitan's death.[4] In a telling reflection of the nascent public sphere already beginning to be felt in nineteenth-century Russian religious culture, the Moscow metropolitan asserted that it was no longer reasonable to expect the public to gain access to Holy Scripture through the medium of the Slavonic text. And in Filaret Drozdov's mind, public accessibility to scripture was a defining issue.

The debate over translation into a common or vernacular language revealed a more serious issue behind the defense of the Slavonic text – namely, the concern of both conservative prelates for retaining a liturgical, biblical language that was identifiably spiritual (*dukhovnyi*) in form and content. In other words, what the two metropolitans shared was a commitment to maintain use of the Church Slavonic as a sacred language for worship, much like the concern among Muslims for retaining the special authority of the Qur'an in Arabic, or among Jews for the authority of the Bible in Hebrew. Metropolitan Filaret Drozdov, no less than Metropolitan Filaret Amfiteatrov, believed in the need to retain the sanctity of God's Word in the Slavonic. Despite his outspoken advocacy for modern Russian biblical translation, Moscow Metropolitan Filaret was uncertain about the capacity of the modern Russian language, especially the clerical Russian of the nineteenth-century Synod chancellery, to convey the inspired Word of God in liturgical worship. As in the subsequent review of the synodal translation (*sinodal'nyi perevod*) in the theological journals of the day, so also in this opening polemic between the two Filarets, the issue of an appropriately "spiritual" or sacred language lay immediately beneath the surface.

The question over what was an appropriately sacred language for modern Russian religious culture continued to be a focus of interest in the twentieth century in the deliberations of the All-Russian Church Council of 1917–18, in the renovationist, "Living Church" movement of the 1920s, and in contemporary debates in Russia and in the emigration. By the end of the nineteenth century, modern translations existed for most liturgical texts, despite continued strict adherence to the use of Slavonic texts in Russian church worship.[5] The concern for an appropriate sacred language for

[4] Chistovich, *Istoriia perevoda Biblii*, 262–4 and 293–4. For the full response, see Filaret, *Sobranie mnenii i otzyvov Filareta, mitropolita moskovskago i kolomenskago po uchebnym i tserkovno-gosudarstvennym voprosam*, IV: 244–59.

[5] B. I. Sobe, "Problema ispravleniia bogosluzhebnykh knig v rossii v XIX–XX vekakh," *Bogoslovskie trudy*, 5 (1970): 25–68.

Russian Orthodox worship was sharply defined in the émigré debate between Father Georges Florovsky and Georgii Fedotov, the latter a church historian formerly of the Leningrad religious underground. The two twentieth-century émigré churchmen essentially reengaged the issue hidden in the debate between the two Filarets in the 1850s. In a defining moment of the later debate, Fedotov argued that Holy Scripture offered divinely inspired narratives of simple fishermen, carpenters, lepers, and nomads. Such narratives did not need to employ obscure or lofty language. As Fedotov concluded:

> Today in the Russian Church there are two deep streams of Russian spirituality vying with each other: the Russian kenotic [sacrificial/suffering] tradition and Byzantine theurgy. They struggle not for destruction, of course, but for predominance and leadership. Who will win? St. Sergei of Radonezh or Areopagus? Upon the outcome of this spiritual duel depends also the fate of Slavonic or Russian liturgics![6]

Fedotov, who frequently wrote about the kenotic side of Russian spirituality, believed that the Russian language was fully capable of conveying God's action in history – simple biblical narratives did not require artificially abstract expression. Florovsky, on the other hand, while not opposed to Russian biblical translation, remained more sensitive to the ascetic, theurgical side of Russian religious culture, and he shared the nineteenth-century concern that holy texts not be transmitted in what might be perceived to be a corrupted language. While the positions of Fedotov and Florovsky were more nuanced than those of their nineteenth-century predecessors, the debate of the two Filarets in the 1850s anticipated precisely this larger discursive issue over appropriate spiritual language. Filaret Amfiteatrov argued that a Russian translation would undermine the sacred language of the Slavonic text. Filaret Drozdov, who was able to carry the Synod with him, argued that a Russian translation would support and clarify the Slavonic text. Neither was prepared to countenance the use of a modern Russian text in liturgical worship.

An equally divisive issue that came to feature in the debate of the Filarets over a renewed modern Russian biblical translation was that of the intra-confessional question of how such a translation would affect the relationship between the Russian church and other Orthodox peoples of the All-Russian Empire (*Vserossiiskaia Imperiia*) and the wider Orthodox East (*pravoslavnyi vostok*). Initially, Metropolitan Filaret of Kiev posed the issue in such a way as to question the textological principles of his Moscow

[6] G. P. Fedotov, "Slavianskii ili russkii iazyk v bogosluzhenii?" *Put'*, no. 57 (August–October 1938): 28.

counterpart. Seeking to discredit earlier Russian OT translations that had used a Hebrew Masoretic textual base, the Kievan prelate argued that a Russian translation based upon the Hebrew Bible parted from the pure Orthodox textological tradition of the Slavonic Bible, grounded as that was upon the Greek Septuagint. But the argument was quickly expanded to note that the current Ecumenical Patriarch of Constantinople, unlike his early nineteenth-century predecessor, had anathematized any effort to render Holy Scripture – OT or NT – into modern Greek. Thus, by engaging in translation of the Bible into modern Russian, the Synod, in the eyes of the Kievan prelate, would be condoning the kind of activity that was elsewhere spurned within Eastern Christendom. With respect to Orthodox Slavs, the argument devolved into a de facto defense of empire, Metropolitan Filaret of Kiev claiming that modern Russian translation would effectively separate Russia from other Slavic peoples (such as Ukrainians, Belarusians, Bulgarians) who were joined to Russia through their common Slavonic biblical/liturgical tradition.[7]

This opposition from Kiev was greeted with a response on three separate levels. First, on the matter of the Greek Septuagint, Metropolitan Filaret Drozdov had already expressed himself during the 1840s in his opposition to the canonization of the Greek Septuagint, and he was equally spirited in his opposition to the canonization of the Slavonic Bible. For the Moscow prelate, the Septuagint was an important OT textual base, but it was not alone in that respect. Earlier having penned his work "On the Dogmatic Value . . . of the Greek Septuagint," Filaret Drozdov argued that the Greek Septuagint *did* have a special place in the Eastern Church, but that the Septuagint remained a translation – the oldest extant translation – from a Hebrew textual tradition that also needed to be embraced. Filaret Drozdov's effort to accommodate both textual traditions came to be reflected in the ultimate synodal translation with use of the Hebrew base text, but with the signature format of variant Septuagint readings footnoted on pages throughout the Russian OT. In the years that followed the publication of the synodal OT in the 1870s, the continuing debate over Hebrew and Greek textological traditions constituted a significant part of a remarkably open and substantive discussion within late nineteenth-century Russian biblical studies.

By raising the issue of the Russian church's relation to the Ecumenical Patriarch, however, the Kievan metropolitan had posed issues of a more transparently political character – issues that generated a candid and

[7] Chistovich, *Istoriia perevoda Biblii*, 270–1.

relatively strident response from the Moscow prelate. Moscow Metropolitan Filaret was known for his principled independence on matters involving Russian ties with the Orthodox East, often defending the Constantinople Patriarchate's position on such matters as Bulgarian church autocephaly over the opposition of powerful pan-Slav sentiment in Russia supporting the Bulgarians. Yet, on the issue of modern Russian biblical translation, Filaret of Moscow saw no need to secure the approval of the current Ecumenical Patriarchate, whose opposition to demotic translation was well known. The metropolitan noted that, even as the Ecumenical Patriarch was not consulted on Russian translations of the Greek church fathers, so also no prior consultation was called for in the case of biblical translation. Aware of the degraded condition of the Patriarchal See under Ottoman authority, Filaret argued that the Greek hierarchy did not have the necessary information on which to base a judgment regarding Russian biblical translation. Concluding his response on the issue, Filaret Drozdov argued that the Constantinople Patriarchate was dependent upon an unbelieving government (the Ottoman Empire) that could depose it at will, and that therefore the Greek hierarchy lacked the full church freedom necessary to judge the issue of Russian biblical translation.[8] Metropolitan Filaret of Moscow believed the issue of modern Russian biblical translation was not a matter for Constantinople to decide, perhaps foreshadowing in the process other significant twentieth-century jurisdictional disputes that have divided the Moscow and Ecumenical Patriarchates.

Even more politically charged was the exchange between the two Filarets over the implications of Russian biblical translation for Ukrainians and Belarusians. Goading the venerable Moscow metropolitan, Filaret of Kiev wrote, "If one is to translate Holy Scripture into Russian, then why not translate also into Ukrainian, Belarusian, and other languages?"[9] Filaret Drozdov responded on three counts, demonstrating in the process his imperial and nationalist sympathies in limiting translation to Russian, but not Belarusian or Ukrainian:

Because the Ukrainian and Belarusian languages are of a small minority and are little developed; because many (but not all) Ukrainians and Belarusians understand Russian and are able to read Holy Scripture in it; and, finally, because for

[8] Moscow Metropolitan Filaret's response, missing from the Chistovich history, can be found in "Konfidentsial'naia zametka o raznoglasii vzgliadov dvukh mitropolitov Filaretov . . . o perevode Sv. Pisaniia," ROGPB, *fond* S.-Peterburgskaia dukhovnaia akademiia, *delo* A.I.80, *ll.* 111–111 ob.

[9] Ibid., *l.* 109 ob. Chistovich, *Istoriia perevoda Biblii*, 275, omits this exchange between the two Filarets.

church and civil unity it is more useful that just the Russian language rule in Ukraine.[10]

Filaret of Kiev had countered that, if the revered Moscow metropolitan really wanted to promote unity, he ought to support the one Slavonic text for both liturgical and home use. "If one is to be concerned about church unity," wrote the Kievan metropolitan, "then it would be more useful for there to be one Slavonic language used by these Slavs and by us in both church worship and home reading."[11] What this exchange between the two metropolitans revealed was the potential manipulation for political ends of the issue of modern Russian biblical translation. Indeed, the exchange raised the tantalizing question of whether high-placed Russian prelates commonly viewed the Slavonic text as serving "imperial" ends. Did part of the importance of the Slavonic Bible rest in its alleged capacity to serve as the architecture for a civil religion of the empire? And, if so, could a Russian text serve in such a capacity for the empire's Ukrainian and Belarusian citizens?

Hidden in the 1850s debate between the two Filarets was yet another issue bearing on modern biblical translation. In the decades prior to the synodal translation, the political aspects of this issue were set within a Russian religious culture that served also as the context for expanded Russian missionary efforts among non-European and non-Christian populations of the empire, the so-called *inorodtsy* or *inovertsy*. Sensitive to the work of popular religious figures such as the Altai missionary Makarii Glukharev, Filaret Drozdov referenced such missionaries in the debate with his Kievan counterpart, offhandedly remarking that, after all, "even the Aleuts have the Gospel in their own common language; ought not Russians to deserve as much?"[12] In short, to accentuate the need for broad public accessibility to Holy Scripture in a demotic or common language, the Moscow metropolitan appealed to the parallelism of Russian missions functioning in minority languages throughout Eurasia.

The background to Filaret Drozdov's appeal to Russian missions was of course to be found not only in the case of the Altai mission, but in a series of missions that dotted the Eurasian landscape in the years immediately preceding and following the Crimean War. By 1865, this missionary enterprise led to the creation of the first formal Russian proselytizing effort – the

[10] "Konfidentsial'naia zametka," *l.* 110; Chistovich, *Istoriia perevoda Biblii*, 290.

[11] "Konfidentsial'naia zametka," *l.* 110.

[12] Chistovich, *Istoriia perevoda Biblii*, 262–3. Filaret's reference is to the Aleut/Russian diglot edition of the Gospel of St. Matthew (1840).

Missionary Society for Assisting the Spread of Christianity among Pagans (Missionerskoe obshchestvo dlia sodeistviia rasprostraneniiu khristianstva mezhdu iazychnikami), renamed in 1870 the Orthodox Missionary Society (Pravoslavnoe missionerskoe obshchestvo). The intellectual center of such activity gravitated to Kazan, where Professor Nikolai Ivanovich Il'minskii (1821–91), a highly regarded authority on the Slavonic Bible, took the lead in preparing missionary biblical translations in Turkic languages, notably in Chuvash and in Kazan Tatar.[13] Il'minskii became convinced that language was the most important instrument of every missionary. Recognizing from his own work that there was a great chasm between the learned Tatar literary language and the everyday conversational language, Il'minskii argued that common, spoken Tatar ought to be the ground for Christian schooling and biblical translation among the Tatars. Often only the mullahs could understand literary Tatar, so heavily infused was it with Arabic and Persian phrases. As Il'minskii wrote in 1858:

> In order to serve effectually for the Christian enlightenment of the baptized Tatars, translations ought to be made in a language entirely comprehensible to them – that is, in a conversational language.[14]

Thus, from the earliest stage in the reopening of modern Russian biblical translation, Orthodox missions offered a parallel argument for modern biblical translation, a parallelism fully embraced by Moscow Metropolitan Filaret. The linkage between Russian missions and modern Russian biblical translation would also be taken up by western Bible societies, notably the BFBS, which seized upon the reopening of modern biblical translation not only to develop the society's own Russian translation, but also to support non-Russian translations commissioned by the society in Kazan and Petersburg. By the time of the Russian missionary conferences of the 1890s, this linkage became so clearly a part of the religio-political culture that it yielded a curious backlash. Orthodox churchmen came to view with increasing alarm the inroads of western, specifically Protestant, Bible Society agencies and colporteurs whose hawking of scripture was seen as a form of dangerous proselytizing that might trigger the growth of sectarianism on the Russian frontier, at the expense of Russian Orthodoxy (see Chapter 6). But, in the debate of the 1850s, the focus of the Moscow

[13] On Il'minskii, see P. V. Znamenskii, *Na pamiat' o N. I. Il'minskom* (Kazan, 1892); and Paul W. Werth, *At the Margins of Orthodoxy: Mission, Governance, and Confessional Politics in Russia's Volga-Kama Region, 1827–1905* (Ithaca, NY: Cornell University Press, 2002).

[14] Quoted internally in Eugene Smirnoff, *A Short Account of the Historical Development and Present Position of Russian Orthodox Missions* (London, 1903), 33.

metropolitan dovetailed closely with the aims of Russian missionaries, who tended to share the metropolitan's desire for translations of Holy Scripture publicly accessible to a mass audience.

SYNODAL ACTION AND PUBLICATION OF THE SYNODAL NEW TESTAMENT

In his July 1857 rejoinder to the Kievan metropolitan, submitted to the Holy Synod, Filaret Drozdov reported that, in the end, despite their differences, Filaret Amfiteatrov had consented to the resumption of Russian biblical translation, but on condition that it not be hurried. Thus, as Chistovich has noted, the reopening of such translation in 1858 ultimately came with the unanimous support of the Holy Synod – a unanimity assured also by the intervening death of the Kievan metropolitan, Filaret Amfiteatrov. Synod support was quickly followed by the emperor's confirmation reopening modern Russian biblical translation. The Synod resolution approved by the emperor specifically called for the translation to be undertaken by theological academy professors under the control of the Holy Synod. Responding to the concern that the process not be rushed, the Holy Synod accordingly called for immediate work on the New Testament, to be followed by a more lengthy period of OT translation during which time alternative Russian OT variants could be published openly in the scholarly journals of the respective theological academies. No doubt with an eye toward the Pavskii affair, Metropolitan Filaret Drozdov recommended that the Russian Psalter of the Bible Society era, which had been translated "with insufficient consideration of the Greek text," should be corrected with appeal to both the Hebrew and Greek texts. Similarly, in the case of the prophetic texts, they were not to be published immediately, but only later, in the academy journals, with allowance for possible corrections recommended from academy scholars.

On the matter of NT translation, the St. Petersburg Theological Academy was given responsibility for translating the Gospel of Matthew; the Moscow Theological Academy responsibility for the Gospel of Mark; the Kazan Theological Academy for the Gospel of Luke; and the Kiev Theological Academy for the Gospel of John. After the initial division of responsibilities proved to be too time-consuming and duplicative, the process was redivided among the academies in 1859 to ensure no duplication of effort.[15]

[15] Chistovich, *Istoriia perevoda Biblii*, 263–5, 314–16. Although Metropolitan Filaret called for the use of both Greek and Hebrew original texts in OT translation ("O dogmaticheskom dostoinstve,"

At each of the academies, translation commissions were formed. In the case of the St. Petersburg academy, for example, the translation commission met from 1858, initially with the goal of completing the translation of the Gospel of Matthew. Commission members included Evgraf Ivanovich Loviagin (1822–1909), instructor in the Greek Department and assistant to the inspector of the academy; Moisei Aleksandrovich Golubev (1824–69), professor in biblical exegesis; and, from 1860, the Metropolitan of Novgorod and St. Petersburg, Isidor (Nikol'skii). Additional commission members were added to handle OT translation. A graduate of the St. Petersburg academy, Isidor had served as rector of Moscow Theological Seminary before his appointment to the episcopate. Having briefly assumed the Kievan diocesan seat following the death in 1858 of Metropolitan Filaret (Amfiteatrov), Isidor was appointed to St. Petersburg in 1860. From that point forward, Isidor personally oversaw the editing of the synodal translation, a position made all the more significant by the intervening death of Metropolitan Filaret Drozdov in 1867.

In revising and retranslating the New Testament, the translators were guided by Filaret Drozdov's injunction to use the authoritative Erasmian Greek *textus receptus* as well as Slavonic biblical tradition.[16] The authorized synodal edition of the four Gospels was published in St. Petersburg in 1860 (see Figure 9).[17] Following a similar process of academy revision under Metropolitan Isidor's editorial oversight, the remaining books of the Russian NT were issued by the Synod in 1862, initially in a diglot edition with the Slavonic text.[18] The publication of the Synod's authorized NT in Russian translation, 1860–2, was a landmark in Russian biblical studies. It signaled not only the effective reopening of Russian biblical translation, but also a renewed opportunity for marketing or disseminating modern biblical texts.

The end product was a compromise text that, like the earlier Bible Society translation, reflected the churchly Russian language of the nineteenth century. As a result, the issue of the authority of the language in biblical translation remained just as problematic in the aftermath of the synodal NT as it

Pribavleniia k izdaniiu Tvorenii Sviatykh Ottsev v russkom perevode, 17 [1858]: 452–84), he sanctioned a process that ultimately gave priority to the original Hebrew Masoretic text with footnoted Septuagint variant readings.

16 The appeal to the Erasmian Greek NT standardized in the Elzevir edition published in Moscow in 1810 became an issue bearing on the evaluation of the textology of the Russian NT (see Afterword).

17 *Gospoda Nashego Iisusa Khrista Sviatoe Evangelie ot Matfeia, Marka, Luki i Ioanna na russkom narechii* (St. Petersburg: Sinodal'naia tip., 1860). See Appendix, no. 43.

18 *Deianiia i Poslaniia Sviatykh Apostolov s Apokalipsisom na russkom narechii* (St. Petersburg: Sinodal'naia tip., 1862) – Appendix, no. 49. There followed in 1863 the complete NT, a rebinding of the two separate parts of the Russian NT with the common title, *Novyi Zavet Gospoda Nashego Iisusa Khrista na russkom narechii* (St. Petersburg: Sinodal'naia tip., 1863) – Appendix, no. 62.

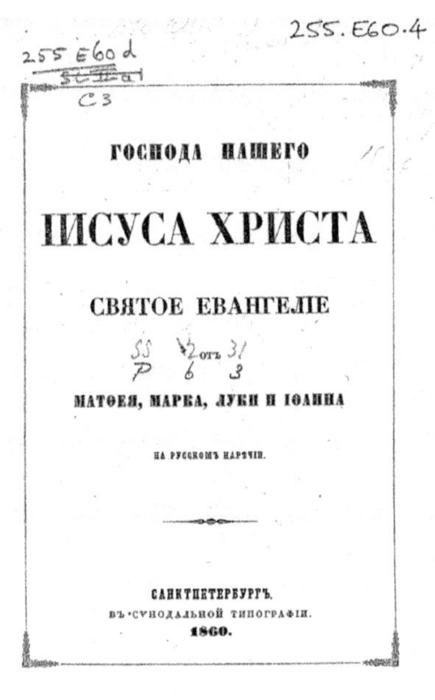

Figure 9. First edition (1860) of the synodal Russian text of the Gospels (Annotated Bibliography, no. 43). Specimen courtesy of BFBS Library collection, Cambridge University Library.

had been in the debate between the two Filarets. A leading biblical textologist of the early twentieth century, Ivan Evseev, summarized the situation by indicating that the Russian Bible was "sufficient for elementary needs in edifying reading, but it cannot satisfy any higher requirements." He pointed to recent crucial developments in both critical Greek NT textology and the modern Russian language, his point being that the synodal translation employed a decidedly "pre-Pushkin" churchly language.[19]

Despite such critical assessments, the Russian *sinodal'nyi perevod* became, from its issuance, the exclusive source base used in biblical commentaries from the 1860s right up to the Bolshevik Revolution. The relative obscurity of the Slavonic text meant that, however

[19] Ivan E. Evseev, *Stoletniaia godovshchina russkogo perevoda Biblii* (Petrograd, 1916), 34. See also Viktor Zhivov, *Kul'turnye konflikty v istorii russkogo literaturnogo iazyka* XVIII*–nachala* XIX *veka* (Moscow: Institut russkogo iazyka, AN SSSR, 1990); and his "Iazyk Feofana Prokopovicha i rol' gibridnykh variantov tserkovnoslavianskogo v istorii slavianskikh literaturnykh iazykov," *Sovetskoe slavianovedenie*, 1985, no. 3: 70–85.

undistinguished the Russian Bible may have seemed to its critics, the new translation, *not* the Slavonic text, found its way into virtually all manuals produced for students of theology in the last fifty years of the Russian Empire. This was also true for most citations to scripture found in literary works of the day.[20] As Francis Thompson has noted, the appearance of the Russian text "inevitably led to questions about the Slavonic text," because of the differences that set the synodal translation apart from its more obscure Slavonic counterpart.[21]

Alongside Professor Evseev's concern over the failure of translators to use a modern Russian literary language, there are two additional observations relevant to the authority of the language used in the synodal Russian NT. The first has to do with the relationship of the synodal text to that of the Russian Bible Society NT issued forty years earlier. Using two of the more readily recognizable passages, it is instructive to compare the two texts (see Table 1).

Allowing for the difference of construction in John 1:3, the two texts are otherwise virtually the same. It may be countered that these are relatively exceptional passages unlikely to be changed radically because they would have been well engrained in the religious culture, or public consciousness. Yet not only does that fail to recognize the broad similarities of the two texts across a wide spectrum of the New Testament, but such a counter-argument indeed makes the very point intended here – namely, that the language of the Russian Bible Society NT, as the received text, significantly influenced, consciously or unconsciously, the structure and formation of the authorized synodal NT. The "pre-Pushkin" language of the RBS New Testament was also the language of the synodal NT.

Lest this judgment somehow be seen to diminish the significance of the modern Russian translations of the nineteenth century, it is well to remember a second point about the language of Russian biblical translation at that time. Despite its archaisms, the churchly language of modern Russian biblical translation in the nineteenth century continued to be "edifying reading" for twentieth-century readers, retaining its communicative value, because in part it also served as a reaction to Soviet "bureaucratese."

[20] On this use of the Russian, rather than the Slavonic text, see Fedor Eleonskii, *Po povodu 150-letiia Elizavetinskoi Biblii: O novom peresmotre slavianskogo perevoda Biblii* (St. Petersburg: A. P. Lopukhin, 1902), 194–212.

[21] Francis J. Thomson, "The Slavonic Translation of the Old Testament," in *Interpretation of the Bible: On the Occasion of the Publication of the New Slovenian Translation of the Bible*, ed. Jože Krašovec (Ljubljana/Sheffield: Slovenian Academy of Sciences and Arts/Sheffield Academic Press, 1998), 713. The issuance of the NT in diglot editions tended also to call attention to these differences.

Table 1

RBS NT, 1819–21	Synodal NT, 1860–2
John 1:1–4	*John 1:1–4*
1. Въ началѣ было Слово, и Слово было у Бога, и Богъ было Слово.	1. Въ началѣ было Слово, и Слово было у Бога, и Слово было Богъ.
2. Оно было въ началѣ у Бога.	2. Оно было въ началѣ у Бога.
3. Все Имъ получило бытіе, и без Него не получило бытія ничто, что ни получило бытіе.	3. Все чрезъ Него начало быть, и безъ Него ни что не начало быть, что начало быть.
4. Въ Нем была жизнь, и жизнь была свѣтъ человѣковъ.	4. Въ Нем была жизнь, и жизнь была свѣтъ человѣковъ.
1 Corinthians 13: 1–2	*1 Corinthians 13: 1–2*
1. Естьли я говорю языками человѣческими и Ангельскими, а любви не имѣю; то я мѣдь звучащая, или кимвалъ звенящій.	1. Если я говорю языками человѣческими и ангельскими, а любви не имѣю; то я мѣдь звучащая, или кимвалъ звенящій.
2. Естьли имѣю даръ пророчества, и знаю всѣ тайны, и имѣю всѣ познанія, и всю вѣру, так что могу и горы переставлять, а не имѣю любви; то я ничто.	2. Если имѣю *даръ* пророчества, и знаю всѣ тайны, и имѣю всякое познаніе и всю вѣру, так что *могу* и горы переставлять, а не имѣю любви; то я ничто.

Similarly, the late Nobel Poet Laureate Czesław Miłosz, when asked why he set about learning Hebrew and retranslating the Psalter into Polish late in his life, replied that one of his reasons for embarking on a translation of the Bible was to address the degradation of the literary language in post-World War II Poland.[22] The appeal of a bygone past, of cherished archaisms, speaks of course to the continuing authority in varying ways of the King James Bible in English, the ancient Grabar text in Armenian and, by extension, both the Slavonic and modern Russian synodal texts.

THE SYNODAL OLD TESTAMENT

With the complete Russian New Testament having been issued in an authorized synodal edition, Moscow Metropolitan Filaret turned to the matter of the Old Testament, using a January 1863 letter to newly appointed Synod Ober-prokuror A. P. Akhmatov as the occasion for reviewing the

[22] Czesław Miłosz, "Problems of Biblical Translation," unpublished lecture at Arizona State University, January 20, 1984. Miłosz noted his concern over language degradation and his parallel commitment to the study of Hebrew in memory of the Holocaust.

principles agreed upon earlier by the full Synod for OT translation. Filaret's letter to the ober-prokuror was accompanied by a note, "On the Continuation of the Translation of Holy Scripture into Russian," that summarized how the matter should proceed.[23] Noting that the original decision of the Synod to proceed with modern Russian translation had not been just a matter of his own personal intervention, but had been unanimously approved by the ten prelates present at the original 1856 meeting of the Synod in Moscow, Metropolitan Filaret reviewed the considerations that would need to be followed as the process moved forward. First, he noted that the Synod had recommended priority be given to the correction and retranslation of the Psalter. The Psalter was one of the most difficult Old Testament books to translate, as Filaret noted, using the occasion also to remind the ober-prokuror of the commitment to employ both the original Hebrew and Greek texts in OT translation. While there was no need to rush the OT translation, the importance of the Psalter was such that it deserved special attention, a precedence that had been recognized earlier in the era of the Russian Bible Society.

Recalling the Synod's decision to permit publication of variant Old Testament translations while work proceeded deliberately on the preparation of the Synod's own approved translation, Metropolitan Filaret reconfirmed the sequence of the work on the Old Testament. In addition to work on the Psalter, initial publication of the Russian Pentateuch should also be attempted, to be followed sequentially by translation of the historical books, then the poetic books, and finally the prophetic books, or books of the major and minor prophets. Filaret's note effectively reconfirmed what had already begun to evolve in practice – namely, a two-track system of translation and publication whereby variant OT readings could be prepared and published in academy or other religious journals, with those publications serving to inform a second track of translation and publication undertaken by a formal translations committee gathered in St. Petersburg to create what would ultimately be the Synod's own authorized Old Testament edition.

KEY PARTICIPANTS IN THE PREPARATION OF THE SYNODAL OT TRANSLATION

Because of its importance for the preparation of the authorized synodal OT, the composition of the translations committee attached to the

[23] "O prodolzhenii perevoda Sviashchennago Pisaniia na russkoe narechie," in *Sobranie mnenii i otzyvov Filareta* (Moscow, 1887), V: 388–90.

St. Petersburg Theological Academy has understandably commanded great attention. Although Moscow Metropolitan Filaret continued to participate in the review of translations right up until his death, local oversight of the translation process, especially in the case of the OT, fell increasingly to Metropolitan Isidor (Nikol'skii) of St. Petersburg and Novgorod, the leading member of the Holy Synod following Metropolitan Filaret's passing in 1867. Known for his even-handed temperament and ability to work through divisive issues, Metropolitan Isidor had earlier served in the diocesan seat of Polotsk and Mogilev where he addressed the conflicted issue of the Uniate or Greek-Catholic population. Similarly, he served as exarch of Georgia during a critical transitional period in the history of Transcaucasia. In each of these posts he was known for his "akkuratnost'," a habit of attention to detail. By the 1860s, following the death of Metropolitan Filaret Drozdov, he held seniority in the Holy Synod, where he brought the kind of conciliatory air and moral influence that also helped advance the OT revision process to completion. Initially appointed to the St. Petersburg and Novgorod diocese in 1860, he inherited oversight of the preexisting St. Petersburg Theological Academy translations committee initially established for translation of the Gospel of Matthew.

With the committee's broadened responsibilities, its membership also expanded. From the outset the committee had included two prominent academy faculty members – Evgraf Ivanovich Loviagin (1822–1909), who taught natural sciences and later assumed the chair in New Testament Greek language and literature, and Moisei Aleksandrovich Golubev (1824–69), who held the academy's professorial chair in biblical exegesis and who knew Hebrew. Loviagin helped guide the translation process in connection with the Greek Septuagint readings and provided his own translation of the OT deuterocanonical books. Golubev's contributions included translations of several historical and poetic books from the Hebrew Masoretic text.

The most important addition to the translations committee for the Synod's Old Testament was Daniil Khvol'son (1819–1911), a professor of Hebrew, Old Syriac, and Chaldean philology in the Oriental Faculty of St. Petersburg University. Khvol'son's translations rest behind an estimated two-thirds of the synodal OT text.[24] The appointment of Daniil Khvol'son for OT translation brought a person with international distinction in Near Eastern languages to the Synod's translation effort. Of Jewish parentage, Khvol'son was born into very modest circumstances in Vilnius. Having come under the tutelage of the Jewish Enlightenment scholar Abraham

[24] See "Khvol'son, Daniil Avraamovich," in *Entsiklopedicheskii slovar'* (St. Petersburg: Brokgauz-Efron, 1903), LXXIII: 136.

Geiger in Breslau, Khvol'son completed his studies at Breslau University in the Faculty of Semitics where in 1850 he defended his doctoral thesis on the Sabaeans. Specializing initially in Arabic religion, he became known for his work in a variety of ancient Semitic languages. He returned to Russia in 1851, working initially in St. Petersburg as a censor for Hebrew books. Regarded as "the most famous Russian Jewish apostate of all time," he converted to Orthodox Christianity in 1855 under the influence of the Near East traveler and Russian Minister of Public Instruction, Avraam Sergeevich Norov, whose name Khvol'son assumed as his own patronymic – Daniil *Avraamovich* Khvol'son.[25] In 1855, he assumed the post at St. Petersburg University, combining his position there with instructional responsibilities in Hebrew and biblical archeology at both the St. Petersburg Theological Academy (1858–83) and the Catholic Theological Academy (1858–84). Although Khvol'son's major scholarly contributions were to Hebraic and specifically biblical scholarship, he was known also for his seminal contributions to Old Syriac, Arabic, and Khazar paleography.[26]

Following the death of Moisei Golubev in 1869, Pavel Ivanovich Savvaitov (1815–95) was added to the translations committee. Savvaitov was the son of a Russian priest from the region of Vologda. A graduate of the St. Petersburg Theological Academy, Savvaitov returned to the academy in 1842 following a brief period as professor of philosophy at Vologda Seminary. At the academy he taught patristics and hermeneutics, the latter field having been developed in Russian theological education only from the period of the 1808 Commission on Ecclesiastical Schools. Savvaitov's work served as an early definition of this field of hermeneutics for Russian biblical exegesis.[27] His

[25] On Khvol'son as "the most famous Russian Jewish apostate," see Michael Stanislawski, *Tsar Nicholas I and the Jews: The Transformation of Jewish Society in Russia, 1825–1855* (Philadelphia, PA: Jewish Publication Society of America, 1983), 146. In his rather unsympathetic portrait of Khvol'son, Stanislawski dismisses the conversion as simple expediency for the purposes of professional advancement. Drawing on Saul M. Ginsburg's study of Russian Jewish converts to Orthodoxy, *Meshumodim in Tsarishn Rusland: Forshungen un zikhroynes vegn Yidishn lebn in amolikn Rusland* ["Apostates in Tsarist Russia"] (New York: Tsiko bikher farlag, 1946), 120–1, Stanislawski attributes to Khvol'son the famous epigram, "I believe that it is better to be a professor in St. Petersburg than a *melamed* in Eishishok."

[26] On Khvol'son, see the tribute by his distinguished student, St. Petersburg Theological Academy professor, Ivan Troitskii, "Professor D. A. Khvol'son," *Zhurnal ministerstva narodnogo prosveshcheniia*, n.s. 34 (1911), no. 8, otd. 4: 90–9; also the biographical entry in Men', *Bibliologicheskii slovar'*, III: 349–50. For Khvol'son's work on the OT text, see "Istoriia vetkhozavetnogo teksta i ocherk ego drevneishikh perevodov," *Khristianskoe chtenie*, 1874, chast' 1: 519–74, chast' 2: 3–74.

[27] Pavel I. Savvaitov, *Bibleiskaia germenevtika*, 2nd edn (St. Petersburg, 1859). First published in 1844, this standard work on biblical hermeneutics has been the subject of controversy. Fedor Eleonskii has claimed that Savvaitov simply translated and revised an earlier work used in seminary instruction, *Delineatio Hermeneticae Sacrae, ad usum studiosorum Sacrae Scripturae accommodata*. See F. G. Eleonskii, "Otechestvennye trudy po izucheniiu Biblii v XIX v.," *Khristianskoe chtenie*, 1901, no. 1:

work sought to carve out a careful line that allowed for biblical exegesis to be guided by church tradition, while at the same time recognizing the appeal to the scripture text as an independent authority in argumentation. At the conclusion of his *Bibleiskaia germenevtika*, Savvaitov's six "rules" for interpreting the Bible included the admonition in the case of historical biblical accounts to "defend the historicity of supernatural occurrences and oppose all false opinions about the miracles of God" – a mark of the degree to which his hermeneutics differed from historico-critical text studies of a later era.[28] Savvaitov's selection for membership on the translations committee may also have been influenced by his earlier work with translation, including his preparation of a Zyrian grammar and dictionary.[29]

The challenge for the translations committee attached to St. Petersburg Theological Academy was to address the differences in the original Hebrew and Greek base texts, while also building upon the achievements already made in Russian OT translation in the first half of the nineteenth century. In balancing the appeal to Hebrew and Greek source texts, the St. Petersburg translations committee ultimately created a composite text that was neither slavishly tied to the Greek Septuagint (or Slavonic Bible), nor consistently in accordance with the Hebrew Masoretic text. Symbolic of that balancing effort was the signature manner in which variant Greek Septuagint readings not accepted by the committee for incorporation into the main Russian translation were occasionally referenced in Russian translated footnotes at the bottom of the relevant page. The meetings of the translations committee were not minuted, but the effort to carve out a middle ground was evident not only in the footnoted entries within the synodal OT, but also in the personal reflections of the committee's most illustrious member. Commenting to a western observer on the potential limitations of such a mixed translation, Daniil Khvol'son described the synodal translation as a "conjectural translation," adding that "it cannot be considered a faithful rendering of the Hebrew text, even though in some instances in which it differs it is sustained by the New Testament."[30] Sensitive to the mixed translation and the critique that followed its issuance

5–28 and no. 5: 633–60. See also the treatment of Savvaitov in Alexander I. Negrov, *Biblical Interpretation in the Russian Orthodox Church: A Historical and Hermeneutical Perspective* (Tübingen: Mohr Siebeck, 2008), 97–102.

28 Savvaitov, *Bibleiskaia germenevtika*, 141.

29 See P. I. Savvaitov, *Grammatika zyrianskogo iazyka* (St. Petersburg, 1849) and his *Zyriansko-Russkii i Russko-Zyrianskii slovar'*, 2 vols. (St. Petersburg, 1849).

30 See Khvol'son to BFBS, received in London, December 8, 1870, BFBS Agents Books (Russia), no. 125, 234 (BSA/D1/7/125). Khvol'son's critique of the synodal OT text needs to be seen, however, in the context of his offer then being considered by the BFBS Petersburg Agency to complete on retainer for the BFBS a parallel Russian OT translation more consistently faithful to the Hebrew original.

in the 1870s, the Holy Synod in 1876 asked Daniil Khvol'son to explain and clarify the footnoted references in the Synod's own Pentateuch.[31] It seems that within a decade of the death of Moscow Metropolitan Filaret, there was already some institutional memory loss over the manner in which the esteemed Moscow prelate had sought to balance Hebrew and Greek textology in the architecture of the Russian OT.

Such balancing, of course, was not required in those cases where the OT text was supported by only one language source base, Greek or Hebrew. Thus, in the pivotal issue of deuterocanonical texts, or the apocryphal readings supported only by the Greek Septuagint, translations from the Greek were inserted directly into the Russian OT. This was not an issue for the translation of the Pentateuch, for which there were no additional deuterocanonical texts, but for the OT historical, poetic, and prophetic sections, translation directly from the Greek Septuagint was overseen primarily by St. Petersburg professor of NT Greek, Evgraf Loviagin, and the deuterocanonical books were inserted into each of the final three sections of the synodal Russian Old Testament.

Meanwhile there were inevitable delays that stalled production of the synodal OT, not the least of them being the untimely death in 1869 of Moisei Golubev, whose translations of OT historical and poetic books were published as supplements to the journal of the St. Petersburg Theological Academy, *Khristianskoe chtenie*, between 1861 and 1869.[32] With the death of Golubev, the primary translator from the Hebrew Masoretic text became Daniil Khvol'son, who submitted his work to the St. Petersburg Theological Academy's translations committee for editorial revision. Khvol'son benefited from the earlier Pavskii and Makarii translations, which were among several OT translations circulating openly in the 1860s.[33] Khvol'son was also able to utilize the unpublished RBS Octateuch, unbound copies of which still existed in Petersburg.

While the work of the translations committee in St. Petersburg was but one of the translation centers established in the four theological academies in Kiev, Kazan, Moscow, and St. Petersburg, the committee operating at the

[31] The synodal questioning is documented in Troitskii, "Professor D. A. Khvol'son," 90–9.

[32] Khvol'son's comments on the delay caused by the death of Golubev were relayed to London BFBS offices by its Petersburg agent William Nicolson. See Nicholson to R. B. Girdlestone, December 3, 1870, BFBS Agents Books (Russia), no. 125, 231 (BSA/D1/7/125).

[33] On St. Makarii's translations, published in *Pravoslavnoe obozrenie*, see Chapter 3, n. 53. The Pavskii OT books were similarly serialized in the journal *Dukh khristianina*, 1862–3 (Appendix, no. 56). Kiev Academy Professor of Hebrew Mikhail Spiridonovich Guliaev published his separate translation of the historical books of the OT, *Istoricheskie knigi Sviashchennago Pisaniia* (Kiev, 1866). See also Leon Mandel'shtam's Russian translation of the Pentateuch published in Berlin in 1862 (Appendix, no. 54).

St. Petersburg Theological Academy incorporated suggestions from other academies. This final revision, which also benefited from the editorial oversight of St. Petersburg Metropolitan Isidor, became the approved synodal version. The resulting authorized synodal Old Testament was published by the St. Petersburg Press of the Holy Synod in four separately bound editions between 1868 and 1875 – the Pentateuch in 1868, the historical books in 1869, the poetical or *uchitel'nye* books in 1872 (including the revised Psalter), and the major and minor prophets in 1875.[34] Thus, even though it was not issued as a single bound volume until 1876, by 1875 the Synod had completed the translation and publication of a modern Russian Bible in an authorized version – the *sinodal'nyi perevod.*

THE BFBS AND THE SYNODAL RUSSIAN BIBLE

Because of its continuing agency presence in St. Petersburg, British and Foreign Bible Society records provide an additional perspective on the synodal translation. As an agency committed to distributing the Bible in the languages of the Russian Empire, the BFBS had an interest in the availability and potential circulation of a modern Russian text. At the same time, the BFBS operated under its own ideological strictures, not the least of which was its insistence on circulating scripture "without note or comment," and without the apocryphal or deuterocanonical texts. The opposition of British evangelicals to circulation of the deuterocanonical texts of the Bible – the Apocrypha controversy – meant that, by 1825, the BFBS was forced to take the position that it would not circulate copies of scripture containing the deuterocanonical books of the Bible. This in turn set the BFBS Petersburg agency on a path toward potential conflict with the translation process under way in reformist Russia. How did the BFBS respond to this reopening of biblical translation in the post–Crimean War period, particularly on the thorny issue of Russian OT translation?

The BFBS had never been far removed from Russian biblical translation and dissemination, even in the period when modern translation had been relegated to the underground. While its Leipzig and London revised editions of Russian Bible Society scripture published between 1838 and 1860 never circulated openly in Russia, agents of the BFBS continued to serve in

[34] The separate parts of the Russian OT prepared by the St. Petersburg committee were published in 1868 (Part I, Pentateuch), 1869 (Part II, historical books of Joshua–Esther), 1871 (Psalter), 1872 (Part III, poetical books, Job–Ecclesiasticus, with the Psalter), and 1875 (Part IV, the prophetic books, Isaiah – 3 Esdras) by the Synodal Press of St. Petersburg and were issued under the general title *Sviashchennyia Knigi Vetkhago Zaveta v russkom perevode* (Appendix, nos. 91, 97, 104, 111, and 121).

Petersburg throughout the period, even during the difficult days of the Crimean War when Russian and English forces faced each other in military combat.[35] Upon publication of the Russian translation of the Gospels in 1860, the Petersburg BFBS agency secured approval from the London home office to market the edition in its Petersburg shop.[36] Archibald Mirrielees, the British merchant in Petersburg who served on the BFBS Petersburg agency committee, wrote to London heralding the significance of the first synodal edition of the Gospels, noting that "the demand has been very great, the shop being literally crowded and the number of copies sold to one applicant limited to 50 as the edition [36,000 copies] was likely to be soon exhausted."[37] The activities of the Petersburg BFBS offices began to outstrip the capacities of the part-time agents who were serving voluntarily for the BFBS while also seeing to their independent commercial interests. The demand for the synodal Russian edition of the Gospels and subsequently for the full New Testament forced the St. Petersburg BFBS agency to reorganize its operations in the decade of the 1860s, adding a full-time agent and launching an ambitious program of colportage. Purchasing stock from the publishing house of the Holy Synod in Petersburg, the BFBS became the largest wholesale and retail outlet for Russian scripture, its agency sales by the close of the century reaching distribution figures of approximately one million copies annually (see Chapter 6).

The commercial success of the BFBS in disseminating the synodal NT, however, could not long camouflage the problems the society would encounter in addressing the Russian Old Testament. The BFBS confronted three intractable situations that ultimately thwarted the effort to circulate a

[35] Richard Knill's role as BFBS agent in Petersburg (1825–33) was perpetuated in a succession of BFBS agents, who oversaw the translation and distribution of biblical texts. Upon the reopening of biblical translation, BFBS agents commissioned the society's own biblical translations, both in Russian and non-Russian languages of the empire. Petersburg agents included: John Brown (1833–40), Thomas Ellerby (1840–53), Archibald Mirrielees (1853–7), and informally thereafter on the BFBS Petersburg agency committee, William Mirrielees (1857–65), Andrew Muir (1860–9), Adalbert Eck (1865–9), William Nicolson (1869–97), and William Keen (1896–1918). See S. K. Batalden, "Revolution and Emigration: The Russian Files of the British and Foreign Bible Society," in *The Study of Russian History from British Archival Sources*, ed. Janet M. Hartley (London: Mansell Publishing for the University of London School of Slavonic and East European Studies, 1986), 147–71.

[36] The BFBS editorial subcommittee undertook only the most perfunctory review, sending a copy of the synodal 1860 Gospels to a former Siberian missionary for the London Missionary Society, Edward Stallybrass, who approved of the text (see BFBS Minutes of the Editorial Subcommittee, vol. 6, June 5, 1860, 105–6; and the note of Stallybrass's support, 114 [BSA/C17/1/6]). A member of the Petersburg agency committee, W. Lee, also forwarded a positive evaluation of the text, but there was no evaluation by a native speaker of Russian (W. Lee to W. H. Ropes, May 31, 1860, St. Petersburg, in BFBS Editorial Correspondence Inwards, no. 1, 322 [BSA/E3/1/4/1]).

[37] A. Mirrielees to H. Knolleke, June 13, 1860, BFBS Editorial Correspondence Inwards, no. 1, 323 (BSA/E3/1/4/1).

Russian Old Testament – namely, difficulty with the textual base of the synodal translation, identification of alternative translators should the society develop its own variant Russian OT text, and the barriers it would encounter to marketing such an alternative BFBS Russian OT text.

The first of these issues involved the conflict noted between the BFBS and the Russian church over OT textology and the placement of notations within biblical editions. On the matter of textology, BFBS editorial superintendents well into the nineteenth century considered the Greek Septuagint to be an inferior, "translated" text, upholding instead exclusive use of the Hebrew Masoretic text for OT translation. Most odious to the Bible Society was the fact that the Greek Septuagint included deuterocanonical texts it had rejected, but that the Synod had included in its OT text. For the BFBS, it mattered little that Russian inclusion of the deuterocanonical books reflected the role of these texts as traditional parts of the established liturgical text, the Slavonic Bible.

Asked to examine the issue more closely, the BFBS Petersburg agent William Nicolson, newly appointed in 1869, contacted Synod translator Daniil Khvol'son, and then reported to London on his "very long conversation over the matter" with Khvol'son:

> He tells us that the Synod's translation is not altogether his work. There was a committee consisting of four persons appointed to examine the work after it passed through the hands of Dr. Chwolson and his coadjuters. He gave, I may remark by the way, no flattering account of the composition of that committee, there being scarcely a Russian ecclesiastic who knows anything of Hebrew. The translation, so far as the Pentateuch is concerned . . . is a sort of hodge-podge between the Hebrew and Septuagint. In many passages, as for example, Gen. 4:7, the Hebrew text has been preferred, while the additions to be found in the Septuagint have been put within brackets. In other portions, however, the version of the Septuagint has been preferred (for example, in Gen. 47:3 and other instances).[38]

Khvol'son's comments on the composition of the Synod committee, though they may have been correct about the command of Hebrew in the translations committee after the death of Moisei Golubev, were almost surely intended to advance his own standing with the BFBS Petersburg representatives.

While the Pentateuch, published in a Synod-authorized Russian edition in 1868, posed no problem over the deuterocanonical books, all subsequent parts, including the second volume of historical books issued in 1869,

[38] Nicolson to R. B. Girdlestone, St. Petersburg, December 3, 1870, BFBS Agents Books (Russia), no. 125, 230 (BSA/D1/7/125).

contained deuterocanonical readings. Thus, by the end of the 1860s, the BFBS London home office recognized that despite mild protestations from British merchants on the Petersburg BFBS agency committee, such as William Mirrielees, who could not quite understand the fuss over deuterocanonical texts, a fundamental obstacle stood in the way of its Petersburg agency's sale of the synodal Russian OT text.

Anticipating this OT impasse, the BFBS London home office had already begun to use early nineteenth-century RBS editions of the Psalter and the first eight books of the Old Testament in published reprintings and edited revisions. Such BFBS Old Testament editions began with the 1852 Psalter printed in Leipzig, and continued with revised publication of the Octateuch in London in 1861.[39] The problems the London home office had in retaining reliable Russian native speaker editors and proofreaders were well illustrated in the case of the Octateuch. In order to prepare copy for the press, the BFBS turned to the noted Russian émigré in London, Alexander Herzen, who in turn recommended his assistant Vasilii Ivanovich Kel'siev, the notorious Russian nihilist revolutionary, who had taken residence at the time in Britain.[40]

Despite these editions of the Russian Octateuch and Psalter published for the BFBS in the West, the BFBS lacked its own reliable Russian text for the majority of the Old Testament at a time when both the Petersburg and Vienna BFBS agencies were experiencing growing demand for such a modern Russian text. Early in 1865, three years before the synodal OT editions began to be published, Andrew Muir, who was then serving as the society's part-time agency representative in Petersburg, responded to this

[39] In preparing the Leipzig Psalter (Appendix, no. 32), BFBS called upon John Paterson's collaborator in the RBS, Ebenezer Henderson, to cleanse the RBS Psalter of its chapter headings, notes, and the 151st Psalm (see BFBS Minutes of Editorial Subcommittee, vol. 4, August 13, 1851, 38; and January 27, 1852, 53–4 [BSA/C17]). The 1852 BFBS Psalter was reissued in London reprintings of 1854 and 1855 (Appendix, nos. 34 and 35) using the stereotype plates purchased from Tauchnitz in Berlin. The London edition of the Russian Octateuch (Genesis–Ruth), *Bibliia; Vosem' knig vetkhago zaveta: Piatiknizhie Moiseevo, Iisus Navin, Sud'i i Ruf'*, was issued in 1861 and again in 1862 (Appendix, nos. 48 and 50).

[40] On Kel'siev and his collaboration with the BFBS, see S. K. Batalden, "Revolutionaries and Evangelicals in Concert: Alexander Herzen, Vasilii Kel'siev, and the British and Foreign Bible Society," paper delivered to the Russian-Speaking Society, Cambridge, UK, February 10, 2004. Kel'siev, whom Herzen refers to as "a nihilist in the surplice of a deacon" in *My Past and Thoughts* (London: Chatto & Windus, 1968): III: 1333, was also the pseudonymous "Vadim," who created his own independent Russian translation of the Pentateuch in a version that renders OT names in Russian with Hebrew pronunciation (Moshe, rather than Moisei). For his controversial Pentateuch, see Appendix, no. 40. Kel'siev also proofread for the BFBS a revised small 24mo edition of its London Russian Psalter issued in 1860 (and reprinted in 1862) – an edition that became known as the "imperative Psalter" for its prodigious use of exclamation points (see Appendix, nos. 42 and 53).

demand by suggesting that the BFBS add its own competing Russian OT text to those then surfacing in Russia:

I annex a list of new translation of parts of the Old Testament into Modern Russ, which have lately appeared. As there seems no prospect of the Old Testament being published as a whole by the Synod here, and your ordinary editions of the Pentateuch [*sic*] might be revised if a competent person could be found, you could thus with little difficulty complete the work. Your doing this would perhaps hasten the movements of the Synod.[41]

Muir thought that western involvement in Russian biblical translation and publication might stimulate competitive Synod action. On the translation process itself, Muir reasoned somewhat simplistically that all the BFBS needed to do was contract with a local Russian scholar to provide a complete OT text by combining revisions of the existing BFBS edition of the Octateuch and Psalter with revisions of one or another of the formerly clandestine Russian OT texts then openly being published in the religious journals of Alexander II's Russia. To that end, Muir recommended that the BFBS contact Leon Mandel'shtam, a distinguished polyglot scholar who despite the restrictive atmosphere of Nicholas I's Russia, had been the first Jewish graduate of the University of St. Petersburg in 1843. Mandel'shtam was then in Berlin, but had earlier been employed by the Russian government to compose a Hebrew/Russian lexicon. According to Muir, Mandel'shtam might even be willing to relocate to London to undertake such an assignment.[42]

In the end, after BFBS Vienna agent Edward Millard raised questions about the appropriateness of employing a Jew for BFBS translations, the decision was made to employ a Jewish convert to Christianity, Vasilii Levison, for preparation of an independent BFBS edition of the modern Russian Old Testament in potential competition with the synodal translation already in preparation.[43] With the hire of Levison the BFBS

[41] A. Muir to H. Knolleke, St. Petersburg, January 3, 1865, BFBS Editorial Correspondence Inwards, no. 3, 309 (E3/1/4/3). The reference should be to the BFBS Octateuch, not Pentateuch.

[42] Muir to Knolleke, St. Petersburg, January 3, 1865 (BSA/E3/1/4/3). For the 1862 Mandel'shtam Hebrew/Russian diglot of the Pentateuch, or Torah, see Appendix, no. 54, and the discussion in Chapter 5. Mandel'shtam's preface to the diglot is addressed to Jewish schoolteachers, exhorting them to train their children to read the Bible and to be good citizens of the Russian Empire. See also the 1872 reprinting (Appendix, no. 108). Mandel'shtam prepared a separate Hebrew/Russian diglot of the Psalter (see Appendix, no. 109). The personal library of Leon Mandel'shtam today rests at the foundation of the New York Public Library Judaica collection.

[43] Millard to Knolleke, Vienna, February 17, 1865, BFBS Editorial Correspondence Inwards, no. 4 (BSA/E3/1/4/4). Millard cautioned against Mandel'shtam, referencing in coded language Mandel'shtam's Jewish identity – "my experience of birds of this feather is such as to advise great caution." After correspondence with BFBS agents in Vienna, Petersburg, and Odessa in winter and

committed itself to the preparation of its own rival Russian OT text. The profile of Vasilii Levison represents a particularly interesting case of Jewish conversion to Russian Orthodoxy.[44] Following his conversion at the age of twenty-five, Levison moved from his German homeland to Russia, where he taught Hebrew from 1840 to 1860 in Catholic and Orthodox seminaries in Petersburg. Then he accompanied the Russian mission to Jerusalem where he also came to the attention of missionaries from the London Society for Promoting Christianity among the Jews. Having translated several works of theology into German for the private reading of the Russian empress, the German wife of Nicholas I, Levison ingratiated himself with the imperial family. Despite his knowledge of Hebrew, however, Levison had an insecure command of modern Russian. Thus he hired a Russian native speaker, his former seminary student Petr Ivanovich Bogoliubov (d. 1880), to assist him throughout the translation process. Bogoliubov had taught church history and Greek at the St. Petersburg Theological Seminary (not to be confused with the postgraduate Petersburg Theological Academy) before becoming director in 1854 of the St. Petersburg Home for the Upbringing of Poor Children (Dom vospitaniia bednykh detei). In addition, the BFBS Petersburg agency arranged for a two-person team of Russian correctors, Professors Hoffman and Nikolai Astaf'ev (the latter a founding director of the Society for the Dissemination of Holy Scripture in Russia), to review the translation and proofread the resulting publications to be printed in London.

Arriving in Petersburg in 1869, BFBS Petersburg agent William Nicolson (see Figure 10) lamented the terms of the agreement whereby Levison was paid a lavish monthly salary, rather than specific remuneration for completed work. But despite delays in completing his Russian translations, Levison managed to translate and the BFBS managed to publish in London the OT books of 1 and 2 Samuel, Proverbs, and all the major and minor prophetic books well in advance of the parallel work under way on the synodal translation.[45] Upon the sudden death of Vasilii Levison in 1869,

spring 1865, the BFBS editorial subcommittee in London authorized the hiring of Vasilii Levison in April 1865 at a salary of 200 rubles per month. See BFBS Minutes of the Editorial Subcommittee, vol. 8, April 19, 1865, 56–8 (BSA/C17/1/8).

44 On Levison, see the attestation of Gottlieb Abramsohn to BFBS agent Millard, Berlin, December 31, 1864, BFBS Editorial Correspondence Inwards, no. 3, 312–13 (BSA/E3/1/4/3); also "Levison, Vasilii Andreevich," *Evreiskaia entsiklopediia* (repr. Moscow: Terra, 1991), x: 117–18.

45 For London publication of these Levison/Bogoliubov Russian OT editions, see Appendix, nos. 81–2, 84–5, 93–4, and 102. Upon his arrival in Petersburg, BFBS agent William Nicolson assessed the work of Levison and Bogoliubov rather negatively (see Nicolson to BFBS, November 2, 1881, BFBS Editorial Correspondence Inwards, no. 16, 133–41 [BSA/E3/1/4/16]). His assessment not only reflected the advice he had received from the subsequent BFBS translator Daniil Khvol'son, it also reflected the

Figure 10. William Nicolson, BFBS agent in St. Petersburg, 1869–97. Photo courtesy of the BFBS, 1879 photograph album, BFBS Archive, Cambridge University Library.

the BFBS Petersburg agency was again faced with having to locate a reliable translator to complete its own Russian OT edition.

By 1869, however, the Holy Synod had commenced publication of its authorized Russian OT edition, thus raising the question for the BFBS offices in Petersburg and London of the feasibility of proceeding with a separate BFBS Russian Old Testament. The unwillingness of the BFBS to circulate a synodal OT that included the deuterocanonical books meant that, in the end, it was obliged to hire a new translation team to complete the BFBS Russian Old Testament. Within weeks of Levison's passing, BFBS Petersburg agency committee representative William Mirrielees wrote to BFBS editorial superintendent Girdlestone in London noting the recent progress of the Holy Synod in translating and publishing its

critical evaluation of the Levison/Bogoliubov BFBS texts by Moscow Theological Academy Professor Nikol'skii in the Russian journal, *Pravoslavnoe obozrenie* (M. Nikol'skii, "Russkii perevod Biblii i znachenie evreiskoi filologii," *Pravoslavnoe obozrenie*, 1876 [April]: 645–72). Nicolson ultimately recommended BFBS revision of the Levison translations to make them conform to the subsequent BFBS translations undertaken by Daniil Khvol'son and Pavel Savvaitov.

own Russian OT, which included apocryphal readings. Then, in a move that would commit the BFBS to the completion of its parallel Russian OT, Mirrielees proposed that the BFBS hire the Synod's translator, Daniil Khvol'son, to complete the BFBS translation of the Russian OT from the Hebrew.[46] The London BFBS editorial subcommittee readily agreed that the Petersburg agency should engage the services of Khvol'son, a process that after protracted negotiation led to the hiring of Khvol'son and his Russian colleague, Pavel Savvaitov for the completion of the BFBS Russian OT translation.[47]

As a result, by 1871 the very same translators who were at work preparing the synodal Russian Old Testament translation had also been engaged to prepare the BFBS Russian OT translation, the only ostensible difference being the more exclusive Hebrew Masoretic source base used in the BFBS translations. There followed in fairly prompt succession the translations by Khvol'son/Savvaitov of those OT portions that had not previously been translated by either the Russian Bible Society or the team of Levison and Bogoliubov. Added to this were revisions of the Russian Psalter and the Octateuch to bring them into conformity with the translation exclusively from the Hebrew Masoretic text.[48] Although Khvol'son urged the BFBS Petersburg agency to revise also those books that had been translated by Levison and Bogoliubov (including the major and minor prophets) in order to bring them into conformity with the language and translation practices of Khvol'son and Savvaitov, the BFBS postponed such action, preferring to bring its completed BFBS Old Testament out quickly in a single volume in 1875 shortly before the complete 1876 synodal Russian Old Testament.

[46] W. S. Mirrielees to R. B. Girdlestone, St. Petersburg, July 15, 1869, BFBS Editorial Correspondence Inwards, no. 7 (BSA/E3/1/4/7). The death of Levison came prior to the arrival in Petersburg of BFBS agent William Nicolson. Thus Khvol'son's initial contact within the BFBS agency was William Mirrielees.

[47] After some haggling over what rate should be paid for the translation and whether the existing BFBS Russian Pentateuch needed revision, the terms of Khvol'son's engagement were confirmed in early 1871. See Nicolson to Girdlestone, St. Petersburg, January 4, 1871, BFBS Agents Books (Russia), no. 125, 253–4 (BSA/D1/7/125); and BFBS Minutes of the Editorial Subcommittee, vol. 10, February 1, 1871, 71 (BSA/C17/1/10).

[48] The remaining books were published in 1873 (Appendix, nos. 112–15). The revision of the Psalter (no. 114) included, for the first time, the renumbering of the Psalms according to the Hebrew numbering system. In order to issue the complete OT, BFBS also needed to reissue its Octateuch (Genesis–Ruth) in a compatible 12mo format. To do so BFBS utilized the services of Khvol'son and Savvaitov, seeking a consistent translation from the Hebrew Masoretic text and eliminating all bracketed Septuagint footnotes present in London editions of the Octateuch. The resulting revised BFBS Russian Octateuch (Appendix, no. 126) effectively brought to completion the BFBS translation of the Russian OT, which the society proceeded to combine with the NT text in a bound 1875 complete edition of the Russian Bible (Appendix, no. 128), issued just prior to the Synod's complete bound edition of 1876 (Appendix, no. 130).

While the BFBS had managed to identify and engage competent, internationally recognized Petersburg translators to complete a BFBS edition of the Russian OT in a uniform format by 1875, there remained the hurdle of securing rights to the circulation and sale of its own or an appropriately modified synodal translation. BFBS Petersburg agent Nicolson managed to secure a contract for publication by the Synodal Press of an edition of the BFBS Russian Old Testament without the deuterocanonical readings, but this one-time edition issued in 1882 created lasting animus at the Holy Synod where Ober-prokuror Konstantin Pobedonostsev argued that the Synod ought not to be publishing editions of scripture in competition with its own. Given its strict policy of not circulating texts including the deuterocanonical books, the BFBS Petersburg agency was obliged to limit its circulation of Russian scripture, for the most part, to NT printings of the *sinodal'nyi perevod*. The one exception to this policy involved the circulation of an OT diglot edition in Hebrew and Russian. Having been given the authority to circulate these diglot editions for the Jewish population in the Pale of Settlement, the Vienna BFBS agency issued several printings throughout the remainder of the nineteenth and early twentieth centuries.[49]

What conclusion can be drawn from this picture of competing Russian translations in the years following the Crimean War when modern biblical translation was again possible in the Russian Empire? At the time of the RBS closure in 1826 all the major questions of authority surrounding biblical translation and dissemination remained unresolved: What source texts were to be considered authoritative for translation of Holy Scripture? Who had the authority to translate Russian scripture? Who had the authority to disseminate such Russian texts? And, what linguistic medium was to be considered authoritative for biblical translation? By proscribing modern biblical translation, Nicholas I had artificially closed off all official translation, leaving these issues of authority essentially unresolved.

The reopening of modern biblical translation was accompanied by a flurry of publication, particularly of Old Testament texts that had been circulating underground during the thirty-year hiatus in modern Russian translation. Indeed, for a while it appeared as though there might be a more

[49] This Hebrew/Russian Vienna diglot (Appendix, no. 132) employed the BFBS, not the synodal, Russian OT text. While this diglot could circulate through the BFBS Petersburg agency, BFBS outlets in the Russian Empire were never permitted to circulate the BFBS Russian Bible in a Russian-only edition, even though the Vienna BFBS agency produced such a text. The first printing of the BFBS Russian-only biblical edition was issued in 1877 (Appendix, no. 134). Despite the proscription against circulation, some copies of the full BFBS Russian Bible circulated clandestinely in regions of Ukraine adjacent to Austro-Hungarian territory. Lacking synodal blessing, however, the BFBS Russian-only OT text never circulated openly in the Russian Empire.

open religious marketplace, a "public sphere," in which multiple translations published in religious journals would be evaluated within an increasingly diversified Russian Orthodox religious culture. The debates on the pages of the religious journals about the merits of one or another translation seemed to anticipate such a gradual transformation of the Russian religious marketplace. Even Russian state authorities were thought to encourage the new religious marketplace, when they granted rail concessions to BFBS representatives who were transporting the society's stock of scripture to depots, and to colporteurs who were traveling the Eurasian frontier.

Yet in the years following the 1867 death of Moscow Metropolitan Filaret, conservative circles within the Russian church hierarchy, including the church's lay ober-prokuror, sought to maintain narrow churchly authority over the translation and publication of Holy Scripture, yielding state sanction for the authorized synodal translation, and limiting the dissemination of alternative texts. By the time of Alexander II's assassination in 1881, even though the Russian church had completed its landmark authorized Russian Bible, ecclesiastical leadership personified by Ober-prokuror Konstantin Pobedonostsev had come to fear modernist forces and retreated into a period of more conservative, hierarchical control. Nevertheless, public accessibility to the Russian Bible opened a period of significant debate over texts as the sophistication of biblical studies in the Russian theological academies advanced in the nineteenth century.

No doubt it was this development of the field of biblical studies in late imperial Russia in which the war over rival translations ultimately yielded its greatest impact.[50] Within the emergent field of Russian biblical studies, the impact of western scholarship and western Bible societies continued to be felt, especially in the theological academies. The BFBS-sponsored Old Testament translation may well have sped to completion the Synod's own translation, and in doing so contributed to the ongoing debate over textology, especially OT textology. Long after the variant translations were being issued in the 1870s, Ivan Troitskii, the student of Daniil Khvol'son and successor to Khvol'son in the chair of Hebraic studies at St. Petersburg University and the St. Petersburg Theological Academy, confided to BFBS Petersburg agent William Nicolson that he even considered the BFBS translation to be superior. Nicolson shared the news with his London home office:

> I have to report an interview with Prof. Troitsky, Dr. Chwolson's successor as Professor of Hebrew in the St. Petersburg University, and an able Hebraist, as

[50] See, in particular, Repp, "In Search of an Orthodox Way"; also Eleonskii, "Otechestvennye trudy po izucheniiu Biblii"; and Negrov, *Biblical Interpretation.*

becomes a pupil of Chwolson's, in which he, a native Russian and Orthodox believer, testified, I confess somewhat to my surprise, that our translation is decidedly *better* [Nicolson's italics] than the Synod's – less wordy, simple and more idiomatic. He tells me in his own words that the Synod's is more paraphrastic.[51]

Yet, in the debate over the authority of source texts, over the language of translation, and over circulation, the landmark publication of the Bible in Russian, the *sinodal'nyi perevod*, failed to resolve the issues of authority posed by modern biblical translation. Some of the most important rounds of the Bible wars in Russia lay ahead. Two of the controversies, in particular, illumine the significance and reception of the Russian Bible in the last decades of the nineteenth century.

SCHOLARLY DEBATE SPAWNED BY THE RUSSIAN BIBLE

The first such debate spawned by the issuance of the Russian Bible was not at all new, but was rather a continuation of the longstanding polemic over the authority of source texts – specifically, the decision to use the Hebrew Masoretic text in the modern Russian biblical translation. Even before the bound synodal translation of the Bible had been issued in 1876, the question was once again enjoined by Bishop Feofan of Vladimir (Feofan Govorov, 1815–94; Feofan Zatvornik following his canonization in 1988), who used the pages of *Dushepoleznoe chtenie* and *Domashniaia beseda* to reassert the distinctive authority of the Septuagint text for the Orthodox church, and to emphasize the inauthentic status of the Hebrew Masoretic text.[52] He argued that the Septuagint was the infallible translation from the original Hebrew text, and thus should itself be considered the original OT text. The Hebrew Masoretic text was, by contrast, a corrupted text, thus explaining the differences between the Greek and Hebrew originals. Bishop Feofan alleged that the differences between the Hebrew Masoretic text and its

[51] Nicolson to Wright, St. Petersburg, June 7, 1894, BFBS Editorial Correspondence Inwards, no. 32, 77 (BSA/E3/1/4/32).

[52] See the critical articles by Bishop Feofan (Govorov) directed against the synodal translation and use of the Hebrew Masoretic text: "Po povodu izdaniia sviashchennykh knig Vetkhago Zaveta v russkom perevode," *Dushepoleznoe chtenie*, 1875, chast' 3, no. 11 (November): 342–52; "Pravo-slovo ob izdanii sviashchennykh knig Vetkhago Zaveta v russkom perevode," *Domashniaia beseda*, 1875, vyp. 47 (November 22); "Ob upotreblenii novago perevoda vetkhozavetnykh pisanii," *Dushepoleznoe chtenie*, 1876, no. 9 (September), chast' 3, 100–6; "O nashem dolge derzhat'sia perevoda 70 tolkovnikov," *Dushepoleznoe chtenie*, 1876, chast' 2, no. 5 (May): 3–21; "Reshenie voprosa o mere pravoslavnago upotrebleniia evreiskago nyneshniago teksta, po ukazaniiu tserkovnoi praktiki," *Domashniaia beseda*, 1876, vyp. 2; and "Bibliia po perevodu semidesiati tolkovnikov est' zakonnaia nasha Bibliia," *Domashniaia beseda*, 1876, vyp. 20–4.

Greek Septuagint counterpart were to be explained by mistakes in the Masoretic transcription, and in what amounted to a veiled anti-Semitic conspiracy theory, he insisted these mistakes were introduced intentionally by Jews to undermine Christianity's claim to being the natural heir to the Old Testament covenant. Those supporting the use of the Hebrew original to address obscurities in the Slavonic and Septuagint readings were mistaken, he maintained, because such obscurities as existed merely reflected how divine action is often beyond the capacity of humans to comprehend. Thus it was important that the obscurities be preserved.[53]

The critique from Bishop Feofan Govorov triggered an immediate response in the pages of *Pravoslavnoe obozrenie* from Pavel Ivanovich Gorskii-Platonov (1835–1904), a distinguished former student of Gerasim Pavskii and professor of Hebrew and biblical archeology at Moscow Theological Academy.[54] Drawing on the late Moscow Metropolitan Filaret's treatise "O dogmaticheskom dostoinstve," Gorskii-Platonov challenged Bishop Feofan's argument that the Orthodox church held the Septuagint to be inviolable. Responding to the claim that because the Slavonic text was taken from the Septuagint, only the Greek text should be used in Old Testament translation, the Moscow theology professor reminded the bishop of Vladimir and Suzdal that the Orthodox church had never declared the Greek text inviolable, and indeed had often engaged in the correction of its own texts, not infrequently appealing to the use of the Hebrew original for that purpose. He also cited the case of the ancient Syrian church that translated scripture from the Hebrew rather than the Greek, and yet no one challenged the essential Orthodoxy of the Syrian church.

As regarded the books and passages in the Septuagint that were not in the Hebrew Masoretic text, Gorskii-Platonov noted that, contrary to the force of the bishop's position, the Apocrypha were not considered by the Orthodox church to be canonical. Moreover, with respect to the textual differences between the Greek and Hebrew original texts, he reckoned that for every one hundred words of text, there were only five on which the two texts differed, and that there was no reason to assume in each and every case that the Greek text should be given priority.

[53] Bishop Feofan, "Po povodu izdaniia sviashchennykh knig vetkhago zaveta v russkom perevode," 343–8. On the polemical exchange between Bishop Feofan and Professor Gorskii-Platonov, see also Repp, "In Search of an Orthodox Way," 137–44.

[54] P. I. Gorskii-Platonov, "Neskol'ko slov o stat'e episkopa Feofana: 'Po povodu izdaniia sviashchennykh knig Vetkhago Zaveta v russkom perevode' (*Dushepoleznoe chtenie*, 1875, no. 11)," *Pravoslavnoe obozrenie*, series 2, 1875, no. 11 (November), chast' 3: 505–40; see also his "O nedoumeniiakh, vyzyvaemykh russkim perevodom sv. knig Vetkhago Zaveta," *Pravoslavnoe obozrenie*, 1877, pt. 1 (January): 69–104, (February): 260–84, and (April): 681–702.

Gorskii-Platonov was most disparaging of Bishop Feofan's appeal to the purity of the Septuagint text, and the claim that the Hebrew Masoretic text had been corrupted. The reason for scholarly attention to biblical textology, he claimed, was that there had been errors of transmission in all texts, and that any claim for textual purity was inappropriate and unfounded. Even had Bishop Feofan wanted to translate the Russian Old Testament exclusively from the Septuagint, he would encounter variant readings of the Greek Septuagint. As for Feofan's red herring that "to defend the Hebrew is to become Protestant," Gorskii-Platonov countered that the printed texts of the Septuagint had been produced using rational scholarly methods, so that in using one or another Septuagint variant, advocates such as Feofan would inevitably be drawn into the very kind of reasoned choices for which they had accused others of Protestant sympathies.[55]

Finally, on the matter of Feofan's scurrilous claim regarding the intentional corruption of the Hebrew text by Jews for polemical purposes against Christianity, Gorskii-Platonov argued that if Jews had really sought to change the Hebrew text to defend themselves against Christianity, one would assume that the passages they would have changed would have been those appealed to in early Christian writing against Jews. Yet, as Gorskii-Platonov noted, that had not been the case. He reasoned therefore that changes in the Hebrew text had nothing to do with anti-Christian polemics. In his summary statement, he concluded that "the notion of intentional or partly intentional corruption of the Hebrew text should be discarded like an old weapon which is now completely useless."[56]

In the continuing debate, Bishop Feofan proposed that the synodal translation be abandoned and that there be a new Russian Old Testament translation based exclusively on the Greek Septuagint. By the 1890s, that proposal had in fact begun to be addressed, with publication in the pages of the Kazan Theological Academy journal, *Pravoslavnyi sobesednik*, of a Russian OT translation directly from the Septuagint.[57] While the translation by P. A. Iungerov of the Kazan Academy never reached the audience captured by the *sinodal'nyi perevod*, its very production reflected the ongoing debate in Russian biblical studies spawned by the modern

[55] Gorskii-Platonov, "O nedoumeniiakh, vyzyvaemykh russkim perevodom," 691.

[56] Gorskii-Platonov, "Neskol'ko slov," 533. The passage is cited also in Repp, "In Search of an Orthodox Way," 143.

[57] The Iungerov translations included an initial 1890 Kazan University Press publication of the book of Micah (Appendix, no. 185). Iungerov's translations were serialized in *Pravoslavnyi sobesednik*, and then published separately by Kazan University Press. In addition to Micah, the Iungerov translations (see bracketed entries by year in Appendix) included: Amos (1897); Proverbs (1908); Jeremiah (1910); Ezekiel (1911); Daniel (1912); Job (1914); and the Twelve Minor Prophets (1913).

translation of the Bible. Arthur Repp rightly sees the debate in Russian biblical studies between Bishop Feofan and Professor Gorskii-Platonov as the continuation of the earlier debate between the two Filarets, a debate in which two very different visions of Russian Orthodoxy were being advanced – one an appeal to a timeless and unchanging tradition, the other an appeal to tradition that sought to accommodate modern biblical historico-critical methodology.[58] In retrospect, however, the Feofan–Gorskii-Platonov polemic, while it reflected the lively public discussion associated with the development of biblical studies in modern Russia, has today been superseded by the Qumran discoveries of the Dead Sea Scrolls. These discoveries have tended to neutralize the charges and counter-charges over scribal and translator error, revealing instead the existence of significantly varying biblical text traditions at a much earlier stage (150 BCE to 70 CE) than was conceivable at the time of the late nineteenth-century debate over the textology of the Russian Bible.

Within the polemical world of nineteenth-century Russian biblical studies, however, one dispute captured particularly wide attention, for it involved a key translator of the *sinodal'nyi perevod*, Daniil Khvol'son. The conflict arose in connection with the publication by Khvol'son of a straightforward historico-critical text analysis relating to the Gospel accounts of the Last Supper.[59] The Khvol'son work has received considerable attention in western scholarship because of its challenge to traditional Christian accounts of the Pharisees and Sadducees in the New Testament. Such traditional accounts, often based on the synoptic Gospels that were probably compiled after 70 CE, offer a negative portrait of the Pharisees as legalistically preoccupied with purity and man-made laws, as opposed to Jesus Christ's concern with God's unconditional love. Khvol'son challenged this binary opposition between the followers of Christ and the Pharisees, noting that in the first century, ties between Christians and Jews of Pharisaic disposition were characterized by close loving relationships. Indeed, some of the teachings of Christ, as in the Sermon on the Mount, were consistent with the teaching of the Pharisees and with later rabbinical thought. Ironically, it was rather the Sadducees, largely composed of priestly and aristocratic families, with whom early Christian followers experienced the

58 Repp, "In Search of an Orthodox Way," 144.

59 D. A. Khvol'son, "Posledniaia paskhal'naia vecheria Iisusa Khrista i den' ego smerti [The Last Passover Supper of Jesus Christ and the Day of his Death]," *Khristianskoe chtenie*, 1875 and 1877. Responding to challenges to his article, Khvol'son restated his conclusions in an article by the same title in *Khristianskoe chtenie* in 1878. The work was republished under separate cover in St. Petersburg in 1892.

greatest conflict. The subsequent negative depiction of the Pharisees, according to this view, may well have reflected attitudes present during a later period when the Gospels were written, and when Christianity was more focused on its Roman Gentile world, and less closely associated with its early Jewish roots. The Khvol'son recasting of Pharisees and Sadducees is widely accepted today in the historical-critical text literature.

Khvol'son's reframing of the picture of Pharisees and Sadducees in early Christian and rabbinical text traditions constituted but one part of his article. It was to another part of his work that most attention came to be riveted – namely, his effort to explain the discrepancy in the synoptic Gospels over the date of the Last Supper.[60] The Gospels of Matthew, Mark, and Luke all recorded the Last Supper as occurring on "the first day of Unleavened Bread" – the fourteenth day of the month of Nisan in the Jewish calendar. In the Gospel of John, however, the Last Supper was placed on the thirteenth day of Nisan, the eve of the day of Unleavened Bread. Khvol'son, whose article offered a solution to this supposed conflict, sought to quiet those rationalist critics who would challenge the authority of the Gospels based upon such internal discrepancies. Khvol'son's argument accepted as a starting point that the similarity of the three Gospel accounts was based upon the use by the Gospel writers Mark and Luke of the Gospel of Matthew, which was originally written in Aramaic or old Syriac.

Khvol'son arrived at his solution to the dating discrepancy while reading an old Syriac NT edition, for it became clear to Khvol'son in the reading of the relevant passage in the old Syriac Gospel of Matthew that the source of the differing dates was likely owing to scribal error. The original Matthew text (26:17) went as follows:

> Now on the first day of Unleavened Bread the disciples came to Jesus, saying, "Where will you have us prepare for you to eat the Passover?"

But, Khvol'son came to recognize that the passage in the original Aramaic of the Gospel of Matthew most likely read:

> Now as the first day of Unleavened Bread *approached*, the disciples *came* to Jesus, saying, "Where will you have us prepare for you to eat the Passover?"

In the Aramaic original, the italicized words would have been identical, leading Khvol'son to suspect that in copying the original manuscript the first of the duplicative verbs was likely omitted. If so, Matthew's original

60 For a recounting of Khvol'son's dating of the Last Supper, see Repp's interpretive account, "In Search of an Orthodox Way," 145–53.

Aramaic account would have been in full agreement with the Gospel of John that the Last Supper occurred on the thirteenth day of Nisan, the eve of the day of Unleavened Bread.[61]

Khvol'son proceeded to explain why Jesus would have celebrated the Passover on the thirteenth day of Nisan, rather than on the fourteenth day as stipulated in Mosaic law. From his study of Mosaic law, including the Jewish interpretations that preceded those represented in the Mishnah and Talmud (authorities for rabbinical Jewish tradition), Khvol'son found an indication that when the fourteenth day of Nisan fell on a Friday, as it did in the year of Jesus' death, the feast was shifted to the previous day so as not to conflict with the observance of the Sabbath when the sacrifice of a lamb would have been prohibited.

While Khvol'son's exercise in historico-critical text analysis was hailed by reviewers – Repp notes that the Kazan Theological Academy's journal, *Pravoslavnyi sobesednik*, labeled it one of the finest articles of the year – it also met with virulent opposition from Archimandrite Vitalii Grechulevich (1822–85), a popular author of Gospel harmonies and publisher of the journal *Strannik*.[62] Archimandrite Vitalii claimed the Khvol'son article contained fabrications that were scandalous to Christians. He argued that "the first day of Unleavened Bread" in Jesus' day meant not only the fifteenth day of Nisan, but the fourteenth as well. Stooping to ad hominem and anti-Jewish rhetoric, he suggested that Khvol'son, as a convert to Christianity from Judaism, considered rabbinical literature more authoritative than Christian tradition. Unwilling to accept any possibility of corruption of scriptural texts, Archimandrite Vitalii was incensed over what he considered an anti-Orthodox attempt to challenge the inerrancy of Gospel texts.

Khvol'son's response to the diatribe of Vitalii Grechulevich was to restate his views, noting in the process that the rule found in rabbinical sources that the Passover celebration was to take precedence over the Sabbath was not necessarily followed in Jesus' time. As for the matter of Vitalii Grechulevich's claim identifying the first day of Unleavened Bread as incorporating both the fourteenth and fifteenth day of Nisan, Khvol'son noted that there was nothing in three thousand years of Jewish writing to support such a claim. Finally, Khvol'son rather ingeniously noted how his

[61] Khvol'son, "Posledniaia paskhal'naia vecheria," *Khristianskoe chtenie*, 1875 (February): 462; and Repp, "In Search of an Orthodox Way," 147.

[62] Repp, "In Search of an Orthodox Way," 148; for the article by Vitalii Grechulevich, see [A.V.], "Posledniaia paskhal'naia vecheria Iisusa Khrista i den' ego smerti," *Strannik*, 1876, no. 11: 97–126 and no. 12: 185–289.

solution to the dating of the Last Supper indirectly supported the Eastern Orthodox practice of using leavened bread in the celebration of the Eucharist because the eating of unleavened bread would have awaited the next night. It must have been rather galling for the patriotic Russian clergyman to read that his solution for the dating of the Last Supper supported western, rather than Eastern Orthodox liturgical practices.

The mismatched polemic between the historico-critical text scholar and the popular cleric reflected, as Repp has noted, a "growing divide" between the modern Russian biblical scholarship of the academy – unleashed as it was by the reopening of Russian biblical translation – and the less-well-trained audience of clergy and laypeople for whom, ironically, the Russian Bible was intended.[63]

There was also a dark side to the Bible wars of the last half of the nineteenth century – the specific attempt by some to turn legitimate textological disputes over biblical sources into ad hominem and anti-Semitic attacks against Russia's increasingly sophisticated Hebraic scholars. Conversely, as documented in Chapter 5, it was these Russian scholars in the field of Hebraic studies – the architects of the modern Russian OT – who effectively challenged one of the greatest threats to Jewish–Christian relations in Eurasia, the scurrilous charge of blood libel.

[63] Repp, "In Search of an Orthodox Way," 153.

CHAPTER 5

Russian biblical translation and the Jewish Question

While the lively debate over alternative Hebrew and Greek textual bases for the Russian Old Testament continued to dominate critical evaluation of the synodal translation, there were two other compelling issues that linked Russian OT translation with what came to be called Russia's "Jewish Question." The Jewish Question arose in the aftermath of the partitions of Poland in the last quarter of the eighteenth century when approximately half a million Jews were incorporated into the Russian Empire. By the end of the nineteenth century the number of Jews in the Russian Empire had grown to more than five million. The resulting "Russian–Jewish encounter" not only entailed a variety of Russian bureaucratic practices for managing, or mismanaging, this large Jewish minority population, but it also became the arena for the complicated "passage to modernity" of the largest community of Jewish population in the world.[1]

[1] Reference to "Russian–Jewish encounter" and "passage to modernity" reflects the language of Benjamin Nathans, *Beyond the Pale: The Jewish Encounter with Late Imperial Russia* (Berkeley: University of California Press, 2002). Nathans's work is part of a rich and growing western literature on the history of Jews in the Russian Empire. See, in particular, the studies of John Klier, *Imperial Russia's Jewish Question, 1855–1881* (Cambridge University Press, 1995); Michael Stanislawski, *Nicholas I and the Jews* (New York: Jewish Publication Society of America, 1983), his *For Whom Do I Toil: Judah Leib Gordon and the Crisis of Russian Jewry* (Oxford University Press, 1988), and his *A Murder in Lemberg: Politics, Religion, and Violence in Modern Jewish History* (Princeton University Press, 2007); Brian Horowitz, *Jewish Philanthropy and Enlightenment in Late-Tsarist Russia* (Seattle: University of Washington Press, 2009), and his *Empire Jews: Jewish Nationalism and Acculturation in 19th- and Early 20th-Century Russia* (Bloomington, IN: Slavica Publishers, 2009); Darius Staliunas, *Making Russians: Meaning and Practice of Russification in Lithuania and Belarus after 1863* (Amsterdam: Rodopi, 2007); Theodore Weeks, *From Assimilation to Anti-Semitism: The Jewish Question in Poland, 1850–1914* (DeKalb: Northern Illinois University Press, 2006); and Jonathan Frankel, especially his *Prophecy and Politics: Socialism, Nationalism and the Russian Jews, 1862–1917* (Cambridge University Press, 1981).

JEWISH TRANSLATIONS FROM THE HEBREW BIBLE INTO RUSSIAN

The Jewish Question intersected with modern Russian biblical translation in the first instance because leading figures in the Jewish Enlightenment – the *maskilim* or Russian Jewish leaders of the Haskalah – undertook their own translations into Russian of portions of the Hebrew Bible, including two specific editions of the Torah or Pentateuch. These Russian translations, intended for a Jewish audience and reflecting a nuanced accommodation to Russian imperial rule, constituted an important chapter in the history of the Russian Bible. At the opposite end of the spectrum, Russian scholars of Hebrew – the key translators of the Russian Old Testament – responded collectively to one of the most notorious blood libel cases in nineteenth-century Russia, the so-called Saratov affair, by formulating an historic refutation of the anti-Semitic blood libel charge. In both these instances – the *maskilim* translations and the Russian Hebraic scholars' refutation of the blood libel allegation – the controversies attending biblical translation illustrated the complexity of the Russian–Jewish encounter in late imperial Russia.

The major translations of the Torah into Russian in the late imperial era were tied to centers of Jewish Enlightenment in the empire's northwest, Vil'na and St. Petersburg. These Russian translations originated in the very heart of the Russian Jewish *maskilim*. In an effort to sort out the variety of Jewish Enlightenment responses to Russian rule in the last half of the nineteenth century, John Klier has identified four varying intellectual streams. These range from what he calls the "old *maskilim*" – those who came out of the tradition of Moses Mendelssohn in eighteenth-century Germany – to a "new *maskilim*," who were much more intent on developing Russian-language training and enriching the curriculum of traditional Jewish state schools, to an even more secular Russian Jewish intelligentsia that was prepared to integrate Jewish schooling within mainstream Russian schools. At the extreme end of this spectrum were those whom Klier labeled the "total assimilationists," such as Daniil Khvol'son, who converted to Christianity and sought full integration into mainstream Russian professions.

As Klier noted, one and the same person often moved across the spectrum of these varying positions. Whether it be the Gintsburg family and other wealthy notables who led the first generation of the Society for the Promotion of Enlightenment among the Jews of Russia (Obshchestvo dlia rasprostraneniia prosveshcheniia mezhdu evreiami v Rossii [OPE], founded in Petersburg in 1863), or the official school inspectors and aides to local governors-general (the so-called Jewish experts, or *uchenye evrei*) in provincial postings, Jewish enlighteners believed that emancipation, with its increased rights and privileges, would require a transformation of Jews themselves. The transformation necessitated rejection of "Jewish fanaticism," a charge commonly brought by Russian officials seeking to equate Jewish identity with traditional Talmudic training. Central to such transformation sought by Jewish enlighteners was the embrace of the Russian language, recognized by even the older *maskilim* as an instrument for advancement that needed to be cultivated alongside the traditional study of Hebrew.

It is these nineteenth-century enlighteners – the *maskilim* and the evolving Jewish intelligentsia – who initiated distinctive Russian translations of the Hebrew Bible in the last half of the nineteenth century. In assessing the historic place of these *maskilim*, Michael Stanislawski has cautioned that these complicated enlighteners not be viewed merely as a momentary phenomenon, a temporary way-station toward some more fully formed nationalist or socialist Jewish intelligentsia:

> We have an image of the ideological development of East European Jewry as a neat case of doctrinal succession: traditional Judaism yielding to the Haskalah, whose naïve, optimistic view of the world crashes on the shores of anti-Semitism and radicalism and is transmuted into the more realistic and long-lived ideologies of modern Jewish nationalism and socialism.[2]

For Stanislawski, the problem with such a paradigm is that "the vast majority of Jews in Russia ... never became Zionists or Bundists or Autonomists or any other 'ists.'"[3] Like Klier's reference to Jewish enlighteners who moved along a spectrum of accommodation to Russian rule, Stanislawski sees most Jewish writers in Russia prior to 1917 as having one foot in their own traditional world and the other outside of this world as they sought to respond to the challenges of modernity. It is from such a world of the *maskilim* and the emergent Russian Jewish intelligentsia that the Jewish translators of the Russian Bible came.

The earliest of the translators was Leon Mandel'shtam, the first Jewish graduate of the University of St. Petersburg. Born in the province of Vil'na in 1819, Mandel'shtam had initially enrolled at the University of Moscow in 1840 – the first Jew to enroll there as well. Transferring to St. Petersburg, he graduated from its Faculty of Law in 1844 and was shortly thereafter hired by Sergei Uvarov, the Russian Minister of Public Instruction, as a "Jewish expert" for the Ministry. Mandel'shtam embodied that characteristic

[2] Stanislawski, *For Whom Do I Toil*, 5. [3] Ibid.

ambivalence of the new *maskilim* who were rooted in traditional Talmudic training, but at the same time sought to advance their fellow Russian Jewish compatriots by encouraging secular study for the professions. He later wrote:

I love my country and the language of my land [i.e. Russian] but, at the same time, I am unfortunate because of the misfortune of all my fellow Jews. Their rigidity has enraged me, because I can see it is destroying their gifts. But I am bound to their affliction by the closest of ties of kinship and feeling. My purpose in life is to defend them before the world and to help them to be worthy of that defense.[4]

Mandel'shtam briefly held the position of supervisor of Jewish schools in Russia before abandoning the Russian Empire in 1865 for a period of residency in Germany. Prior to his departure for Germany, he completed his Russian translation of the Torah, as well as his Hebrew/Russian, Russian/Hebrew dictionary. Unable to publish his translation of the Pentateuch in Russia, ostensibly because of Synod concern that the church had yet to issue its own authorized Russian edition of the Pentateuch, Mandel'shtam published his 1862 Hebrew/Russian diglot of the Pentateuch in Berlin.[5] Not insignificantly, the Mandel'shtam translation also apparently met with stiff resistance from Orthodox rabbis who considered translation of the Torah blasphemous.[6]

The 1862 Russian Pentateuch was prefaced by a lengthy note in Russian, "To Jewish Instructors." The note indicated he wished to dedicate the work to teachers of Jewish schoolchildren, enjoining the teachers to help "turn Jews into real Russian citizens." The *maskilim* spirit behind the translation was also clear from the analogy Mandel'shtam sought to draw between his own translation into Russian and earlier translations of Saadia Gaon (d. 942, an early writer in both Hebrew and Arabic) and Moses Mendelssohn (1729–86, Jewish Haskalah translator of the Hebrew Bible into German). As Mandel'shtam put it, "If Saadia Gaon found the need to translate Holy Scripture into Arabic, and if Moses Mendelssohn did so into German, and by means of such translations Jews were brought together and became close

[4] Quoted internally in Zvi Gitelman, *A Century of Ambivalence: The Jews of Russia and the Soviet Union, 1881 to the Present* (New York: Viking Press, 1988), 6.

[5] See Appendix, no. 54. On synodal objection to its printing in Russia, see Horowitz, *Jewish Philanthropy and Enlightenment in Late-Tsarist Russia*, 45.

[6] Horowitz, *Jewish Philanthropy*, 252 n. 21. Horowitz cites Il'ia Trotskii's account of the opposition to the Mandel'shtam translation from Orthodox rabbis ("Samodeiatel'nost' i samopomoshch'," in *Kniga o russkom evreistve ot 1860-kh godov do revoliutsii 1917 g.: Sbornik statei* [New York: Soiuz russkikh evreev, 1960], 473).

to their neighboring people . . . is it possible for there to be any doubt of the need for Jews of a Russian translation of the Bible?"[7]

Mandel'shtam's translation was a literal translation from the Hebrew, and its issuance as a diglot was clearly intended to serve the dual functions of religious training and language acquisition, much as the Mendelssohn translation had inspired German-language acquisition among the Jews of Germany from the eighteenth century onward. The Society for the Promotion of Enlightenment Among the Jews of Russia (OPE) subsequently subsidized an 1872 reprinting of the Mandel'shtam translation, buying up several thousand copies. Despite the interest among the *maskilim* in this early Russian biblical translation for the Jewish community, sales of the volume apparently lagged, with the OPE ending up some 4,000 rubles in the red on its purchase.[8] Some years later, Mandel'shtam returned to St. Petersburg, dying there in relative poverty in 1889. Only after his death was his substantial personal library sold to the New York Public Library where it became the foundation for the rich NYPL Judaica collection.

In the preface to his Hebrew/Russian diglot of the Pentateuch, Leon Mandel'shtam also noted that the diglot was to serve as a "preliminary work," until a future translation of the Bible could be undertaken "in a more elegant Russian language."[9] The problem confronting translation and publication of a Russian text of the Bible for Jews did not, however, turn on the elegance of its Russian language. What transpired instead was that the OPE purchase of part of the 1872 edition of the Mandel'shtam diglot followed a quite dramatic internal conflict within the Russian Jewish community – one that set the stage for all subsequent Russian Jewish biblical translation and publication in the late imperial era. Following the initial 1862 publication of the Mandel'shtam Torah diglot in Berlin, there had been several efforts by OPE to secure Orthodox church permission to circulate the text in Russia. In the face of the routine denial of these requests, Daniil Khvol'son (see Figure 11), who was not only an OPE member but also a professor of Near Eastern languages, a Jewish convert to Christianity, and the lead translator of both the synodal and BFBS editions of the Old Testament then still in preparation, proposed a compromise solution to overcome the impasse. At his recommendation, the OPE would suggest to the Holy Synod that the Synod permit OPE to adopt as its own a modified synodal Russian edition, reordering the books

7 L. Mandel'shtam, "Evreiskim nastavnikam," in *Thora, t.e. Zakon, ili Piatiknizhie moiseevo* (Berlin: K. Schultz, 1862), v.

8 Horowitz, *Jewish Philanthropy*, 45.

9 Mandel'shtam, "Evreiskim nastavnikam," iii.

Figure 11. Daniil Avraamovich Khvol'son, 1819–1911, translator of the BFBS and synodal Russian Old Testaments from Hebrew.
Source: http://www.lechaim.ru/ARHIV/210/tabak.htm.

in such a way as to make them conform to the Hebrew canon and introducing modest revisions of the translation so as to conform with Jewish practice. Little did OPE leadership know that Khvol'son had made essentially the same proposal to the British and Foreign Bible Society, which upon the untimely death of BFBS lead translator Vasilii Levison took up Khvol'son's offer at the end of the 1860s to revise the BFBS Old Testament translation exclusively from the Hebrew original. In May 1869, the OPE adopted Khvol'son's compromise suggestion, petitioning the Holy Synod for permission to revise the Synod's own edition, then still under preparation (by Khvol'son, among others), for distribution among the Jews of Russia. In September 1869, the Synod granted OPE permission to prepare such a Jewish version of the synodal text.[10]

Had the proposal become reality, the enterprising Petersburg orientalist Daniil Khvol'son would, in effect, have been working simultaneously on three separate, though very closely related, Russian translations of the

[10] This account of the OPE appeal to the Holy Synod is drawn from Klier, *Imperial Russia's Jewish Question*, 251–4, which in turn is based on I. M. Cherikover, *Istoriia Obshchestva dlia rasprostraneniia prosveshcheniia mezhdu evreiami v Rossii, 1863–1913 gg.* (St. Petersburg, 1913).

Hebrew canon – one for the Holy Synod's Russian Old Testament, one for the BFBS Russian Old Testament, and one for an OPE Russian edition of the Hebrew Bible. No sooner had the Synod granted permission to OPE for a Jewish revision of the synodal text than open conflict broke out within the Jewish community over the very idea. The hostilities ultimately became so widespread that the idea was abandoned. The Odessa newspaper *Den'* attacked the proposal, claiming that the Jews of Russia deserved their own translation, not a Jewish version of a Russian Orthodox text. In his own defense, Khvol'son indicated he doubted whether the Synod would ever permit publication of such a rival Jewish translation, arguing that his own motives were pragmatically those of advancing the command of Russian among the Jews of Russia.[11]

By the spring of 1870, the conflict had taken an ad hominem and conspiratorial turn, with one OPE member, D. Slonimskii, claiming that Khvol'son was secretly trying to convert Jews to Christianity.[12] Given the prominent status of Daniil Khvol'son within the Jewish community and his stalwart defense of Russian Jews on the blood libel issue noted later in this chapter, the attempt to tarnish Khvol'son personally would normally have been disregarded by OPE notables. Nevertheless, because widespread concern had been expressed about the Khvol'son proposal, the Society for Promotion of Enlightenment among the Jews of Russia ultimately abandoned the idea. Khvol'son's accommodationist proposal had taken the OPE, and even its more secular *maskilim*, one step too far. After the dust cleared, OPE did gain Synod authorization to purchase and sell several thousand copies of the 1872 Berlin reprinting of the Mandel'shtam Pentateuch diglot. But it was the poor sales of those very copies that left the OPE budget in the red.

Despite the flurry of controversy attending Jewish Russian biblical translation and despite the weak sales of the Mandel'shtam diglot, two additional Hebrew/Russian Pentateuch diglots were issued in the last decades of imperial Russia. The first of these diglots, published in 1875 by the Jewish press of M. P. Romm in Vil'na, was prepared by a distinguished team of Russian Jewish intellectuals: Judah Leib Gordon, Iona Gershtein, and Lev Levanda.[13] Edited by Gordon, who also translated the book of Exodus, this 1875 Pentateuch diglot answered the original call of Mandel'shtam for a translation "in a more elegant Russian language." Not only had the Vil'na-born Gordon (1830–92) already established a reputation as a leading nineteenth-century Hebrew poet and as one of the most

[11] Klier, *Imperial Russia's Jewish Question*, 252–3. [12] Ibid. [13] See Appendix, no. 123.

passionate exponents of the Jewish Enlightenment in Russia, but his move to St. Petersburg in 1872 to assume the position of OPE secretary also opened up new resources for the project.[14] As noted on the title page of the diglot, OPE ended up supporting the printing of the volume.

Iona Gershtein (1827–91) was also well known to Jewish Enlightenment circles in Russia, having been one of the first to complete the Vil'na Rabbinical School, itself a product of the Haskalah. Following graduation, Gershtein was appointed to the position of Jewish expert in the office of the Vil'na governor-general, a position that permitted him to work with school affairs in the region. Alongside his official duties, he also compiled (with Lev Levanda) a work that became a standard Russian textbook for Jewish schoolchildren, *Pervye uroki russkoi gramoty*.[15] The third member of this translation team, Lev Levanda (1835–88), had served, like Gershtein, as an *uchenyi evrei* at the Vil'na governor-general's office from 1860, but achieved his fame in Petersburg where he became known as a writer of popular fiction, particularly for his novels, *Hot Times* and *Confessions of a Wheeler-Dealer*.[16]

As Michael Stanislawski has noted, the Gordon-edited diglot was the first Russian edition of the Pentateuch to follow Jewish exegetical traditions.[17] Since the Mandel'shtam editions had been printed in Germany, the new Vil'na diglot of 1875 (it secured censorial approval in 1874) was indeed the first Hebrew/Russian diglot of the Pentateuch published in the Russian Empire specifically for Jews. The Russian text of the diglot draws upon previous Russian translations, but contains no Septuagint readings. The text is closest to the original translation printed in sheets by the Russian Bible Society in 1824. The preface to this 1875 Vil'na edition notes that the translators have closely followed the Masoretic Hebrew text, while at the same time utilizing existing Russian translations of scripture, which were appealed to when those translations fitted the purposes of its Jewish audience. The Russian pronunciation of names from the Septuagint was used if those names had become common in the practical life of Jewish people. Otherwise, Hebrew names were rendered in Russian orthography, but with Hebrew pronunciation.

[14] Stanislawski, *For Whom Do I Toil*, especially Chapter 7, "St. Petersburg: Culture and Politics, 1872–1877."

[15] The fifth edition of Gershtein's popular grammar was published in Vil'na in 1875. On Gershtein, see "Gershtein, Iona Gerasimovich," *Evreiskaia entsiklopediia* (Moscow: Terra reprint edition, 1991), VI: 428.

[16] On Levanda, see B.A. Gol'dberg, *L. O. Levanda kak publitsist: Po sluchaiu 40-letnego iubileia voznikonoveniia russko-evreiskoi pechati* (Vil'na, 1900). For brief descriptions of *Hot Times* (*Goriachee vremia*, St. Petersburg, 1875) and *Confessions of a Wheeler-Dealer* (*Ispoved' del'tsa*, St. Petersburg, 1880), see Nathans, *Beyond the Pale*, 130–3 and 215–16.

[17] Stanislawski, *For Whom Do I Toil*, 117.

In assessing the appeal of these Russian/Hebrew diglots, Brian Horowitz has noted that all the OPE-supported religious publications in Russian lost money for the society, even while Jewish interest in the Russian language continued to grow, and texts on more secular subjects – economics, politics, mathematics, and natural history – sold well.[18] This may in part reflect the more secular orientation of those involved in the Jewish Enlightenment, as well as the traditional value placed on Hebrew in the case of biblical texts. But another part of the explanation for the relatively weak sales of Russian-language religious texts among the Jewish population of the empire involved the increasing competition among distributors of Russian-language religious literature intended for a Jewish audience. From 1876 onward, BFBS secured authority from the Holy Synod to distribute in Russia its own Russian/Hebrew diglot of the Pentateuch, editions of which were published in much larger circulation runs of 5,000 copies in each printing beginning in 1876.[19] This ability to distribute the BFBS Russian Old Testament, which did not carry alternative Septuagint readings as in the synodal Russian OT, was conditional on its limited distribution to Jews of the Russian Empire. The publication of these BFBS editions was handled in Vienna, and the text used was that of the BFBS Russian OT as revised by Daniil Khvol'son and Vasilii Levison (see Chapter 4). So as not to conflict with the Holy Synod's sale of its own Russian OT text, the BFBS printings in Vienna carried on the title page the notice that the editions were *dlia upotrebleniia evreiam* (for the use of Jews).

Into this relatively competitive market, there came yet a fourth major Russian/Hebrew diglot of the Pentateuch – the 1901–2 Vil'na revision prepared by a commission under the leadership of Yehoshua (Oshaya) Shteinberg (1830–1908).[20] Shteinberg was a distinguished Hebraist, lexicographer, and biblical scholar, whose work reflected the growing sophistication of biblical studies within the Russian Jewish Enlightenment. Following his graduation from the Vil'na Rabbinical School, Shteinberg served as a rabbi in Belostok, before assuming a position as teacher of Hebrew and Chaldean languages at his alma mater and at the Vil'na Jewish Teachers' Institute. His reputation as a lexicographer and Hebraic scholar was established in major publications of Hebrew grammars, dictionaries, and textbooks, including his Hebrew and Chaldean etymological dictionary (1878), his Russian/Hebrew dictionary (1880, revised in 1888), his encyclopedia of

[18] Horowitz, *Jewish Philanthropy*, 45–6. [19] See Appendix, nos. 131, 132, and 133.

[20] See Appendix, no. 200, *Piatiknizhie Moiseevo* (Vil'na: Romm and Pirozhnikov Presses, 1901, 1902). This edition was reprinted in 1913–14 in Vil'na (Appendix, no. 234).

the Hebrew language with explanations in Russian and German (1896), his Hebrew grammar (1884), and his school textbooks for Chaldean (1872) and Hebrew (1889).[21]

The Russian text of the Shteinberg Pentateuch diglot follows closely the text published in 1875 by Gordon, Gershtein, and Levanda, and it is similarly formatted. The volume also includes Shteinberg's extended explanatory comments at the bottom of each page (also in two columns). The translation and commentary were intended for study of the Hebrew text as much as for study of the Russian, inasmuch as Jewish educational institutions had begun to face the twentieth-century reality that many of their students had a command of Russian, but lacked a parallel command of Hebrew. The title page of the 1901 edition noted that the Pentateuch and commentary had been approved for publication by a "scholarly committee of the Russian Ministry of Public Instruction for use in Jewish educational institutions."

Using a section of the Genesis creation narrative (Genesis 1:26–7), it is instructive to follow the genealogy of these Russian translations of the Pentateuch.

English New Revised Standard Version

1:26 Then God said, "Let us make humankind in our image, according to our likeness; and let them have dominion over the fish of the sea, and over the birds of the air, and over the cattle, and over all the wild animals of the earth, and over every creeping thing that creeps upon the earth."
1:27 So God created humankind in his image, in the image of God he created them; male and female he created them.

Russian Bible Society Octateuch (St. Petersburg, 1825)

1:26 И сказалъ Богъ: "сотворимъ человѣка по образу Нашему, [и] по подобію Нашему; и да владычествуютъ они надъ рыбами морскими и надъ птицами небесными, [и надъ звѣрями], и надъ скотомъ, и надъ всею землею, и надъ всѣми гадами, пресмыкающимися по землѣ!"
1:27 И сотворилъ Богъ человѣка по образу Своему, по образу Божію сотворилъ его; мужчину и женщину сотворилъ ихъ.

[21] On Shteinberg, see ""Shteinberg, Ioshua," *Evreiskaia entsiklopediia*, reprint edn (Moscow: "TERRA," 1991), XVI: 97–8. The *Evreiskaia entsiklopediia* entry identifies the Pentateuch diglot as the result of a "commission" of which Shteinberg was a member, but the title page of the actual diglot specifically identifies Shteinberg by name as the translator.

British and Foreign Bible Society Revised Russian Old Testament, 1875

1:26 И сказалъ Богъ: "создадимъ человѣка по образу Нашему, по подобію Нашему; и да владычествуютъ они надъ рыбами морскими и надъ птицами небесными, и надъ скотами, и надъ всею землею, и надъ всѣми гадами, пресмыкающимися по землѣ!"
1:27 И сотворилъ Богъ человѣка по образу Своему, по образу Божію сотворилъ его; мужчиною и женщиною сотворилъ ихъ.

Synodal Old Testament

1:26 И сказалъ Богъ: "сотворимъ человѣка по образу Нашему, (и) по подобію Нашему; и да владычествуютъ они надъ рыбами морскими и надъ птицами небесными, (и надъ звѣрями), и надъ скотомъ, и надъ всею землею, и надъ всѣми гадами, пресмыкающимися по землѣ!"
1:27 И сотворилъ Богъ человѣка по образу Своему, по образу Божію сотворилъ его; мужчину и женщину сотворилъ ихъ.

Mandel'shtam Pentateuch (Berlin, 1862)

1:26 И Богъ сказалъ: "Содѣлаемъ человѣка въ оттѣнкѣ Нашемъ и по думѣ Нашей: и да владѣетъ рыбою морскою, птицею небесною, и скотомъ, и всею землею, и всякимъ пресмыкающимся, ползающимъ по землѣ!"
1:27 И сотворилъ Богъ человѣка, въ оттѣнкѣ Своемъ, въ оттѣнкѣ Божіемъ сотворилъ Онъ его; мужчиною и женщиною сотворилъ Онъ ихъ.

Gordon/Gershtein/Levanda Pentateuch (Vil'na, 1875)

1:26 И сказалъ Богъ: "сотворимъ человѣка по образу Нашему, по подобію Нашему, и да владычествуютъ они надъ рыбами морскими и надъ птицами небесными, и надъ скотомъ, и надъ всею землею, и надъ всѣми гадами, ползающими по землѣ!"
1:27 И сотворилъ Богъ человѣка по образу Своему, по образу Божію сотворилъ его, мужчину и женщину сотворилъ ихъ.

Shteinberg Pentateuch (Vil'na, 1901)

1:26 И сказалъ Богъ: "создадимъ человѣка по образу Нашему, по подобію Нашему, и да владычествуютъ они надъ рыбою морскою и надъ птицами небесными, и надъ скотомъ и надъ всею землею и надъ всѣми гадами, пресмыкающимися по землѣ!"
1:27 И сотворилъ Богъ человѣка по образу Своему, по образу Божію сотворилъ его, мужчину и женщину сотворилъ ихъ.

Even though the Genesis passage constitutes but one small isolated example, it conforms to a wider pattern – namely, the importance of the *textus primus* originally prepared by Gerasim Pavskii for the 1825 RBS Octateuch.[22] The bracketed Septuagint readings that were introduced in the 1825 Octateuch were retained in the BFBS and synodal editions, but are absent from all three Jewish editions. Otherwise, allowing for minor changes in vocabulary – more so in the less polished Mandel'shtam edition than in the subsequent two Jewish editions – the structure and vocabulary of the first Russian translation of 1825 were largely followed in subsequent editions. Despite the furor ignited over Khvol'son's recommended adoption of a revised synodal text, the "Bible wars" within the Jewish Enlightenment had yielded a text remarkably similar to that of the synodal translation.

RUSSIAN BIBLICAL TRANSLATION AND THE BLOOD LIBEL ISSUE

Behind the controversy over Russian translation of the Hebrew Bible there lay another compelling story in which the development of Hebraic studies in Russia had also come to impact the wider Jewish Question. In the middle of the nineteenth century, parallel with the reopening of Russian biblical translation, the same Hebraic scholars who had translated the Russian Old Testament for the Russian Bible Society and the Holy Synod became leading defenders of Russian Jewry in a notorious instance of blood libel that continued to reverberate into the twentieth century. In the infamous Saratov affair, enlightened nineteenth-century Russian Hebraists – the main translators of the Russian Old Testament – launched one of the most significant challenges to the scourge of blood libel in modern European history, further linking the history of Russian biblical translation with the Jewish Question in modern Russian history.

22 Appendix, no. 23.

The development of Hebraic studies in nineteenth-century Petersburg was closely identified with the work of three prominent translators of the Russian OT – Gerasim Pavskii, Vasilii Levison, and Daniil Khvol'son – all of whom taught Hebrew at one time or another at the St. Petersburg Theological Academy. Gerasim Pavskii and Daniil Khvol'son also taught at the University of St. Petersburg. What brought the careers of these linguists momentarily together in the nineteenth century, however, was not their translation efforts, but their common involvement in the fate of modern Jewry in the Russian Empire. In a unique and largely forgotten instance of collaboration, these three Russian Hebraists – two of them Jewish converts to Russian Orthodoxy – came to share joint membership on a special commission convened in 1855 to investigate the allegation in Saratov that there had been Jewish use of Christian blood for ritual religious purposes. With attention to scholarly detail, Pavskii, Levison, and Khvol'son came to the defense of Russian Jewry, fearlessly challenging the prejudicial charges levied against the local Jews of Saratov. To place the significance of their combined effort in perspective it is necessary to revisit the events and the wide-ranging investigations associated with the Saratov affair.[23]

In December 1852, a ten-year-old Saratov boy, Feofan Sherstobitov, failed to return home from school; seven weeks later an eleven-year-old, Mikhail Maslov, vanished in the same town. Saratov, a major port city on the south-central stretch of the Volga River, was far removed from the more restricted zone of Russian Jewish residence – the Pale of Settlement – but it was a city of mixed ethnic population, owing to its importance as having been one of the centers of Volga German population in the Russian Empire. In March 1853, the bodies of the two boys were found. A local examination led to the allegation that the boys had been crudely circumcised, and then beaten to death. Further inflamed by the anti-Jewish sermon of a local cleric and by conflicts over the destruction of a Jewish cemetery in the region, public outrage – based on rumor – led the authorities to launch an interrogation of all the Jews of Saratov, a relatively small population that included military personnel. The first individual to be arrested was an army private by the name of Shlifferman, identified as the sole person who conducted circumcision among local Jews. There was no evidence, however, linking Shlifferman with the time and place of the two disappearances.

[23] On the "Saratovskoe delo," the most reliable secondary account, because of its appeal to the manuscript record of the investigations, is that of Iu[lii] Gessen, "Saratovskoe delo," in *Evreiskaia entsiklopediia* (St. Petersburg, 1914), XIV: 2–8. See also Gessen's work, *Istoriia evreev v Rossii* (St. Petersburg, 1914); and P. Ia. Levenson, "Eshche o saratovskom dele," *Voskhod*, 1881, no. 4: 163–78.

When news of the disquieting events reached Petersburg, the Ministry of Internal Affairs (hereafter MVD) sent one of its officials (*chinovniki*), N. S. Durnovo, to investigate the matter. With his mind already made up by earlier MVD reports about the ritual use of Christian blood by Jews, Durnovo presupposed the guilt of local Jews in the killing of the two boys and proceeded to direct a broad police surveillance of all Jews of the surrounding district, including baptized Christians of Jewish parentage.

Durnovo's attitude toward the question of ritual Jewish use of Christian blood was clearly influenced by the 1844 report of Vladimir Ivanovich Dal', *An Inquiry concerning the Murdering by Jews of Christian Boys and the Use of Their Blood* (*Rozyskanie ob ubienii evreiami khristianskikh mladentsev i upotreblenii krovi ikh*).[24] A Lutheran convert to Orthodoxy in his later years, Vladimir Dal' is mainly known in Russian history and philology because of his monumental four-volume dictionary of the Russian language, published in the 1860s. Having been trained originally as a surgeon, however, he had worked in that capacity in the province of Orenburg under the direction of Count Vasilii Alekseevich Perovskii, brother of Emperor Nicholas I's future minister of internal affairs. Shortly after Lev Alekseevich Perovskii assumed the ministerial post in 1841, Dal' followed him to Petersburg, where from 1843 to 1849 he participated in most major undertakings of the Perovskii MVD. The anti-Semitism of Dal', visible in entries in his dictionary, was deeply embedded in his 1844 *Rozyskanie*, which posed as an objective history of what were, in fact, unsubstantiated cases of ritual use of Christian blood by Jews from the time of Constantine the Great to the Velizhkoe affair of 1823. The attention accorded the Dal' *Rozyskanie* profoundly affected subsequent MVD proceedings, including the investigation at Saratov headed by the decidedly junior N. S. Durnovo.[25]

[24] V. I. Dal', *Rozyskanie ob ubienii evreiami khristianskikh mladentsev i upotreblenii krovi ikh* (St. Petersburg: Suvorin Press – "Novoe Vremia," 1913). For his four-volume Russian dictionary, see *Tolkovyi slovar' zhivago velikorusskogo iazyka* (Moscow, 1863–6). On Dal', including his involvement in the blood libel issue, see A. Cherkas, "Vladimir Ivanovich Dal'," *Russkii biograficheskii slovar'* (St. Petersburg, 1905), VI: 42–8.

[25] For an account of how Durnovo's Saratov investigation was affected by the prejudicial work of Dal', see Aleksandr Alekseev, *Upotrebliaiut-li evrei khristianskuiu krov's religioznoiu tsel'iu?* (Novgorod, 1886), 10–12. Alekseev, an Orthodox Christian of Jewish parentage, was present in Saratov during much of the investigation. One can also trace the genealogy of the Dal' report in subsequent MVD writing on blood libel. Utilizing the report nearly word for word, Valerii V. Skripitsyn, director of the MVD Department of Spiritual Affairs for Foreign Confessions, prepared an *otnoshenie* for Nicholas I on the Saratov affair, "Svedeniia ob ubiistve evreiami khristian dlia dobyvaniia krovi" (Information on the Murder by Jews of Christians for Obtaining Blood). Skripitsyn's slanderous and unfounded charges were later published in the 1878 volume of *Grazhdanin*, 23–8. The Skripitsyn–Dal' polemic set the tone for much subsequent anti-Semitic propaganda. The Dal' *Rozyskanie* was republished posthumously in the

In the Durnovo proceedings in Saratov, a succession of witnesses, incited by rumors of "ritual crimes" by local Jews, pointed the finger of blame at local Jewish military personnel and others of the small Jewish community. Typical was the case of Private Bogdanov, a discredited drunkard and thief, who testified that he had disposed of the body of one of the boys after blood had been drawn from the child at the home of a local Jewish furrier, Iankel Iushkevicher. Bogdanov's internally conflicting testimony led to his own arrest and that of Iushkevicher. The expanding Durnovo investigation extracted ever more incredible testimony, such as that from retired *guberniia* secretary Kriuger, slandering local Jewish citizens of Saratov. In the atmosphere established by Durnovo, the probe inevitably became broader still with predictable "findings" of wholesale kidnapping of young boys.

In the end, the Saratov prisons and police department jails were unable to hold all those arrested in the affair, with the result that private premises were rented for the incarceration of local citizens. Reporting to Internal Affairs Minister Bibikov of his difficulty in containing the affair, Durnovo was finally told to close his investigation. The ministry declared the preliminary investigation closed in November 1853.

In order to judge the guilt or innocence of those arrested, a committee of ministers, with the approval of Emperor Nicholas I, established in July 1854 a judicial commission (*sudebnaia komissiia*) under the presidency of Aleksandr Karlovich Giers, a section head for special affairs in the MVD and future minister of finance. The professional leadership that A. K. Giers brought to the judicial commission contrasted sharply with that provided earlier in the Saratov investigation by Durnovo. The Giers judicial commission, which met from September 1854 to June 1856, had three main charges:

1. to determine the facts surrounding the killing of Maslov and Sherstobitov;
2. to ascertain whether there was collaboration in this affair by Private Bogdanov, former Secretary Kriuger, or other local officials; and
3. to investigate whether there were any secret dogmas of Jews that might explain their use of Christian blood.[26]

wake of the celebrated Beilis affair. Another work relating to the allegation of Jewish ritual use of Christian blood is the disturbing volume compiled by Ivan O. Kuz'min that perpetuates the old myths, *Materialy k voprosu ob obvineniiakh evreev v ritual'nykh prestupleniiakh* (St. Petersburg, 1913).

[26] See Gessen, "Saratovskoe delo," 5. The contrasting styles of MVD bureaucratic response reflected in the widely differing leadership exercised in the Saratov affair by Giers and Durnovo were not uncommon in the MVD. See, in this regard, the analysis of Daniel T. Orlovsky, *The Limits of Reform: The Ministry of Internal Affairs in Imperial Russia, 1802–1881* (Cambridge, MA: Harvard University Press, 1981), 204–5. Orlovsky notes "the ideological conflict within the bureaucracy itself."

It was with respect to the last of the charges bearing on Jewish dogmas that Giers decided to convene in late 1855 an internal "special commission" (*osobaia komissiia*). This special commission was attached to the MVD's Department of Spiritual Affairs for Foreign Confessions (departament dukhovnykh del inostrannykh ispovedanii). Its composition included Giers (who presided), Daniil Khvol'son, Vasilii Levison, Gerasim Pavskii, and one of Pavskii's students Fedor Sidonskii, a graduate of St. Petersburg Theological Academy. Thus, in 1855, the major St. Petersburg Hebraists responsible for modern Russian Old Testament translation were drawn together "to examine carefully whether in books or manuscripts anything could be found relating to the Jewish use of Christian blood for religious purposes."[27]

Following a period of research into Hebrew sources, as well as into local lore, Pavskii, Levison, and Khvol'son each submitted findings to Giers's special commission. On the basis of these findings, the special commission reported to the wider Saratov judicial commission that there was no documentary or other evidence whatsoever in the Hebrew tradition for the use of Christian blood in Jewish ritual observances. Indeed, it concluded that such a practice was in complete violation of Mosaic laws, which specifically forbade killing. In the most exhaustive effort undertaken by any commission member, Daniil Khvol'son prepared a lengthy report entitled *Concerning Some Medieval Accusations against Jews: Historical Source-based Research* (*O nekotorykh srednevekovykh obvineniiakh protiv Evreev: Istoricheskoe izsledovanie po istochnikam*). First published in 1861, the Khvol'son work was issued in three subsequent editions, as well as in German translation. Frequently cited in German as well as in Russian literature on the blood libel question, the Khvol'son work is the most authoritative examination of sources ever consulted on the question, including the use of works from the pre-Christian era down to the nineteenth century.[28] None of the members of the Giers special commission found any

[27] The charge to the internal *osobaia komissiia* may also be found in Gessen, "Saratovskoe delo," 7–8. For a more complete account of this charge to the special commission, see also the preface to the 1880 edition of Daniil Khvol'son's work, *O nekotorykh srednevekovykh obvineniiakh protiv Evreev: Istoricheskoe izsledovanie po istochnikam* (St. Petersburg: Tip. Tsederbauma i Gol'denbliuma, 1880).

[28] Khvol'son's work was first issued in the journal *Biblioteka dlia chteniia*, 1861, 164 (March): 1–56, (April): 1–48; and 165 (May): 1–60. The 1861 bound edition was expanded to 386 pages in the 1880 edition, including the preface concerning the Saratov events. The German edition, *Die Blutanklage und sonstige mittelalterliche Beschuldigungen der Juden: Eine historische Untersuchung nach den Quellen*, was published in Frankfurt (J. Kauffmann Press, 1901), although it was printed in Vienna (L. Beck & Son). Gerasim Pavskii issued his own response, similar in tone to that of Khvol'son, but much shorter. For the Pavskii response, see N. I. Barsov, "Mnenie protoiereia G. P. Pavskago po voprosu ob upotreblenii evreiami khristianskoi krovi dlia religioznykh tselei," *Tserkovnyi vestnik*, 1879, no. 20.

credible evidence for the Saratov allegations, nor for the longstanding mythical notion of Jewish use of Christian blood.

In addition to this longer scholarly study, Khvol'son later prepared a separate brochure for a more popular audience, reviewing the findings of the Saratov special commission.[29] Khvol'son indicated that the special commission had also reviewed all the testimony offered before the Saratov judicial commission, and had found no support for the charges leveled against local Jews. Khvol'son's recounting included one curious misuse of documentary evidence gathered during the preliminary investigation in Saratov – an illustrated Amsterdam publication found amongst local Saratov Jews purporting to show the Jewish killing of a Christian boy. In the absence of anyone able to decipher the Hebrew inscription under the illustration, no less a prominent figure than the historian Nikolai Ivanovich Kostomarov later argued that the illustration conclusively proved the practice of Jewish use of Christian blood. Khvol'son recalled that when he and Levison first set eyes on the illustration, they were driven to laughter despite the seriousness of the charges, for the inscription, which employed Hebrew orthography, ironically retold the biblical story of the killing of a *Jewish* boy by the Egyptian pharaoh who had been advised to do so to cure himself of his own illness.[30] In this case, as in the formal reports arising out of the Giers special commission, Pavskii, Khvol'son, and Levison were able to use their expertise in Hebraic and biblical studies to defend the Saratov Jews against the scurrilous anti-Semitic charges.

The Saratov events did not end, however, with the findings of Pavskii, Levison, and Khvol'son. Their findings were included when, in June 1856, Giers's wider judicial commission referred the entire affair to the sixth department of the State Senate in Moscow. Although the judicial commission recommended that the Saratov Jews Shlifferman, Iushkevicher, and Iushkevicher's son be held in jail pending final judgment on the matter, its report included the finding that the judicial commission had discovered no evidence of guilt on their part. The commission also found the testimony of Bogdanov and Kriuger contrived and internally contradictory. The Senate department in Moscow confirmed the Giers judicial commission findings, and called for the immediate liberation of all Jews confined in Saratov.[31]

[29] D. A. Khvol'son, *Upotrebliaiut-li evrei khristianskuiu krov'?* [Do Jews Use Christian Blood?] (St. Petersburg, 1879), 69pp. An expanded edition, printed in Kiev in 1912 shortly after Khvol'son's death, incorrectly identifies the author as A. D. Khvol'son.

[30] Khvol'son, *Upotrebliaiut-li evrei khristianskuiu krov'?*

[31] Gessen, "Saratovskoe delo," 5–6.

The matter then passed to the State Council in Petersburg, which had been created in 1810. Within this council, the highest advisory body to the emperor, a committee of three ministers reviewed the previous findings, and despite the call from Minister of Justice Zamiatin for the unconditional acquittal of Shlifferman and the Yushkevichers, the State Council reversed the Moscow Senate department's recommendation, voting by a margin of twenty-two to two to keep the falsely charged Jews under arrest. Emperor Alexander II added his name to the majority, thereby officially closing the matter in 1860.[32] The State Council's reversal of the Giers commission and the Moscow Senate findings sadly confirmed the precedent of the earlier ritual murder case, the notorious Velizhskoe affair, in which Emperor Nicholas I had determined that, even if Jewish ritual use of Christian blood could not be proven, there may have been some deviant Jewish sect that retained responsibility.

What particularly troubled Professor Khvol'son in this matter was the news he received from his close acquaintance, Minister of Education Avraam Sergeevich Norov. Norov informed Khvol'son that the report of the Pavskii–Levison–Khvol'son "special commission" regarding the spurious charge of ritual use of Christian blood by Jews was conspicuously missing from the file reviewed by the State Council on the Saratov affair. Emboldened by the discovery of this omission, Khvol'son committed himself to the full publication of his own findings on the matter. Indeed, it was in this context that Khvol'son moved quickly to secure such publication for his work. Shortly thereafter it appeared as "O nekotorykh srednevekovykh obvineniiakh protiv Evreev," in the journal *Biblioteka dlia chteniia*.[33]

Later, following the deaths of Pavskii and Levison and in the aftermath of yet another set of blood libel allegations – the Kutaissi affair (*Kutaisskoe delo*), Khvol'son republished his work against blood libel and issued his more popular brochure challenging the repeated, unfounded charges in the slanderous works of his contemporaries, Ippolit Liutostanskii and N. I. Kostomarov.[34] Responding in *Novoe vremia* to Kostomarov, Khvol'son

[32] Ibid., 6. On the *memoriia* of the State Council, Alexander II simply wrote alongside the position of the 22, "i ia" [and I].

[33] See note 28 above. Khvol'son's acquaintance with Norov dates from the time of Khvol'son's conversion to Russian Orthodoxy.

[34] Ippolit Liutostanskii, basing his study on the work of Skripitsyn and Dal' (see note 3), first issued his anti-Semitic polemic under the title, *Vopros ob upotreblenii evreiami-sektantorami khristianskoi krovi dlia religioznykh tselei v sviazi s voprosom ob otnosheniiakh evreistva k khristianstvu voobshche* (Moscow, 1876). This broadside prompted Khvol'son to republish *O nekotorykh srednevekovykh obvineniiakh protiv Evreev* in 1880. Khvol'son also issued for a more popular audience his *Upotrebliaiut-li evrei khristianskuiu krov'?* In turn, Liutostanskii issued an expanded two-volume edition of his 1876 work under the slightly revised title, *Ob upotreblenii evreiami (talmudistskimi sektantorami) khristianskoi krovi dlia religioznykh tselei, v sviazi s voprosom ob otnosheniiakh evreistva k khristianstvu voobshche*

was particularly offended by two charges, the first an ad hominem attack, and the other directed more broadly at the Russian intelligentsia. On the ad hominem charge raised by Kostomarov that Khvol'son was merely driven by support for his fellow Jews, Khvol'son responded by saying:

Mr. Kostomarov alludes to my "patriotism" and speaks about my "partiality toward Jews." Yes, I admit that I nourish empathy for Jews, for I know not only their dark, but also their bright side. And I think that it is far more honest to defend those of my fellow race and my former religion from erroneous accusations than to slander them with various fabrications and with false representation of the most innocent facts. To be sure, a defender of Jews cannot count upon the approbation of the majority who invariably throw in their lot with the slanderers of Judaism. But why does an honest man need such approbation? I hold true to my conscience in struggling for justice and for truth.[35]

To this Kostomarev countered that, in the end, truth always wins out, and the very stridency of Khvol'son's defense of Russian Jewry cast doubt upon his case. Khvol'son's rejoinder constituted an appeal to the duty of the Russian intelligentsia:

Mr. Kostomarov says that "the light of truth by itself scatters the darkness of delusion." Unfortunately, I am not such an historical optimist as Kostomarov . . . Truth is not a material force, operating according to general physical laws. It is a spiritual power that does not act by itself, but requires assistance. If the intelligentsia quietly lays down its hands and awaits the "power of truth," surely this power will never be made manifest "by itself." For as the Saviour said, "If indeed the salt has lost its taste, how shall its saltness be restored." [Matt. 5:13].[36]

Daniil Khvol'son and his fellow Old Testament translators effectively challenged prevailing nineteenth-century superstitions directed against Russian Jewry. One of the more sensational instances of the impact of Khvol'son's reasoned refutation of the blood libel charge involved the case of his highly polemical opponent, Ippolit Liutostanskii. A student of the Moscow Theological Academy, Liutostanskii had been a Catholic priest prior to his conversion to Russian Orthodoxy. Persuaded of the error of his own position, Liutostanskii issued in 1882 a remarkable defense of Jews on the blood libel allegation, entitled *Sovremennyi vzgliad na evreiskii vopros*

(Moscow, 1880). This edition devoted a new preface, i–xviii, to a personal attack on Khvol'son. In his more popular 1879 work, Khvol'son also responded to the historian Kostomarov, who had repeated in the pages of *Novoe vremia* the charge of Jewish ritual use of Christian blood. See, within Khvol'son's *Upotrebliaiut-li evrei khristianskuiu krov'?* the third appendix, "Otvet na zamechanie N. I. Kostomarova, 'po povodu broshiury, izdannoi g. Khvol'sonom: upotrebliaiut-li evrei khristianskuiu krov'?'" Khvol'son's response addressed the criticism that Kostomarov first directed at him in the newspaper *Novoe vremia*, no. 1172 (June 5, 1879).

[35] Khvol'son, "Otvet na zamechanie N. I. Kostomarova," (Kiev, 1912), 77. [36] Ibid., 74–5.

(A Contemporary View on the Jewish Question), in which he recanted all of his former writings on the subject.[37] Khvol'son's published refutation remained into the twentieth century among the most significant European scholarly challenges to the charge of blood libel, defending Jews against the scurrilous claim of ritual murder.

In the end, it may not have been coincidental that the architects of Hebraic studies in Orthodox Russia – Gerasim Pavskii, Daniil Khvol'son, and their students – should have become such outspoken defenders of Jews against the blood libel myth. For, as Ronald Hsia has noted in the case of Germany, so also in the case of Russia, the systematic scholarly refutation of the ritual murder charge invariably accompanied the advance of serious Hebraic studies in the academy.[38] The tradition of outstanding Hebrew scholarship in Petersburg continued well into the twentieth century. The last major student of Khvol'son, Pavel Konstantinovich Kokovtsev (1861–1942), taught exclusively at Petersburg University, subsequently Leningrad State University, not at the Theological Academy. Kokovtsev's later years were spent at the Leningrad Division of the Institute of Oriental Studies of the Soviet Academy of Sciences.

The once great authority of the Russian Orthodox Church in Hebraic studies, seen preeminently in the contributions of Petersburg scholars Pavskii, Levison, Khvol'son, and Khvol'son's students Ivan Troitskii and Pavel Kokovtsev, collapsed in the Soviet era, and is only today reviving. The linkage of Russian Old Testament translation and Hebraic studies with the scholarly refutation of ritual murder nevertheless constituted an important hidden chapter linking the politics of the modern Russian Bible with the Jewish Question in modern Russian history.

[37] Ippolit Liutostanskii, *Sovremennyi vzgliad na evreiskii vopros* (St. Petersburg, 1882). On Liutostanskii, see the entry under his name in *Entsiklopedicheskii slovar'* (St. Petersburg, 1896), XXXV: 265.

[38] On the linkage of the refutation of ritual murder accusations with the development of Hebraic studies, see Ronald Po-chia Hsia, *The Myth of Ritual Murder: Jews and Magic in Reformation Germany* (New Haven, CT: Yale University Press, 1988).

CHAPTER 6

Colportage, sectarianism, and Russian Bible publication

Holy Synod publication of the modern Russian Bible in the third quarter of the nineteenth century reopened virtually all the issues of the distribution and marketing of scripture that had been handled by the Russian Bible Society in the first quarter of the century. At stake in such marketing was a fundamental issue of authority that had been left unresolved in the aftermath of the society's 1826 closure: namely, who had the right to disseminate Holy Scripture. In the fifty years following the 1862 publication of the Russian New Testament, the politics of the modern Russian Bible shifted increasingly to this issue of distribution rights. In the *publication* of the Russian scriptural text, the Holy Synod had assumed monopoly rights at the time of the closure of the Bible Society. Although it permitted open publication of variant Old Testament versions in the 1860s, the Holy Synod never authorized other domestic presses to publish synodal editions once the Synod's own translation was published (1862 in the case of the NT; 1876 in the case of the OT).

However, in the matter of *distribution* after 1862, the Holy Synod and its press were unprepared to address the wider demands of the religious marketplace. Instead, what grew up alongside the Holy Synod's printing establishment was an independent system for mass dissemination of Holy Scripture marked by a unique arrangement for colportage operating largely outside official Russian Orthodox circles. The resulting mass peddling of scripture that followed in the decades prior to World War I – a phenomenon largely overlooked in western treatments of Russian religious culture – served as a powerful mechanism for the expansion of literacy and popular piety. So effective and far-reaching was this new marketing system that, by the 1890s, fears began to be expressed at the highest levels of the church bureaucracy that popular religious piety was increasingly developing at the fringes of, and indeed outside, established Orthodox state institutions.

Colportage was very much present in earlier periods of Russian history, as in the oral transmission of spiritual values by wandering holy men (*stranniki* or *stranstvuiushchie*). The early nineteenth-century Russian Bible Society had developed a new empire-wide network of sales through branch societies. After the closure of these branches and auxiliaries, moral and religious tracts continued to be peddled through Petersburg booksellers like K. I. Meier and G. B. Blister, as well as the BFBS Petersburg agency. But the specific use of colportage for Russian biblical distribution originated with the founding of the Society for the Dissemination of Holy Scripture in Russia in 1863, less than a year after publication of the Holy Synod's New Testament.[1]

The Society for the Dissemination of Holy Scripture in Russia (ORSPR, Obshchestvo dlia rasprostraneniia Sv. Pisaniia v Rossii) had eight founding members, but was primarily the inspiration of Nikolai Astaf'ev, a Petersburg history instructor who served also as a corrector on the BFBS Petersburg OT revision committee.[2] Astaf'ev's private apartment became the first meeting place of the ORSPR, and he served as the chronicler of the society's history until his death in 1906, by which time the society's activity had been largely subsumed within the BFBS St. Petersburg agency. In June 1863, shortly after the founding of the ORSPR, it sponsored the first planned trip of one of its members, the long-time Dutch resident of Petersburg, Otton Bogdanovich Forkhgamer (Forschammer), for the purpose of marketing Holy Scripture at the Nizhnii Novgorod trade fair. In securing copies of the synodal Russian New Testament, Astaf'ev turned to his Petersburg BFBS contact, Adalbert Eck.[3] Having maintained its agency in Petersburg following the RBS closure in 1826, the BFBS continued to be a major supplier of scripture in modern languages within the Russian Empire, and it welcomed the overture of Astaf'ev's ORSPR.

Despite later strains, the early alliance of the ORSPR with the Petersburg BFBS agency turned out to be crucial in several respects. Most importantly, the BFBS Petersburg agency, subvented by its London parent offices, was in a position to provide discounted copies of Holy Scripture to the fledgling society, first at a 12.5 percent markdown, and ultimately at what came to be a standard 20 percent reduction. BFBS agencies also could provide scripture in other ancient and modern languages. In the case of the Russian New

[1] On ORSPR, see N. A. Astaf'ev, *Obshchestvo dlia rasprostraneniia sv. Pisaniia v Rossii (1863–1893): Ocherk ego proiskhozhdeniia i deiatel'nosti* (St. Petersburg: Tip. E. Evdokimova, 1892). The society published an annual *Otchet.*

[2] Astaf'ev was professor of history at the St. Petersburg Historico-Philological Institute. See "Astaf'ev, Nikolai Aleksandrovich," in the Brokgauz-Efron *Entsiklopedicheskii slovar'* (St. Petersburg, 1890), III: 333–4. Astaf'ev's Protestant/sectarian leanings were later held against the society during the 1890s missionary conferences.

[3] Astaf'ev, *Obshchestvo*, 5. Adalbert Eck was employed by the BFBS agency from 1860, heading the Petersburg agency from 1865 to 1869.

Testament, the Synodal Press initially did the printing for the BFBS Petersburg agency, which in turn passed along discounted copies for Astaf'ev's society. As conflicts later arose over the distribution of free copies by the ORSPR – a potential undercutting of the BFBS's own retail sales network – each group, the BFBS agency and the ORSPR, developed its own separate sales force of colporteurs. Astaf'ev's society also began to purchase directly from the Synodal Press at what became the established discounted rate of 20 percent off the retail sales price.[4]

By the end of the nineteenth century, BFBS agents were directing an empire-wide operation out of central agencies and sub-agency depots that dotted the Eurasian landscape. The BFBS had added agencies in Odessa, Ekaterinburg, and Tiflis during the course of the nineteenth century. More cautious than its counterpart Society for the Dissemination of Holy Scripture in avoiding the charge of fomenting sectarianism, BFBS agencies weathered the political storms of the 1880s and 1890s that placed Astaf'ev's ORSPR under threat. Yet, in the 1860s, during the reform-oriented administration of Emperor Alexander II, Astaf'ev's society had managed to gain the support of well-placed Russian ministerial officials, and this support offered a convenient cover for the expanded operations of the BFBS's own agencies. Aided by the pious Russian rail minister, Aleksei Pavlovich Bobrinskoi, who headed the Russian Railways Ministry (Ministerstvo putei soobshcheniia), both ORSPR and BFBS secured free rail passage for those who were peddling scripture. Containers of scripture as heavy as 500 *pood* (approximately 18,000 pounds) were permitted to ride the rails without charge. Operating under imperial charter from 1871, Astaf'ev's society distributed more than 1.5 million volumes of scripture in the first thirty years of its operation.[5]

As scriptural texts became available in additional languages of the empire and publication of the Russian synodal translation expanded to include both the Old and New Testaments, the size and scope of BFBS operations, particularly in purchasing and distribution at discount to individual colporteurs, greatly increased. In 1880, the first year for which published BFBS colportage statistics were broken down, thirty-three colporteurs had sold

[4] Ibid., 256. For an example of the friction that occasionally arose between the BFBS agency and Astaf'ev's Society over terms of sale, see William Nicolson to Rev. C. Jackson (St. Petersburg, November 20, 1869), BFBS Agents Books (Russia), no. 125 (BSA/D1/7).

[5] Astaf'ev, *Obshchestvo*, 258. For an account of Bobrinskoi's participation in Pashkovite and Radstock circles in St. Petersburg, see Hans Brandenburg, *The Meek and the Mighty: The Emergence of the Evangelical Movement in Russia* (New York: Oxford University Press, 1977), 106–21.

approximately 47,000 volumes of scripture.[6] Thirty-three years later, on the eve of World War I, the BFBS reported on the individual sales of its 101 colporteurs and hawkers – a 300 percent increase in the force. That colportage network accounted for sales of more than 187,000 volumes of scripture (whole Bibles or portions), a fourfold increase over 1880 colportage figures. Adding other retail sales to the colportage figures, BFBS agencies were reporting annual sales by 1913 of more than 700,000 volumes of the Bible (in whole or in part).[7] Although comparable sales records are not available for the Holy Synod, its publication records bear out a total distribution figure, including BFBS agencies and Holy Synod operations, of approximately one million copies annually by the twentieth century.[8] The cost of such scripture varied widely from the 10-kopeck copy of the Gospels to the most popular 25-kopeck People's (Narodnyi) New Testament to the well-bound Russian/ Slavonic diglot Bible that cost several rubles.[9]

The annual scripture sales figures, although they document the substantial increase in distribution of biblical literature in the period leading up to World War I, need to be set against the even greater expansion of literacy during the same period. Boris Mironov in his *Social History of Russia* calculates that literacy rates in the Russian Empire expanded from roughly 5 percent of the population in 1800 to approximately 40 percent in 1913. Meanwhile, the empire-wide population of approximately 30 million in 1800 had increased to 160 million in 1913. Thus the literate population had increased from approximately 1.5 million in the early nineteenth century to more than 60 million on the eve of the First World War.[10] The annual scripture sales figure of one million copies by the early twentieth century needs to be seen in the context of this greatly expanded literate population. By comparison, the annual RBS scripture circulation figures in the early 1820s following the publication of the first Russian New Testament approximated 200,000 copies. Thus, while the

[6] Beginning in 1881, the BFBS published in its annual reports the colportage figures for each of its overseas agencies, including the names of all colporteurs and hawkers. See *The Seventy-Seventh Report of the BFBS* (London: BFBS, 1881), Appendix A, 245–6.

[7] *The Hundred and Tenth Report of the BFBS* (London: BFBS, 1914), "Supplementary Tables of Circulation," 11–12.

[8] It is possible to reconstruct Holy Synod Press circulation from the archival records of the press. In 1913, for example, the BFBS was the largest single purchaser of scripture from the Holy Synod Press, but there was substantial circulation outside the BFBS network, resulting in total print runs of approximately one million copies (see RGIA *fond* 800, *opis'* 1, *delo* 583 ["Godovoi otchet za 1913"], *l.* 28).

[9] Price figures are listed in the BFBS annual reports, and prices are marked on bound copies within the Bible Society's scripture collection.

[10] See B. N. Mironov, *Sotsial'naia istoriia Rossii (XVIII – nachalo XX v.)*, 2 vols. (St. Petersburg: Izd. "Dmitrii Bulanin," 2003), 1: 377 and 383. Mironov's table (377) provides total population figures for the empire. His ninth table (383) provides approximate literacy percentages for the same period.

annual scripture sales in Russia of one million copies in the early twentieth century greatly exceeded the circulation of the early nineteenth century, the Russian Bible Society of the early nineteenth century nevertheless managed to reach a higher percentage of the literate population (one copy per 7.5 potential readers) than the distribution network put in place by the Holy Synod and its Bible Society distributors in Russia on the eve of the First World War (one copy per sixty potential readers).

Using the annual reports of the BFBS, which assumed primary responsibility for most Eurasian colportage in the last three decades before World War I, it is possible to reconstruct the outlines of the colportage network operating in the Russian Empire in the period after 1880. From 1880 to 1913, more than 550 colporteurs and hawkers were employed in the Russian Empire by the BFBS, and they were identified by name, region, length of service, and sales record.[11] The terms "colporteur" and "hawker" denoted precise distinctions. Colporteurs (*doverennye knigonoshi*) received no fewer than 40 rubles per month as a fixed salary. Hawkers (*vol'nye knigonoshi*) received no more than 25 rubles per month. Both colporteurs and hawkers secured the same 20 percent commission on sales, but colporteurs alone received free rail ticketing and postage.[12] Colporteurs could also participate in a voluntary deposited savings and retirement plan offered by the BFBS.[13] While colporteurs were thus in a far better material position, they nevertheless were obliged to follow a routing predetermined by the respective BFBS agent or depot superintendent. Hawkers were free to follow their own itinerary or schedule.

For the period 1880 to 1913, BFBS agencies employed 386 colporteurs (roughly 70 percent of the total force) and 170 hawkers (30 percent).[14] Although the overwhelming majority involved in colportage were male, there were some notable female *knigonoshi* employed both by the Society for the Dissemination of Holy Scripture in Russia and by BFBS agencies and depots. From 1888 to 1911, the well-known BFBS hawker Mariia Andreeva

[11] Based on the annual *Report of the BFBS* between 1881 and 1914, it is possible to compile cumulative sales records by name for each colporteur and hawker listed.

[12] I. I. Starinin, "Zapiski bibleiskago knigonoshi" (Notes of a Bible Hawker), *Golos minuvshago*, 1914, no. 12: 182.

[13] BFBS established an "Employees' Savings Fund" in December 1880, the terms of which are set forth in Appendix A of *The Seventy-Seventh Report of the BFBS*, 236–7. The BFBS continued to pay pensions to widows of its former employees well into the Soviet period.

[14] The statistics offered here are based upon the author's tabulations of yearly BFBS colportage figures. The statistics have been converted to individual files by name. Analysis of the name files allows for information over time, e.g. regarding the total number of colporteurs and hawkers, their average length of service, sales record by name and region, description of the sales force by gender and ethnicity, etc.

peddled her Bibles through the streets of Moscow selling, during her prime years in the 1890s, almost 5,000 volumes per year. Most *knigonoshi* worked for much shorter periods of time. More than half the hawkers (92) ended up working for less than one year. Most of the remaining hawkers (62) worked less than five years. Colporteurs tended to be employed for longer periods. More than 15 percent (57) of the BFBS colporteurs between 1880 and 1913 served for periods in excess of ten years. The largest single cohort of colporteurs (178) held their posts between one and five years.

Sales varied widely by region. Throughout the thirty-three-year period, 1880–1913, the main BFBS agency was located in St. Petersburg, but in the half-century prior to the Russian Revolution, the BFBS added agencies serviced by full-time agents in Odessa (1867–95), Ekaterinburg (1889–1918), and Tiflis (1879–1920). BFBS depots or sub-agencies were located in Moscow and in numerous cities across Eurasia. While the greatest number of *knigonoshi* were employed within the St. Petersburg agency, relatively few actually worked in the imperial capital itself – no doubt a reflection of the ready availability of scripture in local retail outlets. The St. Petersburg agency included colportage in Finland and the Baltic region, the Polish territories, the Muscovite heartland, and, after the closure of the Odessa agency, Ukraine. Sales in the northern Caucasus and Don–Volga River valleys grew to considerable proportions. The general growth of sales in Siberia after 1896 was also notable, even as far east as Iakutiia. The expansion of colportage into Siberia and the Far East was almost certainly tied to the additional rail service provided by the extension of the Trans-Siberian Railway. Sales in Siberia, although they amounted to more than 70,000 volumes in 1913, never reached the scale of the sales through the European agencies.[15]

By language, the Russian texts were clearly the most popular, amounting in 1913 to more than a third of the sales in European Russia, and more than half of the sales in Siberia. Sales of Russian and diglot Russian/Slavonic texts taken together constituted more than half of all circulation. Sales of Slavonic-only texts trailed well behind with less than 10 percent of the total, followed in declining order by Finnish, German, Polish, Hebrew, Latvian, and Chuvash. Already on the eve of World War I, approximately one-third of all sales involved non-Slavic languages of the empire, and thus mirrored the ethnic diversity of Eurasia. By 1913, portions of the Bible were sold by BFBS agencies of the Russian Empire in more than fifty languages.[16]

The average *knigonosha* tended to reflect the ethnic background of the region where he or she sold. However, there was clearly a disproportionate

[15] For Siberian sales in 1913, see *Hundred and Tenth Report of the BFBS*, 11. [16] Ibid., 12.

Germanic representation within the colportage lists. Such surnames as Annwerdt, Bergmann, Garmasch, Lunge, Morgenfeld, Mueller, Pagge, and Streike were especially prominent among those with more than ten years of service. This Germanic complexion of the colportage lists reflected also the tendency of colporteurs and hawkers to be drawn from awakening evangelical Protestant, sectarian forms of religious piety wherein German settlers had a formative influence.

The predisposition toward sectarian piety – evidenced in such activities as Bible reading, prayer meetings, hymn singing, and revivalist preaching – undoubtedly fed the colportage movement. One such sectarian leader, a certain Zhidkov by name, was the grandfather of Mikhail Iu. Zhidkov, former General Secretary of the Union of Evangelical Christians and Baptists and the Soviet-era pastor of the Central Baptist Church of Moscow. The elder Zhidkov is identified in BFBS records as having served as a colporteur on the lower Volga for eight years before his proselytizing activity led BFBS officials to discharge him in 1885 under the pressure of mounting official scrutiny of colportage.[17] The official charges, not without foundation, stated that colporteurs and hawkers were essentially peddling by day and proselytizing by night. Officials feared that colportage and the Bible reading practices it encouraged were becoming a front for the conversion of mainstream Orthodox believers into adherents of sectarian Protestant groups.

By the 1880s, such official fears led Konstantin Pobedonostsev, the Synod's ober-prokuror, to establish a series of widely publicized "missionary congresses" at which *knigonoshi* were vilified as dangerous enemies of Orthodoxy.[18] In this climate, Astaf'ev's Society for the Dissemination of Holy Scripture in Russia found itself particularly threatened. The agencies and depots of the BFBS survived the crisis, but only because of vigorous efforts by BFBS agent William Nicolson, who forcefully sought to disassociate the British and Foreign Bible Society from any proselytizing. The BFBS mission, after all, was a commercial one – the sale of scripture – and could not be allowed to be threatened by colporteurs who engaged in nefarious proselytizing activity. The credibility of the BFBS, in that regard, tended to be quite high, despite the excesses of some of its earlier Odessa agents. This reflected the manner in which the BFBS

[17] The elder Zhidkov is listed in BFBS published colportage statistics under the name "Schidkoff." For the ongoing controversy surrounding proselytizing and the case of Zhidkov in particular, see the unpublished BFBS Minutes of the Committee for the 1880s and 1890s when the charge of proselytism directed against the BFBS Petersburg agency was frequently brought to the attention of the committee by its Petersburg agent, William Nicolson (BSA/B1).

[18] For a discussion of these congresses from the point of view of the affected colporteurs, see Starinin, "Zapiski bibleiskago knigonoshi," 180–1. Starinin recounts confronting an instance of overt hostility from the wave of public vilification.

Russian agencies were essentially run as commercial enterprises, much like the parent British agency in London itself.[19]

Despite the attempt to vilify colportage as an exclusively Protestant outgrowth, the colportage movement in Russia clearly appealed beyond sectarianism, for it was rooted in a popular piety that spread to traditional Orthodox peasants and workers alike.[20] The nature of this popular piety was well represented in the only known memoir of a BFBS hawker, Ivan Ignat'evich Starinenko, whose "Zapiski bibleiskago knigonoshi" (Notes of a Biblical Colporteur) were serialized in 1914 in the popular journal, *Golos minuvshago*.[21] BFBS annual reports document Starinenko's ten-year period as a hawker out of the Moscow depot from 1887 to 1896. With the exception of a brief period in 1889–90 when he was persuaded by BFBS agent Nicolson to become a colporteur in Vladimir, Starinenko confined his activity to hawking in Moscow and its environs. A relatively successful hawker, he sold on an annual basis an average of more than 2,000 volumes, and his sales reached more than 2,400 volumes in 1892 and 1893. From 1891 to 1895, Starinenko's hawking also involved supplying scripture in ancient and modern languages to students of the Moscow Theological Academy.[22]

According to Starinenko's "Notes," there were distinctly varying responses to his attempts to sell biblical texts. Openly hostile were the monastic authorities, whom he portrayed as being unwilling on occasion even to let him enter monastery grounds to exhibit his books. At monasteries where he was permitted to sell, he reported "decidedly no success among the monastic brethren."[23] Starinenko, however, noted the sharply contrasting reception he was accorded at women's monasteries, where he met with a warm welcome

[19] The BFBS commercial, entrepreneurial mission is set in sharp relief in Howsam's *Cheap Bibles*. The entrepreneurial management of BFBS Russian operations owed much to the leadership of its Petersburg agent, William Nicolson, who spoke Russian and was resident in Petersburg from 1869 to 1897. His letters and reports are heavily represented in the BFBS Archive, particularly in BFBS Agents Books (Russia), 4 vols. (nos. 125, 137, 142, and 149), 1869–74 (BSA/D1/7).

[20] This popular piety has been the focus of recent western writing. See, for example, Vera Shevzov, *Russian Orthodoxy on the Eve of Revolution* (New York: Oxford University Press, 2004); Page Herrlinger, *Working Souls: Russian Orthodoxy and Factory Labor in St. Petersburg, 1881–1917* (Columbus, OH: Slavica, 2008); Nadieszda Kizenko, *A Prodigal Saint: Father John of Kronstadt and the Russian People* (University Park: Pennsylvania State University Press, 2000); Gregory L. Freeze, "Dechristianization in Holy Rus'?: Reports from Vladimir Diocese on Popular Piety," in *Faith and Story: Orthodox Narratives in Imperial Russia*, ed. Heather Coleman (Bloomington, IN: Indiana University Press, forthcoming); and the collection of articles in Valerie A. Kivelson and Robert H. Greene, eds., *Orthodox Russia: Belief and Practice under the Tsars* (University Park: Pennsylvania State University Press, 2003).

[21] Starinin, "Zapiski bibleiskago knigonoshi," 1914, no. 10: 150–85; no. 11: 167–211; no. 12: 166–97. These "Notes" were published under the name I. I. Starinin, a pseudonym for Starinenko, after his arrest by the Okhrana following a two-year period of surveillance in Moscow during his years as a hawker. This surveillance is discussed openly in the Starinin, "Zapiski," no. 12: 195.

[22] Starinin, "Zapiski," no. 12: 179. [23] Ibid., no. 12: 170.

and was frequently invited to join the nuns for coffee. Starinenko related that his most hostile reception came from Roman Catholic priests (*ksendzy*). Curiously, he thought the hostility of Catholic clergy to the dissemination of scripture almost matched that of Old Believer priests, although he found the priestless Old Believers (*bezpopovtsy*) to be more open to his sale of biblical texts.

Going door to door, Starinenko found that the best purchasers were, predictably, Russian sectarians. While he appreciated the respect they showed him as a *knigonosha*, he maintained some reservations about Protestant beliefs, based on local evangelical meetings he had attended. He mentioned in this regard a particular gathering at which Dr. Frederick Wilhelm Baedeker (1823–1906), the renowned British evangelical, had preached.[24]

Despite the good sales and respect he received from sectarians, Starinenko felt "the warmest and most brotherly welcome" from factory workers in industrial plant settings. Such workers invited him to stay for dinner, gave him a bed for the night, and engaged him in "soul talk" (*pogovorit' po dusham*). Starinenko noted that "the religious question among workers was at the time a large and difficult issue. Each of them had some more or less agonizing misapprehension over dogmas and rites."[25] He hesitated to respond to the questions of these workers, but advised them to seek counsel in the scriptures. Invariably upon leaving a workers' quarter, he would be asked by one of the residents to write to someone in the person's family in an outlying village. Starinenko's memoir thus demonstrated, quite unintentionally, how the *knigonosha* served as a connecting link to the religious and family traditions that existed in the distant villages from which these workers had come.

The result of this interaction between *knigonoshi* and a popular mass audience was undoubtedly the advancement of social processes already well under way. For example, the colportage movement, by its sheer volume of sales, encouraged the growth of literacy in both urban and rural parts of the Russian Empire. While diglossia was perpetuated in the sale of Slavonic scripture – and there were still those whose literacy developed out of contact with Slavonic texts – the mass purchase of the modern Russian Bible, or biblical text in a comparable national language, contributed to literacy, while posing new problems for an Orthodox church nurtured in the Slavonic liturgy.

Among these new problems, one of the most nettlesome for church leaders was surely the growth of Protestant sectarianism. Russian sectarians

[24] Ibid., no. 10: 173. Frederick Baedeker was the son of the German publisher Karl Baedeker, whose travel guides, including *Baedeker's Russia*, set the standard for authoritative tourist guidebooks.

[25] Starinin, "Zapiski," no. 12: 175.

were uniquely positioned to benefit from colportage. The mass distribution of Holy Scripture met an audience caught in the disruptive process of urbanization. For this audience, the Protestant appeal to the authority of the printed word may well have been heightened in a political culture within which the ability to read was valued and the authority of the printed word went almost unquestioned. At the same time, sectarianism provided a natural outlet for the pervasive anticlericalism of workers and peasants of the Russian Empire. Such anticlericalism was found even among *knigonoshi* themselves, at least judging from the language of Starinenko's memoir, published eighteen years after he abandoned the sale of Bibles.

Colportage and its practice in the late Russian Empire served to reinforce two dominant themes relating to the politics of the modern Russian Bible. First, colportage and the official response to *knigonoshi* reflected the continuing sensitivity of the issues of authority posed by biblical translation. What was at stake here was the authority to distribute sacred texts. Caught between the desire to limit sectarianism and a commitment to the dissemination of the new Russian Bible, Russian religious and political authorities waffled in their response. On the one hand, generous subsidies were allowed to colporteurs in the form of free rail ticketing and discounted purchases. On the other hand, at least until the edicts of toleration addressed to Protestants and Old Believers in 1904 and 1905, the Holy Synod under the leadership of Konstantin Pobedonostsev sought to vilify and impede those who would hawk by day and proselytize by night. Facing not only this pressure from church leaders but also the oversight activities of the Okhrana secret police, Starinenko abandoned colportage in 1896.[26]

The other reality emerging out of the colportage phenomenon was the subtle manner in which the marketplace had reinserted itself into the arbitration of modern Russian religious culture. Just as in the days of the Russian Bible Society, when the effective marketing of modern biblical texts momentarily threatened even to exceed the limits of a literate public audience, so also in the period of intense colportage, it was the appeal of the marketplace – the interaction between hundreds of hawkers and colporteurs and a newly urbanized population of workers and ex-peasants – that began to stretch the limits of official arbitration of popular Russian religious consciousness. Insofar as this involved not just domestic actors, but also external commercial interests such as those of the British and Foreign Bible Society, it fitted a wider pattern in which religiously inspired movements could become the unwitting modernizing agents of what Charles Taylor calls "a secular age."

[26] See Starinin's reference to Okhrana secret police monitoring of his hawking efforts, ibid., no. 12: 180, 195.

AFTERWORD

Russian biblical translation in the twentieth century

Despite the debates that swirled over the authority of the textual sources and the language employed in modern Russian biblical translation, the Bible wars of the nineteenth century yielded a Synod-authorized version of the Russian Bible that circulated widely throughout the empire in the decades prior to the 1917 Bolshevik Revolution. Mass distribution of this Russian Bible signaled the engagement of Russian religious culture in an emergent public sphere that required new types of commercial marketing characterized by commissions to hawkers and colporteurs and the negotiated waiver of rail shipping charges. Although the authority of the Slavonic text in liturgical worship continued to go largely unchallenged, the circulation of biblical texts in modern versions of other, non-Russian languages, including Ukrainian and Polish, reflected the increasingly complicated multinational status of the Russian Empire. Even in the Russian language, the *fin de siècle* publication of Iungerov's Russian Old Testament translations from the Septuagint and the publication of Pobedonostsev's revised New Testament translation in 1906 challenged the monopoly of the Holy Synod's authorized edition.

In this encounter of Russian religious culture with modernity, the increasingly sophisticated field of Russian biblical studies came to serve as the locus for early twentieth-century debate over Russian biblical translation. Although biblical studies (*bibliologiia*) was introduced into theological academy instruction in the early nineteenth century, its maturation as a discipline within theology followed the renewal of Russian biblical translation in the latter half of the nineteenth century. The advance of Russian biblical studies and its impact upon biblical translation were typified in the contributions of three of its leading practitioners within the theological academies of turn-of-the-century Russia – Fedor G. Eleonskii, Nikolai N. Glubokovskii, and Ivan E. Evseev. As was the case with most theological academy professors, all three rose out of the ranks of the clerical estate in the latter half of the nineteenth century. While they were unlike many of the "popovichi" who abandoned an ecclesiastical vocation, they nevertheless reflected the same secular, modern identity depicted in Laurie Manchester's *Holy Fathers, Secular Sons.*[1] The works of Eleonskii, Glubokovskii, and Evseev exemplify the sophistication of Russian biblical studies and the theological academy professoriate on the eve of the Russian Revolution.

Fedor Gerasimovich Eleonskii (1836–1906) was a graduate of the St. Petersburg Theological Academy who returned to the academy in 1870 to become professor of biblical history with a special research interest in the history of the Bible. His doctoral thesis focused on the history of the Israelites in Egypt, but his contribution to the history of Russian biblical studies and to the study of the Slavonic Bible was of equal importance.[2] Eleonskii was part of a new generation of academy professors who were well read in western, particularly German, Protestant biblical criticism. He was optimistic about the future of biblical studies in Russia, noting that Russian scholars of the Bible had the opportunity to learn from, and therefore not repeat, the mistakes of their German counterparts. Fully conversant with the work of Ferdinand Baur and the Tübingen school of biblical studies, Eleonskii shared the Tübingen school's embrace of historico-critical text study – the need to ground Christian faith and scripture in historical context – but he remained skeptical about some of the conclusions of his German counterparts, particularly as regarding the alternative authorship of many of the Pauline epistles.[3] In Eleonskii, Russian biblical studies had reached a level of sophistication that superseded the earlier polemics of the 1870s. In his study of the Elizabeth Slavonic Bible, Eleonskii called for a major scholarly reexamination of the eighteenth-century text commonly used in Russian liturgical worship.

Like Eleonskii and most other theological academy professors, Nikolai Nikanorovich Glubokovskii (1863–1937) shared the theological academy training of his counterparts, having graduated from Moscow Theological Academy in 1889. A New Testament scholar and theologian, Glubokovskii was known both for his works on the Apostle Paul and his leadership in the

[1] Laurie Manchester, *Holy Fathers, Secular Sons: Clergy, Intelligentsia, and the Modern Self in Revolutionary Russia* (DeKalb: Northern Illinois University Press, 2008),

[2] See F. G. Eleonskii, "Otechestvennye trudy po izucheniiu Biblii v XIX veke," *Khristianskoe chtenie*, 81 (1901), no. 1: 5–28 and no. 5: 633–60; *Po povodu 150-letiia Elizavetinskoi Biblii: O novom peresmotre slavianskogo perevoda Biblii* (St. Petersburg: A. P. Lopukhin, 1902); *Sledy vliianiia evreiskogo teksta i drevnikh, krome grecheskogo LXX, perevodov na drevnii slavianskii perevod knig Bytiia i Iskhoda* (St. Petersburg, 1905); and his articles "Bibliia v Rossii" and "Bibleiskie obshchestva v Rossii" in *Pravoslavnaia bogoslovskaia entsiklopediia*, ed. A. P. Lopukhin (St. Petersburg, 1901), II: 490–544 and 575–97.

[3] On the Tübingen school, see Horton Harris, *The Tübingen School: A Historical and Theological Investigation of the School of F. C. Baur* (Oxford University Press, 1975).

interconfessional ecumenical movement.[4] Commanding a western Pauline literature that tended to be divided between those who interpreted Paul as coming out of rabbinical Judaism and those who saw him as a product of the Hellenistic Judaism of the diaspora, Glubokovskii's encyclopedic work served both as a critique of this literature and as a faithful introduction to it. Glubokovskii was also among the finest pre-revolutionary scholars of New Testament Greek. He reviewed the latest critical western editions of the Greek New Testament, documenting in the process how NT Greek scholarship had advanced well beyond the earlier Erasmian Greek *textus receptus* that had been employed in the synodal translation.[5] Addressing the language of the New Testament, an issue very much in dispute following issuance of the synodal Bible, Glubokovskii noted the simplicity of the original Greek NT in contrast with the Attic Greek of the period. He wrote that the language of the original biblical text "embodied the heightened understanding of the Jewish and Christian faith in a language that provided accessibility for busy people … It didn't lose the respect of the educated public, but was still the language of everyday life."[6] Following the Bolshevik Revolution and the closure of the theological academy, Glubokovksii taught briefly at the Petrograd Theological Institute and at Petrograd University before emigrating in 1921. His later years were spent as a professor of theology at the University of Sofia in Bulgaria, where he was also honored with corresponding membership in the Bulgarian Academy of Sciences.

The advances in Russian biblical studies culminated in the pre-revolutionary period in the work of Ivan Evseevich Evseev (1868–1921), a distinguished paleographer and scholar of the Slavonic Bible.[7] Evseev graduated from St.

[4] N. N. Glubokovskii, *Lektsii po Sv. Pisaniiu Novago Zaveta* (St. Petersburg, 1906); and *O vtorom poslanii sv. Ap. Pavla k Fessalonikiitsam* (Petrograd, 1915). On Glubokovskii, see the recent study by T. A. Bogdanova, *N. N. Glubokovskii: Sud'ba khristianskogo uchenogo* (St. Petersburg, 2010).

[5] N. N. Glubokovskii, "Novosti bogoslovskoi literatury," *Khristianskoe chtenie*, 1901 (December): 988–1002. Here Glubokovskii analyzed the works of two critical western scholars of the NT Greek text: Caspar René Gregory, *Textkritik des Neuen Testaments* (Leipzig, 1900); and Eberhard Nestle, *Einführung in das Griechische Neue Testament*, 2nd edn (Gottingen, 1899). Not only does he applaud the work of Nestle and Gregory, but he decries the "primitive" stage of Russian investigations with respect to critical text study of the Slavonic Bible (1001): "It is time also for us to participate in the search for original readings of the New Testament … The book of Professor Nestle can serve as a fine guide to our helpless position, and is worthy of the serious attention of all who value not the abstract Bible, but the Word of God in its original expression." Glubokovskii's position was in striking contrast to that of subsequent uncritical Soviet-era defenders of the Erasmian *textus receptus* underlying the synodal NT.

[6] N. N. Glubokovskii, "Bibleiskii grecheskii iazyk v pisaniiakh Vetkhago i Novago Zaveta," *Trudy kievskoi dukhovnoi akademii*, 1913 (February): 216.

[7] On Evseev, see the works of his disciple, the late Konstantin Logachev, writing in *Zhurnal moskovskoi patriarkhii*: "Professor I. E. Evseev: K 50 letiiu so dnia konchiny," 1971, no. 12, "Trudy I. E. Evseeva po istorii slavianskoi Biblii," 1972, no. 8, and "Raboty prof. I. E. Evseeva po russkomu perevodu Sv.

Petersburg Theological Academy in 1893, and early in his career became preoccupied with the study of biblical translation. He ultimately occupied the St. Petersburg Academy chair of Russian and Church Slavonic languages and paleography. As Aleksandr Men' has noted in his *Bibliologicheskii slovar'*, Evseev "energetically spoke out on the reconsideration of the Russian translation of the Bible." Evseev considered the closure of the Russian Bible Society in 1826 a "deplorable historical mistake" that delayed Russian biblical translation and set back the development of Russian biblical studies. The most important future requirement for the Russian Bible, according to Evseev, was that of modernizing its language.[8]

In 1911, Evseev proposed to the Holy Synod a project to undertake the preparation of a scientific edition of the Slavonic Bible. The Synod delayed action on the recommendation, but finally in 1915 created what became the Commission for the Scientific Edition of the Slavonic Bible (Komissiia po nauchnomu izdaniiu Slavianskoi Biblii). Under Evseev's direction, the commission, which continued to function during World War I and the Russian revolutions of 1917, worked to prepare a critical scientific edition of the Slavonic Bible with variant readings. Its meetings gathered the leading biblical scholars of the day, and its proceedings, which were minuted, documented the last promising pre-revolutionary effort to advance both Slavonic and Russian biblical translation.[9] In 1918, shortly after the Russian Revolution, the commission was placed under the authority of the Academy of Sciences. Following the death of Evseev in 1921, the commission limped on until its final closure in 1929, leaving an archival legacy for future scholars of the Slavonic Bible.

These representative portraits of Fedor Eleonskii, Nikolai Glubokovskii, and Ivan Evseev document the vitality and international stature of Russian biblical studies on the eve of the First World War and the Russian Revolution. Biblical studies had become a core part of the theological academy curriculum by the twentieth century. Theological academy scholars from a range of disciplines (patristic studies, philology, paleography, ancient Greek and Hebrew studies, biblical archeology, and history) enjoyed close communication with their counterparts in western Europe, and were occupied with

Pisaniia," 1973, no. 2. For Evseev's own work, see *Ocherki po istorii slavianskogo perevoda Biblii: Cherty bytovoi istorii slavianskoi Biblii s kontsa XV do XVIII veka*, vol. II, pt. I (Petrograd: M. Merkushev, 1916) and vol. II, pt. 2, published in *Komissiia po nauchnomu izdaniiu Slavianskoi Biblii (Russkaia Bibleiskaia Komissiia), 1915–1929*, ed. K. Logachev (Leningrad State University Press, 1990), 20–78; also Evseev's *Stoletniaia godovshchina russkogo perevoda Biblii* (Petrograd, 1916) and *Sobor i Bibliia* (Petrograd, 1917).

[8] "Evseev, Ivan Evseevich (1868–1921)," in Men', *Bibliologicheskii slovar'*, I: 418.

[9] The Evseev Commission's proceedings are housed in the Archive of the Academy of Sciences in St. Petersburg. For a guide to the collection, see *Komissiia po nauchnomu izdaniiu Slavianskoi Biblii*.

reframing all of the issues of authority – the authority of texts, of translators, and of the linguistic medium – that had been central to the Bible wars of the nineteenth century. The Russian Revolution ended that inquiry, and with it Russian biblical translation in Eurasia. Renewed interest in biblical translation would not resurface in Eurasia until the recovery of religious identities associated with the late Soviet and post-Soviet era.

The hiatus in translation activity did not extend, however, to the Russian emigration. In a landmark revival of modern Russian translation, scholars associated with the St. Sergius Theological Institute in Paris, most notably the rector Bishop Kassian (Sergei Sergeevich Bezobrazov, 1892–1965), launched with the support of the British and Foreign Bible Society an original Russian New Testament translation in the years immediately following World War II. The political context for this translation was to be found in World War II Britain, where in late 1941, the BFBS "postwar planning subcommittee" met with Nicholas Zernov, a prominent figure in Russian émigré circles.[10] From the encouragement offered by Zernov, to further exploratory conversation with George Fedotov in the United States, and from the United States back to the St. Sergius Theological Institute in Paris, BFBS translations personnel found a broad interest in the emigration for renewed Russian biblical translation. As a result, BFBS began to express its interest not only in supporting a good Russian text closer to the common language, but also one that could command the political backing of all Russian church jurisdictions. In the end, it secured neither. In the process, however, there came into being the first Russian New Testament translation since the Bolshevik Revolution, a work that constituted only the second such translation (along with that published by Konstantin Pobedonostsev in 1906) since the synodal Bible.

There was caution from all sides in entering into such a project. An initial proposal made in 1946 by one of Zernov's émigré acquaintances, Yury Bezsonov, never secured BFBS support.[11] But the later involvement of Paul Anderson, a prominent American Russianist attached to the Paris YMCA, advanced the process significantly by linking Bible Society interests with Russian religious émigré circles in Paris. Anderson inquired of Father

[10] On the conversation with Zernov, see BFBS Minutes of the Postwar Planning Special Subcommittee, October 23, 1941, in BFBS Editorial Correspondence, Russian, file 2 (BSA/E3/3); also Batalden, "Revolution and Emigration," 156–61.

[11] The Bezsonov correspondence with the BFBS (1946–9) includes an unpleasant exchange in *The Times* following the BFBS abandonment of the project. See BFBS Editorial Correspondence, Russian, file 2 (BSA/E3/3). Bezsonov's escape from the USSR and conversion to Christianity can be followed in his popular interwar books, *Dvadtsat' shest' tiurem i pobeg s Solovkov* (Paris: Impr. de Navarre, 1928; London: J. Cape, 1929) and *Partiia sil'nykh* (Paris: Les Éditeurs Réunis, 1942).

Georges Florovsky and representatives of the Paris Institute, reporting back to the American Bible Society general secretary, Eric North, in the spring of 1950 that "they [the St. Sergius Institute colleagues] all quite agree that a new translation is desirable."[12] Not to be outdone by its American counterpart, the BFBS soon sent its translations secretary to Paris to meet all the interested parties. These meetings, held in September 1950, yielded approval for the new translation. BFBS translations secretary Wilford J. Bradnock returned to London prepared to have the British and Foreign Bible Society underwrite the enterprise, even though the Moscow Patriarch's western European representative, Archimandrite Ieremin, had already withdrawn from the project on instructions from Moscow. Despite this, the project was broadened at Bradnock's suggestion to constitute a completely new translation, not a mere "russification" to remove archaisms in the 1862 synodal New Testament.[13]

During Bradnock's Paris visit he had met with a committee from the St. Sergius Theological Institute headed by its rector and professor of New Testament studies, Bishop Kassian. From that meeting Bradnock came away confident that there was suitable expertise to undertake the project. Bishop Kassian would be the chief translator from the Greek, and a committee of as wide an interconfessional cross-section as possible would review and revise Kassian's Russian text. Work began with the Gospel of Matthew under the expectation that a New Testament would be completed within two or three years. The BFBS agreed to pay Bishop Kassian's salary for two and a half years of released time, and it allotted substantial support for secretarial services and travel costs for Bishop Kassian and the other revision committee members. Donald Lowrie, the replacement for Paul Anderson at the Russian YMCA Press, attended and took minutes of the sessions of the revision committee as a local representative in Paris for the BFBS.[14]

12 Copy of Anderson to North, April 4, 1950, BFBS Editorial Correspondence, Russian, file 3 (BSA/E3/3).

13 W. J. Bradnock, "To the Members of the [BFBS] Translations and Library Subcommittee," October 2, 1951, BFBS Editorial Correspondence, Russian, file 3 (BSA/E3/3).

14 Lowrie to Bradnock, Paris, January 26, 1951, and Bradnock to Lowrie, London, January 29, 1951, BFBS Editorial Correspondence, Russian, file 3 (BSA/E3/3). On the Russian YMCA Press, see Matthew L. Miller, "A Hunger for Books: The American YMCA Press and Russian Readers," *Religion, State, and Society*, 38, no. 1 (March 2010): 53–75. Lowrie and Anderson were significant interpreters of the Russian church and the Russian religious émigré community for a western audience. See Donald Lowrie, *St. Sergius in Paris: The Orthodox Theological Institute* (New York: Macmillan, 1951) and *The Light of Russia: An Introduction to the Russian Church* (Prague: YMCA Press, 1923); also Paul B. Anderson, *People, Church, and State in Modern Russia* (New York: Hyperion Press, 1980).

Bishop Kassian (Bezobrazov) had graduated from Petrograd University in 1914, teaching briefly in the History Faculty of Petrograd University in 1917 before leaving for Central Asia where he joined the Faculty of Religious History at the newly formed Turkestan University in Tashkent. Returning to Petrograd in 1922, he served briefly as a professor of church history at Petrograd Theological Institute before emigrating to Yugoslavia where he taught in the Russian Serbian School (Russko-Serbskaia Shkola), 1922–4. Following his move to Paris, he became one of the founders of the St. Sergius Theological Institute and was appointed to its chair of New Testament studies in 1925. In 1932, Kassian was tonsured into a monastic vocation, assuming along with several of the St. Sergius professors a position within the jurisdiction of the Ecumenical Patriarchate, rather than within either of the two competing Russian Orthodox communities – the western European diocese of the Moscow Patriarchate or the Munich-based Russian Orthodox Church Abroad. Elevated to the status of bishop by the Ecumenical Patriarch of Constantinople, Kassian spent much of World War II on Mount Athos. A popular teacher among the St. Sergius students, Bishop Kassian was a specialist on the Gospel of John, a Gospel that had served as the basis for his doctoral thesis.[15]

The selection of Bishop Kassian to lead the translation effort ultimately undermined BFBS interests in the creation of an easily readable translation, for Bishop Kassian was slavishly committed to a literal translation of the Greek text. Kassian's commitment to the Greek text extended to his belief, occasionally followed in practice, that it was possible to replicate the original Greek word order in the Russian text, as in his Russian rendering of the Gospel of John.[16] No one on the St. Sergius revision committee was fully able to counteract this Russian linguistic usage problem. BFBS translations secretary Bradnock, who deferred to Lowrie and his successor Robbins Strong in the meeting-to-meeting details, did not know Russian. Even though Bradnock soon grasped the nature of the problem and sought to give greater authority to an internal literary panel led by Boris Zaitzeff and Wladimir Weidle, Bishop Kassian's archaic use of Russian and his fixation on Greek word order were never entirely overcome. It proved to be the single greatest liability of the text. Anthony Bloom, the Moscow Patriarchate's

[15] On Kassian, see "Kassian (Sergei Sergeevich Bezobrazov, 1892–1965)," in Men', *Bibliologicheskii slovar'*, II: 35–7.

[16] See the revision committee minutes in BFBS Editorial Correspondence, Russian files, beginning with 1951 (BSA/E3/3). For the Gospel of John, see the copy of Kassian's notes in BFBS microfilms: "Russian, NT Notes of Bishop Kassian," 2 rolls, 1957–8.

esteemed Bishop of Sourozh in Britain, responded to a request for his evaluation of the initial text of the Gospel of Matthew, writing to the BFBS:

> Everyone is deeply disappointed by this translation and is convinced that it would have been better not to publish it . . . badly needed is a translation which would bring to conscience and heart all the richness of the Greek text, the many-sided shades of the Greek words. It is impossible to achieve this with the usual method – translation of each word by one single word. This impoverishes the text.[17]

Despite the problematic use of Russian in Bishop Kassian's literalism, there were several interesting elements in this BFBS Russian émigré project, including its roster of participants, the textology employed in the translation, and the actual production of what came to be referred to as the "Kassian New Testament." Although the Moscow Patriarchate officially withdrew from the project, and the Munich-based Russian church-in-exile showed little interest in the effort, the translation project commanded broad interest among the Russian religious émigré intelligentsia. The revision committee roster at the St. Sergius Theological Institute read as a "who's who" of first-wave Russian émigré religious leaders. The special ties of Constantinople Ecumenical Patriarch Athenagoras with the St. Sergius Institute and with Bishop Kassian personally were evidenced in a letter of blessing that he sent to the project.[18] Many other clerical and lay leaders attached themselves to the project as corresponding members. Alongside Bishop Kassian, the revision committee included at one time or another the following scholars: Wladimir Weidle, N. A. Koulomzin, Boris Zaitzeff, Vladimir Lossky, Vladimir Rayevsky, Anton Kartasheff, John Meyendorff, Dimitri Obolensky, Alexei Kniazeff, Ilia Melia, and A. P. Wassilieff (the committee's only Protestant member).[19] When word reached Russian evangelical circles of the new translation project, appeals came to the BFBS for adequate Protestant representation in the preparation of the new text. Pastor A. P. Wassilieff, a leading Russian Protestant and Bible school superintendent in Brussels, was quickly added to the committee.[20]

The Protestant issue was not unrelated to a subsequent crisis that threatened to abort the whole project, namely the conflict over capitalization of

[17] Rev. Anthony Bloom to BFBS, London, November 27, 1953, BFBS Editorial Correspondence, Russian, file 5 (BSA/E3/3).

[18] Copy of Patriarch Athenagoras to Bishop Kassian, Constantinople, April 24, 1951, BFBS Editorial Correspondence, Russian, file 3 (BSA/E3/3).

[19] For the complete list of members, see Lowrie to Bradnock, Paris, February 22, 1951, BFBS Editorial Correspondence, Russian, file 3 (BSA/E3/3).

[20] On the organized appeal of Russian evangelicals and Wassilieff's inclusion on the revision committee, see ibid.

pronominal references to Mary, the mother of Jesus. While seemingly a matter of splitting hairs, the issue of pronominal Marian references (e.g. она, её, ея) had earlier arisen in the pre-revolutionary circulation of the 1862 Synod New Testament.[21] Most Orthodox members of the St. Sergius Institute revision committee were adamant in their insistence upon capitalization of all Marian references, claiming that in a day when Soviet authorities were seeking to denigrate religious belief by using lower case references even to "god," failure to capitalize pronominal references to Mary would be interpreted as caving in to Soviet disbelievers. Wassilieff, on the other hand, was equally adamant in his claim that to capitalize such Marian references was to capitulate to Roman Catholic Mariology. Ultimately unable to resolve their differences, the BFBS was forced to issue two variants of a "trial edition" (*probnyi vypusk*) of the Gospel of Matthew. The capitalized version was issued with red lettering on the paperback cover and a small notation on the title page verso, "u. c. edition." The non-capitalized version was issued with orange lettering on the paperback cover and a small notation on the title page verso, "l. c. edition."[22] The two differently colored editions of the Gospel of Matthew came to be called in London "the tentative Matthew."

In contrast to the problems over literal translation and pronominal Marian references, the textology of the Kassian NT proved to be its greatest contribution to New Testament text study, influencing both Soviet and post-Soviet scholarship. Bishop Kassian was conversant with the latest Greek textological scholarship and used as the basis for his translation a revised critical Greek text compiled by Eberhard Nestle.[23] The Nestle critical edition reflected variant readings from more than two thousand extant fragments of the Greek New Testament. By contrast, the synodal NT had been based on an adapted Erasmian Greek New Testament, the *textus receptus*, that drew upon a mere half-dozen Greek texts available to the sixteenth-century humanist, Desiderius Erasmus of Rotterdam. Beginning in 1954, faculty members from the Moscow and Leningrad theological academies wrote extended articles in the official *Journal of the Moscow Patriarchate* reviewing the "tentative Matthew," defending in the process

[21] From 1882 (Appendix, no. 150), the Holy Synod began to introduce occasional capitalization of pronominal references to the Virgin Mary in its NT editions, notably in the inexpensive octavo "people's edition" (e.g. Appendix, no. 191). The Synod had no clear precedent for handling pronominal Marian references, because the traditional Slavonic text was typically printed with a Slavonic font that made no distinction between upper- and lower-case letters.

[22] On the issue of pronominal Marian references, see BFBS Editorial Correspondence, Russian, file 3 (BSA/E3/3). For these trial editions of the Gospel of Matthew, see Appendix, no. 291.

[23] The 1945 Nestle edition was used – *Novum Testamentum graece, cum apparatus critico*, ed. Eberhard Nestle and Erwin Nestle, 17th edn (Stuttgart: Württembergische Bibelanstalt, 1945).

the nineteenth-century synodal translation and its use of the *textus receptus.*[24] As if to give greater force to its challenge to the translation efforts under way in Paris, the Moscow Patriarchate issued a new printing of the synodal Bible in 1956, one of the relatively few reprintings of the *sinodal'nyi perevod* in the Soviet period.[25] The defensiveness of Soviet scholars in the revived theological academies of post-World War II Moscow and Leningrad included the curious claim that the Erasmian text was somehow more "Orthodox" than later critical Greek NT scholarship. This intense interest in the émigré translation of the St. Sergius Institute nevertheless showed how attentive Soviet scholars were to the Russian emigration. The published responses in the *Journal of the Moscow Patriarchate* also documented the degree to which Russian biblical studies in Moscow and Leningrad had deteriorated during the intervening years, since the generation of Eleonskii, Glubokovskii, Evseev, and their pre-revolutionary academy peers.

In July 1955, a delegation of visiting Soviet churchmen was fêted at the BFBS London offices, at which time Bradnock gave the Leningrad Theological Academy rector (the future Metropolitan Nikodim [Boris Georgievich Rotov] of Leningrad) and the Archbishop of Minsk copies of Kassian's notes offering Greek textual justifications for the departures from the *sinodal'nyi perevod.* Later, in response to the interest expressed by Bishop Nikodim, a more complete set of Kassian's notes was prepared in a microfilm edition that was hand-delivered to Bishop Nikodim during his 1960 visit to Paris.[26] The same Bishop Nikodim, later Metropolitan

[24] The opposition campaign waged in the pages of *Zhurnal moskovskoi patriarkhii* included articles by I. Alekseev, "K voprosu o novom perevode na russkii iazyk *Evangeliia ot Matfeia,*" 1954, no. 2: 76–7; A. Osipov, "K izdaniiu russkoi Biblii," 1955, no. 8: 58–66, and "Ob odnom novom zagranichnom izdanii russkoi Biblii," 1955, no. 10: 48–53; A. I. Ivanov: "K voprosu o vosstanovlenii pervonachal'nogo grecheskogo teksta Novogo Zaveta," 1954, no. 3: 38–50, "Novyi perevod na russkii iazyk *Evangeliia ot Matfeia,*" 1954, no. 4: 45–5 and no. 5: 38–47, "Novoe izdanie grecheskogo Novogo Zaveta [a review of the 1952 edition of the Nestle critical Greek NT]," 1954, no. 12: 69, "Novoe kriticheskoe izdanie grecheskogo teksta Novogo Zaveta," 1956, no. 3: 49–58, no. 4: 49–58, and no. 5: 43–52. These articles consistently referred to the Erasmian *textus receptus* as the appropriate "Orthodox" text of the Greek NT. One of the more curious contributions to the campaign against the new translation effort was a short piece submitted by a contributor claiming to be a leader of an Old Believer community – I. Vakon'ia, "Bestsennoe bogatstvo russkikh perevodov Slova Bozhiia i tserkovnoi literatury," 1955, no. 6: 65–7. The authenticity of Vakon'ia's Old Believer sympathies may be subject to question in light of his defense of the synodal translation, writing as he did that "the love and sympathy of Old Believers must be completely on the side of the traditional Russian translation prepared for us by the Russian Orthodox Church."

[25] *Bibliia, ili Knigi Sviashchennogo Pisaniia Vetkhogo i Novogo Zaveta* (Appendix, no. 203 [1956]). Like earlier reprintings, the 1956 Bible perpetuated the practice of footnoted variant OT Septuagint readings.

[26] On the 1955 visit, see Bradnock to Wilkinson, London, November 4, 1955, BFBS Editorial Correspondence, Russian, file 9 (BSA/E3/3). The 1960 transmission is confirmed in Anderson to Bradnock, Paris, December 21, 1960, ibid.

of Leningrad, launched in the 1960s a Russian Biblical Commission at the Leningrad Theological Academy, a commission that survived into the 1990s, when under the leadership of Konstantin I. Logachev, it became the Northwest Bible Commission (Severo-zapadnaia bibleiskaia komissiia), loosely affiliated with the Philological Faculty of St. Petersburg University.[27] The late Russian biblical scholar and churchman Aleksandr Men' continued this interest in the Kassian translation, even using modified citations from the Kassian NT in his *Syn chelovecheskii*.[28]

Intended for speedy completion during a two- to three-year period, the project faced interminable delays over disputed passages, with Bishop Kassian and the Paris revision committee working on the project continuously from 1951 onward, even carrying the translation to its completion after the tragic death of Bishop Kassian in 1965. To advance the translation Kassian would retire to his seaside hideaway in Javea, Spain, for periods of concentrated work on the project. His death, which happened when a rip current pulled him out to sea during one of his daily swimming exercises, came after he had completed the translation of the New Testament, but before the revision committee had managed to complete its review of the final books, from the Epistle to the Galatians through the book of Revelation.[29] Following committee revision, the BFBS published the text in separate installments – the trial edition of Matthew (1953), an edition of the Gospels (1958), the Gospels with the Acts of the Apostles (1963), and the complete NT (1970).[30] The rather hostile reception accorded the "tentative Matthew" tended to limit BFBS publishing interest. That loss of interest, coupled with the delays in the work of the revision committee, meant that publication of the entire Russian New Testament did not follow until 1970, five years after Bishop Kassian's death.

27 See K. Logachev, "Khristianskoe Sviashchennoe Pisanie v Rossii," in *Bibliia i vozrozhdenie dukhovnoi kul'tury russkogo i drugikh slavianskikh narodov: K 80-letiiu Russkoi/Severo-Zapadnoi Bibleiskoi Komissii (1915–1995)*, ed. P. Dmitriev *et al.* (St. Petersburg: Petropolis, 1995), 114–26; also Stephen Batalden, "The Contemporary Politics of the Russian Bible: Religious Publication in a Period of Glasnost," in *Seeking God*, 232–43.

28 Aleksandr Men', *Syn chelovecheskii* (Moscow: Slovo Publishers, 1991). Writing of the Kassian work, Men' notes, "this translation, unfortunately, is far from perfect, but its advantage lies in the fact that the achievements of modern textual criticism are taken into account. In citing certain of the Savior's utterances in this translation, the text is arranged in accordance with the rules of sacred Biblical poetry" (222).

29 To speed his translating Kassian took residence at the Javea seaside resort community from whence his occasional correspondence to BFBS translations secretary Bradnock is dated. Upon completion of the draft translation from the Greek, Kassian became involved as an observer at the Vatican Council. His failing health meant that committee revisions from the Epistle to the Galatians onward were done without the translator.

30 For the complete NT, see *Novyi Zavet Gospoda Nashego Iisusa Khrista* (London: BFBS, 1970) – Appendix, no. 312.

The Kassian Russian New Testament demonstrated the degree to which the Bible wars of the nineteenth century continued to cast their shadow over twentieth-century Russian religious culture. In this case, the conflicts were not only about language and textology, but also reflected the new divisions of the Soviet era. Since World War II, when Stalin's overture to the Russian church (in return for patriotic support of the war effort) led to the reopening of theological academies in Moscow and Leningrad, there was renewed state authorization for carefully controlled theological training. But the price of this officially sanctioned higher religious education was to be seen in the artificially induced conflict between the spokesmen of the Moscow Patriarchate and the Russian religious émigré community. Bishop Kassian and the members of the St. Sergius Theological Institute revision committee were the heirs of pre-revolutionary scholarship in Russian biblical studies – the followers of Eleonskii, Glubokovskii, and Evseev. In rejecting the Kassian New Testament, contributors to the *Journal of the Moscow Patriarchate* were not only commenting on the debilitating literalism and advanced textology of the Paris/BFBS project, but they were also reflecting the underlying uneasiness of official church authorities in the Soviet Union toward the Russian religious diaspora.

While there continue to be significant internal battles over authority within post-Soviet religious institutions, the recovery of pre-revolutionary Russian scholarship in biblical studies, marked symbolically by the publication of Aleksandr Men's posthumous *Dictionary of Biblical Studies* (*Bibliologicheskii slovar'*, 3 vols., Moscow, 2002), demonstrates how far-reaching is the cultural transformation under way in post-Soviet society.

The Bible wars of nineteenth-century Russia were fought over fundamental issues of authority – the authority of source texts, the authority of the linguistic medium, and the authority of translators, publishers, and purveyors. The defenders of modern Russian biblical translation – Archpriest Gerasim Pavskii, Archimandrite Makarii (Glukharev), Metropolitan Filaret (Drozdov), local and international Bible societies, and a generation of late nineteenth-century academic scholars – were invariably those most attuned to international scholarship in the field of biblical studies. The opponents – from Archimandrite Fotii in the era of the Russian Bible Society to Kievan Metropolitan Filaret (Amfiteatrov) in the era of the Great Reforms, to the Soviet-era opponents of the Kassian New Testament – sought to protect the purity of a set of traditions they identified exclusively with the Slavonic Bible. In the arbitration of that conflict, there was an early and ultimately abortive effort to let the marketplace determine the outcome of the Bible wars – leading to the rapid outpouring of modern biblical translations in multiple languages and in unprecedented circulation runs facilitated by the RBS stereotype press in the decade after the Napoleonic wars. Following the RBS closure in 1826, arbitration of the Bible wars fell to the Holy Synod and a Russian church hierarchy that encouraged Emperor Nicholas I's prohibition of all translation and publication of modern Russian scripture. In the era of the Great Reforms, under the leadership of Moscow Metropolitan Filaret, there was the resumption of Russian biblical translation, yielding in installments from 1860 to 1875 a complete, authorized churchly translation of the Bible, the *sinodal'nyi perevod.* That translation, although it was undertaken by scholars of the theological academies, was advanced under the authority of the Russian Orthodox Church.

While publication of the synodal translation constituted a landmark in the history of modern Russian religious culture, it did little to resolve the fundamental questions of authority that divided modern Russian religious culture and drove the Bible wars of the nineteenth century. The churchly language of the nineteenth-century translations continued to be at odds with the evolving post-Pushkin Russian literary language. Indeed, even the exclusive use of the Slavonic text in liturgical worship would be challenged in the twentieth century, especially from within the ranks of the renovationist movement.[31] Moreover, the source bases for the synodal translation continued to be challenged, not only in the case of the Old Testament for which use of the Hebrew Masoretic text remained controversial, but also in the case of the New Testament for which an antiquated Erasmian Greek *textus receptus* had been employed alongside use of the Slavonic text. In marketing the new synodal text, the church pivotally yielded some of its hegemonial authority in return for increased profit from sales, in the process granting to Bible societies, their colporteurs and hawkers, wide latitude and significant precedent for the open marketing of Holy Scripture.

Despite the church leadership of Metropolitan Filaret Drozdov and, after his death, that of St. Petersburg Metropolitan Isidor (Nikol'skii), arbitration of the Bible wars, especially following the issuance of the synodal translation, moved increasingly from the church hierarchy to the theological academies where scholars trained in modern biblical text criticism assumed a new secular authority over biblical scholarship. The Holy Synod's 1915 creation of a Commission for the Scientific Edition of the Slavonic Bible

[31] See Edward E. Roslof, *Red Priests: Renovationism, Russian Orthodoxy, and Revolution, 1905–1946* (Bloomington: Indiana University Press, 2002); and Mikhail V. Shkarovskii, *Obnovlencheskoe dvizhenie v Russkoi Pravoslavnoi Tserkvi XX veka* (St. Petersburg: "NESTOR," 1999).

(Komissiia po nauchnomu izdaniiu Slavianskoi Biblii) effectively symbolized the transfer of the church's authority to arbitrate the debate over biblical translation to a commission of professional theological academy scholars. The new commission, while it was by no means still-born, was nevertheless soon undermined by the Bolshevik Revolution and the ensuing closure of the theological academies. As a result, by the end of World War II, the momentum for Russian biblical translation shifted temporarily to the emigration and to a group of émigré scholars at St. Sergius Theological Institute who were both the heirs to the Bible wars of the nineteenth century and students of prerevolutionary Russian biblical scholarship in the theological academies.

The Bible wars of the nineteenth century reflected the engagement of Russian religious culture with what Charles Taylor has termed "a secular age." In the concern for public accessibility to sacred texts and in the commercial marketing of Holy Scripture, the advocates of Russian biblical translation – Russian archpriests, monks, church hierarchs, academy professors, and agents of international Bible societies – sought to mobilize the religious culture for a modern marketplace, the public sphere. In the process they not only produced the *sinodal'nyi perevod*, but they also created the foundation for Russian biblical studies and, not coincidentally, provided a powerful scholarly refutation to the charge of blood libel. In opposing Russian biblical translation, some churchmen – the fundamentalists of their day – became the advocates of the inviolability or purity of the Slavonic text, while others believed the use of Hebrew in Russian translation conflicted with churchly tradition, and yet others objected to the popular marketing of sacred texts, especially if it advanced sectarian interests. The Bible wars that ensued challenged the traditional hierarchical arbiters of religious authority in Russia, laying the groundwork for modern Russian biblical studies.

The politicization of modern scriptural translation also reflected the state's remarkable exercise of authority in modern Russian religious culture. Thus the original Russian Bible Society, 1812–26, was closed by imperial decree. Following a thirty-year period of clandestine translation, official translation of the Russian Bible was reopened only with the blessing of Emperor Alexander II. The effort by state authorities to control the publication and distribution of the Russian Bible became far more pronounced in the Soviet era, even though some renovationist church circles sought to introduce the Russian Bible into Orthodox liturgical worship.

Today, in the "post-atheist" Russian state, although significant conflict over religious language in liturgical worship continues, the Russian Bible wars have largely abated. In 2011, following a generation of relatively tranquil post-Soviet scholarly biblical translation and revision – a period nevertheless punctuated by the violent 1990 assassination of a leading Russian biblical scholar, Aleksandr Men' – the post-Soviet Russian Bible Society issued a new edition of the Russian Bible, the first complete biblical text since the synodal translation of the 1870s.[32] One of the predictable ironies of this conclusion to the Russian Bible wars is that the reception of this latest biblical text is now perhaps just as likely to be determined by the purchasing preferences of a newly emerging Russian marketplace as by the efforts of religious or political elites to impose their authority over modern Russian religious culture.

[32] *Bibliia: Sovremennyi russkii perevod* (Moscow: Rossiiskoe bibleiskoe obshchestvo, 2011), 1408pp. The lead NT translator, Valentina Nikolaevna Kuznetsova, a classical philology graduate of Moscow State University, worked with an editorial commission created in the 1980s at the initiative of the late Aleksandr Men'. The OT, parts of which began to be issued from 1999, was translated from the Hebrew by a team of scholars who divided the responsibility for the translation of individual books. Separate complete editions of the OT have been produced for those wishing the inclusion/exclusion of deuterocanonical books. The primary difference between the new Russian Bible Society translation and the nineteenth-century synodal translation is the elimination of archaisms and phrases unclearly translated from the Hebrew and Greek original.

APPENDIX

Annotated bibliography of the Russian Bible, 1794–1991

The only previously published bibliography of Russian biblical imprints is found within the standard multivolume work of T. H. Darlow and H. F. Moule, *Historical Catalogue of the Printed Editions of Holy Scripture*, 2 vols. in 4 (London, 1903–11), hereafter abbreviated DM. It includes a short descriptive list (vol. II, 1299–1351) of the "Great Russian" biblical imprints located in the library of the British and Foreign Bible Society (BFBS). Even though the DM entries do not include the actual Russian titles and most often lack annotations, it is a useful starting point for a bibliography of the Russian Bible. Subsequent BFBS librarians have added new Russian entries, particularly those imprints after 1911, in an unpublished working catalogue in the BFBS Library now housed within the Cambridge University Library in the UK. There has been no other systematic bibliography of Russian biblical imprints.

While there are multiple reprintings not included in this annotated bibliography owing to the limited holdings of Russian library collections consulted in its preparation, the goal of the bibliography has been to identify and analyze all major editions of Russian scripture. "Edition" is used here to mean an original translation or format, as opposed to the multiple subsequent reprintings of individual texts. In addition to the inclusion of all major Russian published editions of scripture, all available reprintings of these editions have been cited, along with information on their print runs. Thus the bibliography clarifies issues raised in this volume about the circulation of modern Russian scripture.

The richest repository of Russian scripture outside the Russian Federation is the BFBS Library. The locations registered below reveal that BFBS holdings often exceed those of the Russian National Library in St. Petersburg (RNB), the major Russian collection used for this bibliography. Because the BFBS Library was used in compiling the bibliography, there may be some exaggeration of the role played by the BFBS in the publication and dissemination of Russian scripture in both the nineteenth and twentieth centuries. Still, the significant role of the BFBS in Russian biblical publication has been poorly understood, and the annotations for each item seek to provide a balanced perspective regarding western-sponsored and more exclusively Russian synodal or Patriarchal printings of Old Testament (OT) and New Testament (NT) texts. Annotations include references to BFBS archival records that document circulation runs and other publication information.

Entries are listed chronologically through 1991, the end of the Soviet period. Title and imprint information is accompanied by a description of the collation and physical size of each volume in centimeters. The annotations that follow address translatorship, format, comparisons with other printings of the same edition, circulation run if available, and other information of interest concerning the entry. Each entry closes with a reference to known location ("Loc") in a library consulted in compiling the bibliography. Almost all entries have been viewed by the author, but a few bibliographical entries are provided by date in the case of *non de visu* imprints. In such cases, the entry is usually unnumbered and placed within brackets [ ]. In addition to the Bible Society Library within the Cambridge University Library, listings are provided for items in the RNB, the Oxford University Bodleian Library (OX), the British Library (BL), and the Cambridge University Library (CUL).

1. 1794. NEW TESTAMENT. EPISTLE TO THE ROMANS

Къ римлянамъ посланіе святаго апостола Павла.
Moscow: Synodal Press, 1794.
Title, preface, VIII; text, 136pp.

Translation by Archimandrite Mefodii (Mikhail Alekseevich Smirnov, 1761–1815), later archbishop of Pskov, accompanied by a commentary on the epistle. The volume was reissued in 1799 and 1814. On Mefodii Smirnov, see the entry in the *Russkii biograficheskii slovar'*. See also, *Сводный каталог русской книги гражданской печати XVIII века* (Moscow, 1964), vol. II, 240.
Loc: *Non de visu.*

2. 1818. PSALTER

Псалтирь въ стихахъ съ приложеніемъ при каждомъ псалмѣ содержащагося въ немъ историческаго, таинственнаго или нравственнаго смысла.
St. Petersburg: Imperial Foundling Home Press, 1818.

Title, censor's permit [2]; preface, IV; Part I half-title, verso blank [2]; Part I text (Psalms 1–75), 1–246; Part II half-title, verso blank [2]; Part II text (Psalms 76–151), 3–255.
21.5 × 13.

A free Russian translation in metrical verse by Gavriil Pakatskii, parish priest of Sts. Konstantin and Helen Church in St. Petersburg. A historical introduction inserted before each Psalm, and explanatory footnotes are added. The 151st Psalm is included, and the numbering of Psalms follows the Septuagint numbering system. Text is in one column on the page without numbering of verses. Preface includes translator's expression of appreciation for the support of Count Dmitrii N. Sheremet'ev.
Loc: BL (3434.e.47)

3. 1819. NEW TESTAMENT. SLAVONIC/RUSSIAN GOSPELS DIGLOT

Господа Нашего Іисуса Христа Святое Евангеліе отъ Матфея, Марка, Луки и Іоанна, на славянскомъ и русскомъ нарѣчіи.
St. Petersburg: Printed at the Press of Nikolai Grech for the RBS, 1819.
Title, verso blank [2]; preface ("K khristoliubivym chitateliam"), iii–vii; imprimatur [2]; text, 402.
24.5 × 14.5.

First Russian edition of the Gospels printed with the Slavonic. Russian and Slavonic texts are in parallel columns on the page with paragraph indention of verses. Archimandrite Filaret (St. Filaret [Drozdov], 1782–1867), then rector of the St. Petersburg Theological Academy, oversaw preparation of the translation for the Holy Synod's Commission on Ecclesiastical Schools. He contributed the translation of the Gospel of John. Gerasim P. Pavskii (1787–1863), Hebrew instructor at the St. Petersburg Theological Academy and archpriest at Kazan Cathedral in St. Petersburg, translated the Gospel of Matthew; Archimandrite Polikarp Gaitannikov, inspector of the St. Petersburg Theological Academy, translated the Gospel of Mark; and Archimandrite Moisei Bogdanov-Platonov, rector of the Kiev Theological Academy, translated the Gospel of Luke. The preface is signed by Mikhail, Metropolitan of Novgorod and St. Petersburg; Serafim, Metropolitan of Moscow and Kolomna; and Filaret, Archbishop of Tver and Kashin. The preface is dated March 30, 1819, and includes the imperial decree of February 23, 1816 authorizing RBS publication of the NT in Russian. Printed in 5,000 copies (see letter of John Paterson, November 8, 1818, *Monthly Extracts*, no. 20: 78; Chistovich offers no documentation for his claim of 10,000 copies [I. A. Chistovich, *Istoriia perevoda Biblii na russkii iazyk*,

2nd edn (St. Petersburg, 1899), 30]). A price of "7r" (7 rubles) is marked on the title page of the BFBS copy.
Loc: BFBS

4. 1819. NEW TESTAMENT. SLAVONIC/RUSSIAN GOSPELS DIGLOT

Господа Нашего Iисуса Христа Святое Евангелiе отъ Матфея, Марка, Луки и Iоанна, на славянскомъ и русскомъ нарѣчiи.
St. Petersburg: Printed at the Press of Nikolai Grech for the RBS, 1819.
24.5 × 14.5.

Reprinting of no. 3 identified on the title page as the "second edition." Despite minor typesetting changes, pagination is identical to the first printing. Last page is incorrectly numbered 363. This printing circulated in 10,000 copies (see John Paterson, letter of April 30, 1819, in *Monthly Extracts*, no. 26: 27). Price of 10 rubles is on title page of BFBS copy.
Loc: BFBS

5. 1820. NEW TESTAMENT. SLAVONIC/RUSSIAN GOSPELS AND ACTS DIGLOT

Господа Нашего Iисуса Христа Святое Евангелiе отъ Матфея, Марка, Луки и Iоанна и Деянiя Святыхъ Апостоловъ, на славянскомъ и русскомъ нарѣчiи.
St. Petersburg: Printed at the Press of Nikolai Grech for the RBS, 1820.
Title, verso blank [2]; preface, III–VII; imprimatur in Slavonic [2]; text, 523pp.
23.5 × 14.5.

First edition of the Acts of the Apostles in Slavonic and Russian with reprinting of the Gospels diglot (no. 3 above). Translation done under the supervision of the Commission on Ecclesiastical Schools. Title page identifies this as the third edition of the Gospels. Pagination for the Gospels identical with nos. 3 and 4 above. The text of Acts, in Slavonic and Russian parallel columns, follows the Gospels with continuous pagination (403–523) and paragraph indention of verses. Preface and imprimatur are identical with nos. 3 and 4. Price of 3 rubles, 50 kopecks is on the title page of BFBS copy.
Loc: BFBS; CUL (8100.c.1095)

6. 1820. NEW TESTAMENT. GOSPELS, ACTS OF THE APOSTLES, AND TEN EPISTLES IN SLAVONIC/RUSSIAN DIGLOT

Господа Нашего Іисуса Христа Святое Евангеліе отъ Матфея, Марка, Луки и Іоанна и Деянія Святыхъ Апостоловъ, на славянскомъ и русскомъ нарѣчіи.
St. Petersburg: Printed at the Press of Nikolai Grech for the RBS, 1820.
Title, imprimatur [2]; preface, III–VII; text, 703pp.
23.5 × 14.5.

First edition of the Catholic or general epistles (James; 1 and 2 Peter; 1, 2, and 3 John; and Jude), Romans, and 1 and 2 Corinthians in Slavonic and Russian is accompanied by a reprinting of the Gospels and Acts of the Apostles (see no. 5 above). The ordering of the general epistles before the Pauline epistles follows the practice employed in the Slavonic NT. The title page identifies this as the "fourth edition" (i.e. fourth printing) of the Gospels and the "second edition" (i.e. second printing) of the Acts of the Apostles. The pagination for the Gospels and Acts is identical with nos. 3, 4, and 5 above. The ten epistles follow in consecutive pagination (524–703). Price of 4 rubles is marked on title page of BFBS copy.
Loc: BFBS

7. 1821 [1822]. NEW TESTAMENT IN SLAVONIC AND RUSSIAN

Господа Нашего Іисуса Христа Новый Завѣтъ, на славянскомъ и рускомъ языкѣ.
St. Petersburg: RBS, 1821 [1822].
Title, table of contents verso [2]; preface, III–VI; imprimatur in Slavonic, verso blank [2]; text, 820pp.
[27 × 16].

First Russian edition of the complete NT and the first Russian edition printed at the press of the RBS. The text is in two parallel columns on each page, Russian and Slavonic. Preface and imprimatur are identical to those used in earlier printings, but the table of contents backing the title page is new. The text of the Gospels, Acts of the Apostles and first ten epistles is taken from no. 6 above. This edition contains the first Russian translations of the Epistles to the Galatians, Ephesians, 1 and 2 Thessalonians, 1 and 2 Timothy, Titus, Philemon and Hebrews, as well as the book of Revelation. This circulated in 5,000 copies (see Robert Pinkerton letter, February 20,

1822, *Monthly Extracts*, no. 57: 109). According to Pinkerton, it was bound for Alexander I in December 1821, but open circulation did not occur until 1822. Collation based upon entry no. 8 below.
Loc: *Non de visu.*

8. 1822. NEW TESTAMENT IN SLAVONIC AND RUSSIAN. 27 × 16

Господа Нашего Іисуса Христа Новый Завѣтъ, на славянскомъ и рускомъ языкѣ.
St. Petersburg: RBS, 1822.

A second printing of no. 7. The collation, format, and text are identical. Printed in 20,000 copies (see Robert Pinkerton letter, January 28, 1822, in *Monthly Extracts*, no. 57: 107). The BFBS copy contains pre-cut irregular-sized pages in a binding of later date.
Loc: BFBS; BL (2 copies: 842.k.8 and 3042.dd.3); OX (N.T.Russ.d.2)

9. 1822. NEW TESTAMENT IN SLAVONIC AND RUSSIAN 24.5 × 14.5

Господа Нашего Іисуса Христа Новый Завѣтъ, на славянскомъ и рускомъ языкѣ.
St. Petersburg: RBS, 1822.

A third printing of no. 7. The sequence of matter before the text is altered (title, logotype of RBS verso [2]; preface, III–VI; imprimatur [1]; table of contents [1]; text). Title page includes printed price of "four rubles bound," in Russian. There are two variant printings of this third impression. They are identical until p. 640, at which point the signatures change, with the number of lines per column after p. 652 becoming greater in one variant. By the end of the text, one variant has 818 pages of text, the other 820 pages.
Loc: BFBS (both variants); BL (three copies of 818-page variant: 1004.k.5, 3061.d.11, and 3061.e.5); CUL (two copies of 818-page variant: 1.40.21 and 1.40.22); OX (818-page variant: N.T.Russ.d.1); and personal copy (818-page variant)

10. 1822. NEW TESTAMENT IN SLAVONIC AND RUSSIAN

Господа Нашего Іисуса Христа Новый Завѣтъ, на славянскомъ и рускомъ языкѣ.
St. Petersburg: RBS, 1822.

Fourth printing of no. 7. This reprinting on different paper is the same as the 818-page variant of no. 9 above. Title page includes printed price of 4 rubles.
Loc: BFBS

11. 1822. PSALTER

Книга Хваленій или Псалтирь на россійскомъ языкѣ.
St. Petersburg: Printed at the Press of Nikolai Grech [for the RBS], 1822.
Title, verso blank [2]; preface, I–XI; verso blank [1]; text, 195pp.
19 × 11.5.

First Russian edition (along with no. 12) of the Psalter, issued without parallel Slavonic text. Translation was done by Gerasim Petrovich Pavskii. Undated preface signed by Serafim, Metropolitan of Novgorod and St. Petersburg; Filaret, Archbishop of Moscow; and Simeon, Archbishop of Iaroslav. Preface explains how the translation drew from both the Greek Septuagint, the basis for the Slavonic Psalter, and the Hebrew "original." Examples are provided of cases in which the translation from the Hebrew was given precedence. Although included in all subsequent RBS printings of the Russian Psalter, the 151st Psalm was omitted in this first edition. The RBS supported the use of the Hebrew text alongside the Septuagint in translations of the OT. Septuagint numbering of the Psalms was retained in RBS editions of the Russian Psalter. Verses are numbered and indented. This first edition circulated in 15,000 copies (see Pinkerton letter, January 28, 1822, in *Monthly Extracts*, no. 57: 108). More than 100,000 copies of the Russian Psalter circulated before the closure of the RBS in 1826 (see nos. 12–18 and 22).
Loc: BFBS

12. 1822. PSALTER

Книга Хваленій или Псалтирь на россійскомъ языкѣ.
Moscow: Printed at the Synodal Press for the RBS, Moscow Section, 1822.
Title, verso blank [2]; preface, I–XI; text, 249pp.
18.5 × 11.5.

Like no. 11, this printing of the Russian Psalter is identified on the title page as the "first edition." The preface is identical with no. 11. This Moscow printing does not include the indention of each verse, and verse numbers are rather inserted in exterior margins. The Moscow edition includes the 151st Psalm. BFBS copy lacks page 249.
Loc: BFBS; BL (3089.d.9)

13. 1822. PSALTER

Книга Хваленiй или Псалтирь на россiйскомъ языкѣ.
St. Petersburg: RBS, 1822.
Title, RBS logotype [2]; preface, I–IX; text, 172pp.
19 × 12.

Third printing of the Russian Psalter, incorporating corrections introduced by Gerasim Pavskii, and the 151st Psalm. The text is in one column on the page with paragraph indention of each verse. This third printing was the first issued from the RBS's own press. Price of 1 ruble, 50 kopecks is printed on the title page. The two CUL copies bear the signatures of their owners: "Nikolai Aleksandrovich Sablukov, 13 Avgusta 1822" and "John Koitnitsky, London, February 10, 1840." The Koitnitsky copy includes on the inside back cover the Russian imprint of the RBS's British binder, "E. Renni, perepletchik" [i.e. Ebenezer Rennie, binder].
Loc: CUL (2 copies: 8100.d.2649 and 8100.d.2796)

14. 1822. PSALTER

Книга Хваленiй или Псалтирь на россiйскомъ языкѣ.
St. Petersburg: RBS, 1822.
19 × 11.5.

Identified on title page as the "fifth edition," this is a stereotype reprinting of the Russian Psalter identical with no. 13. Price of 1 ruble, 50 kopecks is printed on title page.
Loc: BFBS

15. 1822. PSALTER

Книга Хваленiй или Псалтирь на россiйскомъ языкѣ.
St. Petersburg: RBS, 1822.
20 × 11.5.

A stereotype reprinting of nos. 13 and 14 identified on the title page as the sixth edition. Some copies include a price of 1 ruble on title page. The 151st Psalm was included, but the Oxford copy has a piece of paper glued over the 151st Psalm so that it cannot be seen.
Loc: BFBS; BL (1016.g.2); OX (Ps.Russ.e.1)

16. 1822. PSALTER

Книга Хваленій или Псалтирь на россійскомъ языкѣ.
St. Petersburg: RBS, 1822.
19 × 12.

Seventh stereotype reprinting of the RBS Psalter. Collation, format, and text are identical to nos. 13–15 above. Price of 1 ruble is printed on title page.
Loc: OX (Ps.Russ.e.3)

17. 1823. PSALTER

Книга Хваленій или Псалтирь на россійскомъ языкѣ.
St. Petersburg: RBS, 1823.
19 × 11.5.

A stereotype eleventh reprinting uniform with nos. 13–16.
Loc: BFBS

18. 1823. PSALTER

Книга Хваленій или Псалтирь на россійскомъ языкѣ.
St. Petersburg: RBS, 1823.
19 × 12.

A twelfth stereotype reprinting of the RBS Psalter, uniform in title, pagination and format with nos. 13–17. Price of 1 ruble is printed on title page. The BL copy has a blank page glued over page 172 to obliterate the 151st Psalm. The OX copy has removed the blank page, revealing Psalm 151. Copies of the Psalter sent to London appear to have been routinely altered by the BFBS to omit/cover the 151st Psalm not found in the Hebrew canon.
Loc: BL (3089.c.25); OX (Ps.Russ.e.1)

19. 1823. NEW TESTAMENT IN SLAVONIC AND RUSSIAN

Господа Нашего Іисуса Христа Новый Завѣтъ, на славянскомъ и рускомъ языкѣ.
St. Petersburg: RBS, 1823.
23 × 14.5.

A sixth stereotype reprinting of the Russian NT diglot uniform with the fourth printing (no. 10). Price of 4 rubles is printed on title page.
Loc: BFBS

20. 1823. NEW TESTAMENT

Господа Нашего Іисуса Христа Новый Завѣтъ.
St. Petersburg: RBS, 1823.
Title, verso blank [2]; imprimatur [2]; first preface, v–x; second preface, xi–xiv; table of contents, verso blank [2]; text, 620pp.
20 × 11.5.

First edition of the NT issued in Russian only without parallel Slavonic text. The title page contains the RBS logotype. Title page includes blank space for pricing ("Bound value is ___rub., ___kop."). Imprimatur is in Russian, not Slavonic. A new second preface dated October 25, 1823 is signed by Serafim, Metropolitan of Novgorod and St. Petersburg; Filaret, Archbishop of Moscow and Kolomna; and Iona, Archbishop of Tver and Kashin. Second preface indicates that publication of the NT without the Slavonic text is for easier use and so that it could be sold more cheaply. The second preface responds to charges arising over differences in the Slavonic and Russian texts. Using an example from Luke 9:23, the signatories show how differences in the Russian can be accounted for by the need to be true to the Greek original. Text is printed in one column on the page in paragraphs with verse numbering in outside margins.
Loc: BFBS; BL (1003.e.20); CUL (F182.d.14.2); OX (N.T. Russ.e.1)

21. 1823. NEW TESTAMENT

Господа Нашего Іисуса Христа Новый Завѣтъ.
St. Petersburg: RBS, 1823.
19.5 × 12.

Second stereotype reprinting of the NT in Russian only, uniform in collation, text, and format with no. 20. Title page includes price of 2 rubles, 25 kopecks.
Loc: CUL (8100.d.2795)

22. 1824. PSALTER

Книга Хваленій или Псалтирь на россійскомъ языкѣ.
St. Petersburg: RBS, 1824.

Title, logotype of RBS verso [2]; preface, i–ix; text, 284pp.
19 × 11.

A new printing of the Russian Psalter using larger typeface. Preface and text are identical to earlier printings. Title page identifies this as the

thirteenth edition. The two BFBS copies are bound differently. One has a printed price of 1 ruble, 25 kopecks on the title page. The other, with finer binding, has a printed price of 1 ruble, 75 kopecks.
Loc: BFBS (two copies)

23. [1824–5.] OLD TESTAMENT. GENESIS–RUTH

[*Библія. Восьмикнижіе.*]
[St. Petersburg: RBS, 1824–5.]
Text, 424pp.
23.5 × 14.5.

First Russian edition of the Octateuch – the Pentateuch, plus Joshua, Judges, and Ruth – overseen by the RBS translations committee, with original translation from Hebrew into Russian by Archpriest Gerasim Pavskii. The text includes bracketed passages translated from the Septuagint, a practice continued in subsequent Russian OT editions. The edition was printed in sheets, but never published. Separately bound copies later surfaced. The spine of one BFBS copy carries the title bracketed above. The volumes lack a title page and other prefatory matter. Printed in 1824–5, the text remained unbound in 10,000 copies at the time of the 1826 RBS closure. Circulation remained forbidden in Russian in the 1850s (see Ellerby to Knolleke, May 25, 1850, BFBS Foreign Correspondence Inwards, 1850, no. 1, 257). For London reprintings of the Octateuch, see nos. 48 and 50.
Loc: BFBS (two copies); RNB (18.98.3.10)

24. 1838. NEW TESTAMENT

Господа Нашего Іисуса Христа Новый Завѣтъ.
Leipzig: Karl Tauchnitz Press, 1838.
Title, verso blank [2]; table of contents, verso blank [2]; text, 620pp.
8.5 × 11.5.

New 12mo printing of the Russian NT text of the RBS. Title page includes the logotype of the old RBS and a note in Russian that the "edition is made exactly according to the legal edition published by the RBS in St. Petersburg in 1823" (no. 20). The text is in paragraphs with verse numbering in the margins. BFBS agent Robert Pinkerton arranged for publication in 2,000 copies, purchasing 1,000 of them for Bible Society distribution, and keeping BFBS identification secret (see Pinkerton to Jackson, February 21, 1839, BFBS Foreign Correspondence Inwards, 1839, no. 1, 119). See nos. 31 and 33 for reprintings. This is the first publication of Russian scripture

outside the Russian Empire, reflecting BFBS frustration over the publication ban on Russian scripture imposed by Emperor Nicholas I.
Loc: BFBS; BL (3061. cc. 5); OX (N. T. Russ. e. 2)

25. 1838–41. OLD TESTAMENT. JOB. PROVERBS, ECCLESIASTES, SONG OF SONGS, AND THE MAJOR AND MINOR PROPHETS

[*Книги священнаго писанія ветхаго завѣта*]
[Lithographed by St. Petersburg Theological Academy students in three printings: 1838–41]

Gerasim Pavskii's Russian translation from the Hebrew of the poetic and prophetic books of the OT (exclusive of the Psalter that had been published by the RBS). Petersburg Theological Academy students compiled the translation from lecture notes of their Hebrew course taken under Pavskii's tutelage. The translations were lithographically reproduced by academy students in three separate printings. Academy students were authorized to lithograph lecture notes, thus making the printings technically legal at a time when translation and publication of the Bible in Russian were otherwise forbidden. In all, 490 copies were lithographed in three separate printings, 1838–41. The lithographed text is in handwritten script, normally in a single column on the page. The leaves are thicker than normal printed pages, with text on only one side of the leaf. Pagination varies in the three lithographings, some leaves being without pagination. The work is variously bound, occasionally excluding one or more books. The five RNB copies all constitute differing compilations. The only complete set of the five is RNB no. 18.173.3.8. For an account of this translation and the "Pavskii affair," see Chapter 3 and S. K. Batalden, "Gerasim Pavskii's Clandestine Old Testament: The Politics of Nineteenth-Century Russian Biblical Translation," *Church History*, 57, no. 4 (December 1988): 486–98.
Loc: RNB (five copies: 18.173.3.8; 18.296.1.11–19; V.P. 7256; V.P. 7257; and V.P. 7258)

26. 1840. NEW TESTAMENT. GOSPEL OF MATTHEW IN ALEUT/RUSSIAN DIGLOT

Господа Нашего Іисуса Христа Евангеліе, написанное Апостоломъ Матфеемъ. [Half-title: *Евангеліе отъ Матфея на алеутско-лисьевскомъ и русскомъ языкахъ.*]
Moscow: Synodal Press, 1840.

Half-title, verso blank [2]; imprimatur [1]; Aleut/Russian titles on facing pages, verso blank [3]; first preface, I–V; second preface, VI–XIV; text, 247pp; verso blank [1]; appendix 1 (Gospel of St. John in Aleut, 1:1–17; 20:24, 30–1; and 21:25) [3]; appendix 2 [4–21].
26.5 ×17.

A diglot Gospel of St. Matthew in Russian and Aleut. The Russian text is taken from the RBS edition. Title page indicates that the translation was done from Russian to "Aleut-Lis'ev" (i.e. Aleut-Fox) by Ioann Veniaminov (later Metropolitan Innokentii of Moscow) in 1828, and was corrected in 1836. It also notes that Iakov Netsvetov added the clarifying notes at the bottom of the text for the Aleut residents of Atkha. The first preface is written by Father Ioann Veniaminov, dated Novo-Arkhangel'sk, August 26, 1838. Veniaminov notes that the translation was initially done in 1828 with the assistance of Ivan Pan'kov. Subsequently, Petr Burenin also examined the text and assisted Veniaminov in its correction. In a second preface, Netsvetov notes that the translation of Veniaminov follows the same prelate's earlier translation into Aleut of the Catechism. For both the Catechism and this Gospel Netsvetov indicates that he has added variant Atkha readings because of the differences in Unalashkan and Atkhan Aleut. In contrast to the text of Matthew, an appendix containing passages from the Gospel of St. Luke and the Acts of the Apostles is, according to Netsvetov's note, in Atkhan Aleut with alternative Unalashkan readings footnoted. The translator of the passages in the appendix is Iakov Netsvetov. The Aleut is in Cyrillic script. This rare Aleut/Russian diglot constituted a unique exception to the ban on Russian biblical publication in the reign of Nicholas I.
Loc: BFBS; BL (3068. f. 29)

27. 1843. READINGS FROM THE GOSPELS AND ACTS OF THE APOSTLES

Чтенія изъ четырехъ евангелистовъ и изъ книги деяній апостольскихъ для употребленія въ училищахъ.
St. Petersburg: Imperial Academy of Sciences Press for the Department of Public Instruction, 1843.
Title, verso blank [2]; preface [2]; text, 188pp.
20.5 × 13.

Selected readings from the Gospels and Acts of the Apostles grouped by topic heading, such as "The birth of Jesus Christ." The readings were intended for use in schools. The scripture extracts were compiled in St. Petersburg in 1819 from the French by William Swan, William Allen, Walter Venning, John Venning, Stephen Grellet, John Paterson, and Jean

Paterson. After the headings were fixed and the French texts pasted underneath, the project was given over to Archimandrite Filaret (Drozdov) for Russian translation. The Russian extracts were then published with Emperor Alexander I's financial support (see Paterson, *The Book for Every Land*, 1857, 309–12). Even though the RBS Russian Gospels would have been available to Filaret in 1819, the text of these extracts does not always follow the RBS Gospels. Parts of the translation were probably rendered directly from the French, as also in nos. 28–30 below. The BFBS copy includes the note on the title page, "tenth printing," confirming that these NT readers for school children escaped the official ban on the publication of biblical texts in modern Russian during Nicholas I's reign. The price of 23 silver kopecks is printed on the title page. Because of the non-scriptural text headings, the BFBS agency committee later forbade distribution of the volume within the Petersburg agency despite the fact that the book had earlier been compiled with the assistance of the Bible Society's own representatives (see BFBS Minutes of Committee, vol. 36, June 19, 1848, 212–13).
Loc: BFBS

28. 1845. READINGS FROM THE OLD TESTAMENT

Историческія чтенія изъ книгъ ветхаго завѣта. Для употребленія въ училищахъ.
St. Petersburg: Imperial Academy of Sciences for the Department of Public Instruction, 1845.
Title, verso blank [2]; text, 133pp.
20.5 × 14.

Selected "historical readings from the books of the Old Testament" in Russian translation "for use in schools." A companion volume to no. 27 compiled in the same manner. Included are selections from Genesis, Exodus, Joshua, Judges, 1 and 2 Kings, Daniel, 1 Esdras and, as a supplement, a NT selection from the book of Hebrews referring to the OT. The Russian text is not from the RBS Octateuch (no. 23), rather being a separate translation from the French as in no. 27. Price of 17 silver kopecks is printed on title page.
Loc: BFBS

29. 1849. READINGS FROM THE GOSPELS AND THE ACTS OF THE APOSTLES

Чтенія изъ четырехъ евангелистовъ и изъ книги деяній апостольскихъ для употребленія въ училищахъ.

St. Petersburg: Department of Public Instruction at the Press of the Academy of Sciences, 1849.
Title, publication authorization [2]; preface [2]; text, 188pp.
21 × 14.

Eleventh reprinting of no. 27. The title page verso contains the note that "the right to publish this book belongs to the Department of Public Instruction." Typsetting differences confirm that the multiple printings of these readers were not stereotyped. Page 17 of this eleventh printing is transposed "71."
Loc: BFBS

30. 1849. READINGS FROM THE OLD TESTAMENT

Историческія чтенія изъ книгъ ветхаго завѣта. Для употребленія въ училищахъ.
St. Petersburg: Published by the Department of Public Instruction at the Press of the Academy of Sciences, 1849.
20.5 × 13.5.

Reprinting of no. 28. Pagination and text are the same.
Loc: BFBS

31. 1850. NEW TESTAMENT

Господа Нашего Iисуса Христа Новый Завѣтъ.
Leipzig: Karl Tauchnitz Press [for BFBS], 1850.
Title, verso blank [2]; table of contents, verso blank [2]; text, 620pp.
22 × 13.5.

Second stereotype reprinting of no. 24. The collation and format are identical with the 1838 printing, but the BL copy has wider margins. One thousand copies were printed for the BFBS (see BFBS Minutes of Committee, vol. 38, June 3, 1850, 193–4).
Loc: BL (3035.aa.16); OX (N.T.Russ.e.3)

32. 1852. PSALTER

[*Псалтирь или Книга Хваленій на россійскомъ языкѣ.*]
[Leipzig: Karl Tauchnitz Press for BFBS, 1852.]

A rare edition of the RBS Psalter reprinted outside Russia. Having received funding to prepare stereotype plates of the Russian NT and

Psalms (see entry no. 33 for Hubbard donation), the BFBS editorial subcommittee commissioned Ebenezer Henderson to ready the RBS Psalter for republication, eliminating the headings, notes, preface, and Psalm 151. A new title page was also prepared, and the text was submitted to the Tauchnitz Press for printing. See BFBS Editorial Subcommittee Minutes, vol. 4, August 13, 1851, 38; and January 27, 1852, 53–4. This RBS Psalter as revised by Henderson was published in an edition of 1,000 copies (see Pinkerton to Browne, May 28, 1852, BFBS Foreign Correspondence Inwards, 1852). The title page purposely avoided mention of BFBS involvement in this western reprinting of the RBS Psalter. The stereotype plates were sent to London following publication. See no. 34 for a stereotype reprinting.
Loc: *non de visu*

33. 1854. NEW TESTAMENT

Господа Нашего Іисуса Христа Новый Завѣтъ.
London: [W. M. Watts for BFBS], 1854.
18.5 × 11.

Stereotype reprinting of no. 24. Except for the title page, the reprinting is identical to the Leipzig 1838 edition. In January 1851, an offer was made to BFBS by William E. Hubbard to fund a stereotype edition of the Russian Bible in whole or in part for inexpensive distribution at one shilling per copy for circulation among Russian prisoners during the Crimean War. Using the Hubbard donation, the BFBS purchased from Karl Tauchnitz the stereotype plates used in the 1838 and 1850 Leipzig printings (see BFBS Minutes of the Printing and Depository Subcommittee (PDSC), vol. 4, February 3, 1851, 154). This BFBS 1854 printing was executed by W. M. Watts in 5,000 copies (see BFBS DPSC Minutes, vol. 5, February 27, 1854, 17) using the Tauchnitz plates. A further run of 10,000 copies was printed in 1854 to permit continued free distribution to Russian prisoners of war (see BFBS DPSC Minutes, vol. 5, October 9, 1854, 42–3).
Loc: BFBS

34. 1854. PSALTER

Псалтирь или Книга Хваленій на россійскомъ языкѣ.
London: [W. M. Watts for BFBS], 1854.
Title, verso blank [2]; text, 155pp.
18 × 11.

Stereotype reprinting of no. 32 from plates cast by the Tauchnitz Press in Leipzig. Five thousand copies were published in 1854 (see BFBS DPSC Minutes, vol. 5, October 30, 1854, 44). BFBS copy is bound with no. 33.
Loc: BFBS

35. 1855. PSALTER

Псалтирь или Книга Хваленій на россійскомъ языкѣ.
London: [W. M. Watts Press for BFBS], 1855.
18 × 11.

Stereotype reprinting uniform with nos. 32 and 34.
Loc: OX (Ps.Russ.e.4)

36. 1855. NEW TESTAMENT

Господа Нашего Іисуса Христа Новый Завѣтъ.
London: [W. M. Watts for BFBS], 1855.
18.5 × 11.

Stereotype reprinting of no. 33. At least 10,000 copies were printed in 1855 (see the annual "Editions of the Scriptures" in *The Fifty-First Report of the BFBS*, 53, and *The Fifty-Second Report of the BFBS*, 57).
Loc: BFBS

37. 1858. NEW TESTAMENT

Господа Нашего Іисуса Христа Новый Завѣтъ.
London: Printed by W. M. Watts [for the BFBS], 1858.
Title, printer's imprint [2]; table of contents, verso blank [2]; text, 601pp.
14.5 × 9.

A new small 24mo edition of the RBS NT with smaller font, and verse numbering in the left-hand margins. Edward Stallybrass, former London Missionary Society missionary to Siberia, corrected and proofread the text, which was intended to conform to the earlier Leipzig and London stereotype edition (see Stallybrass to Phillips, December 17 and 24, 1857, BFBS Miscellaneous Editorial Correspondence, File B, 1851–60). According to the "Editions of Scriptures" section of *The Report of the BFBS* for 1858 and 1859, 5,000 copies were printed. BFBS has two copies, one of which is marked with corrections by W. L. [Lee]. The edition was severely criticized for its

proofreading errors, including occasional use of the Cyrillic "*B*" (pronounced "V") in rendering the word for God (thus "Vog," instead of "Bog").
Loc: BFBS

38. 1858. OLD TESTAMENT. SONG OF SOLOMON

Пѣсни Пѣсней Царя Соломона.
London: [Printed for Prince L. L. Bonaparte], 1858.
Title, verso blank [2]; text, 5–22.
14 × 11.

A free translation of the Song of Solomon into Russian. The translator is not identified. DM indicates a press run of 250 copies. BL copy is bound with translations of the Song of Solomon done for Prince Louis Bonaparte into other languages, 1859–62.
Loc: BFBS (three copies); BL (3022.aa.14.4)

39. 1859. OLD TESTAMENT. JOB

Іовъ: Свободное подражение священной книгѣ Іова.
St. Petersburg: Korolev and Co. Press, 1859.
Title, censor's permit [2]; dedication, verso blank [2]; translator's preface, iii–viii; half-title, verso blank [2]; Job text, 171pp; translator's poem, 172–3.
25 × 17.

A free translation of the book of Job by F. Glinka with dedication to the translator's wife. A preface identifies notable readings of the book of Job, including a reading at the death of Markos Botsaris in Greece and readings in Jewish communities of the Russian Empire. The "epilog" is the translator's own poem. The text of Job, centered in one column on the page, is in metrical verse by chapter without verse numbering.
Loc: BL (11586.h.7.[3.])

40. 1860. OLD TESTAMENT. PENTATEUCH

Библія. Священное Писаніе Ветхаго и Новаго Завѣта переведенное съ еврейскаго независимо отъ вставокъ въ подлинникѣ и отъ его измѣненій, находящихся въ греческомъ и славянскомъ переводахъ. Ветхій Завѣтъ. Отдѣлъ первый заключающій въ себѣ Законъ или Пятикнижіе.
London: Trubner and Co., 1860.

Title, copyright notice and printer imprint [i–ii]; preface, iii–xiv; list of the OT books, verso blank [2]; text of Genesis, 1–81; verso blank [82]; Exodus

half-title, verso blank [2]; Exodus title, printer imprint verso [2]; Exodus text, 83–149; verso blank [150]; Leviticus and Numbers half-title, verso blank [2]; Leviticus and Numbers title, printer imprint verso [2]; Leviticus text, 151–201; verso blank [202]; Numbers text, 203–72; Deuteronomy title, printer imprint verso [2]; translator statement, verso blank [2]; Deuteronomy half-title, verso blank [2]; Deuteronomy text, 273–335.
22 × 13.5.
A free Russian translation from Hebrew by "Vadim" (i.e. Vasilii I. Kel'siev, see no. 42 below). The preface to the volume indicates the translator's desire to follow with greater accuracy the use of names and related vocabulary of the Hebrew original. Kel'siev, an itinerant émigré attached to Alexander Herzen in London, introduced the Roman letter "J" into his Russian script. He credits the work of Dr. Abraham Benisch, whose *Jewish School and Family Bible* (2nd edn, London, 1852) he considers the most accurate rendering of the Hebrew original. The translator further notes that he has not utilized the Pavskii text, which was unavailable. But he criticizes the Pavskii text for using Septuagint readings alongside the Hebrew text.
Loc: BL (3061.cc.19)

41. 1860. OLD TESTAMENT. JOB

Книга Iова въ русскомъ переводѣ съ краткимъ объясненiемъ.
Viatka: K. Blinov Press, 1860.
Title, imprimatur [2]; preface, 1–19; text with notes, 22–319.
26.5 × 17.

A Russian translation from the Hebrew by Ieromonakh Agafangel (Aleksei Fedorovich Solov'ev, 1812–76). Before assuming the position of rector of Kazan Theological Academy, Agafangel was among those drawn into the Pavskii affair. Agafangel's preface comments on the inferior quality of previous translations from the Greek Septuagint. Occasionally, in footnoted commentary, a translation from the Septuagint is added (see, for example, the note on Job 1:21, p. 27). The preface claims that the Slavonic text of Job follows more closely the Hebrew original than the Septuagint. A second printing of this volume was issued in 1861 in Viatka at the same press (see no. 46). DM mistakenly identifies this translation as the work of Mikhail Spiridonovich Guliaev, a professor at Kiev Theological Academy who participated in the preparation of the Holy Synod's Russian OT prior to his death in 1866.
Loc: BFBS; BL (3062.bb.1)

42. 1860. PSALTER

Псалтирь или Книга Хваленій на россійскомъ языкѣ.
London: Printed by W. M. Watts for BFBS, 1860.
Title, printer's imprint [2]; text, 149pp.
14 × 10.

A small 24mo edition of the Russian Psalter uniform in size and format with the BFBS 1858 NT (no. 37). The text is taken from the original RBS Psalter. Edward Stallybrass was retained to see the text through the press. A Russian émigré associate of Alexander Herzen then in London, Vasilii Ivanovich Kel'siev, was appointed on the recommendation of Herzen to collaborate in the proofreading (see BFBS Editorial Subcommittee Minutes, vol. 6, December 7, 1859, 65–6). The appointment of a paid Russian assistant to Stallybrass was, in part, a response to the criticism registered over the quality of Stallybrass's work on the 1858 NT (no. 37). Neither Stallybrass nor the BFBS appears to have been aware that Kel'siev was the pseudonymous "Vadim," translator of the controversial Russian Pentateuch published in 1860 in London (no. 40 above). Kel'siev's BFBS employment provided the destitute émigré a modest income (BFBS Ledger no. 4 [April 1855 – March 1865], 93, 201, records cash payments to Kel'siev and Stallybrass of 160 pounds sterling). It also alerted Kel'siev to the renewal of OT translation in Russia. As a consequence, Kel'siev abandoned his ambitious project to complete a Russian translation of the Hebrew Bible for which his Pentateuch (no. 40) was to have been "part one." During the course of the preparation of this 1860 Psalter for press, Stallybrass complained to the BFBS that Kel'siev was altering punctuation, introducing too many exclamation marks, and modernizing unnecessarily the Russian orthography (see Stallybrass to Meller, December 16, 1859, BFBS Miscellaneous Editorial Correspondence, File B, 1851–60). Some, if not all, of Kel'siev's changes were sustained, for this small-size Psalter introduces punctuation and orthographical changes not present in earlier western reprintings cast by Tauchnitz in Leipzig (for example, no. 32). Five thousand copies of the Psalter were printed (see BFBS DPSC Minutes, vol. 6, October 10, 1859, 67). This 1860 edition was reprinted in 1862 (no. 53).
Loc: BFBS

43. 1860. NEW TESTAMENT. GOSPELS

Господа Нашего Іисуса Христа Святое Евангеліе отъ Матфея, Марка, Луки и Іоанна на русскомъ нарѣчіи.

St. Petersburg: Synodal Press, 1860.
Title, synodal blessing verso [2]; text, 224pp.
22.5 × 15.

First edition of the Holy Synod's Gospels in Russian. The Russian text follows closely, but is distinct from, the RBS edition first published in 1819. This is the first portion of the Bible issued by the Holy Synod after its decision to recommence modern Russian biblical translation in 1856. The text is in two columns on the page with each verse constituting a new paragraph. In a practice commonly employed in subsequent printings of the NT in octavo, each page of text is placed within a rectangular border (17.5 × 11) with uniform engravings at the corners. Andrew Muir, the BFBS representative in Petersburg, reported that this first edition of the Synod's Russian Gospels was issued in 36,000 copies (see BFBS Editorial Subcommittee Minutes, vol. 6, July 18, 1860, 113–14).
Loc: BFBS

44. 1860. NEW TESTAMENT. GOSPELS AND ACTS IN SLAVONIC AND RUSSIAN

Господа Нашего Іисуса Христа Святое Евангеліе отъ Матфея, Марка, Луки и Іоанна и Деянія Святыхъ Апостоловъ, на славянскомъ и русскомъ нарѣчіи.
St. Petersburg: Synodal Press, 1860.
Half-title, verso blank [2]; title, synodal blessing verso [2]; text, 1–476.
22.5 × 15.

A "second edition" (i.e. second printing) of the Gospels and Acts of the Apostles in a Slavonic/Russian diglot employing the 1860 synodal Russian text. The first edition of this diglot, also dated 1860, is not represented in the library collections used for this bibliography. The Slavonic and Russian texts are alongside each other in two separate columns on the page within a rectangular border. The format of this octavo synodal diglot was followed in multiple reprintings of the later nineteenth and early twentieth centuries.
Loc: BL (3061.cc.18)

[1860. OLD TESTAMENT. JEREMIAH AND LAMENTATIONS. A translation by Archimandrite Makarii (Glukharev), published posthumously in *Pravoslavnoe obozrenie.* For full entry to the publication of Archimandrite Makarii's translations, see no. 57 (1863).]

45. 1861. NEW TESTAMENT. GOSPELS AND ACTS

Господа Нашего Iисуса Христа Святое Евангелiе отъ Матфея, Марка, Луки и Iоанна и Деянiя Святыхъ Апостоловъ.
St. Petersburg: Synodal Press, 1861.
22 × 14.5.

A reprinting of no. 43 with identical title, collation and text. Title page indicates this is the fourth printing.
Loc: BFBS; BL (03025.ff.26)

46. 1861. OLD TESTAMENT. JOB

Книга Iова въ русскомъ переводѣ съ краткимъ объясненiемъ.
Viatka: K. Blinov Press, 1861.
26.5 × 17.

A reprinting of no. 41.
Loc: BFBS

47. 1861. OLD TESTAMENT. JOB

Книга Iова (Опытъ переложенiя на русскiй языкъ.)
Moscow: Katkov and Co. Press, 1861.
Half-title, verso blank [2]; title, censor's permit verso [2]; text, 5–102pp.
23.5 × 15.5.

A translation of the book of Job from the Hebrew by the Altai missionary St. Makarii (Archimandrite Makarii [Mikhail Iakovlevich Glukharev, 1792–1847]). This posthumous publication is an offprint from *Pravoslavnoe obozrenie*, 1861, no. 5. The text is divided by chapters with internal verse numbering and occasional brief footnotes. Makarii's text follows closely the Hebrew original unlike the freer translation of Ieromonakh Agafangel (nos. 41 and 46 above).
Loc: BFBS

48. 1861. OLD TESTAMENT. GENESIS–RUTH

Библiя. Восемь книгъ ветхаго завѣта. Пятикнижiе Моисеево, Иiсусъ Навинъ, Судьи и Руфь.
London: Printed by W. M. Watts for BFBS, 1861.
Title, verso blank [2]; text, 653pp; printer's imprint verso [654].
13.5 × 9.5.

A small 24mo edition of the Octateuch, formatted in conformity with the BFBS 1858 NT (no. 37) and the 1860 Psalter (no. 42). The text is from the RBS translation (no. 23). As in the case of the 1860 Psalter, Stallybrass and the Russian émigré V. I. Kel'siev (see notation under no. 42) saw the edition through the press. Ironically, in retaining Kel'siev, the BFBS was employing the pseudonymous "Vadim" whose rival free translation of the Pentateuch (no. 40, London, 1860) specifically sought to discredit this Russian translation from the Hebrew. Five thousand copies were printed (see BFBS DPSC Minutes, vol. 6, October 10, 1859, 67), and the edition was reprinted in 1862 (no. 50).
Loc: BFBS; BL; CUL; OX

[1861. OLD TESTAMENT. EZEKIEL, DANIEL, AND HOSEA–MALACHI. Archimandrite Makarii Glukharev's translations from the Hebrew published in 1861 in *Pravoslavnoe obozrenie*. For the full entry to the posthumous publication of Archimandrite Makarii's translations, see no. 57.]

[1861. OLD TESTAMENT. GENESIS–RUTH, ECCLESIASTES. D. A. Khvol'son's translations of Genesis–Ruth and Ecclesiastes were first serialized in *Khristianskoe chtenie* in 1861. See the full entry under no. 73. This translation, which follows closely the 1824–5 RBS text of the Octateuch, served as the basis for the Holy Synod's authorized OT.]

49. 1862. NEW TESTAMENT. ACTS–REVELATION

Деянія и Посланія Святыхъ Апостоловъ съ Апокалипсисомъ на русскомъ нарѣчіи.
St. Petersburg: Synodal Press, 1862.
Title, synodal blessing [2]; text, 276pp.
22.5 × 15.

The Holy Synod's first edition of Acts–Revelation, marking the completion of the synodal translation of the NT. The format – text in double columns within a rectangular border – is identical to the Synod's 1860 Gospels (see no. 43). The BFBS copy cited here is bound with no. 45, a fourth printing of the synodal Gospels, to constitute a complete NT.
Loc: BFBS

50. 1862. OLD TESTAMENT. OCTATEUCH (GENESIS – RUTH)

Библія. Восемь книгъ ветхаго завѣта. Пятикнижіе Моисеево, Іисусъ Навинъ, Судьи и Руфь.

London: [William Clowes and Sons for BFBS], 1862.
14.5 × 9.

A stereotype reprinting of no. 48. Ten thousand copies were printed (see BFBS DPSC Minutes, vol. 7, May 26, 1862, 11).
Loc: BFBS

51. 1862. NEW TESTAMENT AND PSALTER

Господа Нашего Iисуса Христа Новый Завѣтъ
[and]
Псалтирь или Книга Хваленiй на россiйскомъ языкѣ.
London: [W. M. Watts for BFBS], 1862.
18.5 × 11.

A reprinting of the Leipzig/London octavo NT (see nos. 24, 31, and 33) and the Leipzig/London octavo Psalter (see nos. 32, 34, and 35) bound together in 5,000 copies (see BFBS DPSC Minutes, vol. 6, February 10, 1862, 192). Text, collations and titles are uniform with previous printings. There is no general title page. A separate title page for the Psalter follows the NT. This reprinting was undertaken while BFBS revision of the NT was also under way (see no. 52 below) because the BFBS supply of Russian NTs was exhausted.
Loc: BFBS (one NT and Psalter bound together; one copy of Psalter alone)

52. 1862. NEW TESTAMENT

Господа Нашего Iисуса Христа Новый Завѣтъ.
London: W. Clowes and Sons [for BFBS], 1862.
Title, printer's imprint [2]; table of contents, verso blank [2]; text, 595pp.
14.5 × 9.

A small 24mo BFBS edition of the Russian NT. Although the title page identifies this as an edition "done exactly according to the edition printed by the RBS in St. Petersburg in 1823," this pocket-size NT is a product of the editing and correcting done by Edward Stallybrass and V. I. Kel'siev. While Kel'siev and Stallybrass were readying this revised NT for publication, using the 1823 RBS edition, the Holy Synod issued its first edition of the Gospels in St. Petersburg, 1860 (no. 43). Following a favorable review of the Synod text by BFBS representatives in Petersburg and London, it was decided to use the 1860 Synod Gospels rather than the RBS Gospels. Thus, this BFBS

1862 NT constitutes a combination of the 1860 Synod text for the Gospels and the 1820 RBS text for Acts–Revelation. Proofreading and corrections were handled by Kel'siev under the supervision of Stallybrass. BFBS, "Editions of the Scriptures" (see *The Report of the BFBS* for 1861 and 1863) shows an increase in the number of Russian NTs issued by the society between March 30, 1861 (22,339) and March 30, 1863 (43,139), a reflection of the circulation run of this 24mo edition.
Loc: BFBS

53. 1862. PSALTER

Псалтирь или Книга Хвалений на россійскомъ языкѣ.
London: W. Clowes and Sons [for BFBS], 1862.
Title, verso blank [2]; text, 149pp.
14.5 × 9.

A stereotype reprinting of no. 42. Printer is identified on p. 149.
Loc: BFBS

54. 1862. OLD TESTAMENT. PENTATEUCH

Тора, т.е. Законъ, или Пятикнижіе Моисеево. Буквальный переводъ въ пользу русскихъ евреевъ.
Berlin: K. Schultz Press, 1862.
Title, Deuteronomy 31:12 verso [2]; preface, III–XVI; Genesis text, 130 columns.
27.5 × 18.5.

A quarto edition of the book of Genesis translated from the Hebrew by Lev [Leon] Iosifovich Mandel'shtam (1819–89) for use by Russian Jews. The title indicates that the entire Torah, or Pentateuch, is included, but the BL copy contains only the book of Genesis. Mandel'shtam's preface is addressed to Jewish schoolteachers, exhorting teachers to train their children to read the Bible and to teach them to be good citizens of the Russian Empire. The text is similar to D. A. Khvol'son's 1861 translation in *Khristianskoe chtenie* (see no. 73), but there are significant differences in the poetic parts such as Chapter 49. The text is in two columns on the page with paragraph indention of verses. Each column is paginated. A statistical register of the number of verses is on the last page of the text. Bound with the BL copy is a biblical lectionary compiled by Mandel'shtam and published by Korneg Press in Berlin in 1862 (*Filologicheskii slovar' k russkomu perevodu Biblii*). The lectionary constitutes chapter-by-chapter translator notes on the book of Genesis.
Loc: BL (3061.e.2)

55. 1862. NEW TESTAMENT. ACTS–REVELATION IN SLAVONIC/RUSSIAN DIGLOT

Деянія и Посланія Святыхъ Апостоловъ съ Апокалипсисомъ.
St. Petersburg: Synodal Press, 1862.
Title, synodal blessing [2]; table of contents, verso blank [2]; text, 583pp.
22 × 15.

First diglot edition of the Holy Synod's translation of Acts–Revelation in Slavonic and Russian. The texts are opposite each other in two columns on the page within a rectangular border in format identical to no. 44.
Loc: BFBS

56. 1862. OLD TESTAMENT. 1 AND 2 CHRONICLES; PROVERBS; EZRA; NEHEMIAH; ESTHER

Первая книга Паралипоменонъ (У Евреевъ – Дневныя Записки).
[and]
Вторая книга Паралипоменонъ (У Евреевъ – Дневныя Записки).
[and]
Притчи Соломона
[and]
Эздра
[and]
Неемія [and] *Эсфирь.*
St. Petersburg: Lermantov and Co. Press [for *Dukh Khristianina*], 1862.
25.5 × 16.5.

Publication of Archpriest G. P. Pavskii's previously banned translations from the Hebrew of OT books. The Pavskii translations were issued serially in the journal, *Dukh Khristianina*, 1862–3. BFBS holds copies of these separate offprints from the serialized 1862 publications. See also the 1863 offprints (no. 64). The text in each case is in a single column on the page with paragraph indention of verses. Verses are numbered in the left-hand margin.
Loc: BFBS

57. 1863 [1860–3]. OLD TESTAMENT. ISAIAH–MALACHI

Пророческія Книги Ветхаго Завѣта (Опытъ переложенія на русскій языкъ.).
Moscow: Moscow University Press, 1863.

General title, verso blank [2]; Isaiah title, censor's permit verso [2]; Isaiah text, 3–113; Jeremiah title, censor's permit [2]; Jeremiah text, 3–123; Lamentations heading followed by Lamentations text, 125–34; Ezekiel half-title, verso blank [2]; Ezekiel title, censor's permit verso [2]; Ezekiel text, 5–116; Daniel title, censor's permit verso [2]; Daniel text, 3–38; Hosea title, censor's permit verso [2]; Hosea–Malachi text, 3–96.
22.5 × 14.5.
A bound edition of the OT prophetical books translated from the Hebrew by St. Makarii (Archimandrite Makarii [Glukharev]). The bound volume dates to 1863, but constitutes an offprint of translations published posthumously in *Pravoslavnoe obozrenie*, 1860–3. Jeremiah and Lamentations were issued in 1860, no. 8; Ezekiel in 1861, no. 1; Daniel in 1861, no. 4; Hosea–Malachi in 1861, no. 10; and Isaiah in 1863. See also Archimandrite Makarii's translations of Job (no. 47), the Pentateuch (no. 59), Song of Solomon, Ecclesiastes and Proverbs (no. 58), Joshua and Judges (no. 78), 1 Samuel – 2 Kings (no. 83), and 1 Chronicles–Esther (no. 92). The preface to the book of Isaiah (p. 4) addresses Archimandrite Makarii's translation activity in the 1830s (see Chapter 3 above). The text in a single column is divided by chapter without separate verse indention, and with verse numbering internal within the paragraph. Brief footnotes accompany the text.
Loc: BFBS; RNB (72–5/3570)

58. 1863. OLD TESTAMENT. SONG OF SOLOMON, ECCLESIASTES AND PROVERBS

Пѣснь Пѣсней, Экклезіастъ и Притчи.
Moscow: Moscow University Press, 1863.
Offprint title, censor's permit verso [2]; text, 98pp.
25 × 16.

An offprint edition of Archimandrite Makarii's translation from Hebrew of Song of Solomon, Ecclesiastes, and Proverbs parallel with no. 57. From the journal, *Pravoslavnoe obozrenie*, 1863, nos. 1–7.
Loc: BFBS

59. 1863. OLD TESTAMENT. PENTATEUCH

Законъ или Пятикнижіе Моисея.
Moscow: Moscow University Press, 1863.
Title, censor's permit verso [2]; text, 426pp.
22.5 × 15.5.

An offprint edition of Archimandrite Makarii's translation from the Hebrew of the Torah, or Pentateuch, parallel in format with nos. 57 and 58, published originally in *Pravoslavnoe obozrenie*, 1863, nos. 8–12. Archimandrite Makarii's text follows closely that of G. P. Pavskii in the RBS edition (see no. 23), including bracketed Septuagint readings.
Loc: BFBS

60. 1863. NEW TESTAMENT. GOSPELS

Господа Нашего Iисуса Христа Святое Евангелiе отъ Матфея, Марка, Луки и Iоанна на русскомъ нарѣчiи.
St. Petersburg: Synodal Press, 1863.
Title, synodal blessing verso [2]; text, 280pp.
13.5 × 8.5.

A printing of the Holy Synod's text of the Gospels but in reduced pocket size. The text is in double columns on the page with paragraph indention of verses. The BFBS copy lacks a front cover, but the back cover shows a printed price of 7 kopecks.
Loc: BFBS

61. 1863. NEW TESTAMENT. ACTS–REVELATION

Деянiя и Посланiя Святыхъ Апостоловъ съ Апокалипсисомъ на русскомъ нарѣчiи.
St. Petersburg: Synodal Press, 1863.
Title, synodal blessing verso [2]; text, 346pp.
13 × 8.

A printing of the Holy Synod's Acts–Revelation in reduced pocket size. The format is identical with no. 60. This was bound with the Gospels and issued as a complete NT (no. 62).
Loc: BFBS (bound as a part of no. 62)

62. 1863. NEW TESTAMENT

Новый Завѣтъ Господа Нашего Iисуса Христа на русскомъ нарѣчiи.
St. Petersburg: Synodal Press, 1863.
Title, synodal blessing verso [2]; Gospels title, synodal blessing verso [2]; Gospels text, 280pp; Acts–Revelation title, synodal blessing verso [2]; Acts–Revelation text, 346pp; NT table of contents, verso blank [2].
13 × 8.

A small-size edition of the synodal NT constituting a rebinding of nos. 60 and 61 with new title leaf and table of contents.
Loc: BFBS

63. 1863. NEW TESTAMENT. GOSPELS

Господа Нашего Іисуса Христа Святое Евангеліе отъ Матфея, Марка, Луки и Іоанна на русскомъ нарѣчіи.
St. Petersburg: Synodal Press, 1863.
21.5 × 14.5.

A fifth printing from stereotype plates of no. 43, the Holy Synod's octavo Gospels, bound with a second printing of Acts–Revelation (no. 66) to constitute a complete NT.
Loc: BFBS

64. 1863. OLD TESTAMENT. JOSHUA, JUDGES, AND RUTH

Книга Іисуса Сына Навина.
[and]
Книга Судей Израилевыхъ [and] *Руфь.*
St. Petersburg: Lermantov and Co. Press, 1863.
25.5 × 16.5.

An offprint edition of G. P. Pavskii's translations from Hebrew of the books of Joshua, Judges, and Ruth originally published in *Dukh Khristianina.* The format is the same as no. 56. Pavskii's translation corresponds to the text of the earlier 1824–5 RBS edition (no. 23), but eliminates bracketed Septuagint readings.
Loc: BFBS

65. 1863. PSALTER

Священныя Пѣснопѣнія древняго Сіона, или стихотворное переложеніе псалмовъ, составляющихъ Псалтирь.
St. Petersburg: D. I. Kalinovskii Press for N. Shigin, Bookseller, 1863.
Blank page, David with harp verso [2]; title, printer's imprint verso [2]; extract from a Slavonic preface [2]; index to drawings [4]; Psalter text, 330pp + 20 illustrations.
21.5 × 14.

"Second edition" of a Russian Psalter in free translation done by an unidentified translator. The text is in metrical verse without verse numeration. Each Psalm has an extended heading. The translation is from the Slavonic

and includes the 151st Psalm. Each of the accompanying Sadovnikov illustrations features the figure of David in a flowing robe and beard.
Loc: BL

66. 1864. NEW TESTAMENT. ACTS–REVELATION

Деянія и Посланія Святыхъ Апостоловъ съ Апокалипсисомъ на русскомъ нарѣчіи.
St. Petersburg: Synodal Press, 1864.
21.5 × 14.5.

A second stereotype printing of no. 49, with identical title and collation. The Holy Synod frequently reprinted Acts–Revelation and the Gospels separately, combining the reprintings as needed to form whole NTs. BFBS holdings include, in addition to this separately bound copy, copies bound with three printings of the Gospels (nos. 63, 67, and 79).
Loc: BFBS (four copies as noted above)

67. 1864. NEW TESTAMENT. GOSPELS

Господа Нашего Іисуса Христа Святое Евангеліе отъ Матфея, Марка, Луки и Іоанна.
St. Petersburg: Synodal Press, 1864.
21.5 × 14.5.

A stereotype reprinting of the synodal Gospels. The title page identifies this as the "fifth edition" printed in 1864, even though an 1863 reprinting (no. 63) is also identified as the "fifth edition." The BFBS copy is bound with no. 66 to form a complete NT.
Loc: BFBS

68. 1864. NEW TESTAMENT

Господа Нашего Іисуса Христа Новый Завѣтъ.
London: W. M. Watts, printer, for BFBS, 1864.
Title, printer's imprint verso [2]; table of contents, verso blank [2]; text, 489pp.
11.5 × 7.

A BFBS edition of the synodal Russian NT in small 24mo size. The title page inaccurately describes this as an "edition done exactly according to the edition legally printed by the RBS in St. Petersburg in 1823." Rather, the edition was prepared verbatim from the 1862 synodal NT (see BFBS Editorial Subcommittee Minutes, vol. 7, November 26,

1862, 56–7), the first such London BFBS printing. The BFBS had earlier appropriated the text of the synodal Gospels, but from this point forward utilized the entire synodal NT for its editions. Printed in 5,000 copies, the edition was proofread and corrected by James Heard and his brother, natives of Russia but of English parentage (see BFBS Editorial Subcommittee Minutes, vol. 7, April 15, 1863, 82). The format is similar to no. 52 with a single column to the page without paragraph indention of verses, and verse numbering in the left-hand margin. There is no record documenting BFBS purchase of the rights to the synodal NT.
Loc: BFBS

69. 1864. NEW TESTAMENT AND PSALTER

Господа Нашего Іисуса Христа Новый Завѣтъ [and] Псалтирь или Книга Хваленій на россійскомъ языкѣ.
London: W. M. Watts, printer, for BFBS, 1864.
NT title, printer's imprint verso [2]; NT table of contents, verso blank [2]; NT, 489pp; Psalter half-title, verso blank [2]; Psalter title, verso blank [2]; Psalter text, 3–127.
11.5 × 7.

A binding of the BFBS 1864 NT (no. 68) with a reprinted small 24mo Psalter. The NT and Psalter are each paginated separately. The text of the Psalter is the same as in the Kel'siev–Stallybrass corrected edition of 1860 (no. 42). Since there is no common title page for the NT and Psalter, it is likely that the Psalter was reissued only for binding with the NT (see BFBS DPSC Minutes, vol. 7, December 8, 1862, 35–6). The 1864 BFBS Psalter is not bound separately.
Loc: BFBS; BL (3061.a.3); CUL (8100.e.286); OX (N.T.Russ.g.1)

70. 1864. NEW TESTAMENT. GOSPELS

Господа Нашего Іисуса Христа Святое Евангеліе отъ Матфея, Марка, Луки и Іоанна.
St. Petersburg: Synodal Press, 1864.
Title, synodal blessing verso [2]; text, 280pp.
13 × 8.

A reprinting of the synodal Gospels uniform with no. 60. It is bound also with an 1864 complete NT (see no. 71).
Loc: BFBS

71. 1864. NEW TESTAMENT

Новый Завѣтъ Господа Нашего Иисуса Христа.
St. Petersburg: Synodal Press, 1864.
Title, synodal blessing verso [2]; text, 626pp; table of lessons title, verso blank [2]; table, 23pp; verso blank [1]; table of contents, verso blank [2].
13 × 8.5.

A printing of the synodal NT in the same format and small size as no. 62. The Gospels reprint of 1864 (no. 70) has been incorporated in this complete NT printing. There is, however, consecutive pagination for the entire NT text. This is the first edition of the synodal NT to append tables of lessons. There is a table of Gospel readings (pp. 1–12) and a table of epistle readings (pp. 13–23).
Loc: BFBS

72. 1864. NEW TESTAMENT. GOSPELS IN GEORGIAN/RUSSIAN DIGLOT

Господа Нашего Іисуса Христа Святое Евангеліе отъ Матфея, Марка, Луки и Іоанна на грузинскомъ и русскомъ языкахъ.
Tiflis: Enfiadzhiants and Co., printer, for the Society for the Reestablishment of Christianity in the Caucasus, 1864.
Georgian/Russian half-title, Georgian title verso, Russian title, society's authority verso [4]; text, 633pp.
21 × 14.

A diglot edition of the Gospels in Georgian and Russian. Each page has two columns with parallel Georgian and Russian text. Paragraph indention is used for each verse. The text is set within a rectangular border (17 × 11). The Russian text is that of the synodal Gospels.
Loc: BFBS

73. 1865 [1861–5]. OLD TESTAMENT. VOL. I: GENESIS–RUTH, ECCLESIASTES. VOL. II: 1 SAMUEL – 2 CHRONICLES, ECCLESIASTES, SONG OF SOLOMON, AND PROVERBS

Книги Священнаго Писанія Ветхаго Завѣта въ русскомъ переводѣ.
St. Petersburg: Press of the Provincial Department, 1861–5.
Vol. 1: half-title, verso blank [1–2]; Genesis title (1861), censor's permit [3–4]; Genesis text, 5–160; Exodus half-title, verso blank [161–2]; Exodus text, 163–292; Leviticus half-title, verso blank [293–4]; Leviticus text, 295–388; Numbers half-title, verso blank [389–90]; Numbers text, 391–520; Deuteronomy half-title, verso blank

[521–2]; Deuteronomy text, 523–635; verso blank [1]; Joshua half-title, verso blank [1–2]; Joshua text, 3–78; Judges half-title, verso blank [79–80]; Judges text, 81–154; Ruth half-title, verso blank [155–6]; Ruth text, 157–67; verso blank [1]; Ecclesiastes title (St. Petersburg, 1861), censor's permit [1–2]; Ecclesiastes text, 3–28. 23.5 × 15.

Vol. II: half-title, verso blank [1–2]; 1 Samuel title, censor's permit [3–4]; 1 Samuel text, 5–103; verso blank [104]; 2 Samuel half-title, verso blank [105–6]; 2 Samuel text, 107–87; verso blank [188]; 1 Kings half-title, verso blank [189–90]; 1 Kings text, 191–287; verso blank [288]; 2 Kings half-title, verso blank [289–90]; 2 Kings text, 291–382; 1 Chronicles half-title, verso blank [383–4]; 1 Chronicles text, 387 [*sic*]–476; 2 Chronicles half-title, verso blank [477–8]; 2 Chronicles text, 479–585; verso blank [586]; Ezra half-title, verso blank [587–8]; Ezra text, 589–620; Ecclesiastes half-title, verso blank [2]; Ecclesiastes text (also in vol. 1), 3–28; Song of Solomon half-title, verso blank [29–30]; Song of Solomon text, 31–47; verso blank [1]; two blank leaves [4]; Job fragment of Job, 71–110; Proverbs half-title, verso blank [111–12]; Proverbs text, 113–203. 23.5 × 15.

A reissue of Russian OT translations done from the Hebrew by Daniil Khvol'son, and first published in the journal *Khristianskoe chtenie*, 1861–5. Even though there are fewer bracketed Septuagint readings in these original Khvol'son translations than in the ultimate synodal authorized text, this text served as the basis for the OT later adopted by the Holy Synod and published in the 1870s. There are frequent footnoted references to variant readings. Format is that of one column on the page either with verse numbering in the left-hand margin or, more commonly, with paragraph indention of each verse. BL copy was rebound in 1940.
Loc: BL (Ac.2059/2.[3])

74. 1865. NEW TESTAMENT. GOSPELS

Господа Нашего Iисуса Христа Святое Евангелiе отъ Матфея, Марка, Луки и Iоанна.
St. Petersburg: Synodal Press, 1865.
13 × 8.

A reprinting of nos. 60 and 70, with uniform collation, text, format, and size. Bound also as part of no. 75.
Loc: BFBS

75. 1865. NEW TESTAMENT

Новый Завѣтъ Господа Нашего Иiсуса Христа.
St. Petersburg: Synodal Press, 1865.
13 × 8.5.

A reprinting of no. 71. There are two variants of this 1865 reprint. One excludes the table of lessons, the other includes the table of lessons and inserts the table of contents leaf immediately following the title leaf. All other matters are uniform with no. 71.
Loc: BFBS (both variants)

76. 1865 [1866]. NEW TESTAMENT. GOSPELS

Господа Нашего Іисуса Христа Святое Евангеліе отъ Матфея, Марка, Луки и Іоанна, на русскомъ нарѣчіи.
Moscow: Synodal Press, 1865 [1866?].
Title, synodal blessing verso [2]; text, 3–298; table of Gospel lessons, 12pp.
25.5 × 16.5.

A Moscow edition of the synodal Gospels in large type. The title page identifies this as the "sixth edition" (i.e. sixth printing). The text is in one column on the page with paragraph indention of each verse. There is no rectangular border on the page as in octavo editions of the synodal Gospels. A green paper cover notes the date of publication in Moscow as 1866, despite the title page date of 1865. The back cover leaf has a price of 30 kopecks printed on it. Includes a table of Gospel lessons.
Loc: BFBS

77. 1865 [1866?]. NEW TESTAMENT. ACTS–REVELATION

Дѣянія и Посланія Святыхъ Апостоловъ съ Апокалипсисомъ, на русскомъ нарѣчіи.
Moscow: Synodal Press, 1865 [1866?].
Title, synodal blessing verso [2]; text, 3–364; table of readings, 11pp.
25.5 × 15.5.

A large-type Moscow edition of the synodal translation of Acts–Revelation formatted like no. 76. Title page identifies this as a "first edition." As with no. 76, the green paper cover has an 1866 publication date, despite 1865 on the title page. A price of 32 kopecks is printed on the back cover. Includes a table of epistle readings.
Loc: BFBS

78. 1866 [1865]. OLD TESTAMENT. JOSHUA AND JUDGES

Книги Іисуса Навина и Судей Израилевыхъ.
Moscow: Moscow University Press (Katkov and Co.), 1866.

Title, censor's permit verso [2]; text, 104pp.
22 × 15.

An offprint edition of Archimandrite Makarii's Russian translation of the books of Joshua and Judges from Hebrew. First published in the journal *Pravoslavnoe obozrenie* in 1865. The format is uniform with other OT translations of Archimandrite Makarii (Glukharev) published posthumously in *Pravoslavnoe obozrenie* (nos. 47, 57, 58, and 59).
Loc: BFBS

79. 1866. NEW TESTAMENT. GOSPELS

Господа Нашего Іисуса Христа Святое Евангеліе отъ Матфея, Марка, Луки и Іоанна.
St. Petersburg: Synodal Press, 1866.
21.5 × 14.5.

Reprint of the synodal Gospels uniform with no. 67. Title page identifies this as the sixth printing. The BFBS copy is bound with no. 66 to form a complete NT.
Loc: BFBS

80. 1866. NEW TESTAMENT. GOSPELS IN SLAVONIC/RUSSIAN DIGLOT

Господа Нашего Іисуса Христа Святое Евангеліе отъ Матфея, Марка, Луки и Іоанна, на славянскомъ и русскомъ нарѣчіи.
St. Petersburg: Synodal Press, 1866.
Title, synodal blessing [2]; text, 476pp; table of lessons, 477–88.
21.5 × 14.5.

Seventh printing of the Slavonic/Russian Gospels diglot identical to no. 44. Russian table of Gospel lessons is appended. One of the BFBS copies is bound with no. 55 to form a complete NT diglot.
Loc: BFBS (two copies)

81. 1866. OLD TESTAMENT. PROVERBS

Книга Притчей Соломона, переведенная съ еврейскаго текста.
London: W. M. Watts, printer, for BFBS, 1866.
Title, verso blank [2]; text, 3–44.
18.5 × 11.
Russian edition of the book of Proverbs translated from Hebrew for the BFBS by Vasilii Andreevich Levison and P. I. Bogoliubov. Commissioned

by BFBS to translate the OT into modern Russian, St. Petersburg Theological Academy Hebrew instructor Levison prepared literal translations from Hebrew which were then brought into conformity with literary Russian by P. I. Bogoliubov, Levison's assistant and former pupil. As in subsequent Levison and Bogoliubov translations, BFBS agents in Petersburg submitted the Proverbs translation to local "revisors," Dr. Hoffman and Professor Astaf'ev, for editing. Final copy was transmitted to London for publication, but proofreading was handled in Petersburg. The book of Proverbs and subsequent BFBS-commissioned OT translations were published in 12mo format with two columns to the page and paragraph indention of verses. This edition of Proverbs was published in 5,000 copies (see BFBS DPSC Minutes, vol. 7, December 4, 1865, 218).
Loc: BFBS; BL (three copies: 3061.b.8, bound with 3061.bb.5, and bound with 3068.aa.21)

82. 1866. OLD TESTAMENT. ISAIAH

Книга Пророка Исаіи, переведенная съ еврейскаго текста.
London: W. M. Watts, printer, for BFBS, 1866.
Title, printer's imprint [2]; text, 3–94.
18.5 × 11.

Russian edition of Isaiah translated from Hebrew for the BFBS by Levison and Bogoliubov. Format is uniform with no. 81. Five thousand copies were published (see BFBS DPSC Minutes, vol. 7, January 26, 1866, 226).
Loc: BFBS; BL (bound with 3061.bb.5)

83. 1867 [1865–6]. OLD TESTAMENT. 1 SAMUEL – 2 KINGS (I.E. 1–4 KINGS).

Четыре Книги Царствъ.
Moscow: Moscow University Press (Katkov and Co.), 1867 [1865–6].
Title, censor's permit [2]; 1 Samuel text, 1–68; 2 Samuel – 2 Kings text, 1–189.
22 × 15.

Russian edition of 1 Samuel – 2 Kings (1–4 Kings, in Russian) translated from Hebrew by Archimandrite Makarii (Glukharev). The offprint is dated 1867, even though the translations were first published in the journal *Pravoslavnoe obozrenie* in 1865 and 1866. A note at the end of 1 Samuel (p. 68, first pagination) indicates that that book was published in the journal in 1865, nos. 7–10. The remaining books were published in 1866. The

format is uniform with other translations of Archimandrite Makarii published in *Pravoslavnoe obozrenie* (see nos. 47, 57, 58, 59, and 78).
Loc: BFBS

84. 1867. OLD TESTAMENT. JEREMIAH AND LAMENTATIONS

Книга Пророка Іереміи, переведенная съ еврейскаго текста.
London: W. M. Watts, printer, for BFBS, 1867.
Title, verso blank [2]; text, 3–117.
18.5 × 11.

Russian edition of Jeremiah and Lamentations translated from Hebrew for BFBS by Levison and Bogoliubov. Format is uniform with nos. 81 and 82. Two thousand five hundred copies were printed (see BFBS DPSC Minutes, vol. 8, March 27, 1867, 34). Although not in the title, Lamentations (*Plach Ieremii*) is included in consecutive pagination (109–117) following Jeremiah.
Loc: BFBS; BL (bound with 3061.bb.5)

85. 1867. OLD TESTAMENT. EZEKIEL

Книга Пророка Іезекіиля, переведенная съ еврейскаго текста.
London: W. M. Watts, printer, for BFBS, 1867.
Title, verso blank [2]; text, 3–99.
18 × 11.

Russian edition of Ezekiel translated from Hebrew for the BFBS by Levison and Bogoliubov. Format is uniform with nos. 81, 82, and 84. Two thousand five hundred copies were printed (see BFBS DPSC Minutes, vol. 8, August 30, 1867, 38).
Loc: BFBS; BL (bound with 3061.bb.5)

86. 1867. NEW TESTAMENT

Новый Завѣтъ Господа Нашего Іисуса Христа.
St. Petersburg: Synodal Press, 1867.
Title, synodal blessing [2]; table of contents, verso blank [2]; text, 626pp.
13 × 8.

A reprinting of the synodal NT in the same small format as nos. 62 and 71. Table of contents is inserted between the title leaf and the first text page.
Loc: BFBS; OX (N.T.Russ.f.2)

87. 1867. NEW TESTAMENT. GOSPEL OF JOHN

Отъ Іоанна Святое Благовѣствованіе.
London: W. M. Watts, printer, for BFBS, 1867.
Title [1]; text, 168–217; printer's imprint [1].
11 × 7.

A stereotype reprinting of the synodal Gospel of John from the 24mo 1864 BFBS NT (no. 68). Five thousand copies were printed for sale at one penny each, and for free distribution at the Paris Exhibition of 1867 (see BFBS DPSC Minutes, vol. 8, February 22, 1867, 10–11).
Loc: BFBS

88. 1867. NEW TESTAMENT. ROMANS, 1 AND 2 CORINTHIANS AND GALATIANS

Къ Римлянамъ, Коринфянамъ и Галатамъ Посланія святаго Апостола Павла.
London: W. M. Watts, printer, for BFBS, 1867.
Title [1]; text, 314–90; printer's imprint [1].
11 × 7.

Stereotype reprinting of selected NT epistles formatted as no. 87. Five thousand copies were printed for free distribution at the Paris Exhibition. Title is embossed on the cover. Onto the binding is glued a seal with the Russian translation of Acts 16:31. The same inscription is found on the binding of no. 90.
Loc: BFBS

89. 1867. OLD TESTAMENT. PSALTER

Псалтирь или Книга Хваленій на россійскомъ языкѣ.
London: W. M. Watts, printer, for BFBS, 1867.

Reprint of the BFBS 24mo Psalter (see no. 69), uniform in format and cover with nos. 87–8, for free distribution at the Paris Exhibition. Printed in 5,000 copies.
Loc: *Non de visu.*

90. 1867. NEW TESTAMENT. GOSPEL OF JOHN

Евангеліе отъ Іоанна.
[St. Petersburg: Synodal Press?], 1867.
Half-title, verso blank [2]; text 3–64.
13.5 × 9.5.

A printing of the synodal Gospel of John. The text is in two columns to the page with paragraph indention of verses. Embossed on the cover is the note in Russian, "Gift from the Paris Exhibition, 1867," along with the title and a quote in Russian from Acts 16:31, as in no. 88. This printing in Russia paralleled the BFBS Gospel of John (no. 87), which also was distributed gratis at the Paris Exhibition. Its Holy Synod Press publication appears to have been commissioned by N. A. Astaf'ev's Russian Society for the Dissemination of the Holy Scriptures.
Loc: BFBS

91. 1868. OLD TESTAMENT. PENTATEUCH

Священныя Книги Ветхаго Завѣта въ русскомъ переводѣ. 1. *Пятикнижіе Моисеево.*
St. Petersburg: Synodal Press, 1868.
Title, synodal blessing [2]; text, 320pp.
24.5 × 15.5.

First edition of the Holy Synod's Pentateuch, and its first officially authorized Russian OT translation. The synodal OT, which was launched with contributions from Moscow, Kiev, and St. Petersburg Theological Academies, underwent revision by a committee appointed from the St. Petersburg Theological Academy: M. A. Golubev, P. I. Savvaitov, D. A. Khvol'son, and E. I. Loviagin. Translation from the Hebrew was overseen by the Hebraist Khvol'son, whose version of the OT began circulating in the journal of the St. Petersburg Theological Academy (*Khristianskoe chtenie*) from 1861 (see no. 73). This is the first portion to be printed at the Synodal Press with the synodal blessing affixed. The text is placed in two columns to the page with paragraph indention for each verse. Variant readings supported only by the Greek Septuagint are placed in brackets in the text, as explained in a note at the bottom of the first page of text. A price of 40 kopecks is printed on the back cover. This first part of the synodal OT was published in seventeen separate reprintings between 1868 and 1916. RNB in Petersburg contains this first printing, as well as the second (1869, RNB 82–5/2706), fourth (1875, RNB 18.40.5.76) and eighth (1897, RNB 18.195.3.59) through seventeenth (1916, RNB 38.73.1.35). The later RNB holdings are *non de visu*.
Loc: BFBS; RNB (18.54.5.75)

92. 1868. OLD TESTAMENT. I CHRONICLES–ESTHER

Историческія Книги Ветхаго Завѣта (Вторая Часть). I и II Книги Паралипоменонъ, Книги Нееміи, Эздры и Эсфирь.

Moscow: Moscow University Press (Katkov and Co.), 1868.
Title, censor's permit [2]; text, 196pp.
22 × 15.

A Russian edition of the books of 1 and 2 Chronicles, Nehemiah, Ezra and Esther translated from the Hebrew by Archimandrite Makarii (Glukharev). The format is uniform with that of nos. 47, 57, 58, 59, 78, and 83. OT translations of Archimandrite Makarii were issued separately as offprints following posthumous publication in *Pravoslavnoe obozrenie*. Published even as the St. Petersburg OT translation committee was readying the synodal OT, these translations demonstrate how critical evaluation of variant Russian OT texts continued well into the 1860s.
Loc: BFBS

93. 1868. OLD TESTAMENT. DANIEL

Книга Пророка Даніила, переведенная съ еврейскаго текста.
London: W. M. Watts, printer, for BFBS, 1868.
Title, verso blank [2]; text, 3–32.
18.5 × 11.

Russian book of Daniel translated from the Hebrew for the BFBS by Levison and Bogoliubov. Format is uniform with nos. 81–2 and 84–5. Two thousand five hundred copies were printed (see BFBS DPSC Minutes, vol. 8, November 29, 1867, 50). BFBS holds two copies – one bound with Ezekiel (no. 85); the other bound with all Levison/Bogoliubov translations, Proverbs and Isaiah–Malachi (nos. 81–2, 84–5, and 94).
Loc: BFBS (two copies); BL (bound within 3061.bb.5)

94. 1868. OLD TESTAMENT. HOSEA – MALACHI

Книги Двѣнадцати Пророковъ: Осіи, Іоиля, Амоса, Авдія, Іоны, Михея, Наума, Аввакума, Софоніи, Аггея, Захаріи и Малахіи, переведенныя с еврейскаго текста.
London: W. M. Watts, printer, for BFBS, 1868.
Title, verso blank [2]; text, 3–81.
18.5 × 11.

A Russian edition of the twelve minor prophets translated from the Hebrew for the BFBS by Levison and Bogoliubov. The text is uniform in format and size with nos. 81–2, 84–5, and 93, with which numbers it is also bound. Two thousand five hundred copies were printed (see BFBS DPSC Minutes, vol. 8, November 29, 1867, 50).
Loc: BFBS; BL (bound with 3061. bb. 5)

95. 1869. NEW TESTAMENT

Господа Нашего Іисуса Христа Новый Завѣтъ.
London: W. M. Watts for BFBS, 1868.
Title, printer's imprint [2]; table of contents, verso blank [2]; text, 506pp.
18.5 × 11.

A BFBS printing of the synodal Russian NT in 5,000 copies seen through the press by James Heard, Russian consular employee and proofreader used by the BFBS. For circulation, see BFBS DPSC Minutes, vol. 8, April 24, 1868, 77–8. Format is similar to previous BFBS NT editions. The text is in a single column on the page divided by paragraphs, with numbering of verses in the left-hand margin.
Loc: BFBS (two copies; one bound separately, the other bound as part of no. 128)

96. 1869. NEW TESTAMENT

Господа Нашего Иісуса Христа Новый Завѣтъ.
London: W. M. Watts, printer, for BFBS, 1869.
Title, printer's imprint [2]; table of contents, verso blank [2]; text, 624pp.
15.5 × 11.

First BFBS edition of Russian synodal NT with marginal references. Text is printed in two columns on the page with references in the outside margins. Text and marginal references are enclosed within a rectangular border (13.5 × 9.5). The marginal references accompanying the text were prepared by the Russian evangelical Madame Marie de Peuker, who adapted the references of the English Authorized Version to the modern Russian NT (see BFBS Editoral Subcommittee Minutes, vol. 8, April 18, 1866, 133–4; and November 28, 1866, 192). A Russian-speaking émigré, H. Gersoni, was employed in London to prepare Madame de Peuker's references for typesetting (see H. Gersoni to BFBS, BFBS Miscellaneous Editorial Correspondence, File C, 1861–70). Proofreading was undertaken in Petersburg by a Mr. Beletskii who resigned after not being allowed to make substantive changes in the Synod's NT text. Proofreading was subsequently carried out by a Mr. Treumann, assistant to BFBS St. Petersburg agent Adalbert Eck (see Eck to Girdlestone, July 3/15, 1867, BFBS Miscellaneous Editorial Correspondence, File C, 1861–70). Printed in 5,000 copies (see BFBS DPSC Minutes, vol. 8, January 7, 1867, 1).
Loc: BFBS; BL (3061.aaa.13)

97. 1869. OLD TESTAMENT. JOSHUA–ESTHER

Священныя Книги Ветхаго Завѣта въ русскомъ переводѣ. 2. Книга Іисуса Навина – Книга Эсфирь.
St. Petersburg: Synodal Press, 1869.
Title, synodal blessing [2]; table of contents, verso blank [2]; text, 496pp.
24.5 × 15.5.

First authorized synodal edition of the second part of the Russian OT, Joshua–Esther. Translation follows closely the text first published in *Khristianskoe chtenie*, and is largely the work of D. A. Khvol'son. Uniform in format with part one (no. 91). Septuagint readings are in brackets.
Loc: BFBS

98. 1869. OLD TESTAMENT. THE PSALTER

Псалтирь или Книга Хвалений на россійскомъ языкѣ.
London: W. M. Watts for BFBS, 1869.
Title, verso blank [2]; text, 509–636.
18.5 × 11.

A printing of the BFBS Russian Psalter, with text identical to nos. 42 and 53. Pagination continues that of the BFBS NT (no. 95) with which it was meant to be bound. Printed in 5,000 copies (see BFBS DPSC Minutes, vol. 8, April 24, 1868, 77–8). BFBS and BL copies are bound with a collection of other BFBS OT texts printed in London between 1866 and 1873.
Loc: BFBS; BL (bound with 3068.aa.21)

99. 1870. OLD TESTAMENT. JOB

Книга Іова.
St. Petersburg: Synodal Press, 1870.
[1], 42pp.

First authorized synodal Russian edition of Job, translated from the Hebrew by D. A. Khvol'son and a committee from St. Petersburg Theological Academy. This translation became the first book of part three of the Synod's authorized OT edition (no. 111, 1872). The DM 7847 entry is a Khvol'son translation of Job dated 1869 (St. Petersburg), which is most likely an 1870 imprint.
Loc: RNB (82–6/3350, *non de visu*)

100. 1870. NEW TESTAMENT. GOSPELS IN SLAVONIC AND RUSSIAN

Господа Нашего Iисуса Христа Святое Евангелiе отъ Матфея, Марка, Луки и Iоанна на славянскомъ и русскомъ нарѣчiи.
St. Petersburg: Synodal Press, 1870.
22.5 × 15.

A ninth printing of the synodal Gospels Slavonic/Russian diglot uniform with no. 80. BFBS copy has been bound with no. 55, Acts–Revelation, to form a complete NT diglot. The rebound NT lacks an overall title page.
Loc: BFBS

101. 1870. NEW TESTAMENT

Новый Завѣтъ Господа Нашего Iисуса Христа.
St. Petersburg: Synodal Press, 1870.
Title, verso blank [2]; table of contents, verso blank [2]; Gospels title, synodal blessing verso [2]; Gospels text, 222pp; Acts–Revelation title, synodal blessing verso [2]; Acts–Revelation text, 269pp.
21.5 × 14.5.

Reprint of the synodal NT uniform with no. 43 and subsequent reprintings. Unlike prior reprints, the Gospels text has been reduced to 222 pages. The Gospels and Acts–Revelation have separate title leaves and pagination. Gospels title page indicates "seventh printing."
Loc: BFBS

102. 1870. OLD TESTAMENT. 1 AND 2 SAMUEL

Книги Самуила, или Первыя Двѣ Книги Царствъ, переведенныя съ еврейскаго текста и изданныя Обществомъ Распространенiя Библiи въ Британiи и другихъ странахъ.
London: W. M. Watts for BFBS, 1870.
Title, verso blank [2]; text, 3–119.
18.5 × 11.

BFBS Russian translation of 1 and 2 Samuel from the Hebrew by Levison and Bogoliubov. Uniform in format and size with nos. 81–2, 84–5, and 93–4. BFBS copy has been rebound with no. 126.
Loc: BFBS

103. 1870. NEW TESTAMENT. GOSPELS

Господа Нашего Іисуса Христа Святое Евангеліе отъ Матфея, Марка, Луки и Іоанна на русскомъ нарѣчіи.
St. Petersburg, Synodal Press, 1870.
13 × 8.

Reprint of synodal Gospels uniform with nos. 60, 70, and 74. A note on the inside cover page indicates that this printing was prepared for the 1870 St. Petersburg Exhibition. A Russian stamp on the title page of the BFBS edition reads: "All-Russian Manufacturing Exhibition, 1870."
Loc: BFBS

104. 1871. PSALTER

Псалтирь.
St. Petersburg: Synodal Press, 1871.
Title, synodal blessing verso [2]; text, 283pp.
15.5 × 10.5.

First Synod-authorized Russian Psalter prepared by the St. Petersburg Theological Academy committee identified under entry no. 91. The text is in a single column on the page with paragraph indention of verses, and text is placed within an inset rectangular border (12 × 8). The synodal edition includes the 151st Psalm.
Loc: BFBS; RNB (18.121.6.54)

105. 1871. OLD TESTAMENT. JOSHUA–ESTHER

Священныя Книги Ветхаго Завѣта въ русскомъ переводѣ. 2. Книга Іисуса Навина – Книга Эсфирь.
St. Petersburg: Synodal Press, 1871.

Second printing of no. 97, part two of the synodal OT – the historical books – in identical format and pagination. The BFBS copy is rebound with part 1 (third printing, 1873), part 3 (first printing, 1872), and part 4 (first printing, 1875).
Loc: BFBS

[1871. OLD TESTAMENT. LAMENTATIONS. Reflecting the role in OT translation of Mikhail Spiridonovich Guliaev, professor of Hebrew at Kiev Theological Academy, this Kiev 1871 edition of the *Kniga Plach Ieremii* or the book of Lamentations contributed to the synodal OT (no. 121 below). *Non de visu.*]

106. 1872. NEW TESTAMENT. GOSPELS

Господа Нашего Іисуса Христа Святое Евангеліе отъ Матфея, Марка, Луки и Іоанна на русскомъ нарѣчіи.
St. Petersburg: Synodal Press, 1872.
13 × 8.

Reprint of the synodal Russian Gospels uniform with previous printings, nos. 60, 70, 74, and 103. BFBS copy bears the stamp in Russian of the Moscow Society of the Lovers of Spiritual Enlightenment.
Loc: BFBS

107. 1872. NEW TESTAMENT

Новый Завѣтъ Господа Нашего Іисуса Христа.
St. Petersburg: Synodal Press, 1872.
13.5 x 8.5.

Reprint of small pocket-size synodal Russian NT uniform with no. 86.
Loc: BFBS

108. 1872. OLD TESTAMENT. PENTATEUCH IN HEBREW/RUSSIAN DIGLOT

Тора, т.е. Законъ, или Пятикнижіе Моисеево. Буквальный переводъ Л.И. Мандельштама, кандидата С. Петербургскаго Университета. Третье изданіе.
Berlin: Zittenfel'd Press, 1872.
[Collation back to front:] Half-title, full Hebrew title verso, Russian title [3]; text [3–276].
26.5 × 18.

Third printing of Leon I. Mandel'shtam's Hebrew/Russian diglot of the Torah or Pentateuch (see no. 54, 1862). Hebrew text provides Arabic numbering of verses in left- and right-hand margins. The Russian title page identifies the volume as a literal translation and identifies Mandel'shtam as a "kandidat" from St. Petersburg University – he had been the first Russian Jew to graduate from the university in 1844. A tabulation of the number of total verses follows the Russian text. In January 1865, BFBS Petersburg agent Andrew Muir wrote the London home offices identifying Mandel'shtam as a learned Jew who had been employed for a time by the Russian government in compiling a lexicon of Hebrew and Russian. Muir noted that Mandel'shtam had by then (1865) moved to Berlin, but that he was a gifted linguist who might be consulted in connection with BFBS efforts to complete its own edition of the Russian

OT (Muir to Knolleke, January 3, 1865, BFBS Editorial Correspondence Inwards, vol. 3, 309–10). The biographical entry on "Mandel'shtam" in the *Evreiskaia entsiklopediia* (vol. X, Moscow 1991 reprint edition, 592) indicates that, by virtue of an 1869 Russian imperial decree, this third edition was for the first time permitted to circulate openly in the Russian Empire.
Loc: BFBS

109. 1872. PSALTER. HEBREW/RUSSIAN DIGLOT

Псалмы. Буквальный переводъ Л.И. Мандельштама, кандидата С. Петербургскаго Университета. Третье изданіе.
Berlin: Zittenfel'd Press, 1872.
[Collation from back to front:] Half-title page blank, Hebrew title verso, Russian title [3]; text [columns 1–84]; table verso [1].
26.5 × 18.

Third printing of L. I. Mandel'shtam's Hebrew/Russian diglot of the Psalter. Similar in format to no. 108 above, the Hebrew text is printed in two columns to the page, but without Arabic verse numerals. The Russian text is also in two columns without paragraph indention of verses. Each Psalm constitutes one paragraph in the Russian and Hebrew texts. A tabulation of total verses (2527) in the Psalter is placed at the end of the Russian text.
Loc: BFBS

110. 1872. OLD TESTAMENT. 1 AND 2 KINGS

Первая Книга Царей, или Третья Книга Царствъ. Переведенная съ еврейскаго текста и изданная Обществомъ Распространенія Библіи въ Британіи и другихъ странахъ.
London: Gilbert and Rivington Press for BFBS, 1872.
Title, verso blank [2]; text, 3–11.
18.5 × 11.

BFBS Russian edition of 1 and 2 Kings translated from Hebrew by D. A. Khvol'son and P. I. Savvaitov. Following the death of V. A. Levison in 1869, the BFBS contracted with Khvol'son to complete for the society its own Russian translation of the OT. In this effort, Khvol'son was assisted by a native-speaking Russian associate Savvaitov (Khvol'son and Savvaitov were both also on the official committee preparing the Synod's OT in St. Petersburg). The first product of the Khvol'son–Savvaitov BFBS collaboration was this translation of 1 and 2 Kings (although the title refers only to 1 Kings). Astaf'ev and Hoffman, revisors/correctors for the previous Levison/Bogoliubov BFBS translations (see the note under no. 81 above), continued to

correct and proofread for the society. The format is uniform with nos. 81–2, 84–5, 93–4, and 102. Printed in 2,500 copies (see BFBS DPSC Minutes, vol. 9, March 24, 1871, 3). BFBS copy later rebound with Genesis–Ruth (no. 126).
Loc: BFBS

111. 1872. OLD TESTAMENT. JOB, PSALTER, PROVERBS, ECCLESIASTES, SONG OF SOLOMON, WISDOM OF SOLOMON, AND ECCLESIASTICUS (WISDOM OF JESUS, SON OF SIRAKH)

Священныя Книги Ветхаго Завѣта въ русскомъ переводѣ. 3. [*Книга Іова, Псалтирь, Книга Притчей Соломоновыхъ, Книга Экклезіаста или Проповѣдника, Книга Пѣсни Пѣсней Соломона, Книга Премудрости Соломона, Книга Премудрости Іисуса, сына Сирахова*]
St. Petersburg: Synodal Press, 1872.
Title, synodal blessing [2]; table of contents, verso blank [2]; text, 283pp.
23.5 × 15.

Part three of the authorized synodal Russian OT translation, uniform with parts one and two (nos. 91 and 97). The Psalter from this part had been previously issued in an authorized 1871 synodal edition (no. 104). The BFBS copy has been rebound with part one (Pentateuch, third printing, 1873), part two (Joshua–Esther, second printing, 1871), and part four (Isaiah – 3 Ezra, first printing, 1875).
Loc: BFBS

112. 1873. OLD TESTAMENT. I CHRONICLES–ESTHER

Книги Паралипоменонъ, Эздры, Нееміи и Эсфирь: У евреевъ, Лѣтописи.
London: Gilbert and Rivington for BFBS, 1873.
Title, verso blank [2]; text, 3–183.
18.5 × 11.

BFBS Russian edition of 1 and 2 Chronicles, Ezra, Nehemiah, and Esther translated from Hebrew by D. A. Khvol'son and P. I. Savvaitov. The text reflects revisions of previous translations undertaken by Khvol'son (e.g. no. 73) and revisions of the Synod's version. Format is uniform with nos. 81–2, 84–5, 93–4, 102 and 110. Two thousand five hundred copies were printed (see BFBS DPSC Minutes, vol. 9, January 26, 1872, 56). For OT books, earlier translated by Khvol'son and the Synod's committee, the BFBS revision entailed the elimination of bracketed Septuagint readings and other related changes bringing the text into closer conformity with

the Hebrew original. The BFBS copy is rebound with Genesis–Ruth (no. 126).
Loc: BFBS; BL (3061.bb.3.)

113. 1873. OLD TESTAMENT. JOB

Книга Іова.
London: Gilbert and Rivington for BFBS, 1873.
Title, verso blank [2]; text, 3–50.
18.5 × 11.

BFBS Russian edition of Job translated from Hebrew by D. A. Khvol'son and P. I. Savvaitov, constituting a revision of Khvol'son's earlier translation of Job, first published in *Khristianskoe chtenie* (no. 73). Format is uniform with nos. 81–2 and subsequent BFBS OT translations. Printed in 2,500 copies (see BFBS DPSC Minutes, vol. 9, March 28, 1873, 132). BFBS copy was bound with nos. 85, 98, and 115, and was subsequently rebound with the entire BFBS Bible (no. 128).
Loc: BFBS; BL (bound with no. 3068.aa.21)

114. 1873. PSALTER

[*Книга Псалмовъ или Псалтирь*].
[London: Gilbert and Rivington for BFBS, 1873.]
Title leaf missing [2]; text, 3–122.
18.5 × 11.

BFBS Russian edition of the Psalter revised by D. A. Khvol'son and P. I. Savvaitov. The title leaf is lacking because the edition was rebound with the BFBS Bible (no. 128). By 1873, numerous editions of the Psalter were in circulation – the RBS Pavskii edition as revised by the BFBS, the new synodal edition, plus editions by Makarii (Glukharev), and indeed by Khvol'son himself. The BFBS agreed to Khvol'son's recommendation to revise the Psalter, eliminating the Septuagint readings and renumbering according to the Hebrew system. The revision, which constituted a distinctly different text from any other circulating at the time, was approved for publication in April 1873 (see BFBS Editorial Subcommittee Minutes, vol. 9, April 2, 1873, 1). Only 1,000 copies were published because the Bible Society was negotiating with the Holy Synod to use the Synod's version without the 151st Psalm (see no. 117 below). The format is uniform with nos. 81–2 and subsequent BFBS OT editions.
Loc: BFBS

115. 1873. OLD TESTAMENT. ECCLESIASTES AND SONG OF SOLOMON

Экклезіастъ и Пѣснь Пѣсней.
London: [Gilbert and Rivington for] BFBS, 1873.
Title page, verso blank [2]; text, 3–24.
18.5 × 11.

BFBS Russian edition of Ecclesiastes and Song of Solomon translated from Hebrew by D. A. Khvol'son and P. I. Savvaitov. Format is uniform with no. 114 and similar printings of the BFBS Russian OT. By the time of their publication these books had already been issued in an 1872 authorized synodal edition (see no. 111), but the Khvol'son revision was carried through by the BFBS to complete its OT and eliminate all Septuagint readings. One BFBS copy is bound with nos. 81, 98, and 113; the other is bound with the full BFBS Bible, no. 128.
Loc: BFBS (2 copies); BL (no. 3068.aa.21)

116. 1873. NEW TESTAMENT

Новый Завѣтъ Господа Нашего Іисуса Христа.
St. Petersburg: Synodal Press, 1873.
21.5 × 14.5.

Reprint of the synodal NT identical in format and pagination to no. 101. The Gospels reprint is identified as the eighth printing. Acts–Revelation is identified as the fourth printing.
Loc: BFBS

117. 1873. PSALTER

Псалтирь.
St. Petersburg: Synodal Press [for the BFBS], 1873.
Title, synodal blessing verso [2]; text, 251pp.
15.5 × 11.

A 16mo edition of the synodal Psalter similar to no. 104. However, this edition excises the 151st Psalm and prints with smaller type yielding a work of thirty-two fewer pages. The Holy Synod printing of this edition was negotiated by BFBS Petersburg agent William Nicolson, with the BFBS agreeing to purchase 100,000 copies which they distributed at 20 kopecks each (see BFBS Editorial Subcommittee Minutes, vol. 10, October 2, 1872,

189). The price is stamped on the back cover. In addition to the copy held by the BFBS, RNB holds eighteen additional printings of this 16mo edition issued between 1877 (RNB: 18.55.9.52, *non de visu*) and 1917 (RNB: 17.148.4.8, *non de visu*). Printings issued for direct synodal sale include p. 252 with the 151st Psalm. The Synodal Press in Petersburg issued two other standard Russian Psalters, one in 183-page format, the other in 130-page format. Only this 251-page format was printed without Psalm 151. The RNB holds fifty-six such printings in the three formats, 1873–1917, with a total circulation amounting to several million copies, not including Psalter editions published in Moscow and Kiev.
Loc: BFBS; RNB (18.91.5.13)

118. 1874. NEW TESTAMENT

Новый Завѣтъ Господа Нашего Iисуса Христа.
St. Petersburg: Synodal Press, 1874.
Title, synodal blessing verso [2]; text, 626pp; table of contents [1].
13 × 8.

Reprint of the synodal NT uniform in format, title, and pagination with the pocket-size nos. 71 and 75. Table of contents inserted at the conclusion, rather than between the title leaf and text.
Loc: BFBS

119. 1874. NEW TESTAMENT. THE GOSPELS

Господа Нашего Iисуса Христа Святое Евангелiе отъ Матфея, Марка, Луки и Iоанна.
St. Petersburg: Synodal Press, 1874.
13.5 × 8.5.

Reprint of the pocket-size synodal Gospels uniform with no. 74.
Loc: BFBS

120. 1874. NEW TESTAMENT IN SLAVONIC/RUSSIAN DIGLOT

Новый Завѣтъ Господа Нашего Iисуса Христа на славянскомъ и русскомъ нарѣчiи.
St. Petersburg: Synodal Press, 1874.
Title, synodal blessing verso [2]; table of contents, verso blank [2]; Gospels title, synodal blessing verso [2]; Gospels text, 476pp; Acts–Revelation title, synodal blessing verso [2]; Acts–Revelation text, 548pp.
21.5 × 14.5.

Reprint of the Slavonic and Russian NT diglot uniform in format with previous diglot printings of the Gospels (no. 80) and Acts–Revelation (no. 55). This printing contains its own title page. The Gospels, identified on the title page as the twelfth edition, have the same pagination as no. 80 (1866). Acts–Revelation, identified as the second edition (i.e. second printing), has been reduced in length from the first edition of 1862 (no. 55). The same double-column Slavonic/Russian format enclosed in a rectangular inset border is employed.
Loc: BFBS

121. 1875. OLD TESTAMENT. ISAIAH – 3 ESDRAS

Священныя Книги Ветхаго Завѣта въ русскомъ переводѣ. 4. [*Книга пророка Исаіи – Третья книга Эздры*].
St. Petersburg: Synodal Press, 1875.
Title, synodal blessing verso [2]; table of contents, verso blank [2]; text, 509pp.
24.5 × 15.5.

First edition of part four of the Synod's authorized Russian OT text, comprising prophetic books, Isaiah – 3 Ezdras. The text of part four includes deuterocanonical books. Format is uniform with parts one through three (nos. 91 [1868], 97 [1869], and 111 [1872]). The BFBS copy is rebound with the 1873 third edition of part one, the 1871 second edition of part two, and the 1872 first edition of part three. With the exception of the text of Lamentations (*Kniga Plach Ieremii*), which was drawn from the 1871 translation done in Kiev and published in the journal, *Trudy kievskoi dukhovnoi akademii* (1871, vol. 4, October–November), the translations in part four were prepared in St. Petersburg and readied for the press by the translations committee of the Petersburg Theological Academy. While issuing this fourth part separately, the Holy Synod also rebound this part with the other parts to form its first complete edition of the OT in 1875 (see no. 125).
Loc: BFBS (2 copies); RNB (bound with 82–5/2706)

122. 1875. OLD TESTAMENT. PENTATEUCH

Священныя Книги Ветхаго Завѣта въ русскомъ переводѣ.
1. *Пятикнижіе Моисеево*.
St. Petersburg: Synodal Press, 1875.
22 × 14.5.

Fourth printing of the Synod's Pentateuch, uniform in format, title, and pagination with no. 91.
Loc: BFBS (2 copies); RNB (18.40.5.76, *non de visu*)

123. 1875. OLD TESTAMENT. PENTATEUCH IN HEBREW AND RUSSIAN

Пятикнижіе Моисеево въ еврейскомъ текстъ и дословномъ русскомъ переводъ для Евреевъ.
Vil'na: Tip. M. P. Romma, 1875.
ii, 486pp.

Diglot edition of the Pentateuch in Russian and Hebrew intended for Jews of the Russian Empire. The text is presented in two parallel columns on each page – Russian on the left-hand side, Hebrew on the right. The title page carries the inscription in Russian that this was "printed with the support of the Society for the Promotion of Enlightenment Among the Jews of Russia." The translators are identified as "Iona Gerasimovich Gershtein, Lev Levanda, and Judah Leib Gordon." In his biographical account of Gordon, *For Whom Do I Toil: Judah Leib Gordon and the Crisis of Russian Jewry* (New York: Oxford University Press, 1988), Michael Stanislawski identifies Gordon as the translator for the book of Exodus and editor for the other four books, as well as the author of the two-page preface. On the collaborating role of the popular Jewish writer Lev Levanda and of Iona Gerasimovich Gershtein, see the biographical entry on "Gershtein" in the pre-revolutionary Russian Jewish dictionary, *Evreiskaia entsiklopediia* (1991 Moscow reprint), vol. VI, 428. The Russian text is original, but follows closely the RBS and synodal translations, but without bracketed alternative Septuagint readings. The text is closest to the original RBS translation (no. 23), and its London BFBS revision in 1861 (no. 48). The preface notes that the translators have closely followed the Masoretic Hebrew text, while at the same time taking into consideration existing Russian translations of scripture, especially when those translations fitted the purposes of this edition for the Jewish people. Russian rendering of names from the Septuagint is retained when those names had become common in the practical life of Jewish people. Otherwise, Hebrew pronunciation is rendered in Cyrillic script.
Loc: BL (1903.ee.1)

124. 1875. OLD TESTAMENT. ISAIAH IN HEBREW AND RUSSIAN

Книга пророка Исаіи съ дословнымъ русскимъ переводомъ.
Vil'na: Press of L. L. Mats, 1875.
[4], 112pp.

Diglot Russian/Hebrew edition of Isaiah translated into Russian from Hebrew by O. N. Shteinberg, with Russian and Hebrew parallel text in two columns on the page (Hebrew on the right; Russian on the left). Shteinberg, an inspector at the Vil'na Jewish Teachers' Institute, translated into Russian other portions of the Hebrew Bible for publication in diglot editions. See his Pentateuch published in Vil'na in 1901–2 (no. 200) and 1913–14 (no. 234).
Loc: BL (1945.g.16.); RNB (18.75.3.85)

125. 1875. OLD TESTAMENT

Священныя Книги Ветхаго Завѣта въ русскомъ переводѣ.
St. Petersburg: Synodal Press, 1875.
Title, synodal blessing verso [2]; table of contents [2]; title (Genesis–Deuteronomy), synodal blessing verso [2]; text, 320pp; title of part two, synodal blessing verso [2]; table of contents, verso blank [2]; text, 496pp; title of part three, synodal blessing verso [2]; text, 283pp; verso blank [1]; table of contents for part three, verso blank [2]; title of part four, synodal blessing verso [2]; text of part four, 509pp; verso blank [1]; table of contents for part four, verso blank [2].
23.5 × 15.

First edition of the Holy Synod's authorized Russian OT having consecutive pagination and its own title page. The edition is a compilation of the four separate parts already issued. Part one is the fourth printing of no. 91. Part two is the third printing of no. 97. Part three is the second printing of no. 111. Part four is the first edition, no. 121. Deuterocanonical books are included, and the order and internal numbering of books agrees with the Septuagint. Publication of the entire Russian OT in an authorized synodal edition marks the completion of Russian biblical translation work reopened under synodal direction in 1856.
Loc: BFBS; BL (3061.g.2.); RNB (18.54.5.75)

126. 1875. OLD TESTAMENT. GENESIS–RUTH

Книги Священнаго Писанія Ветхаго Завѣта переведены съ еврейскаго текста и изданы Обществомъ Распространенія Библіи въ Британіи и Другихъ Странахъ. Томъ первый.
London: Gilbert and Rivington for BFBS, 1875.
Title, printer's imprint verso [2]; text, 3–484.
18.5 × 11.

A new edition of the Octateuch revised by D. A. Khvol'son and P. I. Savvaitov, and printed for the BFBS in a 12mo, double-column format

uniform with nos. 81–2, 84–5, 93–4, 102, 110, and 112–14. The revision was done from the Synod's version, nos. 91 and 97, not from the BFBS 1861 text (no. 48). This revision eliminated bracketed Septuagint readings from the Synod's text. There are additional corrections unrelated to the deletion of the Septuagint. Printed in 1,000 copies (see BFBS DPSC Minutes, vol. 9, August 29, 1873, 161).
Loc: BFBS (three copies bound with other OT parts)

127. 1875. OLD TESTAMENT. JOB–MALACHI

Книги Священнаго Писанія Ветхаго Завѣта переведены съ еврейскаго текста и изданы Обществомъ Распространенія Библіи въ Британіи и Другихъ Странахъ. Томъ второй.
London: Gilbert and Rivington [and Spottiswoode and Co.] for BFBS, 1875.
Title, printer's imprint version [2]; table of contents, verso blank [2]; text of Job, 3–50; text of the Psalter, 3–122; text of Proverbs, 3–44; text of Ecclesiastes and Song of Solomon, 3–24; text of Isaiah, 3–94; text of Jeremiah–Malachi, 1223–1543.
18.5 × 11.

Reprint of BFBS Russian translation of Jeremiah–Malachi bound with nos. 113, 114, 81, 115, and 82 to comprise the second half of the BFBS Russian OT, Job–Malachi. Jeremiah–Malachi (nos. 84, 85, 93, and 94) has a single pagination. One thousand copies of Jeremiah–Malachi were printed for rebinding in this volume (see BFBS DPSC Minutes, vol. 9, September 6, 1875, 294; and September 24, 1875, 296–7).
Loc: BFBS

128. 1875. BIBLE

London: Gilbert and Rivington, printers, for BFBS, 1875.
19 x 11.

A rebinding of the BFBS Russian OT with no. 95 (the BFBS edition of the synodal NT) to form a complete BFBS Russian Bible. There is no title page for the rebound collection, but separate titles, contents pages, and pagination for each part. The NT in single-column paragraph format is not consistent with the double column format of the OT. DM 7861 identifies the ten separately paginated OT sections that have been revised by Khvol'son. This is the first BFBS bound edition of the entire Russian Bible, and the first complete edition of the Russian OT according to the Hebrew canon.
Loc: BFBS; BL (3061.c.11/1–2)

129. 1876. OLD TESTAMENT

Священныя Книги Ветхаго Завѣта въ русскомъ переводѣ. [2 vols.]
St. Petersburg: Synodal Press, 1876.

Reprint of the synodal OT uniform with no. 125, except that it is published in two parts instead of four. There is a single title page, but two separate paginations. The first 816-page part corresponds to the first two sections of no. 125. The second 784-page part corresponds to the last two sections of no. 125.
Loc: RNB (82–5/2880)

130. 1876. BIBLE

Библія, или Книги Священнаго Писанія Ветхаго и Новаго Завѣта въ русскомъ переводѣ.

St. Petersburg: Synodal Press, 1876.
[2], II, 1602, 392pp.
First bound edition of the complete Russian translation of the Bible in an authorized synodal edition. The text and format of the OT are uniform with no. 129 and previous printings in parts. Although all parts of the synodal Bible had been published separately by 1875, this was the first edition to combine the OT and NT in a single volume with a common title and pagination, marking the formal completion of the synodal translation. RNB contains 1878 and 1882 reprintings of this complete Bible.
Loc: RNB (18.121.7.47)

131. 1876. OLD TESTAMENT. PENTATEUCH IN HEBREW/RUSSIAN DIGLOT

[Vienna: A. Holzhausen, printer, for BFBS, 1876.]

First edition of Russian/Hebrew diglot of the Pentateuch using the BFBS Russian OT text as revised by Khvol'son and Savvaitov (see no. 126). Several of these BFBS diglot editions were issued in the years following 1876 for distribution out of the Vienna BFBS offices to Jewish communities on the borders of the Russian Empire. According to BFBS Vienna agent Edward Millard, an edition of this diglot in 5,000 copies was printed in October 1876 (see BFBS FDSC Minutes, vol. 2, June 27, 1877, 46–7). See also no. 133.
Loc: *Non de visu.*

132. 1876. OLD TESTAMENT IN HEBREW/RUSSIAN DIGLOT

Священныя Книги Ветхаго Завѣта переведенныя съ еврейскаго текста. Для употребленія евреямъ.
Vienna: A. Holzhausen, printer, for A. Reichardt and Co. [BFBS], 1876.

Hebrew/Russian diglot of the OT employing the BFBS Russian text as revised by D. A. Khvol'son (no. 128), and the format as in nos. 131 and 133. BFBS Vienna agent Edward Millard noted sale of 5,300 Russian OTs with parallel Hebrew text (see BFBS Editorial Correspondence Inwards, vol. 14, copy of Millard to BFBS, November 26, 1878, 183).
Loc: RNB (38.80.7.133, *non de visu*)

133. 1877. OLD TESTAMENT. PENTATEUCH IN HEBREW/RUSSIAN DIGLOT

Священныя Книги Ветхаго Завѣта, переведенныя съ еврейскаго текста. Для употребленія евреямъ. Томъ I [*Пятикнижіе Моисеево*].
Vienna: A. Holzhausen, printer, for A. Reichardt and Co. [BFBS], 1877.
[Pagination and text from back to front:] blank page, Russian title verso [2]; Hebrew title, printer's imprint verso [2]; Russian half-title [1]; text.[1, 1–350].
20.5 × 12.5.

Reprint of the Pentateuch in Russian and Hebrew. Single-column format on each page with Russian and Hebrew parallel texts on facing pages. Russian text is broken only by chapter with Arabic verse numbering in the margins. Russian text is drawn from the revised BFBS text (no. 126). This second printing issued in 10,000 copies (see BFBS FDSC Minutes, vol. 2, June 27, 1877, 46–7). Hebrew text is drawn from the 1874 Letteris text printed in Vienna. Publication of the Hebrew/Russian diglot was part of a strategy both to expand sales to Jews of the Austrian Empire, and to secure permission for sales in the Russian Empire on the grounds that such sales addressed a non-Russian, Jewish audience.
Loc: BFBS (three copies)

134. 1877. BIBLE

Священныя Книги Ветхаго и Новаго Завѣта.
Vienna: A. Holzhausen, printer, for BFBS, 1877.
Title, imprint verso [2]; OT table of contents, verso blank [2]; OT text, 864pp; title of NT, verso blank [2]; NT table of contents, verso blank [2]; NT text, 260pp.
23.5 × 15.

First Vienna edition of complete BFBS Russian biblical text (no. 128) in octavo. Format is consistent throughout with two columns to the page and paragraph indention of verses. Only OT books of the Hebrew canon are included. Arrangements were made with A. Holzhausen for inexpensive publication of what became the standardized BFBS Russian edition. Ten thousand copies were printed (see BFBS Editorial Subcommittee Minutes, vol. 11, January 5, 1876, 205). The South Slav scholar, Franjo Miklošić, saw the printing through the press. "Mr. Vinogradov," attached to the Russian chaplaincy in Vienna, assisted in proofreading. The volume was printed from stereotype plates and went through multiple reprintings. Vienna BFBS agent Eduard Millard voiced objections over punctuation used in the BFBS text, noting examples especially of exclamation marks in Genesis 1. Despite Khvol'son's defense of his own punctuation, this 1877 edition and subsequent Vienna printings were altered in accordance with Millard's recommendations and the request of the London offices that the punctuation conform more to that of the synodal text (see BFBS Editorial Correspondence Inwards, vol. 12, letters of E. Millard and W. Nicolson, February–April 1876, 31–3, 38, 39, 48–50, 81).
Loc: BFBS; RNB (37.75.4.53)

135. 1877. NEW TESTAMENT

Новый Завѣтъ Господа Нашего Іисуса Христа.
Moscow: Synodal Press, 1877.
Title, synodal blessing verso [2]; text, 3–658; table of contents, verso blank [2]
25.5 × 16.

A quarto edition of the Synod's NT employing large font. Format is a single column on the page. Each verse is indented as a separate paragraph.
Loc: BFBS

136. 1877. NEW TESTAMENT. GOSPELS

Господа Нашего Іисуса Христа Святое Евангеліе отъ Матфея, Марка, Луки и Іоанна.
St. Petersburg: Synodal Press [for the BFBS], 1877.
12.5 × 8.

Reprint of the synodal Gospels in small-size format, title, and pagination uniform with no. 70 and subsequent reprintings. Back cover of BFBS copy gives price of "12 kop."
Loc: BFBS; BL (3042.a.22)

137. 1877 [1878]. NEW TESTAMENT

Новый Завѣтъ Господа Нашего Іисуса Христа.
St. Petersburg: [Synodal Press], 1877 [1878].
21.5 × 14.5.

A rebinding of the NT, composed of the tenth printing (1875) of the Gospels and a fifth printing (1878) of Acts–Revelation. Pagination, format, and title are identical to no. 101. Although the fifth printing of Acts–Revelation is dated 1878, the NT title page imprint reads 1877.
Loc: BFBS

[1878. BIBLE. See annotation under no. 130 regarding reprintings of the synodal Bible, including a second printing in 1878 (RNB, 18.24.8.1). *Non de visu.*]

138. 1878. NEW TESTAMENT. GOSPELS AND ACTS OF THE APOSTLES

Господа Нашего Іисуса Христа Святое Евангеліе и Деянія Апостоловъ. Съ С. Петербургскаго изданія Св. Синода.
Vienna: A. Holzhausen Press for BFBS, 1878.
Title, printer's imprint verso [2]; table of contents, verso blank [2]; text, 286pp.
12.5 × 8.

A 32mo pocket-size Vienna printing of the synodal Gospels and Acts of the Apostles. Text is printed in two columns on the page with paragraph indention of verses. Cross-references to OT passages have been inserted in parentheses at the end of individual NT verses, as in Synodal Press editions. *The Seventy-Fourth Report of the BFBS* (London, 1878, 40) notes publication of 60,000 copies of portions of the NT of which this edition of the Gospels and Acts was a component. In *The Seventy-fifth Report of the BFBS* (London, 1879, 39), the extensive distribution of small NTs and portions was attributed to circulation among Russian soldiers in the Russo-Turkish War. In Romania and Bulgaria alone, 242,382 copies were "distributed among the troops." Adding sales from the BFBS Odessa depot, close to a half million copies were distributed during the war, with primary circulation from Vienna and regions adjacent to the Black Sea.
Loc: BFBS

139. 1878. BIBLE

Священныя Книги Ветхаго и Новаго Завѣта.
Vienna: A. Holzhausen for BFBS, 1878.
23.5 × 15.
Third stereotype printing of no. 134. Printed in 10,000 copies (see BFBS FDSC Minutes, vol. 2, 105–6).

Loc: BL (3062.b.1); CUL (8100.c.1539); OX (Bib.Russ.d.1); RNB (122/451)

140. [1878.] NEW TESTAMENT

[Vienna: A Holzhausen, printer, for BFBS, 1878.]
[12.5 × 8.].
A printing of the popular pocket-size Vienna 32mo edition of the synodal NT distributed during the Russo-Turkish War. Format is uniform with no. 138.
Loc: *Non de visu.*

141. 1878–9. OLD TESTAMENT. PENTATEUCH

Священная Лѣтопись... Изданіе второе исправленное. 3 vols.
Vol. I: *Священная Лѣтопись первыхъ временъ мира и человѣчества ... Вступленіе и книга Бытія съ примѣчаніями и картою.*
St. Petersburg: Tovarishchestvo "Obshchestvennaia Pol'za" Press, 1879.
Title, censor's permit verso [2]; Holy Synod actions, I–II; Pentateuch essay, 1–130; table of contents for essay, verso blank [2]; Genesis half-title (1878), verso blank [2]; Genesis text, 3–390; Genesis table of contents, I–IV; list of misprints [2] + I–III; Middle East map.
28 × 18.5.
Vol. II: *Священная Лѣтопись. Вторая и третья книги Моисеевы. Исходъ и Левитъ съ картою и рисунками.*
St. Petersburg: Tovarishchestvo "Obshchestvennaia Pol'za," 1878.
Title, censor's permit verso [2]; misprints, I–II; Exodus half-title, verso blank [2]; introduction to Exodus, 3–6; Exodus text, 7–268; supplement to Exodus, 269–351; verso blank [352]; Leviticus half-title, verso blank [2]; Leviticus text, 3–169; verso blank [170]; tables of contents for Exodus and Leviticus, I–IV, I–II; Leviticus misprints [1].
28 × 18.5.
Vol. III: *Священная Лѣтопись. Четвертая и пятая книги Моисеевы. Числа и Второзаконіе съ указателемъ пятикнижія.*
St. Petersburg: Tovarishchestvo "Obshchestvennaia Pol'za" Press, 1878.
Title, censor's permit verso [2]; Numbers half-title, verso blank [2]; introduction to Numbers, 3–5; verso blank [6]; Numbers text, 7–230; table of contents to

Numbers, I–III; verso blank [I]; Numbers misprints, I–II; Deuteronomy half-title, verso blank [2]; introduction, 3–5; verso blank [6]; Deuteronomy text, 7–183; verso blank [I]; Deuteronomy table of contents, I–III; verso blank [I]; Deuteronomy misprints, I–II; half-title of Pentateuch index, verso blank [II]; index, III–XXXIV.
28 × 18.5.

A printing of the synodal Russian text of the Pentateuch accompanied by a second edition of Georgii Vlastov's extended notes and commentary. The first printing of this Vlastov commentary, according to the opening essay, was in 1877–8.
Loc: BL (3061.g.4)

142. 1879. NEW TESTAMENT AND PSALTER

Новый Завѣтъ Господа Нашего Іисуса Христа и Псалтирь въ русскомъ переводѣ.
St. Petersburg: Synodal Press [for BFBS], 1879.
Title, synodal blessing verso [2]; table of contents, verso blank [2]; text, 619pp.
21.5 × 14.5.

An octavo printing of the synodal NT and Psalter for distribution by the BFBS agency in St. Petersburg. The NT format – paragraph indention of verses with two columns per page set within an inset rectangular border – is uniform with no. 137 and previous printings. This is the first time, however, that the Synod's Psalter appears in the same page format as the Gospels, and with a single consecutive pagination. The Psalter omits the 151st Psalm, but retains Septuagint numbering of the Psalms. From the mid 1870s, BFBS Petersburg agent William Nicolson negotiated terms of special printing orders with the Synodal Press business office such that BFBS circulation of Russian scripture (in whole or in part) inside Russia reached 180,000 copies annually by 1878 (see *The Seventy-fourth Report of the BFBS*, London, 1878, 86, 93). Throughout the 1870s, individual print orders ranged up to 100,000 or more at a time.
Loc: BFBS

143. 1879. NEW TESTAMENT

Новый Завѣтъ Господа Нашего Іисуса Христа.
St. Petersburg: Synodal Press, 1879.
13 × 8.

A printing of the small-size Russian synodal NT uniform in format with the Gospels edition of no. 70 and subsequent reprintings.
Loc: BFBS

144. 1880. NEW TESTAMENT

Новый Завѣтъ Господа Нашего Іисуса Христа.

St. Petersburg: Synodal Press, 1880.
Title, synodal blessing verso [2]; table of contents, verso blank [2]; Gospels text, 22pp; Acts–Revelation title, synodal blessing verso [2]; Acts–Revelation text, 269pp.
22 × 15.

Reprint of the synodal NT with formatting similar to nos. 101 and 137. The overall title page gives St. Petersburg as the place of publication, although the separate title page of Acts–Revelation identifies that portion as the sixth edition published at the Moscow Synodal Press, 1878. The rectangular inset border of the Moscow Acts–Revelation is slightly larger than the inset border for the Gospels of this printing.
Loc: BFBS

145. 1881. NEW TESTAMENT

Новый Завѣтъ Господа Нашего Іисуса Христа.
St. Petersburg: Synodal Press, 1881.
13 × 8.

Reprint of the pocket-size synodal NT uniform with no. 143 and previous printings.
Loc: BFBS

146. 1881. NEW TESTAMENT. GOSPEL OF JOHN

Господа Нашего Іисуса Христа Святое Евангеліе отъ Іоанна.
St. Petersburg: Synodal Press, 1882.
Title, synodal blessing verso [2]; Gospel text, 64pp.
12 × 8.

A printing of the Synod's Gospel of John in small format uniform with the NT format for no. 145.
Loc: BFBS

147. 1881. NEW TESTAMENT IN SLAVONIC AND RUSSIAN

Новый Завѣтъ Господа Нашего Іисуса Христа на славянскомъ и русскомъ нарѣчіи.
St. Petersburg: Synodal Press, 1881
[2], 1122, 21pp.

First printing of what became a standard Slavonic/Russian diglot of the Synodal NT. The parallel texts are set in two opposing columns on the page with paragraph indention of verses. According to the RNB card catalog, this diglot went through seventeen printings prior to 1917, the seventeenth printing coming in 1915 (RNB, 38.55.4.57, *non de visu*). The collation includes an appended 21-page lectionary.
Loc: RNB (18.145.7.8)

148. 1882 [1881–2]. BIBLE

[There is no title leaf.]
St. Petersburg: Synodal Press for BFBS, 1882 [1881–2].
Genesis–Deuteronomy title, synodal permission verso [2]; Genesis–Deuteronomy text, 1–233; table of contents verso [1]; Joshua–Esther title, synodal "permission" verso [2]; Joshua–Esther text, 233–542; table of contents for Joshua–Esther, verso blank [2]; Job–Song of Solomon title, synodal "permission" verso [2]; Job–Song of Solomon text, 543–683; table of contents for Job–Song of Solomon [1]; Isaiah–Malachi title, synodal "permission" verso [2]; Isaiah–Malachi text, 683–928; table of contents for Isaiah–Malachi, verso blank [2]; NT title, synodal "blessing" verso [2]; NT text, 1–286; NT table of contents, verso blank [2].
24.5 × 14.5.

Revised large octavo edition of the synodal Russian Bible prepared by the Synodal Press for BFBS distribution in Russia. The OT was printed with only the books of the Hebrew canon and without the variant Septuagint readings in parentheses. The Psalter contained only 150 Psalms. The format is that of two columns to the page with paragraph indention of verses. The work is divided into five sections each with its own title and table of contents: Genesis–Deuteronomy, Joshua–Esther, Job–Song of Solomon, Isaiah–Malachi, and the NT. Each of the four OT sections is dated 1882. The NT is dated 1881 and has separate pagination. After prolonged negotiations in which BFBS Petersburg agent William Nicolson sought Synodal Press publication of a Russian OT text without deuterocanonical and other Septuagint readings, the Synod agreed to publish this edition in 20,000 copies (see BFBS Editorial Subcommittee Minutes, vols. 13–14; also BFBS Editorial Correspondence Inwards, vol. 16). Professor Nikolai A. Astaf'ev was engaged in Petersburg to bring the synodal OT into conformity with BFBS concerns and to see the corrections and proofreading through the press. The OT sections each bear on the title page verso the inscription (in Russian) "with the permission of the Most Holy Ruling Synod for the English Bible Society." But the NT title page verso bears the more usual inscription, "with the blessing of the Most Holy Ruling Synod." Following

publication of this modified edition of the Holy Synod's Russian OT, authorization for this OT revision was withdrawn by synodal Oberprokuror K. P. Pobedonostsev. Given BFBS unwillingness to circulate OT editions that included deuterocanonical texts, the synodal decision to curtail publication of this revised OT text meant that BFBS agencies in Russia were limited largely to circulation of the synodal NT. The BL copy has been bound without page trimming, leaving wider margins and a larger bound copy (30 × 20.5). The RNB copy contains only the 1882 revised OT.
Loc: BFBS; BL (3061.h.5); RNB (82–7/699)

[1882. BIBLE. Third printing of the complete synodal Russian Bible (RNB, 18.145.4.1, *non de visu*). See annotation under no. 130.]

[1882. NEW TESTAMENT. Acts–Revelation. Moscow: Synodal Press, 1882 (see no. 171).]

149. 1882. NEW TESTAMENT. ACTS–REVELATION IN SLAVONIC AND RUSSIAN

Деянія и Посланія Святыхъ Апостоловъ с Апокалипсисомъ на славянскомъ и русскомъ нарѣчіи.
St. Petersburg: Synodal Press, 1882
Title, synodal blessing verso [2]; text, 548pp.
21.5 × 14.5.

Third printing of the Synod's Slavonic/Russian diglot of the Acts of the Apostles–Revelation. Format is similar to the first edition, no. 55 (1862), but this printing completes the Slavonic and Russian texts in 35 fewer pages (548, not 583) than the first edition.
Loc: BFBS

150. 1882. NEW TESTAMENT

Новый Завѣтъ Господа Нашего Іисуса Христа.
Kiev: Pecherskaia Lavra Press, 1882.
Title, synodal blessing verso [2]; text, 660pp; table of Gospel readings, 1–14; table of epistle readings, 15–27; table of contents verso [1].
14 × 10.

A Kievan printing of the synodal NT in small size with format similar to no. 70 and subsequent reprintings (two columns to the page, verse indentions, etc.), although pagination is different. A table of Gospel and epistle lessons is

appended. This is the first printing of the synodal Russian NT to capitalize pronominal references to the Virgin Mary ("Она," "Ея," etc.). The Slavonic Bible offered no clear guidance on the matter of pronominal capitalization. The decision of the Kievan press to capitalize pronominal references to Mary appears to have been taken without appeal to synodal authority, for there is no record of the matter before the Synod in the Russian State Historical Archive in Petersburg (RGIA). The St. Petersburg Synodal Press began occasional use of pronominal capitalization later, in the 1890s, but no consistent pattern appears to have been established.
Loc: BFBS

151. 1883. NEW TESTAMENT

Новый Завѣтъ Господа Нашего Іисуса Христа.
St. Petersburg: Synodal Press, 1883.
21.5 × 14.5.

A reprinting of the synodal NT in a format uniform with no. 144 and previous printings. Acts–Revelation, printed in Moscow, is identified on the title page as the "sixth edition" (see no. 144).
Loc: BFBS

[1883. NEW TESTAMENT. The so-called "People's Edition" of the NT was first published in 1883 (RNB, 18.216.7.28, *non de visu*). For a full description of the "People's Edition," which went through forty-five printings, see no. 155.]

152. 1883. PSALTER

Псалтирь.
St. Petersburg: Synodal Press [for BFBS], 1883.
15 × 11.

A reprinting uniform with no. 117, an edition that excised the 151st Psalm. BFBS agencies in the Russian Empire continued to procure copies of this adjusted Psalter even after permission had been rescinded for reprinting the 1882 OT without Septuagint readings (no. 148).
Loc: BFBS

153. 1883. NEW TESTAMENT. GOSPEL OF MARK

Господа Нашего Іисуса Христа Святое Евангеліе отъ Марка.
St. Petersburg: Synodal Press, 1883.
Title, synodal blessing verso [2]; text, 1–50.
12.5 × 8.

A printing of the Synod's Gospel of Mark circulated by BFBS agencies in Russia in small format uniform with no. 146.
Loc: BFBS

154. 1884. NEW TESTAMENT

Новый Завѣтъ Господа Нашего Іисуса Христа.
Moscow: Synodal Press, 1884.
26.5 × 17.5.

A quarto printing of the synodal Russian NT uniform with the 1877 Moscow NT (no. 135). This text is set within a rectangular inset border (21.5 × 13).
Loc: BFBS

155. 1885. NEW TESTAMENT

Новый Завѣтъ Господа Нашего Іисуса Христа въ русскомъ переводѣ.
St. Petersburg: Synodal Press [for BFBS], 1885.
Title, synodal blessing verso [2]; table of contents, verso blank [2]; text, 508pp.
16.5 × 11.5.

A third printing of a popular, inexpensive octavo synodal NT – what came to be called the "People's Edition." The text is set in double columns on the page with paragraph indention of verses. The "People's Edition" was the most popular item sold by colporteurs and hawkers out of BFBS agencies in the Russian Empire. It sold for 25 kopecks, and went through forty-five printings between 1883 and 1917. *The Eighty-Second Report of the BFBS* (London, 1886, 112) records that the first two printings of this volume were of 50,000 copies each. This third printing of 100,000 copies was received from the Synodal Press in November 1885. A fourth printing of 100,000 copies was then on order. The BL copy has the original binding which reads on the back cover, "Dlia russkago naroda [for the Russian people], 25 k [kopecks]." Since all printings after the initial two were ordered by the BFBS Petersburg Agency in lots of 100,000, the circulation of the "People's Edition" exceeded four million copies between 1883 and 1917. The format of this stereotyped edition changed only slightly over the course of the forty-five printings. The 1904 twenty-ninth edition (RNB: 38.38.7.33, *non de visu*) introduced a 514-page format. With the thirty-sixth printing in 1909 (RNB: 38.58.9.20, *non de visu*), a 440-page format became standard.
Loc: BFBS, BL (3061.aaa.16); RNB (18.216.7.29)

156. 1885. NEW TESTAMENT. GOSPELS AND ACTS IN RUSSIAN AND KOMI-ZYRIAN

Святое Евангеліе отъ Матфея, Марка, Луки и Іоанна и Деянія Святыхъ Апостоловъ. На зырянскій языкъ перевелъ Г.С. Лыткинъ, преподаватель Спб. шестой гимназіи.
St. Petersburg: Synodal Press, 1885.
Title, synodal blessing verso [2]; text 558pp.
19 × 12.5.

An octavo diglot edition of the synodal Gospels and Acts with a Komi-Zyrian translation. The parallel texts are on two opposing columns on the page with paragraph indention of verses. The title page identifies this as a translation by G. S. Lytkin, a teacher at the St. Petersburg Sixth Gymnasium. Lytkin was employed by the BFBS (for 100 rubles and 200 copies of the printed outcome) to "transliterate" the Zyrian Gospel of Matthew from the old Cyrillic into the Russian civil script (see BFBS Editorial Subcommittee Minutes, vol. 13, April 2, 1879, 102). The original Zyrian text had been translated by A. Shergin for the RBS (St. Petersburg, 1823, DM 9810). The Shergin Zyrian Gospel of Matthew in Lytkin's transliterated civil script was printed in 5,000 copies for the BFBS by the Academy of Sciences in Petersburg (DM 9812, 1882). This 1885 edition of the Gospels and Acts incorporates the Shergin translation of Matthew (as transliterated by Lytkin) and adds the remaining Gospels and Acts along with the parallel Russian text. Unlike the 1882 Matthew in Zyrian, this 1885 diglot was printed at the Synodal Press and carries the inscribed blessing of the Synod. The 1882 Academy of Sciences/BFBS Zyrian Gospel of Matthew was again reprinted in a 1973 facsimile edition by the Institute for Bible Translation in Stockholm. In 1979 the Stockholm Institute published a complete Zyrian NT. Komi-Zyrian, an Altai language, is still spoken by a majority of the people in the Komi Republic of the Russian Federation.
Loc: BFBS

157. 1885. PSALTER IN RUSSIAN/KOMI-ZYRIAN DIGLOT

Псалтирь/Ошкансыломъ на русскомъ и зырянскомъ языкахъ. Зырянскій переводъ составленъ Г.С. Лыткинымъ.
St. Petersburg: Synodal Press, 1885.
Title, synodal blessing verso [2]; text, 249pp.
19 × 12.5.

A diglot edition of the Psalter in Russian and Komi-Zyrian uniform in format with no. 156. The translation was compiled by G. S. Lytkin. The Russian and Zyrian texts include the 151st Psalm.
Loc: BFBS

158. 1886. NEW TESTAMENT. GOSPEL OF MATTHEW IN GREEK, SLAVONIC, RUSSIAN AND LATIN

Новый Завѣтъ Господа Нашего Іисуса Христа на четырехъ языкахъ: Эллинскомъ, Словенскомъ, Россійскомъ и Римскомъ, съ параллельными мѣстами. Книга первая. Отъ Матфея Святое Благовѣствованіе [Title in Cyrillic orthography]
St. Petersburg: Synodal Press, 1886.
Title, synodal blessing verso [2]; preface [2]; half-title [1]; parallel texts, 2–235; verso blank [1]; variant readings, 3–8.
24.5 × 16.

A polyglot edition of the Gospel of Matthew including Greek, Slavonic, and Latin, along with the synodal Russian text. According to the preface, the Greek text is drawn from the 1861 Greek edition published by the Synodal Press in St. Petersburg. The Latin text follows the Vulgate except for those "inadequacies" in comparison to the Greek that are filled in by bracketed passages from the text of Theodore Beza. The Synod's Slavonic and Russian texts are used. The texts are printed in two columns on the page, the four parallel texts on facing pages (from left to right: Greek, Slavonic, Russian, and Latin). As in the case of no. 150, this is one of the early instances of capitalized pronominal references to the Virgin Mary. Parallel references are placed after each chapter. The appendix of variant readings constitutes longer additions to the reference notes at the end of each chapter. These variant readings are drawn largely from the Moscow and Kiev *Naprestol'nye Evangeliia* and Beza's Latin version. The volume is identified as the first book of a series intended among other uses as an aid for young people studying the languages.
Loc: BFBS; OX (N.T.Polyg. d.9/1)

159. 1887. PSALTER

Псалтирь.
St. Petersburg: Synodal Press [for BFBS], 1887.
15.5 × 11.

Reprint uniform with nos. 117 and 152.
Loc: BFBS

160. 1887. NEW TESTAMENT. THE GOSPEL OF MARK

Господа Нашего Iисуса Христа Святое Евангелiе отъ Марка.
St. Petersburg: Synodal Press, 1887.
12.5 × 8.

Reprint of no. 153.
Loc: BFBS

161. 1887. NEW TESTAMENT. GOSPELS

Господа Нашего Iисуса Христа Святое Евангелiе отъ Матфея, Марка, Луки и Iоанна.
St. Petersburg: Synodal Press, 1887.
12.5 × 8.

A reprint of no. 60. Inscribed on the back cover is a price of 19 kopecks.
Loc: BFBS

162. 1887. NEW TESTAMENT. GOSPELS

Господа Нашего Iисуса Христа Святое Евангелiе отъ Матфея, Марка, Луки и Iоанна.
St. Petersburg: Synodal Press, 1887.
21.5 × 14.5.

Eleventh printing of the synodal Gospels in the original format of no. 43 (1860). Pagination, however, follows that of the 1870 seventh printing (no. 101).
Loc: BFBS

163. 1887. NEW TESTAMENT. GOSPEL OF MARK IN GREEK, SLAVONIC, RUSSIAN, AND LATIN

Новый Завѣтъ Господа Нашего Iисуса Христа на четырехъ языкахъ: Эллинскомъ, Словенскомъ, Россiй скомъ и Римскомъ съ параллельными мѣстами. Книга вторая. Отъ Марка Святое Благовѣствованiе.
St. Petersburg: Synodal Press, 1887.
Title, synodal blessing verso [2]; half-title [1]; text, 2–147.
24.5 × 16.5.

Polyglot edition of the Gospel of Mark, uniform in format with no. 158. The Russian text of Mark is that of the synodal edition. The Oxford copy is bound with nos. 158 and 164.
Loc: OX (N.T.Polyg. d.9/1)

164. 1888. NEW TESTAMENT. GOSPEL OF LUKE IN GREEK, SLAVONIC, RUSSIAN, AND LATIN

Новый Завѣтъ Господа Нашего Іисуса Христа на четырехъ языкахъ: Эллинскомъ, Словенскомъ, Россій скомъ и Римскомъ съ параллельными мѣстами. Книга третья. Отъ Луки Святое Благовѣствованіе.
St. Petersburg: Synodal Press, 1888.
Title, synodal blessing verso [2]; half-title [1]; text, 2–253.
24.5 × 16.5.

Polyglot edition of the Gospel of Luke uniform in format with no. 163. For the Gospel of John in uniform format, see no. 179. Oxford copy is bound with nos. 158 and 163.
Loc: OX (N.T.Polyg. d.9/1)

165. 1888. NEW TESTAMENT

Новый Завѣтъ Господа Нашего Іисуса Христа.
Moscow: Synodal Press [for BFBS], 1888.
Title, synodal blessing verso [2]; text, 3–922; table of contents [2].
22.5 × 15.

An octavo edition of the synodal NT in large type. Format is similar to the 1884 quarto edition (no. 154), but the rectangular border within which the single-column text is set is smaller (17.5 × 11), as is the page size. This Moscow large-font edition was identified by BFBS Petersburg agent William Nicolson as "one of the most numerously circulated of our Russ editions" (*The Eighty-Sixth Report of the BFBS*, London, 1890, 95).
Loc: BFBS

166. 1888. NEW TESTAMENT AND PSALTER

Новый Завѣтъ Господа Нашего Іисуса Христа и Псалтирь въ русскомъ переводѣ.
St. Petersburg: Synodal Press [for BFBS], 1888.
Title, synodal blessing verso [2]; table of contents, verso blank [2]; text, 783pp.
12.5 × 8.

A printing of the pocket-size synodal NT and Psalms. The NT text (pp. 1–626), has the same format and pagination as no. 71 (1864) and subsequent small-size printings. This edition includes the Psalter with consecutive pagination. The Psalter omits Psalm 151. The last page is mistakenly numbered "159," not 783.
Loc: BFBS

167. 1888. OLD TESTAMENT. GENESIS–JUDGES AND I SAMUEL – 2 KINGS IN HEBREW AND RUSSIAN

Священныя Книги Ветхаго Завѣта переведенныя съ еврейскаго текста. Для употребленія евреямъ.
Vienna: A. Holzhausen, printer, for BFBS, 1888.
[Collation back to front:] blank page, Russian title verso [2]; Hebrew title, printer's imprint verso [2]; Russian half-title for Pentateuch [1]; text, 1, 1–350, 350; verso blank [1]; Russian/Hebrew title for Joshua – 2 Kings [text for Ruth is missing] [1]; text, 352, 352–660, 660; verso blank [1].
21.5 × 13.

Reprint of the first two parts of the BFBS Hebrew/Russian diglot of the OT uniform in title, format, and pagination with no. 132. Although the title page indicates a complete OT, the BFBS copy lacks the last two parts. As in no. 132, this diglot used the BFBS Russian OT text. Its intended audience was the Jewish population of the Russian Empire, and its circulation was through BFBS agencies in Vienna, Odessa, and St. Petersburg. Because of its intended audience, this diglot edition was able to be sold out of the BFBS St. Petersburg Agency even though it did not contain the synodal text. Thirteen thousand copies were issued in 1888 (see BFBS FDSC Minutes, vol. 3, December 16, 1887, 256).
Loc: BFBS

168. 1889. NEW TESTAMENT. GOSPEL OF MATTHEW

Господа Нашего Іисуса Христа Святое Евангеліе отъ Матфея.
St. Petersburg: Synodal Press, 1889.
Title, synodal blessing verso [2]; text, 80pp.
12.5 × 8.

A printing in small format of the Gospel of Matthew, with format identical to small-size printings of the Gospels of Mark and John (nos. 146, 153, and 160).
Loc: BFBS

169. 1889. NEW TESTAMENT. THE GOSPEL OF LUKE

Господа Нашего Іисуса Христа Святое Евангеліе отъ Луки.
St. Petersburg: Synodal Press, 1889.
Title, synodal blessing verso [2]; text, 86pp.
12.5 × 8.

A printing in small format of the Gospel of Luke, uniform with the printings of the Gospels of Matthew, Mark and John circulated by BFBS agencies in Russia (see nos. 146, 153, 160, and 168).
Loc: BFBS

170. 1889. NEW TESTAMENT. GOSPEL OF JOHN

Господа Нашего Іисуса Христа Святое Евангеліе отъ Іоанна.
St. Petersburg: Synodal Press, 1889.
12.5 × 8.

Reprint of no. 146.
Loc: BFBS

171. 1889. NEW TESTAMENT

Новый Завѣтъ Господа Нашего Іисуса Христа.
St. Petersburg [and Moscow]: Synodal Press, 1889 [1882; 1889].
21.5 × 14.5.

Reprint of the synodal Gospels uniform in title, format, and pagination with no. 144 (1880) and previous printings. The internal subtitle page for Acts–Revelation indicates that it is the sixth printing (Moscow, 1882), here rebound with an 1889 printing of the Gospels.
Loc: BFBS

172. 1889. BIBLE

Библія или Книги Священнаго Писанія Ветхаго и Новаго Завѣта въ русскомъ переводѣ съ параллельными мѣстами. Изданіе первое.
St. Petersburg: Synodal Press, 1889.
Title, synodal blessing verso [i–ii]; table of contents [iii]–iv; OT text, 1–1219; verso blank [1220]; NT half-title, verso blank [1221–2]; NT text, 1223–1525; table of OT lessons, 1526–35; table of NT readings, 1536–48.
24.5 × 16.

First edition of an octavo synodal Bible with references and appended tables of OT and NT readings. Pagination is consecutive throughout. The text is in two columns on the page with paragraph indention of verses. References are placed at the bottom of the page. The OT includes bracketed passages from the Septuagint, as well as the deuterocanonical books of the OT not in the Hebrew canon. The NT does not capitalize pronominal references to the Virgin Mary. There is a note on page 1 of the text

indicating that the references have been taken from an earlier 1882 Moscow edition (*non de visu*), although this edition is specifically noted on the title page as the first. This reference edition went through thirteen printings (13th printing, RNB, 17.154.3.5, *non de visu*).
Loc: BFBS; RNB (18.173.6.14)

173. 1889. NEW TESTAMENT AND PSALTER

Новый Завѣтъ Господа Нашего Іисуса Христа и Псалтирь въ русскомъ переводѣ.
Moscow: Synodal Press [for the BFBS], 1889.
Title, synodal blessing verso [2]; NT text, 3–922; NT table of contents, verso blank [2]; Psalter title page, synodal blessing verso [2]; Psalter text, 3–242.
23 × 15.

Reprint of the synodal NT and Psalter in a Moscow large-type format uniform with no. 165. The Psalter has been added to this printing in uniform format, but with separate pagination. The 151st Psalm is omitted. Pronominal references to Mary are, for the first time, capitalized in an edition prepared for BFBS agency circulation in the Russian Empire.
Loc: BFBS

174. 1889. NEW TESTAMENT IN SLAVONIC AND RUSSIAN

Новый Завѣтъ Господа Нашего Іисуса Христа на славянскомъ и русскомъ языкахъ.
St. Petersburg: Synodal Press, 1889.
Title, synodal blessing verso [2]; text, 1121pp; table of contents verso [1].
15.5 × 11.

Third printing of the synodal NT diglot uniform with no. 147 (1881). The parallel texts are set in two opposing columns on the page with paragraph indention of verses. This is one of seventeen printings issued between 1881 and 1915.
Loc: BFBS

175. 1889. BIBLE

Священныя Книги Ветхаго и Новаго Завѣта.
Vienna: A. Holzhausen, printer, for BFBS, 1889.
23.5 × 14.5.

A fourth printing from stereotype plates of the Vienna BFBS Bible compiled from the synodal NT and the BFBS translation of the OT (see

no. 134 [1877] and no. 139 [1878]). The title, collation, and format are identical with earlier printings. According to BFBS FDSC Minutes (vol. 4, February 24, 1988, 17), Three thousand copies were printed.
Loc: BFBS; RNB (B9–7/3383)

176. 1889. OLD TESTAMENT. PENTATEUCH IN HEBREW/RUSSIAN DIGLOT

Vienna: A. Holzhausen for BFBS, 1889.
Stereotype reprint uniform of no. 131. According to BFBS FDSC Minutes (vol. 4, February 24, 1888, 17), Three thousand copies of the diglot were printed from the society's stereotype plates.
Loc: BFBS

177. 1889. NEW TESTAMENT

Новый Завѣтъ Господа Нашего Іисуса Христа въ русскомъ переводѣ.
Изданіе седьмое.
St. Petersburg: Synodal Press for BFBS, 1889.
17 × 12.

A seventh printing of the "People's Edition" of the synodal Russian NT uniform in title, collation, and format with no. 155 (1885). Circulation in 100,000 copies brought the total number of copies printed of this edition to 600,000.
Loc: BFBS

178. 1890. NEW TESTAMENT IN SLAVONIC/RUSSIAN DIGLOT

Новый Завѣтъ Господа Нашего Іисуса Христа на славянскомъ и русскомъ языкахъ.
St. Petersburg: Synodal Press, 1890.
Title, synodal blessing verso [2]; table of contents, verso blank [2]; Gospels text, 3–478; Acts–Revelation text, 548pp.
21.5 × 14.5.

A printing of the synodal NT in a Slavonic and Russian diglot similar in format to no. 120, with two columns of parallel texts and paragraph indention of verses set within a rectangular border. On the back cover (BFBS copy) the sale price of 1 ruble, 50 kopecks is inscribed. This is the first St. Petersburg Synodal Press imprint to capitalize pronominal references to the Virgin Mary.
Loc: BFBS

179. 1890. NEW TESTAMENT. GOSPEL OF JOHN IN GREEK, SLAVONIC, RUSSIAN AND LATIN

Новый Завѣтъ Господа Нашего Іисуса Христа на четырехъ языкахъ: эллинскомъ, словенскомъ, россійскомъ и римскомъ съ параллельными мѣстами. Книга четвертая отъ Іоанна святое благовѣствованіе.
St. Petersburg: Synodal Press, 1890.
Title, synodal blessing verso [2]; half-title [1]; text, 2–193.
24.5 × 16.

Polyglot edition of the Gospel of John uniform in format to no. 164.
Loc: OX (N.T.Polyg. d.9/2)

180. 1890. NEW TESTAMENT. GOSPELS

Господа Нашего Іисуса Христа Святое Евангеліе отъ Матфея, Марка, Луки и Іоанна.
St. Petersburg: Synodal Press [for BFBS], 1890.
12.5 × 8.5.

Reprint uniform with no. 60 (1863) and numerous subsequent reprintings. This popular item sold in BFBS agencies at 12 kopecks (see back cover of BFBS copy).
Loc: BFBS

181. 1890. NEW TESTAMENT. GOSPELS IN SLAVONIC/RUSSIAN DIGLOT

Господа Нашего Іисуса Христа Святое Евангеліе отъ Матфея, Марка, Луки и Іоанна на славянскомъ и русскомъ языкахъ. Изданіе тридцать девятое.
St. Petersburg: Synodal Press, 1890.
Title, synodal blessing verso [2]; text, 3–478.
21.5 × 14.

Reprint of the synodal Gospels in parallel Slavonic and Russian text, uniform in format with the Gospels section of no. 178 (1890). Title page identifies this as the thirty-ninth printing of the Gospels diglot. Back cover of BFBS copy gives price of 50 kopecks. DM 7880 mistakenly identifies this as the thirty-second printing. This printing continues the capitalization of pronominal references to Mary first introduced in the 1890 St. Petersburg entry no. 178.
Loc: BFBS

182. 1890. NEW TESTAMENT AND PSALTER

Новый Завѣтъ Господа Нашего Іисуса Христа и Псалтирь въ русскомъ переводѣ.
St. Petersburg: Synodal Press [for BFBS], 1890.
13 × 8.

Reprint of synodal NT and Psalter uniform in all respects with no. 166 (1888). A handwritten note on the flyleaf of the BFBS copy indicates the cost to the Bible Society was 32½ kopecks per bound copy. The selling price is not marked.
Loc: BFBS

183. 1890. NEW TESTAMENT. GOSPEL HARMONY

Краткое Изложеніе Евангелія.
[Geneva, 1890]

A paraphrastic translation by Leo Tolstoy. For complete annotation, see no. 202 (1901).
Loc: *Non de visu.*

184. 1890. PSALTER

Псалтирь.
St. Petersburg: Synodal Press [for BFBS], 1890.
Title, synodal blessing verso [2]; text, 3–159.
12.5 × 8.

A printing of the pocket-size Psalter similar in format to the Psalter bound in no. 166 (1888). The pagination is different, although the last page is misnumbered, as in no. 166. Psalm 151 is omitted. The BFBS Petersburg Agency purchased 20,000 copies of this work from the Synod for distribution through BFBS agencies in Russia (BFBS FDSC Minutes, vol. 4, November 14, 1890, 225).
Loc: BFBS

185. 1890. OLD TESTAMENT. MICAH [AND OTHER OT BOOKS]

Книга пророка Михея. Библіологическое и экзегетическое изслѣдованіе.
Kazan: University Press, 1890.
[4], lxvi, 372, vii pp.

Russian translation of Micah from the Septuagint, the first of P. Iungerov's published translations of OT books. Iungerov's commentary accompanies his translation. Over the course of twenty-six years, Iungerov published several other OT translations from the Greek Septuagint. Listed below are the Iungerov translations represented within RNB holdings. Most of the translations were first published in the journal of the Kazan Theological Academy, *Pravoslavnyi sobesednik*, and subsequently issued separately:

Amos, Kazan University Press, 1897 (RNB: 20.85.6.6)
Proverbs, Kazan University Press, 1908 (RNB: 38.5.9.60)
Jeremiah, *Pravoslavnyi sobesednik*, 1910 (RNB: 38.77.7.78)
Ezekiel, *Pravoslavnyi sobesednik*, 1911 (RNB: 37.30.8.201)
Daniel, *Pravoslavnyi sobesednik*, 1912 (RNB: 20.98.8.201)
The Minor Prophets, *Pravoslavnyi sobesednik*, 1913 (RNB: 20.38.9.57)
Job, *Pravoslavnyi sobesednik*, 1914 (RNB: 37.55.6.381)
Loc: RNB (18.220.4.39)

186. 1892. OLD TESTAMENT. PENTATEUCH

Библія или Книги Священнаго Писанія Ветхаго и Новаго Завѣта въ русскомъ переводѣ съ параллельными мѣстами. Томъ I. Изданіе второе, вновь просмотрѣнное.
St. Petersburg, Synodal Press, 1892.
Title, synodal blessing verso [2]; table of contents, verso blank [2]; text, 1–248.
25 × 16.

Reprint of the synodal Pentateuch uniform in format with the 1889 Petersburg Bible (no. 172). A note on page 1 of the text indicates that the references are drawn from the 1890 Moscow Bible, references that were unchanged from the 1882 Moscow and 1889 St. Petersburg printings. The BFBS circulated the synodal Pentateuch in their agencies inasmuch as it contained no deuterocanonical texts, and could be bound separately.
Loc: BFBS

187. 1892. PSALTER

Псалтирь.
St. Petersburg: Synodal Press [for BFBS], 1892.
15.5 × 10.5.

Reprint of the Synodal Psalter without the 151st Psalm, uniform with no. 117 (1873) and subsequent reprintings done for the BFBS. A printing of

20,000 copies was ordered in June 1891 (see BFBS FDSC Minutes, vol. 5, June 12, 1891, 5).
Loc: BFBS

188. 1892. NEW TESTAMENT

Библія или Книги Священнаго Писанія Ветхаго и Новаго Завѣта въ русскомъ переводѣ съ параллельными мѣстами. Томъ V: [*Новый Завѣтъ Господа Нашего Іисуса Христа.*] Изданіе второе, вновь просмотрѣнное.
St. Petersburg: Synodal Press, 1892.
Title, synodal blessing verso [2]; table of contents, verso blank [2]; half-title, verso blank [2]; text, 1223–1525; table of OT readings, 1526–35; table of NT readings, 1536–48.
25.5 × 17.

A "newly revised second edition" of the synodal NT with references, uniform with the first edition of 1889 (no. 172). "Newly revised" refers to Synodal Press capitalization for pronominal references to Mary in this edition. Otherwise, the edition is the same as that of 1889. Pagination reflects the fact that this fifth part of the full Bible was being sold separately as a NT (as in the BL copy). The RNB copy cited below is part of an entire Bible with an 1892 Petersburg imprint.
Loc: BL (3061.g.15); RNB (18.322.2.2, *non de visu*)

189. 1893. BIBLE

Библія или Книги Святаго Писанія Ветхаго и Новаго Завѣта въ русскомъ переводѣ съ параллельными мѣстами.
Kiev: Pecherskaia Monastery Press, 1893.
iv, 1548pp.

First printing of the complete Russian synodal Bible in a Kiev edition. At least four printings were issued before World War I (see also RNB 20.63.3.17 [1899]; RNB 38.10.6.10 [1904]; and RNB 37.33.4.21 [1911]).
Loc: RNB (38.9.3.27, *non de visu*)

190. 1893. BIBLE

Священныя Книги Ветхаго и Новаго Завѣта.
Vienna: A. Holzhausen, printer, for BFBS, 1893.
24 × 15.

Fifth stereotype reprinting of the Vienna BFBS Bible first issued in 1877 (no. 134).
Loc: BFBS; RNB (82–7/700)

[1893. OLD TESTAMENT. PSALTER IN HEBREW AND RUSSIAN

According to the RNB catalog, the Psalter was issued separately in 1893 in a Hebrew/Russian diglot published by A. Holzhausen of Vienna.]

191. 1893. NEW TESTAMENT

Новый Завѣтъ Господа Нашего Іисуса Христа въ русскомъ переводѣ.
Изданіе двѣнадцатое.
St. Petersburg: Synodal Press [for BFBS], 1893.
16 × 11.5.

A twelfth printing of the "People's Edition" of the synodal NT uniform with no. 155 (1885) and subsequent printings. According to the report of St. Petersburg BFBS agent William Nicolson, the 100,000 copies of this 1893 printing brought BFBS circulation of the "People's Edition" to more than one million (*The Ninetieth Report of the BFBS*, London, 1894, 103). The Synodal Press had introduced capitalization of pronominal references to Mary between the seventh printing (no. 177, 1889) and this twelfth printing.
Loc: BFBS

192. 1893. OLD TESTAMENT. THE PSALTER

Псалтирь въ русскомъ переводѣ с греческаго Еп. Порфирія.
St. Petersburg: Synodal Press, 1893.
242pp.

A translation of the Psalter from the Greek Septuagint done by Bishop Porfirii (Uspenskii, 1804–85). Published posthumously, this is the first published translation of the Psalter into Russian based exclusively upon the Septuagint, and reflects the continuing debate over the synodal translation within the Russian church.
Loc: RNB (18.267.5.40)

193. 1894. NEW TESTAMENT

Новый Завѣтъ Господа Нашего Іисуса Христа въ русскомъ переводѣ.
Изданіе четырнадцатое.
St. Petersburg: Synodal Press [for BFBS], 1894.
16 × 11.5.

Fourteenth printing of the "People's Edition" of the synodal Russian NT uniform with no. 191 (1893). Fifty thousand copies were printed (see *The Ninety-First Report of the BFBS*, London, 1895, 105).
Loc: BFBS

194. 1896. NEW TESTAMENT AND PSALTER

Новый Завѣтъ Господа Нашего Iисуса Христа съ указателемъ евангельскихъ и апостольскихъ чтенiй.
Moscow: Synodal Press, 1896.
NT title, synodal blessing verso [2]; NT table of contents [2]; NT text, 621pp; verso blank [1]; table of readings, 1–30; Psalter text, 152pp.
15.5 × 12.

A smaller printing of the synodal Russian NT and Psalms with a table of Gospel and epistle lessons. The text is set in two columns on the page with paragraph indention of verses. The Psalter includes the 151st Psalm, but the NT does not capitalize pronominal references to Mary. The title of the Psalter is not on the general title page, but is included on the spine of the BFBS copy. The back cover lists a price of 40 kopecks, and includes in Russian the seal of Astaf'ev's Society for the Dissemination of the Holy Scriptures in Russia, which purchased scripture through the BFBS Petersburg agency at reduced rates.
Loc: BFBS

195. 1896. BIBLE

Библiя или Книги Святаго Писанiя Ветхаго и Новаго Завѣта въ русскомъ переводѣ, съ параллельными мѣстами и указателемъ церковныхъ чтенiй. Въ трехъ частяхъ.
Moscow: Synodal Press, 1896.
Title, verso blank [2]; table of contents [2]; title (Genesis–Esther), synodal blessing verso [2]; Genesis–Esther text, 1–710; title (Job – 3 Ezra), synodal blessing verso [2]; Job – 3 Ezra text, 1–686; title (NT), synodal blessing verso [2]; NT text, 1–354; table of readings, 355–70.
31 × 23.

A printing of the synodal Russian Bible in larger format. The format is similar to no. 172 (1889), but the font is larger. There is irregular capitalization of pronominal references to Mary. The CUL copy includes an inscription to the Cambridge University Library from Archbishop Antonii of Finland (St. Petersburg, August 28, 1897).
Loc: CUL (20.6.b.85.2)

[1897. BIBLE. A third printing of the synodal reference Bible uniform with nos. 172 and 199 (RNB, 20.97.1.25, *non de visu*).]

196. 1897. NEW TESTAMENT AND PSALTER

Новый Завѣтъ Господа Нашего Іисуса Христа и Псалтирь въ русскомъ переводѣ.
St. Petersburg: Synodal Press [for BFBS], 1897.
Title, synodal blessing verso [2]; NT text, 3–838; NT table of contents [2]; Psalter title, synodal blessing verso [2]; Psalter text, 3–220.
23 × 15.5.

An octavo printing of the synodal Russian NT and Psalter in large type, similar to the Moscow large-print editions of 1888 (no. 165) and 1889 (no. 173). This St. Petersburg edition has fewer pages than the Moscow edition. This volume circulated widely through BFBS agencies in Russia. BFBS agent William Nicolson ordered 35,000 copies (BFBS FDSC Minutes, vol. 6, 264; and vol. 7, 10, 37). The edition includes capitalized pronominal references to Mary, but excludes the 151st Psalm.
Loc: BFBS

197. 1897. NEW TESTAMENT

Новый Завѣтъ Господа Нашего Іисуса Христа въ русскомъ переводѣ.
Изданіе двадцатое.
St. Petersburg: Synodal Press [for BFBS], 1897.
16 × 11.5.

Twentieth printing of the "People's Edition" of the synodal NT, uniform with no. 191 (1893).
Loc: BL (3061.de.44)

[1897. OLD TESTAMENT. AMOS. P. Iungerov's Russian translation from the Septuagint of the book of Amos, published at Kazan University Press in 1897 (RNB: 20.85.6.6, *non de visu*).]

198. 1898. PSALTER

Псалтирь.
St. Petersburg: Synodal Press [for BFBS], 1898.
15 × 11.

Reprint of the synodal Psalter uniform with no. 117 (1873). A price of 25 kopecks is on the back cover. Commonly circulated by BFBS agencies in Russia, 10,000 copies were ordered in November 1897 (BFBS FDSC Minutes, vol. 7, 91).
Loc: BFBS

199. 1898. BIBLE

Библія или Книги Святаго Писанія Ветхаго и Новаго Завѣта въ русскомъ переводѣ съ параллельными мѣстами. Изданіе четвертое.
St. Petersburg: Synodal Press, 1898.
Title, synodal blessing verso [2]; table of contents [2]; OT text, 1–1219; verso blank [1220]; NT half-title, verso blank [1221–2]; NT text, 1223–1525; table of lessons, 1526–48.
25.5 × 16.

Fourth printing of the synodal Bible with references and a table of readings in larger octavo format uniform with the 1889 edition (no. 172, see also the bracketed listing for 1897). Pronominal references to Mary are not uniformly capitalized throughout. See fifth stereotype reprinting of 1900 immediately below.
Loc: CUL (20.6.c.90.1); RNB (20.105.2.35)

[1900. BIBLE. A fifth printing of the St. Petersburg reference Bible uniform with no. 199 (RNB, 20.65.7.3, *non de visu*) and a second printing of the Moscow reference Bible (uniform with no. 195) were both issued in 1900.]

200. 1901, 1902. OLD TESTAMENT. PENTATEUCH IN RUSSIAN/HEBREW DIGLOT

Пятикнижіе Моисеево съ дословнымъ русскимъ переводомъ и съ комментаріями русскимъ еврейскимъ, объясняющими текстъ, также исторію, географію и археологію библейскаго мира. Чч. 1–5.
Vil'na: Tip. Vdovy i Br. Romm, 1901; and Vil'na: Tip. I. I. Pirozhnikova, 1902.
Title pages for parts 1–2, censor's approval verso; Genesis, 1–134; Exodus, 1–112; title pages for parts 3–5, censor's approval verso [i–iv]; preface [v]–xxx; Leviticus, 1–88; Numbers, 1–114; Deuteronomy, 1–110.

A rebinding of two separately published portions of the Pentateuch prepared by O. [Osei] N. Shteinberg, inspector of the Vil'na Jewish Teachers' Institute. The separate portions are the 1901 publication of Genesis and Exodus, and the 1902 publication of Leviticus, Numbers,

and Deuteronomy. The preface, which is located at the beginning of the 1902 publication, includes sections on "the most ancient testament in general," "the five books of Moses (Torah) in particular," and "the language of Holy Scripture and its Translations: Aramaic, Greek, Samaritan, Syrian, Arabic, Persian, Latin, and Church-Slavonic." The text, which follows closely the text of Gordon, Gershtein, and Levanda (no. 123), is in two columns on the page – right-hand side Hebrew, left-hand side Russian – but also includes extended explanatory comments intended for students at the bottom of each page (also in two columns). The translation and commentary were intended for study of Hebrew and of the Torah in Jewish educational institutions. The 1901 title page records that this Pentateuch with the commentary was approved by a "scholarly committee of the Russian Ministry of Public Instruction for use in Jewish educational institutions."
Loc: BL (ORB30/1359); RNB (34.3.1.126, *non de visu*)

201. 1901. NEW TESTAMENT. ROMANS–COLOSSIANS IN SLAVONIC/RUSSIAN DIGLOT WITH COMMENTARY

Общедоступное объясненіе первыхъ семи посланій Святаго Апостола Павла.
St. Petersburg: Synodal Press, 1901.
Title, censor's permit verso [2]; table of contents, verso blank [2]; general preface, 1–9; preface to Romans, 9–13; table, 14; Romans text, 15–138; 1 Corinthians half-title, verso blank [139–40]; preface, 141–5; table, 146; 1 Corinthians text, 147–255; verso blank [256]; 2 Corinthians half-title, verso blank [257–8]; preface, 259–61; table, 262; 2 Corinthians text, 263–340; Galatians half-title, verso blank [341–2]; preface to Galatians, 343–6; Galatians text, 347–98; Ephesians half-title, verso blank [399–400]; preface to Ephesians, 401–5; verso blank [406]; Ephesians text, 407–51; verso blank [452]; Philippians half-title, verso blank [453–4]; preface to Philippians, 455–9; table, 460; Philippians text, 461–95; verso blank [496]; Colossians half-title, verso blank [497–8]; preface, 499–506; Colossians text, 507–48.
25.5 × 16.5.

A diglot edition of Romans–Colossians in parallel Slavonic and Russian synodal texts with extended commentary prepared by Bishop Nikanor. The text is in two columns on the page with the lengthy commentary at the foot of the page. Each epistle is preceded by a preface. On the general title page of the BFBS copy is a handwritten note to Rev. [Arthur] Taylor, General Secretary of the BFBS, from Bishop Nikanor. A note on the back

cover gives a price of 3 rubles. In the twentieth century, the synodal text began to be issued with extended commentaries.
Loc: BFBS

202. 1901. NEW TESTAMENT. GOSPEL HARMONY

L. N. Tolstoy. *Изложеніе Евангелія съ примечаніями взятыми изъ книги «Соединеніе и переводъ 4-хъ Евангелій».*
Christchurch, UK: Izdanie "Svobodnago Slova," no. 61, by A. Tchertkoff, 1901.

A second edition of the Gospel harmony prepared by the Russian writer Leo Tolstoy and published with the assistance of his colleagues in Britain, Anna and Vladimir Chertkov. Pages 1–103 of this compendium constitute the Tolstoy paraphrase of the four Gospels. The paraphrase was first published in Geneva in 1890 (see no. 183). Each verse of the paraphrase is numbered consecutively, and the numbers are then correlated at the end of the volume (pp. 214–22), with verse references to the synodal Gospels. Republication of this Gospel harmony dates to the Chertkovs' Tolstoyan activity in Britain.
Loc: BL (3227.ee.17)

203. 1902 [1901–2]. NEW TESTAMENT. 1 THESSALONIANS–HEBREWS IN SLAVONIC/RUSSIAN DIGLOT

Общедоступное объясненіе первыхъ семи посланій Святаго Апостола Павла.
St. Petersburg: Synodal Press, 1902 [1901–2].
General title, verso blank [2]; title for 1 and 2 Thessalonians, censor's permit verso [2]; preface, 3–9; verso blank [10]; 1 Thessalonians text, 11–48; 2 Thessalonians half-title, verso blank [49–50]; preface, 51–4; 2 Thessalonians text, 55–74; title for Timothy, Titus and Philemon, censor's permit verso [2]; preface, 1–8; Timothy text, 9–52; 2 Timothy half-title, verso blank [53–4]; preface, 55–7; verso blank [58]; 2 Timothy text, 59–92; Titus half-title, verso blank [93–4]; preface, 95–9; verso blank [100]; Titus title, 101–19; verso blank [120]; Philemon half-title, verso blank [121–2]; preface, 123–5; verso blank [126]; Philemon text, 127–35; verso blank, 136; title for Hebrews, censor's permit verso [2]; preface, 1–8; Hebrews text, 9–149.
25.5 × 16.5.

A diglot edition of 1 Thessalonians–Hebrews in Slavonic and Russian synodal texts with extended commentary by Bishop Nikanor. Uniform with no. 201.
Loc: BFBS

[1902. NEW TESTAMENT. SELECTIONS. Selections of a NT translation prepared by the Russian poet Vasilii Zhukovskii may be found in the Russian journal, *Strannik* (1902, no. 4)]

[1902. BIBLE. RNB holdings include a sixth printing of the St. Petersburg Bible with references issued in 1902 (20.72.6.28, *non de visu*) uniform with no. 172.]

[1902. BIBLE. RNB holdings include a 1902 stereotype reprinting of the Vienna BFBS Bible (82–5/2867, *non de visu*) uniform with nos. 134 and 190.]

204. 1903. OLD TESTAMENT. THE PROPHETS AND THE WRITINGS IN HEBREW/RUSSIAN DIGLOT

Священныя Книги Ветхаго Завѣта въ переводѣ съ еврейскаго текста. 2 vols. in 1.
Vienna: Trowitsch and Sons [Berlin] for BFBS, 1903.
[Collation from back:] blank page, Russian title verso [2]; Hebrew title, printer's imprint verso [2]; list of later prophets [1]; Russian/Hebrew, 663, 663–987, 987; verso blank [988]; Hagiographa half-title [989]; text, 990, 991–1384, 1384.
21.5 × 13.

Stereotype reprint of the Hebrew/Russian diglot of the later prophets and Hagiographa using the BFBS Russian OT text. The format is uniform with diglots earlier printed for the BFBS by the Viennese printer Holzhausen (see nos. 133 and 167).
Loc: BFBS

205. 1903. OLD TESTAMENT. THE FORMER PROPHETS (JOSHUA, JUDGES, 1 SAMUEL – 2 KINGS) IN HEBREW/RUSSIAN DIGLOT

Пророки первые переведенные съ еврейскаго текста. Для употребленiя евреямъ.
Vienna: Trowitzsch and Sons [Berlin] for BFBS, 1903.
[Collation from back:] blank page, Russian title verso [2]; Hebrew title, printer's imprint verso [2]; Former Prophets half-title [1]; text, 352, 352–660, 660.
22 × 13.5.

Stereotype reprint of the Former Prophets in Hebrew and Russian. The Russian OT text is that of the BFBS and the format is uniform with no. 167.

This is a portion of the OT diglot ordered in 5,000 copies, but bound in separate parts (see BFBS FDSC Minutes, vol. 10, 2).
Loc: BFBS

206. 1903. NEW TESTAMENT. GOSPELS

Господа Нашего Іисуса Христа Святое Евангеліе отъ Матфея, Марка, Луки и Іоанна. Изданіе первое.
St. Petersburg: Synodal Press [for BFBS], 1903.
Title, synodal blessing verso [2]; text, 230pp.
16 × 12.

A printing of the synodal Russian Gospels in small format uniform with that of the "People's Edition." Thirty thousand copies were ordered by the BFBS Agency in Petersburg (BFBS FDSC Minutes, vol. 10, 99). DM 7883 indicates this printing was later bound for free distribution by BFBS colporteurs to "Russian troops proceeding to the Far East during the Russo-Japanese War," 1904–5. The back cover has a Russian logotype for the BFBS and the note, "for free distribution." A front flyleaf label in Russian says the volume "is given by the British and Foreign Bible Society." Although the title page describes this as a "first edition" and DM 7883 calls it a "special edition," the format is uniform with the Gospels in the "People's Edition" of the NT. Pronominal references to Mary are capitalized.
Loc: BFBS (two copies)

[1904. BIBLE. RNB holdings include a seventh printing of the St. Petersburg Russian reference Bible (38.67.2.39, *non de visu*) uniform with no. 172.]

[1904–13. Толковая Библія или Комментаріи на всѣ книги св. Писанія Ветхаго и Новаго Завѣта. Between 1904 and 1913, this twelve-volume interpreter's Bible was published as a supplement to the journal *Strannik* under the editorship of A. P. Lopukhin. The biblical text was that of the synodal translation. See no. 340 for the 1987 reprint edition commissioned to mark the millennium of Christianity in Russia. RNB holds this first edition (*Non de visu*).]

207. 1904. PSALTER

Псалтирь.
St. Petersburg: [Synodal Press for BFBS] 1904.
Title, verso blank [2]; text, 130pp.
16 × 12.

An octavo edition of the synodal Russian Psalter uniform in format with the "People's Edition" of the NT. Psalm 151 is omitted. The title page does not include the Synodal Press imprint, nor is the Synod's blessing on the title page verso. The binding of the BFBS copy is similar to that of no. 206, and the purpose of the special printing was identical (free distribution to troops).
Loc: BFBS; RNB (38.62.9.19)

208. 1904. NEW TESTAMENT. GOSPELS

Господа Нашего Іисуса Христа Святое Евангеліе отъ Матфея, Марка, Луки и Іоанна на русскомъ языкѣ.
St. Petersburg: Synodal Press, 1904.
Title, synodal blessing verso [2]; text, 3–285; verso blank [286]; index of readings, 287–99.
24.5 × 17.

An octavo large-font edition of the synodal Gospels similar in format to the Moscow large-print NT (no. 165, 1888), but with an ornate rectangular inset border and new pagination. A table of readings is added in consecutive pagination.
Loc: BFBS

209. 1904. NEW TESTAMENT. GOSPELS

Господа Нашего Іисуса Христа Святое Евангеліе отъ Матфея, Марка, Луки и Іоанна.
St. Petersburg: Synodal Press, 1904.
Title, synodal blessing verso [2]; text 322pp.
13.5 × 9.

An edition of the small pocket-size synodal Russian Gospels similar in format to the edition of no. 60 (1863) and other reprintings, but with different pagination. The new format adds a rectangular inset border. There are two columns to the page with paragraph indention of verses. Pronominal references to Mary are capitalized.
Loc: BFBS

210. 1904. NEW TESTAMENT IN SLAVONIC/RUSSIAN DIGLOT

Новый Завѣтъ Господа Нашего Іисуса Христа на славянскомъ и русскомъ языкахъ. Изданіе тринадцатое.
St. Petersburg: Synodal Press, 1904.

Title, synodal blessing verso [2]; text, 1–1121; table of contents [1]; table of readings, 3–30.
15 × 10.5.

Thirteenth printing of the Slavonic/Russian synodal NT diglot in small format. The text is set in two columns, Slavonic and Russian, on each page with paragraph indention of verses. The Russian text includes pronominal capitalization of references to Mary.
Loc: BL (3062.a.2)

211. 1905. BIBLE

Священныя Книги Ветхаго и Новаго Завѣта.
Vienna: A. Holzhausen, printer, for BFBS, 1905.
23.5 × 15.

Stereotype reprinting of the Vienna Russian Bible employing the BFBS OT text, uniform with no. 134 (1877) and subsequent reprintings. Five thousand copies were printed (BFBS FDSC Minutes, vol. 11, 21).
Loc: BFBS

212. 1905. NEW TESTAMENT. ACTS OF THE APOSTLES AND CATHOLIC EPISTLES

Дѣянія Святыхъ Апостоловъ и соборныя посланія въ новомъ русскомъ переводѣ.
St. Petersburg: Synodal Press, 1905.
Title, synodal statement verso [2]; table of contents, verso blank [2]; Acts half-title, introduction verso [1–2]; text, 3–91; verso blank [92]; James half-title, introduction verso [93–4]; text, 95–104; 1 Peter half-title, introduction verso [105–6]; text, 107–16; 2 Peter half-title, introduction verso [117–18]; text, 119–25; verso blank, 126; 1 John half-title, introduction verso [127–8]; text, 129–38; 2–3 John half-title, introduction verso [139–40]; text, 140–4; Jude half-title, introduction verso [145–6]; text, 147–9.
22 × 15.

A new Russian translation of the Acts of the Apostles and the Catholic epistles done by Konstantin P. Pobedonostsev, ober-prokuror of the Holy Synod, 1881–1905. The text follows closely the synodal edition, replacing Slavonic archaisms with modern Russian words or phrases. The text is printed in one column on the page in paragraphs without individual verse numbering. The title page verso reads in Russian, “printed on the order of the ober-prokuror of the Holy Synod in a small number of copies not for public circulation.” The Bodleian Library copy is bound with nos. 213 and 214 below.
Loc: OX (Birkbeck e.53)

213. 1905. NEW TESTAMENT. GALATIANS, EPHESIANS, PHILIPPIANS, COLOSSIANS AND 1–2 THESSALONIANS

Посланія Апостола Павла въ новомъ русскомъ переводѣ. [Часть 1]
St. Petersburg: Synodal Press, 1905.
Title, synodal statement verso [2]; table of contents, verso blank [2]; translator's introduction [2]; Galatians half-title, introduction verso [2]; text, 1–12; Ephesians half-title, introduction verso [13–14]; text, 15–25; verso blank [26]; Philippians text, 29–37; verso blank [38]; Colossians half-title, introduction verso [39–40]; text, 41–8; 1–2 Thessalonians half-title, introduction verso [49–50]; text, 51–65.
22 × 15.

A new Russian translation of the Pauline epistles (first part) by K. P. Pobedonostsev, with format identical to no. 212. Title verso statement regarding non-circulation to the public is as in no. 212. The Oxford Bodleian copy bears an inscription on the title page signed by Pobedonostsev to the "most beloved Ivan (i.e. John) Birkbeck, 26 September 1905." Opening preface is dated July 1905.
Loc: OX (Birkbeck e.53)

214. 1905. NEW TESTAMENT. 1–2 CORINTHIANS, ROMANS, 1–2 TIMOTHY, TITUS, PHILEMON, AND HEBREWS

Посланія Апостола Павла въ новомъ русскомъ переводѣ. [Часть 2]
St. Petersburg: Synodal Press, 1905.
Title, synodal statement verso [2]; table of contents, verso blank [2]; 1 Corinthians half-title, introduction verso [2]; text, 3–36; 2 Corinthians half-title, introduction verso [37–8]; text, 39–62; Romans half-title, introduction [63–4]; text, 65–99; verso blank [100]; 1–2 Timothy half-title, introduction verso [101–2]; text, 103–19; verso blank [120]; Titus half-title, introduction [121–2]; text, 123–7; verso blank [128]; Philemon half-title, introduction [129–30]; text, 131–2; Hebrews half-title, introduction verso [133–4]; text, 135–61.
22 × 15.

The Pauline epistles (second part) translated into Russian by K. P. Pobedonostsev, uniform in format with nos. 212 and 213. Again, the title verso notes that the edition is not for circulation to the public. Pobedonostsev's Russian NT translation was issued in 1905–6 as an experiment intended to introduce a more easily readable text for domestic use. For the full NT text, see no. 217.
Loc: OX (Birkbeck e.53)

215. 1905. NEW TESTAMENT. GOSPELS

Господа Нашего Іисуса Христа Святое Евангеліе отъ Матфея, Марка, Луки и Іоанна на русскомъ языкѣ.
Tokyo: Printed for the Russian Spiritual Mission in Japan, 1905.
Title, bishop's imprint verso [2]; text, 3–382; table of lessons, 383–95.
15.5 × 11.

A printing of the synodal Russian Gospels in a photolithographic, reduced-size format. The text is taken from the Moscow 1889 large-print edition (no. 173, 1889). The appended lessons are reproduced in reduced size from an edition identical in format to that at the end of no. 208 (St. Petersburg, 1904). The title verso says that the volume was "reprinted from the Russian synodal edition by a phototypographical method." The name of "Bishop Nikolai, Superintendent of the Russian Spiritual Mission in Japan," is printed on the title page verso. The BFBS copy contains a note entered by a Russian prisoner of war in Japan who says that the copy was given personally by Bishop Nikolai on September 8, 1905. DM 7887 notes the edition was "intended for Russian prisoners in Japan during the Russo-Japanese war."
Loc: BFBS

216. 1906. NEW TESTAMENT

Новый Завѣтъ Господа Нашего Іисуса Христа.
Moscow: Synodal Press, 1906.
22.5 × 15.

A reprinting of the Moscow large-type synodal NT uniform with nos. 154 (1884) and 165 (1888). CUL copy is bound with the 1910 Psalter (no. 227). A table of NT readings, pp. 1–18, is appended following the Psalter.
Loc: CUL (28.6.c.90.1)

217. 1906. NEW TESTAMENT

Новый Завѣтъ Господа Нашего Іисуса Христа въ новомъ русскомъ переводѣ: Опытъ къ усовершенствованію перевода на русскій языкъ священныхъ книгъ Новаго Завѣта.
St. Petersburg: Synodal Press, 1906.
Title, synodal permission verso [2]; translator's preface, I–VI; Gospels text, 1–301; verso blank [302]; Acts half-title, verso blank [303–4]; introduction to epistles and Acts [305–6]; Acts–Revelation text, 307–629; verso blank [1]; table of contents, verso blank [2].
20.5 × 14.5.

Complete edition of Konstantin Pobedonostsev's Russian translation of the NT in octavo. See portions under nos. 212–14. Pobedonostsev's text is the first new Russian text of the NT since publication of the 1862 synodal edition. As Pobedonostsev indicates in his preface, the attempt was to modernize Russian usage, replacing Slavonic phrases for which there were adequate Russian equivalents. Several examples of this modernization are provided in the preface. Pronominal references to Mary are capitalized. Aside from the lexical changes, the text follows closely the phrasing and structure of the synodal NT. The text is printed in one column on the page. The Gospels and Revelation have separate paragraph indention for each verse. The Acts of the Apostles and the epistles are set in longer paragraphs with verse numbering in the margins. The Catholic epistles precede the Pauline epistles. Brief introductory notes at the beginning of each NT section address authorship and reasons for changes from the synodal edition. Title page verso includes a note that the edition is printed with synodal "permission," as opposed to the normal "blessing" in standard printings of the synodal translation.
Loc: OX (N.T.Russ. e.4); RNB (82–3/4998)

[1907. NEW TESTAMENT. RNB holds a second printing (37.1.5.42, *non de visu*) of no. 217, with a 1907 imprint.]

218. 1907. NEW TESTAMENT

Новый Завѣтъ Господа Нашего Іисуса Христа въ русскомъ переводѣ. Изданіе тридцать третье.
St. Petersburg: Synodal Press for BFBS, 1907.
Title, table of contents verso [2]; text, 514pp.
16 × 11.5.

Thirty-third printing of the "People's Edition" of the synodal NT, with format similar to no. 193 (1894) and other printings. Synodal blessing is found on the title page with the table of contents verso.
Loc: BFBS

219. 1907. BIBLE

Библія. Книги Священнаго Писанія Ветхаго и Новаго Завѣта (каноническія) въ русскомъ переводѣ съ параллельными мѣстами.
St. Petersburg: Synodal Press for BFBS, 1907.
Title, Synod "permission" verso [2]; table of contents [2]; OT text, 682pp; NT title, synodal "blessing" verso [2]; NT text, 208pp.
21.5 × 14.5.

An edition of the complete Russian synodal Bible with marginal references prepared for the BFBS Petersburg Agency by the Holy Synod Press. The OT was based on the synodal text, but excluded books not in the Hebrew canon and eliminated bracketed Septuagint passages as in the St. Petersburg 1882 edition for the BFBS (no. 148). The Psalter does not contain the 151st Psalm. The edition retained capitalization of pronominal references to Mary, an increasingly uniform feature of all synodal printings. The OT title verso contains the note "printed for the British Bible Society" and indicates that it is "with the permission [not the "blessing"] of the Most Holy Synod." By contrast, the NT title verso contains the standard synodal blessing. The text is in two columns on the page with references in the left and right margins without paragraph indention of individual verses. Permission was granted for printing of 25,000 copies (see *The Hundred and Fourth Report of the BFBS*, London, 1908, 121). An electroplate reprinting of this edition was issued by the American Bible Society in 1918. The RNB also holds a stereotype reprint of this edition bearing a 1917 Petrograd imprint (130/4232, *non de visu*).
Loc: BFBS; RNB (37.21.4.64)

[1908. BIBLE. RNB holdings include an eighth printing (38.72.7.26, *non de visu*) of the St. Petersburg Russian reference Bible uniform with no. 172.]

[1908. BIBLE. RNB holdings include a reprinting of the Moscow Russian reference Bible (37.1.2.2., *non de visu*) uniform with no. 195.]

[1908. OLD TESTAMENT. PROVERBS. A Russian translation from the Greek Septuagint of the OT book of Proverbs done by P. Iungerov, published by Kazan University Press, 1908 (RNB: 38.5.9.60, *non de visu*). See no. 185 for a listing of the Iungerov translations.]

220. 1908. BIBLE

Библія или Книги Священнаго Писанія Ветхаго и Новаго Завѣта въ русскомъ переводѣсъ параллельными мѣстами.
St. Petersburg: Synodal Press, 1908.
Title, synodal blessing verso [2]; OT half-title, verso blank [2]; OT text, 1–728; NT half-title, verso blank [729–30]; NT text, 731–908; index readings, 909–30; table of contents [931–2].
18.5 × 12.5.

An octavo printing of the synodal Bible in small type with marginal references. Format is similar to no. 219 prepared for the BFBS Petersburg Agency, but is smaller in page and font size and has fewer pages. There are two columns to the page. Each chapter constitutes one paragraph with

numbering of verses within the paragraph. The text includes all the books of the synodal edition, including deuterocanonical books of the OT and the 151st Psalm. Other Septuagint readings are footnoted in brackets. Curiously, in contrast to the 1907 edition prepared for BFBS (no. 219), this is one of the few St. Petersburg editions after 1890 not to capitalize pronominal references to the Virgin Mary.
Loc: BFBS; RNB holds a stereotype reprint of this edition with a Petrograd imprint of 1915 (37.66.2.15, *non de visu*).

221. 1908. NEW TESTAMENT. GOSPEL OF MATTHEW

Господа Нашего Іисуса Христа Святое Евангеліе отъ Матфея.
St. Petersburg: [Synodal Press for BFBS] 1908.
Title with synodal blessing, verso blank [2]; text, 92pp.
13 × 9.

Reprint of the synodal Gospel of Matthew uniform in format with the small-size 1904 Gospels (no. 209). The back cover lists a price of 3 kopecks. See also nos. 222–4. These small-size Gospels were distributed gratis by BFBS agencies in Russia. Each of these single Gospels was printed in 20,000 copies (see BFBS FDSC Minutes, vol. 13, 196).
Loc: BFBS

222. 1908. NEW TESTAMENT. GOSPEL OF MARK

Господа Нашего Іисуса Христа Святое Евангеліе отъ Марка.
St. Petersburg: [Synodal Press for BFBS] 1908.
Title, verso blank [2]; text, 58pp.
13 × 9.

Reprint of the synodal Russian Gospel of Mark uniform with no. 221 above.
Loc: BFBS

223. 1908. NEW TESTAMENT. GOSPEL OF LUKE

Господа Нашего Іисуса Христа Святое Евангеліе отъ Луки.
St. Petersburg: [Synodal Press for BFBS] 1908.
Title, verso blank [2]; text, 98pp.
13 × 9.

Reprint of the synodal Russian Gospel of Luke uniform with nos. 221–2.
Loc: BFBS

224. 1908. NEW TESTAMENT. GOSPEL OF JOHN

Господа Нашего Іисуса Христа Святое Евангеліе отъ Іоанна.
St. Petersburg: [Synodal Press for BFBS] 1908.
Title, verso blank [2]; text, 74pp.
13 × 9.

Reprint of the synodal Russian Gospel of John uniform with nos. 221–3.
Loc: BFBS

225. 1909. NEW TESTAMENT AND PSALTER

Новый Завѣтъ Господа Нашего Іисуса Христа и Псалтирь въ русскомъ переводѣ.
Piatigorsk: Parovaia Press of K. K. Kibardin, 1909.
Title, table of contents verso [2]; text, 606pp; errata [2].
17.5 × 11.

An edition of the synodal Russian NT and Psalter with marginal references published in Piatigorsk for Russian Baptists. The text is printed in a single column on the page with paragraph indention of each verse. References are placed in the outside margins. Psalm 151 is omitted, as is capitalization for pronominal references to Mary. There is a note in the hand of BFBS Petersburg agent William Kean inserted in the BFBS copy, which reads: "As this book has been issued without a permit from the Holy Synod, legal proceedings are being taken against the printer (November 1909)."
Loc: BFBS; RNB (38.78.8.47)

226. 1909. NEW TESTAMENT

[*Новый Завѣтъ Господа Нашего Іисуса Христа въ русскомъ переводѣ.*]
[St. Petersburg: Synodal Press for BFBS, 1909.]

Thirty-seventh printing of the "People's Edition" of the synodal Russian NT. The BFBS working catalog of Russian imprints indicates that the 1915 "People's Edition" (no. 240) was drawn from this prior 1909 thirty-seventh printing (*non de visu*). See DM 7894.

[1910. BIBLE. RNB lists a ninth printing in 1910 (38.79.3.78, *non de visu*) of no. 172, the St. Petersburg Russian reference Bible.]

[1910. OLD TESTAMENT. JEREMIAH. A Russian translation from the Greek Septuagint of the book of Jeremiah done by P. Iungerov, first published in Kazan in *Pravoslavnyi sobesednik* (RNB: 38.77.7.78, *non de visu*).]

227. 1910. PSALTER

Псалтирь въ русскомъ переводѣ.
Moscow: Synodal Press, 1910.
22.5 × 15.

Reprint of the Moscow large-font octavo synodal Psalter. Collation and format follow the 1889 printing (no. 173). CUL copy is bound with the 1906 NT (no. 216) and a table of NT readings, pp. 1–18.
Loc: CUL (28.6.c.90.1)

228. 1910. OLD TESTAMENT. SONG OF SOLOMON

Пѣснь Пѣсней Соломона. Переводъ съ древне-еврейскаго и примѣчанія А. Эфроса. Предисловіе В. Розанова. Изданіе второе, исправленное и дополненное.
St. Petersburg: "Panteon" Book Publishers, 1910.
Title, verso blank [2]; Rozanov preface, 1–22; half-title, engraving, 23–4; translator's introduction, 25–8; text, 29–80; 1:1–3 notation, verso blank [2]; half-title to critical literature, engraving, 81–2; Efros "Predislovie," 83–9; engraving, 90; commentary, 91–9; engraving, 100; title for Feofan Prokopovich's "Razsuzhdenie," engraving verso, 101–2; text, 103–16; Herder's essay, 117–35; engraving, 136; Renan extracts, 137–53; engraving, 154; Olesnitskii extract, 155–66; half-title to the anthology on Song of Songs, foreword verso, 167–8; Russian poetry, 169–215; Engel' essay, 216–24; Efros's essay, 225–8; Efros's notes, 229–63; engraving, 264; table of contents, engraving note verso [2].
25 × 19.

Second printing of Abram Efros's Russian translation from the Hebrew of the Song of Songs. The text is accompanied by Vasilii Rozanov's preface. Musical notation and critical comments are added by Iu. Engel'. Extracts from works by Prokopovich, Herder, Renan, and Olesnitskii on the Song of Solomon are also included. The anthology of Russian poetry related to the Song of Solomon includes works by Derzhavin, Pushkin, Fet, Mei, Feofanov, Baturlin, Zarin, Iaffe, Lokhvitskaia, V. Briusov, G. Chulkov, and S. Solov'ev. Efros's notes demonstrate his fidelity to the Hebrew text. He references passages when his translation differs from the synodal and BFBS OT translations. A final note on the last page indicates that the unusual engravings have been taken from old Hebrew parchments according to the publication of D. Gintsburg and V. Stasov, *L'Ornement Hébreu* (Leipzig: K.W. Hiersemann, 1905).
Loc: BL; CUL (Ub.8.212)

229. 1911. NEW TESTAMENT. RUSSIAN/ENGLISH DIGLOT GOSPEL OF LUKE

Евангеліе отъ Святаго Луки.
London: Trowitzsch & Son [Berlin], printer, for BFBS, 1911.
Blank page, English title verso [2]; Russian title, verso blank [3–4]; text, 5–115; printer's imprint verso [1].
16 × 12.

A diglot Russian/English edition of the synodal Russian Gospel of Luke. The text is in double columns, English and Russian on the same page, with paragraph indention of each verse. The BFBS edition included capitalization of pronominal references to Mary. This is one of several English diglots requested by W. B. Cooper, BFBS Canadian agent "for immigration work" (BFBS Minutes of the Committee, January 2, 1911, vol. 112, 615). Inexpensive printing was done in Berlin, although the title page bears a London imprint. Five thousand copies were printed (*The Hundred and Eighth Report of the BFBS*, London, 1912: appendix, [25]), and another 5,000 copies were issued in 1912 (see BFBS FDSC Minutes, vol. 16, 2).
Loc: BFBS

230. 1911. OLD TESTAMENT. ECCLESIASTICUS

Книга Премудрости Іисуса сына Сирахова. Введеніе, переводъ и объясненіе по еврейскому тексту и древнимъ переводамъ.
St. Petersburg: M. Merkushev Press, 1911.
Title, verso blank [I–II]; introduction, III–XCVIII; half-title, verso blank [2]; text, 805pp; verso blank [1]; table of contents, I–IV; errata, verso blank [2].
25 × 16.

A translation from the Hebrew of the deuterocanonical book of Ecclesiasticus with introduction and commentary by Archpriest A. P. Rozhdestvenskii. In his introduction, Rozhdestvenskii notes that the synodal Russian translation of Ecclesiasticus, like the early freer translation of Bishop Agathangel (1859), was done from the Greek. Rozhdestvenskii, while accepting some appropriate phrasing when possible from the synodal text, had done his translation from a Hebrew text that was discovered fifteen years previously (he references the discoveries of Lewis and Gibson, *The Expositor*, July 1896). Rozhdestvenskii's translation, divided into sections and rarely broken at chapter endings, precedes each chapter of "text and commentary." A lengthy explanatory essay

follows each section. The text is in a single column on the page with verse numbering in the left margin.
Loc: BL (3042.cc.8)

231. 1911. OLD TESTAMENT. GENESIS–LEVITICUS

Толковая библія. Книги: Бытіе, Исходъ, Левитъ. Томъ 1.
Beijing: Pekinskaia dukhovnaia missiia, 1911.
[2], 349pp.

A printing of the synodal Russian text of Genesis–Leviticus with commentary. Published in Beijing, the title corresponds to the first part of the multivolume interpreter's Bible edited by A. P. Lopukhin (see bracketed entry for 1904–13). *Non de visu.*
Loc: RNB (37.32.2.8)

[1911. OLD TESTAMENT. EZEKIEL. A Russian translation from the Greek Septuagint of the book of Ezekiel by P. Iungerov, first published in Kazan in *Pravoslavnyi sobesednik* (RNB: 37.30.8.201, *non de visu*).]

232. 1912. NEW TESTAMENT IN SLAVONIC/RUSSIAN DIGLOT

Новый Завѣтъ Господа Нашего Іисуса Христа на славянскомъ и русскомъ языкахъ.
Moscow: Synodal Press [for BFBS], 1912.
Title, synodal blessing verso [2]; text, 3–1172; table of readings, I–XVIII; table of contents [2].
16.5 × 11.5.

A printing of the synodal Russian NT in Slavonic/Russian diglot edition. The texts are in two parallel columns on the page with paragraph indention of verses. Pronominal references to Mary are capitalized in the Russian text. A table of readings and a table of contents are appended. This diglot was routinely sold by BFBS agencies in Russia. Fourteen thousand copies were ordered from the Holy Synod in 1912 (see BFBS FDSC Minutes, vol. 15, 241, 285, and 332; and vol. 16, 42). The BFBS copy has a front cover seal indicating that it comes from the separate stock of the Society for the Dissemination of Holy Scripture in Russia (located on Vasil'evskii Island, at Pervaia liniia 34, apt. 5). Opposite the seal is affixed a printed poem by

Emperor Alexander II's nephew Konstantin Konstantinovich on the value of the word of God.
Loc: BFBS; RNB (82–2/1439)

[1912. OLD TESTAMENT. DANIEL. A Russian translation from the Greek Septuagint of Daniel by P. Iungerov, first published in Kazan in *Pravoslavnyi sobesednik*, 1912 (RNB: 20.98.8.201, *non de visu*).]

[1913. BIBLE. RNB holdings include an eleventh printing (37.47.2.2, *non de visu*) of the St. Petersburg Russian reference Bible uniform with no. 172.]

233. 1913. NEW TESTAMENT

Новый Завѣтъ Господа Нашего Іисуса Христа. Съ С.-Петербургскаго изданія Св. Синода.
Vienna: A. Holzhausen, printer, for BFBS, 1913.
Title, printer's imprint verso [2]; table of contents, verso blank [2]; text, 490pp. 13 × 18.5.

Small pocket-size synodal Russian NT published in Vienna for the BFBS. The text is in two columns on the page with paragraph indention of each verse. Pronominal references to Mary are not capitalized. Five thousand copies were ordered in late 1912 (BFBS FDSC Minutes, vol. 16, 51). Another printing of the NT with the Psalter was executed from these BFBS plates in Berlin (no. 255, 1921). RNB holds an earlier 1906 printing of this edition uniform in collation (38.42.2.14, *non de visu*). This Vienna imprint was reissued in an electroplate printing by the American Bible Society in 1918 for circulation to Russians in the emigration. For a copy of the 1918 printing, see RNB (18.75.6.57, *non de visu*).
Loc: BFBS

[1913. OLD TESTAMENT. THE MINOR PROPHETS. A Russian translation from the Greek Septuagint of the Minor Prophets by P. Iungerov, first published in Kazan in *Pravoslavnyi sobesednik* (RNB: 20.38.9.57, *non de visu*).]

234. 1913–14. OLD TESTAMENT. PENTATEUCH IN RUSSIAN/HEBREW DIGLOT

Vol. I: *Пятикнижіе Моисеево съ дословнымъ русскимъ переводомъ и съ комментаріями русскимъ и еврейскимъ, объясняющими текстъ, также исторію, географію и археологію библейскаго мира.*
Vil'na: B. Tsionson Press, 1914.
[Collation from back:] Hebrew half-title, Hebrew title [I–II]; blank page, Russian title verso [III–IV]; Russian preface, V–XIV; Hebrew preface, XV–XXX; Hebrew half-title, verso blank [2]; Genesis diglot, 1–134; Hebrew half-title, verso blank [2]; Exodus diglot, 1–112.
23 × 16.5.
Vol. II: *Пятикнижіе Моисеево, съ дословнымъ русскимъ переводомъ.*
Vil'na: B. Tsionson Press, 1913.
[Collation from back:] Hebrew title, Russian title verso [2]; Leviticus diglot, 1–88; Numbers diglot, 1–114; Deuteronomy diglot, 1–110.
23 × 16.5.

A reprinting of the diglot Pentateuch in Hebrew and Russian, the Russian being a literal translation from the Hebrew by O. N. Shteinberg. The diglot was for use by students in Jewish schools. Shteinberg is identified on the title page as inspector of the Vil'na Jewish Teachers' Institute. Volume II, comprising Leviticus, Numbers, and Deuteronomy, carries an imprint date prior to volume I. The text is printed in two parallel columns on each page, the left-hand column in Russian, the right-hand in Hebrew. There are lexical notes at the foot of each page. The preface includes a section on how literary figures – Goethe, Herder, Lamartine, *et al.* – valued the beauty of the OT. There follows a chronological table. For the earlier 1901–2 edition of the same diglot printed in Vil'na, see no. 200. RNB holdings also include Shteinberg's translation of 2 Samuel published at the same Tsionson Press in 1913 (37.55.4.161, *non de visu*) and the book of Judges published in Vil'na by I. A. Katsenelenboigen in 1914 (37.55.4.304, *non de visu*).
Loc: OX (O.T.Heb.d.34)

235. 1914. BIBLE

Священныя Книги Ветхаго и Новаго Завѣта.
Vienna: A. Holzhausen, printer, for BFBS, 1914.
24 × 15.

Stereotype reprint of no. 134 (1877), the Vienna BFBS Bible, issued in 6,000 copies (see BFBS FDSC Minutes, vol. 16, June 12, 1913, 159).
Loc: BL (3042.cc.6)

[1914. OLD TESTAMENT. JOB. Russian translation from the Greek Septuagint of the book of Job by P. Iungerov, first published in Kazan in *Pravoslavnyi sobesednik* (RNB: 37.55.6.381, *non de visu*)]

236. 1914. NEW TESTAMENT. GOSPEL OF JOHN

Господа Нашего Іисуса Христа Святое Евангеліе отъ Іоанна.
St. Petersburg: Synodal Press for BFBS, 1914.

Reprint of no. 224 (1908). William Kean, the BFBS Petersburg agent, ordered 40,000 copies of single Gospels, including this reprinting, from the Holy Synod in June 1914 (BFBS FDSC Minutes, vol. 16, 340).
Loc: BFBS

237. 1914. NEW TESTAMENT. GOSPELS IN SLAVONIC AND RUSSIAN

Господа Нашего Іисуса Христа Святое Евангеліе отъ Матфея, Марка, Луки и Іоанна на славянскомъ и русскомъ языкахъ. Изданіе семьдесятъ четвертое.
St. Petersburg: Synodal Press, 1914.
Title, synodal blessing verso [2]; text, 3–464; table of readings, 1–8.
21.5 × 14.5.

Seventy-fourth printing of the synodal octavo Gospels in Slavonic/Russian diglot. Formatting is uniform with no. 181 (1890), but this printing has a slightly different collation and includes a table of readings at the end. Owing to stereotype plates dating from before 1890, pronominal references to Mary are not capitalized. The front cover bears an inscription indicating that copies were presented to those completing primary school by the St. Petersburg city duma (May 30, 1914). The large number of such presentational school copies explains the frequent reprintings of this popular diglot.
Loc: CUL (9100.c.2790)

238. 1915. NEW TESTAMENT. GOSPELS

Господа Нашего Іисуса Христа Святое Евангеліе отъ Матфея, Марка, Луки и Іоанна.
Petrograd: Synodal Press [for BFBS], 1915.
14 × 9.

A printing of the Gospels similar to no. 209 (1904), without capitalized pronominal references to Mary. The text is set in two columns on the page with paragraph indention of verses. Although BFBS agency circulation reached a record in 1915, the procurement of scripture was increasingly handicapped by wartime supply shortages. This 1915 Petrograd reprint was one of the more popular items sold by BFBS Russian agencies. The total 1915 circulation for all editions sold in BFBS Russian agencies exceeded 837,000 volumes (*The Hundred and Twelfth Report of the BFBS*, London, 1916, 66, 90).
Loc: BFBS

239. 1915. NEW TESTAMENT AND PSALTER

Новый Завѣтъ Господа Нашего Іисуса Христа и Псалтирь въ русскомъ переводѣ.
Petrograd: Synodal Press [for BFBS], 1915.
Title, table of contents [2]; NT text, 550pp; Psalter title, synodal blessing [2]; Psalter text, 3–139.
12.5 × 8.

A printing of the synodal NT and Psalter in small pocket-size format similar to no. 166 (1888). The NT was condensed into 550 pages of text as opposed to 626 pages in the 1888 printing. Pronominal references to Mary are capitalized. The same two-column format is followed, but there is no rectangular border as in no. 209. The Psalter is similarly reduced in size, with format similar to no. 184 (1890). Psalm 151 is omitted.
Loc: BFBS

240. 1915. NEW TESTAMENT

Новый Завѣтъ Господа Нашего Іисуса Христа въ русскомъ переводѣ. Изданіе сорокъ третье.
Petrograd: Synodal Press [for BFBS], 1915.
Title, synodal blessing verso [2]; table of contents, verso blank [2]; text, 1–440.
16.5 × 11.5.

Forty-third printing of the "People's Edition" of the NT, similar in format to no. 155 and subsequent printings, but employing a smaller font. The text does not capitalize pronominal references to Mary.
Loc: OX (N.T.Russ.e.5)

[1916. BIBLE. RNB holdings include a twelfth printing (34.105.2.45, *non de visu*) of the St. Petersburg Russian reference Bible uniform with no. 172.]

241. 1916. NEW TESTAMENT AND PSALTER

Новый Завѣтъ Господа Нашего Іисуса Христа [NT title only]. Специіальное изданіе перепечатанное съ помощью фотографическихъ снимковъ съ изданій Св. Правительствующаго Синода.
Berne: Galvag Press for Princess A. A. Golitsyna, 1916.
NT title, approvals verso [2]; NT text, 626pp; Psalter half-title, approval verso [2]; Psalter text, 3–183; press imprint verso [1].
12.5 × 8.

A photographically produced printing of the pocket-size synodal NT and Psalter prepared for Russian prisoners of war in memory of Prince Sergei Mikhailovich Golitsyn (d. Lausanne, June 9/22, 1915) by his widow. The NT text is based on the 626-page small-size edition of 1863 (no. 62), but includes capitalized pronominal references to Mary. The Psalter, which omits the 151st Psalm, is formatted like the NT, but has more pages than the 1888 printing (no. 166) and subsequent variants.
Loc: BFBS

[1917. BIBLE. RNB holdings include a thirteenth printing (17.154.3.5, *non de visu*) of the St. Petersburg Russian reference Bible uniform with no. 172.]

242. 1917. NEW TESTAMENT. GOSPELS IN SLAVONIC/RUSSIAN DIGLOT

Господа Нашего Іисуса Христа Святое Евангеліе отъ Матфея, Марка, Луки и Іоанна на славянскомъ и русскомъ языкахъ.
Petrograd: Synodal Press, 1917.
Title, synodal blessing verso [2]; text, 3–464.
21.5 × 14.5.

Eightieth printing of the synodal Russian Gospels in Slavonic and Russian diglot similar to no. 80 (1866), but with fourteen fewer pages. The format is the same – two columns parallel text on each page. The text is set within a rectangular border (17 × 11). Pronominal references to Mary are not capitalized. Fifty thousand copies were ordered (see BFBS FDSC Minutes, vol. 15, 241).
Loc: BFBS

243. 1918. BIBLE

Russian Bible/Библія. Книги Священнаго Писанія Ветхаго и Новаго Завѣта. Каноническія. Въ русскомъ переводѣ съ параллельными мѣстами.

New York: American Bible Society, 1918.
18.5 × 12.5.

An electroplate 12mo reprinting of no. 219 (1907). Pagination and format are identical, but the size of the printed page has been reduced. Opposite the original title page is an English title, "Russian Bible: Special Edition," with the publisher's imprint and date. The American Bible Society (ABS) in 1918–19 produced electroplates through a photo-reproduction process used in reprinting Bulgarian, Hungarian, Finnish, Lithuanian, Ukrainian, Czech, and Russian Bibles (*One Hundred and Fourth Annual Report of the American Bible Society*, New York, 1920, 41). A set of the Russian electroplates, which retained the pre-revolutionary Russian orthography, was also furnished to the BFBS (see no. 252, 1920). This 1918 American printing was circulated in 25,000 copies to Russian heritage speakers in the United States (*One Hundred and Third Annual Report of the American Bible Society*, New York, 1919, 46). The ABS later sought authority to reprint from these electroplates for distribution in Vladivostok (BFBS Minutes of the Committee, vol. 119, January 5, 1920, 395).
Loc: BFBS

[1918. NEW TESTAMENT. See annotation for no. 233 regarding this Vienna pocket-size reprinting. RNB holds this 1918 edition (18.75.6.57, *non de visu*).]

244. 1918. NEW TESTAMENT

Новый Завѣтъ Господа Нашего Iисуса Христа.
London: Billing and Sons, Ltd., Guildford, for BFBS, 1918.
Title, synodal blessing verso [2]; table of contents, verso blank [3–4]; text, 390pp; printer's imprint, verso blank [2].
14.5 × 9.

A 16mo printing of the synodal NT commissioned by the BFBS to compensate for the inability of the Petersburg Synodal Press (renamed after the Russian Revolution the "Second State Press") to supply adequate copies for distribution in Russia and among new émigrés. The initial 1918 printing called for 15,000 copies of the NT, 2,000 copies of the NT and Psalter, and 10,000 copies of the Psalter alone. There was also a separate printing of 10,000 copies of the four Gospels, and 10,000 copies of each Gospel bound separately. On these London printings, see BFBS DPSC Minutes, vol. 17, November 9, 1917, 262. These editions were proofread and corrected in London by Margaret Burstow, daughter of BFBS Siberian agent Walter Davidson (see BFBS Editorial Correspondence: Russian, File 1). Pronominal references to Mary are not

capitalized. The text is set in two columns to the page with paragraph indention of each verse. All these issues, nos. 244–9, retained the pre-revolutionary orthography and used the familiar statement of synodal blessing on the title verso, although the Synod had ceased to exist. The 1918 printings were reissued in the 1920s.
Loc: BFBS

245. 1918. NEW TESTAMENT. GOSPELS

Господа Нашего Іисуса Христа Святое Евангеліе отъ Матфея, Марка, Луки и Іоанна.
London: Billing and Sons, Ltd., Guildford, for BFBS, 1918.
Title, synodal blessing verso [2]; table of contents, verso blank, 3–[4]; text, 5–313; printer's imprint verso [1].
12.5 × 8.5.

A small 16mo edition of the synodal Gospels published by the BFBS for distribution in Russia and the West uniform in format to no. 244. Ten thousand copies were printed. Format follows the synodal Gospels of 1915 (no. 238).
Loc: BFBS; BL (3061.a.36); CUL (ccc.21.9.94); OX (N.T.Russ.f.1)

246. 1918. NEW TESTAMENT. GOSPEL OF MATTHEW

Господа Нашего Іисуса Христа Святое Евангеліе отъ Матфея.
London: Billing and Sons, Ltd., Guildford, for BFBS, 1918.
Title, synodal blessing verso [2]; text, 3–90; printer's imprint [1].
12 × 8.5.

A printing in 10,000 copies of a separate small-size Gospel of Matthew drawn from no. 245.
Loc: BFBS

247. 1918. NEW TESTAMENT. GOSPEL OF MARK

Господа Нашего Іисуса Христа Святое Евангеліе отъ Марка.
London: Billing and Sons, Ltd., Guildford, for BFBS, 1918.
Title, synodal blessing verso [2]; text, 3–57; printer's imprint [1].
12 × 8.5.

A printing in 10,000 copies of a separate small-size Gospel of Mark drawn from no. 245.
Loc: BFBS

248. 1918. NEW TESTAMENT. GOSPEL OF LUKE

Господа Нашего Іисуса Христа Святое Евангеліе отъ Луки.
London: Billing and Sons, Ltd., Guildford, for BFBS, 1918.
Title, synodal blessing verso [2]; text, 3–95; printer's imprint [1].
12 × 8.5.

A printing in 10,000 copies of a separate small-size Gospel of Luke drawn from no. 245.
Loc: BFBS

249. 1918. NEW TESTAMENT. GOSPEL OF JOHN

Господа Нашего Іисуса Христа Святое Евангеліе отъ Іоанна.
London: Billing and Sons, Ltd., Guildford, for BFBS, 1918.
Title, synodal blessing verso [2]; text, 3–73; printer's imprint [1].
12 × 8.5.

A printing in 10,000 copies of a separate small-size Gospel of John drawn from no. 245.
Loc: BFBS

250. 1918. NEW TESTAMENT AND PSALTER

Новый Завѣтъ Господа Нашего Іисуса Христа [*(и) Псалтирь въ русскомъ переводѣ*].
London: Billing and Sons, Ltd., Guildford, for BFBS, 1918.
NT title, synodal blessing verso [2]; table of contents, verso blank, 3–[4]; NT text, 5–390; printer's imprint, verso blank [2]; Psalter title, synodal blessing verso [2]; Psalter text, 3–96.
14.5 × 9.

A binding of the synodal NT with the Psalter according to the note under no. 244. The Psalter, issued separately, is here added to the NT with separate pagination. The Psalter omits the 151st Psalm. The text throughout is in two columns with paragraph indention of verses. Reprinted in 1919 (no. 251).
Loc: BFBS

251. 1919. NEW TESTAMENT AND PSALTER

Новый Завѣтъ Господа Нашего Іисуса Христа [*(и) Псалтирь въ русскомъ переводѣ*].
London: Billing and Sons, Ltd., Guildford, for BFBS, 1919.
14 × 9.

Stereotype reprinting of no. 250 in 50,000 copies (see BFBS DPSC Minutes, vol. 17, August 18, 1919, 391). As in no. 250, the title page is for the NT only. Pre-revolutionary orthography is retained.
Loc: BFBS

252. 1920. BIBLE

Библія. Книги Священнаго Писанія Ветхаго и Новаго Завѣта. Каноническія. Въ русскомъ переводѣ съ параллельными мѣстами.
London: BFBS [Oxford University Press], 1920.
18 × 12.5.

Reprint of the 1907 BFBS/Holy Synod Russian Bible (no. 219) with marginal references, utilizing the electrotype plates given to the BFBS by the American Bible Society (see annotation for no. 243). Because of the machinery needed for printing from electrotype plates, the BFBS turned to Oxford University Press for printing 10,000 copies (see BFBS DPSC Minutes, vol. 18, August 6, 1920, 48). The imprint on the title pages reads London, BFBS (in Russian). Title verso reads in English, "The Holy Bible in Russian." Oxford University Press was commissioned to reprint this volume in 25,000 copies in 1922 (see BFBS DPSC Minutes, vol. 18, 168). See the Berlin reprint of 1922 (no. 259).
Loc: BFBS; BL (03068.ee.41); RNB (58–2/1885)

253. 1921. NEW TESTAMENT

[*Новый Завѣтъ Господа Нашего Іисуса Христа.*]
[London: Billing and Sons, Ltd., Guildford, for the American Bible Society, 1921.]

Reprint of no. 244 in 10,000 copies for the ABS (see BFBS Editorial Correspondence: Russian, File 1).
Loc: *Non de visu.*

254. 1921. NEW TESTAMENT AND PSALTER

Новый Завѣтъ Господа Нашего Іисуса Христа [*(и) Псалтирь въ русскомъ переводѣ*].
London [Sortavala]: Home Mission Society Press of the Finnish Church, Sortavala (Serdobol), for BFBS, 1921.
NT title, note verso [2]; table of contents, verso blank [3–4]; NT text, 5–390; imprint, verso blank [2]; Psalter title, note verso [2]; Psalter text, 3–96.
14.5 × 9.5.

A reprinting of the NT and Psalter based on no. 250. The printing was executed for the BFBS by the Finnish Home Mission Society, directed by Dean Aarnisalo. Eighty thousand copies were printed for an expected BFBS return to Petrograd (*The Hundred and Eighteenth Report of the BFBS*, London, 1922, 94). The title page verso alters the standard synodal blessing to read, "printed from the edition issued with the blessing of the Most Holy Ruling Synod." Walter Davidson, BFBS Northeast European agent in Helsinki, oversaw publication.
Loc: BFBS

255. 1921. NEW TESTAMENT AND PSALTER

Новый Завѣтъ Господа Нашего Іисуса Христа [*(и) Книга Псалмовъ*].
Berlin: Trowitzsch and Sons, printer, for the BFBS, 1921.
NT title, note verso [2]; table of contents, verso blank [2]; NT text, 490pp; Psalter title, verso blank [2]; Psalter text, 3–125; printer's imprint verso [1].
13 × 8.

Reprint of the small synodal NT and Psalter similar in format to no. 239. In April 1921, Albert Hartkopf, the BFBS Berlin agent, received authorization to print 10,000 copies of the NT and 10,000 copies of this NT with Psalms (BFBS FDSC Minutes, vol. 21, 47). Hartkopf's agency was handling requests for Russian scriptures coming from W. L. Jack, a Russian Baptist émigré leader in the organization, "Light to the East" (*Svet vostoku*). The seal of the Society for Dissemination of the Gospel, Wernegerode am Hartz, is on the inside cover of BFBS copy.
Loc: BFBS

256. 1921. NEW TESTAMENT. GOSPEL OF JOHN

Господа Нашего Іисуса Христа Святое Евангеліе отъ Іоанна.
Berlin: Trowitzsch and Sons, printer, for BFBS, 1921.
Title, note verso [2]; Gospel text, 3–59.
13.5 × 9.

An edition of the synodal Gospel of John printed in small size and using the new Russian orthography for the first time in printings of Russian scripture. Albert Hartkopf, BFBS Berlin agent, with the assistance of a Russian affiliated with W. L. Jack's "Light to the East" organization, saw this specimen Gospel through the press. The manuscript was prepared by Mrs. V. Bulmer for the BFBS (see BFBS Editorial Correspondence: Russian, File 1). This specimen Gospel was printed in an edition of 20,000 copies (BFBS FDSC Minutes,

vol. 21, February 17, 1921, 1). Pronominal references to Mary are capitalized. The text is in two columns to the page with paragraph indention of verses.
Loc: BFBS

257. 1921. OLD TESTAMENT. SONG OF SOLOMON

Пѣснь Пѣсней.
Vienna: Mechitharisten-Buchdruckerei, 1921.
Blank leaf, title, printer's imprint verso [4]; preface, 5–6; translator's preface, 7–16; Brodovskii preface, 17–24; poem half-title, verso blank [25–6]; poem, 27–8; Song of Solomon half-title, verso blank [29–30]; text, 31–82; Iaroshevskii poem, 83–4.

A third printing of Lev Iaroshevskii's Russian free verse translation of the Song of Solomon. The accompanying prefaces by M. A. Kuz'min, the translator Iaroshevskii, and G. Brodovskii date to 1916. The translator dismisses the conservatism of Abram Efros's translation of the Song of Solomon (see no. 228), rather envisioning the Song of Solomon as a poem expressing the feelings between two young lovers.
Loc: BL (3061.f.14)

258. 1922. NEW TESTAMENT

Новый Завѣтъ Господа Нашего Іисуса Христа въ русскомъ переводѣ.
Prague: International YMCA (Mezhdunarodnyi Komitet Khristianskikh Soiuzov Molodykh Liudei), 1922.
Title, publisher imprint [2]; text, 440pp; table of contents, verso blank [2]. 17.5 × 12.5.

A reprinting of the synodal NT based upon no. 226 (1909). This "People's Edition" circulated before 1917 in numerous printings. The text is in two columns on the page with paragraph indention of verses. Pronominal references to Mary are not capitalized. The YMCA arranged a printing of 50,000 copies in anticipation of possible circulation in Russia. In 1924, most of the copies then stored in Stettin were handed over to the BFBS for circulation (see BFBS Editorial Correspondence: Russian, File 1). Pre-revolutionary orthography was employed.
Loc: BFBS; RNB (82–3/4997)

259. 1922. BIBLE

Библія. Книги Священнаго Писанія Ветхаго и Новаго Завѣта. Каноническія.
Berlin: BFBS, 1922.
17.5 × 12.

Photographically reproduced printing of the 1907 synodal text prepared for the BFBS (no. 219). Twenty-five thousand copies were printed (see BFBS FDSC Minutes, vol. 20, July 13, 1922, 37). The general title page and NT title bear the Berlin imprint. BFBS Berlin agent Albert Hartkopf arranged for this printing at the request of W. L. Jack's Russian Protestant "Light to the East" Society.
Loc: BFBS; RNB (34–2/126)

260. 1922. BIBLE

Библія или Книги Священнаго Писанія Ветхаго и Новаго Завѣта въ русскомъ переводѣ съ параллельными мѣстами.
Philadelphia: The Judson Press, [1922].
24.5 × 15.5.

A photographic reproduction of the 1892 synodal reference Bible (see no. 188). Although the 1892 NT introduced capitalization of pronominal references to the Virgin Mary, the American Baptist Publication Society's Judson Press chose this for its edition. For dating, see Neil to Kilgour [BFBS], November 15, 1922, BFBS Editorial Correspondence: Russian, File 1).
Loc: BFBS

261. 1925. OLD TESTAMENT. RUTH

Книга Руфь.
Moscow: "Mospoligraf," the sixteenth press, for M. and S. Sabashnikov, 1925.
Blank leaf [2]; half-title, printer's imprint [3–4]; blank page, engraving [5–6]; title, translator's dedication verso [7–8]; Chapter 1 heading, engravings [9–10]; text, 11–32; "Posleslovie," verso blank [33–4]; afterword, 35–42.
25.5 × 20.

An edition of the book of Ruth translated from the Hebrew by Abram Efros with eight engravings by V. Favorskii. The text is printed in one column on the page with verse numbering in the left-hand margins. The translation follows the Hebrew text closely and should not be confused with free or loose translations of OT texts. Personal names are transliterated from the Hebrew, differing in this respect from synodal and BFBS translations. The new Soviet orthography is employed. The afterword is the translator's discussion of the significance and dating of the book of Ruth.
Loc: BFBS; BL (3041.f.3); RNB (20.89.1.109)

262. 1926. BIBLE

Библия. Книги Священного Писания Ветхого и Нового Завета. Канонические. В русском переводе с параллельными местами.
Leningrad: Tsentroizdat Press (Ekateringofskii Prospekt 87), for I. S. Prokhanov and Ia. I. Zhidkov, 1926.
Title, printer's imprint [2]; table of contents [2]; OT text, 752pp; NT title, verso blank [2]; NT, 3–237; verso blank [1]; 5 maps.
21.5 × 14.

A Leningrad edition of the synodal reference Bible in the new orthography adapted from the 1907 synodal edition prepared for the BFBS (no. 219). References and text are the same as the 1907 edition, including the capitalization of pronominal references to Mary. The font is larger than the 1907 edition, thus explaining the greater number of pages. The edition was printed in Leningrad with funds provided to I. S. Prokhanov by the American Bible Society. The cost of the plates (estimated $10–15,000) was provided by the ABS with the proviso that the plates be prepared in Leningrad, that the 1907 edition be followed (except for paragraph indention of verses if desired), that the name of the ABS not in any way be attached to the edition, that the plates subsequently be made available to other groups in the Soviet Union desiring to publish scripture, and that the book should bear an imprint to the effect that it was produced from an edition approved by the Synod (see Dr. Haven, ABS to C. H. K. Boughton, BFBS, December 18, 1925, BFBS Editorial Correspondence: Russian, File 1). The title verso notes a circulation run of 25,000 copies. The edition followed paragraph indention of verses, unlike the 1907 edition. Five thousand seven hundred copies of this edition were to be the property of the BFBS for use in its Leningrad depot, which continued to operate into the 1920s.
Loc: BFBS; RNB (22/981)

263. 1926 [1927]. BIBLE

Библия. Книги Священного Писания Ветхого и Нового Завета. Канонические. В русском переводе с параллельными местами.
Kiev: "Gostrest Kiev-Pechat," printer, for Kiev Oblast' Union of Evangelical Christians, 1926 [1927].
17.5 × 12.

A photolithographically reproduced printing of no. 262 (1926) in reduced page size with identical collation, format, title, and orthography. The general title page bears the imprint of the Kiev Regional Union of

Evangelical Christians, 1926. However, the NT title bears an imprint date of 1927. The general title page verso includes the notation that the work is "from an edition printed with the permission of the Holy Synod," and adds that the volume was printed at the Photolithographic Press No. 1 in an edition of 5,000 copies. The printer, "Ukrglavlit, Gostrest, Kiev Pechat'" was the Ukrainian State Trust Printing Association, Kiev. The Kiev Union of Evangelical Christians was the regional representative of I. S. Prokhanov's All-Russian Union of Evangelical Christians.
Loc: BFBS (2 copies); RNB (49/405)

264. 1927. BIBLE

Священныя Книги Ветхаго и Новаго Завѣта.
Berlin: BFBS, 1927.
23.5 × 15.

Stereotype printing of the BFBS Vienna Russian Bible incorporating the BFBS OT without bracketed or other Septuagint readings, and employing pre-revolutionary Russian orthography. Collation is identical to earlier pre-1917 printings (see no. 134). This is the first such printing to bear a Berlin imprint.
Loc: CUL (20.6.c.90.1)

265. 1927. NEW TESTAMENT AND PSALTER

Новый Завет Господа Нашего Иисуса Христа и Псалтирь в русском переводе.
Leningrad: Tsentrizdat Press for I. S. Prokhanov and Ia. I. Zhidkov, 1927.
Title, printer's imprint [2]; table of contents, verso blank [2]; text, 5–584; appendix, 1–8; 2 maps.
14 × 10.

A pocket-size synodal NT and Psalms similar to no. 255 (1921) in the new orthography printed in Leningrad with funds provided to the All-Russian Union of Evangelical Christians (I. S. Prokhanov and Ia. I. Zhidkov) by the American Bible Society (see Haven to Kilgour, December 12, 1927, BFBS Editorial Correspondence: Russian, File 1). The title page verso notes a circulation run of 25,000 copies. The text is in two columns on the page with paragraph indention of verses. The Psalter follows directly after the NT with continuous pagination. The NT text includes capitalization of pronominal references to Mary. The appendix provides historical tables and measures for NT money, etc. The publication is cited in Ia. Glan, *Antireligioznaia literatura za 12 let (1917–1929)* (Moscow, 1930), item 2253.
Loc: BFBS; RNB (41/2408)

266. 1927. NEW TESTAMENT

Новый Завѣтъ Господа Нашего Іисуса Христа.
London: The Whitefriars Press, Ltd., for the Trinitarian Bible Society, 1927.
Title, table of contents [2]; text, 3–[722].
14.5 × 10.

Reprint of the synodal NT in the old orthography, photographically reduced and reproduced from a pre-war large-type printing. The text is in one column on the page with paragraph indention of each verse, a format similar to the Moscow large-type printings (see, for example, no. 165), but there are fewer pages in this printing than in previous large-type editions. Pronominal references to Mary are capitalized.
Loc: BFBS

267. [1930.] NEW TESTAMENT. GOSPEL OF MATTHEW

Господа Нашего Иисуса Христа Святое Евангелие от Матфея.
New York: American Bible Society, [1930].
Title, note verso [2]; text, 3–61; photos [3].
11.5 × 7.5.

A specimen pocket-size synodal Gospel of Matthew in the new orthography. The text is in one column on the page with paragraph indention of verses. Like the specimen Gospel of Mark (no. 268), this is a 1930 publication. These ABS Gospels are set in variable size type so that the length of each constitutes precisely sixty-four pages of print. According to Gilbert Darlington's report prepared in the 1960s (see Darlington duplicated materials in four ring-binders, BFBS Archive), these Gospel specimens were printed in more than 1,200,000 copies (300,000 of each Gospel) between 1930 and 1953. In 1967, approximately 350,000 copies of the four specimens remained unsold.
Loc: BFBS

268. [1930.] NEW TESTAMENT. GOSPEL OF MARK

Господа Нашего Иисуса Христа Святое Евангелие от Марка.
New York: American Bible Society, [1930].
Title, verso blank [2]; text, 3–62.
11.5 × 7.5.

A pocket-size Gospel of Mark in the new orthography uniform with no. 267.
Loc: BFBS

269. [1930.] NEW TESTAMENT. GOSPEL OF LUKE

Господа Нашего Иисуса Христа Святое Евангелие от Луки.
New York: American Bible Society, [1930].
Title, credits verso [2]; text, 3–64.
11.5 × 7.5.

A pocket-size Gospel of Luke in the new orthography uniform in format with nos. 267 and 268.
Loc: BFBS

270. [1930.] NEW TESTAMENT. GOSPEL OF JOHN

Господа Нашего Иисуса Христа Святое Евангелие от Иоанна.
New York: American Bible Society, [1930].
Title, credits verso [2]; text, 3–63; photo.
11.5 × 7.5.

A pocket-size Gospel of John in the new orthography uniform in format with nos. 267–9.
Loc: BFBS

271. 1931. BIBLE

Священныя Книги Ветхаго и Новаго Завѣта.
Berlin: BFBS, 1931.
24 × 15.

Reprint of no. 264, uniform in format and pagination.
Loc: BL (X.100/6012)

272. 1940. NEW TESTAMENT AND PSALTER

Новый Завет Господа Нашего Иисуса Христа.
London: Lowe and Brydone, printers, for BFBS, 1940.
Title, imprint verso [2]; table of contents, verso blank [2]; NT text, 3–237; verso blank [1]; Psalter title [1]; Psalter text, 240–98; blank page, printer's imprint [2].
16.5 × 12.

Photographic reprint of the Russian NT and Psalter in the new orthography, using the NT and Psalter text of the 1926 Leningrad imprint (no. 262). The table of contents erroneously gives the starting page of the Psalter as 440, instead of 240. The first printing of this 1940 NT and Psalter, a run of 10,140 copies, was largely destroyed by a World War II bombing

attack that hit the Watkins Bindery. A subsequent reprinting of 19,250 copies was prepared in 1942 (see BFBS Version Book no. 27, October 9, 1941, 59; and no. 274 below).
Loc: BFBS

273. [1941.] NEW TESTAMENT AND PSALTER

Новый Завет Господа Нашего Иисуса Христа.
New York: American Bible Society, 1941.
17 × 11.5.

Photographic reprinting of no. 272. The starting page number listed for the Psalter in the table of contents has been corrected. The title page verso indicates the volume was "printed in the United States of America." The circulation run of 10,000 copies and the 1941 publication date are noted at the bottom of the contents page.
Loc: BFBS

274. 1942. NEW TESTAMENT AND PSALTER

Новый Завет Господа Нашего Иисуса Христа.
London: Lowe and Brydone, printers, for the BFBS, 1940.
16.5 × 12.

Reprint of no. 272, copies of which had been destroyed by fire (see annotation for no. 272).
Loc: BFBS

275. 1943. NEW TESTAMENT. GOSPELS

Господа Нашего Иисуса Христа Святое Евангелие по синодальному тексту с введением, приложением и объяснительными примечаниями.
Paris: "Istina" Press with the "permission of Roman Catholic Diocesan Administration," 1943.
Half-title, verso blank [2]; title, permit verso [3–4]; introduction, 5–41; verso blank [1]; half-title, verso blank [2]; Gospels text, 3–275; map verso [1]; supplement [1–33].
15.5 × 9.5.

A small octavo edition of the Russian synodal Gospels with references and notes published by the Roman Catholic "Istina" Press in Paris. The introduction reviews the textology of the Gospels and their translation into Slavonic and modern Russian. A "list of canonical books" recognized by the Council of Trent with their abbreviations concludes the introduction. The

text is in one column on the page, divided into paragraphs according to subject matter, with headings introduced into the text. Verse numbering occurs within each paragraph. Explanatory notes and references are at the foot of each page. The supplement contains a geographical, political and social guide to Palestine at the time of Christ. There is a supplemental Gospel harmony table and a table of daily Gospel readings. This Roman Catholic publication of the Gospels curiously does not capitalize pronominal references to the Virgin Mary.
Loc: BFBS

276. 1944. NEW TESTAMENT. GOSPEL OF LUKE IN ENGLISH/RUSSIAN DIGLOT

Господа Нашего Иисуса Христа Святое Евангелие от Луки
New York: American Bible Society, 1944.
Half-title, English title verso [2]; Russian title [1]; text, 1, 1–44, 44.
16.25 × 11.

A diglot edition of the Gospel of Luke in English and Russian. The Russian text is drawn from the synodal edition. The texts are printed in two columns on the page with paragraph indention of verses. The English and Russian texts are on facing pages – the Russian on the recto side. The Russian is in the new orthography. This diglot was part of a larger project of the American Bible Society to produce its own carefully proofread version of the synodal text introducing the new orthography. The principal Russian assistant seeing these editions through the press was Ivan V. Neprash (see copies of ABS Versions Committee Minutes, February 8, 1944, 10, in BFBS Translations Department Papers). The Russian text of Luke includes capitalization of pronominal references to Mary.
Loc: BFBS

277. 1945. NEW TESTAMENT

Новый Завет Господа Нашего Иисуса Христа.
London: Williams, Lea & Co., Ltd., printer, for the Scripture Gift Mission, 1945.
Title, verso blank [2]; table of contents, printer's imprint [2]; NT text, 446pp; publisher's address [1].
16 × 10.

A printing of the synodal Russian NT text for distribution by the Scripture Gift Mission. The text is in one column on the page without

verse numbering. A note on the table of contents verso indicates words printed in italics are not found in the original Greek, but are necessary for clear interpretation of the Greek. The use of italics is the same as in other editions of the synodal NT. The pronominal references to Mary are not capitalized, and the ordering of epistles (Catholic epistles before the Pauline epistles) is retained as in most synodal editions.
Loc: BFBS

278. 1945. NEW TESTAMENT. GOSPEL OF JOHN

Евангелие от Св. Иоанна.
Kutna Hora (Czechoslovakia): Dr. Ed. Gregr and Son, printer (Prague), for Czech Bible Work, 1945.
Title page, verso blank [2]; text, 3–64.
16 × 11.

A printing of the synodal Russian Gospel of John undertaken by "Česká Biblická Práce" in 1945. The text is printed in two columns on the page with paragraph indention of verses. Pronominal references to Mary are capitalized. References are included in small print at the end of each relevant verse. The printing is in the new orthography.
Loc: BFBS

279. [1945.] NEW TESTAMENT AND PSALTER

[*Новый Завет Господа Нашего Иисуса Христа.*]
[New York: American Bible Society, 1945.]

A first printing of the American Bible Society's synodal NT and Psalter in the new orthography, with corrections and proofreading by Ivan V. Neprash. For collation and description, see second printing (no. 280).
Loc: *Non de visu.*

280. [1946.] NEW TESTAMENT AND PSALTER

Новый Завет Господа Нашего Иисуса Христа.
New York: American Bible Society, [1946].
NT title, credits verso [2]; table of contents, verso blank [2]; NT text, 1–331; verso blank [1]; Psalter title [1]; Psalter text, 332–413; verso blank [1]; maps.
16.5 × 11.

A second printing of the ABS's revised synodal NT and Psalter in the new orthography. Proofreader was Ivan V. Neprash. The text is printed in two columns on the page with paragraph indention of each verse. The Psalter omits the 151st Psalm. According to the ABS Darlington Materials, BFBS Archive, 27,900 copies were printed.
Loc: BFBS

281. 1946. BIBLE

Библія или Книги Священнаго Писанія Ветхаго и Новаго Завѣта въ русскомъ переводѣ съ параллельными мѣстами.
Uppsala: Almqvist & Wiksell Press for the UBS [American Bible Society], 1946.
Blank page, synodal blessing [2]; title, printer's imprint [2]; table of contents [2]; OT text, 1–1002; NT title, verso blank [1003–4]; NT text, 1005–1307.
17.5 × 11.5.

A photo-offset reprint of the synodal Bible employing the eleventh printing of the Synod's text published in large five-part octavo (see no. 172 and subsequent printings) in the pre-revolutionary orthography. Pagination is identical to the earlier printings, as is the two-column format with references at the foot of the page. The total number of pages is smaller because OT books not in the Hebrew canon have been excised. However, chapters 13 and 14 of the Book of Daniel and bracketed OT Septuagint readings remain. The page size has been reduced. NT includes capitalization of pronominal references to Mary. Although the "United Bible Societies" is cited as the publisher on the title page, funding was from the American Bible Society. Following the formation of the United Bible Societies in May 1946, the UBS imprint could be used for "situations in which it is better to use a non-national imprint" (see *Minutes of the First Executive Committee*, London: UBS, 1947, 77). The American Bible Society printed 50,000 copies in 1946 (*One-hundred and Thirty-first Annual Report of the ABS*, New York, 1947, 53).
Loc: BFBS

282. [1947.] BIBLE

Библия. Книги Священного Писания Ветхого и Нового Завета. Канонические. В русском переводе с параллельными местами.
New York/Geneva/London: UBS [i.e. American Bible Society], [1947].
Title, notes verso [2]; table of contents, verso blank [2]; OT text, 1–925; verso blank [1]; NT title, verso blank [2]; NT text, 1–292; maps.
19.5 × 13.5.

First edition of the United Bible Society's revised synodal Bible in the new orthography with references and chapter headings, and separate Bracketed Septuagint references are omitted as is the 151st Psalm. The NT capitalizes pronominal references to Mary. The text is in two columns on the page divided by a central section of references. Chapter headings identifying special topics are introduced. According to ABS Versions Committee Minutes, October 1, 1947, 8 (see BFBS Translations Department papers), the chapter headings were prepared by J. Oscar Boyd, Eric North, and Eugene Nida, and translated into Russian by Ivan Neprash. Neprash also proofread the text and entered the center-margin references in Russian. The references are from the 1892 Russian synodal printing (no. 188). The NT title page bears the imprint in Russian of the American Bible Society. This UBS/ABS edition became a standardized version issued on both sides of the Atlantic in numerous printings. With few revisions, this edition circulates to the present. The first printing was in 25,000 copies. By 1964, the BFBS had also adopted the text, publishing about 50,000 copies between 1964 and 1968 (see BFBS printing card for "Russian Bible F' cap 8vo, offset," code 043x). Special plates and printings of this edition were also prepared for the All-Union Council of Evangelical Christians in Moscow (no. 295, for example).
Loc: BFBS

283. 1947. NEW TESTAMENT. GOSPEL OF MATTHEW

Евангелие от Матфея.
Stockholm: Gummessons Boktryckeri AB [Slaviska Missionen], 1947.
Title, printer's imprint [2]; text, 1–54.
15.5. × 10.5.

A specimen synodal Russian Gospel of Matthew employing new orthography, with references in small type immediately following the verse. The text is set in two columns on the page with paragraph indention of verses. Pagination and format are continued in nos. 284–6. Pronominal references to Mary are capitalized. This setting of the Gospels was undertaken by the Protestant Slaviska Missionen, a Stockholm-based "Society for the Proclamation of the Gospel Among Slavic People" (see entry no. 1138 in *The Encyclopedia of Modern Christian Missions: The Agencies*, ed. B. L. Goddard [Camden, NJ: Thomas Nelson and Sons, 1967], 565). These specimen Gospels were later reissued in a NT and Psalter published by the same organization in 1962, 1966, and 1967.
Loc: BFBS

284. 1947. NEW TESTAMENT. GOSPEL OF JOHN

Евангелие от Иоанна.
Stockholm: Gummessons Boktryckeri AB [Slaviska Missionen], 1947.
Title, printer's imprint [2]; text, 143–84.
15.5 × 10.5.

Synodal Russian Gospel of John uniform with no. 283.
Loc: BFBS

285. 1948. NEW TESTAMENT. GOSPEL OF MARK

Евангелие от Марка.
Stockholm: Gummessons Boktryckeri AB [Slaviska Missionen], 1948.
Title [1]; text, 54–87; printer's imprint [1].
15 × 10.5.

Russian synodal Gospel of Mark uniform with nos. 283–4.
Loc: BFBS

286. 1948. NEW TESTAMENT. GOSPEL OF LUKE

Евангелие от Луки.
Stockholm: Gummessons Boktryckeri AB [Slaviska Missionen], 1948.
[Cover title]; text, 88–142.
15 × 10.5.

Russian synodal Gospel of Luke uniform with nos. 283–5.
Loc: BFBS

287. 1948. BIBLE

Библия или Книги Священного Писания Ветхого и Нового Завета. Канонические. В русском переводе с параллельными местами.
New York: ABS, 1948.
19.5 × 13.5.

Second and third reprintings of the UBS/ABS Russian Bible, uniform in collation, format, and text with no. 282. The ABS imprint was used on the title page. The combined printings in 1948 came to approximately 100,000 copies (see the ABS Darlington Materials, BFBS Archive). This large press run was done as part of a shipment sent to the Soviet Union following the visit of Leningrad Metropolitan Grigorii to the American Bible Society in 1947.
Loc: *Non de visu.*

288. 1948. NEW TESTAMENT AND PSALTER

Новый Завет Господа Нашего Иисуса Христа [*(and) Псалтирь.*]
New York: ABS, 1948.
16.5 × 11.

Third and fourth reprintings of the UBS/ABS Russian NT and Psalter, uniform with no. 279 (in 23,500 and 200,000 copies respectively, according to ABS Darlington Materials, BFBS Archive). The fourth printing incorporated a gift of 190,000 copies to the Moscow Patriarchate, as arranged by Leningrad Metropolitan Grigorii during his 1947 visit to the United States.
Loc: BFBS; BL (X.108/8016)

289. 1950. NEW TESTAMENT. GOSPEL HARMONY

Четвероевангелiе: Текстъ четырехъ Евангелiй, поставленный параллельно, въ хронологическомъ порядкѣ.
Jordanville, New York: Iov Pochaevskii, printer, at the Holy Trinity Monastery, 1950.
Blank leaf [2]; title, publisher imprint [3–4]; preface, 5–7; verso blank [8]; half-title, verso blank [9–10]; Part I half-title [11]; text, 12–43; verso blank [44]; Part II half-title [45]; text, 46–385; verso blank [386]; Part III half-title [387]; text, 388–475; verso blank [476]; table of contents, 477–86.

A Gospel harmony utilizing the synodal text and divided by subject into three parts: (1) the coming of Jesus Christ into the world; (2) the servanthood of Jesus Christ through Wednesday of Holy Week; and (3) the last days of the life of Christ. In each of the parts, the four Gospel texts are presented in parallel columns on facing pages (Matthew and Mark on the left, Luke and John on the right). Subject headings introduce each part. Verses are indented as paragraphs. The texts were compiled and arranged by A. S. Anan'in. The preface, notes, and subject headings were done by M. Pol'skii. As in other Jordanville publications, pre-revolutionary orthography is retained.
Loc: BL (3110.e.1)

290. 1950. PSALTER IN SLAVONIC/RUSSIAN DIGLOT

Псалтирь на славянском и русском языках.
Rome: Vatican Press for the Russian Pontifical College, 1950.
Blank page, illustrated verso [2]; title, publisher's imprint [3–4]; preface [5–6]; introduction, vii–viii; prayers, ix–xx; Psalter half-title, 1; Psalter diglot, 2–487;

verso blank, 488; supplement half-title, verso blank [489–90]; appendices, 491–[502]; table of contents [503].
17 × 11.5.

A new printing of the synodal Russian Psalter in a Slavonic/Russian diglot prepared by the Pontifical Biblical Institute in Rome. The Slavonic text is from a 1906 Moscow Synodal Press edition. The Russian synodal text is reprinted from the printing of the NT and Psalms done by the Synodal Press in Petrograd, 1917. New headings and notes for the text were prepared by the Pontifical Biblical Institute, although the notes prepared by D. A. Khvol'son for his synodal translation are also printed in italics. The parallel texts are printed on opposite pages, the Slavonic on the left and the Russian on the right, with paragraph indention of verses. The Slavonic text is published in the old orthography, but the Russian is printed in the post-1917 orthography. The Pontifical Institute's notes are taken from the 1945 *Liber Psalmorum.* The introduction offers a history of various Psalter texts.
Loc: OX (Ps.Slav.f.2)

291. 1953. NEW TESTAMENT. GOSPEL OF MATTHEW

Евангелие от Матфея.
London: Wm. Clowes and Sons, printer, for BFBS, 1953.
Title, imprint verse [ii]; preface, iii–vii; verso blank [viii]; text, 9–67; printer's imprint [1].
18.5 × 13.5.

First "trial edition" (*probnyi vypusk*) of the Gospel of Matthew newly translated from the Greek into Russian by Bishop Cassian (Kassian; Sergei Sergeevich Bezobrazov, 1893–1965) and prepared with the assistance of a committee working at St. Sergius Theological Institute under the sponsorship of BFBS. The translation project, of which this is the first specimen, operated with the blessing of Ecumenical Patriarch Athenagoras of Constantinople. The committee was composed of V. N. Rayevsky, A. V. Kartashev, N. A. Koulomzine, B. K. Zaitseff, A. P. Wassilieff, V. N. Lossky, D. Obolensky, J. Meyendorff, W. Weidle, and A. Kniazeff, among others, along with international representatives of the Paris YMCA – Paul Anderson, Donald Lowrie, and Robbins Strong. As noted in the preface, the translation is the first to utilize textological advances in Greek NT studies, Bishop Cassian having based his translation upon the Eberhard Nestle critical Greek edition of 1949. For subsequent installments of this translation project funded by the BFBS, see nos. 296, 300, and 312. The text is printed in one column on the

page with verse numbers in the left-hand margin. There is no paragraph indention by verse. The new orthography is employed. Because of a dispute within the committee over the capitalization of pronominal references to Mary, two separate printings were issued of this trial edition, one with pronominal references to Mary capitalized, one with the references in lower case (the bindings were color coded to differentiate between the printings). Two thousand copies were printed without capitalization (see BFBS Versions Book no. 33, 27) and 1,875 copies with capitalization (BFBS Versions Book, no. 32, 318). For an account of this translation project, see S. K. Batalden, "Revolution and Emigration: The Russian Files of the British and Foreign Bible Society, 1917–1970," in Janet Hartley, ed., *The Use of British Archives for the Study of Russian History* (London, Mansell Publishing, for the University of London School of Slavonic and East European Studies, 1986).
Loc: BFBS (capitalized version only); BL (capitalized version, 3061.l.3; lower case version, 3061.l.2); CUL (with capitals, 1953.7.5759; lower case, 1953.7.5760); OX (with capitals, N.T.Russ.e.6; lower case, N.T.Russ.e.7)

292. 1954. BIBLE

Библія или Книги Священнаго Писанія Ветхаго и Новаго Завѣта въ русскомъ переводѣ съ параллельными мѣстами.
Philadelphia: The Judson Press, 1954.
24.5 × 15.5.

Reprint of no. 260, the Russian synodal Bible drawn from an 1892 printing (no. 188). Published in 1922 by Judson Press, this reproduction is one of the unusual post-World War II texts employing the old pre-1917 orthography.
Loc: BL (3062.b.2)

293. 1956. BIBLE

Библия или Книги Священного Писания Ветхого и Нового Завета, в русском переводе, с параллельными местами и указателем церковных чтений.
Moscow: Moscow Patriarchate, 1956.
Title, patriarchal blessing [2]; OT half-title, verso blank [3–4]; OT text, 5–993; verso blank [994]; NT half-title, verso blank [995–6]; NT text, 997–1252; tables of readings half-title, verso blank [1253–4]; tables, 1255–71; table of contents [1272]; maps.
26.5 × 20.

A large octavo printing of the synodal text of the Russian Bible in the new orthography with references, tables of OT and NT readings, and maps.

This is the first printing of the Russian Bible undertaken by the Moscow Patriarchate since its reestablishment during the 1917–18 Russian Church Council. The OT includes the entire synodal text (*kanonicheskie* and *nekanonicheskie*), as well as bracketed Septuagint readings, the 151st Psalm, and Chapters 13 and 14 of the book of Daniel. The format follows closely that of large octavo synodal printings before 1917. The text is in two columns on the page with references at the foot of each page. There is paragraph indention of verses. The NT also follows the synodal text. Pronominal references to Mary are capitalized. Post-1917 Soviet orthography is employed. Unlike most Soviet publications, no information is provided regarding the circulation run. Walter Sawatsky, "Bibles in Eastern Europe since 1945," *Religion in Communist Lands*, Supplementary Paper no. 3: 13, states that this edition circulated in 50,000 copies, basing his figure on an oral interview with Archbishop Pitirim.
Loc: BFBS; BL (3062.bb.2 – incorrectly catalogued as 1964 imprint); CUL (20.6.b.95.1); OX (Bib.Russ.d.2); GPB (R40. G-7/5)

294. 1956. NEW TESTAMENT AND PSALTER

Новый Завет Господа Нашего Иисуса Христа и Псалтирь.
Moscow: Moscow Patriarchate, 1956.
Title, patriarchal blessing [2]; NT half-title, verso blank [3–4]; NT text, 5–416; blank page, two maps, blank page, map, blank page [6]; Psalter half-title, verso blank [417–18]; Psalter text, 419–524; table of readings, 525–43; table of contents, 544.
22.5 × 14.5.

A large 16mo edition of the synodal NT and Psalter in the new orthography published by the Moscow Patriarchate. The Psalter includes the 151st Psalm. The text is set in two columns to the page with paragraph indention of verses. References are at the foot of each page, and are identical with synodal editions of the turn of the century. No circulation figure or other imprint information is provided. The Oxford Bodleian copy includes the signatures of Archimandrite Nikodim, Archimandrite Philaret, and Father Bartholomew, dating from their visit to Oxford, June 20, 1960.
Loc: CUL (20.6.c.95.1); OX (Bib.Russ.e.1)

295. 1957. BIBLE

Библия или Книги Священного Писания Ветхого и Нового Завета. Канонические. В русском переводе. С параллельными местами.
Moscow: All-Union Council of Evangelical Christians-Baptists, 1957.
22.5 × 14.

A reprint of no. 282 with identical collation, format, and text. The plates for this printing were provided by the American Bible Society through the mediation of the BFBS.
Loc: BFBS

296. 1958. NEW TESTAMENT. GOSPELS

Господа Нашего Иисуса Христа Святое Евангелие от Матфея, Марка, Луки и Иоанна.
London: William Clowes and Sons, Ltd. for BFBS, 1958.
Title, English imprint [2]; table of contents, verso blank [3–4]; table of abbreviations [5–6]; text, 7–234.
15.5 × 11.

A new edition of the Gospels in Russian translated by Bishop Cassian and a revision committee as noted under no. 291. The text is in one column on the page with verse numbering within the text. Marginal references have been added. The typeface is smaller than in the trial edition of Matthew, no. 291. The printer's imprint is at the bottom of the last page of text. Two thousand copies were printed in 1958, and another 5,000 copies in 1960 (see BFBS Versions Book, no. 35: 92; and no. 36: 30).
Loc: BFBS; BL (3055.a.19); CUL (1959.6.126); OX (N.T.Russ.f.3)

297. 1959. NEW TESTAMENT. GOSPEL HARMONY AND ACTS OF THE APOSTLES

Слово Жизни Вечной. Евангельское повествование.
Brussels: A. Rosseels, printer, "Life with God" Publishers, 1959.
Two blank leaves [4]; title, permission verso [2]; preface, 5–16; table of canonical books, 17–18; table of hours, 19; map, 20; text, 21–433; note on Palestine, 434–52; index of verses, 453–63; alphabetical index, 464–86; comments of notable people, 487–92; table of contents, 493–508; printer's imprint, verso blank [2].
15.5. × 10.5.

A compilation of texts from the Gospels and from the Acts of the Apostles prepared by the Roman Catholic priest Ioann Kornievskii. The texts constitute compilations from all four Gospels ordered by theme. The passages from the Acts of the Apostles are in a final section on "The Church." A Russian synodal text in a single column on the page fits the intended harmony of the Gospel texts. A note in the preface indicates that the text reproduces the editions published in Rome of the Gospels (1944) and Acts–Revelation (1946). The harmonization of the four Gospels follows that published by Ieromonakh

Ioann Robal'd, Milan (Barnabites Society), 1954. The book appears to have been printed for the Brussels exhibition. The title of the volume in English is "The Word of Eternal Life."
Loc: BFBS

298. 1959. NEW TESTAMENT. GOSPELS OF MARK AND JOHN

Сокрытые сокровища и Новая Жизнь: Археологические открытия и Евангелие.
Bruges, Belgium: P. Verbeke, printer, Friendship Publications (Izdaniia Druzhba), 1959.
Half-title, verso blank [2]; title, verso blank [2]; map, verso blank [2]; list of illustrations, verso blank [2]; half-title, verso blank [2]; text on discoveries, 11–60; half-title to two Gospels, verso blank [61–2]; Mark text, 63–115; John text, 116–180; postscript, 181–93; verso blank [1]; list of outlets [2].
17.5 × 12.

A printing of the synodal Russian text of the Gospels of Mark and John with an introductory essay on the discoveries of the Dead Sea biblical texts. The Gospel texts are in one column on the page with verse numbering internal within the text. Authorship of the introductory essay and notes to the Gospels is not identified. The illustrations are photos from the Holy Places and Sinai region.
Loc: BFBS

299. 1962. NEW TESTAMENT AND PSALTER

Новый Завет Господа Нашего Иисуса Христа в русском переводе с параллельными местами. [*Псалтирь* is on a separate internal title page.]
Stockholm: "Tryckt hos Evangeliipress," Örebro, for the Slavic Mission Society [Slaviska Missionen], 1962.
Title, printer's imprint [2]; table of contents, verso blank [2]; NT text, 1–412; Psalter half-title, verso blank [2]; Psalter text, 1–105.
14.5 × 9.

A printing of the synodal NT and Psalter drawn from a synodal printing of 1917 (see note on title page verso), uniform in format with the single Gospels of the Stockholm Slaviska Missionen, nos. 283–6. There is a separate title page for the Psalter as well as separate page numbering. Pronominal references to Mary are capitalized as in the synodal 1917 printing. The 151st Psalm is not included.
Loc: UBS Europe Regional Centre

300. 1963. NEW TESTAMENT. GOSPELS AND ACTS OF THE APOSTLES

Господа Нашего Иисуса Христа Святое Евангелие от Матфея, Марка, Луки и Иоанна и Деяния Апостолов.
London: Wm. Clowes and Sons, Ltd., printer, for BFBS, 1963.
Title, English imprint [2]; table of contents, verso [3–4]; abbreviations for references [5–6]; Gospels text, 7–234; blank leaf [235–6]; Acts text, 237–304.
15.5 × 11.

A rebinding of Bishop Cassian's translation of the Russian Gospels (no. 296) with his translation of the Acts of the Apostles in a format uniform with the 1958 Gospels. Marginal references are included. BFBS ordered the printing of 3,300 copies of Acts of the Apostles, reflecting the fact that only about 3,500 of the 7,000 printed copies of the Gospels had been sold, the remainder then being rebound as a part of this volume (see BFBS Versions Book, no. 38: 42).
Loc: BFBS; BL (X.108/66); CUL (1964.6.20); OX (N.T.Russ.f.4)

301. 1964. BIBLE

Библия. Книги Священного Писания Ветхого и Нового Завета. Канонические. В русском переводе с параллельными местами.
London: Lowe & Brydone, Ltd., printers, for the "Bible Societies," 1964.
16.5 × 11.

A photographically produced reprinting of the UBS/ABS 1947 synodal Bible (no. 282), the first reprinting of this format by the BFBS. The collation, text, chapter headings, etc., are identical to no. 282. The printer's imprint, located on the first of two blank leaves at the end, gives the date of 1964. According to BFBS records (see BFBS Versions Book no. 39: 8), 3,000 copies were printed in 1964. For other reprintings of this format between 1964 and 1968, see the annotation for no. 309.
Loc: CUL (1964.6.19); OX (Bib.Russ.e.2)

302. [1965.] NEW TESTAMENT

[*Новый Завет Господа Нашего Иисуса Христа.*]

[Brussels: "Life with God" Publishers, 1965.]
The BFBS working catalog of biblical editions cites this 1965 NT printing as a Roman Catholic edition corresponding to an earlier Rome edition of 1944/1946. *Non de visu.* See also no. 305.

303. 1966. NEW TESTAMENT AND PSALTER

Новый Завет Господа Нашего Иисуса Христа в русском переводе с параллельными местами [*и Псалтирь*].
Stockholm: Evangeliipress, Orebro, for Slaviska Missionen, 1966.
10.5 × 7.

A reduced pocket-size reprint of no. 299 (1962), identical in collation and format. Publication information is on the second blank leaf following the Psalter.

Loc: BFBS

304. 1967. NEW TESTAMENT AND PSALTER

Новый Завет Господа Нашего Иисуса Христа в русском переводе с параллельными местами [*и Псалтирь*].
Orebro, Sweden: Tryckt hos Tryckcentralen, printer, for Ryska Bibelsallskapet [Slaviska Missionen], 1967.
14 × 9.

A larger reprint of no. 299 (1962) uniform in collation, format, and page size. Publication information is on the final blank leaf, as in no. 303.
Loc: BFBS

305. 1967. NEW TESTAMENT

Новый Завет Господа Нашего Иисуса Христа.
Brussels: "Life with God" Publishers, 1967.
Title, blessing/publisher's imprint [2]; preface, verso blank [3–4]; NT text, 5–508; tables, 509–27; list of synodal text variants and errata, 528–32; table of contents [533]; maps.
14.5 × 9.5.

A pocket-size Roman Catholic reproduction of a Rome 1944/6 edition of the synodal Russian NT with introductions to each book and text notes. The volume was published in 5,000 copies by the Brussels Catholic publishing house, "Life with God," for free distribution at the Montreal exhibition of 1967. The text and introductions are printed in paragraph style, one column to the page. Verse numbering is internal within paragraphs. A list of variant readings from the synodal text is added (pp. 528–30) along with several supplementary tables. The imprint on the title page remains "Rome, 1944 and 1946," but the Brussels imprint is on the title verso.
Loc: BFBS

306. 1967. NEW TESTAMENT. GOSPEL OF LUKE

Благая весть: Евангелие от Луки.
[New York:] UBS [by the American Bible Society], 1967.
Title, publisher imprint verso [2]; Luke text, 3–31; full-page illustration verso [32].
23 × 17.5.

An illustrated edition of the Gospel of Luke utilizing the synodal Russian text. Paragraph headings are included. The illustrations are photos from the Holy Land. Fifty thousand copies of this edition were published by the American Bible Society under the United Bible Societies imprint (see the Darlington Materials, BFBS Archive), with a portion of the print run sent to the Soviet Union as a Christmas gift to the Moscow Patriarchate. This specimen Gospel was later incorporated into a printing of the four Gospels (no. 311).
Loc: BFBS

307. 1968. NEW TESTAMENT AND PSALTER

Библия. Книги Священного Писания Нового Завета и Псалтирь.
Moscow: Moscow Patriarchate, 1968.
Title, patriarchal blessing [2]; NT half-title, table of contents [2]; NT text, 1–336; Psalter half-title, Psalter text, 1–62.
20 × 13.

A reprinting of the Russian synodal NT and Psalter by the Moscow Patriarchate. A note on the title verso indicates that the text is drawn from the synodal Bible printed in 1912 (the same note is printed in no. 308). The text is in two columns on the page with footnoted references. The Psalter is printed with a smaller typeface. Pronominal references to Mary are capitalized and the 151st Psalm is included. Circulation information is lacking. This printing was reissued in a pirated photo-offset edition published in New Delhi, India, in the 1980s. The New Delhi printing bears the inscription in Russian, "Published by the Partnership Mission."
Loc: BFBS

308. 1968 [1969]. BIBLE

Библия: Книги Священного Писания Ветхого и Нового Завета.
Moscow: Moscow Patriarchate, 1968 [1969].
Title, patriarchal blessing [2]; OT half-title, table of contents verso [3–4]; OT text, 5–987; table of OT readings, 988–98; appended notes, 999–1002; maps [1003–8]; NT half-title, table of contents [1009–10]; NT text, 1011–1346; table of

readings, 1347–60; appended notes, 1361–72; list of illustrations, verso blank [2]; six icons.
22 × 14.5.

An octavo printing of the synodal Russian Bible published from a 1912 text (see title page verso). The text is in two columns to the page in paragraphs with internal verse numbering. According to the printer's imprint (p. 1372), the volume was not actually submitted for printing until late 1969, hence the 1969 date alongside the 1968 title page entry. The OT contains the full synodal text and bracketed Septuagint readings. The NT contains capitalization of pronominal references to Mary. The notes introduced between the OT and NT address disputes over the Septuagint text and deuterocanonical books, among other issues. References are again placed at the bottom of each page. The font is considerably smaller than in the 1956 printing (no. 293), hence the smaller size of the volume.
Loc: CUL (20.6.c.95.2); OX (Bib.Russ.e.3)

309. 1968. BIBLE

Библия: Книги Священного Писания Ветхого и Нового Завета. Канонические. В русском переводе с параллельными местами.
London: Lowe & Brydone, Ltd. for the Bible Societies, 1968.
16 × 11.

A photographic reprinting of the Russian synodal Bible with collation and format identical to the standard western Bible Societies edition (no. 282, 1947). Page and type size have been reduced. The 1968 reprinting was in 20,000 copies. All subsequent reprintings of this edition bear the imprint of the United Bible Societies (e.g. no. 310). Center-column marginal references and specially prepared chapter headings date from 1964 (no. 301). From 1964 until UBS takeover of printing responsibility, the text was printed by Lowe & Brydone of London. According to BFBS Versions Books, circulation runs of the various reprintings were as follows: 3,000 copies in 1964 (BFBS Versions Book no. 39, 8); 3,000 copies in 1965 (BFBS Versions Book no. 39, 159); 7,000 copies in 1966 (BFBS Versions Book no. 39, 335); 5,000 copies in 1967 (BFBS Versions Book no. 40, 339); 1,000 copies in a first 1968 printing (BFBS Versions Book no. 41, 69); and this printing of 20,000 copies (*United Bible Societies Bulletin*, no. 79: 135). Although some copies reached a Soviet audience, the majority served a western émigré readership.
Loc: BFBS

310. [1968, 1969.] BIBLE

Библия: Книги Священного Писания Ветхого и Нового Завета. Канонические. В русском переводе с параллельными местами.
[Stuttgart?]: UBS, [1968, 1969].
15 × 10.

Although page and type size were reduced from no. 309, this is a photographic reprinting with collation and format identical to the 1968 printing. By 1968, the United Bible Societies had established a "European Production Fund" (EPF) for scripture publication for Eastern Europe. This is the first printing of the Russian Bible to be undertaken directly at the expense of its EPF. The *United Bible Societies Bulletin*, no. 80, 1969: 181, notes a contribution to the Fund from the Finnish Bible Society of paper for a press run of 10,000 copies of the Russian Bible. The 1969 date is based upon the *Bulletin* article.
Loc: BFBS

311. 1969. NEW TESTAMENT. ILLUSTRATED GOSPELS

Четвероевангелие от Матфея, Марка Луки и Иоанна в русском переводе с греческого, одобренном священным синодом, Москва, 1956.
New York: UBS [American Bible Society], 1969.
Title, French imprint verso [2]; Matthew title, note verso [2]; Matthew text, 3–31; illustration [32]; Mark title, note verso, 33–4; Mark text, 35–63; illustrations [64]; Luke title, note verso, 65–6; Luke text, 67–95; illustration [96]; John title, note verso, 97–8; John text, 99–127; illustration [128].
23.5 × 18.

An illustrated edition of the four Gospels in paragraph format with text drawn from the Moscow 1956 synodal Russian edition (no. 293). Fifty thousand copies were published by the American Bible Society under the UBS imprint for presentation as a gift to the Moscow Patriarchate. The illustrations are photos from Jerusalem and surrounding regions.
Loc: BFBS

312. 1970. NEW TESTAMENT

Новый Завет Господа Нашего Иисуса Христа.
London: William Clowes and Sons, Ltd., printer, for BFBS, 1970.
Title page, publisher imprint [2]; table of contents, verso blank [3–4]; abbreviations [5–6]; text, 7–513.
15.5 × 11.

First complete edition of the Russian NT translation of Bishop Cassian and the revision committee (see no. 291), with marginal references. Format is uniform with nos. 296 and 300. The western order of the epistles is followed, Pauline epistles preceding Catholic epistles. Publication of the entire Cassian Bezobrazov NT was delayed until five years after Bishop Cassian's death because of BFBS concern over demand. The initial press run was only 3,000 copies. There followed a second electroplate printing of 3,000 copies in 1972 (see BFBS Versions Book no. 42, 61, 350). The 1970 imprint is on both printings. The Bezobrazov text was subsequently pirated by the Slavic Gospel Association in a 1977 diglot (see no. 322). The popularity of the translation was limited from the outset by its rather stiff Russian language, evidenced in Bishop Cassian's effort to maintain the original Greek word order in his translation of the Gospel of John.
Loc: BFBS; BL (X.208/1270); CUL (9100.e.82); OX (N.T.Russ.f.5)

313. [1970?] NEW TESTAMENT. PARAPHRASE OF EPISTLE TO THE ROMANS

Пробудись к жизни; Парафраз Послания к Римлянам.
Wheaton, IL: Youth for Christ ("Living Letters Overseas"), [1970?].
Title, publisher's imprint, half-title, illustrations, preface [8]; Romans paraphrase, 9–62.
21 × 13.5.

Russian translation of a 1964 English paraphrase of the Epistle to the Romans done by Kenneth N. Taylor. Identity of the Russian translator of Taylor's paraphrase is not provided. The "Living Letters" series includes paraphrases done by the literature division of Youth for Christ (Wheaton, IL), Living Bibles International. The estimated 1970 publication date is based upon the date of BFBS Library acquisition.
Loc: BFBS

314. [1973–4.] NEW TESTAMENT IN MICRO-EDITION

Новый Завет Господа Нашего Иисуса Христа.
Manila: Far East Broadcasting Corporation, Marshburn Press, [1973–4].
1 leaf.

A printing of the synodal Russian NT in "micro" format such that the entire NT fits onto both sides of one sheet of paper foldable to letter size. The BFBS Library contains magnified xeroxes of two separate versions.

One is a micro-edition of the NT based on the American Bible Society 1947 edition with center column references (no. 282). The other, in slightly larger magnification, employs the text setting of no. 282, but has spliced out the chapter headings and marginal references so as to allow for a larger typeface. In an undated cover letter with the BFBS copies, Marshburn Press manager Bud Jillson explains how the entire text was printed on two sides of a special, thin paper, 23" × 36". The first two printings, in October 1973, were in 3,000 copies each, the third printing was in 55,000 copies, printed at the rate of 15,000 copies per hour.
Loc: BFBS

315. 1973. OLD TESTAMENT. SELECTIONS

"Древнееврейская литература," in *Поэзия и проза Древнего Востока*, 537–652; 652; 713–27.
Moscow: Khudozhestvennaia Literatura, 1973.

This collection of OT texts ("early Hebrew literature") consists of the following subsections of a larger anthology of early oriental prose and poetry:

(a) "Drevneevreiskaia literatura," an essay by Igor M. D'iakonov, pp. 537–50.
(b) "Iz 'Knigi Bytiia,'" a translation of Genesis 6–8 (the flood), by S. Apt, pp. 551–4.
(c) "Kniga Ruf'," a translation of the book of Ruth, by I. Braginskii, pp. 557–63.
(d) "Kniga Iova," a translation of the book of Job, by S. Averintsev, pp. 563–625.
(e) "Pesn' pesnei," a translation of the Song of Solomon, by Igor D'iakonov, pp. 625–38.
(f) "Kniga Ekklesiast," a translation of the book of Ecclesiastes, by Igor D'iakonov, pp. 638–52.
(g) "Primechaniia," notes for the above subsections, pp. 713–27.

Original translations of OT texts from Hebrew into Russian by leading scholars of the Soviet Academy of Sciences who applied modern historico-critical textology to ancient texts. Sergei Averintsev, for example, drew upon ancient texts of Job in Greek and Hebrew, and noted in that connection the importance of the Qumran finds. He also utilized an unpublished work on "The Book of Job" [in Russian] by M. I. Rizhskii. The texts were produced in one column on the page with poetical or quoted sections indented. Verse numbering, when employed, is in the margins. The text is in paragraphs undivided by verse, but with clear chapter divisions. The translations follow closely the traditional text so that, even though the Russian texts depart significantly from the synodal edition, they cannot be said to be "free" translations. In the case of

passages in which the synodal translation includes bracketed Septuagint readings (for example, lengthy phrases in Gen. 6:19 and Gen. 8:7), there is no fixed pattern in the new translation. Some Septuagint readings are translated into Russian, but there are no bracketed Septuagint passages as in the synodal OT. These OT selections are published as articles within a bound 1973 anthology.
Loc: BFBS; OX, CUL

316. 1974. NEW TESTAMENT AND PSALTER

Новый Завет Господа Нашего Иисуса Христа [(and) *Псалтирь*].
Moscow: Moscow Press No. 5 for the All-Union Council of Evangelical Christians-Baptists, 1974.
Title, printer's imprint [2]; table of contents, verso blank [2]; NT text, 1–331; verso blank [1]; Psalter title [1]; Psalter text, 332–413; verso blank [1]; maps.
17 × 11.

A subsidized Moscow reprinting of the synodal Russian NT and Psalter for the All-Union Council of Evangelical Christians-Baptists, reproduced from the American Bible Society printings of 1945/6 (nos. 279 and 280). According to the United Bible Societies "Background Paper," September 1977, 20,000 copies were printed.
Loc: BFBS

317. 1975. OLD TESTAMENT. PENTATEUCH (TORAH) IN HEBREW/RUSSIAN DIGLOT

Пять Книг Торы. Vol. I of III.
Jerusalem: Sivan Press for Mossad Harav Kook, 1975.
[Collation from back:] half-title, Hebrew title [ii]; Russian title, publisher's imprint [iii–iv]; publisher imprint in Russian [v]; letter from Minister of Religion Itzhak Raphael, vi–viii; Russian translation, ix–xi; blank page [1]; list of editors/translators in Hebrew and Russian, verso blank [2]; Russian pronunciations, verso blank [2]; Torah half-title [1]; Hebrew/Russian diglot, 1–271.
22 × 14.

A new Jerusalem Russian translation of the Pentateuch, or Torah, done by Rabbi David Iosifon and an editorial committee composed of Iosifon's assistant, Avraam Melamed, and four others: Maiia Osovysheva, Barukh Burshtein, Galiia Kats, and Professor Aaron Shulov (this last a consultant on zoological questions). The Hebrew text is drawn from a Leningrad Hebrew Masoretic manuscript text provided by Keter Aram Tsova. That text, published here for the first time, was prepared for publication in Jerusalem by Mordecai Broer.

Publication was made possible by the support of the Ministry of Absorption (in charge of placement of Soviet Jewish émigrés) and the Ministry of Religion. The Minister of Religion, then Itzhak Raphael (son of Rabbi Shemueil Tsyva), describes the translation in a prefatory letter. The texts are in single columns on facing pages, the left in Russian, the right in Hebrew. Verse numbering is in the outer margins. The translation follows the Hebrew text closely, does not incorporate the Synod's bracketed Septuagint readings, and introduces transliterated Hebrew names for otherwise common Russian OT names. This project (see also nos. 325 and 326) constituted the first new Russian translation of the OT from the Hebrew since 1875.
Loc: BFBS

318. 1976. BIBLE

Библия: Книги Священного Писания Ветхого и Нового Завета.
Moscow: Moscow Patriarchate, 1976.

Stereotype reprint of the 1968/9 Moscow Bible (no. 308). According to Keston College News Service (March 11, 1983), 100,000 Bibles were printed by the Russian Orthodox Church in 1976 on the centenary of the synodal Bible. The RNB also holds a 1979 photographic reprinting (no. 328) of the same edition.
Loc: RNB (77–5/185)

319. 1976. NEW TESTAMENT [AND PSALTER?]

[*Библия: книги священного писания нового завета и Псалтирь.*]
[Moscow: Moscow Patriarchate, 1976.]

According to Keston College News Service (March 11, 1983), 70,000 copies of the NT and Psalter were printed by the Moscow Patriarchate in 1976 for the centenary of the synodal Bible.
Loc: *Non de visu.*

320. 1976. NEW TESTAMENT. GOSPEL OF JOHN PARAPHRASE

Полноценная жизнь: Пересказ Евангелия от Иоанна.
[Wheaton, IL:] International Living Bible, 1976.
Half-title, publisher's imprint [2]; title page [3]; preface, 4–7; blank page [8]; John paraphrase, 9–91; illustrations [2]; statements [1].
19 × 13.

Russian translation of Kenneth N. Taylor's English paraphrase of the Gospel of John. Translator is not identified. The paperbound volume is illustrated with contemporary photos. "International Living Bible" publishers issued a similar paraphrase of the Epistle to the Romans (no. 313).
Loc: BFBS

321. 1977. NEW TESTAMENT AND PSALTER

Новый Завет Господа Нашего Иисуса Христа [*(и) Псалтирь*].
Stuttgart: UBS, 1977.
NT title, table of contents [2]; NT text, 1–292; blank leaf, Psalter title, verso blank [293–6]; Psalter text, 297–367; verso blank [1]; maps.
16 × 10.5.

Reprint of the Russian synodal NT and Psalms uniform with the UBS 1947 Bible (no. 282), with minor errata corrected in the plates since the previous 1968 BFBS reprint (no. 309) and the 1969 UBS printing (no. 310). The United Bible Societies, which adopted this edition with chapter headings and center-margined references, undertook the corrections of errata based upon a list of some eighty or more typographical errors compiled from the 1947 stereotype edition (see BFBS Editorial Correspondence: Russian, June 1970). Format and collation are identical with the previous printings of no. 282. According to the UBS note enclosed in the BFBS copy, 2,000 copies were printed for the "European Production Fund." This corrected 1977 printing remained the version most commonly sold by western Bible societies into the twenty-first century.
Loc: BFBS

322. [1977?] NEW TESTAMENT IN RUSSIAN/ENGLISH DIGLOT

Новый Завет Господа Нашего Иисуса Христа. Новый перевод с греческого подлинника.
Wheaton, IL: Slavic Gospel Association, Inc. (New American Standard Bible, English text by the Lockman Foundation, La Habra, CA), [1977?].
Blank leaf [2]; blank page, Russian title [2]; English title, copyright verso [2]; foreword [2]; explanation, verso blank [2]; table of contents, verso blank [2]; text, 1–769; Russian NT glossary, 770–81.
16.5 × 11.5.

A Russian/English diglot of the NT. The Russian text is pirated from the BFBS translation of Bishop Cassian Bezobrazov (no. 312). The volume is undated.
Loc: UBS Europe Regional Centre

323. [1978.] BIBLE

Библия: Книги Священного Писания Ветхого и Нового Завета. Канонические. В русском переводе с параллельными местами.
Moscow [i.e. Stuttgart]: All-Union Council of Evangelical Christians-Baptists [i.e. UBS], 1968 [i.e. 1978].
16 × 10.5.

A reprinting of the standard ABS/BFBS Russian synodal Bible (see nos. 282, 309, and others) with corrections introduced in 1977 to the NT and Psalter (no. 321). This printing follows the text, format, and collation of no. 309 and previous printings. According to the United Bible Societies "Background Paper," February 1979: 5, a printing of Bibles was undertaken in Stuttgart in 1978 for the Moscow All-Union Council of Evangelical Christians-Baptists, which had authority to import 25,000 Bibles. Because the corrections introduced into the 1977 printing (no. 321) are also in this reprinting, the photographic 1968 imprint date on the title page is in error. Dating conforms to the All-Union Council's 1978 import permit.
Loc: BFBS

324. 1978. NEW TESTAMENT. GOSPEL OF JOHN

Евангелие по Иоанну в новом русском переводе: Вариант, параллельный переводу Евангелия в Новой Английской Библии.
Brussels: Headley Brothers, Ltd., printers (London), for the United Bible Societies, 1978.
Title, publisher imprint [ii]; preface, iii–v; verso blank [vi]; John text, 1–39; printer's imprint.
21 × 14.5.

Experimental Russian translation of the Gospel of John prepared in Leningrad by Konstantin Ivanovich Logachev with the permission of Leningrad Metropolitan Nikodim (d. 1978). Logachev is identified in the preface as a scholarly consultant to the Leningrad Theological Academy. The text was an attempt to create an easily readable Russian text parallel to that produced by modern textual scholarship in the New English Bible. Publication was arranged officially in cooperation with the United Bible Societies, which published 2,000 copies as a supplement to its periodical, *The Bible Translator*. The "BFBS" acronym is on the title page verso. The work in Leningrad was part of a wider translation effort supported by Metropolitan Nikodim and documented in an interview with the then rector of the Leningrad Academy, Bishop Kirill (currently Patriarch of Moscow). For the interview, see Elizabeth Pond, "In Soviet Russia – A New Bible

Translation," *Christian Science Monitor*, June 22, 1976, 14. The text is printed in one column on the page in paragraphs. Verse numbering is internal within the text. The title page verso includes the unfortunate English short title, "Russian John." Notes regarding variant English and Greek readings are at the foot of the text. The text of John 7:53–8:11 is translated as an appendage and placed at the end of the Gospel.
Loc: BFBS; CUL (Uc.1.2387)

325. 1978. OLD TESTAMENT. JOSHUA, JUDGES, 1–2 SAMUEL, 1–2 KINGS, ISAIAH, JEREMIAH, EZEKIEL, AND HOSEA–MALACHI IN HEBREW/RUSSIAN DIGLOT

Первые и последние пророки.
Jerusalem: Sivan Press for Mossad Harav Kook, 1978.
Half-title, Hebrew title verso [2]; Russian title, publisher's imprint [2]; Russian publisher's imprint [1]; Hebrew preface [1]; Russian preface, verso blank [2]; list of translators, verso blank [2]; list of books, verso blank [2]; Joshua half-title [1]; Hebrew/Russian diglot of Joshua through Twelve Later Prophets, 1–494.
22 × 14.

The second volume of the Jerusalem Russian translation of the Hebrew Bible, or Tanakh. The format for this edition of the earlier and later prophets is uniform with the 1975 Jerusalem translation of the Pentateuch (Torah), no. 317. The translation was undertaken by Rabbi David Iosifon in collaboration with an editorial revision committee. In the case of the book of Isaiah, Avraam Melamed translated Chapters 1–9, and Shimshon Midbari translated Chapters 10–52. For Ezekiel, the translation is credited both to Rabbi Iosifon and Natan Faingol'd. Of the twelve later prophets, Hosea, Joel, and Amos were translated by Avraam Melamed. The format is uniform with no. 317. In addition to the financial support of the Israeli Ministries of Absorption and of Religion, support for the translation came from the Memorial Fund for Hebrew Culture.
Loc: BFBS

326. 1978. OLD TESTAMENT. PSALMS, PROVERBS, JOB, SONG OF SOLOMON, RUTH, LAMENTATIONS, ECCLESIASTES, ESTHER, DANIEL, EZRA, NEHEMIAH, AND 1–2 CHRONICLES IN HEBREW/RUSSIAN DIGLOT

Кетувим.
Jerusalem: Sivan Press for Mossad Harav Kook, 1978.
Half-title, Hebrew title verso [2]; Russian title, publisher's imprint [2]; Russian publisher's imprint, Hebrew preface [2]; Russian preface, verso blank [2]; Hebrew/

Russian editorial committee, verso blank [2]; half-title list of books, verso blank [2]; Psalter half-title [1]; Hebrew/Russian diglot (Psalter – 1, 2 Chronicles), 1–394. 22.5 × 13.5.

The third volume of the Jerusalem Russian translation of the Hebrew Bible in a Russian/Hebrew diglot uniform with nos. 317 and 325. Volume III is the Hagiographa or "Sacred Writings." The chief translator is again Rabbi David Iosifon, but the five books of the Megilloth were translated into Russian by Shimshon Midbari. Daniel, Ezra, and Nehemiah were translated by Professor Shimon Ben-Baruch. In addition to the members of the editorial committee listed under no. 317, Avraam Below-Ellinson, Professor Shimon Ben-Baruch, Felix Dektor, Ioseif Lishchinskii, Esteir Lomovskaia, Professor B. Massis, and Aleksandr Rozen participated in the revision of the text. The supporting agencies listed in no. 325 underwrote production.
Loc: BFBS

327. 1979. BIBLE.

[*Библия: Книги Священного Писания Ветхого и Нового Завета.*]
[Moscow: All-Union Council of Evangelical Christians-Baptists, 1979.]

A reprinting of the Russian synodal Bible uniform with no. 323. According to the United Bible Societies' "Background Paper," February 1981: 21, the monies recovered by the All-Union Council of Evangelical Christians-Baptists from their distribution of the 25,000 Bibles received from the UBS in 1978 (no. 323) "enabled the Baptist Church to print a further 20,000 copies in the USSR. These were completed in 1979."
Loc: *Non de visu.*

[1979. NEW TESTAMENT. (MOSCOW: MOSCOW PATRIARCHATE, 1979). According to an article in the *American Bible Society Record*, March 1984 ("More Bibles for Russia"), 50,000 NTs were printed by the Moscow Patriarchate in 1979. *Non de visu.*]

328. 1979. BIBLE

Библия: Книги Священного Писания Ветхого и Нового Завета.
Moscow: Moscow Patriarchate, 1979.
Reprint of no. 318 in 50,000 copies.
Loc: RNB (77–5/185)

329. 1981. BIBLE

Библия: Книги Священного Писания Ветхого и Нового Завета. Канонические. В русском переводе с параллельными местами.
Stuttgart: UBS, European Production Fund, 1981.
23 × 16.

According to the American Bible Society's *International Division Report* (1981), 4,000 copies of the UBS Russian Bible were printed in July 1981 in a larger size. The collation and format remained the same despite the larger font.
Loc: *Non de visu.*

330. 1981. NEW TESTAMENT. GOSPEL OF LUKE IN BRAILLE

Библия для слепых: Евангелие от Луки.
Yucaipa, CA: Lutheran Braille Association for the UBS, 1981.
71 leaves.

An edition of the Russian synodal text of the Gospel of Luke in Braille for use by the blind. The external cover, which is not in Braille, identifies the edition as the work of the Lutheran Braille Association on the order of the United Bible Societies' European Production Fund. The UBS arranged production in response to a 1980 order from the USSR All-Union Council of Evangelical Christians-Baptists. According to the cover, 500 copies were printed. A note in the *UBS World Report*, March 1984, indicates the UBS European Production Fund "since September 1981 has supplied to Moscow 1,000 copies each of the Russian braille version of the Gospels of Matthew, Luke, John and the Acts of the Apostles" (see nos. 332–4). The Gospel of Mark in Russian Braille was also completed in 1984. Production for the UBS was carried out by the Lutheran Braille Association in the USA and by the Torch Trust in Britain. Further editions of Romans, 1 and 2 Corinthians, Hebrews, Galatians, and the Psalms, the *World Report* noted, were transcribed into Russian Braille by computer.
Loc: BFBS

[1982. BIBLE WITH REFERENCES (STOCKHOLM: INSTITUTE FOR BIBLE TRANSLATION, [1982]). According to an article in the Eastern European Mission's *Gospel Call* (Walter E. Zurfluh, "An Improved Russian Reference Bible Goes to Press," January/February 1984), 20,000 copies of "the Goetze Bible," an interwar reference Bible using the synodal text, were published approximately two years previously for distribution to Russian pastors and Christian workers. The 1982 edition is the second printing, the original "Goetze Bible" having been published in 1939. According to East/West News Service (January 1, 1982), Underground Evangelism (UE) underwrote the Stockholm publication. *Non de visu.*]

331. 1982. NEW TESTAMENT ON CASSETTE TAPES

[Новый завет.] Audio edition.
[Wheaton?]: Slavic Gospel Association, 1982.

According to the Missionary News Service (September 15, 1982), the Slavic Gospel Association completed in 1982 a two-year project to record on cassette tapes the synodal version of the Russian NT. The recording was done by Vera Enutine, a former Moscow radio broadcaster resident in the United States. The recording is on a twenty-four-cassette tape album.
Loc: *Non de visu.*

332. 1982. NEW TESTAMENT. GOSPEL OF MATTHEW IN RUSSIAN BRAILLE

[*Библия для слепых: Евангелие от Матфея.*]
[Yucaipa, CA: Lutheran Braille Association for the UBS, 1982.]

A Braille edition of the synodal Russian Gospel of Matthew printed in 1,000 copies (*UBS World Report*, October 1983), uniform with no. 330.
Loc: *Non de visu.*

333. 1983. NEW TESTAMENT. GOSPEL OF JOHN IN RUSSIAN BRAILLE

[*Библия для слепых: Евангелие от Иоанна.*]
[Yucaipa, CA: Lutheran Braille Association for the UBS, 1983.]

A Braille edition of the synodal Russian Gospel of John printed in 1,000 copies, uniform with nos. 330 and 332.
Loc: *Non de visu.*

334. 1983. NEW TESTAMENT. ACTS OF THE APOSTLES IN RUSSIAN BRAILLE

[*Библия для слепых: Деяния Апостолов.*]
[Yucaipa, CA: Lutheran Braille Association for the UBS, 1983.]

A Braille edition of the synodal Russian Acts of the Apostles printed in 500 copies, uniform with nos. 330 and 332–3.
Loc: *Non de visu.*

335. 1983. BIBLE. BIBLICAL SELECTIONS AND PARAPHRASES FOR CHILDREN

Детская Библия.
Stockholm: Institute for Bible Translation, 1983.
Half-title, publisher imprint [2]; title, verso blank [3–4]; preface [5–8]; half-title [9]; text and illustrations, 10–379; verso blank [1]; maps.
19 × 12.5.

A selection of Russian biblical passages and paraphrases for children prepared by the Institute for Bible Translation in Stockholm. Internal quotes (e.g. NT sayings of Jesus) are taken directly from the synodal Russian translation, but otherwise the text is loosely paraphrased. The publication was issued in 5,000 copies, and used as a basis for translation for children's Bibles in non-Russian languages of the Soviet Union.
Loc: BFBS

[*1983. Bible. Библия: Книги Священного Писания Ветхого и Нового Завета. (Moscow: Moscow Patriarchate, 1983).* According to an article in the *American Bible Society Record* (March 1984, "More Bibles for Russia"), the Moscow Patriarchate issued another printing of its Bible (no. 308) in 70,000 copies in 1983. The account is based upon remarks by Archbishop Pitirim, head of the publishing department of the patriarchate, while visiting Finland as a guest of the Lutheran Church. *Non de visu.*]

336. 1983. BIBLE

Библия: Книги Священного Писания Ветхого и Нового Завета в русском переводе с приложениями.
Brussels: "Life with God" Publishers, 1983.
Title, imprint verso [2]; introduction, 3–17; Vatican II excerpts, 18–22; biblical text, 1–[1844]; supplements [1845]–2535.
17 × 10.5.

Second printing with new supplements of a Roman Catholic edition of the Russian synodal text of the Bible with marginal references. For earlier printings of the NT by the same press, see nos. 302 and 305. According to the introduction, the text follows that of the Moscow Patriarchate 1968

edition (no. 308). Accordingly, all the Septuagint texts are used, including the following texts not normally included in the Catholic canon: the third book of Maccabees, the third book of Esdras, the prayer of Manasses, Psalm 151, and the Syriac ending of the book of Job. Septuagint readings are, as in the Russian synodal editions, printed within parentheses in the OT text. The text is published in a single column on the page with references on the outer margin of each page. Chapter numeration is at the margin, but verse numeration is within the text. The text is published in paragraphs with subheadings. The title page verso contains the note that the edition is published "with the permission of church authorities" (*s razresheniia tserkovnykh vlastei*). This popular edition circulated in the emigration through the Paris YMCA Press and other outlets.
Loc: Personal copy

337. 1984. BIBLE

Библія. Книги Священнаго Писанія Ветхаго и Новаго Завѣта. Каноническія.
[Stockholm: Institute for Bible Translation, 1984.]
Title, imprint verso, table of contents [1–5]; OT text, 6–892; NT title, table of contents [2]; NT text, 3–306; appendices, [1]–178; maps.
13.5 × 21.5

Third printing with an additional map and enlarged appendices of the so-called "Goetze Bible" with references (see the bracketed note above for 1982). The text follows the synodal edition, and utilizes a modified combination of old and new orthography, incorporating the use, for example, of "ѣ" and "i" from the old orthography. The expanded appendices in this edition include the lengthy article by D. A. Khvol'son, "Bibleiskie perevody," reprinted from the pre-revolutionary *Entsiklopedicheskii slovar'*, 139–63, followed by the article on "Bibliia u Slavian" taken from the same encyclopedia. The first printing of this Goetze edition was issued in 1939. Bernhard Goetze was born in Poland in 1888. He had the idea of publishing a study Bible in Russian. To do this he engaged several coworkers and consulted with Russian pastors, missionaries, priests, and others. In July 1939, after several years' work, two months before the German invasion of Poland, 10,000 copies of Goetze's Bible were printed in the Polish town of Bydgoszcz. Four thousand copies were distributed; the remaining 6,000 copies were destroyed by the Gestapo, along with thousands of copies of other Russian and Polish books Goetze had published. According to an article in *Gospel Call* (Walter E. Zurfluh, "An Improved Russian Bible Goes

to Press," January/February 1984), only 2,000 copies of the earlier 1982 printing remained in stock, so the East European Mission in Canada and USA commissioned the printing of a further 10,000 copies. The costs were covered by the East European Mission, the newly reconstituted Russian Bible Society, World Christian Ministries (Canada), and Rev. D. Kiritch (Canada). The reprint was done by the Institute for Bible Translation in Stockholm, as noted on the title page verso.
Loc: BFBS

338. [1984?] NEW TESTAMENT AND PSALTER

Moscow: All-Union Council of Evangelical Christians-Baptists, [1984?].

According to the European Baptist Press Service (July 28, 1983), the All-Union Council of Evangelical Christians-Baptists printed 20,000 NTs with the Psalter for distribution in 1984 in honor of the one hundredth anniversary of the Baptist Union founded in Novo-Vasil'evka in 1884.
Loc: *Non de visu.*

339. 1984. GOSPELS, ACTS OF THE APOSTLES, ROMANS, AND FIRST EPISTLE OF JOHN

Начала Христианской Веры: Пересказ семи книг Нового Завета.
Naperville, IL: Living Bibles International, 1984.
Title, imprint verso, table of contents, text of seven NT books, [2]–500; appendices, 502–15.
11.5 × 15.5.

A paraphrase Russian edition of the Gospels, Acts of the Apostles, Epistle to the Romans, and the First Epistle of John, uniform with the earlier 1976 Living Bible edition of the Gospel of John (no. 320).
Loc: BFBS

340. 1987. BIBLE

Толковая Библія, или комментаріи на всѣ книги св. Писанія Ветхаго и Новаго Завѣта. 3 vols.
Stockholm: Reprinted by Institute for Bible Translation, 1987.
Vol. 1: Original title page, Stockholm imprint verso, preface, table of contents [i–vi]; internal title, table of contents, introductions [i–xvi]; text/commentary for Pentateuch, 1–[671]; Joshua, Judges, Ruth, and the books of Kings [viii], 1–585; 1 and 2 Chronicles, 1 and 2 Esdras, Nehemiah, Tobit, Judith, and Esther, 1–442; Job, Psalms, Proverbs, and the Books of Solomon, 1–502.
15 × 23.

Vol. II: Original title page, Stockholm imprint verso, table of contents [iv]; internal title/text for Ecclesiastes, Song of Songs, Wisdom of Solomon, Ecclesiasticus, and Isaiah, 1–548; title/text for Jeremiah, Lamentations of Jeremiah, Epistle of Jeremiah, Ezekiel, and Baruch, 1–544; Daniel, Hosea, Joel, Amos, Obadiah, Jonah, Micah, Nahum, Habbakuk, Zephaniah, Haggi, Zechariah, and Malachi, 1–341.
15 × 23.
Vol. III: Original title page, Stockholm imprint verso, table of contents [iv]; internal title/text for Matthew, 1–478; title/text for Mark, Luke, and John, 1–505; title/text for Acts of the Apostles, Epistles of James, Peter, John, Jude, and the Epistle of Paul to the Romans, 1–519; maps [vi]; title/text for Epistles of Paul to Corinthians, Galatians, Ephesians, Philippians, Colossians, Thessalonians, Timothy, Titus, Philemon, Hebrews, and the book of Revelation, 1–609; maps.
15 × 23.

A three-volume reprint of the interpreter's Bible – a study Bible originally prepared by A. P. Lopukhin in twelve parts, 1904–13 – incorporating the synodal Russian Bible and commentary. This large three-volume edition was published by the Institute for Bible Translation in Stockholm as a gift to the Russian Orthodox Church from the churches of the Nordic countries of Denmark, Norway, Finland, Sweden, Greenland, Iceland, and the Faroe Islands on the occasion of the celebration of the millennium of Christianity in Russia at the end of the 1980s. A brief introductory essay by Boris Arapovich, director of the Stockholm Institute, identifies the work of the original editor, Aleksandr Pavlovich Lopukhin, and his collaborators/successors who carried the project forward after Lopukhin's death in 1904. Each of the three reprinted volumes contains four of the original twelve parts. Ten thousand copies of the three-volume set were printed.
Loc: BFBS, OX, CUL

341. 1988. BIBLE

Библия. Книги Священного Писания Ветхого и Нового Завета.
Moscow: Press of the Moscow Patriarchate, 1988.
14 × 22.

Stereotype reprint of the Moscow Patriarchate's synodal Russian Bible of 1968 (no. 308) and 1976 (no. 318), with identical format and pagination.
Loc: BFBS

342. 1990. BIBLE

Библия. Книги Священного Писания Ветхого и Нового Завета. Канонические. С иллюстрациями Гюстава Доре. 2 vols.
Leningrad: Northwest Bible Commission, 1990.

Vol. I: Title, Northwest Bible Commission preface, internal title [4]; text, 5–565; illustrations, 566–7; tables [5].
24 × 17.
Vol. II: Title, preface, internal title [4]; text, 5–607; illustrations, 608–13; tables, 615–21.
24 × 17.

This two-volume edition includes the OT text of the canonical books only, as in the 1907 OT prepared by the Holy Synod for BFBS distribution. There are no marginal references, but there are chapter headings. The novelty of the edition is its inclusion of illustrations from the illustrated Bible of Gustave Doré (1833–83), whose biblical illustrations were popular additions to western biblical texts of the 1860s. The edition was prepared by Konstantin Logachev's Russian Northwest Bible Commission, as he notes in the brief preface on the title page verso.
Loc: BFBS

343. 1990–1. BIBLE

Библия. Том первый: Ветхий Завет от Бытия до Книги Премудрости Иисуса, сына Сирахова. Том второй: Ветхий Завет от Книги Пророка Исайи до Третьей Книги Эздры; Новый Завет. 2 vols.
Leningrad: Dukhovnoe prosveshchenie [for the Northwest Biblical Commission], 1990–1.
Vol. I: title, imprint verso, patriarchal greeting [iv]; Logachev note, v–viii; internal OT title and table of contents [1–2]; text, 3–468; explanatory matter, 469–72.
24 × 17.5.
Vol. II: title, imprint verso, table of contents, [1]–4; text, 5–483; explanations, 468–95.
24 × 17.5.

A two-volume edition of the synodal text of the Russian Bible bearing the blessing of the future Patriarch of Moscow Aleksii, who in 1990 was the Metropolitan of Leningrad and Novgorod. The text includes the deutero-canonical books of the OT. In addition, the Logachev commission moved the alternative Septuagint readings traditionally found in bracketed notes at the margins of the page in synodal editions directly into the text itself, making this a more hybrid translation combining Hebrew and Greek originals. Metropolitan Aleksii's preface cited the seventy-fifth anniversary of the work of the Russian Biblical Commission launched by I. E. Evseev in 1915 and noted the symbolic importance of the publication for biblical studies in the Leningrad Metropolia.
Loc: BFBS

344. 1990. BIBLE. BIBLICAL SELECTIONS AND PARAPHRASES FOR CHILDREN

Детская Библия.
Stockholm: Institute for Bible Translation, 1990.
19 × 12.5.

An expanded 519-page edition of the children's Bible issued initially in 1983 (no. 335). The format is identical, with similar binding and with illustrations and text on facing pages.
Loc: BFBS

345. 1990. OLD TESTAMENT

Библия. Книги Священного Писания. Канонические. В русском переводе с параллельными местами.
[Stuttgart]: UBS, 1990.
18.5 × 12.

Reprint of the standard UBS text of the OT, identical in format with earlier UBS biblical editions, such as no. 282 (1947), and nos. 309 and 310. This is a publication of the OT books only. The text has chapter headings and reference notes between two columns on each page. Only the canonical books of the OT are included. The 151st Psalm is excluded.
Loc: BFBS

346. 1990. BIBLE

Библия. Книги Священного Писания. Канонические. В русском переводе с параллельными местами.
[Stuttgart]: UBS, 1990.
15 × 9.5.

Reprint of the standard UBS edition of the synodal Russian Bible, uniform with no. 310 (1969) and other printings. Included are only the canonical books of the OT. NT pronominal references to the Virgin Mary are capitalized.
Loc: BFBS

347. 1991. NEW TESTAMENT

Новый Завет Господа Нашего Иисуса Христа.
Swindon: BFBS, 1991.
Title, imprint verso, table of contents [4]; text, 7–21.
14.5 × 8.5.

A reprinting in small font of the Cassian Bezobrazov NT translated from the Greek original and first published in 1970 (no. 300). The title page

identifies the publisher as the "Bible Societies," but the title page verso identifies the continuing BFBS copyright and publication in Britain.
Loc: BFBS

348. 1991. NEW TESTAMENT. GOSPELS

Евангелие. Перевод с древнегреческого священника Православной Церкви о. Леонида Лутковского.
Moscow: "Druzhba narodov," 1991.
Front matter, title page, imprint [6]; translator introduction, 7–9; icons, table of contents [10]–18; text, 19–282; notes, 283–6; Logachev essay, 287–95; Mumrikov essay, 296–301; table of contents, publication information [302–3].
22 × 14.5.

A new translation of the four Gospels by the Russian priest, Leonid Lutkovskii, first published in 1990 in the pages of the journal, *Literaturnaia ucheba*, which had a large circulation (900,000). This work was then issued separately in this 1991 edition in 300,000 copies. The text is presented in a single column on the page with indention of each new verse. Like the Cassian Bezobrazov work of the 1950s and 1960s, this translation sought a more literal rendering closer to the Greek original. The Lutkovskii text, however, lacked the accuracy and fidelity of the Cassian Bezobrazov NT.
Loc: BFBS

349. 1991. NEW TESTAMENT AND PSALTER

Новый Завет Господа Нашего Иисуса Христа и Псалтирь.
[Stuttgart: UBS, 1991]

A photographic reprint of the synodal Russian NT and Psalter (no. 321, 1977), reflecting the standardization of the NT and Psalter printings distributed by the United Bible Societies after World War II. The 151st Psalm is excluded, and pronominal references to the Virgin Mary are capitalized.
Loc: BFBS

350. 1991. NEW TESTAMENT. GOSPEL OF MATTHEW

Господа Нашего Иисуса Христа Святое Евангелие от Матфея.
[St. Michel's of Finland for the Northwest Bible Commission and UBS], 1991.
Title, imprint verso, patriarchal note, Logachev introduction [i]–xvii; text, 1–134; index of names [14].
17.5 × 12.

A modern Russifying of the nineteenth-century synodal translation of the Gospel of Matthew prepared by Konstantin Logachev and his Northwest Bible Commission with the blessing of Patriarch Aleksii. The main contribution of the text is its effort to remove archaisms in the synodal text. The text is one column on the page with indention of each verse.
Loc: BFBS

Select bibliography

The following Russian abbreviations are used here and in the notes:

kn. = book
otd. = section
vyp. = issue or no.
chast' = part
smes' = a mix or collection; this typically refers to a subsection of a journal with separate pagination.

UNPUBLISHED ARCHIVAL COLLECTIONS

1. RUSSIAN STATE HISTORICAL ARCHIVE (ROSSIISKII GOSUDARSTVENNYI ISTORICHESKII ARKHIV, RGIA), ST. PETERSBURG, RUSSIA

The RGIA contains state records of the Russian imperial government and church records for the period from Peter the Great to 1917. The archive also contains the papers of the Russian Bible Society and the Commission on Ecclesiastical Schools. Footnote citations to these collections include reference to the *fond* or collection, the *opis'* or descriptive index, the *delo* or file, and the *list* or leaf.

Fond 796, "The Chancellery of the Holy Synod" (Kantseliariia Sinoda)

This is the single largest set of files covering the actions of the Holy Synod during the imperial period. Its companion collection is that of the "Holy Synod Ober-prokuror," *fond* 797. Chapter 3 of this study draws heavily upon the secret files (*tainye dela*) relating to the Pavskii affair, found within *fond* 796, *opis'* 205. *Fond* 796, *opis'* 137 (1856) and *opis'* 143 (1863), contain files on the translation of the New and Old Testament into Russian.

Fond 800, "The Press of the Holy Synod" (Tipografiia Sinoda)

This collection documents the activities of the Holy Synod's press, particularly its operations in St. Petersburg. The annual reports (*godovye otchety*) of the Synodal

Press have been consulted as a basis for comparison with biblical circulation figures reported in the statistical supplements to the annually published *Report of the BFBS*.

Fond 802, "The Commission on Ecclesiastical Schools" (Komissiia dukhovnykh uchilishch, 1808–39)

Charged with overseeing modern Russian translation of the Bible during the Bible Society era, this commission has its own archive, including files on Gerasim Pavskii, Archimandrite Makarii, and Metropolitan Filaret (Drozdov). On this *fond*, see the published description, *Opis' dokumentov i del khraniashchikhsia v arkhive Sviateishago Pr. Sinoda, s ukazateliami k nei: Dela kommissii dukhovnykh uchilishch, 1808–1839* (St. Petersburg, 1910).

Fond 808, "The Russian Bible Society" (Rossiiskoe bibleiskoe obshchestvo)

This collection contains the records of the RBS from its founding in 1812 to the period immediately following its closure in 1826. Subcommittee reports are included along with the reports of John Paterson to the society's governing committee. The *fond* contains Paterson's original reports in English, along with the Russian copies read to the committee. Extensive files also document the activities of the Bible Society's press and its young apprentices. The materials within this *fond* complement the holdings of the BFBS Archive, particularly the BFBS "Deposited Papers of John Paterson."

Fond 832, the Papers of Metropolitan Filaret (Drozdov)

II. ROSSIISKAIA NATSIONAL'NAIA BIBLIOTEKA, RUKOPISNYI OTDEL. (MANUSCRIPTS DIVISION, STATE PUBLIC LIBRARY, RNB), ST. PETERSBURG, RUSSIA

Fond 194, Papers of N. N. Glubokovskii. Professor, St. Petersburg Theological Academy

Opis' 1, *dela* 53–9, contains Professor Glubokovskii's "Notes on the Four Gospels (1892–1897)."

Fond S. Peterburgskaia dukhovnaia akademiia

Delo A.1.80, "Sbornik statei o raznykh predmetakh." 381 leaves.

III. BRITISH AND FOREIGN BIBLE SOCIETY ARCHIVE (BSA), CAMBRIDGE UNIVERSITY LIBRARY, CAMBRIDGE, UK

The BFBS archive, along with its library of biblical imprints, was moved (1984–5) from the London BFBS offices to the Cambridge University Library, where it is housed on permanent loan. The organization of materials that follows is described more fully in Kathleen Cann, "A Summary Catalogue of the BFBS Archives (BSA)," in *Sowing the Word: The Cultural Impact of the British and Foreign Bible Society*, ed. Stephen Batalden, Kathleen Cann, and John Dean (Sheffield: Phoenix Press, 2004), 344–59; see also Stephen K. Batalden, "Revolution and Emigration: The Russian Files of the British and Foreign Bible Society, 1917–1970," in *The Use of British Archives for the Study of Russian History*, ed. Janet M. Hartley (London: Mansell Publishing, for the University of London School of Slavonic and East European Studies, 1986), 147–71. The principal series used for this study are as follows.

Minutes of the Committee (BSA/B1), 1807–1939 (vols. 3–129)

The BFBS committee, also known as the general committee, was the principal governing body of the society. The Minutes of the Committee are cited without abbreviation.

Minutes of the Printing and Depository Subcommittee (BSA/C10), 1817–1939 (21 vols.)

This subcommittee supervised the technical side of the society's Bible production, including statistical records of the size of print runs. The minutes of this subcommittee are abbreviated in the appendix as "DPSC Minutes." Print runs for Russian Bibles issued by the society after World War II can be verified in the BFBS Versions Books.

Minutes of the Editorial/Translations Subcommittee (BSA/C17), 1830–1939 (65 vols.)

Continued as the Society's Translations and Library Subcommittee, 1939–72 (10 vols.). The minutes are abbreviated in this study as "ESC Minutes."

Minutes of the Foreign Depots Subcommittee (BSA/C20), 1852–1939 (29 vols.)

This subcommittee monitored the stocks and the printings of Bibles overseas. The minutes are abbreviated in this study as "FDSC Minutes."

Agents Books (BSA/D1/7), 1867–77 (36 vols.)

Numbered 117–52, this is an incomplete series of copybooks or letterbooks reflecting reports and correspondence from BFBS agents in foreign countries. The original correspondence upon which these volumes are based is no longer extant. Presumably there were letterbooks predating these volumes, but only the thirty-six volumes remain in the BFBS archive. Four of the thirty-six volumes are letterbooks of the Russian BFBS agents in Petersburg and Odessa for the years 1869–74. These four books are cited as "Agents Books (Russia)" with the relevant volume number.

Deposited Personal Papers (BSA/F3)

The BFBS archive contains separate collections of the papers of some of the society's foreign agents. Among these "Deposited Papers" are the "Paterson Papers." Substantial portions of the personal memoirs and papers of BFBS agent John Paterson (1776–1855) were published posthumously as *The Book for Every Land* (London, 1857).

Editorial Correspondence, Incoming (BSA/E3/1/4), 1858–97 (35 vols.)

These thirty-five letterbooks contain copies of incoming letters on matters of translation. The original letters, with the exception of the "Miscellaneous Editorial Correspondence" cited below, are no longer extant. The BFBS archive also contains copies of the corresponding "Foreign and Editorial Correspondence Outwards."

Editorial Correspondence: Russian (BSA/E3/3), 1910–71

Twentieth-century Russian correspondence of BFBS editorial superintendents. Alongside the renaming of the editorial subcommittee noted above, the editorial superintendent assumed the title of "translations secretary" from 1939. The end of these files marks the effective date when Russian editorial correspondence is no longer conducted by the BFBS, but is rather subsumed within the Europe Regional Centre of the United Bible Societies (UBS).

Foreign Correspondence Inwards (BSA/D1/2), 1804–56
and 1901–5 (150 boxes)

Original incoming letters for which the BFBS archive includes an index of writers for the period 1804–56.

Miscellaneous Editorial Correspondence (BSA/E3/5), 1811–80 (5 files)

Original letters on translation not included in the main series of copybooks.

Secretaries' Correspondence: Russia (BSA/D8/8), 1919–1967 (3 files)

The correspondence both inward and outward of the general secretaries. These papers continue BFBS "Foreign Correspondence Inwards and Outwards."

Versions Books (BSA/E2/3/8), 1935–1969 (nos. 21–41)

Volumes of standardized forms giving circulation records on BFBS biblical imprints.

PUBLISHED PRIMARY SOURCES

Birrell, Charles M., ed. *The Life of the Rev. Richard Knill of St. Petersburgh; being selections from his reminiscences, journals, and correspondence, with a review of his character by the late Rev. John Angell James*, 2nd edn. London: James Nisbet & Co., 1859.

British and Foreign Bible Society (BFBS). *Report*, 1805–.
Monthly Extracts from the Correspondence of the BFBS, 1817–58.
Brown, Rev. J. C. "Historical Sketch of the Church of Christ at St. Petersburg." *Evangelical Magazine and Missionary Chronicle*, 17, n.s. (1839): 446–7.
Filaret (Drozdov), Metropolitan of Moscow. *Sobranie mnenii i otzyvov Filareta, mitropolita moskovskogo i kolomenskogo po uchebnym i tserkovno-gosudarstvennym voprosam*, 6 vols. Moscow, 1885–8.
Henderson, Ebenezer. *An Appeal to the Members of the British and Foreign Bible Society on the Subject of the Turkish New Testament printed at Paris in 1819.* London, 1824.
Biblical Researches and Travels in Russia. London: James Nisbet, 1826.
Henderson, Thulia S. *Memoir of the Rev. E. Henderson, including his labours in Denmark, Iceland, Russia, etc., etc.* London: Knight, 1859.
Memorials of John Venning, Esq. (formerly of St. Petersburgh, and late of Norwich), with numerous notices from his manuscripts relative to the Imperial family of Russia. London: Knight & Son, 1862.
Makarii (Glukharev), Archimandrite. *Pis'ma Arkhimandrita Makariia.* Kazan, 1905.
"Predstavlenie sv. sinodu o neobkhodimosti izdaniia Biblii na russkom iazyke." *Chteniia v imperatorskom obshchestve istorii i drevnostei rossiiskikh pri moskovskom universitete*, 1862, kn. 3: [167]–78.
Paterson, John. *The Book for Every Land: Reminiscences of Labour and Adventure in the Work of Bible Circulation in the North of Europe and in Russia.* London: John Snow, 1857.
A letter to the Rev. H. H. Norris, A.M., Perpetual Curator of St. John's Chapel, Hackney, etc. containing animadversions on his "Respectful letter to the Earl of Liverpool," on the subject of the Bible Society. London, 1823.
Paterson, John, and Ebenezer Henderson. *Extracts of Letters from the Rev. John Paterson and the Rev. Ebenezer Henderson during their respective tours through the East Sea Provinces of Russia, Sweden, Denmark, Jutland, Holstein, Swedish Pomerania, etc., to Promote the Object of the British and Foreign Bible Society.* London, 1817.
Pinkerton, Robert. *Russia: Or, Miscellaneous Observations on the Past and Present State of that Country and its Inhabitants.* London, 1833.

PUBLISHED SECONDARY WORKS

Ackroyd, P. R., and C. F. Evans, eds. *The Cambridge History of the Bible*, 3 vols. Cambridge University Press, 1970.
"Agafangel" [Aleksei Fedorovich Solov'ev]. In *Russkii biograficheskii slovar'.* St. Petersburg, 1896, 1: 52–4.
Aleksandrovich, N. "Girs, Aleksandr Karlovich." In *Russkii biograficheskii slovar'.* Moscow, 1916, [v]: 230–3.
Alekseev, Aleksandr. *Upotrebliaiut-li evrei khristianskuiu krov's religioznoiu tsel'iu?* Novgorod, 1886.
Alekseev, Anatolii A. "O grecheskoi osnove slavianskikh bibleiskikh perevodov." *Paleobulgarica*, 8, no. 1 (1984): 3–22.

"Printsipy istoriko-filologicheskogo izucheniia literaturnogo naslediia Kirilla i Mefodiia." *Sovetkoe slavianovedenie*, 2 (1984): 94–106.

"The Slavonic Bible and Modern Scholarship." *Jews and Slavs*, 1 (1993): 44–75.

Alekseev, I. "K voprosu o novom perevode na russkii iazyk Evangeliia ot Matfeia." *Zhurnal moskovskoi patriarkhii*, 1954, no. 2: 76–7.

Altbauer, Moshé. "Contacts between Christians and Jews in the Field of Bible Translations." *Harvard Ukrainian Studies*, 12–13 (1988–9): 194–9.

Some Methodological Problems in Research of the East-Slavic Bible Translations: Vilnius codex 262. Jerusalem: Israeli Slavists' Committee, 1968.

Amburger, Erik. *Geschichte des Protestantismus in Russland.* Stuttgart: Evangelisches Verlagswerk, 1961.

Anderson, Paul B. *People, Church, and State in Modern Russia.* New York: Hyperion Press, 1980.

Arkhangel'skii, A. N. *Aleksandr I.* Moscow: Vagrius, 2000.

Astaf'ev, Nikolai A. *Obshchestvo dlia rasprostraneniia sv. Pisaniia v Rossii (1863–1893): Ocherk ego proiskhozhdeniia i deiatel'nosti.* St. Petersburg, 1895.

Opyt istorii Biblii v Rossii v sviazi s prosveshcheniem i nravami. St. Petersburg: V. V. Komarov, 1892.

Zhizn' i trudy pervago knigonoshi Obshchestva dlia rasprostraneniia Sv. Pisaniia v Rossii: O. B. Forkhgamera po ego avtobiografii i pis'mam. Moscow: M. Borisenko Press, 1902.

"Astaf'ev, Nikolai Aleksandrovich." In *Entsiklopedicheskii slovar'.* St. Petersburg: Brokgauz-Efron, 1890, III: 333–4.

B–v, A. "Iz otzyvov i vospominanii P. S. Kazanskago o mitropolite Filarete." *Pravoslavnoe obozrenie*, 1882 (August): 723–33.

Bakounine, Tatiana. *Répertoire biographique des francs-maçons russes (XVIIIe et XIXe siècles).* Collection historique de l'Institut d'Études slaves, XIX. Paris: Institut d'Études Slaves, 1967.

Baron, Sabrina Alcorn, Eric N. Lindquist, and Eleanor F. Shevlin, eds. *Agent of Change: Print Culture Studies after Elizabeth L. Eisenstein.* Amherst: University of Massachusetts Press, and Washington, DC: Center for the Book, 2007.

Barskov, Ia. "Lopukhin, Ivan Vladimirovich." In *Russkii biograficheskii slovar'.* St. Petersburg, 1914, [X]: 650–82.

Barsov, N. I. *Istoricheskie, kriticheskie i polemicheskie opyty.* St. Petersburg, 1879.

"Mnenie prot. G. P. Pavskago po voprosu ob upotreblenii evreiami khristianskoi krovi dlia religioznykh tselei." *Tserkovnyi vestnik*, 1879, no. 20.

"Protoierei Gerasim Petrovich Pavskii: Ocherk ego zhizni po novym materialam." *Russkaia starina*, 27 (1880), kn. 1–4 and 28 (1880), kn. 1–2 [discontinuous pages].

"Vzgliad na zhizn' i deiatel'nost' mitr. Filareta Moskovskago." In *Neskol'ko izsledovanii istoricheskikh i razsuzhdenii o voprosakh sovremennykh*, 42–9. St. Petersburg: Tip M. M. Stasiulevicha, 1899.

Barsov, T. V. "Sviateishii sinod vo vremia ministerstva dukhovnykh del i narodnago prosveshcheniia." *Khristianskoe chtenie*, 1895 (May–June): 505–26.

Barton, Peter F. *Ignatius Aurelius Fessler: Vom Barockkatholizismus zur Erweckungsbewegung*. Vienna/Cologne: Hermann Böhlaus, 1969.

Batalden, Stephen K. "The Contemporary Politics of the Russian Bible: Religious Publication in a Period of Glasnost." In *Seeking God: The Recovery of Religious Identity in Orthodox Russia, Ukraine, and Georgia*, ed. Stephen K. Batalden. DeKalb: Northern Illinois University Press, 1993, 232–43.

"Gerasim Pavskii's Clandestine Old Testament: The Politics of Nineteenth-Century Russian Biblical Translation." *Church History*, 57, no. 4 (1988): 486–99.

"Musul'manskii i evreiskii voprosy v Rossii epokhi Aleksandra I glazami shotlandskogo bibleista i puteshestvennika." *Voprosy istorii*, 2004, no. 5: 46–63.

"Nineteenth-Century Russian Biblical Translation and the Jewish Question." In *Kirchen im Kontext unterschiedlicher Kulturen: Auf dem Weg ins dritte Jahrtausend*, ed. K. C. Felmy *et al.* Göttingen: Vandenhoeck & Ruprecht, 1991, 577–87.

"Revolutionaries and Evangelicals in Concert: Alexander Herzen, Vasilii Kel'siev, and the British and Foreign Bible Society." Unpublished paper delivered to the Russian-Speaking Society, Cambridge, UK, February 10, 2004.

Bawden, Charles. *Shamans, Lamas, and Evangelicals: The English Missionaries in Siberia*. London: Routledge & Kegan Paul, 1985.

"Bazhanov, Vasilii Borisovich, 1800–1883." In *Russkii biograficheskii slovar'*. St. Petersburg, 1900, II: 402–3.

[Bebb, L.] "The Russian Bible." *Church Quarterly Review*, 41 (1895–6): 203–25.

Belliustin, I. S. *Description of the Clergy in Rural Russia*, trans. and intro. Gregory L. Freeze. Ithaca, NY: Cornell University Press, 1985.

Berger, Peter. *Modernisation and Religion: The Fourteenth Geary Lecture*. Dublin: Economic and Social Research Council, 1981.

The Sacred Canopy. Garden City, NJ: Doubleday, 1967.

Bezhanidze, G. V. "Ober-prokuror Sviateishago Sinoda A. P. Akhmatov i sviatitel' Filaret (Drozdov)." In *Tserkov' v istorii Rossii*, Sbornik 8. Moscow, 2009, 85–100.

Bezhanidze, G. V. and P. Khondzinskii, eds. *Bibliograficheskii ukazatel' opublikovannykh trudov sviatitelia Filareta, mitropolita Moskovskogo i Kolomenskogo, i literatury o nem*. Moscow, 2003.

Bezsonov, P. "Vospominaniia o Labzine (iz zapisok M. A. Dmitrieva)." *Russkii arkhiv*, 4 (1866), no. 1: 817–36; no. 2: 837–55; no. 3: 855–60.

Bezsonov, Vassili. "A. F. Labzin." *Russkii arkhiv*, 6 (1868): 833.

Bezsonov, Yurii. *Dvadtsat' shest' tiurem i pobeg s Solovkov*. Paris, 1928; London, 1929.

Partiia sil'nykh. Paris, 1942.

"Bibleiskie obshchestva." In *Khristianstvo: Entsiklopedicheskii slovar'*. Moscow: "Bol'shaia Rossiiskaia entsiklopediia," 1993, I: 229–30.

Birdsall, J. Neville. "Georgian Translations of the Bible." In *Interpretation of the Bible: On the Occasion of the Publication of the New Slovenian Translation of the Bible*, ed. Jože Krašovec. Ljubljana/Sheffield: Slovenian Academy of Sciences and Arts/Sheffield Academic Press, 1998, 387–91.

Blagovidov, F. V. *Ober-prokurory sv. sinoda v XVIII i v pervoi polovine XIX stoletiia*. Kazan, 1899.

Blane, Andrew. "The Relations between the Russian Protestant Sects and the State, 1900–1921." Ph.D. dissertation, Duke University, 1964.

Bobrovnikov, A. A. "Ocherk religioznago sostoianiia kalmykov." *Pravoslavnoe obozrenie*, 1865 (July): 335–52 and (August): 495–510.

Bodianskii, O., ed. *Pis'ma moskovskago i kolomenskago mitropolita Filareta k Gavriilu, arkhiepiskopu riazanskomu i zaraiskomu*. Moscow University Press, 1868.

Bogdanova, T. A. *N. N. Glubokovskii: Sud'ba khristianskogo uchenogo*. St. Petersburg, 2010.

Brandenburg, Hans. *The Meek and the Mighty: The Emergence of the Evangelical Movement in Russia*. New York: Oxford University Press, 1977.

Brilliantov, A. I. "Preosviashchennyi Innokentii (Smirnov), episkop penzenskii i saratovskii." *Khristianskoe chtenie*, 1912 (December): 1375–1410.

Brodskii, L., ed. *Mneniia, otzyvy, i pis'ma Filareta, mitropolita moskovskogo i kolomenskogo, po raznym voprosam za 1821–1867 gg*. Moscow, 1905.

Brooks, Jeffrey. *When Russia Learned to Read: Literacy and Popular Literature, 1861–1917*. Princeton University Press, 1985.

Browne, George. *A History of the British and Foreign Bible Society, from its Institution in 1804, to the Close of its Jubilee in 1854*, 2 vols. London: BFBS, 1859.

Bukharev, A. M. "O Filarete. . . ." *Pravoslavnoe obozrenie*, 1884 (April): 717–49.

Bukharev, Fedor. *O novom zavete Gospoda nashego Iisusa Khrista*. St. Petersburg.: Tip. I. Orisko, 1861.

Butkevich, T. I. *Obzor russkikh sekt i ikh tolkov*, 2nd edn. Petrograd, 1915.

Protestantstvo v Rossii. Khar'kov, 1913.

Calder, R. F. "Robert Haldane's Theological Seminary." *Congregational Historical Society Transactions*, 13, no. 1 (September 1937): 53–63.

Cann, Kathleen. "The Archives of the British and Foreign Bible Society." In *Sowing the Word: The Cultural Impact of the British and Foreign Bible Society*, ed. Stephen Batalden, Kathleen Cann, and John Dean. Sheffield: Phoenix Press, 2004, 14–21.

Canton, William. *A History of the British and Foreign Bible Society*, 5 vols. London: J. Murray, 1904–10.

Casanova, José. *Public Religions in the Modern World*. University of Chicago Press, 1994.

Cassian (Bezobrazov), Bishop. "The Revision of the Russian Translation of the New Testament." *The Bible Translator*, 5, no. 1 (January 1954): 27–35.

Cherkas, A. "Dal', Vladimir Ivanovich." In *Russkii biograficheskii slovar'*. St. Petersburg, 1905, [VI]: 42–8.

Chistiakov, G. "Slavianskaia Bibliia kak istochnik dlia budushchego russkogo perevoda." *Mir Biblii*, 1, no. 3 (1995): 104–9.

Chistovich, Ilarion A. "Ispravlenie teksta slavianskogo perevoda Biblii pered izdaniem 1751 g." *Pravoslavnoe obozrenie*, 1860 (April–May): 495–507.

Istoriia perevoda Biblii na russkii iazyk. St. Petersburg, 1873; 2nd edn, 1899.

"Istoriia perevoda Biblii na russkii iazyk: Perevod vetkhozavetnykh knig s evreiskago iazyka na russkii Arkhimandrita Makariia." *Khristianskoe chtenie*, 1872 (March): 1–49.

Istoriia sanktpeterburgskoi dukhovnoi akademii. St. Petersburg, 1857.

Rukovodiashchie deiateli dukhovnago prosveshcheniia v Rossii v pervoi polovine tekushchago stoletiia. St. Petersburg, 1894.

Cimosa, Mario. "Translating the Old Testament." In *Interpretation of the Bible: On the Occasion of the Publication of the New Slovenian Translation of the Bible*, ed. Jože Krašovec. Ljubljana/Sheffield: Slovenian Academy of Sciences and Arts/ Sheffield Academic Press, 1998, 1341–57.

Clark, Christopher M. *The Politics of Conversion: Missionary Protestantism and the Jews in Prussia, 1728–1741.* Oxford: Clarendon Press, 1995.

Clogg, Richard. "Enlightening 'A Poor, Oppressed, and Darkened Nation': Some Early Activities of the BFBS in the Levant." In *Sowing the Word: The Cultural Impact of the British and Foreign Bible Society, 1804–2004*, ed. Stephen K. Batalden, Kathleen Cann, and John Dean. Sheffield: Phoenix Press, 2004, 234–50.

Collins, David N. "Colonialism and Siberian Development: A Case-Study of the Orthodox Mission to the Altai, 1830–1913." In *The Development of Siberia: People and Resources*, ed. Alan Wood and R. A. French. New York: St. Martin's Press, 1989, 50–71.

"The Role of the Orthodox Mission in the Altai: Archimandrite Makarii and V. I. Verbitskii." In *Church, Nation, and State in Russia and Ukraine*, ed. Geoffrey A. Hosking. New York: St. Martin's Press, 1989, 76–107.

Cooper, Henry R., Jr. "The Origins of the Church Slavonic Version of the Bible: An Alternative Hypothesis." In *Interpretation of the Bible: On the Occasion of the Publication of the New Slovenian Translation of the Bible*, ed. Jože Krašovec. Ljubljana/Sheffield: Slovenian Academy of Sciences and Arts/Sheffield Academic Press, 1998, 959–74.

Slavic Scriptures: The Formation of the Church Slavonic Version of the Holy Bible. Madison, NC: Fairleigh Dickinson University Press, 2003.

Crews, Robert. "Empire and the Confessional State: Islam and Religious Politics in Nineteenth-Century Russia." *American Historical Review*, 108, no. 1 (2003): 50–83.

Dal', Vladimir Ivanovich. *Rozyskanie ob ubienii evreiami khristianskikh mladentsev i upotreblenii krovi ikh.* St. Petersburg: Suvorin Press "Novoe Vremia," 1913.

Darlow, T. H., and Horace Frederick Moule. *Historical Catalogue of the Printed Editions of Holy Scripture in the Library of the British and Foreign Bible Society*, 2 vols. in 4. London: BFBS, 1903–11.

"Deiatel'nost' obshchestva rasprostraneniia knig sv. pisaniia v Rossii v 1883 godu." *Pravoslavnoe obozrenie*, 1884, 3 (October): 425–6.

Delicostopoulos, Athan. "Major Greek Translations of the Bible." In *Interpretation of the Bible: On the Occasion of the Publication of the New Slovenian Translation of the Bible*, ed. Jože Krašovec. Ljubljana/Sheffield: Slovenian Academy of Sciences and Arts/Sheffield Academic Press, 1998, 297–316.

Delitsyn, P. S. "Protoierei Petr Spiridonovich Delitsyn (Nekrolog)." *Pravoslavnoe obozrenie*, 1863 (December): 219–25.

"Derzhavin, Ioann Semenovich." In *Russkii biograficheskii slovar'.* St. Petersburg, 1905, [v]: 323.

deWaard, Jan. "Old Greek Translation Techniques and the Modern Translator." *The Bible Translator*, 41 (1990): 311–12.

deWaard, Jan, and Eugene A. Nida. *From One Language to Another: Functional Equivalence in Bible Translation.* Walton-on-Thames: T. Nelson & Sons, 1986.

Dmitriev, P., *et al.*, eds. *Bibliia i vozrozhdenie dukhovnoi kul'tury russkogo i drugikh slavianskikh narodov: K 80-letiiu Russkoi/Severo-Zapadnoi Bibleiskoi Komissii (1915–1995).* St. Petersburg: Petropolis, 1995.

Dmitriev, P., Konstantin Logachev, and G. Safronov, eds. *Perevody Biblii i ikh znachenie v razvitii dukhovnoi kul'tury slavian: Materialy mezhdunarodnoi bibleiskoi konferentsii 1990 g., posviashchennoi semidesiatipiatiletiiu Russkoi Bibleiskoi Komissii.* St. Petersburg: Sankt-Peterburgskii Universitet, 1994.

Dobonravin, Konstantin (Protoierei). "Rossiiskoe bibleiskoe obshchestvo." *Strannik*, 1869 no. 8 (August): 49–67.

"Dokhody (gosurdarstvennye)." In *Entsiklopedicheskii slovar'.* St. Petersburg, 1893, XXI: 85.

"Donesenie po povodu perevoda na russkii iazyk sv. Marka v mosk. dukh. Akademii." *Dushepoleznoe chtenie*, 1880, pt. 3, no. 1: 128.

Donnachie, Ian, and George Hewitt. *Historic New Lanark: The Dale and Owen Industrial Community since 1785.* Edinburgh University Press, 1993.

Dooley, Allan C. *Author and Printer in Victorian England.* Charlottesville: University Press of Virginia, 1992.

Drozdov, N. M. "V zashchitu svobodnago nauchnago izsledovaniia v oblasti bibliologii." *Trudy kievskoi dukhovnoi akademii*, 1902 (October): 300–31 and (November): 461–90.

Dubrovin, N. F. "Nashi mistiki-sektanty: Aleksandr Fedorovich Labzin i ego zhurnal *Sionskii vestnik.*" *Russkaia starina*, 82 (1894), no. 9: [145]–203, no. 10: [101]–26, no. 11: [58]–91 and no. 12: [98]–132; and 83 (1895), no. 1: [56]–91 and no. 2: [35]–52.

ed. *Sbornik istoricheskikh materialov, izvlechennykh iz arkhiva sobstvennoi ego Imperatorskago Velichestva Kantseliarii*, vol. XII. St. Petersburg, 1903.

E. "Predpolagaemoe izdanie vetkhozavetnoi Biblii v russkom perevode s primechaniami." *Chteniia v obshchestve liubitelei dukhovnogo prosveshcheniia*, 1877 (March), otd. 1.

Edgerton, William B. "Leskov, Pashkov, the Shtundists, and a Newly Discovered Letter." In *Orbis Scriptus: Dmitrij Tschizhewskij, zum 70. Geburtstag*, ed. Dietrich Gerhardt, Wiktor Weintraub, and Hans-Jürgen zum Winkel. Munich: Wilhelm Fink Verlag, 1966, 187–99.

Edling, Roksandra. *Mémoires de la Comtesse Edling (née Stourdza), Demoiselle d'Honneur de Sa Majesté L'Impératrice Élisabeth Alexéevna.* Moscow: Archives Russes, 1888.

Eisenstein, Elizabeth L. *The Printing Press as an Agent of Change: Communications and Cultural Transformation in Early Modern Europe.* Cambridge University Press, 1979.

Ekshtut, S. A. *Aleksandr I: Ego spodvizhniki, dekabristy – V poiske istoricheskoi al'ternativy.* St. Petersburg: "Logos," 2004.

Eleonskii, Fedor G. "Bibleiskie obshchestva v Rossii" and "Bibliia v Rossii." In *Pravoslavnaia bogoslovskaia entsiklopediia*, ed. A. P. Lopukhin. St. Petersburg: A. P. Lopukhin, 1901, II: 575–97 and 490–544.

"Otechestvennye trudy po izucheniiu Biblii v XIX veke." *Khristianskoe chtenie*, 81 (January 1901): 5–28, and (May 1901): 633–60.

Po povodu 150-letiiu Elizavetinskoi Biblii: O novom peresmotre slavianskogo perevoda Biblii. St. Petersburg: A. P. Lopukhin, 1902.

"Sledy vliianiia evreiskogo teksta i drevnikh, krome grecheskogo LXX, perevodov na drevnii slavianskii perevod knig Bytiia i Iskhoda." *Khristianskoe chtenie*, 85 (1905): 26–38.

"Sravnitel'noe dostoinstvo grekoslavianskogo i evreiskoslavianskogo perevodov Byt. 2:5." *Khristianskoe chtenie*, 85 (1905): 173–93.

Eleonskii, N. A. "Svidetel'stva o proiskhozhdenii perevoda LXX i stepen' ikh dostovernosti." *Chteniia v obshchestve liubitelei dukhovnago prosveshcheniia*, 1875 (January): 3–47.

Erikhsen, O. "Sidonskii, Fedor Fedorovich (protoierei)." *Russkii biograficheskii slovar'*. St. Petersburg, 1904, [XVIII]: 418–21.

Escott, Harry. *A History of Scottish Congregationalism*. Glasgow: Congregational Union of Scotland, 1960.

Evseev, Ivan E. "Bibliograficheskaia zametka: Moskovskoe izdanie grecheskoi biblii 1821 g." *Bogoslovskii vestnik*, 11, no. 1 (January 1902): 207–11.

Ocherki po istorii slavianskogo perevoda Biblii: Cherty bytovoi istorii slavianskoi Biblii s kontsa XV do XVIII veka, vol. II, pt. 1. Petrograd: M. Merkushev, 1916; vol. II, pt. 2. In *Komissiia po nauchnomu izdaniiu Slavianskoi Biblii (Russkaia Bibleiskaia Komissiia), 1915–1929: Sbornik arkhivnykh materialov*, ed. K. L. Logachev. Leningrad State University Press, 1990, 20–78.

Sobor i Bibliia. Petrograd, 1917.

Stoletniaia godovshchina russkogo perevoda Biblii. Petrograd, 1916.

ed. *Otchet o deiatel'nosti komissii po nauchnomu izdaniiu slavianskoi Biblii za 1915-i god*. Petrograd, 1916.

Faggionato, Raffaella. "From a Society of the Enlightenment to the Enlightenment of Society: The Russian Bible Society and Rosicrucianism in the Age of Alexander I." *Slavonic and East European Review*, 79, no. 3 (July 2001): 459–87.

A Rosicrucian Utopia in Eighteenth-Century Russia: The Masonic Circle of N. I. Novikov. Dordrecht: Springer, 2005.

Fedotov, G. P. *Litso Rossii: Sbornik statei, 1918–1931*. Paris: YMCA Press, 1967.

"Slavianskii ili russkii iazyk v bogosluzhenii?" *Put'*, no. 57 (August–October 1938): 3–28.

Feofan (Georgii Vasil'evich Govorov, 1815–94), Bishop of Vladimir and Suzdal. "Bibliia po perevodu semidesiati tolkovnikov est' zakonnaia nasha Bibliia." *Domashniaia beseda*, 1876, vyp. 20–4.

"O nashem dolge derzhat'sia perevoda 70 tolkovnikov." *Dushepoleznoe chtenie*, 1876, chast' 2, no. 5 (May): 3–21.

"Ob upotreblenii novago perevoda vetkhozavetnykh pisanii." *Dushepoleznoe chtenie*, 1876, chast' 3, no. 9 (September): 100–6.

"Po povodu izdaniia sviashchennykh knig Vetkhago Zaveta v russkom perevode." *Dushepoleznoe chtenie*, 1875, chast' 3, no. 11 (November): 342–52.
"Pravo-slovo ob izdanii sviashchennykh knig Vetkhago Zaveta v russkom perevode." *Domashniaia beseda*, 1875, vyp. 47 (November 22).
"Reshenie voprosa o mere pravoslavnago upotrebleniia evreiskago nyneshniago teksta, po ukazaniiu tserkovnoi praktiki." *Domashniaia beseda*, 1876, vyp. 2.
Filaret (Drozdov), Metropolitan of Moscow. "O dogmaticheskom dostoinstve i okhranitel'nom upotreblenii grecheskogo sedmidesiati tolkovnikov i slavenskogo perevodov Sviashchennogo Pisaniia." *Pribavleniia k tvoreniiam Sviatykh Ottsev v russkom perevode*, 32 (1858): 452–84.
Pis'ma k vysochaishim osobam i raznym drugim litsam, 2 vols. Tver, 1888.
Pis'ma mitr. Filareta k ober-prokuroru Sv. sinoda Nechaevu. St. Petersburg: Tip. Akademii nauk, 1895.
Pis'ma mitr. moskovskago Filareta k A. N. M., 1832–1867. Kiev, 1869.
"Pis'ma mitropolita moskovskago Filareta k Evseviiu arkhiepiskopu Mogilevskomu s 1841–1867: Materialy dlia istorii russkoi tserkvi." *Chteniia v obshchestve liubitelei dukhovnago prosveshcheniia*, 1882, chast' 2, nos. 11–12.
Sobranie mnenii i otzyvov Filareta mitropolita moskovskago, 6 vols. Moscow, 1885–8.
Izbrannye trudy, pis'ma, vospominaniia. Moscow, 2003.
Trudy mitropolita Moskovskago i Kolomenskago Filareta po perelozheniiu Novago Zaveta na russkii iazyk. St. Petersburg: Sinodal'naia Tip., 1893.
Zapiski na knigu Bytiia, rukovodstvuiushchiia k razumeniiu pismeni eia, i k ispytaniiu dukha eia, pri posredstve slicheniia perevodov s podlinnikom, mnenii svotets i tolkovatelei, 2nd edn. Moscow, 1835.
Filimonov, D. D. *Materialy dlia biografii osnovatelia altaiskoi missii Arkhimandrita Makariia*, 2nd edn. Moscow: V. F. Rikhter, 1892.
Finke, Roger. "The Consequences of Religious Competition: Supply-side Explanations for Religious Change." In *Rational Choice Theory and Religion: Summary and Assessment*, ed. Lawrence A. Young. New York: Routledge, 1997, 45–64.
Florovsky, Georges. *Puti russkogo bogosloviia, 2nd edn.* Paris: YMCA Press, 1981.
Ways of Russian Theology, trans. Robert L. Nichols. In *Collected Works of Georges Florovsky*. Belmont, MA: Nordland Press, 1979, vol. v, pt. 1.
Flynn, James T. *The University Reform of Tsar Alexander I, 1802–1835.* Washington, DC: Catholic University Press of America, 1988.
Freeze, Gregory L. "Die Lutherisch-Evangelische Kirche in Russland, 1800–1914." In *Handbuch der baltischen Geschichte*, vol. 11 of 3 vols., ed. Konrad Maier, Karsten Brueggerman, and Ralph Tuchtenhagen (Stuttgart: A. Hiersemann, forthcoming).
The Parish Clergy in Nineteenth-Century Russia: Crisis, Reform, Counter-Reform. Princeton University Press, 1983.
The Russian Levites. Cambridge, MA: Harvard University Press, 1977.
Galakhov, I. A. "Obzor misticheskoi literatury v tsarstvovanie Imperatora Aleksandra I." *Zhurnal ministerstva narodnago prosveshcheniia*, 182 (November 1875): [87]–175.

Gavriil, Archbishop. "Pis'mo Preosviashchennago Gavriila Arkhiepiskopa Tverskago (v posledstvii mitropolita Novgorodskago) k Filaretu, mitropolitu moskovskomu, o chtenii sviashchennago pisaniia (pisano 12 dekabria 1844 goda)." *Pravoslavnoe obozrenie*, 1861 (June): 3–18.

Gavrilov, A. V. *Ocherk istorii S.-Peterburgskoi sinodal'noi tipografii v 1711–1839 gg.* St. Petersburg, 1911.

Gennadi, Grigorii Nikolaevich, ed. *Spravochnyi slovar' o russkikh pisateliakh i uchenykh umershikh v XVIII i XIX stoletiiakh i spisok russkikh knig s 1725 po 1825*, vols. I–II: Berlin, 1876–80; vol. III: Moscow, 1908; reprint, The Hague: Mouton, 1969.

Gessen, Iulii. *Istoriia evreev v Rossii.* St. Petersburg, 1914.

"Saratovskoe delo." In *Evreiskaia entsiklopediia.* Reprint, Moscow: Terra, 1991, XIV: 2–8.

Ginsburg, Saul M. *Meshumodim in Tsarishn Rusland: Forshungen un zikhroynes vegn Yidishn lebn in amolikn Rusland* [Apostates in Tsarist Russia]. New York: Tsiko bikher farlag, 1946.

Girdlestone, R. B. *Suggestions for Translators, Editors, and Revisors of the Bible.* London: Hatchards, 1877.

Glinskii, B. "Zhukovskii, Vasilii Andreevich." In *Russkii biograficheskii slovar'.* Petrograd, 1916, [VII]: 60–117.

Glubokovskii, N. N. "Bibleiskii grecheskii iazyk v pisaniiakh Vetkhago i Novago Zaveta." *Trudy kievskoi dukhovnoi akademii*, 1913 (February): 213–26.

Lektsii po Sv. Pisaniiu Novago Zaveta. St. Petersburg, 1906.

"Novosti bogoslovskoi literatury." *Khristianskoe chtenie*, 1901 (December): 988–1002.

O vtorom poslanii sv. Ap. Pavla k Fessalonikiitsam. Petrograd, 1915.

Russkaia bogoslovskaia nauka v ee istoricheskom razvitii i noveishem sostoianii. Warsaw, 1928.

Vysokopreosviashchennyi Smaragd (Kryzhanovskii), Arkhiepiskop Riazanskii: Ego zhizn' i deiatel'nost'. St. Petersburg, 1914.

Golitsyn, Aleksandr. "Most Submissive Memorial to His Imperial Majesty from the Director-General of the Clerical Concerns of Members of Foreign Faiths." In *Religious Intelligence.* London: BFBS, 1813, 193–8.

Golitsyn, N. N. *Upotrebliaiut-li evrei khristianskuiu krov'?* Warsaw, 1879.

Golitsyn, N. S. "Evgenii Bolkhovitinov, Mitropolit kievskii: Zametka k stat'e prof. N. I. Barsova, 'Protoierei G. P. Pavskii.'" *Russkaia starina*, 29 (1880): 197.

Golubinskii, Evgenii Evsigneevich. *Vospominaniia.* Kostroma, 1923.

Gorfunkel', A. Kh., and L. E. Strel'tsova. *Gosudarstvennyi istoricheskii arkhiv Leningradskoi oblasti: Kratkii putevoditel'.* Leningrad, 1960.

Gorskii, Aleksandr Vasilievich. "Iz vospominanii pokoinago Filareta, mitropolita moskovskago." *Pravoslavnoe obozrenie*, 26 (August 1868): 507–42.

Gorskii-Platonov, P. I. "Neskol'ko slov o stat'e episkopa Feofana: 'Po povodu izdaniia sviashchennykh knig Vetkhago Zaveta v russkom perevode' (*Dushepoleznoe chtenie*, 1875, no. 11)." *Pravoslavnoe obozrenie*, series 2, 1875 (November): chast' 3: 505–40.

"O nedoumeniiakh, vyzyvaemykh russkim perevodom sv. knig Vetkhago Zaveta." *Pravoslavnoe obozrenie*, 1877 (January): 69–104, (February): 260–84, and (April): 681–702.

"Gossner, Ioann, 1773–1858." In *Entsiklopedicheskii slovar'*. St. Petersburg, 1893, XVII: 388.

Grech, Nikolai. *Zapiski o moei zhizni*. Moscow: I. Zakharov, 2002.

Gregory, Caspar René. *Textkritik des Neuen Testaments*. Leipzig, 1900.

Hansard, Thomas Curson. *Typographia*. London, 1825.

Harris, Horton. *The Tübingen School: A Historical and Theological Investigation of the School of F. C. Baur*. Oxford University Press, 1975.

Harrison, J. F. C. *Robert Owen and the Owenites in Britain and America: The Quest for the New Moral World*. London: Routledge and Kegan Paul, 1969.

Hechter, Michael. "Religion and Rational Choice Theory." In *Rational Choice Theory and Religion*, ed. Lawrence A. Young. New York: Routledge, 1997, 147–60.

Herrlinger, Page. *Working Souls: Russian Orthodoxy and Factory Labor in St. Petersburg, 1881–1917*. Columbus, OH: Slavica, 2008.

Herzen, Alexander. *My Past and Thoughts, 4 vols*. London: Chatto & Windus, 1968.

Hollingsworth, B. "John Venning and Prison Reform in Russia, 1819–1830." *Slavonic and East European Review*, 48 (1970): 537–56.

Horn, Johan von [Jean de Horn]. *Konspekt filosoficheskago ekzamena, proizvedennago v dukh. akad. Ivanom fon Gornom, professorom filos. nauk i vostoch. iazykov*. St. Petersburg, 1812.

Mémoire sur ma carrière civile et militaire en Russie. London: Mitchell & Sons, 1843.

Howsam, Leslie. *Cheap Bibles: Nineteenth-Century Publishing and the British and Foreign Bible Society*. Cambridge University Press, 1991.

Hrovat, Jasna, Marijan Smolik, and Anica Zadnikar. "Bibliography of Slovenian Translations of Biblical Texts." In *Interpretation of the Bible: On the Occasion of the Publication of the New Slovenian Translation of the Bible*, ed. Jože Krašovec. Ljubljana/Sheffield: Slovenian Academy of Sciences and Arts/Sheffield Academic Press, 1998, 1075–1107.

Iakimov, I. S. *Otnoshenie grecheskago perevoda LXX tolkovnikov k evreiskomu mazoretskomu tekstu v knige proroka Ieremii*. St. Petersburg, 1874.

Ieronim (Arkhimandrit). *Istoriia permskoi dukhovnoi seminarii posle preobrazovaniia 1840 g. do pozdneishago vremeni*. Perm, 1876.

Ignat'ev, A. "Pamiati Prof. Nikolaia Nikanorovicha Glubokovskogo." *Zhurnal moskovskoi patriarkhii*, 1966, no. 8: 57–77.

Il'minskii, N. "Iz Kazani: Ob obrazovanii inorodtsev posredstvom knig, perevedennykh na rodnoi iazyk." *Pravoslavnoe obozrenie*, 10 (March 1863): "Zametki," 136–41.

"Religioznoe sostoianie kreshchenykh tatar: predislovie k Dnevniku starokreshchenago tatarina." *Pravoslavnoe obozrenie*, 18 (October 1865): 13–147.

"Shkola dlia pervonachal'nago obucheniia detei kreshchenykh tatar v Kazani." *Pravoslavnoe obozrenie*, 15 (December 1864): "Zametki," 155–62; 16 (February 1865): "Zametki," 77–82; 17 (May 1865): "Zametki," 26–40; and 18 (November 1865): "Zametki," 88–93.

"The Immanent Frame: Secularism, Religion, and the Public Sphere." See http://blogs.ssrc.org/tif/ (accessed October 9, 2010).

Innokentii (Pavlov), Igumen. "Bibleiskoe obshchestvo v Russii v proshlom i teper'." *Slavianovedenie*, 4 (1995): 84–8.

"Patriarshaia i sinodal'naia bibleiskaia komissiia." *Mir biblii*, 1 (1993): 105–6.

Ismailov, F. F. "Zapiski." *Pravoslavnoe obozrenie*, 1870 (February): 114.

Istoricheskiia chteniia iz knig vetkhago zaveta: Dlia upotrebleniia v uchilishchakh. St. Petersburg: Imperial Academy of Sciences for the Department of Public Instruction, 1845.

Iungerov, P. A. *Obshchee istoriko-kriticheskoe vvedenie v sviashchennye vetkhozavetnye knigi.* Kazan, 1910.

Ivanov, A. I. "K voprosu o vosstanovlenii pervonachal'nogo grecheskogo teksta Novogo Zaveta." *Zhurnal moskovskoi patriarkhii*, 1954, no. 3: 38–50.

"Novoe izdanie grecheskogo Novogo Zaveta." *Zhurnal moskovskoi patriarkhii*, 1954, no. 12: 69.

"Novoe kriticheskoe izdanie grecheskogo Novogo Zaveta." *Zhurnal moskovskoi patriarkhii*, 1956, no. 3: 49–58 and no. 5: 43–52.

"Novyi perevod na russkii iazyk Evangeliia ot Matfeia." *Zhurnal moskovskoi patriarkhii*, 1954, no. 4: 45–55 and no. 5: 38–47.

Ivanov, Petr. "Zakonouchitel' imp. Aleksandra II-go i mitr. Filaret." *Vozrozhdenie* (Paris), 1954, no. 35 (September–October): 148–64.

Izbrannyia mesta knig Vetkhago Zaveta na sviashchennom iazyke, dlia obuchaiushchikhsia semu iazyku v dukhovnykh uchilishchakh. Edited, translated, and with an introduction by G. P. Pavskii. Moscow: Sinodal'naia tipografiia, 1828.

Izvestiia o deistviiakh i uspekhakh bibleiskikh obshchestv v Rossii i drugikh gosudarstvakh. No. 10. St. Petersburg: Tip. Nikolaia Grecha, 1824.

Jakobson, Roman. "The Beginnings of National Self-Determination in Europe." *Review of Politics*, 7, no. 1 (1945): 29–42.

Jellicoe, S. *The Septuagint and Modern Study.* Oxford: Clarendon Press, 1968.

Jones, M. V. "The Sad and Curious Story of Karass, 1802–1835." *Oxford Slavonic Papers*, n.s. 8 (1975): 53–81.

Jung-Stilling, Johann Heinrich. *The Autobiography of Heinrich Stilling*, trans. Samuel Jackson, 3rd edn. London: John Wright & Co., 1844.

Theory of Pneumatology; in Reply to the Question, What Ought to be Believed or Disbelieved concerning Presentiments, Visions, and Apparitions according to Nature, Reason, and Scripture, trans. Samuel Jackson. New York: Redfield, Clinton Hall, 1851.

Kahle, Wilhelm. *Evangelische Christen in Russland und der Sowjetunion: Ivan Stepanovich Prochanov (1869–1935) und der Weg der Evangeliums-Christen und der Baptisten.* Wuppertal: Oncken Verlag, 1978.

Kailo, Uriel. *Sanan Lähettiläs: John Patersonin elämä ja työ.* Helsinki: Agricola-Seura, 1962.

Kamen, Michael L. "The Science of the Bible in Nineteenth-Century America: From 'Common Sense' to Controversy, 1820–1900." Ph.D. dissertation,

University of Notre Dame, 2004. Available at: http://etd.nd.edu/ETD-db/theses/available/etd-04142004-064458/unrestricted/KamenML042004.pdf.

Karpov, A. "A. M. Bukharev (Arkhimandrit Fedor)." *Put'*, no. 22 (June 1930): 24–51 and no. 23 (August 1930): 25–47.

"Kassian (Sergei Sergeevich Bezobrazov, 1892–1965)." In *Bibliologicheskii slovar'*, ed. Aleksandr Men'. Moscow: Fond im. Aleksandra Menia, 2002, II: 35–7.

Katz, David S. "The Phenomenon of Philo-Semitism." In *Christianity and Judaism*, ed. Diana Wood. Studies in Church History, XXIX. Oxford: Basil Blackwell for the Ecclesiastical History Society, 1992, 327–61.

Katz, Jacob. *From Prejudice to Destruction: Anti-Semitism, 1700–1933*. Cambridge, MA: Harvard University Press, 1980.

Kazanskaia dukhovnaia akademiia. *Idealy pravoslavno-russkogo inorodcheskago missionerstva*. Kazan, 1901.

Missionerskoe protivomusul'manskoe otdelenie. *Missionerskii protivomusul'manskii sbornik*. Vyp. 12, 1876.

Kazanskii, P[etr Simonovich]. "Mysli i chuvstvovaniia m. Filareta po delu otobraniia litogr. perevoda knig Vetkhago Zaveta po pis'mam ego k o. Antoniiu." *Pravoslavnoe obozrenie*, 1878 (January): 106–18.

Kean, William. *The Bible in Russia*. Centenary Pamphlet, 7. London: BFBS, 1904.

Kharlampovich, Konstantin Vasil'evich. *Archimandrite Makarii Glukharev: Founder of the Altai Mission*, trans. and with an interpretive essay by James Lawton Haney. Studies in Russian History, VI. Lewiston, New York: Edwin Mellen Press, 2001.

"Makarii Glukharev i tobol'skie dekabristy." *Russkii arkhiv*, 42 (February 1904): 235–43.

"Ucheno-literaturnye trudy arkhim. Makariia Glukhareva." *Khristianskoe chtenie*, 1905 (December): 794.

ed. *Pis'ma arkhimandrita Makariia Glukhareva, osnovatelia altaiskoi missii, s biograficheskim ocherkom, portretami, vidom i dvumia faksimile*. Kazan, 1905.

ed. *Pis'mo pokoinago missionera Arkhimandrita Makariia, byvshago nachal'nikom altaiskoi dukhovnoi missii, k sinodal'nomu chlenu, vysokopreosviashchenneishemu Filaretu mitropolitu moskovskomu, ot 23 dnia marta 1834 goda, o potrebnosti dlia rossiiskoi tserkvi*. Moscow, 1861.

Khvol'son, D. A. "Bibleiskiia obshchestva v Rossii." In *Entsiklopedicheskii slovar'*. St. Petersburg: Brokgaus-Efron, 1891, VI: 696–708.

Die Blutanklage und sonstige mittelalterliche Beschuldigungen der Juden: Eine historische Untersuchung nach den Quellen. Frankfurt: J. Kauffmann Press, 1901.

"Istoriia vetkhozavetnago teksta i ocherk drevneishikh ego perevodov po ikh otnosheniiu k podlinniku i mezhdu soboiu." *Khristianskoe chtenie*, 1874 (January): 519–74 and (February): 3–74.

O nekotorykh srednevekovykh obvineniiakh protiv Evreev: Istoricheskoe izsledovanie po istochnikam. St. Petersburg, 1861; 2nd edn, St. Petersburg: Tip. Tsederbauma i Gol'denbliuma, 1880.

"Otvet na zamechanie N. I. Kostomarova." In *Upotrebliaiut-li evrei khristianskuiu krov'?* St. Petersburg, 1879; 3rd edn, Kiev, 1912.

"Posledniaia paskhal'naia vecheria Iisusa Khrista i den' ego smerti." *Khristianskoe chtenie*, 1875, nos. 9–10: 430–88; 1877, nos. 5–6: 821–76; 1878, nos. 3–4: 352–419. Published separately St. Petersburg, 1892.

Upotrebliaiut-li evrei khristianskuiu krov'? St. Petersburg, 1861; 3rd edn, Kiev, 1912.

Kiselev, N., and Iu. Samarin, eds. *Zapiski, mneniia i perepiska A. S. Shishkova*, 2 vols. Berlin, 1870.

Kizenko, Nadieszda. *A Prodigal Saint: Father John of Kronstadt and the Russian People*. University Park: Pennsylvania State University Press, 2000.

Komissiia po nauchnomu izdaniiu Slavianskoi Biblii (Russkaia Bibleiskaia Komissiia), 1915–1929: Sbornik arkhivnykh materialov, ed. K. Logachev. Leningrad State University Press, 1990.

Konstantinos tou ex Oikonomon. *Peri ton o ermeneuton tēs palaias Theias grafēs vivlia*, 4 vols. Athens, 1844–9.

Korsunskii, Ivan Nikolaevich. "Filaret (Vasilii Mikhailovich Drozdov)." In *Russkii biograficheskii slovar'*. St. Petersburg, 1901, XXI: 83–93.

Mitropolit Filaret Moskovskii v ego otnosheniiakh i deiatel'nosti po voprosu o perevode Biblii na russkii iazyk. Moscow, 1886. Serialized initially in *Pravoslavnoe obozrenie*, 1884 (November, December): 561–87, 750–86 and 1885 (April, November, December): 666–98, 533–68, 657–92.

"O podvigakh Filareta, mitropolita Moskovskago, v dele perevoda Biblii na russkii iazyk: Istoriko-kriticheskoe izsledovanie." In *Sbornik izdannyi obshchestvom liubitelei dukhovnago prosveshcheniia, po sluchaiu prazdnovaniia stoletniago iubileia so dnia rozhdeniia (1782–1882) Filareta, Mitropolita Moskovskago*. Moscow: L. F. Snegirev, 1883, II: 215–666.

Pamiati sviatitelia Filareta, mitropolita moskovskago: K istorii redaktsii russkago perevoda Sviashchennago Pisaniia. Moscow: Universitetskaia tip., 1894.

Perevod LXX: Ego znachenie v istorii grecheskago iazyka i slovesnosti. Moscow: Sv. Troits. Sergieva Lavra, 1897.

Preosviashchennyi Feofan, byvshii Mitropolit Vladimirskii i Suzdal'skii. Moscow: L. F. Snegirev, 1895.

"Sud'by katikhizisov Filareta mitropolita moskovskogo." *Russkii vestnik*, 163, no. 1 (1883): 322–83

"Trudy moskovskoi dukhovnoi akademii po perevodu Sv. Pisaniia i tvorenii Sv. Ottsev na russkii iazyk za 75 let eia sushchestvovaniia (1814–1889 gg.)." *Pribavleniia k tvoreniiam Sviatykh Ottsev v russkom perevode*, 56 (1889), kn. 4: 419–587; 57 (1890), chast' 1, kn. 2: 341–405; 57 (1891), chast' 2, kn. 2: 483–614.

ed. *Trudy mitropolita Moskovskago i Kolomenskago Filareta po perelozheniiu Novago Zaveta na russkii iazyk*. St. Petersburg, 1893.

Kostomarov, N. I. "*Upotrebliaiut li evrei khristianskuiu krov'?*" *Novoe vremia*, no. 1172 (June 5, 1879).

Kotovich, A. N. "Cherty i usloviia razvitiia russkoi bogoslovskoi mysli v epokhu Nikolaia I." *Khristianskoe chtenie* (November 1906): 644–68 and (December 1906): 854–77.

Dukhovnaia tsenzura v Rossii, 1799–1855 gg. St. Petersburg: Tip. "Rodnik," 1909.

Krachkovskii, Ignatii Iulianovich. "P. K. Kokovtsev v istorii russkogo vostokovedeniia, 1861–1942." In *Izvestiia otdeleniia literatury i iazyka Akademii Nauk*. Moscow: Akademiia nauk, 1944, III: 274–79.

Kr[asnyi], G. [Ia.]. "Biblii: Perevody i izdaniia v Rossii." In *Evreiskaia entsiklopediia*. St. Petersburg; reprint, Moscow: Terra, 1991, XIV: 526–34.

Krašovec, Jože. "Slovenian Translations of the Bible." In *Interpretation of the Bible: On the Occasion of the Publication of the New Slovenian Translation of the Bible*, ed. Jože Krašovec. Ljubljana/Sheffield: Slovenian Academy of Sciences and Arts/Sheffield Academic Press, 1998, 1039–74.

Kuzmič, Peter. *Vuk-Daničićevo Sveto Pismo i Biblijska Društva na južnoslavenskom tlu u XIX stoljeću*. Zagreb: Kršćanska Sadašnjost, 1983.

Kuz'min, Ivan O. *Materialy k voprosu ob obvineniiakh evreev v ritual'nykh prestupleniiakh*. St. Petersburg, 1913.

L – g., S. "O liuteranskikh i reformatskikh tserkvakh v S.-Peterburge." *Pravoslavnoe obozrenie*, 1863 (December): 286–315.

Lahaye, Tim F., and Jerry B. Jenkins. *Left Behind: A Novel of the Earth's Last Days*. Carol Stream, IL: Tyndale House Publishing, 1995.

Latimer, Robert Sloan. *Dr. Baedeker and his Apostolic Work in Russia, with introductory notes by Her Highness Princess Nathalie Lieven of St. Petersburg and the Right Hon. Lord Radstock*. London: Morgan and Scott, 1908.

Leskov, Nikolai. "Sentimental'noe blagochestie." *Pravoslavnoe obozrenie*, 1876 (March): 526–51.

"Velikosvetskii raskol: Grenvil' Val'digrev Lord Redstok, ego zhizn', uchenie, i propoved'." *Pravoslavnoe obozrenie*, 1876 (December) and 1877 (February): 294–334.

Levenson, P. Ia. "Eshche o saratovskom dele." *Voskhod*, 1881, no. 4: 163–78.

Levin, Eve. *Sex and Society in the World of the Orthodox Slavs, 900–1700*. Ithaca, NY: Cornell University Press, 1989.

Levison, Vasilii A. *Ierusalimskiia pis'ma 1858 g*. St. Petersburg, 1864.

"Levison, Vasilii Andreevich." In *Evreiskaia entsiklopediia*. St. Petersburg; reprint, Moscow: Terra, 1991, X: 117–18.

Lindenmeyr, Adele. *Poverty Is Not a Vice: Charity, Society and the State in Imperial Russia*. Princeton University Press, 1996.

Liutostanskii, Ieromonakh Ippolit. *Ob upotreblenii evreiami (talmudistskimi sektantorami) khristianskoi krovi dlia religioznykh tselei, v sviazi s voprosom ob otnosheniiakh evreistva k khristianstvu voobshche*. Moscow, 1880.

Sovremennyi vzgliad na evreiskii vopros. St. Petersburg, 1882.

Vopros ob upotreblenii evreiami-sektatorami Khristianskoi krovi dlia religioznykh tselei, v sviazi s voprosom ob otnosheniiakh evreistva k Khristianstvu voobshche. Moscow, 1876.

"Liutostanskii, Ieromonakh Ippolit." In *Entsiklopedicheskii slovar'*. St. Petersburg: Brokgauz-Efron, 1896, XXXV: 265.

Lobko, L. "O perevodakh sv. pisaniia: Neskol'ko slov po povodu stat'i g-na Bezsonova o knige: *Opisanie rukopisei sinodal'noi biblioteki* (pis'mo k redaktoru)." *Russkaia beseda*, 3, kn. 11, otd. v (1858): 129–36.

Logachev, Konstantin. "Bibleiskaia gruppa pri Leningradskoi dukhovnoi akademii." *Zhurnal moskovskoi patriarkhii*, 1974, no. 9: 78–80.

"Bibleiskaia komissiia i izuchenie istorii Biblii u slavian (po neopublikovannym dokumentam Komissii)." *Zhurnal moskovskoi patriarkhii*, 1974, no. 7: 76–80.

"Chto stoit za 'programmoi ottorzheniia' Russkoi Biblii 1876 goda." In *Bibliia i vozrozhdenie dukhovnoi kul'tury russkogo i drugikh slavianskikh narodov: K 80-letiiu Russkoi/Severo-Zapadnoi Bibleiskoi Komissii (1915–1995)*, ed. P. Dmitriev et al. St. Petersburg: Petropolis, 1995, 236–48.

"Izdaniia russkikh perevodov Biblii." *Zhurnal moskovskoi patriarkhii*, 1975, no. 7: 72–8; no. 11: 73–80; no. 12: 44.

"Khristianskoe Sviashchennoe Pisanie v Rossii." In *Bibliia i vozrozhdenie dukhovnoi kul'tury russkogo i drugikh slavianskikh narodov: K 80-letiiu Russkoi/Severo-Zapadnoi Bibleiskoi Komissii (1915–1995)*, ed. P. Dmitriev *et al.* St. Petersburg: Petropolis, 1995, 114–26.

Kirillo-mefodievskie perevody u iuzhnykh i vostochnykh slavian. Leningrad State University Press, 1988.

"The Problem of the Relationship of the Greek Text of the Bible to the Church Slavonic and Russian Text." *The Bible Translator*, 25 (1974): 313–18.

"Problema kriticheskogo izdaniia pervogo pis'mennogo pamiatnika kirillo-mefodievskoi traditsii." *Sovetskoe slavianovedenie*, 5 (1982): 66–73.

"Professor I. E. Evseev (k 50-letiiu so dnia konchiny)." *Zhurnal moskovskoi patriarkhii*, 1971, no. 12: 64–8.

"Raboty prof. I. E. Evseeva po russkomu perevodu Sv. Pisaniia." *Zhurnal moskovskoi patriarkhii*, 1973, no. 2.

"Russkaia Bibleiskaia Komissiia i znachenie ee idei i metodov v nashi dni." In *Perevody Biblii i ikh znachenie v razvitii dukhovnoi kul'tury slavian: Materialy mezhdunarodnoi bibleiskoi konferentsii 1990 g., posviashchennoi semidesiatipiatiletiiu Russkoi Bibleiskoi Komissii*, ed. P. Dmitriev, K. Logachev, and G. Safronova. St. Petersburg: Sankt-Peterburgskii Universitet, 1994, 10–15.

"Russkii perevod Novogo Zaveta (k 15-letiiu izdaniia)." *Zhurnal moskovskoi patriarkhii*, 1969, no. 11: 61–8.

"Trudy I. E. Evseeva po istorii slavianskoi Biblii." *Zhurnal moskovskoi patriarkhii*, 1972, no. 8: 76–7.

Lopukhin, Ivan Vladimirovich. *Nekotoryia cherty o vnutrennei tserkvi, o edinom puti istiny i o razlichnykh putiakh zabluzhdeniia i gibeli.* St. Petersburg, 1798; English translation, *Some Characteristics of the Interior Church*. Mesa, AZ: Scriptoria Books, 2009.

Some Characteristics of the Interior Church, trans. D. H. S. Nicholson. London: Theosophical Publishing Society, 1912.

Lovegrove, Deryck W. *Established Unity, Sectarian People: Itinerancy and the Transformation of English Dissent, 1780–1830*. Cambridge University Press, 1988.

"Unity and Separation: Contrasting Elements in the Thought and Practice of Robert and James Alexander Haldane." In *Protestant Evangelicalism: Britain, Ireland, Germany and America, c. 1750–c.1950: Essays in Honour of W. R. Ward,* ed. Keith Robbins. Studies in Church History, VII. Oxford: Basil Blackwell, for the Ecclesiastical History Society, 1990, 153–77.

Loviagin, Evgraf I. *Ob otnoshenii pisatelei klassicheskikh k bibleiskim po vozzreniiu khristianskikh apologetov*. St. Petersburg, 1872.

Lowrie, Donald. *The Light of Russia: An Introduction to the Russian Church*. Prague: YMCA Press, 1923.

St. Sergius in Paris: The Orthodox Theological Institute. New York: Macmillan, 1951.

Makarii (Glukharev), Archimandrite. "Otryvki iz pis'ma arkhimandrita Makariia o perevode biblii na russkii iazyk." *Pravoslavnoe obozrenie*, 1861 (October), "Zametki": 273–9.

Malov, E. A. "Prikhody starokreshchennykh i novokreshchennykh tatar v kazanskoi eparkhii." *Pravoslavnoe obozrenie*, 17 (August 1865): 449–94.

Manchester, Laurie. *Holy Fathers, Secular Sons: Clergy, Intelligentsia, and the Modern Self in Revolutionary Russia*. DeKalb: Northern Illinois University Press, 2008.

"Mandel'shtam, Leon Iosifovich, 1819-1889." In *Evreiskaia entsiklopediia*. St. Petersburg; reprint, Moscow: Terra 1991, x: 591–2.

Marker, Gary. "Primers and Literacy in Muscovy: A Taxonomic Investigation." *Russian Review*, 48, no. 1 (1989): 1–19.

Publishing, Printing, and the Origins of Intellectual Life in Russia, 1700–1800. Princeton University Press, 1985.

[Markon, I.] "Troitskii, Ivan Gavriilovich." In *Evreiskaia entsiklopediia*. St. Petersburg; reprint, Moscow: Terra, 1991, XV: 27.

Martin, Alexander. *Romantics, Reformers, Reactionaries: Russian Conservative Thought and Politics in the Reign of Alexander I*. DeKalb: Northern Illinois University Press, 1997.

Martin, David. *On Secularization: Towards a Revised General Theory*. Burlington, VT: Ashgate Publishing, 2005.

Martin, Roger H. *Evangelicals United: Ecumenical Stirrings in Pre-Victorian Britain, 1795–1830*. Metuchen, NJ, and London: Scarecrow Press, 1983.

Masonstvo v ego proshlom i nastoiashchem, ed. S. P. Mel'gunov and N. P. Sidorov, 2 vols. [Moscow]: Izdanie "Zadrugi" i K. F. Nekrasova [1914–15].

Meletii (Ieromonakh). "Zapiski zabaikal'skago missionera za 1864 god." *Pravoslavnoe obozrenie*, 17 (June 1865): 198–220.

Men', Aleksandr (Protoierei), ed. *Bibliologicheskii slovar'*, 3 vols. Moscow: Fond im. Aleksandra Menia, 2002.

"K istorii russkoi pravoslavnoi bibleistiki." *Bogoslovskie trudy*, 28 (1987): 272–89.

Metallinos, Geōrgios. *To zētēma tēs metaphraseōs tēs Agias Graphēs eis tēn neoellēnikēn kata ton 19 aiōna*. Athens, 1977.

Metzger, Bruce M. *The Text of the New Testament, its Transmission, Corruption, and Restoration*, 2nd edn. Oxford University Press, 1968.

Michatek, N. "Kridener, Baronessa Varvara-Iuliia." In *Russkii biograficheskii slovar'*. St. Petersburg, 1903, [IX]: 435–41.

Miller, Matthew L. "A Hunger for Books: The American YMCA Press and Russian Readers." *Religion, State, and Society*, 38, no. 1 (March 2010): 53–75.

Miłosz, Czesław. "Problems of Biblical Translation," lecture delivered at Arizona State University (Tempe), January 20, 1984.

Mironov, B. N. *Sotsial'naia istoriia Rossii (XVIII – nachalo XX v.): Genezis lichnosti, demokraticheskoi sem'i, grazhdanskogo obshchestva iz pravovogo gosudarstva*, 2 vols. St. Petersburg: Izd. "Dmitrii Bulanin," 2003.

"Mnenie preosviashchennykh mitropolitov novgorodskago Serafima i kievskago Evgeniia o bibleiskom obshchestve." In *Sbornik istoricheskikh materialov, izvlechennykh iz arkhiva sobstvennoi ego Imp. Vel. Kantseliarii*, ed. N. F. Dubrovin. St. Petersburg, 1903, vol. XII: 376–8.

Moore, R. Laurence. *Selling God: American Religion in the Marketplace of Culture*. New York: Oxford University Press, 1994.

Moroshkin, M. Ia., ed. "K istorii bibleiskikh obshchestv." *Russkii arkhiv*, 6 (1868): 940–51.

Nachertanie zhizni i deianii sv. prav. sinoda chlena Mefodiia [Smirnova], arkhiepiskopa pskovskago. Moscow, 1823.

Nadezhdin, Aleksandr. *Istoriia sanktpeterburgskoi pravoslavnoi dukhovnoi seminarii*. St. Petersburg, 1885.

Negrov, Alexander I. *Biblical Interpretation in the Russian Orthodox Church*. Beiträge zur historischen Theologie, CXXX. Tübingen: Mohr Siebeck, 2008.

Nekrasov, Aleksandr A. "Po povodu predpolagaemago peresmotra russkago perevoda novozavetnago teksta." *Pravoslavnyi sobesednik*, 1895, no. 3: 265–79.

"Vsegda li russkii perevod s evreiskago teksta tochno peredaet soderzhanie vetkhozavetnykh knig?" *Pravoslavnyi sobesednik*, 1898, no. 1: 153–61.

"Zamechaniia k pervym dvum glavam russkago perevoda Evangeliia ot Matfeia." *Pravoslavnyi sobesednik*, 1884, no. 1: 151–64.

"Zamechaniia otnositel'no tekh mest russkago novozavetnago teksta, kotoryia ne vpolne sootvetstvuiut tekstam grecheskomu i slavianskomu." *Pravoslavnyi sobesednik*, 1884, no. 1: 17–23.

Nestle, Eberhard. *Einführung in das Griechische Neue Testament*, 2nd edn. Göttingen, 1899.

Nichols, Robert L. "*Metropolitan Filaret of Moscow and the Awakening of Orthodoxy*." Ph. D. dissertation, University of Washington, 1972.

Nikanor (Preosviashchennyi). *Avtobiograficheskie materialy*, ed. Fr. S. Petrovskii. Odessa, 1900.

Nikitenko, A. V. *Zapiski i dnevnik*. St. Petersburg, 1893.

Nikol'skii, M. "Britanskii perevod Sv. Pisaniia Vetkhago Zaveta na russkii iazyk." *Pravoslavnoe obozrenie*, 1877, pt. 1 (February): 335–45.

"Russkii perevod Biblii i znachenie evreiskoi filologii." *Pravoslavnoe obozrenie*, 1876, pt. 1 (April): 645–72.

"Uspekhi nashei bibleiskoi nauki." *Pravoslavnoe obozrenie*, 1877, pt. 1 (March): 574–82.

Nikon. "Magisterial Dispute (Study of the Archives of the Altaic Orthodox Mission, 1830–1920)." *Journal of the Moscow Patriarchate*, 1989, no. 6: 23–34.

Nord, David. "Free Grace, Free Books, Free Riders: The Economics of Religious Publishing in Early Nineteenth-Century America." In *Religion, Media, and the Marketplace*, ed. Lynn Schofield Clark. New Brunswick, NJ: Rutgers University Press, 2007, 37–66.

Norris, H[enry] H[andley]. *A respectful letter to the Earl of Liverpool, K.G., First Lord of His Majesty's treasury, occasioned by the speech imputed to His Lordship at the Isle of Thanet Bible Society meeting, Oct. 17, 1821*. London: F. C. & J. Rivington, 1822.

Novum Testamentum graece, cum apparatu critico curavit, ed. Eberhard and Erwin Nestle, 17th edn. Stuttgart, 1945.

"Ob izdanii Biblii v russkom perevode v Londone (pis'mo iz-za granitsy)." *Pravoslavnoe obozrenie*, 3 (November 1860): 381–91.

"Ob odnom novom zagranichnom izdanii russkoi Biblii." *Zhurnal moskovskoi patriarkhii*, 1955, no. 10: 48–53.

Obraztsov, I. Ia. "Opisanie dokumentov otnos. k istorii izdaniia Elisavetinskoi Biblii." In *Opis' dokumentov i del khraniashchikhsia v arkhive Sviateishago Pr. Sinoda, s ukazateliami k nei: Dela kommissii dukhovnykh uchilishch, 1808–1839*. St. Petersburg, 1910, vol. III, no. 38.

Obshchestvo dlia rasprostraneniia Sv. Pisaniia v Rossii. *Otchet*. St. Petersburg, 1863–1902.

Okenfuss, Max. *Discovery of Childhood: The Evidence of the Slavic Primer*. Newtonville, MA: Oriental Research Partners, 1980.

Orlov, Aleksandr F. *Protoierei Gerasim Petrovich Pavskii*. St. Petersburg, 1863.

Orlovsky, Daniel T. *The Limits of Reform: The Ministry of Internal Affairs in Imperial Russia, 1802–1881*. Cambridge, MA: Harvard University Press, 1981.

Orthodox Russia: Belief and Practice under the Tsars, ed. Valerie A. Kivelson and Robert H. Greene. University Park: Pennsylvania State University Press, 2003.

Osipov, A. "K izdaniiu russkoi Biblii." *Zhurnal moskovskoi patriarkhii*, 1955, no. 8: 58–66.

Osipov, V. O. "Russkaia knigotorgovaia bibliografiia v pervoi polovine XIX veka." *Sovetskaia bibliografiia*, 1973, no. 2: 44–57.

"Otchet o deiatel'nosti obshchestva rasprostraneniia sv. pisaniia v Rossii za 1885 god." *Pravoslavnoe obozrenie*, 1887 (January): 210–13.

Pagels, Elaine. *The Gnostic Gospels*. New York: Random House, 1979.

Partridge, C. S. *Stereotyping*, 2nd edn. Chicago and New York: Inland Printer, 1909.

Pavlov, A. A. "Zapiska o kramolakh vragov Rossii." *Russkii arkhiv*, 6 (1868): 1329–91.

Pavskii, Gerasim P. *Bibleiskie drevnosti dlia razumeniia sv. pisaniia*. St. Petersburg, 1884.

Filologicheskie nabliudeniia nad sostavom russkago iazyka, 4 vols., 2nd edn. St. Petersburg, 1850.

"Kniga Pesn' Pesnei [1825] v perevode Gerasima Petrovicha Pavskago," introduction by N. I. Barsov. *Russkaia starina*, 30 (1881): 467–86.

"Mysli zakonouchitelia protoiereia G. P. Pavskogo o religioznom uchenii i vospitanii e. i. v. gosudaria velikago kniazia … Aleksandra Nikolaevicha, izlozhennyia v 1826 godu." *Sbornik imperatorskago russkago istoricheskago obshchestva*, 30 (1881): 61–8.

"Ob"iasnenie na primechaniia, sdelannyia protiv knizhek, 'Khristianskoe uchenie v kratkoi sisteme' i 'Nachertanie tserkovnoi istorii.'" *Chteniia v imperatorskom obshchestve istorii i drevnosti pri moskovskom universitete*, 1870, kn. 2, otd. 5: 175–208.

"Religiia." *Khristianskoe chtenie*, 1821 (January): 43–56.

"Pavskii, Protoierei Gerasim Petrovich (nekrolog)." *Pravoslavnoe obozrenie*, 10 (April 1863), "Zametki": 242–4.

Pečírková, Jaroslava. "Czech Translations of the Bible." In *Interpretation of the Bible: On the Occasion of the Publication of the New Slovenian Translation of the Bible*, ed. Jože Krašovec. Ljubljana/Sheffield: Slovenian Academy of Sciences and Arts/Sheffield Academic Press, 1998, 1167–1200.

Petri, Hans. *Ignaz Lindl und die Bauernkolonie Sarata in Bessarabien*. Munich: R. Oldenbourg, 1965.

Piatidesiatiletie Vysochaishe utverzhdennoi komissii po razboru i poslaniiu arkhiva sviateishago sinoda, 1865–1915: Istoricheskaia zapiska. Petrograd: Sinodal'naia tip., 1915.

Pinkerton, Robert. *Russia, or Miscellaneous Observations on the Past and Present State of that Country and its Inhabitants*. London, 1833.

Pisarev, S. "K voprosu ob ispravlenii teksta slavianskoi Biblii." *Pravoslavnoe obozrenie*, 1876 (January): 56–72.

Pitcher, Harvey. *Muir & Mirrielees: The Scottish Partnership That Became a Household Name in Russia*. Cromer, Norfolk: Swallow House Books, 1994.

Pogodin, M. *Utro*, 3 vols. Moscow, 1859–68.

Pond, Elizabeth. "In Soviet Russia - A New Bible Translation." *Christian Science Monitor*, 22 (June 1976): 13–14.

Popov, K. D. "Iur'evskii arkhimandrit Fotii i ego tserkovno-obshchestvennaia deiatel'nost'." *Trudy kievskoi dukhovnoi akademii*, 1875 (February): 373–84 and (June): 696–817.

"Portret Gerasima Petrovicha Pavskago, s zhivopisnago portreta, pisannago v 1842 g. khudozhnikom N. S. Volkovym, risoval na dereve K. O. Brozh. Graviroval vo Frantsii Akademik L. A. Seriakov." *Russkaia starina*, 29 (1880): inset between pp. 222 and 223.

Pravoslavnaia entsiklopediia, 25 vols. to date. Moscow, 2000–.

Prokhanoff, I. S. *Atheism, or the Gospel in Russia, Which? The Religious Situation in Russia and the Activities of the All-Russian Evangelical Christian Union*. New York: All-Russian Evangelical Christian Union, [1933].

In the Cauldron of Russia, 1869–1933: Autobiography of I. S. Prokhanoff, Founder and Honorary President of the All-Russian Evangelical Christian Union. New York: All-Russian Evangelical Christian Union, 1933.

Triumph of the Gospel in the Heart of Russia, or the Great Evangelical Reformation in Russia. New York: All-Russian Evangelical Christian Union, [1929].

Protopopov, Sergei V. "Protoierei Gerasim Petrovich Pavskii (Materialy dlia ego biografii)." *Strannik*, 17 (1876), no. 1: 3–45, no. 2: 101–37, and no. 3: 213–24.

Protoierei G. P. Pavskii. St. Petersburg, 1876.
Protopopov, V. (Protoierei). *Ob upotreblenii evreiami khristianskoi krovi dlia religioznykh tselei*. St. Petersburg: Tip. Landau, 1880.
Pypin, A. N. "Bibleiskaia sekta 20-kh godov." *Vestnik Evropy*, 2, kn. 3 (1871): 248–82.
Izsledovaniia i stat'i po epokhe Aleksandra I, vol. III: *Obshchestvennoe dvizhenie v Rossii pri Aleksandre I*, 5th edn. Petrograd: OGNI, 1918; reprint, 2001.
"Rossiiskoe bibleiskoe obshchestvo." In *Izsledovaniia i stat'i po epokhe Aleksandra I*, vol. I: *Religioznyia dvizheniia pri Aleksandre I*, ed. and with new intro. and notes by N. K. Piksanov. Petrograd, 1916.
Russkoe masonstvo XVIII i pervaia chetvert' XIX v. Petrograd, 1916; reprint, 1997.
R., S. G. "Krinitskii, Pavel Vasil'evich." In *Russkii biograficheskii slovar'*. St. Petersburg, 1903, [IX]: 444.
Raeff, Marc. *Michael Speransky: Statesman of Imperial Russia, 1772–1839*, 2nd edn. The Hague: Martinus Nijhoff, 1969.
The Well-Ordered Police State: Social and Institutional Change through Law in the Germanies and Russia, 1600–1800. New Haven, CT: Yale University Press, 1983.
Repp, Arthur C. "In Search of an Orthodox Way: The Development of Biblical Studies in Late Imperial Russia." Ph.D. dissertation, University of Illinois at Chicago, 1999.
Reusch, Franz Heinrich. "Lindl, Ignaz." In *Allgemeine Deutsche Biographie*. Leipzig, 1883, XVIII: 698–9.
Rizhskii, Mikhail Iosifovich. *Istoriia perevodov Biblii v Rossii*. Novosibirsk, 1978.
Roberts, Bleddyn J. *The Old Testament Text and Versions*. Cardiff: University of Wales Press, 1951.
Rodosskii, Aleksei S. *Biograficheskii slovar' studentov pervykh xxviii–li kursov sanktpeterburgskoi dukhovnoi akademii, 1814–1869 gg*. St. Petersburg, 1907.
[R., A.] "Bogoliubov, Konstantin Ioannovich, 1821–1888." In *Pravoslavnaia bogoslovskaia entsiklopediia*. Petrograd, 1903, II: 748–9.
Rossiiskoe bibleiskoe obshchestvo. *Otchet*, vols. I–X. St. Petersburg, 1814–23.
Rosslyn, Wendy. *Deeds, Not Words: The Origins of Women's Philanthropy in the Russian Empire*. Birmingham Slavonic Monographs, XXXVII. Birmingham: Centre for Russian and East European Studies, 2007.
Runkevich, S. "Agafangel (Solov'ev), 1812–1876." In *Pravoslavnaia bogoslovskaia entsiklopediia*. Petrograd, 1900, I: 256–7.
"Platon (Levshin)." In *Russkii biograficheskii slovar'*. St. Petersburg, 1905, [XIV]: 49–54.
Sadov, A. "Nekrolog Evgrafa Ivanovicha Loviagina, 1822–1909." *Khristianskoe chtenie*, 1910 (September): 1147–62.
Savvaitov, Pavel Ivanovich. *Bibleiskaia germenevtika*, 2nd edn. St. Petersburg, 1859.
Grammatika zyrianskogo iazyka. St. Petersburg, 1849.
Ob izdanii Ostromirova Evangeliia i o sodeistvii Mosk. mitr. Filareta. Moscow, 1884.

Zyriansko-Russkii i Russko-Zyrianskii slovar', 2 vols. St. Petersburg, 1849.

"Savvaitov, Pavel Ivanovich, 1815–1895." In *Entsiklopedicheskii slovar'*. St. Petersburg: Brokgauz-Efron, 1900, LVI: 27.

Sawatsky, Walter. *Soviet Evangelicals since World War II*. Scottdale, PA: Herald Press, 1981.

Sbornik izdannyi obshchestvom liubitelei dukhovnago prosveshcheniia, po sluchaiu prazdnovaniia stoletnaiago iubleia so dnia rozhdeniia (1782–1882) Filareta, Mitropolita Moskovskago. Moscow: Tip. L. F. Snegireva, 1883.

Schmidt, Ute. "Germans in Bessarabia: Historical Background and Present-Day Relations." *South-East Europe Review*, 3 (2008): 307–17.

[Serafim (Glagolevskii), Metropolitan of St. Petersburg]. "K istorii bibleiskikh obshchestv v Rossii." *Russkii arkhiv*, 6 (1868): 940–51.

Serdechnyi privet: Sbornik statei, izdannykh S.-Peterburgskoi dukhovnoi akademiei v pamiat' piatidesiatiletiia sviatitel'skogo sluzheniia vysokopreosviashchenneishago Isidora Mitropolita Novgorodskago, S-Peterburgskago i Finliandskago. St. Petersburg, 1884.

Sergii (Vasilevskii), Arkhimandrit. *Vysokopreosviashchennyi Filaret (Amfiteatrov), m. kievskii i galitskii i ego vremia*, 3 vols. Kazan, 1888.

Severo-zapadnaia bibleiskaia komissiia. *Pravda o russkoi Biblii*. Leningrad: Severo-zapadnaia bibleiskaia komissiia, 1991.

Shevchenko, I. "Three Paradoxes of the Cyrillo-Methodian Mission." *Slavic Review*, 23 (1964): 226–32.

Shevzov, Vera. *Russian Orthodoxy on the Eve of Revolution*. New York: Oxford University Press, 2004.

Shil'der, N. K. *Imperator Aleksandr Pervyi, ego zhizn' i tsarstvovanie*, 4 vols. St. Petersburg, 1897–8.

Shishkov, A. S. "Razsuzhdenie A. S. Shishkova o bibleiskikh obshchestvakh voobshche i v osobennosti o rossiiskom bibleiskom obshchestve." In *Sbornik istoricheskikh materialov, izvlechennykh iz arkhiva sobstvennoi ego Imp. Vel. Kantseliarii*, ed. N. F. Dubrovin. St. Petersburg, 1903, XII: 348–76.

"Sobstvennoruchnaia zapiska o bibleiskikh obshchestvakh." In *Sbornik Istoricheskikh materialov, izvlechennykh iz arkhiva sobstvennoi ego Imp. Vel. Kantseliarii*, ed. N. F. Dubrovin. St. Petersburg, 1903, XII: 339–48.

Shkarovskii, M. V. *Obnovlencheskoe dvizhenie v russkoi pravoslavnoi tserkvi XX veka*. St. Petersburg: Izd. "NESTOR," 1999.

"Shteinberg, Ioshua." In *Evreiskaia entsiklopediia*. St. Petersburg; reprint, Moscow: Terra, 1991, XVI: 97–8.

Skripitsyn, Valerii V. "Svedeniia ob ubiistve evreiami khristian dlia dobyvaniia krovi." *Grazhdanin*, nos. 23–8 (1878).

Slotskii, A. "Protoierei G. P. Pavskii i Mitropolit Filaret." *Russkaia starina*, 1881 (July): 479–86.

Smart, Herbert G. *Electrotyping and Stereotyping: A Record of Effort and Achievement Spread over the Generations*. London: St. Bride Printing Library, 1984.

Smirnoff, Eugene [Evgenii Smirnov]. *A Short Account of the Historical Development and Present Position of Russian Orthodox Missions*. London: Rivertons, 1903.

Smirnov-Platonov, G. "O russkom perevode *Premudrosti Iisusa Syna Sirakhova*." *Pravoslavnoe obozrenie*, 1860 (December): 512–48.

"Russkii perevod biblii." *Pravoslavnoe obozrenie*, 1860 (January): 78–91.

Smith, Douglas. *Working the Rough Stone: Freemasonry and Society in Eighteenth-Century Russia*. DeKalb: Northern Illinois University Press, 1999.

Snegirev, I. M. "Novyi Zavet na serbskom narechii: Ocherk iz epokhi vozrozhdeniia pis'mennosti u pravoslavnykh Serbov." *Pravoslavnyi sobesednik*, 1876, kn. 3, nos. 10–11: 198–240.

Zhizn' Moskovskago mitropolita Platona, 4th edn. Moscow, 1891.

Sobe, B. I. "Problema ispravleniia bogosluzhebnykh knig v rossii v XIX–XX vekakh." *Bogoslovskie trudy*, 5 (1970): 25–68.

Sol'skii, S. M. "Ob uchastii imperatora Aleksandra I v izdanii Biblii na russkom iazyke." *Trudy kievskoi dukhovnoi akademii*, 1878 (January): 172–96.

"Obozrenie trudov po izucheniiu Biblii v Rossii s XV veka do nastoiashchago vremeni." *Pravoslavnoe obozrenie*, 27 (1868) and n.s. 1 (1869): 801–22.

"Upotreblenie i izuchenie Biblii v Rossii." *Pravoslavnoe obozrenie*, 27 (1868): 145–80, 251–70.

Sorokin, Vladimir, and Konstantin Logachev. "Aktual'nye problemy russkogo perevoda sviashchennogo pisaniia." *Bogoslovskie trudy*, 14 (1975): 154–60.

Sowing the Word: The Cultural Impact of the British and Foreign Bible Society, 1804–2004, ed. Stephen K. Batalden, Kathleen Cann, and John Dean. Sheffield: Phoenix Press, 2004.

Stanislawski, Michael. *For Whom Do I Toil: Judah Leib Gordon and the Crisis of Russian Jewry*. New York: Oxford University Press, 1988.

Tsar Nicholas I and the Jews: The Transformation of Jewish Society in Russia, 1825–1855. Philadelphia, PA: Jewish Publication Society of America, 1983.

Starinin, I. I. "Zapiski bibleiskago knigonoshi." *Golos minuvshago*, 1914, no. 10 (October): 150–85; no. 11 (November): 167–211; no. 12 (December): 166–97.

Steeves, Paul D. "*The Russian Baptist Union, 1917–1935: Evangelical Awakening in Russia*." Ph.D. dissertation, University of Kansas, 1976.

Stelletskii, N. *Kniaz' A. N. Golitsyn i ego tserkovno-gosudarstvennaia deiatel'nost'*. Kiev: I. I. Gorbunov, 1901.

Sturdza, A. S. "O sud'be pravoslavnoi tserkvi pravoslavnoi tserkvi russkoi v tsarstvovanie imperatora Aleksandra I." *Russkaia starina*, 1876: 266–88.

Sulotzkii, A. "G. P. Pavskii i mitropolit Filaret." *Russkaia starina*, 31 (1881): 479–86.

Sushkov, Nikolai. "K razskazu o kvakerakh v 'Zapiskakh o zhizni i vremeni sviatitelia Filareta, mitropolita moskovskago.'" *Chteniia v imperatorskom obshchestve istorii i drevnostei rossiiskikh pri moskovskom universitete*, 1870, kn. 1 (January–March), otd. 5 (smes'): 235–40.

ed. *Zapiski o zhizni i vremeni sviatitelia Filareta mitropolita moskovskago (s prilozheniem)*. Moscow, 1868.

Swan, William. *Memoir of the Late Mrs. Paterson, Containing Extracts from her Diary and Correspondence*, 2nd edn. Edinburgh: Waugh & Innes, 1823.

Tal'berg, N. D. *Aleksandr I: Ocherki istorii imperatorskoi Rossii.* Moscow: Izd. Sretenskogo monastyria, 2001.

Taylor, Charles. *A Secular Age.* Cambridge, MA: Harvard University Press, 2007.

Thomson, Francis J. "The Slavonic Translation of the Old Testament." In *Interpretation of the Bible: On the Occasion of the Publication of the New Slovenian Translation of the Bible*, ed. Jože Krašovec. Ljubljana/Sheffield: Slovenian Academy of Sciences and Arts/Sheffield Academic Press, 1998, 605–920.

Tikhon (Shevkunov), Archimandrite, ed. *Bogosluzhebnyi iazyk russkoi tserkvi: Istoriia, popytki reformatsii.* Sretenskii Monastery: Tip. "Molodaia gvardiia," 1999.

Titlinov, B. V. *Dukhovnaia shkola v Rossii v XIX st.*, 2 vols. Vil'na, 1908–9.

Troitskii, Ivan. "Professor D. A. Khvol'son." *Zhurnal ministerstva narodnago prosveshcheniia*, n.s. 34 (1911), no. 8, otd. 4: 90–9.

Troitskii, N. A. *Aleksandr I protiv Napoleona.* Moscow: Iauza/Eksmo, 2007.

Trotter, Mrs. Edward. *Lord Radstock: An Interpretation and a Record,* 2nd edn. London: Hodder & Stoughton, 1914.

Tr[ubetskoi], S[ergei]. "Fessler, Ignatii Avrelii." In *Russkii biograficheskii slovar'.* St. Petersburg, 1901, [XXI]: 59–60.

Tselunova, E. "Psaltyr' 1683g. 'na prostom slovenskom' iazyke." *Kalbotyra*, 39, no. 2 (1988): 112–18.

Psaltyr' 1683 goda v perevode Avramiia Firsova. Slavistische Beiträge, CCXLIII. Munich: Otto Sagner, 1989.

Tserkovnyi vestnik: Offitsial'nyi organ Sv. Sinoda. St. Petersburg, 1875–1916.

Tsvetkov, S. E. *Aleksandr I, 1777–1825: Belletrizirovannaia biografiia.* Moscow: Tsentrpoligraf, 1999.

Twyman, Michael. *Printing, 1770–1970: An Illustrated History of its Development and Uses in England.* London: Eyre & Spottiswoode, 1970.

Uchastkina, Zoya Vasil'evna. *A History of Russian Hand Paper-mills and their Watermarks, ed. and adapted for English by J. S. G. Simmons. Collection of Works and Documents Illustrating the History of Paper*, IX, ed. E. J. LaBarre. Hilversum, Holland: Paper Publications Society, 1962.

Ulybin, V. V. *Aleksandr I: Obratnaia storona tsarstvovaniia – vlast' i tainye obshchestva v 1801–1825 godakh.* St. Petersburg: Aleteiia, 2004.

Urry, James. "John Melville and the Mennonites: A British Evangelist in South Russia, 1837–ca.1875." *Mennonite Quarterly Review*, 1980 (October): 305–22.

Uspensky, Boris A. "The Schism and Cultural Conflict in the Seventeenth Century." In *Seeking God: The Recovery of Religious Identity in Orthodox Russia, Ukraine, and Georgia*, ed. Stephen K. Batalden. DeKalb: Northern Illinois University Press, 1993, 106–43.

[V., A.]. "Posledniaia paskhal'naia vecheria Iisusa Khrista i den' ego smerti." *Strannik*, 1876, no. 11: 97–126 and no. 12: 185–289.

Vakon'ia, I. "Bestsennoe bogatstvo russkikh perevodov Slova Bozhiia i tserkovnoi literatury." *Zhurnal moskovskoi patriarkhii*, 1955, no. 6: 65–67.

Valliere, Paul R. "Russian Orthodoxy and the Challenge of Modernity: The Case of Archimandrite Makary." *St. Vladimir's Theological Quarterly*, 22, no. 1 (1978): 4–15.

Varieties of Secularism in a Secular Age, ed. Michael Warner, Jonathan VanAntwerpen, and Craig Calhoun. Cambridge, MA: Harvard University Press, 2010.

Vasil'evskii, Sergei. *Vysokopreosviashchennyi Filaret v skhimomonashestve Feodosii Amfiteatrov, mitropolit Kievskii i galitskii i ego vremia*, 3 vols. Kazan, 1888.

Veniamin, Bishop of Selenginsk. "Zabaikal'skaia dukhovnaia missiia." *Pravoslavnoe obozrenie*, 16 (April 1865): 343–62.

Verbitskii, Vasilii I. "Ocherk deiatel'nosti Altaiskoi dukhovnoi missii po sluchaiu piatidesiatiletnego eia iubileia (1830–1880)." In *Pamiatnaia knizhka tomskoi gubernii 1885 goda*. Tomsk, 1885, 142–221.

Vinogradov, Aleksei. *Istoriia angliisko-amerikanskoi Biblii, ee alfavita, perevodov, teksta, kanona, revizii, izdanii, literatury, ekzegeza i bibleiskikh obshchestv*, pts. 1–3. St. Petersburg, 1889–91.

Istoriia Biblii na Vostoke: S obzorom metoda i uslovii blagopriiatnykh i neblagopriiatnykh ee perevodam i rasprostraneniiu s khristianskoi tserkov'iu u raznykh narodov. St. Petersburg, 1889–95.

Vol'skii, Arsenii. "Pavskii, Gerasim Petrovich." In *Russkii biograficheskii slovar'*. St. Petersburg, 1902, [XIII]: 103–9.

Vostokov, N. M. "Innokentii, Arkhiepiskop Khersonskii i Tavricheskii, 1800–1857 gg." *Russkaia starina*, 24 (1879): 651–708.

Werth, Paul W. *At the Margins of Orthodoxy: Mission, Governance, and Confessional Politics in Russia's Volga-Kama Region, 1827–1905*. Ithaca, NY: Cornell University Press, 2002.

"Imperial Russia's Multiconfessional Establishment: The Institutional Domestication of the 'Foreign Confessions.'" Available at: www.harrimaninstitute.org/MEDIA/01167.pdf.

Wexler, P. "Christian, Jewish, and Muslim Translations of the Bible and Koran in Byelorussia: Sixteenth to the Nineteenth Centuries." *Journal of Byelorussian Studies*, 6 (1988): 12–19.

Whittaker, Cynthia, ed. and trans. *Alexander Pushkin: Epigrams and Satirical Verse*. Ann Arbor, MI: Ardis, 1986.

Wodecki, Bernard. "Polish Translations of the Bible." In *Interpretation of the Bible: On the Occasion of the Publication of the New Slovenian Translation of the Bible*, ed. Jože Krašovec. Ljubljana/Sheffield: Slovenian Academy of Sciences and Arts/Sheffield Academic Press, 1998, 1201–34.

Wosh, Peter J. *Spreading the Word: The Bible Business in Nineteenth-Century America*. Ithaca, NY: Cornell University Press, 1990.

Young, Lawrence A., ed. *Rational Choice Theory and Religion: Summary and Assessment*. New York: Routledge, 1997.

Zacek, Judith Cohen. "The Imperial Philanthropic Society in the Reign of Alexander I." *Canadian-American Slavic Studies*, 9 (1975): 427–36.

"The Lancasterian School Movement in Russia." *Slavonic and East European Review*, 45, no. 105 (July 1967): 343–67.

"The Prison Reform Movement in the Reign of Alexander I." *Canadian Slavic Studies*, 1 (1967): 196–211.

"The Russian Bible Society and the Catholic Church." *Canadian Slavic Studies*, 5 (Spring 1971): 35–50.

"The Russian Bible Society and the Russian Orthodox Church." *Church History*, 35 (1966): 411–37.

"The Russian Bible Society, 1812–1826." Ph.D. dissertation, Columbia University, 1964.

Zaitsev, Boris."O episkope Kassiane." *Russkaia mysl'*, no. 2283 (March 18, 1965): 2–3.

Zakharov, Vsevolod Valentinovich. "Svedeniia o nekotorykh peterburgskikh tipografiiakh (1810–1830-e gody)." *Kniga: Issledovaniia i materialy*, 26 (1973): 65–79.

"Zamechaniia na vvod chteniia Biblii v Rossii." *Chteniia v imperstorskom obshchestve istorii i drevnostei pri moskovskom universitete*, 1862, kn. 3: 162–6.

"Zamechaniia po povodu novago russkago perevoda Evangeliia ot Mattheia, sostavlennyia monakhom o Antoniem monastyria sv. Savvy v Palestine." *Pravoslavnyi put'*, 1954: 107–14.

"Zametki: Otryvki iz pis'ma arkhimandrita Makariia o perevode biblii na russkii iazyk." *Pravoslavnoe obozrenie*, 6 (October 1861): 273–79.

"Zametki: Perevody sviashchennykh i bogosluzhebnykh knig dlia inorodtsev Rossii." *Pravoslavnoe obozrenie*, 1 (January 1860): 92–4.

Zdravomyslov, K. "Feofilakt." In *Russkii biograficheskii slovar'*. St. Petersburg, 1913, [xxv]: 466–9.

Zernova, A. S., ed. *Svodnyi katalog russkoi knigi kirillovskoi pechati* XVIII *veka*. Moscow, 1968.

Zhivov, Viktor. "Iazyk Feofana Prokopovicha i rol' gibridnykh variantov tserkovnoslavianskogo v istorii slavianskikh literaturnykh iazykov." *Sovetskoe slavianovedenie*, no. 3 (1985): 70–85.

Kul'turnye konflikty v istorii russkogo literaturnogo iazyka XVIII*-nachala* XIX *veka*. Moscow: Institut russkogo iazyka, AN SSSR, 1990.

Zhukova, Iuliia. "Pervaia zhenskaia organizatsiia v Rossii (Zhenskoe patrioticheskoe obshchestvo v Peterburge v period 1812–1826." *Vse liudi – sestry: Biulleten' peterburgskogo tsentra gendernykh problem*, 5 (1996): 38–56.

"Zhukovskii. Vasilii Andreevich." In *Bibliologicheskii slovar'*, ed. Aleksandr Men'. Moscow: Fond im. Aleksandra Menia, 2002, 1: 449–50.

Znamenskii, P. V. *Bogoslovskaia polemika 1860-kh godov ob otnoshenii pravoslaviia k sovremennoi zhizni*. Kazan: Tip. Universiteta, 1902.

Istoriia kazanskoi dukhovnoi akademii za pervyi (doreformennyi) period eia sushchestvovaniia, 1842–1870, vyp. 2. Kazan, 1892.

Na pamiat' o N. I. Il'minskom. Kazan, 1892.

Zykov, V. I. "Iz zhizni imperatorskoi petrogradskoi dukhovnoi akademii: V bibleiskoi kommissii." *Khristianskoe chtenie*, 1916 (March): 361–5.

Index

CPSIA information can be obtained
at www.ICGtesting.com
Printed in the USA
LVOW04s0419170316
479491LV00012B/62/P

9 781316 600924